EUROPE IN THE NINETEENTH AND TWENTIETH CENTURIES
(1789-1950)

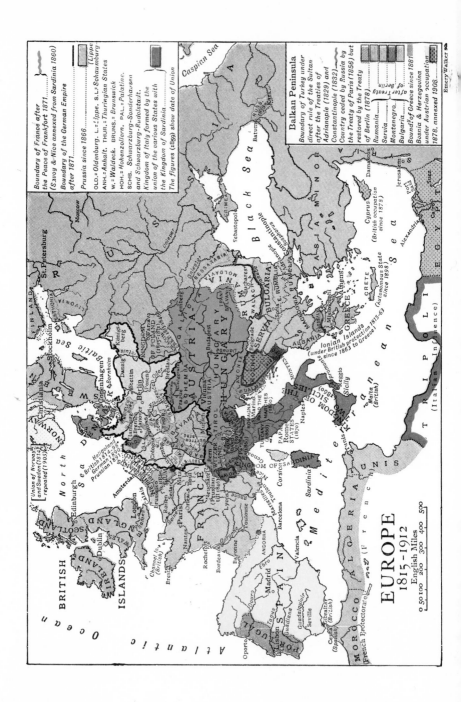

EUROPE
1815-1912
English Miles
0 50 100 200 300 400 500

Emery Walker sc.

Boundary of France after
the Peace of Frankfort 1871............
(Savoy & Nice annexed from Sardinia 1860)
Boundary of the German Empire
after 1871

Prussia since 1866

OLD.= Oldenburg. L.= Lippe. S.L.= Schaumburg
ANH.= Anhalt. THUR.= Thuringian States
W.= Waldeck. BRUNS.= Brunswick
HOH.= Hohenzollern. PAL.= Palatine.
SCHB. Schwarzburg-Sonderhausen
and Schwarzburg-Rudolstadt.

Kingdom of Italy formed by the
union of the various States with
the Kingdom of Sardinia

The figures (1859) show date of Union

Balkan Peninsula

Boundary of Turkey under
direct rule of the Sultan
after the Treaties of
Adrianople (1829) and
Constantinople (1832)
Country ceded by Russia by
the Treaty of Paris (1856) but
restored by the Treaty
of Berlin (1878)
Rumania
Servia
Montenegro.
Bulgaria
Bound of Greece since 1881
Bosnia & Herzegovina
under Austrian occupation
1878, annexed 1908.

after Treaty
of Berlin

Europe in the Nineteenth and Twentieth Centuries
(1789–1950)

BY

A. J. GRANT, M.A., Litt.D.

Professor of History in the University of Leeds, 1897–1927

AND

HAROLD TEMPERLEY, Litt.D.

Professor of Modern History in the University of Cambridge
1931–1939

SIXTH EDITION

REVISED AND EDITED BY
LILLIAN M. PENSON, D.B.E., LL.D., D.Lit.

*Professor of Modern History in the University
of London*

WITH MAPS

LONGMANS

LONGMANS, GREEN AND CO LTD
London and Harlow
*Associated companies, branches and representatives
throughout the world*

BIBLIOGRAPHICAL NOTE

First Edition
  Europe in the 19th Century .   .   .   June 1927
Second Edition .   .   .   .   .   .   June 1928
New Impression   .   .   .   .   .   January 1929
Third Edition   .   .   .   .   .   .   January 1931
Fourth Edition
  Europe in the 19th and 20th Centuries   .   October 1932
New Impressions   May 1933, January 1934, November 1934
                        November 1935, January 1937
Fifth Edition   .   .   .   .   .   .   January 1939
New Impression with Supplementary Section .   April 1940
New Impressions November 1940, January 1942, May 1943,
                March 1944, October 1944, July 1945,
                January 1946, September 1947, January 1948
Sixth Edition   ·   ·   ·   ·   ·   · February 1952
New Impressions June 1956 (with minor corrections) June 1959
                April 1960, July 1961, February 1962,
                September 1963, November 1964, February
                1966, January 1969

PRINTED IN GREAT BRITAIN BY
SPOTTISWOODE, BALLANTYNE AND CO. LTD.
LONDON AND COLCHESTER

NOTE TO THE SIXTH EDITION

THE present edition is in a sense a new venture. It has been extended to June 1950 in accordance with the practice of the original authors who tried as far as possible to keep this book completely up to date. The new material which this has involved has given opportunity not only for the consolidation of the additions made to the previous edition but for the revision of the later part of the book to a very considerable degree. The passage of time, and in particular the events of the War of 1939–45, has led to the necessity for a substantial revision of that part of the book which related to the post-1919 period. At the same time care has been taken to maintain the original wording as far as possible and thus to preserve the original character of the book.

Since the publication of the fifth edition in 1939, both the distinguished historians who were the authors have died. Professor Temperley died in July 1939 just before the events in which he was so closely interested led to the catastrophe of that year. Professor Grant, who was his elder by several years, lived until May 1948 and thus saw both the passage of the war years and the first stages of the new era which has followed them. The present editor, who was closely associated with both the original authors in historical work, was therefore able to discuss with Professor Grant the revision which has now taken place.

The combination of the two authors with their wide but differing experience and their common devotion to European history gave to the book its particular characteristics of individuality and original thought. It was their wish that there should be successive editions which should maintain some at least of these characteristics and at the same time take into account the differing outlook of a new era.

In the note to the fifth edition the authors referred to the personal experience of Professor Temperley in the British Imperial General Staff in the first World War and in the negotiations for peace. They acknowledged also the help given by a number of personal friends, some of whom are no longer available for consultation. In particular, acknowledgment was given for the criticisms made by Field-Marshal Lord Birdwood on the chapter relating to the War of 1914-18, and to Mr. J. M. (later Lord) Keynes for help in dealing with the Reparation and Economic Sections of the Treaty of Versailles. Sir Arnold Wilson had given them advice in connection with all matters upon the then recent history of the East; Mr. L. S. Amery had commented upon the section relating to the reconstruction of democracy after the first World War and Major-General A. C. Temperley (the brother of one of the authors) had given advice on the history of Disarmament and the later developments of the League of Nations.

In the note to the fifth edition the debt of the authors was also acknowledged to Mr. Raymond Postgate who had written part of the chapter which dealt with Marxism and with Russia. The debt to Mr. Raymond Postgate still remains, because much use has been made of the chapter to which he contributed. At the same time it has been necessary in the light of events which have taken place since the fifth edition was prepared to review this chapter and to give it to some extent a new orientation.

The editor of the sixth edition wishes to acknowledge not only the help which was given to the original authors, but also that given by Miss Winifred Bamforth, M.A., who has been of the greatest assistance in the research needed for the new edition. She has taken a substantial part in preparing the volume for the press as well as in the comprehensive checking of the references and quotations.

LILLIAN M. PENSON

July 1950

PREFACE REVISED FOR THE SIXTH EDITION

THE history of the last century and a half, up to and beyond the War of 1939, cannot be compressed into a volume of six hundred pages. At the most a sketch, a few outlines, some impressions can be given. But, as in a Japanese picture, if the right lines are put in, the general effect should be good. The original authors offered this book as their conception of how the main threads of the period cross and interweave with one another, and of how the tapestry was composed. The plan of the work is substantially unaltered, and runs on the following lines. Part I reveals the great explosion of the French Revolution and details how it spread over Europe, and what Napoleon retained, and what he rejected, of this great spiritual and national movement. Part II depicts how the Four Great Powers of Europe, after having overthrown Napoleon, struggled vainly to erect a system of international government. The failure of that attempt was rendered certain by Canning, who favoured the rise of strong national governments, and described the new international system as dangerous and premature. The rise of constitutionalism in France and Spain, of independence in Belgium, and the struggles of latent and suppressed nationality in Poland and Italy are likewise depicted. Part III opens with the tide of revolution breaking strongly over all central and western Europe in 1848. The tragic blunder of the Crimean War, the union of Italy, and the amazing triumphs of Prussia in diplomacy and war are related. The period ends with the revival of France.

Part IV opens with the Russo-Turkish War and the unloosing of passions in the Balkans during the years 1876–86. Chapter XXIII deals with colonial development and overseas empire through the century. The story of the formation of the two great systems of European Alliance is then told and how the Powers gradually grouped themselves in opposite camps. Chapter XXV shows how even England began to abandon her isolation and how she entered into an alliance with Japan, and into ententes with France and Russia. The next chapter deals with Europe on the eve of the War. The story of the three crises at Algeciras, over Bosnia, and at Agadir is told. Finally it is shown how the Balkan Wars increased the friction between Triple Entente and Triple Alliance and how, amid ever-increasing difficulties, the nations of Europe finally plunged into war.

In the period covered in Part IV, from 1878 to 1914, as well as in Part V, a somewhat fuller treatment has been adopted and references added to some of the documentary material available. It was thought desirable in a book such as this to give references to the most readily accessible book wherever possible, but this does not mean that printed or unpublished sources have not been used in the preparation of the work.

Part V deals with the War of 1914–18, the Peace Treaties, and the rise of new nationalities. In Chapter XXIX, the War, the authors departed from their rule and gave a plan and a study of a battle, that of the Marne in 1914. But it was thought that the importance of this crisis justified the exception. The study of the military plans of Germany which failed at the Marne is one of very high interest and has also political and moral implications of a very far-reaching character. Equally instructive is Falkenhayn's view of the military situation during the years 1915–16, and his decision to strike first against Russia and then at Verdun. The direction given to German strategy by Hindenburg and Ludendorff and their reasons for acquiescing in a ruthless submarine campaign are of high interest. It is important again to estimate why the strategy of Ludendorff failed, and that of Haig and Foch triumphed, in 1918. In Chapter XXX the strategy is of peace, not of war. A study of the contrasted temperaments of Wilson, Lloyd George and Clemenceau is not only interesting in itself, but is the real key to the mysteries of the Treaty of Versailles. It does much to explain the importance of the Covenant of the League, the origin of the Mandatory system, and the severity of the terms inflicted upon Germany.

Chapter XXXI deals with nation-making in the new Europe. Nations, not men, are the theme, and their origin and character reveal strange developments in national personality. Attention is also given to the problems raised by the racial and religious minorities scattered over so many of the new states. The Russian civil war is also touched upon. Chapter XXXII deals with the East and seeks to show how the European upheaval affected Asia. It tells how the Turks became a new people, how Armenians survived the appalling calamities inflicted by the Turks, how the Arabs rode from Mecca to Damascus, and how Persia, China and Japan began to work out their strange destinies.

Part VI has been considerably revised and extended to deal with the Powers of Europe after the first World War, with the inter-war years, and with the second World War and its immediate aftermath. In Chapter XXXIII there is some necessary repetition of the previous narrative in order to deal with the general or universal movements of the period. Among the many that might have been related, a few have been distinguished. A study of the growth of Marxism provides the background for a survey of the development of the Soviet Union from the Revolution of 1917 to the outbreak of war in 1939. This is followed by a description of the nature of the totalitarian régimes in Italy and Germany and of the events which led to their growth. The parliamentary governments of France and Britain are also treated in this chapter and some account is given of the political instability of France, which contributed to her collapse in 1940.

Chapter XXXIV opens with the problems which faced the League of

Nations, and records the successive attempts made to deal with them. The hopeful period of the twenties is followed by the preparations for war in the thirties, by the rejection of disarmament, and of the ideals of the League. One international crisis succeeds another until Europe becomes embroiled in the second major war of the century, which is treated in Chapter XXXV.

In Chapter XXXVI, the immediate aftermath of the war is considered, and some account is given of such political settlement as has been effected in Europe since 1945, and of the principles behind the treatment of ex-enemy states by the allied Powers. In the Epilogue, the aspects of movements towards European and international co-operation and unity, which had previously formed part of Chapter XXXIV, have been considerably revised and extended to include the United Nations Organisation.

New maps are included to exhibit Northern Africa and the Mediterranean at the outbreak of war in 1939; the extent of German conquests in Europe by January 1942; Europe in 1945 after the end of the war; and the division of Germany into zones in 1945.

Care has been taken to verify details, and to check dates and statements. But it is hardly possible to hope that some errors have not crept in.

CONTENTS

PART I

THE FRENCH REVOLUTION AND NAPOLEON

CHAPTER I

CHAPTER II

CHAPTER III

xi

PART II

FROM INTERNATIONAL GOVERNMENT TO REVOLUTION, 1814–48

CHAPTER IX

CHAPTER X

PART III

FRENCH, GERMAN AND RUSSIAN IMPERIALISM

CHAPTER XI

CHAPTER XII

PART IV

THE GREAT ALLIANCES AND THE BALANCE OF POWER

CHAPTER XXII

CHAPTER XXIII

CHAPTER XXIV

CHAPTER XXV

PART V

THE WAR AND ITS AFTERMATH IN EUROPE AND ASIA, 1914–23

CHAPTER XXIX

CHAPTER XXX

CHAPTER XXXI

CHAPTER XXXII

PART VI

THE GREAT POWERS OF EUROPE IN THE TWENTIETH CENTURY

CHAPTER XXXIII

MARXISM AND THE SOVIET UNION; ITALY AND GERMANY; BRITAIN AND FRANCE 459

MAPS

PART I

THE FRENCH REVOLUTION AND NAPOLEON

CHAPTER I

MODERN EUROPE

EUROPE is not merely a geographical expression. It implies not only a definite area of the earth's surface, but also a certain type of civilisation. The conceptions of the European states concerning social life and government, concerning religion and art and science, have, underneath all their differences, a certain resemblance which may be difficult to define, but which appears unquestionable when they are compared with the ideas of the old civilisations of Asia or the conditions in Africa or the New World. This basis of common ideas and practices is not the result of a common nationality, for the peoples of Europe are many, and some are widely removed from others; it is the result of the historical development of the European lands. All of them, though some to a greater extent than others, have inherited the science and art and philosophy of Greece. A large part of them was incorporated into the Roman Empire, and even over those who were left outside that Empire the law and the language and the institutions of Rome had a great influence. But it was during the Middle Ages that the greatest advance was made towards something that may be called European unity. The Christian Church, whether in its Eastern or its Western form, took up the task of Rome, though on a strangely different plane. Over all Europe the Christian ideas of faith, morals, and worship were accepted. There were wide differences between East and West, between nation and nation, but a common understanding was established which subsequent revolutions did not entirely destroy.

But though there was a certain common basis of culture in Europe this was very far from availing to keep peace among the different states and races. European history is a record of continual war from the second century A.D. onwards. The central doctrines of the Church recognised the unity of mankind and the blessings of peace; but there were no civil institutions that gave effective encouragement to these ideas and no organisation which could enforce them. Yet here, too, it is important to notice that most persistent efforts to realise the unity of Europe as part of the greater unity of mankind were made during the Middle Ages. The Holy Roman Empire—so much misunderstood and so unfairly criticised—was an affirmation that Europe ought to have a single political organisation

1

and an authority raised above the different states which could decide between them. It fell ludicrously short of that ideal, but it was something that it kept it alive. The organisation of the Church, too, was inevitably international in aim and character. Feudalism, chivalry, trade organisations, universities had an international character greater than anything that we find in the modern world until the nineteenth century.

The passing of the mediaeval world was accompanied, both as cause and effect, by the rise of national feeling and the assertion of the independence of each state. This is plainer among the nations that broke away from communion with Rome, but it is, in truth, a feature common to all. Spain and France were hardly less independent of papal control than England or Germany. The international ideas of the Middle Ages had been wearing very thin for some time; they now disappeared from the world even as an aspiration. From the end of the fifteenth to the end of the eighteenth century we have to look to solitary thinkers—to Sir Thomas More and Rabelais, to Sully and Leibnitz and Kant and Rousseau—to find even an echo of ideas that had once, in whatever strange form, been common—namely, that the Christian nations formed one whole and should have institutions to assert and to maintain their unity.

The nations of Europe, therefore, faced one another as armed and distrustful rivals, recognising no rule of conduct except their own advantage, and entering into transitory alliances on the promptings of fear or gain. These unstable and temporary relationships among the states of Europe have received the name of the Balance of Power. This has been idealised by some as a safeguard for European peace and the protection of the world against despotism; it has been denounced by others as the cause of the wars of Europe. It was, in truth, neither the one nor the other. It is simply a convenient name for the way in which states act towards one another when there is no influence to persuade them to concord, nor force to coerce them, nor any court whose authority they are all prepared to recognise. The working of the system—though indeed it was not a system—is seen at its clearest among the states of Greece in the fifth and fourth centuries B.C. It provides the explanation for the kaleidoscopic politics of Italy in the fourteenth and fifteenth centuries; and in the sixteenth century it passed from Italy to the larger state system of Europe, though during the Middle Ages the working of the same force had often been visible.

The most obvious feature of the state system of Europe under the influence of this idea is the recurring alliance of the weaker powers against any state that seemed to exercise or claim a supremacy in Europe. Thus in the sixteenth century the Spanish power was resisted by a combination of states of which England and France were the chief. The seventeenth century saw the rise of France to the leading position in Europe; it saw, too, the union of her enemies against her, and the early years of the eighteenth century saw her overthrow. The union of forces which defeated the naval supremacy of Great Britain for a time in the eighteenth century and led to the independence of the United States has some features in common with these instances already given.

The end of the eighteenth century sees hardly a shadow of international action or aspiration. But with the French Revolution (it is important to note it) the era of international effort begins again, and in various forms has continued, in spite of wars with which the nineteenth century is filled, until the daring effort of the League of Nations. We shall attempt in this book, while telling the story of the different countries of Europe, not to lose sight of the whole in the parts, and especially to examine the forces which from time to time made for war or peace.

It will be well to begin with a survey of the European Powers towards the end of the eighteenth century. Of Great Britain, it is enough to say that, despite the humiliation of the loss of the American colonies, she still ranked as one of the greatest of the Powers. Her navy had recovered from its momentary eclipse. The industrial revolution, which transformed her life, brought to her great wealth and allowed her to bear the strain of the long contest with France and Napoleon. Her Government was, in spite of names, a narrow oligarchy; but it worked in conjunction with a Parliament which had grown steadily more powerful since the end of the mediaeval period. It had a freer press and was in closer touch with large and important sections of the nation than any government on the Continent, and the large measure of support which it received accounts for its survival when nearly all the governments on the Continent perished in the revolutionary storm.

France had lost her military prestige when she was crushed by the alliance of Great Britain and of Prussia in the Seven Years' War. King Louis XV, who died in 1774, was typical of the monarchical decadence. The French Monarchy owed its strength to the effective leadership which it had given to the nation in war, and he was sunk in vice, without energy or military ardour; and under him the nation had suffered great and irremediable defeats. His grandson, Louis XVI, succeeded in 1774, and in the War of American Independence fortune had returned to the standards of France. But the treasury was alarmingly empty, and the organisation of monarchical France was undermined by aristrocratic opposition, by the growing strength and discontent of the middle classes, and by the new hopes and passions which were spreading throughout the country from the great writers of the time. The revolutionary storm first broke in France; and her Constitution and social life have been often treated as if they were an altogether exceptional example of oppression, incompetence, and social distress. But there was very much in France that was representative of conditions that prevailed throughout Europe. Here was a monarchy which had done great things for the safety and the prosperity of France, which had overthrown all rivals for power—the feudal aristocracy, the legal profession, representative institutions both central, provincial and municipal—which ruled

by 'divine right' without recognising any dependence on, or partnership
with, the body of the nation, and which controlled France through its
officials and its bureaucracy; the richest, the most splendid, and the
most influential of the monarchies of Europe. The vigour and life had
largely passed away from it. The mistakes and the defeats of Louis XIV
and the vices and follies of Louis XV in part account for this. But the
institution of autocratic monarchy no longer corresponded to the ideas
or the needs of the time. The example of the Government of Great
Britain was by reason of its success a great force throughout the century,
and the time was soon coming when it would be necessary for all the
governments in one way or another to take the people into partnership.
On the eve of the Revolution the old system of government in France
was almost without defenders. There was an almost universal aspiration after something new; all classes were touched in different ways by
the new spirit, and the King himself was in sympathy with much of the
humanitarian ideas of the time. What these new ideas were we will
shortly examine. It is plain that the complete victory of the Monarchy
over all rivals itself contributed to its overthrow and to the completeness
of the triumph of the Revolution. When the central government was
once overthrown there was no further resistance possible. The defenders of the old system—of what is usually called the old régime—
were few, and they had no institutions through which they could work.
France was, as it were, dominated by a single fort, and, when that fell,
there was no further resistance.

The social system of France had many features common to many
European states as well as some peculiar to herself. The population was
divided—as most European populations were—into the privileged and
the unprivileged classes. The Clergy, the Nobility, and those connected
with the Court were the privileged and belonged to an exclusive society
from which the rest of the inhabitants of France were shut out. They
did not, indeed, govern France: for the Monarchy had found its most
dangerous rivals in the nobles, and had in its triumph excluded them
from the most important administrative posts. But they and the Clergy
and the courtiers enjoyed very considerable social privileges. They were
exempt from many taxes that were paid by the unprivileged; the nobles
alone were eligible for the higher ranks of the army, and formed the
Court that shone with such great splendour at Versailles. The twentieth
century has outlived most of these conditions; but they were then to be
found, with modifications, in various parts of Europe, in Spain and
Italy, in most of the German States, in Poland, and in Russia. Nor
was the social condition of the people exceptional either in the character
or in the extent of its grievances. The chief burden of the taxation fell
upon the inhabitants of the villages and the peasantry. The peasants
were to a very large extent owners of their farms, for the Revolution,
though it increased the peasant proprietorships of France, did not, by
any means, originate them. This class, which since the Revolution has

been the most contented and conservative in France, was before that event full of bitterness and protest. The peasants owned their lands, but they were burdened by a crushing load of taxes—crushing chiefly because the privileged classes had avoided their proper share of it—and they had also to pay many dues of feudal origin which had once represented their relation to their feudal superiors, but which had now lost all social meaning and were merely irritating burdens. They alone paid the *taille*—a tax on the houses and lands of the unprivileged—and the salt monopoly, which was known as the *gabelle*; and in feudal dues they paid a proportion of their crops, dues for pressing their grapes or grinding their corn, and other burdens. Their position as free proprietors with their lands burdened by meaningless impositions was peculiarly irritating and easily accounts for the part they played in the early scenes of the Revolution. But again we must say of all this that there was nothing exceptional in their lot. Most European states showed something like it. In some, and particularly in Poland, the lot of the peasantry was far worse. The dwellers in the French towns had their own grievances: they found the decaying organisations of their trades guilds a restraint to their progress. They saw with natural jealousy the rapid advance in prosperity made by the commercial classes of England, and when the Revolution had begun they had far the chief share in directing and using it.

The great rival of France before 1789 was the House of Austria; or, to speak more accurately, the lands, various in character and origin, which were ruled, with many differences of method and power, by the great House of Hapsburg. Men spoke of France and Austria sometimes as the two ends of the Balance of Power. From 1500 their wars and rivalries fill a great part of the history of Europe, and France found in Austria her most constant opponent from the outbreak of the revolutionary wars down to the fall of Napoleon. The Austrian territories made a long and variegated list. Many nationalities, languages, and religions were found among the populations. They had been brought together by inheritance, by diplomatic marriages, by war, and even by purchase. The chief divisions or groups were the following:[1] (1) The core of the Hapsburg power was to be found in the German lands in the neighbourhood and to the south-west of Vienna; there was no important difference either in language or race between these lands and those which are more usually classed as Germany. (2) To the north of the capital were Bohemia and Moravia, inhabited mainly by a Czech people, which had played a great part in European history, but which since the close of the Thirty Years' War in the seventeenth century had seemed content to be subordinate to the German Hapsburgs. (3) To the east stretched the great Magyar kingdom of Hungary, where the Magyars maintained their authority over many peoples—Rumanians, Croats, and Serbs. Divided in religion and feudal in the tone of their society, they yielded a grudging obedience to the Hapsburg sovereigns. (4) To

[1] *v.* Map, p. 177.

the south of the Alps the Duchy of Milan, rich and populous, gave them rule over a mass of Italians alien in tradition and character. (5) Far to the west of Europe the accident of birth, in the first instance, and then the result of war had made Austria master of those Netherlands which we now call Belgium, the population of which, part Flemish and part French in population and language, presented a great contrast to the rest of the Austrian dominions.

The rule of these widely scattered and different lands was a difficult problem. The modern feeling that the nation and the state should be identical as far as possible was hardly known in the eighteenth century; but the difficulty of governing such varied elements was already apparent. The Emperor Joseph II (1765–90) had wished, in conformity with the general tendency of the age, to introduce a centralised and unified form of government into his dominions. He had tried to make German the official language everywhere; he had tried to bring all parts of his dominions under the direct rule of his officials, to introduce religious toleration, and to establish the equality of all his subjects under his personal rule. The effort was well meant, but it had broken down completely through the national pride and the religious prejudices of his various peoples. Nowhere were Joseph's projected reforms more revolutionary than in Belgium, where, moreover, he proposed to get rid of the restraints which the jealousy of Great Britain and Holland had for more than a century and a half placed on the navigation of the Scheldt, ruining thereby the prosperity of the great harbour of Antwerp. And nowhere more than in Belgium was there determined resistance to his schemes. The people, devoted for the most part to the Catholic Church, rose in violent protest against the proposals to suppress the monasteries and to secularise education; 'liberals' joined with them through dislike of the Emperor's autocratic schemes. It came to open war. Apparently suppressed in 1788, it flared out again in 1789 and was not suppressed. In 1790 when Joseph II died, the Belgians were demanding, through their delegates at Brussels, a federal republic. Joseph was succeeded by Leopold II, whose caution and love of the old routine was a great contrast to his predecessor's impulsive and imaginative temperament. He adopted the traditional Austrian policy of maintaining order by balancing the different interests against one another; and he gained much success. Yet when we come to speak in the next chapter of the great French Revolution it is well to remember that another revolution had already broken out in the neighbouring Belgian lands, very different indeed from what happened in France, but still a revolution which weakened the power of Austria and encouraged the French to believe that they would find allies on their northern frontier.

We have called Joseph II Emperor. He owed that title to the fact that he was head of the 'Holy Roman Empire,' under which ancient and picturesque title were included little more than the states of Germany. It is of some importance to note that, as emperor, Joseph and his successors had a certain responsibility for what happened in Germany. But, though the title ranked highest in Europe, and though Voltaire's well-known gibe that it was 'neither holy nor Roman nor an Empire' does injustice to its early greatness and ideals, we may neglect it for international relations at the end of the eighteenth century. It had no power. It could not raise a soldier or collect a penny in taxation except by consent of the different German states. It is to these that we must turn.

Germany had been called in the seventeenth century 'a divinely ordained confusion,' and contained at that epoch over 300 'states.' The confusion was partly due to the mistakes of the German Powers themselves; but it had also been carefully and successfully fostered by a succession of French statesmen. The confusion was greatest to the west of Germany. No powerful state held the Rhine or watched the entry into Germany from France. Lorraine and Alsace had been in French hands since the end of the seventeenth century. On the western frontier were to be found the debris of states that had once seemed important: Würtemberg and Baden especially; but the most characteristic feature was the ecclesiastical states on or near the Rhine, where bishops ruled, not cruelly nor oppressively, but very inefficiently and in a fashion which offered little likelihood of resistance to an invader. As we look farther east we find states stronger and better organised: Hanover at the mouths of the Weser and the Elbe, attached to Great Britain by the fact that its Elector was also King of Great Britain; Saxony on the upper course of the Elbe; and, farther south, Bavaria on the upper Danube, strongly Catholic and jealous of its northern neighbour, Prussia. Prussia passed through a fiery trial in the wars with Napoleon, and it seemed at one time as though she might succumb; but Germany for a century past and for more than a century afterwards found her destiny almost identified with that of Prussia. Prussia had no geographical advantages. 'Nature had not foreseen Prussia.' The core of the country lay on the middle waters of the Elbe and the Oder, with Berlin as its capital and Magdeburg and Frankfort-on-Oder as its all-important outposts on the Elbe and the Oder. Without defensive frontiers the country had to rely on military force for self-preservation; and from the seventeenth century there was a tradition of military discipline and efficiency which helps to explain its continued progress. There were great Prussian rulers before Frederick the Great (1740–86), but it was he who raised the country from a second-rate to a first-rate Power. Using with great genius the fine army which he inherited from his father, he fought two long wars against a coalition of European Powers, in which Austria was his constant enemy and first France and then Great Britain his ally. He had won by the sword the rich upper valley of the Oder which is called Silesia. By diplomacy he gained in 1772 the northern part of Poland, which connected the central Mark of Brandenburg with Eastern Prussia: this was the first step in the partitions of Poland which will occupy our attention later. Prussia had, after 1772, a large coherent mass of territory in East Europe; but this was separated from her lands on or near the Rhine (Mark and Cleves, etc.), and in the period covered by this book the Prussian sword would be called on to effect the junction with them. The latter part of Frederick's life had been devoted to peaceful and hard-working administration. The prosperity of the country increased greatly. Her prestige stood higher than that of any other country in Europe. Rulers like Joseph II, writers like Voltaire, looked to Prussia as the model of what a state should be. Her army seemed to possess an unrevealed secret of victory. Her triumphs had been won without taking the people into partnership or recognising the need of liberty. Only a few observers, such as Mirabeau—afterwards so famous in the story of the French Revolution—saw that the greatness of Prussia depended on the personal qualities of her king and prophesied trouble when his strong hand and subtle brain were removed.

Great Britain, France, Prussia, and Austria were the chief Great Powers in Europe, and they were mainly concerned in the outbreak of the war with France in 1792 to which our thoughts will shortly be directed. But Russia came little behind them in importance and, as the struggle went on, her influence—direct and indirect—became more and more important. Her vast and loosely organised population seemed hardly to lie within the circle of European culture. The gap between Russia and Western Europe in temperament and ideas has always been a wide one, and still is so. But in the Middle Ages she had accepted Christianity in its Eastern or Orthodox form, and its traditions and ideas had sunk deep into the national consciousness. Then in the seventeenth century Peter the Great, that strange and sometimes sinister genius, had carried her frontiers to the Baltic and for a time to the Black Sea, and had opened to her the civilising agency of maritime intercourse. He had, too, forced upon her aristocracy something of the external forms and something even of the language and science of Western Europe. It is impossible to think of Russia as lying outside the circle of Europe when she took so continuous and so important a part in its international relationships and in its artistic and philosophical progress. The work of Peter the Great in territorial aggrandisement and in the westernisation of the country had been carried on by the Czarina Catherine II—a German by birth—who sat on the Russian throne from 1762 to 1796.

There was one question which especially attracted her attention—the question of Poland. Poland had held a vast space on the map of Europe at the beginning of the sixteenth century. In language and people she was closely akin to Russia. Yet, while Russia moved forward to political unity and constantly widened her territories, Poland gives us a record of political and military decline hardly to be paralleled in the history of Europe. We can make no attempt here at any diagnosis of 'the Polish disease.' When we look at her towards the end of the eighteenth century we see a constitution that legalised anarchy by giving to any nobleman the power of veto in legislation, a social system that maintained the worst abuses of the feudal system without their excuses or the advantages of that system in the Middle Ages, and which especially condemned its peasant population to a condition of serfdom far worse than anything that was found in France; we see in the mass of the people great moral degradation, and few intellectual interests in the upper ranks of society. The frontiers of the country had no natural defences, and the government had not imitated that of Prussia in remedying this defect by the creation of a strong army. The result was that she was marked out as a prey to her neighbours. The first Partition of Poland had taken place in 1772. The incident was characteristic of the diplomacy of the time. A war threatened in the Balkan peninsula between Austria and Russia. Frederick of Prussia intervened to suggest that the appetites of both Powers should be satisfied by the lands of the entirely inoffensive Polish state, and that he himself should take an equal share—as the idea of the Balance of Power would suggest—for Prussia. Even after that partition had taken place the territories of Poland were still wide and attractive. The appetite of her neighbours had not been satisfied by what they had taken, and they were thinking of a further and even of a final partition. Poland, at last really alarmed, was under her last King—Stanislas Poniatowski—seriously trying to set her house in order. When the French Revolution broke out in 1789, the Polish question was the most urgent matter for Prussia, Russia, and Austria. They were anxious for their booty, jealous of one another, and fearful of being outwitted. The interaction of the Polish problem and the French Revolution gives the clue to much of the diplomacy of the next years.

We must not speak in detail of the smaller Powers of Europe, though they had contributed much to build up the civilisation of Europe and were one and all drawn into the current of the French Revolution and the Napoleonic wars. Spain seemed to have almost stepped aside from the main movement of European progress in which she had once played so important a part, but her people would before long play again a great rôle in the story of Europe. Her monarchy was effete beyond anything that France knew. The royal house was a branch of the Bourbons who ruled in France, and the fate of the country had of late been intimately associated with that of France. Italy was divided into several nominally independent states—the republics of Venice and Genoa, the duchies of Milan, Parma, Modena, and Tuscany, the theocracy of the Papal States, the monarchy of Naples—but in fact the country lay under the influence of the Austrian House, which held Milan as a part of its territories and exercised great indirect influence over the rest of the peninsula. In Holland and the Scandinavian states there was a peaceful, vigorous and prosperous population whose annals had been uneventful of late. They, too, would be drawn gradually and unwillingly into the thick of the European conflict.

1*

The states of Europe, then, towards the eve of the French Revolution, come before us independent and unrelated; pursuing their own advantage without any suspicion that there was any other possibility; arranging their temporary alliances as their immediate advantage and the idea of the Balance of Power seemed to dictate; repudiating in their public life any control of religion and any obligations to mankind. But there was in Europe at the same time a strong and strengthening current of thought and conviction of an entirely contrary kind. Perhaps the most revolutionary feature of the age is to be found in the antithetical contrast between the actions of statesmen and the best and most powerful thought of the age. We must try in a very short space to indicate the general character of this thought.

France held the foremost place in the world of thought, and the intellectual movement is usually treated as though it were solely French. But in reality the French were merely the leaders of a general movement, long heralded by the work of such men as Locke and Leibnitz.   Hume, Gibbon, Robertson, in England; Lessing and Kant, Goethe and Schiller in Germany; Benjamin Franklin in America; they are all part of the same movement with Voltaire and Montesquieu, with Diderot and Rousseau. Is it possible to determine the general characteristics of so widespread a movement? First of all it was universal in its outlook, and in this way was in marked contrast to the prevailing character of the politics of the time. In none of the countries mentioned was the tone of the literature patriotic or nationalist. France and England were at war during nearly the whole of the eighteenth century, but rarely has the intercourse of thought between the two countries been more constant or more useful to both sides. Frederick of Prussia had stirred the German temperament to patriotism, and there was in the literature of the time, in Schiller especially, some echoes of this, but the outlook of the great German authors mentioned was before all things wide and human. The second general characteristic of the thought of the time is its humanity. Never during the Christian era, or before it, was this note entirely absent, but in the eighteenth century it became dominant and essential. It is to the bar of humanity that religion, government, and social customs are brought, and they are for the most part condemned because they are found wanting in this respect. Thirdly and lastly, the thought of the time was critical and even hostile to the claims of the existing Churches and religions. Some of the writers possessed religious natures, but not one of them counted as a supporter of any ecclesiastical organisation or creed.

Voltaire, Montesquieu and Rousseau may be selected as the three most typical and influential men in all the group of writers. Voltaire was of all of them the best known and the widest read. His thought never went deep, and he has made no original contributions of importance to any side of European thought. But he was the most powerful influence in popularising ideas that Europe has ever known. His most sharply barbed shafts were directed against the ideas and practices of the Church; in politics he was neither liberal nor democrat, but regarded the honest and benevolent despotism of Frederick the Great as the form of government that should be imitated elsewhere. Above all he attacked in his writings and by his actions the religious intolerance of his time. The great days of the Inquisition were over, but still the Protestants of France suffered from cruel wrongs which sometimes led even to death. In protesting against all this and in many other ways Voltaire was the spokesman of the conscience of mankind. His wit and his satire, the clearness of his language and the humanity of his appeal, pervade the eighteenth century and the French Revolution.

Montesquieu was a profound student of constitutional problems, and by temperament conservative. His 'Spirit of the Laws' is a general discussion of forms of government and was the armoury from which those who were engaged in political reconstruction—a common task in the ensuing years—drew their ideas. The Constitution of the United States of America was largely influenced by it. Yet the book—as Montesquieu would himself admit with pleasure—was largely influenced by the English Constitution which he, like so many of the Frenchmen of his day, admired immensely. He praised a limited government, a machinery of checks and balances, and especially admired in the English practice what he called the 'Separation of the Powers'—the independence of the legislative, executive, and judicial branches of the state; though we see clearly now that he was wrong in thinking that in England the executive and the legislative were really separate.

Rousseau of all the writers of his age provoked the most opposite sentiments of love and hate, and he is still the most discussed. His emotional and meditative temperament hardly seems to belong to his age; and, though in many ways he is one of the most powerful forces in the main current of his time, in others he seems to throw himself across it and to try to swim against it. His moving style has none of the clarity of Voltaire. He was passionately religious in temperament, but neither Catholic nor Christian. He felt the evils of his age and the sufferings of the people, but none of the remedies proposed obtained his approval. The 'Social Contract,' published in 1762, summarises his ideas on government, but does it in such a way that men still argue as to his essential meaning. He opens with an indignant protest against the tyranny of his time. 'Man is born free and yet everywhere he is in chains.' The state owes its origin to the people; it belongs inalienably to them; the right always is theirs, in spite of all treaties or constitutions, to alter or abolish its forms. Yet he does not think that democracy is possible, except in states of small size; he believes that it may be necessary to have recourse to a dictator, and he ends by insisting on the necessity of religion in a state, and proposes that a simple and civic form of religion should be imposed on all, even by the penalty of death. The influence of his ideas and phrases extended far beyond the students of his works. The French Revolution bears traces of his thought throughout.

No other French writers of the time have attracted so much attention from posterity as these three—Voltaire, Montesquieu, and Rousseau—but there was another group that had great contemporary influence and an important relation to the work of the Revolution. This group is known as the Economists or Physiocrats. They were much influenced by the writings of Adam Smith, the English economist. Their chief representatives in France were Mirabeau, the father of the well-known statesman of the Revolution, Say, and above all Quesnay, the real thinker of the movement, whose obscure and difficult 'Tableau Economique' was hailed by some of them as an infallible remedy for the troubles of France. They cared little for the abstract speculations of the time and failed to win the approval of Voltaire and Montesquieu. We may choose from their voluminous writings the following doctrines as central; that all wealth comes from the application of labour to land; that workmen are the most truly productive, perhaps the only productive, class; that the action of government should be reduced to a minimum; that complete free trade and the establishment of a universal system of education were the reforms most immediately requisite; and that all taxation should be reduced to a single land-tax. These principles, says Mirabeau, would suffice to 'set everything right and renew the age of Solomon.' Turgot was a discriminating disciple of this school, and both as an *intendant* and as a minister he made a great effort to put into practice the teaching of Quesnay. The Economists had a considerable influence on the course of the French Revolution, but never approached the importance of the followers of Rousseau and Voltaire.

When the great change had come the Revolution crystallised its aims in the triple watchword of 'Liberty, Equality and Fraternity.' All three words, but especially the first two, are difficult of definition, and they enlarged their meaning as the movement went on and have not yet ceased to enlarge it. At first by Liberty the French meant the security of the individual as against the action of the State; by Equality they meant equality of rights before the law and the abolition of privilege. The Fraternity that they thought of was chiefly among individuals and was exemplified in many an enthusiastic gathering on the eve of 1789, where nobles and peasants fraternised together. The thinkers of the time were not concerned much with international affairs nor with fraternity among nations. But two thinkers—Kant and Rousseau—saw the urgency of the problem and made some contribution to it. Rousseau wrote in 1756 a treatise on 'Perpetual Peace,' founded on the earlier work of Saint-Pierre, but embodying his own ideas and projects. He looked to a European confederation to establish that peace and security from the horrors of war of which he speaks with a noble emotion. He proposed that the sovereigns of Europe should found a perpetual and irrevocable alliance; that there should be a permanent

Diet of their plenipotentiaries; that all should guarantee each against attack on their rights and territories; that any Power who did so attack should be put to the ban of Europe and crushed by the forces of Europe; that the Diet should work not merely for the preservation of peace, but for the general advantage of the human race. Kant reproduced these suggestions with little essential difference in 1795. It will be seen that they had to wait for more than a century and a half before an attempt was made to realise them in the League of Nations.

CHAPTER II

THE FRENCH REVOLUTION IN PEACE

LOUIS XVI, the last King of France to rule under the conditions of the ancient régime, came to the throne in 1774. He was guillotined rather less than twenty years later, and there is a danger of letting that tragedy and all that it symbolises influence unduly our judgment of the first fifteen years of the reign. We are apt to think that France engrossed the attention of Europe and that the atmosphere was heavy with the coming storm. But, in truth, the overmastering figure in the eyes of Europe was Frederick of Prussia. His wars were over and had left him and his state with a high reputation for discipline and success in war. The military and territorial ambitions of Prussia were, for the time, satisfied. The first partition of Poland, carried out in 1772 without the use of arms, had given more to Prussia than the long and tense struggle of the Seven Years' War. When in 1778 a difficult question arose as to the succession in Bavaria, in which the interests of Austria and Prussia were at variance, the conflict was settled by negotiation. Frederick's chief energies were now devoted to the promotion of commerce and industry, and to the building of the Prussian administrative system—autocratic, rigidly honest, and as efficient as any system can be that does not recognise the necessity of liberty. The new hopes of the age found a good deal of acceptance in Germany. Voltaire had been for some time a resident at the Court of King Frederick, and to Goethe and to Schiller and the thinkers of Germany the writers of France were a stimulus, sometimes to imitation and sometimes to opposition. But the Prussian king went on with his work, cynical and harsh in his manner and speech, but fundamentally in considerable sympathy with the new ideas.

In France the new reign of Louis XVI seemed to mark the coming of a better time. It was with real relief to nearly all classes in France that the reign of Louis XV came to an end. The licence of his Court had not been redeemed by success abroad, and, though France had enjoyed an immense prestige through her writers, the Court and Government had not profited by it, for the thought of France was as unfavourable to the system of Louis XV as it had been friendly to the régime of Louis XIV. The advent of the new king was welcomed because it was in any case a change, but there was also much to make Louis XVI popular. He was himself touched by the humanitarian hopes of the time and was ready for a change of system. He claimed for himself in the early years of his reign and in his last hours that 'he loved the people,' and history sees no reason to reject the claim. His wife, Marie Antoinette, was an Austrian princess, the daughter of Maria Theresa, a kind-hearted, brilliant, and really beautiful woman. Her Austrian origin was a disaster, both to herself and her husband. It made her unpopular in the country when France again came into antagonism with Austria (during the Revolution she was constantly denounced as 'the Austrian woman'), and it prevented her from understanding France or sympathising, as her husband did, with the new ideas; while her will, much clearer and stronger than his, made her a powerful and dangerous counsellor for him in his hours of crisis. But these considerations belong to a much later period. On the accession of Louis XVI France entered on a long and sincere effort under the presidency of the Monarchy to alter the character and aim of the Government, and at first found much enthusiastic support from the governing and the literary classes.

Humanitarianism counted for much in this effort; but the old system was in any case untenable, for the simple reason that it was not able to pay its way. Commerce and industry lagged far behind the great achievements of England. The land of France was rich and productive, but the system of privilege—which relieved the Nobility and the Clergy and those attached to the Court from a large part, though not from all, of the taxation that they should have borne—made it impossible for the Government to use this wealth to meet their liabilities. The Revolution, or some revolution, would probably have come in France in any case; but it is through the channel of the financial needs of the state that it did actually arrive. The expedients employed to meet the expenses of the great wars of the eighteenth century had thrown the financial system of France into hopeless disorder. The first need was to balance income and expenditure, and that, as it turned out, could not be done without a complete change in French methods of government.

In Louis XVI's first Ministry Maurepas held the first position, but the name of Turgot, who was Controller-General of Finance, attracted most attention. He was a disciple of the Economists. His character and his writings had already made him well known, and he had had valuable experience as *intendant* of the province of Limousin. He was only in office some twenty months, and what he did had little permanent effect; but men looked back to this short period as the time when there was a chance that reforms, wisely planned and vigorously carried out, might avert the catastrophe of the Revolution. He wanted to introduce honesty and efficiency into the public services—a real revolution this; to check the dangerously great power of the Church; to introduce a

juster method of taxation; to establish freedom of trade within and beyond the bounds of the kingdom. He did not recognise the necessity of
taking the people into partnership by the calling of any national
assembly, though this was recommended to him by some of his colleagues. He worked at his schemes with a passionate zeal for justice and
humanity. But his proposals aroused alarm in the classes whose interests seemed threatened. A Court cabal was formed against him, in
which Marie Antoinette played a part, and Louis was not strong enough
to uphold his Minister when he had become unpopular. Turgot was
dismissed, and Necker became Controller of the Finances.

Necker was a Genevese banker and a Protestant. His appointment
as Controller of the Finances raised certain difficulties which were overcome by the exercise of the royal prerogative. He made the King's
course easier, too, by renouncing the salary attached to the post. He
was for a long period—down to 1790—the most popular of the public
men of France; his unselfishness, his honesty, the belief that he represented the popular aspirations of the time and his connection with the
literary world all contributed to this. He was a skilful financier, but not
a great statesman. He accepted the administrative and financial system
of France as it stood, and hoped, without introducing fundamental
change, to carry on the government by means of economy and of loans,
which his financial knowledge and reputation allowed him to contract
at a cheaper rate than previously. All these efforts left little permanent
trace on the history of France, and lie outside the limits of this book.
For while he was in office there occurred a great event beyond the
Atlantic, which exercised a powerful influence on European affairs.
The tension between the British Government and the American colonies
led to open rebellion in 1775. The Governments of France and of
Great Britain had been constantly hostile during the eighteenth century,
and in the wars between them France had lost to England nearly the
whole of her colonial and Indian possessions. The memory of her defeats made France ready to seize the opportunity for retaliation that
was thus clearly offered. The Government at first hesitated, fearful of
the expense and afraid of the naval power of its rival. But private enterprise compensated to some extent for the inaction of the Government.
Lafayette—courageous, romantic, and full of noble sympathy for the
American cause—led across a band of volunteers. Americans have
never forgotten this generous adventure, and its memory has been a
force that has never ceased to draw the United States to the side of
France. Public opinion soon forced the French Government to support
Lafayette's effort by the action of the state. What followed is a matter
of the utmost importance for world-history and had an important bearing on the French Revolution. The help of France contributed decisively to the triumph of the American cause. Other European nations
joined in a protest against the naval supremacy of Great Britain. The
British fleet was defeated by the French off the coast of America, and

so—as a direct consequence—came the surrender of Yorktown and the creation of a really New World. There was much in the struggle that left a deep impression on the minds of Frenchmen. An army of citizens had beaten the 'mercenary' soldiers of England. The Constitution of the United States was in process of construction. It was begun by the Declaration of Independence, through which the ideas of Rousseau rang unmistakably; the construction was carried on under the influence of Montesquieu's 'Spirit of the Laws' (the even deeper debt to the English Constitution was naturally kept in the background). The Liberty of which France wrote and talked and dreamed so much had arisen splendid and victorious beyond the Atlantic. The belief was strengthened that the soil of France might see movements and triumphs of the same kind.

But the most immediately serious result of the American War was on the finances of France. Necker's careful economies were insufficient to meet the expenses of the war. He issued a statement of the financial situation of France—his *compte rendu*. Both the accuracy and the motives of this publication have been questioned. But it was an appeal to public opinion, going quite beyond the ordinary administrative circles which had hitherto alone concerned themselves with finance. It was widely read and discussed. The royal circle regarded the step as dangerous, and Necker was dismissed from office (1781)—to return again when the storm was about to burst.

There were still eight years before the Revolution came, and there was nothing in the condition of France that made it impossible for the Government to set the finances in order. The wealth of the country was by no means exhausted. We have said already that there is no ground for thinking that France was distinguished from the other countries of Europe by the poverty and misery of her population. The Monarchy as an institution was still accepted by nearly all, and really popular with a large proportion of the people of France. Frederick the Great of Prussia had shown what might be done by a capable and resolute king in a situation far worse than that of Louis XVI. But Louis XVI was the very antithesis of Frederick the Great. His was a gentle, pious, kindly nature, without any of Frederick's demoniac energy; and the machine of French government was clogged by a long tradition of privilege and corruption. The iron will which alone could have made it work for national ends was altogether lacking in the occupant of the French throne. The charge, often brought against Louis XVI, that he resisted the Revolution too long and thus brought about his tragic end is almost the opposite of the truth. It was not inflexibility but weakness of will that was his bane. Out of weakness and out of genuine humanitarian sympathy he allowed the Revolution to come. When it had come, and in a shape very different from what he expected, he intrigued weakly and treasonably against it. So came for him deposition and prison and the guillotine.

Calonne was Finance Minister from 1783 to 1787. He was popular at the Court, with whose expensive pleasures he did not attempt to interfere; for he believed that an expensive Court made borrowing easier, and he lived by borrowing at an increasingly high rate of interest. Even to Calonne it became plain that the Monarchy could not solve the financial difficulty without taking some part of the people into its confidence. He went back to the traditions of the Monarchy of the sixteenth and seventeenth centuries and summoned a body of 'Notables,' who were men summoned by the King at his own choice to give him advice on any subject he might bring before them. They were not a constitutional body, nor representative in any way. They consisted of members of the privileged classes, and it was hoped that they would suggest the taxation of their order. They declined to do so; and said that the States-General should be summoned as alone capable of dealing with the needs of France.

The States-General—that is to say, a body representative of the Clergy, Nobility and Commons of the whole State, as distinguished from the States-Provincial which only contained representatives of a single province—had not been called since 1614. Their real character therefore was only known to the antiquarian and the historian. When the Monarchy had been weak they had often challenged its power: the triumph of the Monarchy under Richelieu had led to their disappearance. There was widespread enthusiasm for election and representation at the time, and the mind of France turned naturally to the one national institution in her past which had both these characteristics. And yet the States-General, in their traditional shape, were but ill-fitted for dealing with the national emergency. The three Estates—the Clergy, the Nobility, and the Commons—had each sat in separate rooms, and there had thus been two privileged Chambers, while the unprivileged Commons had only one. What was even more important they possessed no powers: they could only put forward demands and make suggestions: the government of France had never conceded them any share in taxation or legislation. Each member brought from his constituency a statement of grievances (*cahier des doléances*). The business of each 'estate' was to draw up a general statement of their wishes and to present it separately to the Crown. When this had been done their work was over. It is a far cry from such a body to the contemporary British Parliament: a still further cry to the omnipotent convention which was soon to direct the destinies of the French Revolution.

Calonne fell in 1787. He was succeeded by Cardinal de Brienne, the last of the long list of Cardinal politicians that the old French Monarchy employed. He advocated a policy which if it had been adopted earlier and carried out vigorously might have led to success. He proposed to use the royal power to impose taxes on the privileged classes: and no constitutional lawyer in France could deny that the royal power extended to taxation. Yet the project failed. A body of lawyers—the strangely named Parlement of Paris—had the duty of registering the King's edicts and until they were thus registered they were not valid. Strong in the assurance of popular support the Parlement refused to register. The King used all the means that had been effective in the past; but in vain. Public opinion had become a real political force as it has never been before in France. Voltaire and his companions in arms had roused the French people to a consciousness of their strength. If there had been a strong King—a Henry of Navarre, a Louis XI or a Louis XIV —the Monarchy might have emerged, changed but strengthened. Yet Louis XVI in face of the popular excitement and opposition took a wise step. He dismissed de Brienne, he recalled Necker, and he announced his intention of summoning the States-General. They were summoned first for 1788: but they actually met at Versailles, some twelve miles from Paris, in May 1789.

A King had been driven by national bankruptcy to call the representatives of his people into council. There was nothing necessarily catastrophic in such a situation; nothing that seemed necessarily to mark a new era in the world's history. England could show how Monarchy and the representatives of the people might work together for the good of the nation. Why should not France reach the same goal?

There were no more critical days during the French Revolution than the first weeks of the States-General. There had been much discussion as to their constitution and procedure: and through the influence of Necker the Commons had got some 600 representatives, while the Clergy and the Nobles had about 300 each. But a difficult question of procedure still remained. How were the 1200 members to sit and debate and vote? Were they to sit in three Chambers and decide questions by a majority of Chambers, or were they to sit all together and decide by a majority of individual votes? The first method would give a majority of two Chambers to one for privilege: the second would secure a large majority for reform, for some of the Nobles and many of the Clergy were in sympathy with the Commons. And further, were they to be, as of old, a Council of advice or a real agency of government? And if they governed were they to be an instrument in the hands of the nobility or of the nation at large? The King's decision would probably have been accepted at first; but he had given no decision when the representatives met at Versailles.

Victory of the completest kind rested with the Commons. It was won by the beginning of July 1789, and in these seven weeks we may note the following decisive stages.

First the Commons refused to co-operate with the Government in any way, until the union of all three estates in one Chamber and 'vote by head' were conceded. They refused even to take the preliminary steps necessary to prove themselves legitimately elected until they were joined by the other orders. This system of passive resistance lasted until June 10. They were weeks of great anxiety to the King and his advisers.

The country was falling into very grave disorder. Taxes were not paid. The States-General might be dismissed as stubborn and disloyal; but the financial difficulty would remain as great as ever. So nothing was done. The inaction of the Government gave the Commons confidence. They began to know their leaders and to understand their powers.

On June 10th the Abbé Siéyès—a member of the third estate, celebrated for his study of constitutional forms—proposed that the Clergy and Nobility should be summoned for the last time to join the third estate in one Chamber; and that in case of the refusal of the Clergy and Nobility the Commons should proceed to constitute themselves, and to take action without Clergy and Nobles. The Commons were determined not to yield to the other estates; they felt themselves strong enough to dominate them. Whatever the decision of the Clergy and Nobles, the Commons were determined to take a large part of the government of France into their own hands, and to assume some title which should announce to all the world the power that they claimed. On June 14 the debate began as to what the title should be. Siéyès proposed that they should call themselves 'The National Assembly'; claiming by this very title that they had the right, even though unsupported by the other orders, to speak and act for the nation. Some, and especially Mirabeau, wanted a less challenging title; but on June 17, by an overwhelming vote (491 to 90), they decided for the 'National Assembly.' It was the French Revolution in miniature. The Commons claimed to act for the nation in despite of the King and the Privileged Classes.

Would the Commons make good their claim? The King and his advisers were at last awake to the danger that threatened them. He was persuaded to use an almost forgotten method of procedure in order to force a change of policy on the Commons. In the old days if the King went down in person to the States-General and held a 'Royal Session' it was incumbent that his word must be obeyed. He would hold a Royal Session now: he would announce his will and France would accept it. But the plan failed entirely. The Commons were in no mood for yielding. They were excluded from their Chamber by the preparations for the Royal Session, but they met in a neighbouring Tennis-Court and swore that they would go on with their meetings, in spite of opposition from whatever quarter, until they had 'made a constitution' (June 20). They were encouraged by the action of the Clergy, who were deeply divided in social origin and in their attitude to the claims of the Commons. The Church is sometimes regarded as the implacable foe of the Revolution; but on June 19, by a majority of one, the Clergy had decided for union with the Commons, and on June 22—the eve of the Royal Session—nearly half of them joined the Commons. In the Royal Session, on June 23, the King announced many important reforms in finance and administration and accepted the States-General as a permanent part of the constitution, but he insisted on the 'three chamber' method of debating and voting. He thus surrendered into the hands of the privileged classes, not of the nation. It was a challenge to the Commons and was supported by a scarcely veiled threat that he would use force to crush opposition. Yet the sequel was amazing. When the Commons resisted by refusing to vacate their Chamber, the King declined to support his words by action. Instead he called upon the Clergy and the Nobles to disobey the orders he had given and to join the Commons. On July 2 all the members of the three estates who attended (there were many absentees) met in one Chamber in which the friends of reform were secure of a considerable majority. The courage and sagacity of the leaders of the Commons and the financial needs of the Crown had been the chief causes of this surprising result. But the divided counsels among the King's advisers had also had an important influence. Among them there were some who held that it was best to yield now in order to strike with more effect later.

There were now three main forces in France. First, there was the King and Court, which had surrendered to the Commons. There were elements in this group—we cannot be wrong in counting among them the Queen Marie Antoinette and the King's youngest brother, the Comte d'Artois—who regretted the necessity of the recent surrender and watched for an opportunity of regaining lost ground. Then there was the Assembly which had at different times three different names. First it was the States-General; then, as we have seen, it became the National Assembly; soon it recognised the framing of a constitution as its all-important task and called itself in consequence the Constituent Assembly. A good many of the Clergy and Nobles continued to sit in it, but it was dominated by the Commons. The representatives of the Commons were all drawn from the middle classes; many of them were prosperous and even rich members of the commercial bourgeoisie; the legal profession was strongly represented; there were no workmen nor special representatives of the working classes. They were determined to draw up a political constitution, and their ideas as to its general features were fairly clear. But in social questions they were much less interested and rarely advanced beyond vague and rather sentimental generalisations. These two forces can be clearly seen, but there was a third, important but difficult to define, sometimes vaguely called the People, or the People of Paris, sometimes the Revolutionary Army. For the victory of the Commons had thrown the machinery of the French Government out of gear. Taxes were not paid. In the country there were scores of attacks on the houses of the nobles and gentry. Trade was bad, unemployment was widespread. There were great numbers of half-starving workmen in Paris, whither they had come at the beginning of the Revolution. They were miserable and discontented, excited by the ideas of the times even if they did not understand them, demanding food first of all and generally better conditions of life. They provided the revolutionaries with a valuable and a dangerous weapon; difficult to control, but sometimes quickly responsive to suggestions. The Assembly, an essentially middle-class body, was carried to victory by its undeclared alliance with this force.

The King (we may use the word as a synonym for the Government: it is impossible to determine Louis XVI's personal share in what was done) determined to strike. Troops were ordered to concentrate on Paris, and their march continued in spite of the protest of the National Assembly. On July 11, 1789, all fears and suspicions seemed justified by the news which reached Paris from Versailles that Necker, the popular idol, was dismissed. A royalist *coup d'état* was clearly coming. Paris was in no mood to wait for it. There was no real municipal government in Paris, but the 'electors'—the large committee that had finally chosen the deputies to the States-General—met together and began to organise a government. They created too a Civic Guard, which soon grew to be the all-important National Guard. It was a body of men midway between policemen and soldiers, citizens armed and drilled for the defence of the rights and the property of the people of Paris. The Hôtel des Invalides was broken into and a great store of weapons taken. So Paris had some means of defence. But of more real use than the Civic Guard were the French Guards, regular soldiers quartered in Paris who had become imbued with the spirit of the Revolution and who now openly joined the Parisians. On July 14 the tumultuous forces of Paris—led, if they could be said to be led by anyone, by Camille Desmoulins, a young lawyer, a brilliant writer and, despite his stammer, an effective speaker—attacked the Bastille. The great fortress had no longer any military importance. The garrison was small, the place unprovisioned. But the name of the Bastille had been the symbol of the old despotism, and it might have been made again a means of coercing Paris. A successful attack would be at once a warning to the Monarchy and a demonstration of the city's power.

The attack made no real impression on the fortress; but the Governor, de Launay, through failure of nerve or hopelessness of relief, surrendered in the afternoon. His life was promised him, but he was murdered in the confusion of the surrender. The Parisian army poured in to the great fortress, and almost at once began to demolish it. Its fall did not in any way alter the military situation, and the forces at the disposal of the King were large enough and loyal enough to crush the Paris rising. But again the King yielded, partly through timidity, but more through real feelings of humanity. He came to Paris to express his official sanction of what had been done, and attended a solemn Te Deum in Notre-Dame Cathedral.

The military importance of the fall of the Bastille, as we have said, was nothing, but its political consequences were enormous. The Commons were for the second time victorious over the King. He had been popular at first, but his popularity declined rapidly. Suspicion and distrust had taken its place. The National Assembly felt more secure in its constitution-building. Most important of all, Paris had come into self-conscious existence and had gained an effective government. A full Municipal Government was organised, and the first Mayor was M. Bailly, an astronomer of great distinction, who had been carried away from his scientific work by the enthusiasm of the hour. The National Guards, too, were fully developed, and the famous Marquis of Lafayette became their first commander. The control of the Revolution by Paris had begun.

The Constituent Assembly—for so we must call the National Assembly now—encouraged by these events went confidently on with its work. We will examine the results of that work in a moment. But first we must notice the strange events which three months later completed the work of the fall of the Bastille.

The general features of the situation had not changed. There was a Court which had yielded reluctantly and watched for a chance of recovery; an Assembly confident and hopeful, but suspicious of the King and hostile to the Court; a populace, hungry, excited, a ready instrument for the hands of conspirators. To what extent there was definite organisation of a royalist reaction on the one side, and definite conspiracy against the Monarchy on the other, it is impossible to say. Certainly the mood of Paris was more dangerous than ever. Newspapers had sprung up. The political newspaper was a new phenomenon in France and exercised a great influence. Clubs had been formed to discuss the questions before the Assembly and to mould public opinion. There were moderate and conservative clubs; but the most important were the revolutionary clubs, such as the Cordeliers and the Jacobins. This last came to be one of the great formative forces in the Revolution, rivalling the Assembly in influence, and sometimes coercing it. The presence of unemployment had led to the opening of public workshops—an expedient always attractive and disappointing. The unemployed of France came in great numbers to Paris, and became an intolerable burden on the straitened finances of the country. The workshops were in consequence closed at the beginning of October, and several thousands of men were thrown on the streets to beg or starve.

The doings at Versailles, where the King and Court still resided, provoked angry comment in Paris. A new regiment—the Flanders regiment, consisting mainly of non-French soldiers—had been brought to Versailles, and its arrival had been made the occasion of ultra-royalist talk at a banquet given to the officers. The opinion gained ground that the Court was preparing a blow against Paris. The desire that the King should live in Paris had been strongly expressed before the opening of the States-General, and it was supported now by the public Press. The time had come to carry the wish into effect.

On October 5, 1789, a crowd, which had first demanded 'Bread' at the Hôtel de Ville, was persuaded to march to Versailles and lay its wishes before the Assembly and the King. It arrived there in the afternoon and was followed by Lafayette and the National Guards, which he commanded. The day passed over with petitions and demonstrations that did not seem of great importance. But soon after midnight the palace was penetrated by the crowd. The King and Queen were in some danger, but the arrival of Lafayette secured their personal safety. But Lafayette had himself presented a request that the King should come to Paris to live. And the King again, as usual, thought it wisest to yield. In the afternoon of October 6 he left Versailles, so closely identified with the glories of the French Monarchy, and came to the Tuileries, once the palace of the mediaeval kings of France, but now ill-provided for his accommodation. The Assembly soon followed. Paris henceforth enveloped and controlled the government of France. The Revolution more and more was concentrated in Paris, and in its character reflected the character of the great city.

That is the chief result of the fall of the Bastille and the march on Versailles. But there is another of great importance. What is known as the 'Emigration' had begun. To explain this we must understand that, though the King had yielded, there were large numbers of the nobles who regarded his concessions with contempt and hatred and fear. They refused to live in a France dominated by principles which they detested, and in consequence they withdrew beyond the frontiers; a few to England, but most to the German states on the Rhine, to Mainz, and to Coblenz. Princes of the royal blood took the lead—the King's brother, the Comte d'Artois and the Prince de Condé—and they were followed by a crowd of nobles. In the German towns where they settled they aped the ceremonies of Versailles, talked of the imminent overthrow of the Revolution, and gathered troops in preparation for the day. They declared that the King's concessions to the Revolution were the result of his necessities, and therefore not binding. Their influence was evil in every way. The best hope for France was that the King and the Revolution should be really reconciled and should treat one another with confidence and respect. The 'Emigration' made this difficult, if not impossible. 'There was no event more disastrous for the Monarchy; none more fatal to the development of the Revolution'—writes the greatest of all historians of the Revolutionary period.

Amidst all these alarms the building of the constitution had gone on unceasingly. There were two important preliminaries. First, it was determined to draw up a Declaration of the 'Rights of Man' which should be the basis of the whole constitution. The Declaration was debated throughout August 1789. The following are some of its most prominent clauses:

The representatives of the French people, constituted as a National Assembly, believing that ignorance, forgetfulness, or contempt of the rights of man are the only causes of public misfortunes and of the corruption of governments, have resolved to set forth in a solemn declaration the natural, inalienable and sacred rights of man; in order that this declaration being constantly before all members of the social body may always recall to them their rights and their duties; in order that the acts of the legislative and executive powers being constantly capable of comparison with the objects of all political institutions may on that account be the more respected; in order that the demands of citizens being founded henceforth on simple and incontestable principles may be always directed to the maintenance of the constitution and the happiness of all.

Consequently the National Assembly recognises and declares in the presence and under the auspices of the Supreme Being the following rights of the man and the citizen.

I. Men are born and remain free and equal in rights. Social distinctions can only be founded on public utility.

II. The aim of every political association is the preservation of the natural and imprescriptible rights of man. These rights are liberty, property, security, and resistance to oppression.

III. The principle of all sovereignty resides essentially in the nation. No body and no individual can exercise authority, if it does not take its origin from the nation.

IV. Liberty consists in being allowed to do whatever does not injure other people. . . .

VI. Law is the expression of the general will. All citizens have the right to take a part personally or through their representatives in its formation. . . .

X. No one should be molested for his opinions, even for his religious opinions, provided that their manifestation does not disturb the public order established by law.

XI. The free communications of thoughts and opinions is one of the most precious rights of man. . . .

XVII. Property being an inviolable and sacred right, no one can be deprived of it except when public necessity, declared by form of law, makes it clearly necessary. . . .

It is easy to criticise this famous document. The practical needs of France were urgent and they were neglected during the interminable discussions on 'human rights.' The twentieth century, moreover, no longer talks of the 'rights of man,' the phrase and the idea belonging rather to the philosophy of the eighteenth century. It turned out, too, that some of the principles, so triumphantly enunciated, were decidedly inconvenient when the details of the constitution came to be arranged. Clause 6, for instance, clearly implied universal suffrage, and the Assembly in its later phase was in no mood to grant that. This disparity between principle and practice gave an opening for attack of which the later revolutionists were quick to avail themselves. But, after all, the Declaration of the Rights of Man is the most characteristic example of the nobler side of the Revolution—without which it would not have been the great event in European history that it is. The contrast with the English Revolution has often been pointed out. While the English Parliament in its Declaration of Right enunciated simply the historic and legal rights of Englishmen against the Crown, France based her action on universal principles, and in her Declaration made herself the spokesman of the human race. It is not strange therefore that, while the English Revolution has seemed to foreigners simply a businesslike and successful rearrangement of the constitution, the French Revolution gave a new starting-point for the hopes and efforts of all races and nations. For a quarter of a century the Declaration of the Rights of Man was the watchword and the charter of all the reformers and revolutionists of Europe.[1]

Next, on August 4, amidst a scene of great excitement and enthusiasm, 'feudalism' was declared to be abolished and the privileged classes themselves co-operated in destroying the legal basis of their position. It was a moment of really noble enthusiasm; but when the 'abolition' had been passed it was difficult exactly to define its import. It amounted to this: the Assembly had a perfectly free hand and an open field in their work of political reconstruction.

The constitutional debates are among the most interesting in the history of Europe. The political philosophy of Montesquieu and Rousseau had now to be translated into actual institutions and there was little in the past of France to help the legislators. They were to some extent influenced by the constitution of the United States; but their chief though undeclared model was the English Constitution. Not a single voice was raised to advocate republicanism; benevolent despotism, such as the Prussian, was no longer in fashion: and in England men saw the one great example of the reconciliation of monarchy with popular institutions.

There were hot debates as to the position which should be accorded to the Monarchy. In the end Louis XVI was declared 'King of the French by the Grace of God and the will of the Nation.' In defining his power the Assembly was much influenced by Montesquieu's theory of the 'Separation of the powers'—the view that is, that the executive, legislative, and judicial elements in the State should be kept entirely separate. The King was the head of the executive: he was to appoint the chief officers of the army and the Ministers of State. But, in accordance with the above-named theory and through distrust of the royal power, the Assembly refused to follow the English plan whereby the Ministers have a seat in the Legislative Assembly and are dependent upon its support for their continuance in office. An unbridged gap was thus created between the representatives of the people and the Ministers of the King. If there was divergence of aim between them they could only be brought into harmony by impeachment or by revolution. This point had been passionately argued by Mirabeau, the most constructive and conservative among the popular leaders, but he had struggled in vain for the adoption of the English system. Nor did better luck attend his efforts to give the King of France the right possessed by the Crown of England to veto all legislation. The King received only a suspensive not an absolute veto: that is, he could delay the passing of a measure but only for the space of a session. The position thus accorded him was

[1] It was, wrote Lord Acton, 'stronger than all the armies of Napoleon.' The text quoted above is taken from that prefaced to the Constitution of September 14, 1791, cp. L. G. Wickham Legg: *Select Documents illustrative of the History of the French Revolution*, vol. II. pp. 216–18 (Clarendon Press, 1905).

one of great dignity and influence, with more real power than belonged to the contemporary English Monarchy. But Louis XVI was the descendant of the most powerful of European kings, and what was offered him seemed a great humiliation. The revolutionary settlement in England had only been made possible by a change of dynasty. There were some who thought it might be well to follow the English example here also and to transfer the Crown to the House of Orleans, whose representative, Duke Philippe, had embraced the popular cause with apparent enthusiasm.

The legislative power was to be entrusted to a single Chamber of 745 members. There had been some question of a second Chamber, but it had been voted down by an overwhelming majority. A second Chamber, it was said, would be either the last refuge of the old aristocracy or the cradle of a new one: and France in her present mood wanted no aristocracy of any kind. The franchise was, in direct conflict with the Rights of Man, limited by a property qualification which excluded from the vote the great majority of the artisans of the towns.

The judicial system of France was re-modelled. The judges were to be elected. Torture was abolished. The jury system was introduced.

A clean sweep was made of the old system of local and provincial government. The old historic provinces of France—Brittany, Normandy, Champagne, Guienne, Burgundy, Provence, etc., names even greater in French history than Yorkshire, Lancashire, Kent, or Cornwall in English history—were abolished. In their place came eighty-three 'departments' called after the natural features that belonged to them, without traditions and making no appeal to local sentiment. It seems to most English observers regrettable, but it was intentionally done. The fine local traditions were part of the past that the Revolution was determined to destroy. They stood, too, in the way of that national unity which the Revolution was determined to achieve and which, later, was emphasised by the motto: 'The Republic, One and Indivisible.'

Lastly, we will note the policy adopted by the Constituent Assembly with regard to religion. The question aroused violent passions. The intellectual movement of the century had been constantly directed against the power and claims of the Church of France. With the coming of the Revolution two sections of religious opinion, which had been driven out of sight by persecution, came again into the light of day. There were many Protestants in the Assembly and they had not forgotten all the injustice and cruelty that had been implied by the Revocation of the Edict of Nantes. The Jansenists too—the Methodists of the French Church, as they have been called—were well represented and were eager to settle old scores with the Church and the Monarchy that had so cruelly and so foolishly oppressed them. The intimate union, moreover, which had, since the beginning of the sixteenth century, existed between the Church and the Crown was now a source of danger to the Church.

Now that the absolute Monarchy had gone, the Church, which had been its chief supporter, could not be left unchanged. The first steps were concerned with the property of the Church. Tithes were regarded as a part of feudalism and had been abolished with the rest of it. Then the vast resources of the Church seemed to offer a means of escape from the bankruptcy which threatened the State. Upon the motion of Talleyrand, Bishop of Autun—who now begins his amazing political career—it was decided that the wealth of the Church should be surrendered to the State, and that the State should undertake to maintain the services of the Church and to pay the clergy. It was disendowment combined with a measure of strict establishment. Then the Assembly took the first step on a dangerous slope which was to lead France again to bankruptcy by issuing paper money (the notes were called *assignats*) on the security of the newly acquired property.

There was some protest against all this, but no danger of religious schism. Next, however, the Assembly turned to reorganise the government of the Church which had thus been taken into the pay of the State. The old dioceses were abolished and new ones were established to correspond with the new departments. The stipends of the clergy were rearranged. The bishops received much less than they were used to: the *curés* somewhat more. Then, worst of all, the method of election by all citizens, irrespective of their faith, was introduced into the appointment both of bishops and priests. It was defended as being a return to primitive custom, but when the question was referred to the Pope he denounced the new arrangements and threatened with excommunication all those who adhered to them. The Assembly did not recoil before the threatened conflict. They answered the denunciation of the Pope by enforcing on all clergy an oath of obedience 'to the King, the Law and the Nation.' The Law would, of course, include the new arrangements which were known as the 'Civil Constitution of the Clergy.' The Church was split into two sections: those who accepted and those who refused the new oath—the Dissidents and the Constitutionalists. At first the State generously accorded a pension to those priests who felt themselves unable to take the oath.

Among the evil consequences of this ecclesiastical legislation two are chiefly to be noted. First, it divided the people of France in their feelings towards the Revolution as they had not been divided before. The nobles who had 'emigrated' had, in effect, declared war upon it; but their opposition would rather strengthen the adhesion of the mass of the people. But now the seeds of division were sown throughout the country and they produced actual civil war before long. Next, the King, who had accepted the Revolution with hesitation, but still had accepted it, now found himself in decided opposition to it. The religious fibre in his nature was very strong. He gave his signature to the Church laws for fear of the storm of protest which his veto would have created; but the denunciation by the Pope made him profoundly uneasy. 'I ask

God,' he wrote, 'to accept my profound repentance for having affixed my name, though against my will, to acts which are in conflict with the discipline and the belief of the Catholic Church.'

The ecclesiastical legislation was among the chief causes which impelled the King to his disastrous flight from Paris. At Easter 1791 he tried to go to his palace of St. Cloud (seven miles from Paris) to avoid receiving the Communion at the hands of a 'constitutional' priest. His way was barred by a suspicious crowd, which refused to give way even to the appeals of Lafayette. After this it was clear that the King was a prisoner in his palace at the Tuileries, and the tone of the press was growing even more hostile and suspicious. The boasting of the emigrant nobles that they would soon come and liberate him was a serious cause of annoyance and danger to the King. It had long been a fixed idea with him that he ought to get away from Paris and revise and alter the constitution. The Marquis of Mirabeau, before his death in April 1791, had strongly urged that the King should boldly and openly go to Rouen, summon the Assembly to his side, and make certain changes in the constitution; but to do all this in such a way that his loyalty to the main principles of the Revolution should be beyond question. But neither the King nor the Queen really trusted Mirabeau. They inclined to think him a demagogue who had come over to the side of the Monarchy for selfish ends. His death destroyed the last chance of his plan being carried out. But more than ever the King was bent on escaping from the hateful restraint of Paris. His design was to get into touch with General Bouillé, who commanded the French armies on the north-eastern frontier, and with the backing of the armies to dictate the changes in the constitution that he desired; especially to annul the ecclesiastical legislation and to grant greater power to the nobility; and if necessary to appeal to the support of the Great Powers of Europe.

It was by no means a wild scheme and it came very near to success. Disguised as a servant of his children's governess, he escaped with the Queen and his children unnoticed from the Tuileries. He found a travelling carriage outside the city, and he reached Varennes, a small town on the Meuse. On the other side of the bridge he would have been in safety, but he had already been detected, and he was arrested by the mayor and an inn-keeper from a neighbouring village.

The greatest alarm prevailed in Paris when the King's flight was known. He had left a letter declaring his refusal to accept the constitution, and a foreign war was believed to be imminent. The news of his capture allayed these fears, but raised problems of the greatest difficulty. What was to be done with a runaway king? The example of James II of England and his fortunate escape suggested to some that it would have been well if Louis XVI, too, had managed to get away. There were some who advocated a change of dynasty and the recognition of the Duke of Orleans as king. But the majority of the Assembly determined to bring the King back to Paris, to suspend him from his royal functions until the constitution had received its last touches, and then to offer it to him for his acceptance. If he accepted he would be King once more; if he refused he would lose the throne, and the question of his successor would have to be faced. Such was the decision taken by the Assembly, but there was a small minority in the Assembly, supported strongly in Paris, which demanded the King's instant deposition and the declaration of a republic. Before this there had hardly been a sign of republican feeling. But now a petition was drawn up by the Cordeliers Club and placed on a table in the Champ de Mars for signature. There was nothing illegal in this; but disorder was feared, and Bailly, the Mayor of Paris, was instructed to disperse the crowd that gathered round the petition. The National Guard was called out and, as the crowd did not disperse at the first summons, a volley was fired and many lives were lost by the shots or in the stampede that followed (July 17, 1791). This became known as the Massacre of the Champ de Mars, and is the starting-point of the movement which in little more than a year made France a republic. Bailly, who had given the order to fire, became the object of the bitter execrations of the populace.

In September 1791 the constitution was completed and was accepted by the King. The Revolution seemed at an end. A constitution analogous to that of Great Britain had been adopted, without much violence or loss of life. Many foreign observers prophesied a peaceful constitutional life for France.

CHAPTER III

THE REVOLUTION AT WAR

IT is impossible to understand the French Revolution if its domestic aspects and developments are considered by themselves. The more its course is examined the clearer does it become that the whole of its later phase was conditioned by the great war which broke out and continued with no real period of peace for twenty-three years. We shall examine in a moment the causes of the war and the steps by which it came upon France. We must first consider the condition of the country at the time of its outbreak.

The new Legislative Assembly came into being in the autumn of 1791. It was decided that no member of the late Constituent Assembly could have a seat in the new one.[1] The fortunes of France were therefore entrusted to a number of men without established reputations or definite party connections. The new Chamber was in consequence weak, and the real influence on the course of events was to be found rather in the newspapers and in the clubs than on its benches.

A great number of the members never definitely belonged to any

[1] v. *supra*, p. 25.

political party, but we may notice the following groupings. The Conservative, or Right, party in the House was known as the Feuillants, and represented in the House the opinions of Lafayette outside. It was perhaps the largest party, but it was soon outstripped in influence by others. The Left, or Radical, side of the House was later on divided into two groups. The first of these groups was known as the Girondists, because several of its leaders came from the Department of the Gironde. They were men, for the most part, young, enthusiastic, and eloquent. Though they accepted the Monarchy for the moment they regarded a republic as the ideal. Their main support was to be found outside of Paris in the provinces and country districts, and later on they came to be the special representatives of the middle class, but at first they were regarded with fear as dangerous and headstrong revolutionaries. Their chief leaders were Brissot, Buzot, Vergniaud, and Roland. The wife of the last named was always an important influence in the councils of the party, and because of her character and her tragic fate she has attracted more attention than any of them. The Jacobins were not distinguished at first from the Girondists. We have already seen the Club from which the party took its name. It was more influential in Paris than in the Chamber, and its leaders—Robespierre, Marat, and Danton—were the most powerful political influences in the city.

The King had the right of appointing a Ministry without regard to the wishes of the Assembly, and he chose his first Ministry from the Conservative, or Feuillant, party. Soon there came violent friction between himself and the Assembly. His flight had destroyed his former popularity, and his influence and his character were alike regarded with distrust by many. Whatever he did was interpreted in the worst sense. When he refused to accept a law condemning to death all emigrant nobles who did not return before January 1792, or when again he refused his consent to a very severe law against the priests who would not take the constitutional oath, this was regarded as a sign of sympathy with the enemies of the Revolution. So strong was the protest against his actions that he thought it best to allow his Conservative Ministry to resign, and he appointed a new one from the ranks of the Girondists. Roland was Minister of the Interior, but the most important name was Dumouriez, who, though not in any way closely connected with the Girondist party, had been appointed to the direction of foreign affairs. And as foreign affairs at this juncture became the all-important question, we must turn to consider them and the way in which France became involved in a foreign war.

The origin of the war has been a matter of dispute ever since it broke out. Some have ascribed it to the ambitions and passions of the Revolution; others to the jealousy and fear of the Great Powers. The situation in Europe had many elements of danger, and yet there was not, certainly at first, any inclination to go to war with France, while France on her side had in her constitution expressly repudiated war except for purposes of defence. Great Britain seemed at first disinclined to renew her age-long struggle with France. At the beginning of the Revolution the general feeling in England had been one of sympathy. It seemed that France was imitating the English example and was choosing a form of government closely resembling our own. A few warning voices were raised, and especially Burke's, maintaining that the spirit of the French Revolution was wholly different from that of the English movement in 1688, and that it threatened by its beliefs and examples the established order in every part of Europe; but such warnings were balanced by the enthusiasm of the poets and the acceptance of statesmen. Both Wordsworth and Coleridge wrote in glowing language of their high hopes when the Revolution broke out. Wordsworth has told us that it was 'bliss in that dawn to be alive' and that 'to be young was very heaven.' Coleridge was so convinced of the greatness of the movement in France that he 'hung his head and wept at Britain's name,' because Britain opposed herself to it. Among statesmen, Pitt was quite ready to co-operate with France, while Fox, on behalf of one section of the Whigs, hailed it with rapture. The English Government was concerned with a movement in Holland, where the governing Stadholder found his authority threatened by revolutionary parties. He entered into an alliance with Great Britain and with Prussia, and as Prussia easily suppressed the revolutionary movement in Holland people attached less importance to the danger from France.

It was in Central Europe that the events were to be found which were soon to lead to war, but even there there was a strong desire to avoid it. The organisation of the Empire was to the last degree inefficient. There was no body which could raise an army or could impose taxes. The Empire was indeed a loose and helpless confederation, and, as we have seen in the first chapter, the strength of Germany was to be found not in the Empire but in the individual states, and especially in Austria and in Prussia. Austria and Prussia were old enemies and still jealous and hostile. The memory of the Seven Years' War and of the humiliation of Austria still rankled at Vienna, and the two Powers did not find it easy to co-operate. Moreover, Austria had many great tasks upon her hands which seemed more urgent than the suppression of the revolutionary movement in France. The career of Joseph II had shaken the social and political condition of the different parts of the loosely constructed Empire, and the immediate need was to bring back calm where at present there was turmoil, and contentment where there was bitter opposition. Belgium was full of revolutionary protest against the attempted changes; Hungary had been on the edge of revolt. There was hardly a province in the Austrian dominions which was not more or less disordered. Austria was most unwilling to add a foreign war to any of these pressing domestic tasks. And more important to her than the development of events in France seemed the crisis in Poland.

We have already seen something of the conditions in Poland, a condition in every way worse than that of France, and we have seen how her weakness had exposed her already in 1772 to the first partition at the hands of Prussia, Austria, and Russia. Since then the prospects of Poland had much improved. Stanislas had been appointed to the Polish throne in 1764 through the influence of the Russian Czarina, Catherine II. He had been the favourite and the lover of the Czarina, but in his new task he displayed real energy and public spirit. He saw that the future of Poland was hopeless while she still possessed her hereditary constitution, which condemned her to anarchy and exposed her helplessly to the assaults of her neighbours. The first thing necessary was to give her a constitution that should really be efficient, that should sweep away the anarchical privileges of the nobility, and be able to pass laws and to direct the foreign affairs of the country. Such a constitution was brought forward by the King and received a certain measure of support, but according to the old constitution it was possible for a very slight opposition to wreck a strongly supported plan. There was no chance of passing the constitution by legal means. Stanislas took the responsibility upon himself and determined to violate the constitution in the interest of the people and the State, and in 1791, by the use of the military forces of the State, he forced through an amended constitution. Poland seemed then to enter upon a more hopeful era, but it was of the essence of the situation that her neighbours did not desire her to grow strong and prosperous. They were themselves the cause of her weakness, and they desired to maintain and increase it. From the time of the adoption of the new constitution, Prussia, Austria, and Russia began to think again of interference and partition. Among these neighbours the most influential in Polish affairs was without doubt Catherine II of Russia. If others had hesitations, she had none. She clearly and self-consciously desired to embroil the other Powers in French affairs in order that, whilst they were occupied in the west, she herself might lay hands upon the Polish provinces that she coveted. The other Powers were not without suspicion of her plans; and the international relations of these all-important months and years were governed by the fact that there were in Europe two critical centres of anxiety. For whilst the Powers watched with alarm the development of revolutionary and republican movements in Paris, they were even more concerned with what was happening in Poland. French events might indirectly threaten their institutions or their power, but they were anxious above all things that Poland should not be dismembered in such a way as to upset the Balance of Power in Europe by giving an unfair share of Polish territory to any one of the Great Powers. Russia, Austria, and Prussia watched one another therefore with the utmost jealousy, and were thus prevented from any effective co-operation against France. This is one clue to the amazing triumph of the French Revolution against the European alliance.

The relations between France and the Empire had been difficult for some time past. Decisions which seemed at first sight to be purely domestic in character had affected the foreign relations of France. The abolition of feudalism, for instance, had taken away feudal dues from German subjects who possessed landed properties within the French frontier. The religious legislation of the Assembly had deprived the Bishops of Cologne and of Mainz of tithes which they had hitherto received from French subjects. The reorganisation of the bishoprics of France had taken from their obedience parishes and districts which had long been theirs. All these were questions which were bound to raise friction between France and her German subjects, and the Empire, as in duty bound, had championed the claims of the Germans who alleged themselves to be injured. Then, too, the French had their grievances against the Empire. We have seen how after the fall of the Bastille, and again after the days of October 1789, a considerable number of the princes and nobles of France had fled, in fear or in disgust, from the hated Revolution, and the majority of them had taken up their residence in the German states on the eastern frontier of France. There at Trier and at Mainz, they kept the semblance of a Court, recruited and drilled soldiers, issued manifestos and talked of the coming restoration of the ancient régime. It was impossible for France to tolerate this challenge, contemptible though it might be. She had called upon the Emperor Leopold to disperse these *émigrés*, and he had expressed his willingness to do so. But they had not left German territory and France still nursed a grievance because of their residence there.

Then there had come the flight of the King from Paris, his arrest at Varennes, his return, his imprisonment, and his humiliation. It was not possible for Leopold to regard these events without anxiety, if only because Marie Antoinette was his sister; and yet he had no desire and no intention to undertake military interference. He hoped that something might be done for the French royal pair by a diplomacy which threatened but did not really intend war. He made overtures to Frederick William, the King of Prussia, a man of strange character and of somewhat unbalanced mind, readily accessible however to the appeal of sentiment and chivalrous ideas. They met at the Castle of Pillnitz (August 27, 1791), not far from Dresden, on the Elbe, and there they first settled various outstanding differences which had kept the two nations from agreement; then turning to French affairs they determined to issue a declaration, the so-called Declaration of Pillnitz, in which they declared that the restoration of order in France was a matter that concerned all European States and that, *provided other European States would co-operate* with them, they would be willing to interfere to secure for Louis and Marie Antoinette a more tolerable position. Under the cautious language of diplomacy, this declaration seemed at first to carry a dangerous threat. It was really something different, for Leopold did not intend to follow it up by any action. He had left himself a loophole

2

in the quoted phrase because he knew that Great Britain would not co-
operate. He said in a letter to his Minister '*then* and *in that case* have
been for me the law and the prophets; if England fails us the cause for
interference does not occur.' But Frenchmen were unaware of the
inner diplomatic meaning of the Declaration. It seemed to them that
the Monarchies of Europe were threatening interference in the domestic
affairs of France, and they were not more inclined to feel kindly to their
King because the threat was made on his behalf.

It was at this juncture that the Girondist Ministry came into office,
and the Girondists were generally in favour of a foreign war. Madame
Roland regarded war as the force that was necessary to raise the feeling
of France into republican enthusiasm and to overthrow the Monarchy.
Dumouriez, the Minister of Foreign Affairs, dreamed of a diplomatic
alliance that should give France an excellent chance of success. He
hoped for the support of Great Britain and of Prussia; he even entertained the idea that the French armies might find in the Prussian Duke
of Brunswick a commander who would lead them to victory according
to the best traditions of the strategy of Frederick the Great. As the
negotiations with Austria progressed the passion of France grew much
inflamed. There was a widespread readiness for war, and an outspoken
opposition was only to be found among those who later came to be
extreme Jacobins, men like Marat, Danton, and Robespierre. No wiser
speech was made during the whole course of the Revolution than that
in which Robespierre argued against the wisdom of the war, expressed
his opinion that immediate success was improbable, and that it could
hardly be fruitful either in France or in Europe of consequences favourable to the Revolution. But it fell on deaf ears, and even the Royalists
in France welcomed the idea of a war. They believed that in war the
need would be felt to strengthen the executive, and that this would make
for the restoration of the royal power to something of its old strength.
Under such circumstances the negotiations with Austria grew more and
more strained and bitter. The Emperor Leopold II died on March 1,
1792. He was succeeded by Francis II, who had neither his experience
nor his soberness of judgment. The demands of the French Foreign
Office were refused, and on April 20, 1792, in accordance with the new
constitution, Louis XVI went down to the Assembly and there, with
tears in his eyes, declared war against Francis, not as Emperor, but as
King of Hungary and Bohemia.

Dumouriez's hopes of alliances were falsified. Great Britain stood
aloof for a time; but Prussia joined herself to Austria. The French had
planned an assault upon the neighbouring Austrian Netherlands, where
they hoped to find sympathetic support for their invasion in consequence
of the revolutionary movements already fermenting there. This, the
first campaign of the revolutionary war, was a complete and humiliating
failure. The troops of France were ill-disciplined; the officers to a large
extent disloyal to the Revolution; the campaign ill-planned. The French

armies penetrated Belgium some little distance, but retreated in disorder to the frontier, and the French had to confess the failure of a campaign on which they had placed high hopes. The failure produced an immediate consequence in Paris. The Ministers and the people entertained great suspicion of the honesty of the King's intentions. They saw in the failure, the consequence not merely of insufficient preparation, but of the treasonous designs of the King. On June 20, 1792, a crowd penetrated the badly guarded palace of the Tuileries, forced itself into the presence of the King and Queen, insulted him by various cries and demands, and held the palace for some little time before it was driven out by the arrival of the National Guard. The incident is in itself without importance, yet it shows us in miniature the causes which led to the overthrow of the Monarchy, and even to the Reign of Terror. There was a dangerous foreign war; there was failure on the frontier; all men felt that the first necessary condition for success was energy and the will to victory in the head of the State. They believed the King lukewarm or treacherous. It seemed essential therefore to force on him a more energetic policy; or, failing that, to remove him from the government of France.

The Legislative Assembly, though not yet one year old, was utterly unable to control the situation. The real leaders of public opinion were not to be found there. It looked on at the development of events, anxious but helpless. In France generally it cannot be doubted that the prevailing feeling of the masses of the people, and especially of the peasantry of the country districts, was conservative, rather than radical. The Revolution had done much for them; it seemed to them to have gone far enough. They were by tradition attached to the Monarchy; they would be unwilling to take any violent action to overthrow the throne. If then action were to come, such action as seemed and probably was necessary for the saving of France, it must come, not from the Assembly, nor from the mass of the people of France, but from a resolute minority. That resolute minority was found among the Jacobins. They were men of various origins, but few, if any, of them were members of the working classes. They differed in opinion on many points and their differences led later to fierce struggles among themselves; but they were united in a fanatical and almost religious devotion to the principles of the Revolution, and in a love for France. It was the pressure of the foreign war and the danger that it brought with it to the principles of the Revolution, which made them determine to overthrow the throne and to seize the government in the interest of the Revolution, and of France, which they regarded as identical. The middle class—the bourgeoisie—had dominated the Revolution so far. Power now passed rapidly into the hands of those who leaned on the support of the Parisian populace; and it was the war that caused this change with all its incalculable results.

The military outlook had grown worse since the failure of the

Belgian campaign. Prussia had joined with Austria, and the Prussian Duke of Brunswick was to lead the combined Austrian and Prussian armies into France. The excitement of Paris under these circumstances can well be imagined. The troops that were raised in the provinces passed in many instances through the capital, and their passage was made the occasion for patriotic demonstrations. Especially was this the case with the troops from Marseilles, who arrived on July 30, and who sang for the first time the patriotic hymn, the 'Marseillaise.'

It is impossible to penetrate all the preparations for the blow that was soon to fall; but we know that a Committee of Insurrection was formed, consisting of some of the less-known Jacobins, and presided over by Danton, who now comes prominently into the story of the Revolution. We know that the assemblies of the forty-eight Sections, which roughly corresponded to the wards of a modern city, were declared 'permanent'—that is, were allowed to sit without any permission from the municipal authority—and that in them, the ultra-revolutionary party had won a predominant influence. We know, too, that the National Guard, once regarded as the mainstay of the middle class, was now thrown open to all citizens and became far more revolutionary in spirit. On July 11 the country was solemnly declared to be 'in danger.' On July 22 further excitement was caused by the hoisting of a black flag over the Hôtel de Ville. On August 3 there was published the manifesto of the Duke of Brunswick, the commander of the invading armies, threatening Paris with total destruction if any further insult were offered to the King. It naturally roused a more aggressive spirit in the people of Paris. The King and Royal family were living all this time in the palace of the Tuileries, and the defence of the palace was entrusted partly to National Guards, whose fidelity was now very doubtful, and partly to Swiss Guards, the traditional mercenary but loyal defenders of the Crown. The expected blow fell in the early hours of August 10, 1792. Then, first, new members elected by the Sectional Assemblies went at one o'clock in the morning and displaced the existing Municipal Council, though many of the old members were retained in the new one. This new Council then summoned Mandat, the commander of the Palace garrison, to report himself at the Town Hall. He was, on his arrival, ordered into arrest, and shortly afterwards murdered. The King early in the morning had reviewed the National Guards, but their cries had shown him how weak a support they would be in the hour of attack. At 8.30 in the morning, when the attack was already visibly threatening, he determined to leave the palace and to throw himself upon the protection of the Assembly. He was admitted into their Debating Hall, and given with his Queen and children a position in the reporters' box. During his absence the attack on the palace took place. The soldiers and the crowd penetrated into the gardens. When they approached the palace they were met by a heavy fire from the Swiss Guards, and would very probably have been driven out of the gardens,

The King, however, from his retreat, heard the firing, and sent orders to the Swiss to surrender, as the struggle was now without meaning. They lowered their arms and began to march off, but a large number of them were killed by the invaders of the palace. After the capture of the palace, the excited mob came to the Assembly, where they demanded the deposition of the King and the declaration of a Republic. It was pointed out that this was impossible under the constitution of 1791; but the King was suspended from his functions, and a new Assembly, to be called the Convention, and to be elected by manhood suffrage, was to come into existence at an early date. It would decide what constitutional change was necessary, but the Republic already existed in all but name.

A little more than three weeks elapsed between the fall of the Monarchy and the September massacres. It is important to see the development of events. First, a new Ministry was appointed by the Assembly, drawn largely from the Girondist party. Roland was Minister of the Interior, Danton was Minister of Justice. We may note, too, that after the receipt of the news of the King's fall, Lafayette attempted to raise an armed protest among the troops. He found, however, that they were not inclined to support the Monarchy against the new revolutionary movement, and he soon felt himself in danger. He left the army, crossed the frontiers, and his part in the history of the Revolution was over. In Paris, meanwhile, the newly appointed Commune or Municipal Council was more important than the Legislative Assembly which was nearly deserted, and had only a few more days of existence. In the Commune Robespierre's was the chief influence. He demanded that the examination of crimes against the State should be attributed to the Commune, and the demand had to be granted. A Committee of Supervision, a kind of special Executive Committee, was also appointed, in which Marat was the guiding force.

The news from the frontier grew worse day by day. The fall of Longwy was known on August 26. It was reported, though prematurely, that the great fortress of Verdun had fallen too. The fever and the suspicion in Paris mounted daily higher. On August 28 Danton, as Minister of Justice, demanded that power should be given to him to search the houses of Paris for enemies of the Revolution, and by this means during the next three days some thousands of suspects were seized, and the city prisons were crowded to overflowing with men of various kinds; some innocent; many doubtless really guilty of conspiracy for the restoration of the Monarchy; all suspect of the crime of opposition to the Jacobin power. The position of the Jacobins was critical in the extreme. Danton in a well-known speech gives us the key of the situation. The Revolution, he said, was between two fires, the enemy at the frontier and the enemy at home. In order to survive, **it** was necessary 'to frighten the enemy.'

On September 2, Sunday, the business of frightening the enemy

began. An extemporised tribunal was established by the Commune in
the prisons of Paris. Prisoners were brought before it, more usually in
batches than singly. They were roughly examined. Some effort was
doubtless made to distinguish between the real enemies of the Revolution and others. If they were thought to be innocent, they were sent
back to prison; if they were regarded as guilty, they were ordered to be
removed to another prison. This was a sentence of death. They were
thrust out into the street and murdered by those who were prepared for
the work. In this way during September 2, and the two following days,
many hundreds of people were killed in Paris; the exact number it is
impossible to calculate. As to the origin, the responsibility and the aim
of the September massacres there has been and there will long be discussion and controversy. It is clear, however, that whoever else was
innocent, Marat was guilty, and that it is to the Committee of Supervision that much of the organisation and execution can be traced, though
the passions of the revolutionary populace, inflamed by the bad news
from the frontier, doubtless made very little organisation or direction
necessary. The massacres sprang rather from passion than from policy;
they were a wild stroke at suspected enemies, at a moment when enemies
were believed to surround the revolutionary leaders on all sides. Very
soon even the most ardent of revolutionaries were anxious to free
themselves from any share in the responsibility for the 'September
Massacres.'

This same month of September 1792, saw also events of the greatest
importance on the frontier. The victory of the Allies seemed assured,
and the early occupation of Paris was confidently prophesied, but quite
apart from the enthusiasm and courage of the French armies there
were secret causes weakening and endangering the Allies. Austria and
Prussia, though united against France, were at variance with regard to
Poland, and it is certain that fears of what might happen in Poland had
prevented the Allied armies from reaching anything like their projected
strength. There was also difference of opinion between the Duke of
Brunswick and King Frederick William of Prussia, as to the conduct of
the campaign, the King urging a rapid stroke, Brunswick advising care
and caution. The armies that France opposed to the invaders consisted
only to a very small degree of the new recruits. The chief command was
in the hands of Dumouriez, and he had to rely chiefly upon the old army
officered to a large extent by men out of sympathy with the Revolution,
and irritated by many grievances, but the rank and file were largely
moved by real enthusiasm for the Revolution. The fortress of Verdun
fell on September 2; the road to Paris seemed open, but the lines of the
Argonne Hills, which lay on the road to the capital, were occupied by
Dumouriez, on instructions from Servan, the Minister of War, and here
for some time the armies faced one another. When at last the invaders
by means of a turning movement got into the rear of the French, they
found themselves opposed to a new French army on the hill of Valmy.

Here, on September 20, 1792, there occurred an action, famous and important because of its results, but not worthy of the name of a great battle. The Prussians cannonaded the hill, and then tried to take it by direct assault. They were repulsed with some loss, but this small event was magnified by what followed into one of the decisive battles of the world. For there followed negotiations between Dumouriez and the Duke of Brunswick, full of subtlety and fraud on both sides. The Duke of Brunswick consented to retire and Dumouriez, believing that the Prussians might even now be induced to separate themselves from Austria, allowed him to reach the frontier in safety. But all this is of little importance compared with the fact that Paris which, on September 20, believed itself in imminent danger of attack and perhaps of blockade, found itself by this stroke liberated and triumphant.

The elections for the new Convention had begun about the time of the September massacres. It was believed at first that the result was a great victory for the moderates. Very many voters had abstained from the poll. Of the members returned only some fifty were declared Jacobins, one hundred and twenty were Girondists, and over six hundred were not definitely attached to either party. The new Convention appointed the Ministers and from the first gave executive power into the hands of committees.

The first thing to be decided was the fate of the King, and the decision came quickly. On September 21, 1792, by a unanimous vote the Monarchy was declared to be abolished and a republic established. Then came the question of the King's trial. There seemed no legal basis for his trial. The constitution had declared the loss of the throne the legal penalty for certain offences and especially for failure to resist a foreign invasion. He had perhaps committed the offence but he had certainly paid the penalty. What further charge could be brought against him?[1] It was clear, however, that the dominant party of the Assembly would not allow legality to bar them from their object, and the King's trial was decided upon. The indictment was presented on December 11, and the King was charged with plotting against the nation, with paying the troops raised by the *émigrés* abroad, and with attempting to overthrow the constitution. He was allowed counsel and was daringly and eloquently defended. The votes of the Assembly were given individually and openly, and by a unanimous vote he was declared to be guilty. By a majority of one only, the capital penalty was decided, and, on January 21, 1793, he was guillotined in what had

---

[1] The two decisive clauses in the constitution are Chapter II, Section I, articles vi and viii [*v.* L. G. Wickham Legg: *Select Documents illustrative of the History of the French Revolution*, vol. II. p. 226 (Clarendon Press, 1905)] :

'If the King puts himself at the head of an army and directs its forces against the nation, or if he does not formally resist such an enterprise when made in his name, he shall be judged to have abdicated the crown. . . . After such abdication, the King shall belong to the class of citizens and may like them be accused and judged *for acts posterior to his abdication.*'

formerly been the Square of Louis XV, now re-named the Square of the Republic.

All the future of the Republic turned upon the war. This is really the decisive influence upon every detail even of the domestic history of France, and in spite of the victory of Valmy, the military outlook became rapidly worse. The most serious blow was that shortly after the execution of the King, Great Britain went to war with France. Many influences produced this result, for war rarely springs from a single cause. English opinion had been outraged by the attack upon the King, and still more by his execution: a powerful section of the people was lending a sympathetic ear to the splendid rhetoric with which Burke denounced the character and the aims of the Revolution: but there were more practical reasons as well. After the Battle of Valmy, the French had gained a series of important victories. They had crossed the Rhine at Mainz; more important still, they had invaded Belgium, and, on November 6, in the battle of Jemmappes (a much greater battle than Valmy), they had overthrown the Austrian army, and had by their victory made themselves masters of the whole country. A few days later Brussels fell into their hands. They then took two important and most questionable steps. On November 19 they solemnly declared that they would grant fraternity and help to all peoples who desired to recover their liberty; and this was a plain invitation to all peoples to rise against their governments and a plain menace to all governments who believed that their peoples were anxious to rise against them. Then a little later acting upon the supposed 'natural right' of a people to the possession of the mouth of a river that flowed through its territory, they declared that the river Scheldt, which as a result of many wars and treaties had been closed to the entrance of great vessels, should now be thrown open to all commerce. Great Britain, probably quite mistakenly, had for long regarded the closure of the Scheldt as a matter of the first importance for her commerce, and it has been asserted that she coveted some of the French West Indian islands. Thus sentiment and assumed commercial interests worked together, and when the news of the King's execution reached England, the French Ambassador was dismissed, and on February 1, France anticipated England by declaring war against England and Holland. Spain joined the belligerents almost immediately.

France was thus at war with a great European coalition, which now numbered in its ranks Prussia, Austria, Great Britain, Holland, Sardinia, and Spain. The spring of 1793 saw dangers and disasters accumulating on almost every frontier. The first serious disaster came in Belgium, which had been the scene of the first decisive victory of the Revolution. There had been some readiness in the country to welcome the invaders, but the popularity of the French was soon effaced by the measures which they took for the government of Belgium. They oppressed the Church; they gave forced currency to their paper money.

Worst of all, on the ground of a few petitions offered to them, they declared the country annexed to France. A probable ally was thus turned into a decided enemy. The policy had been dictated from Paris, and Dumouriez, the commander of the French armies, had protested in vain. Now there came to him from headquarters an order to advance into Holland, which he unwillingly obeyed, believing that Belgium was in too dangerous a condition to be left safely in his rear. The earliest stages of the war were successful, but on March 18, 1793, Dumouriez was forced to retreat in order to protect his Lieutenant, Miranda, who had been attacked by the Austrians. The great battle of Neerwinden was fought, and, after a fierce and for a long time not unequal contest, it resulted in the victory of the Austrians. Defeat coming to the French where they had been accustomed to conquer was bad enough, but it was much worse that their commander began at once to treat with the enemy. We have seen that he was already on bad terms with the Home Government. He had never been in real sympathy with the aims of the revolutionaries. He dreamed now of re-establishing the monarchy and giving the crown to the young Duke of Chartres, whose father, in spite of his royal blood, had thrown himself heartily into the revolution. Some suspicion of all this reached Paris and commissioners were sent to the army, but Dumouriez arrested them and went on with his plans. His army, however, refused to support him. He found himself in danger, and on April 5 fled over to the Austrians. The peril had been a very great one, and it left a very great fear behind. It is the second occasion (we have already seen the action of Lafayette) on which an army chief had attempted to raise the army against the Home Government. Fears of treason amongst the officers were henceforth one of the chief alarms of the revolutionists. In the action of Dumouriez, we may see the shadow of Napoleon beginning to pass menacingly across the Revolution.

The foreign situation was dangerous, and its danger was increased by serious disturbance at home. To the south of the Loire, in the district known as La Vendée, a movement broke out which culminated in civil war, and which for two years taxed all the energies that France could spare from the foreign struggle. La Vendée was different in character from the rest of France. The nobility and gentry were resident on their estates. The peasantry were devoted to the Church and not at enmity with the nobles. The country was, to a large extent, covered with forest, difficult to penetrate and easy to defend. At first the revolutionary movement, though not welcome in this backward part of France, had not been resisted, and some of its results had been popular with the peasantry. It was the demand for military service, and the attempt to enforce that demand, which led to rebellion in February 1793. The movement was stimulated by the priesthood, and found leaders in all ranks of society. The best-known names are Cathelineau, a peasant and a hawker, and La Rochejaquelin, a noble of high descent. A young naval officer called Charette had probably more military capacity than

2*

either of them. The Revolution, hard pressed by foreign war, could spare no troops for the west. The insurgents gained great advantages. In March 1793 Fontenay and Niort fell. The movement was clearly a dangerous one.

Against these accumulating dangers the Convention took resolute measures. They gave concentration to the Government; they gave to it a capacity for secrecy and rapidity of action, pushing aside all laws or institutions which were a check upon its effectiveness; and many Frenchmen accepted the action of the Central Government because it was fighting against the common enemy, even though they disliked what it was doing at home. On March 29, 1793, the Revolutionary Tribunal was appointed to deal, by a special procedure, with all those who were accused of hostility to the Government. On April 6 the Committee of Public Safety was appointed, the body which governed France for more than two years, and to which are to be traced most of those measures which gave the country salvation and victory. The Committee of Public Safety consisted of nine members: they had at their disposal a large amount of money to be used for secret services; they could override the action of the Ministers, who were reduced almost to their subordinate agents; they deliberated secretly, and they were only accountable to the Convention when they reported at stated intervals to that body. About the same time also the system of 'representatives on mission' was instituted. These were men appointed by the Convention, sent into all parts of France, nominally to enforce the general levy for the war, really to establish the supremacy of the Central Government in all parts of France. Thus the Revolution, which began by advocating a looser and decentralised form of government, was now, under the influence of the war, swinging back towards the old traditions of centralisation, characteristic of the French Monarchy during the seventeenth and eighteenth centuries.

It was the Girondist party that had suggested the Committee of Public Safety, but the members of the Committee were chiefly drawn from the Jacobins; and from the first the leading influence in it was Danton, already distinguished for the share that he had taken in the overthrow of the Monarchy. The figure of Danton is a somewhat strange one in the history of the Revolution. He was often regarded as one of the most blood-stained of the Jacobins. He had advocated, in the crisis of August 1792, 'Audacity, Audacity, and always Audacity.' Yet the more his career is scrutinised the more clearly do we see that, though he was capable of violent action when occasion seemed to call for it, his constant effort was to prevent the Revolution from falling into the abyss of anarchy and bloodshed which we know awaited it. He desired to return in many ways to ancient methods; he advocated, at a time when it was dangerous to do so, mercy, authority, and respect for government. Jacobin though he was, it was his aim at first to co-operate with the Girondist party, and he made overtures to them for that end.

They rejected them decisively. They had come to regard the Jacobins as a party, not only of violence, but of brutality, and as the antagonists of all their idealistic and philosophic aims. Rejecting the overtures of Danton, they soon found themselves involved in a fierce contest with the whole Jacobin party. It is the first of those contests among the republicans themselves which continuously brought the government into the hands of smaller groups, until they led to the establishment of the personal despotism of Napoleon. In this struggle the Girondists had many elements of weakness. It was Paris that really dominated the Revolution now, and the Girondists represented the provinces and had little support in Paris. They were charged with 'federalism,' which was taken to mean that they wished at this moment, when France was faced by a European coalition, to break up the unity of the country and establish some looser form of government. Some wild threats that were used by one of their party, Isnard, against the city of Paris certainly tended still further to provoke the capital against them. They were weakened, too, by their connection with Dumouriez, who, since the battle of Neerwinden, was always treated as the great traitor. The newspapers of Paris, edited by such men as Marat and Hébert, were opposed to them. In peaceable times the majority of Frenchmen would probably have voted in their favour, but at this particular moment they had no control over the actual forces that counted. On April 24 they brought the most detested of all the Jacobins, Marat, before the Revolutionary Tribunal, but he was acquitted, and the result of the affair was still further to exasperate the revolutionists of Paris against them. They were constant and loud in protest against the action of the Commune, which they declared was plotting against the liberty of the Convention. There was probably some truth in this, but their protest provoked a further attack. On May 31, 1793, a rising of the Paris populace demanded the arrest of the Girondists as enemies of the Revolution. The first rising was dispersed, but a few days later, on June 2, came another. A Parisian crowd, fairly well armed and competently led, surrounded the hall of the Convention, and imprisoned the members until their demands were granted. It was necessary in the end to bow to popular violence, and a large body of Girondists were decreed under arrest and sent off to prison, there to pass through the Revolutionary Tribunal to the scaffold of the guillotine.

With the fall of the Girondists the Reign of Terror, which really began in August 1792, may be said to have reached its culmination. Its essential meaning is that a minority, and a small minority, of resolute men had seized upon the government in an hour of great crisis, and, dispensing with ordinary constitutional forms, pursued exclusively the defence of the country and the maintenance of power in their own hands. There have been many Reigns of Terror in history—many governments, that is to say, which have held power by violence and by frightening their opponents. What is peculiarly ironic about the position of the Jacobins is that their rule, though it rested upon the Revolutionary Tribunal and the guillotine, was exercised all the time in the name of democracy and the sovereignty of the people.

In 1793 the Convention was dwindling in numbers, and its authority was passing over more and more to the Committees. Many of the members feared responsibility and did not attend. It was still, however, the nominal basis of the government of France, and all that was done by the Committees was submitted to its ratification.

The Committee of Public Safety was the all-important institution of France. It had been dominated by Danton up to July 10, and he had devoted himself to the raising of men and the equipment of the army, and to such diplomatic measures as the Convention and his colleagues allowed him. Even his opponents have admitted that the survival of France was largely due to his energy and devotion. Yet on July 10, when, according to the usual practice, the Committee of Public Safety came up for reappointment in the Convention, Danton's name was omitted. It is an obscure incident, partly to be explained by the rather careless temperament of Danton himself, partly by the eager ambition of his rivals. His place in the Committee was soon taken by Robespierre, who had hitherto been known as a follower of the doctrines of Rousseau, and as a persuasive speaker in the Assembly and in the Jacobin Club. He had taken no very prominent part in the overthrow of the Monarchy, nor ought his name to be closely connected with the September massacres. He had eagerly supported the declaration of the Republic and the execution of the King, and from now onwards, until his death in 1794, his was the most prominent name in the history of the Revolution. He remained to the end an idealist, dreaming of a social structure that should be erected in France when the present dangers were removed—a structure that should rest upon virtue and be supported by religion and should establish peace; but for the present he identified himself with those Jacobins who were for maintaining the Reign of Terror and throwing all the energy of the Government into the war against the foreign and domestic enemies of the Revolution. He was an admirable speaker—according to English taste the finest speaker that the Revolution produced—and some of his speeches are masterpieces both of style and of thought. It was as a speaker in the Assembly and in the Jacobin Club that he had most power. He did not show much capacity for the details of administration, but he had devoted friends and colleagues who supplied what he lacked. The Committee of Public Safety now included twelve names. They may be arranged in the following groups: first, a group of five, led by Carnot, which was almost exclusively concerned with the organisation of the army and navy, and only dealt with domestic affairs when it was necessary to do so in the interests of the war; then came the Triumvirate, as they were called—Robespierre, Couthon, and Saint-Just—of whose aims we have already spoken; lastly, there were three men—Barère,

Billaud-Varenne, and Collot D'Herbois—who pursued a line of their own and were usually in close connection with the Commune.

In 1793 the Jacobins brought forward a new and very democratic constitution. This was passed and presented to the people as an indication of the principles that the Jacobins still advocated, and which would guide their actions when peace allowed them to satisfy their true instincts, but the constitution was hardly brought forward before it was suspended.

During all this time the Revolutionary Tribunal was hard at work, and it was much helped by the Law of Suspected Persons, passed in September 1793, which allowed arrest and imprisonment without any proof of guilt. The prisons were crowded, and constantly men and women were brought before the Revolutionary Tribunal. Acquittals were rare, and the guillotine was the universal penalty. Among the most notable victims was, in October, Queen Marie Antoinette; Danton would have saved her life, for he believed that she might have been of use in bargaining with the enemy. But the passions of the hour were too strong; she was regarded as the chief enemy of the Revolution, and she followed her husband to the guillotine. On the last day of October a large batch of Girondists were executed. On November 6 Philippe, Duke of Orleans, who had championed the Revolution, had lent his palace to the agitators, and voted for the King's death, was nevertheless put to death. His connection with Dumouriez weighed heavily against him. On November 10 Madame Roland was executed, the charming and eloquent lady who had been a social centre for the Girondist party. On November 12 Bailly, astronomer and first president of the National Assembly, met his death for having given the order to fire upon the crowd that petitioned in 1791 for the declaration of the Republic. We may specially note that certain generals, such as Custine and Biron, were guillotined, charged either with treason or with slackness in pursuit of the enemy.

In August 1793 a *levée en masse* was ordered—all citizens were called upon, that is, to give their military services to the State. But by Danton's influence this was reduced to the more manageable shape of the conscription of all between the ages of eighteen and twenty-five. By this measure nearly half a million recruits were added to the army.

Lastly, we may notice that in September 1793 was passed the Law of Forty Sous, whereby this sum was given to all those who attended the political meetings of the Parisian Sections or Wards. It proved a valuable incentive to the support of the Jacobin party.

Thus in Paris was established a government, fierce, resolute and, except for the divisions in its own ranks, strong. It had dangerous enemies to face, both domestic and foreign. A great civil war had broken out in addition to the Vendean war. This had been caused largely by the fall of the Girondist party and the fear that the new Government would be hostile to the provinces. It was believed at first that the greater number of the provinces of France had risen in rebellion against the capital and that an overwhelming majority of the people of the country were prepared to rise and crush the Jacobins. But this civil war was soon reduced to comparatively small dimensions. Lyons was in rebellion, and Toulon had not only declared against the Government but opened the harbour to Admiral Hood and the English fleet. Against both places the Jacobins sent considerable forces. Lyons was stormed in September 1793, and a cruel punishment was exacted from the inhabitants of the city. The army that advanced on Toulon had a harder task to face, for the inhabitants were assisted by the crews of the British and Spanish ships. The French Commander was Dugommier, but the chief attention of posterity has been given to the action of his subordinate Napoleon Bonaparte. The siege lasted some time, but on December 19, 1793, the city was taken and the British fleet forthwith evacuated the harbour, burning the shipping and many of the warehouses before they left.

The Vendean war remained, and was a harder task. In their own country and against the hasty levies that the Republic could send against them, the insurgents proved invincible, and the Republicans were again and again driven back. When, however, victory encouraged them to extend their operations the limits of their powers were soon made apparent. It is true that in June 1793 they managed to take the important town of Saumur on the Loire, and from there they advanced to the attack of Nantes, but the attack on that town was a failure and their leader, Cathelineau, was killed. In July 1793 a much more efficient French army was free to operate against the insurgents, for in that month the city of Mainz capitulated to the Prussians. The garrison was allowed to march out on giving its promise not to fight again against the Allies. This was interpreted as making them free to fight against the Vendeans. When they arrived on the western theatre of war a change was quickly seen. In October 1793 was fought the Battle of Cholet. The Vendeans were thoroughly defeated and their leader slain. Henceforth they struggled against an enemy manifestly superior. They made one more effort to cross the Loire, hoping to penetrate as far as Normandy and secure the help of sympathisers there, but this effort also met with disaster at Angers. The movement would probably have given no further serious trouble if it had not been met with brutal and cruel repression from Carrier, the Jacobin representative. His executions and brutalities stimulated further resistance and the country blazed up more than once into renewed rebellion. When Hoche, one of the new generals who had risen from the ranks, was sent to take charge of the war, he adopted more humane methods. In December of 1794 he granted the Vendeans an amnesty, and in February 1795 the war in the west was brought to an end by the Treaty of La Jaunaie.

The foreign war showed alternations of failure and success; failure in the spring and summer of 1793, and then recovery and victory in the autumn of 1793 and in the years 1794 and 1795. Things were at their worst about midsummer 1793. In July of that year the city of Mainz had been recaptured by the Prussians, whose troops proceeded to invade Alsace. Then, in the same month, the important northern fortress of Condé was taken by the Austrians, Dutch, and English. In August of the same year, as we have seen, the harbour of Toulon was surrendered into the hands of the English Admiral, Hood. Thus the French frontiers were pierced at three important points, and with rebellion active in several districts foreign opinion assumed that the collapse of the revolutionary Government was not far off.

And yet it was not collapse but complete victory that awaited France. Before we glance at the events which show this victory we will briefly consider the question of its causes.

In the first place, France had now an efficient and energetic Government, wholly determined to control the country, and to wage energetic war against the foreign enemy. It was the formation of the Committee of Public Safety, and the control of that Committee by Danton, and the direction of the campaign by Carnot which made the victory of the French armies possible. Carnot had not only infused into the army a new energy, he had also introduced improved weapons, a better discipline, and new ideas in tactics and in strategy. The chief quality of this was the abandonment of a passive defence in favour of a resolute and continued aggressive. The secret of all defence, he said, lay in the counter stroke. It was the adoption in war of Danton's famous phrase, 'Audacity, Audacity, and always Audacity.' New officers, too, were rising from the ranks—men usually drawn from the middle class of society who had been trained indeed in the old army, but who found an opportunity for their talents or their genius in the new conditions. Chief among these were Hoche, Jourdan, Pichegru, and Murat. They were ardent supporters of the Revolution, which alone had allowed them to rise to the highest commands, and they fought against the enemy without any consideration for the Monarchy or the ancient régime. Something of their enthusiasm pervaded all ranks of the army, and enthusiasm counted for much. Yet French military writers are at one in telling us that too much stress must not be laid upon this quality of enthusiasm, that enthusiasm alone will win neither battles nor campaigns, and that the tradition that the French revolutionary wars were won by enthusiasm has on some subsequent occasions materially injured the military plans of France.

To France herself belongs the chief credit for the reversal of the fortune of the war and the winning of complete victory over the Allies. Yet all the causes of this change were not to be found in France. It is most important to recognise that the Allies were by no means a united body; that there was divergence of interest and of aim among them, and that on one question—the future of Poland—the tension between Prussia and Austria was so great as almost in itself to ruin the chances of the campaign. The outline of the Polish question is as follows: the neighbours of Poland had seen with alarm the reorganisation of the State under the rule of King Stanislas. They feared that, if this went on, instead of having as their neighbour a state which they could plunder at their will, they might have to deal with a serious military Power. It was decided in consequence to interfere once more, and again, with or without an excuse, to tear from Poland some of her most valuable provinces. It was in January of the year 1793 that the second partition was agreed upon. Prussia and Russia were to take Polish lands, while Austria was to receive the compensation, which was her due according to the idea of Balance of Power, in Alsace and in Lorraine, when these provinces were won from France. As time went on there was less and less prospect of these provinces being conquered. The attitude of Austria to her allies became therefore one of almost unconcealed hostility, and the three Powers began to think that they might have to use their armies rather on the banks of the Vistula than in the neighbourhood of the Rhine. The second partition was enforced upon the Polish Diet at Grodno in September 1793. Just when a decisive blow was possible against France, Polish affairs rather than French claimed the attention of the Eastern Powers.

It is under these circumstances that the tide of battle turned in favour of France. It is not the object of this book to give any detailed military narrative, but we must notice the outstanding facts. In September 1793 the French army marched to the relief of Dunkirk which was being besieged by an English army under the Duke of York. In the battle fought at Hondschoote the French were completely victorious, and Dunkirk was relieved. It was believed later that if the French Commander, Houchard, had shown greater energy the defeat might have been an overwhelming one, and he was guillotined for his supposed failure. In October 1793 Jourdan gained a victory at Wattignies, and the French troops once more crossed the Rhine. Then in 1794, in June, Jourdan defeated the Allies under the Duke of Coburg at Fleurus. No further effort was made to regain Belgium from the French, and the Prussians, disappointed with their failures and suspicious of the designs of their allies in Poland, were now admittedly anxious to retire from the war. At the end of 1794 the French army was sent again to the conquest of the United Provinces (Holland), which had been attempted in vain by Dumouriez in 1793. This time there was no mistake. The French commander, Pichegru, entered Amsterdam in January; the Dutch navy was ice-bound off the coast and was actually, to the amazement of all Europe, captured by a detachment of French cavalry. The war was not over; but with the spring of 1795 it was fairly clear that France would be able to make terms with, at any rate, some of her enemies.

We must turn from these military triumphs of the French Revolution to its domestic history. The Jacobin party, which had acquired complete victory over its rivals, whether Girondists or Constitutionalists, was now deeply and bitterly divided. We have already seen how, on July 10, 1793, Danton had been left out of the Committee of Public Safety in favour of Robespierre. He still remained an important political figure, but his aims changed with the changed situation, and he who had been reckoned the most vehement and violent of revolutionists became now an advocate of milder measures and of the restoration of order. He was closely associated in these last months of his life with Camille Desmoulins, who was the hero of the attack upon the Bastille, and who, by speech and pen, had been foremost among the advocates of the Revolution in its extremest form. He and Danton, on the benches of the Convention and in the pages of a new journal which they founded —the *Old Cordelier*—recommended, often under the veil of allusion and irony, the abandonment of terror and the return to a system of humanity and of law. These men had a considerable following in the Convention, though they had never again controlled any of the great events of the Revolution.

Another group of politicians consisted of Robespierre, Couthon, and Saint-Just (the so-called Triumvirate), all three of them members of the Committee of Public Safety. They were not chiefly concerned with the management of the war, but rather aimed at controlling the general domestic policy of the Revolution. Robespierre was without question an extremely popular figure in Paris, supported by a large number of admiring and devoted friends. It was the tragedy of his life and the cause of his failure that the attempts which he made for the reconstitution and regeneration of France had to be made in an atmosphere of war and of violence. Their failure was probably in any case certain; it was under the circumstances rapid and almost immediate and fatal to himself. He had, as we shall see, a short hour of triumph, and then immediately came his overthrow. His good qualities must not blind us to his obvious defects; he was a man essentially timid, and like many timid men easily induced to adopt measures of cruelty. He was vain, and his vanity was increased by the admiration of his friends. Thus it comes to pass that the period during which this prophet of humanity and disciple of Rousseau dominated France is also the period when the Reign of Terror was seen at its worst and most destructive.

By the side of these two parties we must place the party that had its chief basis in the Commune or Municipal Council of Paris. The chief names here were Hébert and Chaumette, and from this source emanated many important measures subsequently accepted by the Convention. Not all of their proposals were wild or absurd. It was from them that reforms were introduced into the hospitals and cemeteries of Paris; it was from them that the first idea came of that admirable decimal system of weights and measures which has been adopted by the greater part of the world. This last measure is eminently characteristic of their ideas; they discarded what was traditional; they adopted standards which seemed logical and 'natural': as the unit of measurement, a certain portion of the circumference of the globe; as the unit of weight, a certain portion of its volume. From this party also came the proposal to adopt a new calendar. There was a general feeling that the Revolution marked the beginning of a new epoch. Robespierre himself said that France was 'a thousand years ahead of the rest of Europe.' It was decided to mark the great change therefore by the adoption of a new calendar, and the first day of the first year was to begin with the declaration of the Republic in September 1792. The months were to be re-arranged, and an effort was made, by no means the first in history, to change the curious and unsatisfactory traditional names of the months and to substitute for them titles derived from the physical phenomena associated with them. After the year and the month came the turn of the week; the week of seven days with its Oriental origin and its religious association was to be thrown aside. The year was to be divided into decads, divisions of ten days, of which one day should be a holiday. This new calendar with its many interesting features was maintained in France until the establishment of Napoleon's Empire in 1804. Then there came the idea of the adoption of a new religion. The Christian religion, especially in its Roman Catholic form, was still without doubt the religion of the vast majority of the French people, and the future was to show that hardly anything would be more popular than its restoration to honour and official recognition. But the Revolution in its Jacobin form was decidedly opposed both to Christianity and to Catholicism. There was too a very general feeling that the revolutionary settlement could not be completed unless it were accompanied by a positive religious change, as had been clearly declared by Rousseau in his Social Contract. Before the movement was adopted in Paris it had begun in provincial centres. There was indeed a spontaneous effort among the revolutionaries in various parts of the country to find something which might be substituted for the Catholic Christianity which they were prepared to abandon. The movement, it is important to notice, never became thoroughly national; it is untrue to say that Christianity was abolished in France by the Revolution; it was Paris that was mainly concerned with the new movement. In Paris, during the autumn of 1793, various inducements were offered to priests to abandon their orders and abjure their faith. Early in November the Archbishop of Paris, Gobel, a Constitutional Archbishop, not therefore in communion with Rome, abjured his faith, before the Convention. On November 10 the worship of Reason was celebrated in an absurd ceremony which was held in the desecrated cathedral of Notre-Dame. The new worship was not atheism. It approached more nearly to a very vague form of theism. On November 24 all churches were closed in Paris. The movement spread into the provinces and it is estimated that something like 2400 churches in France were turned into Temples of Reason. The movement was more than questionable as a matter of policy; it offended still further the Catholic sentiments of France, and it by no means satisfied all the revolutionaries themselves. Robespierre and his important following would have nothing to do with the worship of Reason. They rejected the traditional faith of France, but they were anxious to introduce a more definite declaration of theism, and this new ceremony made a wide gulf between Robespierre's group and the party of the Commune, which had important results.

Thus we may see three groups among the Jacobins each with its followers. They are by no means clearly defined. Anything like clearness of definition is certain to be a mistake in the interpretation of these confused years. But these three groups passed from co-operation to bitter rivalry, fought against one another, and in the end sent one another to the guillotine. It is strange that it should be so, for they had long been allies in a great struggle, and the differences of policy between them did not justify the extreme passion that was engendered; but it is the way of revolutions to turn all divisions into fanatical hatreds and to make men believe that their ideas must triumph by the death of their opponents. It was not only enthusiasm or fanaticism that produced these results: it was above all fear. The Revolution had spilt so much blood, it had so often realised its aims by execution and slaughter that all men's nerves were shaken and all were inclined to see in a political rival a potential assassin. As we watch the struggle between these groups it is often very hard to see on what failure or triumph depended. It rested chiefly upon the support of the armed mob of Paris, and that might be secured or it might be lost by a very little thing. Each party struck when it believed itself secure in the support of Paris. It is a strange thing that it was in the end not the energetic Danton, nor the violent Hébert who triumphed, but the unmilitary and idealistic Robespierre. The Hébertists were the first to go. For a time they had seemed likely to triumph and Robespierre had drawn nearer to Danton in resistance to them. The measure which gave to Robespierre and his friends their victory was probably a law suggested by Saint-Just, whereby all the property of those who were arrested on suspicion was to be devoted to the relief of the poor. It was a great bribe to Paris, and the pendulum swung decisively in the direction of Robespierre. On March 17 the Hébertists were arrested, and on March 24 they were executed. There remained now two parties in the centre of the political arena; though we must always remember that in the background there were the soldier-members of the Committee of Public Safety, directing the campaign, thinking of politics in terms of the war, supporting the Terror for the sake of the war, acting more secretly and perhaps more importantly than the others who are better known. Danton and Robespierre were old friends and the reason for the tragic struggle is not clear. The charge against Danton was that he leaned too much towards mercy and conciliation. He was not a danger to the life and power of Robespierre and his friends, yet it was always possible that in the Convention he might have organised some movement against the Terrorists, as he had organised the great movement against the Monarchy. Robespierre felt himself threatened whilst Danton and his associates lived. On March 31, 1794, Danton, Camille Desmoulins and others were arrested. On April 2 they were tried before the Revolutionary Tribunal. Their trial was one of the most famous of the many that have attracted the attention of posterity. It seemed at one moment as though the sight of these famous champions of the Revolution in the dock might make an appeal to public opinion that would result in some serious rising. Orders were therefore sent down from the Committee of Public Safety that the trial should be brought to a speedy end. A verdict of guilty was of course found, and on April 5 Danton and Desmoulins were executed.

After the fall and death of Danton the situation was still obscure. The Committee of Public Safety was the one great force in France, and in it Carnot and the military group devoted themselves with success to the problem of driving out the foreign enemy from France and following him on to his own territory. Robespierre and Saint-Just and Couthon were also members of the Committee, but they interfered little or not at all with the management of the war, and between them and Carnot and his followers there was bitter jealousy. Saint-Just was Robespierre's chief supporter and, like his more famous chief, he dreamed of French society reconstituted on principles suggested partly by Rousseau and partly by the traditions of Greece and Rome; a society that should be simple, pacific, agricultural, where education should train men to devotion to their country and should produce a type very different indeed from the ordinary Frenchman of the eighteenth century.

The worship of Reason, as we have already seen, conflicted with the ideas of Robespierre. He followed Rousseau in desiring a form of religion that should be avowedly though simply theistic. He was now so much master of the situation in all that concerned the domestic policy of France that the Convention which a short time before had decreed the worship of Reason now decreed that that worship should be changed into the recognition of the Supreme Being. On June 8 the festival inaugurating this new and pure and, as Robespierre hoped, permanent religion, was carried out. Robespierre himself was made President of the Convention for the occasion. There was a procession of its members and others to the garden of the Tuileries where there was much allegorical burning of images, and the festival ended with a great deal of speech-making in which Robespierre's vanity was extraordinarily illustrated. It is doubtful whether the movement was really in harmony with the wishes of many Frenchmen, yet it was accepted with some favour because it was hoped that it might bring the cessation of the Reign of Terror. The Reign of Terror, however, could not cease; it rested primarily as we have seen on fear, and although one fear, the fear of the foreign enemy, was rapidly passing away, another fear still remained, the fear that each political leader had of his rivals and of the fatal consequence to himself of failure or overthrow. Instead then of the terror ceasing it became very much hotter than before. On June 10, 1794, a law was passed, known as the Law of Prairial from the revolutionary month in which it was carried, by which the procedure of the Revolutionary Tribunal was changed and quickened. All the citizens were now called upon to denounce traitors; members of the Convention were no longer immune from arrest; the kind of evidence that was permissible was rendered even more vague and dangerous than it had previously been. So the number of victims rose rapidly. From June 10 to July 27, the date of Robespierre's fall, there were at Paris 1376 victims, nearly a half of the total number (2750), and in this number members of the old privileged classes and even of the middle class counted only 650. Thus Robespierre's challenge to his rivals, in the Convention, and to what remained of human sentiment among the revolutionaries, was direct and provocative. It was not long in producing the natural result. Saint-Just had some time back proposed, in accordance with the suggestion of Rousseau's Social Contract, the establishment of a Dictatorship, and although that had not been accepted, it is certain that Robespierre and his friends in council together had determined to establish some more concentrated form of government which should give them more security and allow them to go on to work of social regeneration, which we cannot doubt was really dear to them. On July 26, 1794, Robespierre opened the campaign by a speech in the Convention, —a strange speech, well written and eloquent, as all his speeches are,— defending and even eulogising his own career, speaking of the unfairness of the opposition to him and of the number of enemies by whom he was resisted, but actually mentioning no one. It was probably the vagueness of the attack which led to his failure. Had a list of victims been mentioned the Convention might have accepted their arrest, but these vague phrases might threaten almost any one in the Convention. When Robespierre had finished, the Convention plucked up courage to indicate its disapproval by refusing to have the speech circulated as an official utterance of the Revolution. It was a rebuff such as Robespierre had not known of late. Deeply indignant he went to the Jacobin Club where he repeated the speech amidst universal applause. He determined to strike again; and next day, July 27 (or in the Revolutionary Calendar the 9th Thermidor), he presented himself at ten in the morning at the meeting of the Convention. He no doubt intended to remove the vagueness of his previous utterance and to define his aims; but his enemies, or those who feared him, had already made their preparations and had agreed to refuse him a hearing. When he mounted the tribune from which all speeches were made, his first words were interrupted by a violent uproar which was renewed whenever he attempted to speak. Nor were the attempts of his followers to get a hearing more successful. The scene was one of the greatest possible confusion, passion and violence, for most actors in it must have felt that their lives might be at stake. At last it was moved and carried that Robespierre, Saint-Just and his immediate followers should be declared under arrest. They were handed over to the officers of the Convention to be taken to prison and the struggle seemed to be at an end.

It was, however, by no means at an end. Since the fall of Hébert and Chaumette the organisation of the Commune, or Municipality of Paris, had passed under the influence of Robespierre and his friends, who thus controlled the prisons of Paris. When it was found at the Hôtel de Ville that Robespierre had been imprisoned an order was sent for his liberation, and he was brought back in triumph to the Town Hall. The Convention therefore, when it met again in the afternoon, found that its great enemy was at large, and that the decision would not now rest with decrees or majority votes, but with force and arms. They passed a decree declaring Robespierre an outlaw, and turned to the organisation of the fight.

During the course of July 27 military preparations had been made upon both sides. The defence of the Hôtel de Ville was in the hands of Hanriot, a trusted but hardly a trustworthy supporter of Robespierre. The Convention, on their side, gathered what force they could and marched to the attack of the Hôtel de Ville. There was little real fighting. It may be that Robespierre was really unpopular; that Paris was weary of the Reign of Terror, which it ascribed to his influence, or that Hanriot was incapable in his measures of defence. It is at any rate certain that the defences of the Town Hall were broken through; that the assailants rushed up the staircase towards the room where Robespierre and his friends were in council, and that when they entered they found Robespierre with a shattered jaw, whether self-inflicted or not is uncertain, lying upon the table. Some of his allies had leaped from the window, breaking their limbs or falling into the hands of their enemies outside. As Robespierre had already been declared an outlaw there was no need for any trial; a form of identification was sufficient, and he went, a strange and tragic figure, to the fate to which he had sent so many hundreds.

The fall of Robespierre might perhaps have been simply one incident among many in the Reign of Terror; it might have led up to the rule of some fiercer and less scrupulous terrorist; but, as a matter of historic fact, from the moment of the fall of Robespierre the Reign of Terror began rapidly to pass away. The reasons for this are many. The situation was essentially unstable. The rule of the guillotine could not have been made permanent in eighteenth-century France, and public opinion in Paris was turning clearly and violently against it; but there are two reasons more important than any others which rendered the disappearance of the Reign of Terror at this moment inevitable. The first is that the foreign danger was now rapidly disappearing. We shall return to this at the end of the chapter. It is enough to say that, after the battle of Fleurus, France was herself an aggressive Power, and that the assault upon her frontiers, north and east and south, had proved an entire failure. There was rising up in the country a feeling of military confidence and pride that made the Revolutionary Tribunal and the constant batches of victims for the guillotine seem both criminal and absurd. The Reign of Terror was primarily a military measure, and as the military danger passed away the Reign of Terror passed away with it. And then, though less important, whatever else the fall of Robespierre meant, it meant the victory of the Convention. There had been a direct conflict between the forces of the Convention and the forces of the Commune, between the body that represented France and the body that represented Paris. It was the Convention, it was France, that had won. For the first time in the history of the Revolution an attempt to crush by popular force the elected representatives of France had ended in failure and defeat. The Convention felt itself far more confident than before, and it took measures to secure the power that it had won with such difficulty.

Thus immediately after the fall of Robespierre the Commune was closed and broken up, and its work was delegated to Committees and Commissioners. On August 10 the Revolutionary Tribunal was reorganised so as to bring it more into harmony with the ordinary procedure of French law, and the Law of Prairial was repealed. On September 1 the Executive Committees were reconstituted and brought under the direct control of the Convention. The Committee of Public Safety, although it continued to exist, was no longer the independent body it had been. On November 12 the Jacobin Club, that constant source of revolution, was finally closed. Meanwhile the executions had very much diminished, and with the winter of 1794 the Reign of Terror may be said to have passed away. It was a striking and a symbolic fact that seventy-five of the Girondist party who were in prison were allowed to return to the benches of the Convention, where they strongly reinforced the movement of reaction against the Terror. The storm, however, did not settle into a calm without occasional returns of the old troubles. These were stimulated by the fact that the winter of 1794–1795 was a terribly severe one. The suffering would have been great in any case, but with poverty and dislocation of trade and commerce it was trebly felt. In April of the year 1795 there was a rising of the old kind that Paris had grown to know so well, which, from the revolutionary month in which it took place, is known as the rising of Germinal. The demand of the insurgents was for 'bread and the Constitution of 1793.' It was probably never really dangerous, and it was easily crushed by Pichegru, in command of the armed forces of Paris. Again the Convention had triumphed. Its triumph was marked by further reaction against the Jacobins and the Reign of Terror. Prominent Terrorists were exiled. The National Guards were reconstituted so as to be a defence for the middle class. The property of those who had been guillotined was restored to the relations of the victims.

Another rising took place in May 1795 (the rising of Prairial). This was more definitely political in its aims, and was organised by the members of the old Jacobin party. It was for a time dangerous. The hall of the Convention was occupied by the insurgents; an attempt was made to pass legislation that would have taken France back to the principles of 1793 and 1794; but then there came to the assistance of the Convention, not the National Guards, but the regular troops under the command of Menou and Murat. The insurgents were driven out without difficulty, and further steps were at once taken for the defence of the Convention against such a danger in the future.

Then on June 10, 1795, there came an event which had serious consequences. The little son of Louis XVI, recognised by all Royalists as Louis XVII, died in prison. The details of his piteous and tragic existence need not concern us, but it was of much importance that henceforward the unquestioned heir to the French throne was the late King's brother, the Comte de Provence, who was destined to reign in 1815 as Louis XVIII, but who was at present serving in the armies of the foreign enemy against France. There were many Frenchmen, nominally Royalist, who would be unwilling to support the claims of a national enemy. It was thought wise, therefore, to bring forward a new constitution at once in order to clear up ambiguities as to the nature of the Government and to conciliate those who were capable of being brought over. This is known as the Constitution of the Year Three, which lasted, with very slight change, until it was overthrown by Napoleon in 1799. It opened with the declaration of the duties of the citizen as well as of the rights of man. It established a limited franchise which was dependent upon a term of residence and the payment of certain taxes. It reversed the decision of 1790, whereby the idea of a Second Chamber had been pushed aside, and it established not only a 'Council of Five Hundred,' consisting of representatives over the age of thirty, but also a 'Council of Ancients,' consisting of men over forty, and this Council of Ancients was to have the right of vetoing legislation by the other House for the space of one year. Both Councils could hold their meetings elsewhere than in Paris. This provision was introduced to avoid the dangerous influence of the Paris populace which had been so frequently felt during the Revolution, and it assisted, as we shall see, the rise of Napoleon to power. At the head of the State there was to be, of course, no King; neither was there to be a President nor a Consul. Instead there was to be a Committee, or as it was called a Directorate, of five persons, which was to take the place of the Committee of Public Safety, of whom one was to retire every year. A last regulation was the immediate cause of the next outbreak of violence. It was laid down that one-third of both Councils was to retire every year, but that two-thirds of the first Legislative Councils were to consist of members of the existing Convention. It was against this 'regulation of the two-thirds' that the rising took place; for it meant that the elections could produce no immediate change in the character of the Government, and that the

Convention would prolong its rule, at any rate for a time; and so Jacobins and Girondists and even Royalists were ready to join against this detested regulation. On October 3 there came the last rising that we need note—the rising of Vendémiaire. Paris rose, as so often before, but with rather more organisation than she had usually shown. On the side of the Convention, however, there was great determination and a perfect readiness to meet the popular display of force by appeal to the army. The defence of the Tuileries and of the Convention Hall was put into the hands of Paul de Barras, and he had as his subordinate Napoleon Bonaparte, already distinguished at the siege of Toulon. When, on October 5, the attack upon the Convention took place it was met by artillery fire and was easily beaten off. The extent of the fighting has indeed been very often exaggerated: the total loss of the insurgents seems not to have exceeded 100. The significance is that the Central Government once again, and much more decidedly than ever before, had repressed a popular rising. The name of the people no longer exercised its old paralysing charm. The Government maintained its rights even against the claims of the people. It is a significant event, also, because Napoleon, in recognition of the part that he had played in the repression of the movement, was given the command of the home army, and thus got his foot upon the ladder that was to lead him so far and so high. Soon after this, on October 26, 1795, the Convention came to an end. History knows of no representative body more important than this. Its only rival to an equality of importance is to be found in the English Long Parliament of the seventeenth century.

We must end this chapter by noticing very briefly the military situation. On June 1, 1794, there had come the first important naval action of the war. French ships with supplies were being brought into Brest. The French fleet went out to convoy them and was met by the British fleet under Lord Howe. The battle was not an overwhelming defeat for the French, but it was decisive. For long after this the British naval supremacy in the Channel was not challenged. In June of the next year (1795) the British co-operated with the emigrant nobles in organising an attack upon Brittany. It was hoped that the French force, which was to be landed in Quiberon Bay, would receive the assistance of the scattered remnants of the Vendean war. The French force was landed, but it found itself cooped up in the Quiberon Peninsula by a French army under General Hoche. In the end the Royalists were forced to surrender, and a large number of them were executed. Thus ended all hopes of a successful insurrection in the west against the Revolutionary Government. On land, too, the French arms were almost everywhere successful. There was little fighting of note. The most important fact was that Prussia and Austria, still allies in name, were almost avowed enemies. One cause of this contention between them was to be found, as before, in Polish affairs. The second partition had left the unhappy country totally incapable of managing its own affairs or of sustaining

its position as a European State. Those who had robbed already twice,
determined now to rob a third and a last time. The negotiations for the
third partition took place between Austria and Russia. Prussia was not
admitted to the secret of the negotiations, and although she was given
some share of the spoil, that did not in the least appease her hostile and
suspicious humour. The Prussians for some time past had only been
kept in the field by financial subsidies from the British Government.
Their historians recognise and deplore the humiliation of their position.
Now, in 1795, peace was at last made between Prussia and France—the
Peace of Basel. Its terms, which are important, may be summarised as
follows. Certain terms were publicly announced. France was to occupy
the left bank of the Rhine until the conclusion of the general peace.
Further, France promised to undertake no military operations in
Northern Germany, and to recognise the right of Prussia to act as inter-
mediary for any State which required peace. There were also some
secret terms, and by these Prussia was promised compensation elsewhere in Germany for territory evacuated on the left bank of the Rhine.
she thus consented to indemnify herself at the expense of the smaller
German states for German territory that was to be abandoned to
France. The delimitation of the territory in North Germany, where
France agreed to carry on no military operations, was to be secretly
agreed upon between France and Prussia.

It was for Prussia a humiliating peace, and its terms made it impossible for her for the present to be regarded as in any way the representative or the defender of German interests as a whole. It was an immense
triumph for France. It was victory, though not entirely one of arms,
still victory over the greatest military Power of the Continent. It
seemed to portend a general break-up of all resistance to the Republic.
In May 1795 Holland made terms with France, promised to join her in
war against England, and was annexed to the French Republic in all
but name; and in July 1795 Spain withdrew from the contest, surrendering the island of San Domingo to the Republic and promising
certain further concessions. Austria and England remained alone in the
field. It would take several years of war yet to reduce both of them to
peace, but the triumph already acquired was an amazing one. When
men thought of the confidence with which the speedy overthrow of the
Republic had been anticipated in 1792, and again in 1793, and then
looked at the aggressive action, the novel tactics, the daring strategy,
and the ultimate victory of the French Republican armies, it was clear
that a new Power of an incalculable and dangerous kind had come into
the history of Europe.

CHAPTER **IV**

THE RISE OF NAPOLEON TO POWER

FROM this time the interest of the domestic development of France is rivalled by the story of the victories of the French armies until we are in danger of forgetting what is happening in France altogether, and of fixing our eyes only upon the personal triumphs of Napoleon. Napoleon was without question a man of extraordinary force of brain and character, who under all circumstances and in all countries would have won for himself a high position. He had great powers of work and of organisation, rapid insight, courage, a willingness to accept responsibility, resolution in following out a plan once undertaken—all the qualities of the soldier in their highest development; and with all he had the gift of genius which defies analysis. But his rise is much more than the story of a capable man winning for himself a high place in the world. It reflects also one of the most general laws that may be observed on the surface of history. We can see constantly how a period of confusion and of revolution ends in the establishment of some strong and often of a personal power. The instances that are usually quoted in comparison with Napoleon's life history are the establishment of the Roman Empire by Julius Caesar after a century of confusion and revolution in Rome, and the personal rule of Oliver Cromwell which followed the Puritan revolution. But these are only the most obvious instances. We may see something of the same sort when the Tudor Monarchy follows the Wars of the Roses; when the strong concentration of the French kings under Charles VII and Louis XI brought to an end the long agony and turmoil of the Hundred Years' War in France; or, again, when the Thirty Years' War in Germany is followed very generally by the establishment of personal rule. So general a development must have common causes, and they are not difficult to determine. In the first place societies that have undergone great confusion from whatever cause feel the need of some established order as the first necessity of their social life. If they cannot obtain it by constitutional means, by mutual agreement, and through the employment of liberty, they are willing that it should be secured by the strong hand of a soldier. And again, in a revolution such as that which we have been examining, and in periods of confusion such as the others that we have referred to, we may see the decision slipping into the hands of those who control the largest amount of physical force. In France especially the will of the people and the votes of citizens, though often praised and idealised, had hardly decided any important issue since 1793. The Monarchy had been overthrown by violence, the Republic had been established and had been saved by violence, it was by violence that Robespierre had risen and by violence that he had been overthrown. It was natural therefore that

France should be at last ruled by violence in its highest development; not by the unruly mobs of the Paris streets, but by the trained and victorious legions of France herself. Lastly, we may note that France was growing weary of political and social controversy. The ardent hopes of 1789 had in part been realised, but more generally they had been proved incapable of realisation, and whilst men were growing cynical or hostile to the squabbles of party politicians whose great words and aspirations were never translated into action, they were more and more dazzled by the victories that had been won in the past by the Generals of the Republic, and which were now to be given her in much fuller measure and in a more dazzling form by Napoleon Bonaparte. What Rousseau almost recommended in his 'Social Contract' and Burke had prophesied in a splendid passage of the 'Reflections' was now to come to pass. A movement that had begun in a passionate and even extravagant desire for liberty was to end in the rule of a soldier-dictator.[1]

Napoleon was born in 1769 at Ajaccio in Corsica, of Italian stock. Just a year before, the long connection between Corsica and Italy had been broken and the island had been incorporated with France, in spite of Paoli's effort to maintain independence and the sympathy and occasional support of Great Britain. Thus, Napoleon was from his birth a French citizen. One of a large family, he was destined from an early date for a military career, and in 1779 was sent to a military academy at Brienne. In 1785 he had become sub-lieutenant in an artillery regiment, and was at this time full of enthusiasm for Rousseau and a Republic after the classical model, and for the independence of Corsica. When the Revolution broke out he welcomed it. His enthusiastic admiration was given to the Republicans, and he had a somewhat close friendship with Robespierre's brother. He was out of employment when, on August 10, 1792, the Monarchy was overthrown by the attack of the Paris mob. He saw something of the events of that day, and has left on record his belief that the victorious crowds could have been easily dispersed by trained soldiers. He served a little later in the suppression of a rising in Corsica, and henceforth his local patriotism gave way before

---

[1] Near the end of the *Social Contract* Rousseau had contemplated the necessity of a special act entrusting the care of the State to its most worthy citizen, when the safety of the country is at stake. Earlier in the book he says, 'I have some presentiment that this small island (Corsica) will one day astonish Europe.' This is nothing more than a lucky hit. Burke's words, written at the beginning of the Revolution, to 'a very young gentleman at Paris' are genuine historical prophecy, for they spring from a real understanding of the situation. 'In the weakness of one kind of authority, and in the fluctuation of all, the officers of an army will remain for some time mutinous and full of faction, until some popular general, who understands the art of conciliating the soldiery . . . shall draw the eyes of all men upon himself. Armies will obey him on his personal account. . . . But the moment in which that event shall happen, the person who really commands the army is your master, the master (that is little) of your king, the master of your assembly, the master of your whole republic.' *Reflections on the Revolution in France* (October 1790); *v.* Burke: *Select Works* (Clarendon Press, 1877), vol. II. p. 260).

his ardent devotion to France. In December 1793 he had played an important part, though not so important as has sometimes been represented, in the capture of Toulon from the British, and in September 1795 he had, as we have just seen, saved the Convention from the attack of the Revolutionaries. In 1796, when twenty-seven years of age, he had married a widow, Josephine de Beauharnais, who was then aged thirty-four. She seems to have had no idea at all of the nature of the man whom she had married, and of the career to which he was destined, and refused to accompany him or share in the hardships and the glories of his first great campaign.

The Republic, as we have seen, though it had driven from the field the greater number of its enemies, was still left at war with Great Britain and Austria. Of Great Britain we need hardly speak. It had abandoned, after a series of failures, any attempt to defeat the French on the mainland; but the British control of the sea was a permanent threat to the colonies and the possessions of France, and indirectly of great help to Austria. The Directorate, as the new French Government was called, was now aiming a blow at the very heart of the Austrian power which they hoped would give them victory and peace. With this object the main armies of France were to advance on Vienna, under Generals Moreau and Jourdan, by the well-known route of the Black Forest and the Danube. At the same time another army was to support the chief attack and distract a part of the Austrian army by attacking the Austrian power and possessions in Italy. It was this subordinate attack which was entrusted to Napoleon Bonaparte, and which his genius converted into the most important stroke.

Italy had played for many centuries past no important independent part in European politics, and for a century and a half she had contributed little even to the artistic, literary, and scientific life of Europe. After Napoleon's invasion there would come a new breath to stir the dead atmosphere of the peninsula which would never again quite fall back into its old torpor. Italy consisted of several states. There was first, sitting astride of the western Alps, the strangely named kingdom of Sardinia, the real nucleus of which is to be found not in the island from which its name is taken, but in the upper valleys of the Po, which are known as Piedmont, and in the vigorous military and well-disciplined population of the mountains of Savoy. The geographical situation of this kingdom and the character of its people had made it for a long time past an important pawn in the game of European diplomacy, but there was as yet nothing to mark it out as more liberal than any other state in Italy, nothing certainly to indicate that its monarchs were destined to give to Italy the united and constitutional life which her thinkers had already dreamed of. A little farther east there came the Duchy of Milan, an important appanage of Austria—important by reason of its very great wealth and commercial possibilities; important also because it commanded the road by which Austrian troops would pass through the Tyrol into Italy. The famous quadrilateral—the four fortresses of Mantua, Legnago, Verona, and Peschiera—maintained the connection between Austria and Italy. Again, further east we see the Republic of Venice, the oldest of European states, and in some respects the most notable, now sunk far into decline and soon to be overthrown by an unworthy blow from the great conqueror who was about to enter Italy. A little further south there were the Duchies of Modena, Parma, and Tuscany, all of them by matrimonial or political arrangement closely attached to the House of Austria. In the west was the Republic of Genoa, a less interesting counterpart of her Venetian sister, and like Venice sunk in decay. Across the centre of Italy stretched the Papal States, one of the strangest of European Governments, fulfilling few of the requirements of the modern state, but recognised as an independent state by the public law of Europe, and regarded with special veneration by a large part of Europe on account of its connection with the head of the Roman Catholic Church. The south of Italy was occupied by far the largest state of all, covering as it did not far from one-half of the whole peninsula. The kingdom of Naples and the people of Naples differed so widely from the rest of the country that the union which has incorporated them into a single centralised state has seemed to many unnatural and unwise. The King of Naples was a member of the Bourbon family, and was connected by marriage with the House of Austria. It was thus at once exposed to the special hostility of France, and had a special claim upon the support and friendship of Austria.

The campaign which now opens is one of the most interesting of all those which Napoleon engaged in, and has the special interest that it first gave the measure of Napoleon's genius. It exhibited his daring, his rapidity of decision and of action, and at the same time (what did not fail him until late in his career) the sureness with which he could distinguish between what was possible and what was not. From the merely military point of view we may note the great importance that he attached to the use of artillery, his insistence upon never standing on the defensive, but, even with fewer troops than those of the enemy, conducting the campaign always on aggressive lines. We may note too, as soldiers of the time noted, how the character of his army allowed him to do what other armies could not. It was composed of many elements, but it consisted largely of men who were themselves interested in the cause for which they were fighting, and who did not think of their commander merely as a hard ruler and a grudging paymaster. He could send his men out as scouts singly, or in small parties, with little fear of their desertion, whilst such action was impossible to the troops against which he was fighting. In accordance with the plan of this book we shall devote the least possible attention to the details of these remarkable campaigns, but this neglect of the details must not be taken to imply that the campaigns were not themselves of the utmost importance for the development and future destinies of Europe. To trace the fortunes of the Continent without considering the wars which have so frequently passed across its surface, would be in the highest degree absurd. There is no country the condition of which does not directly depend upon wars that have been lost or won. There is no part of the public life of the Continent that does not bear signs of the influence of war. Neither the commercial nor the intellectual nor the political life of Europe is intelligible without reference to its military history.

When Napoleon took up the command of the French army, it was at Savona to the west of the Italian Alps. There it had been for some time trying in vain to find or force a road across the mountains. Soon after Napoleon took charge of it the road was found. A joint army of Sardinians and Austrians was opposed to Napoleon. He managed, however, to separate them, and in the Battle of Mondovi defeated the Sardinians and drove them to accept the Armistice of Cherasco, (April 28, 1796), whereby they retired from the war and ceded Savoy and Nice to France.

Austria remained, and Napoleon lost no time in coming to blows with her. He marched on to Milan, desiring not only to capture the Milanese but to isolate the Austrians from Piedmont. His first big battle was fought at Lodi on May 10, 1796. It was a great victory, and the Austrians at once retired far to the east of Milan, which was abandoned to the conqueror. He entered amidst immense popular enthusiasm. He seemed at first no conqueror but a liberator, and was accepted not only by the liberals but by the clericals of the city. When the Italians found that Napoleon intended them to pay for the war, when they found that he imposed heavy taxes and sacked their cities if they refused to pay them, their mood soon changed. But, though Italian historians vary in their judgment upon Napoleon, they are at one in recognising in these events the beginning of the movement which led them a little more than sixty years later to unity and liberty. Napoleon next laid siege to the great fortress of Mantua, the central Austrian fortress in Italy, strongly defended with artillery and surrounded for the greater part of it by impassable lakes and morasses. It was understood that the fall of Mantua would mean the fall of the Austrian power in Italy, and the Austrians were as determined to relieve it as Napoleon was tenacious in maintaining his hold upon it. On four different occasions Napoleon had to relax his hold upon the place in order to march to the encounter of Austrian armies. They were defeated over and over again; the last and the decisive blow was delivered on January 14, 1797, when an Austrian army of seventy thousand men under Alvinzi was scattered at the Battle of Rivoli. After that there was no more hope for Mantua, which shortly afterwards surrendered. Peace did not come immediately, and in order to force it Napoleon pressed forward through the north-east of Italy into the eastern Alps and reached the town of Laibach. Napoleon's own position was not without its difficulties. The French advances in Germany had shown nothing in any way corresponding to his own meteoric movements in Italy. It was therefore out of consideration for his own position, as well as for the needs of France, that he appealed to the Austrian Archduke Charles to stop the war. An armistice was arranged at Leoben in April 1797. But though preliminaries were signed they were not developed into a peace for some little time. The Austrians were unwilling to admit defeat; they were watching events in Paris, hoping for a Royalist revolution there, but they were disappointed in their hopes. The French armies were now pressing not only east of the Adriatic, but also on the Danube, and so, on October 17, 1797, the definite Peace of Campo Formio was signed. There were in the Peace open and secret articles. By the open articles, which will have to be a little more fully explained in a moment, the Belgian lands were abandoned to France; a republic was set up in Northern Italy, to be called the Cisalpine Republic; France was to take the Ionian Islands; Austria was to be allowed to hold Venice and all her territory in Italy and the Adriatic. (This policy will be more carefully examined.) Lastly, a congress was to be called at Rastatt, wherein the affairs of Germany were to be settled at conferences of representatives from France and the Empire. Besides these open articles there were secret ones, wherein the Emperor promised to cede to France large districts on the left bank of the Rhine, an abandonment of the defence of the Empire which he would be ashamed to confess publicly. France, too, promised that Austria should receive the important ecclesiastical state of Salzburg and a part of Bavaria; and she promised that, in the settlement of Germany, Prussia, the hated rival of Austria, should receive no compensation at all. Such was the Peace of Campo Formio, very characteristic of the diplomacy of Napoleon, in which he showed himself almost as much a master as in the art of war; characteristic, too, of the way in which the Hapsburg Emperor all through this period was ready to abandon the defence of Germany for the winning of small personal advantages for himself; characteristic, lastly, of the method pursued by Napoleon frequently during his career of appeasing the hostility of his greater opponents by allowing them to absorb the territory of the smaller states of Europe.

We must look now a little more carefully at the settlement of Italy by Napoleon on which so much of its future destiny depends. We have seen how Sardinia was treated by the Armistice of Cherasco. We have seen, too, how by the Peace of Campo Formio the Cisalpine Republic was recognised. This strange title was adopted from the history of Ancient Rome, which made during all this period so strong an appeal to the imaginations of Frenchmen. It consisted at first mainly of the territory of Milan, but then there came risings in the districts further south—in Bologna, Ferrara, Ravenna, and Reggio—all districts loosely attached to the Papal States, and these were by their own wish incorporated into the new Republic. Thus there arose on Italian soil a republican state of the modern pattern influenced by all the political and social ideals of the French Revolution. Its name would soon be changed into monarchy, its character would alter, and it was not destined to survive the battle of Waterloo, but it gave to the Italians ideas of social and political life, and above all the idea of an independent Italian State which never passed away from their imagination. Next the corrupt and antiquated Republic of Genoa was overthrown, democratic principles were introduced, and it was rechristened the Ligurian Republic, the name being again borrowed from classical history. More important than what happened to Genoa is the fate of Venice. This famous Republic had done its utmost to maintain neutrality during the collision between Napoleon and Austria, and to stand quite apart from the war that raged at her frontiers. It has sometimes been maintained that any state that is not armed and pursues a peaceful line of action is safe from the worst consequences of war. If it were so, the history of Europe would be a more pleasing story. The helplessness of Venice only made it a more certain prey to the conqueror, and when Napoleon made peace with Austria and desired to establish good relations with the vanquished enemy he could find no better means of doing so than by throwing to Austria the possessions, the liberties, and the existence of the glorious and inoffensive Republic.

There was no justification for the destruction of Venetian independence any more than there was for the partitions of Poland, which it resembles in character; but some thin excuses were found. There were movements in Brescia and Bergamo against the oligarchical Government of Venice which gave France an opportunity of posing as the champion of 'democracy.' There was a collision between the French garrison and the Italian population at Verona, in which French lives were lost. A French ship entering the harbour of Venice was fired on: Napoleon called it 'the most atrocious affair of the century.' Aware of the danger that threatened them, the Venetian Government accepted a democratic form of government, dismissed their famous Slavonian bodyguard, and admitted a body of French troops. All was in vain. The Treaty of Campo Formio handed them over to Austria, and an effort to bribe the Directors of France failed in its object. Early in 1798 the transference to Austria was accomplished. The French had already burnt the Golden Book in which was kept the list of the Venetian nobles. Now the great arsenal was destroyed and the *Bucentaur*, the ship in which the Doge was wont to 'wed the Adriatic,' rotted away.

> 'Men are we and must grieve, when even the shade
> Of that which once was great is passed away.'

The Papal States had also to pay the price of defeat, but Napoleon was anxious to leave the way open to the renewal of friendly relations with the Pope. By the Peace of Tolentino (February 1797) the Pope ceded Avignon to France, and Bologna, Ferrara, and the Romagna to

3

the Cisalpine Republic. He handed over to Napoleon money, manuscripts, and pictures; but the Directory would have liked still harsher terms, and the Pope was grateful to Napoleon for his escape from a deeper humiliation or even from destruction!

We must return from the campaigns of Napoleon to the domestic difficulties of France. From 1795 to 1799 her internal history loses the interest and importance which attached to it up to the day of Vendémiaire. The struggles among the leaders were for the most part personal and egoistic. The interference of the army occurred from time to time. Military rule drew visibly nearer.

We have seen the nature of the Constitution. A recurrent difficulty was the absence of harmony between the Directors, who formed the executive, and the two legislative Chambers. 'The separation of the powers' was still dear to the minds of French theorists. One-third of the Assemblies retired every year; but only one of the five Directors. The Directory, therefore, was not necessarily in sympathy either with the Assemblies or with the constituencies. The first Directors were Carnot, 'the organiser of victory'; Letourneur, an engineer; Barras, who had shared with Napoleon in the defence of the Convention against the rising of Vendémiaire; Larevellière-Lépeaux, a Girondist; and, most important of all, Rewbell, an Alsatian and a Jacobin, in whose hands lay the chief authority.

The problems that these men had to face were many and difficult. The financial situation seemed hopeless. The *assignats*—the paper money of the Revolution—had sunk to one per cent. of their face value. The religious situation was full of menace. The 'Constitutional Church' set up by the Revolution had no vitality and had almost disappeared. A new religious movement called 'Theophilanthropy'—founded by an Englishman and now patronised by the Directors, and especially by Lépeaux—in spite of the carefully-thought-out ceremonial, the many churches allotted to it, and the financial support, had got no real following. Events were soon to show how popular the Roman Catholicism of the old and proscribed type was, and how ready the mass of the people would be to welcome it again. Then there was the question of the *émigrés*, of whom there were perhaps 300,000. The property of all was confiscated, and in many instances men had been declared to be *émigrés* in order that their property might be seized. Their relatives raised bitter protests against the injustice of the act. The friction between the Assemblies and the Directory, and the interference of the army chiefs: these are the outstanding features of the time and we must note two prominent examples.

In March 1797 the elections took place to fill the places of one-third of the Assemblies. The results showed great gains for the Moderate and anti-Jacobin party, while three out of the five Directors were decidedly Jacobin. Here was a difficult situation. A general election (on a small scale) had decided against the Government, but the Government was not in the least inclined to yield. Many believed that a wave of reaction was about to sweep the country; and the Austrian Government delayed to convert the Truce of Leoben into a Peace until the issue was decided in Paris. It would not be decided now by the populace of Paris but by the army. The Directors first appealed to Hoche, but he declined the part suggested to him. Then they were forced to apply to Napoleon, whose character, genius, and success were already beginning to alarm them. He sent his officer, Augereau, to carry out his instructions. It was not necessary to use force. The appearance of this showy and empty-headed soldier was enough. His orders were obeyed. Carnot, who had made himself the spokesman of the Moderates, was deposed from the Directory. A number of deputies were arrested, and among them Pichegru, a soldier of repute. Then at the order of the Directors the results of 154 elections were annulled. The effort to introduce more tolerant measures was dropped. The religious dissidents and the *émigrés* were treated with all the old rigour. The assumed connection of the reactionaries with the designs of the Austrian Government had been fatal to them. The army had re-established the Jacobins in order to dictate terms to the enemy. This is known as the *Coup d'État* of Fructidor. The future was to show that the alliance between the Jacobins and the military chiefs was not natural or permanent. In the next year something of the same sort happened again, when the elections in thirty departments were annulled because the results were not acceptable to the Directors.

Events in Paris were now directly dependent on the war, and we must turn to that to understand the next great domestic movement in which the army, through its great chief, interfered and swept the Republic and the Jacobins out of France.

Austria had accepted a dictated peace, but Great Britain still remained, victorious and impregnable on the water. The Directory sought to find some vulnerable spot. It seemed at times that they had found it. In 1797 there had broken out the great mutinies in the British fleet at The Nore and at Spithead. It seemed for a moment as if the trident were broken in the hands of Britain, but the mutinies were settled and the sea power of Great Britian not diminished. In 1798 there came the great Irish Rebellion. A French army managed to reach Ireland to support it; but, as so often before, an Irish rebellion proved a great disappointment to the enemies of Britain. The movement collapsed, and the bitter memories that it left behind were of no use to France. How was the land power to inflict a dangerous blow on the sea power? How was the lion to destroy the shark? It seemed to the Directors that they might find in Egypt 'the Achilles' heel of invulnerable England.' France had no cause of war, nor even any grievance which could be seriously alleged against Egypt, which was governed by the military caste of the Mamelukes, nor against the Sultan of Turkey, with whom lay the nominal suzerainty. It was really Britain that was attacked when the French expedition sailed for Egypt. The rapid growth of British influence in India had increased the zeal of Frenchmen for the recovery of their former pre-eminence. A French force in the Isthmus of Suez would threaten the English in India, for France would then be far nearer India than England was. The instructions of Napoleon when he was despatched to Egypt contained as their first point 'to drive the English from all their possessions in the East which he can reach.' There followed other instructions: the Isthmus of Suez was to be cut; the condition of the natives was to be ameliorated; and peace was to be maintained with the Sultan. Napoleon took with him, also, learned Egyptologists to throw light on the monuments and antiquities of the then little-known country. The deciphering of the hieroglyphics was one result of the expedition.

At first all went well with it. The island of Malta surrendered to Napoleon on June 11, 1798; on July 1 he reached the coast of Egypt, and six days later began his march to Cairo. He tried to conciliate the native population, but the Mamelukes fought for their power. On July 21, in a battle fought within sight of the Pyramids, they were entirely defeated, and Napoleon was master of Egypt. A few days later bad news came from the coast. Nelson had found the French fleet at Aboukir Bay and had destroyed it in the Battle of the Nile. Napoleon realised at once the importance of the blow. It meant that there would be no more reinforcements from France, while Britain could send what troops she liked into Egypt. He made light of the situation: 'We must remain in these lands and then come forth great like the ancients'; but the fate of the expedition was sealed by the maritime supremacy of Great Britain which was to decide so many issues in Napoleon's career. Turkey now joined herself definitely to Britain, and Napoleon determined to anticipate an attack from the north by a march into Syria. He spoke later of his design of marching on Constantinople or on India, but those were second thoughts; at the time he thought only of the immediate danger. His Syrian campaign opened well. El Arish fell into his hands; Jaffa was occupied. At Jaffa the slaughter of prisoners, 'after much deliberation,' in order to avenge the murder of a French envoy did much damage to his reputation, and the outbreak of plague in his army seriously weakened his strength. He pushed on, nevertheless, to St. Jean d'Acre and laid siege to it. The town was assisted by Sir Sidney Smith with British ships, and in the end, after the prize had often seemed within his grasp, Napoleon was beaten off. He retreated to Egypt after suffering heavy losses (May 1799). He was still strong enough to destroy a Turkish army which was sent into Egypt, but the outlook for the campaign was not really improved, nor could it be while the British had control of the sea. The news from Europe was disquieting. A new coalition had been formed against France and she had suffered severe defeats. For his own sake and for the sake of France it was best that he should leave Egypt. He sailed from Alexandria on August

23 and, after running great danger of capture, reached France at Fréjus on October 9.

The end of the Egyptian expedition may be quickly summarised. The French army had been left under Kléber and Menou. Kléber at once began to negotiate for terms, but Nelson would grant nothing but surrender at discretion. In June 1800 Kléber was assassinated; and the Turks and British planned a threefold attack on the French in Egypt. It was impossible to resist longer and, in August 1801, 20,000 French troops surrendered at Cairo and Alexandria.

The outlook in Europe had changed very much since Napoleon left for Egypt. The Treaty of Campo Formio had given Europe little more than a year of peace. The cause of the new war—which is just a continuation of the old one—is plain. France was immensely powerful. The force of her arms and the attractiveness of the new political and social principles which she championed won for her great gains even during the period of nominal peace. Before Europe could begin to enjoy the hard-won peace she was stirred to panic again, and once more most of the nations of the Continent united with Great Britain—who was still in arms against France—in another league against a pressing danger.

First there had come a revolution in Rome. The papal power was opposed there by strong elements in the population. These were incited by the agents or the example of France to demand democratic reforms. They were supported by the French general, Berthier, who established a republic with a government vested in seven magistrates who bore the venerable name of consuls. The Pope—Pius VI—was expelled by the French and was deported first to Siena and then to Valence, where he died. But it soon proved that the republic was little more than an agency of France. A French garrison remained, and Rome was treated almost as a conquered country. What happened in Holland was not very different. The Batavian Republic had been declared there, but its form had not yet been determined. The country was much divided in feeling: some desiring the return of the House of Orange; some a federal republic in accordance with the old tradition of the land; others, backed by France, supporting a centralised state after the fashion of France herself. The question was put to the vote, and a large majority of those voting declared for the French model. The majority, however, of the citizens did not vote at all. The influence of France had been apparent throughout, and Holland under the new form was only 'a thinly disguised annexe of the French Republic.' By similar methods France came to control the north of Italy. The Cisalpine Republic showed itself inclined to take an independent course. General Berthier had thereupon 'purged the Council of the Republic' and reduced the Government to complete dependence on France. A little further west a more naked extension of the power of France took place. Piedmont had remained attached to the kingdom of Sardinia after the Armistice of

Cherasco. An excuse was now found to expel the King from his Italian territories, and Piedmont was definitely annexed to France. At the same time the Grand Duke of Tuscany was expelled, and France seemed to threaten the independence of the whole of Italy.

Even more important were the steps by which the French Republic became practically mistress of Switzerland. The Helvetic Confederation—to give the country its correct political title—was ruled by a narrow oligarchy, though there were wide differences in the conditions of the different cantons. The oligarchy of Berne was specially powerful and notorious for its narrow exclusiveness. The Canton de Vaud petitioned France for help against its oppressors. Ever since 1792 the Republic had declared that it was ready to help oppressed peoples against their rulers. In accordance, therefore, with the traditions of the Republic a French army of 15,000 under General Brune entered Switzerland and overthrew with unexpected ease the Confederacy, whose proud boast it was to have maintained its liberties against so many tyrants and aggressors. The Helvetic Republic 'one and indivisible' was set up, centralised and unitary after the pattern generally approved of by France; and, like the other republics set up under French influence, strictly subordinated to France. Swiss independence was at an end and her valleys were again, after a long interval, to be full of the noise of war on a great scale. These events did not pass without protest even in France. Carnot, who held by many of the ideals of the early Revolution, refused to acquiesce in the overthrow of the independence of Switzerland. Wordsworth was prompted by the depressing news to write his great sonnet in which he deplored the extinction of the 'two great voices of liberty'—Venice and Switzerland.

Then came a blow against the kingdom of Naples. King Ferdinand IV—a Bourbon—ruled there and his queen was Marie Caroline, sister of Marie Antoinette. The miserable inefficiency of the Government was notorious, but the population was very backward, resentful of any authority, fanatically superstitious, and unprepared for the ideas of the French Revolution. When the Battle of the Nile had seemed to show that the cause of France was weakening and had brought the English fleet and Nelson into the harbour of Naples, the King despatched his general, Mack (an Austrian), to attack Rome and drive out the hated republicans. The French garrison found itself taken by surprise. Championnet, the French general, had to evacuate Rome, and Ferdinand entered to enjoy a short-lived triumph. Soon French reinforcements restored the balance in their favour. Naples was attacked and occupied; the Neapolitan royal family took refuge on the English fleet; and another republic—the Parthenopean—was set up. One incident may be noted as casting light on forces at work below the surface of Europe, which would ultimately prove too strong even for Napoleon. The armies of Naples had shown their proverbial incompetence and had fled before the French attack. But, when Championnet believed that all resistance was at an end, the despised *lazzaroni* of Naples—the lower classes of the town and country—carried on an irregular warfare that proved more serious than the resistance of the regular troops. It was beaten down in the end, but it is the first hint of popular national resistance to the French, even when they came offering liberty and equality; it is the first appearance of that passionate popular resistance which later in Spain and in the Tyrol, in Russia and Prussia and Germany, wore down the might of Napoleon.

France brought to these sister republics, which she set up, better government, higher ideals of social life, and relief from many burdens. But it is not to be wondered at that the states of Europe saw with alarm the advance of the French flood and looked round for means to resist it. Great Britain, under the guidance of Pitt, was ready with advice, money, and co-operation. But the most eager advocate of war against France was found in an unexpected quarter. In 1796 the Czar Paul had succeeded the Czarina Catherine on the Russian throne. He was probably 'a dangerous madman,' but he took his position in Russia and in Europe very seriously. He had been made Protector of the Order of St. John, from which Napoleon had taken the island of Malta on his road to Egypt, and he dreamed of making Russia an important Mediterranean Power. French schemes in Poland gave him a more justifiable cause for action. In December 1798 he joined hands with Pitt and Britain. England was to pay a large subsidy to the Russian armies, and together Britain and Russia were 'to bring back France to her pre-revolutionary frontiers.' Austria at first hung back, but the French interference in Naples had great influence in making her accept the idea of a new war. Strange events in Germany precipitated Austrian action. A conference had been called at Rastatt to consider the changes that would have to be introduced into Germany in accordance with the Peace of Campio Formio. There were French envoys there, and these, as the situation grew more and more warlike, were ordered to leave Germany. A little outside of the town they were met and attacked. Two were killed; one was seriously wounded. The affair still remains obscure. It is not impossible that the Austrian Government had really a hand in it and that the object of the outrage was the seizure of important papers. The indignation of the French Government was natural, and a condition of war was set up at once.

France had a very serious task to face. Her armies were vastly outnumbered; it is reckoned that at first she had only 170,000 men to oppose to 350,000. Her greatest general was in Egypt; and on the other side there were in command men of real energy and talent. Suvorov, the Russian general—Byron describes him as 'hero, buffoon, half demon and half dirt'—had a fiery energy that sometimes touched genius; and the Archduke Charles of Austria gained important victories. Yet in September 1798 the French had laid the basis of their future success by instituting universal military service. The system could not be brought into operation at once, but it provided the troops that won the victories of Napoleon later.

The war was on a vast scale. Italy and Switzerland were the chief theatres of the war, and at first fortune seemed decisively to favour the enemies of France. The French power was driven from Naples. The French armies were defeated in Switzerland. The most complete victory of all was won by Suvorov in Italy. He utterly defeated the French under Moreau at Novi (August 1799) and the Cisalpine and Roman Republics collapsed at once. The omens were very favourable for the allies. With close union and agreement as to the plan of campaign victory seemed assured.

But union and agreement were lacking. Though the Polish question was no longer there to paralyse the action of the allies, there was wide divergence of aim among them. Austria aimed at annexations in Bavaria and North Italy. The Czar was anxious, above all things, to restore the King of Sardinia to Piedmont and the Bourbons to France. Suvorov was a most difficult man to work with, and he was at cross purposes with the Austrian war council. This led to disaster in October 1799. Suvorov was ordered to enter Switzerland in order to join another Russian general before Zürich. He was most unwilling to leave Italy, but moved at last. The Austrians did not co-operate, and Suvorov believed himself betrayed. His march across the mountains was a great achievement, but he found the army that he was to join already dispersed and with great difficulty escaped from the surrounding French armies. There followed bitter recriminations between the generals and the Governments. The alliance was clearly falling to pieces. All this, it must be noted—both the failures of the French and their recovery from them—had happened while Napoleon was away from France.

We must return to Paris, where the Directory was in great difficulties. Its own character was in part responsible for these, for the Government was full of corruption and scandal. But here again it is the foreign war that decided the domestic issue. It was not the scandals of the Government but the failure of the war that overthrew the Directory. Twice the Directors had used the force or prestige of the army in order to exclude from the Councils representatives elected by the country but hostile to their power. But now in June 1799, in presence of defeat, actual and threatening, the support of the army failed them. The Councils took action: deposed one Director and forced the resignation of two others. The new Directors—the last to hold office—were Siéyès, Barras, Ducos, Moulin, and Gohier. Democratic Jacobinism raised its head again. The country was restless and ready to acclaim anyone who would give them honour and security.

Napoleon reached France in October 1799. He was hailed with immense enthusiasm. The failure of his Egyptian adventure was not reckoned against him. That failure had happened on a distant theatre and under obscure circumstances. Men remembered only the way in which in his Italian campaigns he had forced the Austrians to accept peace. His behaviour increased his reputation. He was modest and reserved. He boasted little of his victories, and associated more with men of science than with soldiers. Yet there can be no doubt that his eyes were always set on his great political enterprise, and that he considered carefully the problem and its solution from his arrival in France.

Some change in the Government was certain. What should be its character? Napoleon entered into close relations with Barras, his old ally; with Siéyès, the political theorist; with Talleyrand, ex-bishop and Jacobin and the subtlest and coolest of intriguers. He listened to them all, but he took chief counsel with himself. His hope was that his popularity with nearly all classes would be so great that he would be spontaneously acclaimed as head of the State. He would thus rule by something as near to constitutional right as could be obtained in revolutionary France, and would not have to draw the sword or shed blood. It makes clearer the great intrigue on which he entered if we realise that it did not work out according to programme: that the show of force was not what he wished; and that the need to display, if not to use, force considerably influenced his future career.

The scheme was helped by the fact that his brother Lucien was President of the Council of Five Hundred. Napoleon hoped that the Councils would use their constitutional right to move their sessions to St. Cloud— for Paris was not a suitable environment, even now, for a counter-revolution; that they would invest him with the command of the Paris troops; and then, meeting in the midst of the troops, would vote for constitutional revision and give him the duty of presiding over and directing the work. He did not doubt that if this were done it would result in something like personal power for himself. The Directors would have to be got rid of, but it was hoped that they could be induced to resign.

The programme was followed up to a certain point. Siéyès and Ducos, who were in the plot (though not as completely as they thought), resigned and hoped that the others would do the same. Barras had hoped for a share in the work and the power, and was deeply chagrined to find that his part was to be a negative one; in the end he, too, resigned. The other two Directors, who refused, were placed under arrest. Early on November 9, 1799, the Council of Ancients voted for the transference of the sessions to St. Cloud and conferred the desired command on Napoleon. November 10 (the 19th of Brumaire in the revolutionary calendar) was the real crisis. Napoleon knew that all his future lay on the event of the day; he said to Siéyès, as they drove to St. Cloud, pointing to the place where the guillotine had stood, 'We end there, or in the Palace of the Luxembourg.' At St. Cloud he addressed the two Councils in turn. But now the programme no longer worked; for the Councils were not so influenced by Napoleon's popularity as to be willing to vote away the Constitution and their own existence. The

3*

Ancients listened to Napoleon's address coldly and declared their devotion to the Constitution and cried 'No Cromwell!' The Council of Five Hundred when he appeared before them drove him, with some show of violence, from their hall. Popularity and fine phrases would not solve the problem; unwillingly Napoleon had to appeal to the sword. When his brother brought him word that the Council was getting out of hand he called upon the troops to enter the hall and drive the councillors out. It was for him a moment of tense anxiety. Would the soldiers of the Republic turn their bayonets against the free Government of France? They obeyed with little hesitation. The majority of the legislators fled. The rump of those who remained, acting in collusion with the chief conspirator, voted for constitutional revision, and appointed three consuls to carry it out. The names of the three were Napoleon, Siéyès, and Ducos. Early on November 11 Napoleon was back in Paris and the *coup d'état* was over. Paris and France accepted it with surprising calm. There was no sympathy with the Councils or with the Directors. The country was ready for a new experiment.

The Revolution of Brumaire had decided that the Constitution was to be revised. But what was to be the nature of the revision? On that there were widely differing ideas among the chief actors in the drama. Napoleon Bonaparte and the Abbé Siéyès had been the chief agents of the *coup d'état*: the one was a soldier, the other a man who had devoted much thought to questions of political theory and had exercised a decisive influence in the early stages of the Revolution. He expected that at this crisis the Government would be remodelled according to his ideas and that the soldier would recognise the thinker's superiority. He had a clear if rather elaborate system of government in his mind. He still held by Montesquieu's doctrine of the 'separation of the powers.' The executive was to be independent of the legislative; the Government was not to rest directly upon the support of the elected representatives of the people. Yet he knew the danger of collision between Ministers and Parliament; the history of the Revolution had made that plain. There was the problem! How to fashion a government that should not depend for its existence on the people and yet should have the confidence of the people? The formula that he adopted—he was fond of formulas—was 'Confidence from below; power from above.' The practical application of it was curious. The people were to draw up lists of men who, in their opinion, were worthy of holding office and who would enjoy their confidence as administrators. These lists were to be drawn up by an elaborate method which we need not follow. Then power was to come from above. A Great Elector was to be appointed at once. He was to be well paid and was to fulfil almost exactly the functions of a constitutional sovereign. His business was to appoint, from the lists sent up to him, all the agents of government and the members of the councils. There were to be two consuls—one for home and the other for foreign affairs. There was to be a council of state to initiate legislation;

a tribunate to discuss legislative proposals; a legislative assembly that was to hear the arguments for and against the proposed measure, and was then to vote without discussion. There was to be a senate with the right of veto.

Napoleon was in agreement with many superficial features of this scheme. He distrusted popular control; he preferred nominated assemblies to elective; he disliked and feared parliamentary discussion. But he was utterly opposed to what was fundamental in Siéyès's proposals. It was a system of checks and balances; the nominal head of the State was to have no real control; the head of the army was to be strictly subordinate. Napoleon desired a strong government, centralised in the hands of the head of the army, moving at once in obedience to a command; a government personal, efficient, and bureaucratic; and he desired that the head of the government should be himself. Here was an antagonism that could not be settled by vague phrases. Siéyès and Napoleon were in conflict, and the issue was not in doubt. It was the soldier's prestige and the soldier's sword that had triumphed at Brumaire, and Siéyès must necessarily yield. Fifty members were chosen from the two Councils to decide between the rival schemes, and Napoleon, of course, triumphed.

There was a good deal of make-believe in the scheme that was adopted. Siéyès's scheme of elective machinery, whereby confidence was to be elicited from below, was maintained in theory though it was never actually applied. The wheels in the machine bore the same names as in Siéyès's plan, but the driving force was utterly different. The executive government was to be vested in the hands of one First Consul, who could be none other than Napoleon himself. There were to be—in partial agreement with Siéyès's suggestion—two other consuls, but these were rather vice-consuls than colleagues. Cambacérès and Lebrun were appointed to these posts. They would not rival the importance of Napoleon. A nominated State Council was to initiate all legislation. Then there was to be a 'Conservative Senate' of sixty members chosen by the consuls. They were to make appointments; fill the consular vacancies; appoint a tribunate of 100 members which was to debate legislative proposals; appoint a legislative assembly of 300 who were to listen to speeches on both sides, and then vote on proposals that had come down from the tribunate. Some of these details are interesting and perhaps useful, but they were all unreal. The victorious leader of the armies of France ruled. Whilst he remained victorious and master of the armies he would rule with what constitution he pleased. He soon dispensed with some of these bodies; his personal power tended to show itself more and more openly. The people of France were pleased to have it so. The scheme was submitted to a plebiscite. It was announced that 3,012,000 votes had been cast for it and only 1562 against it.

CHAPTER V

NAPOLEON, EMPEROR AND STATESMAN

NAPOLEON had won his power in the Revolution of Brumaire as a victorious leader of the French armies, and he well knew that victory alone could maintain the position that he had won. It was a good deal later that he said to a friend, 'I act only on the imagination of the nation. When this means fails me I shall be reduced to nothing, and another will succeed me.' It is a sentence which gives us a clue to much of his history. He could not lay down the power that he had won; he was master, but he was also slave. If the French were not continuously dazzled by victories and glory the old ideals of the Revolution—liberty, equality, and fraternity—would come back to their minds, or they would think again of the high place held in an admiring Europe by the old Bourbon Monarchy.

Austria and Great Britain alone remained under arms against France. The position of Great Britain was at present unassailable. Napoleon made overtures to King George III to find some road to peace. George III only answered that it was necessary to restore to the throne of France her legitimate kings, and laid himself open to the retort that, if legitimate kings were never to be expelled, he himself, owing, as he did, his position to the revolution of 1688, had no right to the English throne. It seemed that peace was only to be won by victory.

A twofold attack was planned against Austria, very much after the fashion of those operations of 1796 which had first made Napoleon's name known in Europe. First, Moreau was to lead an army across the Rhine and into the Danube valley in order to attack Vienna by that well-known route. At the same time Napoleon was to take an army into Italy by the passes of Switzerland, which, since recent changes there, were open to him. This Italian expedition was now, however, no subordinate one; it would be upon it that the failure or success of the French Government would depend.

The French power had nearly gone from Italy. The Cisalpine Republic had collapsed, and with it all the other spheres of influence in Italy which France had established. A French army under Masséna was at this time being besieged in Genoa by the Austrian, Melas, and nothing besides this was left of French power in Northern Italy. Napoleon determined to enter Italy, not by his old route of the Mediterranean shore, but across the pass of the Great St. Bernard. He made much of this march of his across the mountains, and it was compared by his flatterers with the exploits of Hannibal and of Francis I, for Napoleon was not only a great general but also an incomparable journalist. In truth, however, there was no great difficulty in the exploit. There were only five leagues which were impracticable to carriages, and that space was quickly made available by his engineers. He descended into the Val d'Aosta, and came down into Piedmont. He hesitated for a moment as to whether he should march on Milan or Genoa. Had he marched on Genoa the French army under Masséna might perhaps have been saved. Napoleon determined, however, to make for Milan, which he entered without opposition. Masséna was in consequence forced to surrender with his army of twenty thousand men, but by a curious oversight these men were allowed to march out in the direction of Napoleon still bearing their arms. Napoleon advanced towards Alessandria, which was the headquarters of the Austrian force, and on June 14, 1800, the Battle of Marengo was fought in the neighbourhood of Alessandria. This was the first battle fought by Napoleon since his assumption of the new title of Consul, and counts as one of his great victories. In truth, it was very nearly a defeat. The French army was attacked unexpectedly whilst it was divided into three parts. It was driven back with considerable loss, and the Austrian general, wearied with heat and age, retired into Marengo, confident that he had won a victory which he might leave a subordinate to complete. It was at this moment that, with dramatic suddenness, a French force, recently detailed to watch the Austrians at Genoa, arrived under Desaix. He had no instructions from Napoleon, but he heard the noise of the guns and marched straight to them. He arrived to find Napoleon defeated, but in time to win a second battle, and this second battle was a complete French victory. The Austrians withdrew behind the river Mincio; and all the results of the victories of the Austrians and the Russians since 1798 were undone at a blow. Before the end of the year there came another heavy disaster upon them north of the Alps. There Moreau came into conflict with the Austrian army under the Archduke John, at Hohenlinden. A severely contested battle ended in a complete French victory, and Vienna itself was in danger. It would have been necessary in any case for Austria to accept peace after these two staggering blows, but a strange change which passed over Russia at the same time made it still more obviously necessary. The half-mad Czar Paul, who had for some time been a champion of legitimate monarchy and a bitter enemy of the French, had now become an eager partisan of the French and was ready to co-operate with Napoleon. So on February 9, 1801, the Austrians accepted the Peace of Lunéville, which was in many respects a repetition and reinforcement of the Peace of Campo Formio. The chief clauses were these: all the territory on the left bank of the Rhine was to be ceded to France; one-seventh of the population of the Empire was thus lost to it, and some of the most famous of German cities, such as Mainz and Cologne, Aachen and Trier. Next it was laid down that the princes who were dispossessed by these cessions were to receive compensation 'according to arrangements which shall be determined later.' It was clear that this compensation would be at the expense of the smaller powers of Germany. It was laid down that the Emperor should decide for the Empire and should accept the decisions made at the Congress of Rastatt. The Italian stipulations of the Peace of Campo Formio were in the main reaffirmed. The Duchy of Tuscany and the island of Elba were ceded to the Cisalpine Republic, and it was agreed that the Duke of Tuscany should receive in Germany compensation for what he lost in Italy. The independence, it may be noted, of the sister republics which had been set up by France in various parts of Europe was guaranteed.[1]

Great Britain alone now remained, and Napoleon despaired as yet of striking any blow against her through direct action at sea, but cherished for a time the hope that what he could not do directly he might do indirectly. It was well known, and had become quite apparent during the war with the American colonies, that every nation that possessed any maritime power resented the claim of Great Britain to be allowed, in time of war, to search all vessels of whatever kind, even those belonging to neutral Powers, in order to see whether they were carrying goods belonging to the enemies of Britain and to destroy such goods if found. There had been a league of neutrals against this practice at the end of the American War, but the practice still continued. Now, under the direction of Russia, Denmark and Sweden joined with Prussia in a league of protest against this right of search. It seemed possible that a formidable naval Power might be created in the Baltic hostile to Great Britain and capable of serious action against her. Great Britain, however, struck too swiftly. On April 2, 1801, Copenhagen was attacked, the Danish fleet destroyed, and the league broken up. At the same time events in Egypt were obviously leading up to the surrender of the French armies into British hands, which occurred during the summer.

The war seemed as though it might go on for ever. Yet peace was desirable for both parties to it; and in England, where Pitt had resigned owing to his sharp difference with George III about the conditions of the union with Ireland, the new Prime Minister, Addington, was less determined in his prosecution of the war. Negotiations were opened, and the peace of Amiens was signed (March 27, 1802). It is a peace of many clauses, but they may be shortly summarised. All English conquests from France were to be restored, but Ceylon and Trinidad, which had been ceded, the one by Holland and the other by Spain, were to be retained by the British. Malta, which had recently been retaken by the British from Napoleon, was to be restored, not to France but to the Knights of St. John. It is a long clause that lays down the method of this restoration. The independence of the island was to be guaranteed by Great Britain, Austria, Spain, Russia, and Prussia. The King of the Two Sicilies was to garrison the island with two thousand troops. There are other details also. We shall see that they were never carried out; and that Great Britain, on that ground, refused to hand over the

---

[1] These sister republics, it will be convenient to note, were the Batavian (Dutch), the Helvetic (Swiss), the Cisalpine and the Ligurian (Italian).

island. Such was the Peace of Amiens. It was greeted with immense jubilation in France and in Great Britain. It opened Europe again to the visits of English tourists. Many regarded it as the end of the period of war and the establishment of a durable peace, and some were ready to see in Napoleon a great benefactor of mankind. It proved, however, to be only a precarious and deceitful truce. In England the early enthusiasm for it soon passed away. Public opinion, especially among the commercial classes, was irritated because France still held Belgium and Holland—still, therefore, controlled those lands which in the hands of a rival Power seemed to us 'a pistol pointed at the heart of London.' The hopes of trade with France, too, proved illusory; nowhere was trade readily admitted, and in some places it was absolutely prohibited. Such as it was, however, the Peace gave to France a much needed breathing space during which great changes were introduced into her political, social, and religious life.

Before, however, we notice them we will follow the influence of this great shaking of Europe on Germany. Germany, as we have seen, was at the beginning of our period a strange congeries of states large and small, secular and ecclesiastical, free and despotic—free towns, even free villages, being mixed on constitutionally equal terms with great States such as Prussia or Bavaria or Austria—and over this strange collection of states there was no effective power at all. The Emperor was a name and the Empire was a dignity, but it was not a force with the capacity for control. The real power belonged not to the Empire as a whole but to its parts, to the rulers of the states of the Empire, such as Austria, Prussia, Bavaria, Hanover, Saxony, Würtemberg. We have seen how in 1795 Prussia had backed out of the war by the Peace of Basel, and how in October 1797 Austria had made the first of her Peaces with France at Campo Formio. By this Peace it was arranged that a conference was to be called at Rastatt in order to settle the terms of peace between France and the Empire—the Empire, that is to say, as distinguished from Austria. Secret articles regulated in advance certain features of this settlement. France was to have territory on the west bank of the Rhine; Prussia was to be allowed no gains. The secular princes who were dispossessed, but not the ecclesiastical, were to be compensated in a way that should be agreed upon with the French Republic. It was a momentous hour in the history of Germany, and we may see in the shaking and destruction of her mediaeval constitution and life the beginning of the movement which was to lead her forward to unity and power in the latter part of the nineteenth century. But for the present there was neither power nor wise statesmanship to take advantage of the opportunities offered by the situation. The Emperor, Francis II, was a man of some natural shrewdness, interested in music, in the drama, and in natural history, but not a strong man either in intellect or will. He had all the instincts of the despot and feared liberty in every shape. His Minister, Thugut, was a statesman after his own heart, without guiding ideas either for the management of the Austrian possessions or for the reconstruction of Germany. Napoleon said of him that he interfered in everything, mixed himself up with the intrigues of all Europe without following any kind of plan. Nor could guidance for Germany come from Prussia when Austria failed her. The time of Prussia was not yet. The King, Frederick William III, 'the most respectable and the most ordinary man who has ever reigned in Prussia,' believed that the Peace of Basel had added to the strength of Prussia and was utterly opposed to new ideas. There is no trace in his policy of any general German patriotism or of any conception of the general meaning for his own country, or for Germany at large, of the tornado which was sweeping across Europe. There were in the Prussian service wiser heads than his own. His Foreign Minister, Hardenberg, had a sincere and eager patriotism. There were soldiers and statesmen who, when the time came, would co-operate in the revival of Prussia which led to the revival and triumph of Germany.

For the present, Germany, as a whole and in its parts, was inert and politically corrupt, unable and apparently unwilling to resist in any effective way the designs of France. At the same time we must beware of thinking of the German people or of life in Germany as decadent or as exhibiting nothing but weakness. In fact there was in the second half of the eighteenth century a splendid flowering of German thought and art. From the middle of the century onwards a great national revival had taken place in literature and thought, to which the principal contributors were Lessing, Goethe, Schiller, and Kant. The years between 1780 and 1805 were the classical age of German literature, centred in Weimar and dominated by the giant figures of Goethe and Schiller. In music the illustrious line of Bach's successors, Haydn, Mozart and Beethoven, gave to the German-speaking lands pre-eminence in Europe. The magnificence of these achievements stands in marked contrast to the political weakness of the German states in this period.

When the Congress met at Rastatt in December 1797 Germany was represented by a 'deputation' of sixty-seven members. France played from the first a leading part there. Napoleon had been present at first himself, but was then succeeded by four diplomatists. The general aims of France in the negotiations which followed were to secure for herself the left bank of the Rhine, to sow dissensions between Austria and Prussia, and to compensate the secular powers by allowing them to absorb the ecclesiastical states; but before any conclusion could be reached at Rastatt there came events that we have already glanced at— the outbreak of the war with the Second Coalition and the murder of the French envoys. When the Battles of Marengo and of Hohenlinden had forced Austria to the Peace of Lunéville the work of reconstruction in Germany was taken up again. The decrees passed at Rastatt were now to be executed, and without further ado the Emperor was to sign on behalf of Germany. The decisions, however, were brought before another and a much smaller deputation of the Empire. It included, indeed, only eight members, representing respectively Mainz, Saxony, Bohemia, Brandenburg (Prussia), Bavaria, Würtemberg, Hesse-Cassel, and the Knights of the Teutonic Order. The deputation, however, would consent to nothing, and in the end France and her new ally, Russia, intervened as mediating Powers. They dictated terms and made treaties with the separate states. The memory of these days is a humiliation for all German historians. Questions profoundly affecting the destinies of the whole and of the parts of Germany were decided, not by the imperial authority, nor even by the kings and princes of Germany, but almost entirely by French diplomatists. The future of the lands of the Oder and the Elbe and the Vistula depended upon the decisions that were taken in the Foreign Office of Paris; and the rooms of Talleyrand, Napoleon's trusted Foreign Minister, were crowded with German princes and agents each seeking, by whatever means, to secure the favour of the great Minister for himself or his master. It was not until February 1803 that all was over. The settlement agreed on elsewhere was then brought before, and accepted by, the Reichstag. The general characteristics of the settlement of Germany are clear from what we have already said: the strong states gained, the weak states lost. One hundred and twelve so-called states were absolutely annihilated, being absorbed in their greater neighbours. Most of the imperial knights and all but six imperial towns disappeared by this process. The ecclesiastical states were swept away from the map of Europe with one single exception. Mainz had been annexed by France, but the Archbishop of Mainz was Chancellor of the Empire, and it was thought unwise to destroy his power entirely. He was transferred to the bishopric of Ratisbon. The Teutonic Knights and the Knights of St. John still subsisted for a while: four new members received the electoral dignity; but there was a general feeling that the Empire of which they were thus made electors was fading out from the European world.

Austria had clearly lost control of the shadowy Empire. The long possession of the imperial title by the House of Hapsburg, whereby she had converted what was nominally an elective title into practically an hereditary possession, had been largely due to her championship of the Catholic interest; but now the majority of the electors were Protestants, and would be little likely to support a Hapsburg. As some compensation she was allotted the important city of Trent. Bavaria lost much in the west—Juliers, Berg and the Palatinate—but she was more than compensated by the acquisition of Würzburg, Bamberg, Kempten, and Augsburg. It was the settled policy of France to build up Bavaria and to make her a rival to the power of Austria. The Grand Duke of Baden also gained considerable acquisitions of territory. Prussia received an adequate compensation for what she was losing beyond the Rhine. To Prussia, indeed, Napoleon was inclined, at any rate for a space, to be friendly. He aimed at the dividing of Germany into three main groups

—the Prussian, the Austrian, and the South German. He even hinted that he would not be unwilling to see Prussia in possession of Hanover, for such an acquisition would have made friendship and alliance between Prussia and Great Britain impossible.

The new scheme in Germany was accepted without resistance or declared dislike, and along with French influence there came into Germany things which were a great change for the better. In the territories annexed to France were introduced, of course, all the legal and social institutions which France had won as a result of the Revolution. Elsewhere France only acted by example and by influence, but these were very powerful. There was in the Germany of this period a rapid growth of activity in speculation on social and political topics, a change in the tendency of German ideas, a willingness to alter institutions; and, though all these things were used later against France, it cannot be doubted that they owed in their origin very much to France herself.

We must now turn again to the history of France and, neglecting for the present all military events, though these have the closest and most intimate connection with her domestic history, we will trace in outline the great changes that passed over the position of Napoleon, and the institutions and reforms which he introduced into what was soon to be called his empire.

Napoleon ruled France as First Consul. He disregarded the machinery which had been set up after the Revolution of Brumaire. Those institutions had perhaps been useful in the first instance as screens to his personal power, but as he grew more confident and more assured of public support he swept them away and ruled without even pretending to take the people into partnership. Not only did his power tend more and more to become an avowed autocracy: it also, little by little, dropped all trace of its revolutionary origin, and became more conservative and more dependent upon the conservative support of the Church and the peasantry. Napoleon disliked later to be reminded in any way of his early revolutionary connections and beliefs. In December 1800 a bomb was thrown at him as he was going to the opera. It was declared to be the work of the *septembriseurs*, the contemptuous phrase that was now applied to the violent Jacobins. After an inquiry 130 Jacobins were banished, not for the bomb throwing but, as the edict said, 'for the massacres of September 2, May 31, and every subsequent attempt.' The Government made war even upon women, and the widows of Marat and Chaumette were imprisoned. It is noteworthy, as showing Napoleon's old connections, that the sister of Robespierre was awarded a pension.

These attacks on the First Consul were the cause or excuse of a further hardening of the constitution. Then, in March 1802, came the Peace of Amiens, and France saw herself victorious over all her enemies and in the enjoyment of a military prestige that even Louis XIV at the height of his power had never possessed. She seemed to owe all to the marvellous man who had led her from victory to victory. Liberty had few enthusiasts now; personal rule seemed to bring success and might bring prosperity. Doubtless Napoleon desired to secure his personal power on a more durable and unchallenged basis; but the desire of his people seconded and even outstripped his ambition. In gratitude for the Peace it was proposed to extend his consulate to a second period of ten years. It was due to Napoleon himself that this proposal was enlarged and changed into the consulship for life. The office was not to be hereditary, but—in imitation of Roman models—the Consul was to be allowed to choose his own successor. Changes in the constitutional machinery were made at the same time. The State Council became the Privy Council; its members were nominated by the First Consul and it was given the initiative in all proposals. It was only in the Tribunate that any discussion was allowed. There was nothing that Napoleon so much disliked and feared as discussion, whether in an Assembly or in the press. Already, after the attack on his person, the Tribunate had been remodelled: those who were to retire each year were chosen by the First Consul, who could thus get rid of opponents; and strict limitations were placed on their debates. Now the Tribunate was divided into five sections and the deliberations of each were held in secret. The electoral machinery was still kept in name, and even revised; but the electors were not allowed really to influence the Government in any way. France had now a personal government, with fewer checks upon it than had existed in the time of the old Monarchy. All citizens were asked to give their opinion on the new proposals. They supported Napoleon's extended power by three-and-a-half millions of votes to less than ten thousand. The imperial plebiscites are not above suspicion; but it is clear that the people desired that Napoleon should rule.

He was Emperor in all but name. The name came soon, and it will be well to trace the way by which it came without casting more than a rapid glance upon foreign affairs, which had a profound influence on the assumption of the new title. For in May 1803 the Peace of Amiens broke down and the new war, first with Great Britain and then with a wide European alliance, seemed a personal challenge to the power and character of Napoleon. In face of such an attack it was inevitable that France should rally with enthusiasm round the man of her choice. A similar effect was produced by the Cadoudal plot which came to light in February 1804. This was a really serious affair. Georges Cadoudal was a Vendean Royalist and he had sworn to kill Napoleon. Greater names than his were associated with him: Pichegru, the revolutionary general, and Moreau, the victor of Hohenlinden. The English Government, too, was not ignorant that something was in the wind. But a fellow-conspirator revealed the plot. Cadoudal was executed; Moreau was banished; Pichegru died in prison, not without some suspicions of foul play. The plot, too, caused the death of one who was in no way connected with it. The Duc d'Enghien was a prince of the House of Condé and one of the emigrant nobles. He was resident at Ettenheim in Baden, not far beyond the frontier of France. The reason of the outrage that followed is difficult to make out. Napoleon felt himself surrounded by plots. He was exasperated against the confederacy that was growing up against him. He seems to have believed that some invasion of France was preparing in which Enghien was to be assisted by Dumouriez. A body of cavalry rode to Ettenheim, seized the Duke, and brought him first to Strasburg, and then by rapid marches to Vincennes, near Paris. A court-martial was held upon him, and after the mockery of a trial he was shot at once. Nothing has weighed more heavily on the reputation of Napoleon than this crime. Rumbold, the British representative, was about the same time abducted from Hamburg and his life was with difficulty saved from the anger of Napoleon. Several of the German states were forced to dismiss their British representatives.

Plots real and supposed; the frantic hatred of Europe, and especially of Great Britain—these only increased the readiness of France to testify her confidence in Napoleon. A proposal was made in the Tribunate to make the power of Napoleon hereditary. It passed as a matter of course, Carnot alone maintaining a republican attitude of opposition. Then a little later—on May 18, 1804—a decree of the Senate gave him the title of 'Emperor of the French.' The Pope was in official relations with the new Government of France in consequence of the legislation shortly to be examined. He came to Paris and crowned Napoleon and Josephine in the cathedral of Notre-Dame. All the details of the ceremony were carefully considered. Napoleon avoided the recognition of any superiority in the Pope. He took the crown from the Pope's hands and placed it on his own head.

Napoleon's claim to statesmanship, which gives him a unique place among soldiers of genius, rests primarily on the measures of domestic policy of this period. They are numerous and of vital importance in the history not only of France but of Europe as a whole. In their formulation many people besides Napoleon took a significant part, but Napoleon's direct responsibility is great, for his inspiration and influence affected them all.

First, he found a settlement of the religious question which had for so long been a festering sore in France. The challenge of the Revolution to the Catholic sentiment of France and to the organisation of the Catholic Church had been the source of many of the gravest difficulties which had beset her. The attempt to set up a constitutional Catholic Church independent of Rome and the Pope had proved a dismal failure. The constitutional priests had no following. In many cases they had married and adopted a secular life. Theophilanthropy, in spite of the support given to it in Government circles, had been an entire fiasco. Religious France was at heart Catholic, and a greater part of France was religious than is usually assumed.

Napoleon approached the matter from the point of view of statesmanship. His own religious views do not seem to have gone beyond a vague deism. But he had a just instinct of the strength of the Catholic Church and of the danger of collision with a body that commanded the loyalty of so many Frenchmen. He wanted an established church as a support for his throne. 'A state without a religion is like a vessel without a compass,' he said. Even in his first Italian campaigns he had shown himself more friendly to the Papacy than the French Government quite liked. After the Battle of Marengo the *rapprochement* between him and the Papacy was hurried on. The Battle of Marengo was celebrated by a religious thanksgiving. Pope Pius VII was restored to the Papal States. The attitude of the First Consul clearly invited friendly overtures. At the same time hints of threats were not wanting. A French garrison was maintained in Rome and might at any moment make its presence unpleasant. There was some talk, too, of carrying farther the traditional idea of Gallican liberties and erecting in France a Church, Catholic and orthodox, but independent of Rome. So the Concordat was passed and at Easter 1802 France went back in the main to the ecclesiastical constitution which had existed before the Revolution—a constitution the main lines of which had been laid down by the Concordat of Bologna, signed between King Francis I and Pope Leo X in 1516. The Church entered again into communion with Rome. Catholicism was once more the religion of the State. Its services and organisation were to be supported by State funds. On the other hand, all the higher Church dignitaries were to be nominated by the First Consul; the Pope could only reject his nominees on the ground of heresy or immorality, and, if there was no fault to be found with them on these points, was bound to grant canonical investiture. The First Consul would thus be able to maintain authority over the Church by appointing to the important posts men of whose support he could feel sure. This, however, was not the end nor, in the Pope's view, the worst. In the Concordat there occurred the clause that 'worship should be public so long as it conformed to the police regulations, which the Government should judge necessary in the interest of public tranquillity.' These regulations were soon produced. It was declared that no papal bulls were applicable to France; that no synod of the clergy of France could be held without the permission of the First Consul; that no bishop might leave his diocese even if summoned by the Pope. Worst of all, it was laid down that the declaration of Gallican liberties—that is, the special rights and liberties of the Catholic Church in France—were to be taught to all those who were preparing for the priesthood. This declaration, formulated in 1682, had been a matter of long controversy between the old Monarchy of France and the Papacy. In sum it curtailed the authority of the Pope within the Church of France, and declared that that authority was not final until it had been corroborated by the assent of the Church. So bitter was the draught that the Pope hesitated about accepting the Concordat as a whole, now that this declaration had been attached to it; but he accepted it in the end.

Napoleon's central idea in all this was to control a great force that influenced the actions of men through their feelings and beliefs. Other Churches were not left out of account. The Lutheran and the Calvinist Churches were brought under State control and into State pay. Government support was also given to the Jews. The religious life of France was thus to be established and endowed. The throne, though much changed in style, was once again to lean on the altar or altars of France. There have been widely differing judgments on all this from the point of both religion and policy. It is clear that the time had come when the French people must be allowed to enter again into free communion with the Church that they preferred. But was the State control wise? Was it in the long run good for the Church to be thus identified with the interests of Napoleon? And did Napoleon gain any permanent strength from this connection? The spirit of Bossuet was still strong in France, but so was the spirit of Voltaire. The Catholics and the Catholic Church of France were grateful to Napoleon for his services, but they did not forget the connection of his power with the hated Revolution. And revolutionary sentiment in France regarded the Concordat as a direct attack on their central principles. Joseph Bonaparte called it 'a retrograde and thoughtless step.' 'A million men have died,' said another, 'to destroy what you are re-establishing.'

The same period sees also the elaboration and completion of the Napoleonic codes. They are one of Napoleon's greatest claims to be considered a benefactor of mankind. In his exile in St. Helena he claimed that the Civil Code, and not his victories in war, was his most real claim to fame. The French codes, too, were the most effective instrument in carrying over a large part of Europe the ideas of the French Revolution so far as they were accepted and promoted by Napoleon. The idea and the work of codification were not new in France. There was indeed something characteristically French in this effort to carry forward the work of the Roman Empire and to present the laws of France within the smallest possible compass and in a form clear, logical, and complete. Louis XIV had done something towards this end. The Revolution had expressed a desire to see that work carried farther. Such work has always required for its accomplishment the force of a strong government and usually of a powerful single will; and this was supplied in full measure by Napoleon.

Napoleon was the child of the Revolution, but in many ways he reversed the aims and principles of the movement from which he sprang. And this was particularly true of the codes. The Revolution had not only swept away what remained of feudalism and ecclesiastical control of the State, but it had attacked the cherished traditions of the lawyers of France. It had striven, above all things, for equality. It had insisted that the inheritance should be divided in equal shares among the children; it had limited very strictly the power of testamentary bequest; it had offended Catholic sentiment by introducing divorce; it had removed all control over questions arising out of births, deaths, and marriages from the Church. There was much in all this of which Napoleon in his new mood did not approve. He had made friends with the Church. He valued authority. He had little love for equality. He would therefore not merely present the legislation of the Revolution in a short and logical form; he would desire to alter it in important particulars.

Napoleon was not a lawyer, and he approached the questions with the open mind and also with the ignorance of a layman. But his influence was very great. He not only gave the impulse and insisted on the work being carried out: he also presided at many of the sittings, especially of those devoted to the Civil Code, and interfered often with decisive effect. Some utterances of his with regard to the work of lawyers are of sufficient interest to be quoted: 'I first thought that it would be possible to reduce laws to simple geometrical demonstrations, so that whoever could read and tie two ideas together would be capable of pronouncing on them; but I almost immediately convinced myself that this was an absurd idea. . . . I often perceived that over-simplicity in legislation was the enemy of precision. It is impossible to make laws extremely simple without cutting the knot oftener than you untie it.'

There were five codes in all: the Civil Code, the code of civil procedure, the code of criminal procedure and penal law, the penal code, and the commercial code. Before they became binding on France they passed through many stages, but the really decisive agencies were a preliminary committee, in which the project of the Civil Code was drawn up, and the Council of State before which the suggestions were brought, and which was often presided over by Napoleon himself. He took his duties seriously, and was present at thirty-five out of the eighty-seven sittings devoted to the Civil Code. His influence was naturally thrown on the side of authority, in the family as well as the State. He stood for the absolute authority of the father within the family over wife and children alike. He was strongly in favour of the subjection of women. 'The angel told Eve to obey her husband,' he said. 'Morality has written this article in all languages. *A fortiori* should it be written in French in our code.' The code allowed the father even to imprison his children by what was nearly a return to the practice of the old régime. It allowed divorce, but surrounded it with restrictions; it favoured the division of property, insisting on the equal division among the children of at least a large portion of the inheritance. It secured many of the victories that had been won by the Revolution; but Napoleon's personal influence was responsible for the hardening of many provisions and the disappearance of others. He gave a far wider range to the influence of revolutionary principles than they could have hoped to gain otherwise, but he took from them something of their earlier radiance. The other codes are not so important as the Civil Code. The Court of Criminal

Procedure followed in many respects the example of English practice. Yet the institution of the jury was hotly attacked. Many held that it was too favourable to the accused and limited dangerously the power of the Government. In the end, and largely through the influence of Napoleon, it was maintained. Its decisions were given by a majority; trials were to be held in public; counsel was to be allowed in all cases. The characteristic French procedure of a preliminary and largely secret indictment of the accused by the *juge d'instruction* was maintained, in spite of the protest of the revolutionary statesmen against it. In the penal code branding and confiscation of property were allowed as penalties, and the right of association was only allowed under strict limitations. Yet it is wrong to lay exclusive stress on the harder sides of the codes. Mr. H. A. L. Fisher[1] (whose brilliant chapter on the codes has been used throughout) ends with words which cannot be bettered as a summary of the whole matter. In spite of all defects 'the Codes preserve the essential conquests of the revolutionary spirit—civil equality, religious toleration, the emancipation of land, public trial, the jury of judgment.' To Germany and Italy 'they were the earliest message, as well as the most mature embodiment, of the new spirit. In a clear and compact shape, they presented to Europe the main rules which should govern a civilised society.'

Napoleon also reconstituted the general administration of France, and all he did was inspired by the same spirit; he desired in everything the establishment of a central authority—which could only be his own authority—which should direct or control every part of the life of France. He claimed, and it has often been claimed for him, that he was the incarnation of the French Revolution; but in truth in his work there is more of the spirit of Louis XIV than of the Constituent Assembly. Sometimes he used language which recalled the favourite metaphors of 'Le Roi Soleil': 'Government plays the part of the sun in the social system, whose various bodies should revolve round this central luminary, each keeping strictly to its own orbit.' The codes, as we have seen, perpetuated much of the social gains that had been won by the Revolution. Napoleon was always careful to preserve from molestation the rights of the peasantry; he never proposed to re-establish the system of financial privilege; but in most other respects his reign saw a continual reaction towards the ideas and forms and practices of the old Monarchy.

Thus he revived by successive enactments the hierarchy of rank which the Revolution had so resolutely abolished. The beginnings of this may be found in the establishment of the Legion of Honour in 1802. France was then still a republic, and Napoleon spoke the language of the Revolution; but the men of the Convention would have regarded with horror the new distinction which he distributed primarily to soldiers but also to civilians of high achievement in all walks of life. From 1804 onwards a vast and stately hierarchy of rank grew up. Under the princes

[1] *Cambridge Modern History*, vol. IX. chap. 6.

of the imperial family there were established the six 'grand imperial dignitaries'—the Grand Elector, the Arch-Chancellors of the Empire and of the State, the Arch-Treasurer, the Constable, and the Grand Admiral. Then came the Grand Officers of the Empire, ranging from the Marshals of the Empire to the 'Grand Almoner' and the 'Grand Chamberlain' and the 'Grand Huntsman.' In 1808 the full system was completed, and the imperial throne was surrounded by as thick a crowd of 'Princes and Dukes and Counts and Barons and Knights' as had ever supported the throne of Louis XIV. Many of these dignitaries were 'new men' who had been raised from the ranks of the middle or lower classes by the revolutionary storm; but the tendency was for Napoleon to look to the members of the old families for his servants and his titles. The revolutionists could no longer see in him an ally, but the members of the ancient régime felt no loyalty to him and showed him little fidelity.

The Revolution had had aspirations towards the organisation of an educational system in France, but had not found time to do more than make a beginning. Here, too, Napoleon in characteristic fashion, by his powers of energy and will, translated ideas into facts, but altered all according to his own bias towards rigid centralisation and authority. There were to be schools of four grades: primary, secondary, the characteristic semi-military boarding schools, which were called *lycées*, and special schools for technical training. At the head of all and controlling all came the Imperial University, which was definitely constituted in 1808. There was to be one single University for all France, with seventeen subordinate provincial institutions controlled from the centre. It was intended to bring the whole educational system of France under the control of the University. No one was to be allowed to teach who was not a graduate in one of the faculties of the University, but the vast military and political tasks which claimed Napoleon's attention prevented him from reaching his aim, and, when the Empire fell, the majority of the pupils in French schools were under private and voluntary instruction.

The famous *Institut de France* had been established in 1795 for higher study and research. Napoleon's relation to it is curiously significant. He supported it in the main, and was pleased with the work it did in physical science and the fine arts, in mathematics and literature; but he reorganised it. He disliked the study of moral and political sciences, and, by his decree of January 23, 1803, suppressed the department that was devoted to these studies. There is nothing more characteristic of despotism than suspicion of the studies and speculations that touch human life and conduct, and nothing reveals the essential despotism of Napoleon's outlook more than this hostility towards the moralist and the politician.

He was equally opposed to liberty of expression in the press and in literature. Newspapers were strictly censored, and at last almost suppressed. All books had to be submitted to examination before they were published. The theatre, too, was submitted to a peculiarly rigid control.

Napoleon imitated too the better features of the age of Louis XIV with curious closeness. He inaugurated a vast series of public works. Roads were projected and many constructed; canals were cut; French manufactures were fostered by a protective system which had its origins partly in the political and military relations of France with Europe, but also corresponded to Napoleon's own ideas. Colbert—the great Minister of Louis XIV—would have been delighted by the tariffs by which foreign manufactures were excluded, by the regimentation of French industries in guilds once more, and by the steps which were taken to introduce into France some of the methods of the industrial revolution which had made so profound a change in the life of Great Britain. Agriculture was improved by the introduction of new methods from Belgium and England. The Lyons silk industry was revived, partly through the adoption of the new Jacquard loom. Cotton was introduced from the East, and was manufactured by means of the spinning-jenny, which came from England. Gas was adopted as an illuminant. The general condition of France, until the Empire touched its period of ruin, showed an air of prosperity in all classes. The economic situation was indeed thoroughly artificial, and depended in every part on war. Yet work was plentiful and wages good. Those who looked beneath the surface saw that there would be a Nemesis at last.

Napoleon's ministers and agents depended on him alone. Neither popular approval nor popular censure affected their tenure of office. He was at first served by men of great ability, both in the army and in the domestic administration. In the last category two names stand out pre-eminent: Talleyrand for the management of foreign affairs, and Fouché for the maintenance of order at home. They were both men of something like genius in their widely different ways; the one subtle, ironic, a master of finesse, and a skilful reader of the barometer of Europe; the other brutal and corrupt, the head of a network of spies and secret agents, quick to detect and to suppress conspiracies against his imperial master, and not above the suspicion that he sometimes fomented the conspiracies that he discovered. Both men rendered Napoleon most valuable services, but both fell under his suspicion. They probably saw clearly the dangers that threatened his power in spite of his immense victories, and both prepared the way for a favourable reception in the camp of his enemies. Talleyrand is strongly suspected of having communicated with the British Government at the time of the Treaty of Tilsit in 1807. He quarrelled with Napoleon in 1808, and was not employed again as his chief agent in foreign affairs. Fouché's power lasted longer, and he was for a time the chief man in France next to the Emperor. But he was more guilty than Talleyrand of facing both ways and of thinking of a possible refuge when Napoleon's power was gone. He was dismissed in 1810. Henceforward the

Emperor ruled by weaker and more submissive instruments. Like Louis XIV and many other representatives of sovereign power, he became suspicious of great ability in his subordinates, and tried to manage the whole of his vast Empire himself.

In one respect he was less fortunate than the great French king with whom we have compared him. The throne of Louis XIV was glorified and strengthened by the array of men, great in every department of art and thought, who surrounded it and paid willing homage to it. Napoleon was quite awake to the importance of such support, but his Court was always something artificial and exotic, and it was not connected with any high standard of manners or with any great names in the domains of art or thought. The mind and heart of France were active, but they owed little to Napoleon, and expressed no gratitude to him. The greatest names in literature were in decided opposition to his power. One of them was that of Chateaubriand, who had at one time been in the service of the Empire. He exercised a great influence over the mind of his contemporaries, and his book called 'The Genius of Christianity,' published in 1802, had made him famous. He was not persecuted by Napoleon, but all his influence was thrown against the Emperor. The conflict between the Emperor and Madame de Staël was more direct. She was the daughter of Necker, famous at the beginning of the French Revolution, and was the author of novels and treatises. Though she was thoroughly French in her character and in the style of her writings, she had written a book 'On Germany,' in which she analysed and praised the characteristics of the people, and in so doing managed to strike more than one shrewd blow against the methods of Napoleon. She was subjected to supervision and almost to imprisonment at Napoleon's hands, but she escaped and published her book in England. Europe looked on and applauded the daring woman's resistance to the tyrant, and exaggerated her value both as thinker and artist. France had famous names in science and important names in art at this period, but the fifteen years during which Napoleon was the supreme figure in France are not a great period in French literature, art, or thought. The chief strength of the Emperor's Court lay, probably, in the Empress Josephine. She was prodigal of money, and is estimated by Masson, the biographer of Napoleon, to have spent over a million francs a year on dress alone. But she was beautiful, charming, and, to a large extent, popular. Her divorce was prompted by political and international considerations, but it was probably a mistake. France never took her successor into favour, as we shall see on a later page.

It has been claimed that Napoleon was equally great as statesman and as soldier. Can that claim be justified? Doubtless he had no chance of developing all his ideas amid the hardly interrupted storms of war; his domestic policy was throughout subordinated to military necessities. But we must remember that the European situation was largely his own creation, and that his power in France itself was always

intimately bound up with his military prestige and victories. In his social
and political schemes there is very little that is original. For a part of it
the way had been prepared by the Revolution; for another part, by the
old Monarchy. The great feature about his statesmanship is not its
originality, but the immense energy and strength of will and attention
to detail with which he carried it out. It was not so novel, nor perhaps
so well adapted to the needs of the time, as the work of Colbert, which
it so closely resembles. Finally, it is obvious that in all his work he
showed no appreciation of the value of political liberty. That first great
watchword of the Revolution had perhaps at one time appealed to him,
but his early enthusiasm was quite dead. He thought of liberty as a disturbing factor that prevented the efficiency of a state. There is no hint
in anything that he said or wrote that he thought of it as the great force
making for stability, order, and efficiency.

CHAPTER VI

THE DEFEAT OF THE GOVERNMENTS OF EUROPE

THE Peace of Amiens had been welcomed with profound relief by all
the nations of Europe, and nowhere more than in Great Britain. Many
hoped that the storms of the revolutionary period were over, and that
Europe might enjoy at any rate a space of tranquillity and peaceful development; and yet the Peace of Amiens lasted less than two years, and
quickly gave place to a war of greater intensity and longer duration,
which did not really cease until the Battle of Waterloo. What were the
causes of the new war? Though the rupture of the Peace of Amiens has
had many books written about it there are certain points about which
there is still real difference of opinion among the best informed
historians.

Generally, that rupture illustrates the working of the idea of Balance
of Power. The various nations of Europe regarded one another as
potential enemies; the power of one seemed to be the danger of the rest.
With these ideas it was inevitable that the great position which France
had attained before the Peace should seem a real menace to the safety
of the other European States, and the gains which France made after
the Peace were still further unsettling and alarming to the minds of
traditional European statesmen. We must turn, therefore, to notice
what these fresh developments were which were the excuse, and to a
large extent the real cause, for the outbreak of hostilities.

We have already seen the encroachments of the French power upon
her neighbours during the Peace of Lunéville. The same process may
be observed after the Peace of Amiens. France had established six sister
republics in Europe. These were expressly recognised as independent
by the Treaty of Lunéville, but France treated them in such a way as to

imply that they were, in effect, at her disposal. French garrisons were maintained in all of them. The Cisalpine Republic was already in its foreign policy dependent upon the decision of Napoleon. It was now all but openly annexed. Four hundred and fifty representatives from the Republic came to Lyons. There they debated the form of their constitution. It was agreed to adopt one precisely parallel to that of France. The title of the Cisalpine Republic was changed to that of the Italian Republic, and Napoleon was chosen as its President (this was before his own assumption of the imperial title), 'not as being First Consul of France, but as an individual.' The distinction really made no difference: the Italian Republic was closely bound to the fortunes of France. Piedmont, as we have seen, was definitely annexed in September 1802, and no compensation was paid to Sardinia. France had not ceased, moreover, her interference in the affairs of Switzerland. The French troops were not withdrawn, and this gave her the opportunity of deciding on the issue of the internal political strife which now broke out. There was a democratic party at daggers drawn with an oligarchical party. There was one party which desired a centralised government, while another was in favour of a form of federalism. Napoleon declared that Switzerland must be saved from herself, and he imposed upon her a federal constitution in which nineteen cantons took part. Again the independence of Switzerland was declared, but she was bound to contribute troops to France, and her independence, therefore, was a mere form and shadow.

All these things concerned Great Britain and the Powers of Europe equally, but there were certain incidents which touched Great Britain particularly, and which even alarmed her as implying that France and the ruler of France had not yet given up the idea of challenging the colonial and maritime power of Great Britain.

There were strange events in San Domingo. This island, better known to us as Hayti, was inhabited almost entirely by a population of negro origin. The French Revolution had declared slavery abolished throughout French dominions, but the result had not been to procure peace in San Domingo. On the contrary, a violent servile war had broken out, and in this war there appeared Toussaint L'Ouverture, the greatest military general who has ever come of negro stock. He made himself the leader of the insurgent blacks, occupied practically the whole island, and treated it as belonging to him personally. The offers of the English to help were rejected, and their efforts to occupy the island were defeated. Toussaint began, with victory, to ape something of the manners and ceremony of European military command. In 1801 he took to himself the title of consul for life, and gave to the island a constitution on the model of what had been adopted in France. The Constitution, of course, never existed except on paper. When, therefore, the Peace of Amiens gave to France once more the power of despatching ships across the Atlantic the island was practically independent of France and in the occupation of this remarkable negro chief. It was inevitable that the French should try to recover it. Nor does there seem to be any good reason for the objection felt by the English Government to the method in which it was done. General Leclerc, the husband of Pauline Bonaparte, was sent out with an army of twenty thousand men. Against this force Toussaint could make no effective resistance. He showed great energy and some tactical skill; in the end, however, his surrender was obtained, and he was deported to France and imprisoned there. The French army that was left behind was attacked by disease and reduced to a very small force. San Domingo ultimately became again independent of the French Government. Great Britain saw with alarm, however, that France was capable of sending a large expedition across the seas, and believed that General Leclerc's force implied a readiness once more to dispute with the British the control of the West Indies, then so valued a part of the colonial empire of Great Britain.

There were reports also from India which gave ground for anxiety. The French general, De Caen, had been sent out to India to visit the French possessions that still remained there, to revive French influence, and to report upon the general situation. The instructions that were given to him seemed to show that Napoleon did not really contemplate any permanent peace with England. Another French agent, Sebastiani, was sent to the Levant and Syria in order also to report on the prospects of France there; and by some strange oversight—if it was an oversight— his report was published in the official newspaper, the *Moniteur*, and in it occurred the phrase that an army of 6000 Frenchmen would be enough to conquer Egypt. It seemed, then, that through the mind of the First Consul was at any rate passing the idea of taking up again his Egyptian projects. Besides these matters which concerned British interests overseas, there were others that worked also to produce a feeling of exasperation and unrest. The hopes entertained by Great Britain that the peace would open commerce in France proved to be illusory. On the contrary, British commerce was almost totally excluded from the French possessions, and the indignation of the commercial classes in London was very great. Napoleon, on his side, complained bitterly of attacks made upon him in newspapers that were published in England. Certain French *émigrés* were using those for continued and violent attacks upon the First Consul. Napoleon demanded that these papers should be suppressed, and he would not accept as a sufficient excuse the English freedom of the press. He complained at the same time that the English were harbouring on their soil the Bourbon princes, still the claimants to the throne of France, and he called upon the English to expel them; but he called in vain.

There was, then, during the period of the Peace a gradual increase in the tension between the two Powers, and this tension became in the end concentrated on the question of Malta. That island, important by its natural strength and its geographical position, had, as we have seen, first fallen into the hands of Napoleon. It had then been taken from him by the English, and at the Peace of Amiens the promise had been given that it should be restored to the Knights of St. John under certain conditions. These conditions were not fulfilled. Great Britain had, as a result, a reasonable excuse for her refusal to evacuate the island. It must be noted at the same time that no effort was made to procure the fulfilment of these conditions, and that there is strong evidence that Great Britain was determined to maintain her possession of the island on whatever grounds.[1] With the signing of the Peace diplomatic relations were resumed with France, and Lord Whitworth was sent to Paris as British representative. From the instructions which were given to him when he went, it is clear that the British Government had made up its mind to maintain its hold upon Malta. Between Lord Whitworth and the First Consul there ensued a controversy of the most interesting and often of the most dramatic kind, which is presented to us in his despatches. He was a characteristic Englishman of the period, with an Englishman's contempt for France and its ruler, blind to many of the strong points in the French case, but at the same time stiff and determined to do his utmost for the country that had sent him to Paris. Napoleon, on his side, demanded the execution of the Treaty of Amiens. 'The Treaty of Amiens,' he said, 'and nothing but the Treaty of Amiens.' And Lord Whitworth, on his side, took as his ground that the execution of the treaty was dependent upon the condition of Europe when that treaty was signed, and that the execution of the treaty, therefore, could not be claimed in face of the great strides which had been made by the French power since the signature of the treaty. There were efforts, perhaps genuinely meant, on both sides to find some compromise. Napoleon's brother Joseph took a leading part in these overtures. No good result, however, was obtained, and in March 1803, after a scene of great violence at the Tuileries Palace, relations were broken off between Great Britain and France. Napoleon laid hands upon all those Englishmen who in great numbers had availed themselves of the Peace to resume the habit of continental travel, and many of these unfortunate men remained prisoners for ten years.

War had come, but the extent of the war was yet uncertain. It might possibly be confined to the two great Powers whose quarrel had been the cause of it. On both sides there was keen competition for alliances, and in the end practically the whole continent of Europe was involved in the struggle.

---

[1] Lord Hawkesbury in a secret letter of instructions to Lord Whitworth wrote: 'If the French Government should enter into any conversation with you on the subject of the Island of Malta, it is of great importance that you should avoid committing his Majesty as to what may be eventually his intentions with respect to that island. . . . I recommend you, however, to avoid saying anything which may engage his Majesty to restore the island *even if these arrangements could be completed according to the true intent and spirit of the 10th article of the Treaty of Amiens*' (November 14, 1802). *England and Napoleon in 1803*, being the Despatches of Lord Whitworth. (Ed.) O. Browning (London 1887), pp. 9–10.

Napoleon, on his side, maintained at once that the obligations of the Peace of Amiens were at an end. He reoccupied Naples; he sent an army of 30,000 men into Holland; he saw too that he could secure in Germany a valuable pledge against England by seizing Hanover, which was under the English King, though not of course incorporated in the English State. Hanover was overrun with 40,000 men, and Napoleon declared that he would keep Hanover as long as England kept Malta. He made overtures to Russia and to Prussia for alliance; but in Russia the mad Czar Paul, with his passionate admiration for France, had been succeeded by Alexander, a man of different temperament and aims, and the French overtures were decidedly refused. There was a tradition of friendship between France and Prussia which had been maintained with some care since the Peace of Basel, but this was too weak to bring Prussia in on the side of France. It was only with Spain that Napoleon had any real success. The existing Government of Spain was one of the most corrupt and inefficient to be found in all Europe. The chief figures were the King, Charles IV; his Queen, Louisa; and the Minister Godoy, the lover of the Queen, and unquestionably corrupt in his management of the affairs of the kingdom. In March 1801, negotiations between Napoleon and the Spanish Government resulted in the Treaty of Madrid. By this treaty Spain handed over to France Louisiana in America, and promised to make war against Portugal, the age-long ally of Great Britain. Napoleon, on his side, promised to set up a kingdom of Etruria in Italy, and to give it to the Duke of Parma, the son-in-law of Charles IV. In accordance with this treaty Portugal was invaded by Spain, but was not occupied with the thoroughness that Napoleon had desired. After the rupture of the Peace of Amiens, Spain was induced, or in truth forced, to contribute a sum of four million francs a month to the French treasury. Napoleon knew so much about Godoy that he could threaten revelations with regard to his character and practices if he refused to comply with his demands. Spain was, in effect, dragged helplessly at the chariot wheels of France.

On the other side a great coalition soon sprang into being. Pitt emerged from the retirement into which he had gone as the result of his difference with King George III over the Irish union, and, in 1804, he resumed power, eager to strike a blow against France and Napoleon. His knowledge of the diplomacy of Europe was unrivalled, as was also the tenacity with which he struggled against his great enemy. He soon built up a new and powerful coalition against France. First he won over the power of Sweden, which hitherto had not taken an active part in the European wars against France. The King of Sweden was Gustavus IV, who began to rule in 1792. He was a narrow Lutheran in religion and fiercely hated the principles of the French Revolution and Napoleon. Without hesitation he joined the Third Coalition. Russia, too, joined eagerly. The pro-French policy of the Czar Paul had merely been an accidental interlude, and the general bias of Russia was hostile to

French ideas, character, and aims. Nor could Austria remain neutral. Its head, Francis, was beginning to feel his position as Emperor extremely weak and doubtful. He had already taken to himself the title of hereditary 'Emperor of Austria,' in addition to the fast-fading distinction of Holy Roman Emperor. France had crossed the path of Austria at many points and had already inflicted upon Austria two humiliating peaces. The creation first of the Republic and then of the kingdom of Italy was exasperating to the traditions of Austrian statesmanship. It was believed that her finances had been re-established and that the weaknesses of her army had been remedied. She entered the war once more and brought in with her the kingdom of Naples, which was always a dependency of Austria.

An important question was the future action of Prussia. She had remained obstinately neutral since the Peace of Basel in 1795. She saw the advances of French power with real alarm, but she was bitterly jealous of Austria and refused the overtures that were made to her by the Alliance. She declined also the proposal of Napoleon that she should join with him, even though he offered the kingdom of Hanover to her as the price of that alliance.

So, then, the great Alliance faced France and Spain. The declared objects of the Coalition were to reduce France within her ancient limits, to call a congress to settle the various international questions that had arisen during the war, and to draw up a federal system for the maintenance of the peace in Europe. This last clause may be particularly noticed. It shows us how, even so early during the struggle with Napoleon, the notion of finding some settled basis for European order had come to men's minds. We shall see how it was this idea that produced what is known as the Holy Alliance after the overthrow of Napoleon.

The enemy that Napoleon had to face consisted of, firstly, the overwhelming naval power of Great Britain and, secondly, the apparently vast military strength of Austria and Russia. How was he to attack them? He had beaten his enemies on land before, and he had found that that did not lead to the surrender of Great Britain. She was impregnable behind her seas. But if Great Britain could be beaten down he had every reason to think that such a defeat would have a great and probably a decisive effect upon the position of her military allies. His first idea, then, was to settle the war by a direct blow against Great Britain, and by the invasion and the conquest of our islands. Napoleon knew little himself of naval matters, and he may on this account have felt some jealousy of the French navy and its commanders. At this juncture, however, he devoted most seriously his genius and capacity for detail to the organisation of a descent upon the coasts of England. A large fleet of flat-bottomed boats was collected at Boulogne. The manœuvre of embarkation was constantly practised, so that when conditions were favourable the armies might be got on board and taken across the Channel in the shortest possible time. It was at first his hope that the crossing might be effected under some favourable conditions of the weather without a previous battle against the British Navy; but the more he studied the problem the clearer it became that success could not possibly attend such a scheme, and that the Channel must be held by a French naval force before the fleet of transports could with any prospect of success be launched upon the waters. There were three French squadrons: one at Toulon, the second at Rochefort, and the third at Brest. Napoleon projected a scheme for decoying away the English fleet from its watch over the Channel by an attack upon the West Indian Islands. His aim here was a double one: if our West Indian possessions really fell into his hands, that would be a great and most valuable prize; if the British fleet left the Channel in order to protect the West Indian Islands, that might give to Napoleon the period of safety which he required for the crossing of the Channel.

The incidents that follow, culminating in the Battle of Trafalgar, form the most famous chapter in the naval history of Great Britain. The genius of Nelson, the efficient organisation of the British fleet, resting on a long tradition and improved under Rodney's influence after the failure in the war against the United States, and the conspicuous absence of these very qualities in the French navy, are sufficient to account for the victory which established the naval supremacy of Great Britain for the rest of the war. Opinions have differed as to the influence of the battle on the course of the struggle of Europe against Napoleon. It did but reaffirm the strength of British naval power which was clear before; it did not materially increase that supremacy. Napoleon had known before that the British fleet was his greatest enemy, and that conviction was deepened. Had the battle not been fought at all the issue of the struggle would probably not have been seriously altered. And if Napoleon had won? He is reported to have said: 'If I can only be master of the sea for six hours England will cease to exist.' But if he really believed this he was certainly in error. The nation was identified with the Government in Britain as it was not elsewhere among the enemies of Napoleon, and there can be no doubt that a fierce national resistance would have followed under conditions favourable to the defence. If the Grand Army had disembarked on the shores of England it would almost certainly have won victories, but Napoleon would have found himself committed to a struggle that would have anticipated the exhausting war in Spain and might have been as fatal as his march on Moscow.

Before the Battle of Trafalgar had been fought Napoleon had abandoned the enterprise against England and was in full march for Germany. The unprecedented victories that awaited him there soon made Trafalgar appear to contemporaries of little importance. Austria and Russia stood determinedly against him. Prussia watched the course of affairs in alternations of hope and fear. If she would have to fight France some time there was no time so favourable as the present, when she would have the alliance of the Czar and the Emperor. Were the forces of Prussia joined to theirs Napoleon would not dare to undertake his daring march into the heart of Germany. On the other hand, Napoleon would pay highly for Prussian neutrality. Much might be won by dexterous diplomacy. Hanover might be taken from the King of England and attached to Prussia, whose territories it would so valuably increase. Prussia might become the head of North Germany and might even assume the imperial title with the approval of Napoleon himself. The King and Government of Prussia were incapable of clear thought and direct action. The King—so it was said—'hoped to deceive all the world and yet remain an honest man.' So nothing was done when to do nothing was fatal. But though Napoleon failed to win over Prussia he secured the alliance of Würtemberg and Bavaria. Frederick II, the Elector of Würtemberg, was a man 'of ruffianly and suspicious temper,' quite alien in sympathies from the people over whom he ruled. He had been an officer in the Russian and Prussian armies, and preferred the government that he saw established in those countries to the balanced and weak type that was traditional in South Germany. He could not in any case resist Napoleon, and might get from him an increase of territory and the change in the constitution that he desired. An alliance was made, and Napoleon was received with all honour on his arrival. Bavaria had already been cajoled or forced into the same alliance. The Elector Maximilian Joseph had a real admiration for French ideas and for the great ruler of France. His state was already, to some extent, reorganised on a French model. He could not resist France, and Napoleon would not listen to his plea that he should be allowed to remain neutral. The Elector of Baden was drawn over to the same side. So Napoleon entered upon his campaign in Germany with considerable German support.

The victories that he won in 1805 and 1806 are the most amazing of his career. Three great military states were overthrown one after the other—Austria, Russia, Prussia. A new Charlemagne, or even a new Julius Cæsar, seemed to have arisen, and some thought that the future had in store for Europe some new and enduring organisation. Only a few thinkers and patriots could believe that the storm would pass as quickly as it had come, and that for better or worse the old features of European life would reappear. But at the distance of more than a century we can see that what happened had nothing in it miraculous. A general of genius with the best equipped army in the world attacked troops that still followed an old routine. A government, that had sprung from a popular rising and which still identified itself to a very large extent with the interests and aspirations of the people, came into conflict with governments of the old type: governments that were machines rather than organisms, which were in no vital connection with the people, which in consequence inspired little enthusiasm or self-sacrifice.

So the armies of Napoleon marched from victory to victory. The Austrian general, Mack, was in Ulm with a considerable Austrian force. He had spoken confidently of the victories that he was going to win, but he was alarmed by the size of the armies which marched with unexampled rapidity from Boulogne to the Danube. He tried to withdraw when it was too late, but found himself surrounded, and surrendered with a force of about 33,000 men. There was much worse to follow. Vienna was abandoned without a struggle. The Czar Alexander and the Emperor Francis joined their forces near Austerlitz, to the north of Vienna. There, on December 2, 1805, was fought the Battle of Austerlitz—'the battle of the three Emperors,' as it is sometimes called. The armies of Austria and Russia were hopelessly broken. The Austrian armies could not be re-formed again; the Russian army withdrew to the north-east and had still some heavy fighting before it. For the moment Napoleon the soldier had done his task; but there was much for the diplomatist to accomplish.

Germany lay in his hands, though there were strange and ominous movements reported from Berlin, to which we shall come in a moment. What did Napoleon intend to do with Germany and Central Europe? He had already given hints of great changes that he intended to introduce. In a proclamation, when he crossed the Rhine, he had said: 'We will not stop until we have secured the independence of the German Empire.' And to the Elector of Würtemberg he had said: 'The House of Austria does not disguise its intention of getting hold of the Germanic body and destroying all the sovereign houses.' He would endeavour, therefore, to give to his action in Germany the appearance of a war of liberation and pose as the protector of Germany against Austria. Some hoped even that he would give new vigour to the old machinery of the Holy Roman Empire.

But Napoleon was still at heart a revolutionary. He called the Diet 'a miserable monkey-house,' and had no respect for the rusty machinery of the Holy Roman Empire. Germany seemed to him to be entirely at his mercy, and he planned its reconstruction with little regard to its past history or its aspirations. Scheme after scheme was drawn up and thrown aside. The first consideration in all was the interest of France and of her Emperor. But in the details other influences had been at work: the intrigues of the rival German princes; the private views of Talleyrand; the frank bribery of individual princes and cities.

The fate of Germany was decided in two main treaties. First, the Treaty of Pressburg (December 26, 1805). The primary object of this was to regulate the relations of France with Austria and to exclude the House of Hapsburg from Germany and from Italy where it had exercised so great an authority for centuries. The treaty is in effect, though not in name, a declaration that the Holy Roman Empire exists no longer. Large tracts of territory were taken from the Austrian House. It lost nearly three millions of inhabitants and abandoned the recently

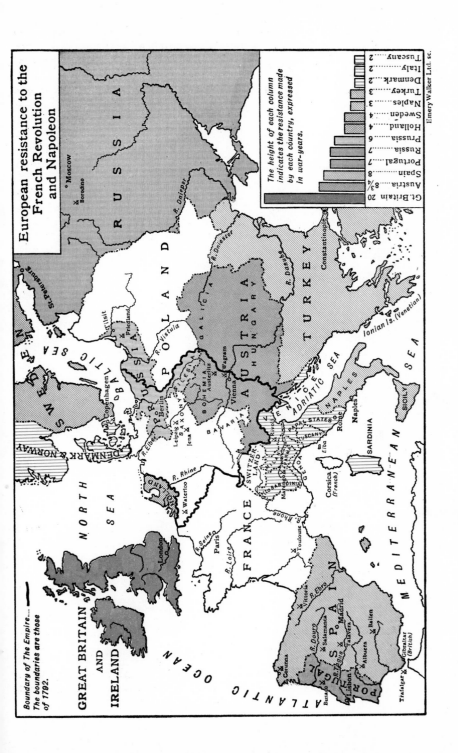

European resistance to the
French Revolution
and Napoleon

The height of each column
indicates the resistance made
by each country, expressed
in war-years.

Gt. Britain 20	
Austria 8¾	
Spain 8	
Portugal 7	
Russia 6	
Prussia 6	
Holland 4	
Sweden 4	
Naples 3	
Turkey 3	
Denmark 2	
Italy 2	
Tuscany 2	

Emery Walker Ltd. sc.

Boundary of The Empire......
The boundaries are those
of 1792.

GREAT BRITAIN
AND
IRELAND

acquired Venetian territories, which went to the kingdom of Italy, as well as much other territory in Italy and in Germany. The seventh article declares that the Electors of Bavaria and of Würtemberg have taken the title of King, and that the Emperor of Germany and Austria will recognise them in that capacity. This adoption of a new title by a member of the Empire without the permission of the Emperor or the Diet was wholly contrary to the tradition and constitution of the Empire. A later article declares that Würtemberg, Bavaria, and Baden—all of which had received great additions of territory at the expense of Austria —are henceforth sovereign bodies; a clause of uncertain meaning, which, however, repudiated any subordination to the old Empire. The rulers of these states interpreted this article as implying that the rulers could henceforth dispense with the traditional constitutions of their states. Their Estates or Parliaments were swept away; centralised despotisms were frankly set up; it was a strange result of the triumph of one who still regarded himself as 'the Revolution.'

Then, on July 12, 1806, came the treaty establishing the Confederation of the Rhine. It was announced by Napoleon as his decision, and the rulers of Germany were called on to give their adhesion or refusal within twenty-four hours. Of those who were concerned only one, and he one of the least important, refused to sign.

The general aim of the Confederation was to break up the German lands into three main bodies. Prussia would still rule in the north, Austria in the south and east would count many millions of German subjects among her variegated populations. But in the west would rise up, under French protection, a new German state independent of both. What was called 'the German Triad' would be constituted. History has shown that Napoleon's creation had not in it the qualities of permanence. In less than ten years the states of Germany would rise against the power of Napoleon in the name of a united Germany that should embrace all German lands and peoples; half a century later Bismarck would give body to those long-cherished aspirations; even the War of 1914–18 and the revolution that followed did not break the sentiment of German unity, but led rather to the greater centralisation of the régime of Hitler. But the era of nationalism had not yet come in 1806, and there was much in the history and racial divisions of Germany which lent support to Napoleon's scheme.

The new arrangement was to be a Confederation not a federal state. The sixteen states which declared themselves detached from the Germanic Empire in order to form part of the new arrangement remained independent and sovereign. A Diet was to sit at Frankfort, where the common interests of the Confederation were to be considered; but the Diet never met, and the constitution of the Confederation remained a dead letter. The members were not to give military service except to the Confederation or its allies. Clause 12 was all-important; the Emperor of the French was declared Protector of the Confederation, and a later article gave him the right of determining the contingents that each member should furnish in case of war. Article 35 declared formally that they were necessary allies in any war that involved either of the parties. This part of the arrangement would be strictly carried out. Any chance of the working of the German Triad vanished when it appeared that the cloud-capped towers and gorgeous palaces of the Holy Roman Empire passed away only to reveal a very efficient and up-to-date modern fortress. But the sword had decided, and no opposition was possible. On August 1, Napoleon notified the Diet of Ratisbon that he had accepted the post of Protector of the Confederation of the Rhine 'with a view to peace,' and that he no longer recognised the existence of the German Constitution. This announcement produced no sensation in Europe. Less than a week later, on August 6, Francis renounced his old imperial title, and the Holy Roman Empire was at an end. It was indeed the 'end of an auld song.'

Western Germany had accepted the French supremacy; Austria could not for the present make any resistance. There remained Prussia —Prussia, which under Frederick the Great had so humiliated France; Prussia, which despite the alien elements in its population had come to be regarded by many—even by Goethe—as the special representative of German nationalism. What would Prussia say to this new organisation of Germany?

Prussia was too much divided to speak with a decisive voice. The weak King was pulled hither and thither by the parties at his Court. On the one side were the 'patriots,' who saw in France the great enemy of Germany and desired to draw the sword to save Prussia and Germany; to this party belonged the Queen Louise, 'the good angel of the good cause,' Hardenberg the Foreign Minister, and Blücher the soldier. But the King himself inclined to seek safety in the friendship of France, and found support from many of his Ministers. It must be remembered that Berlin and Paris were by no means then in that decided antagonism that grew up in the nineteenth century. There was between them a tradition of mutual help and admiration. But the march of Napoleon into Germany and the violation of the Prussian territories of Anspach and Baireuth during that march gave the victory to the war party. The Czar Alexander visited Berlin. He had a solemn interview with the young Prussian King, Frederick William III, at the grave of Frederick the Great. War against Napoleon was determined on; Haugwitz was sent to the French camp with an ultimatum. But the Battle of Austerlitz was fought before the ultimatum was presented; and Prussia in a sudden panic—justified by the situation—sought not war but peace, even at the price of humiliation. Napoleon quite understood the position at Berlin; but he was ready to make concessions to Prussia which were indeed the deepest of humiliations. Hanover was the key of Prussian diplomacy. The Prussian King had promised England to respect the independence and the English connection of Hanover. But now Napoleon offered the bait: Prussia might have not only peace but Hanover as well; and Prussia swallowed the bait. Fox denounced the policy of Prussia as combining 'everything that is contemptible in servility with everything that is odious in rapacity.' She had betrayed Germany, but she hoped she had enlarged her boundaries.

Prussia, however, did not receive the price of her shame. The possession of Hanover was by no means assured. It was known that Napoleon was making a tentative offer to restore the country to England. Then, too, the King of Prussia had formerly received from France the suggestion that he should form a Confederation of North Germany and rule over it with the title of Emperor; but now Napoleon showed no inclination to allow that splendid vision to materialise. And while the gains of Prussia were doubtful, the losses were painful and certain. Napoleon's general, Murat, had been made Duke of Cleves and given a place in the Confederation of the Rhine; he was claiming, as part of his dominions, Essen and Werden and Elten, which were undoubtedly Prussian territory. And meanwhile the patriotic war fever was growing in the army and the country. The army chiefs were confident of victory. The country was excited by an outrage, not in itself of first importance. A pamphlet had been widely circulated called 'Germany in her deep humiliation,' which compared the sufferings of the occupied districts of Germany with the worst that Germany had suffered during the Thirty Years' War. The author could not be discovered, but the publisher, Palm, was caught and executed by Napoleon. Prussia looked round for allies and got promises of help from Russia, which had not been crushed to extinction by Austerlitz, and from her neighbour Saxony. Then an ultimatum demanded that the French troops should be withdrawn west of the Rhine. That could only mean war.

The decision came with amazing suddenness and completeness. On October 14, 1806, the prestige of the Prussian armies was destroyed on the heights of Jena and at Auerstädt, a few miles to the north. No Austrian army had collapsed before Napoleon so completely as these once invincible Prussians. And the battle was clearly no accident; for blow followed upon blow, and Prussia made no further effective resistance. The French entered Berlin, captured fortresses and towns with amazing ease, and at last forced even Blücher to surrender near Lübeck. The King of Prussia had joined the Russian army in the north-east, and the Russians showed something of their old stubborn powers of resistance. At Eylau, in February 1807, they fought against Napoleon a battle that was no real French victory, but, in June 1807, Napoleon struck again at Friedland, and this time he made no mistake. The Russian army could struggle no more after this battle. The Emperor of the French stood at the very height of his power.

We shall examine in the next chapter the new Europe that was rising up under the ruins of the old, and the new economic form which was taken by the Emperor's struggle against Great Britain. That struggle had already begun, and Napoleon was anxious for the support of all Europe in his effort to overthrow by indirect means the Power whose navy he had failed to cope with. He found the Czar of Russia unexpectedly ready to co-operate with him. The Czar had already much of the instability which was to characterise him in later years, and he had his own grievances against the Government of Great Britain. Since the Battle of Jena he had had to bear the chief brunt of the war; he had asked for the guarantee of a loan of six millions from Great Britain, but this had been refused in language that was likely to hurt Russian susceptibilities. He had urged the British Government to make diversions in his favour so as to draw off some part of the French forces; but nothing of importance had been done. The irritation against Great Britain in Alexander's mind boiled up into fierce hatred. He made an armistice with France, held his famous interview with Napoleon in a pavilion built on a raft in the middle of the river Niemen, and established the bases of a peace. Its terms, which concerned Prussia as well as Russia, were subsequently agreed on in a series of meetings held between the Russian, French, and Prussian representatives in the town of Tilsit; but the part played by the Prussians was humiliating in the extreme. Napoleon seemed to delight in insulting the King and Queen of Prussia. The fate of the country was settled by the Russian and French Emperors.

The terms that concerned Prussia were declared in the treaty to be due to the desire of the French Emperor to establish friendship with Russia on unshakable foundations. He implies, therefore, that but for the Czar's mediation the terms would have been even harder. The Prussian provinces on the Rhine were to form a new kingdom, to be called the kingdom of Westphalia, which was to be given to Napoleon's brother Jerome. The greater part of the Prussian territories of Poland was to form a duchy of Warsaw and to be given to the Duke of Saxony; there were many who hoped that this might be the beginning of the restoration of an independent Poland. Prussia lost nearly half her territory, and her population was reduced from ten to five millions.

Russia had no such humiliations to suffer. On the contrary, her territories were increased by Finland and a part of the Polish possessions of Prussia. She was, of course, forced to recognise all the regulations which Napoleon had made for Central Europe. There were secret articles as well as the published ones.[1] It was agreed that Great Britain should be summoned to make peace and to renounce her claims to maritime supremacy; and that, if she refused, Russia and France should make common war against her, and should force Denmark and Sweden and Portugal to close their ports against English merchandise and join in the war against her. Something of the nature of these secret articles was known with extraordinary rapidity in London, and the channel of

---

[1] The full text of the secret articles was not published until 1890. It is to be found in A. Vandal: *Napoléon et Alexandre I.* Vol. I. *De Tilsit à Erfurt* (1891), pp. 499–507.

their revelation is still an unsolved problem. Were there English spies who learned something from high-placed Russians? Or was it Talley-rand who, anxious to make friends with the enemy in case of Napoleon's fall, revealed them to the English Minister, Canning? The British Government acted on the information, however it came. Denmark was summoned to surrender her navy and on her refusal was forced to do so by a naval and military attack on Copenhagen.

The territories of Napoleon received considerable additions after this date. They reached their maximum in the year 1811. But 1807 marks the zenith of his power. Had he died in that year his career would have seemed the most miraculous in the military annals of Europe and per-haps of the world. He had succeeded in every task, overthrown every enemy. He had rearranged Europe according to his liking. He had no military rival, and he was in apparent close and friendly alliance with the Czar of Russia. The French Revolution was left far behind now. It was not France but Napoleon who commanded in Europe. And he had carried with him his family to wealth and fame and power. His mother, once the simple housewife of Ajaccio, was installed as the Empress-Mother in Paris. His eldest brother, Joseph, had just been made King of Naples—from which Ferdinand had been driven in 1806 —and then later he ascended the great historic throne of Spain. His third brother, Louis, was made King of Holland, which had hitherto been treated as an independent republic. Another brother, Jerome, as we have seen, was King of Westphalia. His sister Caroline had married Murat, who was now Duke of Berg, and who would by and by, when Joseph moved to Spain, become King of Naples. Pitt, Napoleon's most determined and most capable enemy, was dead. He seemed a god to kill and to make alive.

<h2 style="text-align:center">CHAPTER VII</h2>

<h2 style="text-align:center">THE RISE OF THE NEW EUROPE</h2>

FOR ten years the personality of Napoleon dominated the life and thoughts of Europe as they had never before been dominated by one man. For any parallel we should have to go back to the careers of Julius Caesar or of Charlemagne, and they can not, for obvious reasons, have exercised the same universal influence that Napoleon did. From 1795 to 1807 it is difficult to take sufficient notice of the affairs of Italy or Germany or Spain. The interest in the domestic affairs of these countries is swallowed up in the great storm that so rapidly spreads from its centre in France. But after 1807 the condition of Europe changes. Napoleon is still the central figure in the drama, and will re-main so until his public life is done; but his armies and his policy no longer monopolise attention. A little below the surface we can see other

4*

forces rising up which oppose a steady resistance to his power and schemes, which make even his greatest victories fruitless, and which soon bring defeat and catastrophe upon him.

Could he have closed his military career at Tilsit? Could he have given to the Europe, that he had made, a permanent settlement and a peaceful development? Are the causes of the nine years of war that still await Europe to be sought in the unsatisfied ambitions of Napoleon, or elsewhere? Was a close alliance between the French Empire, Russia, and Great Britain within the bounds of practical politics, and would such an alliance have given the world a durable peace? It seems certain that the situation in 1807 offered no prospect of peace. Napoleon might have been glad to accept a condition of peace if it gave him a secure position of power at home and in Europe; but, as we have seen, and as he knew, peace was dangerous to his position in France. In Europe, the governments, though so often beaten, had not given up hope of revenge. Below the governments there were the nations, and the national spirit had been stimulated by the French Revolution and the victories of Napoleon. There was no prospect that Germany, Italy, and Russia would for long accept the position of subordination, which was all that a Napoleonic peace would offer them. The governments would soon, in many cases, be reorganised under the impulse of defeat, and Prussia would give the first example of how France could be beaten by the adoption of her own weapons. There was one Power, moreover, that had not been beaten—Great Britain still remained behind her seas, hostile, proud, and confident. Fox, a strong admirer of the French Revolution and of Napoleon, had succeeded Pitt, but his effort to establish peace had failed. On his death in 1806 the Tory party was soon in power again, and carried on the war against France with the support of the vast majority of the nation.

The struggle with England had taken a new character which profoundly modified the course of European affairs until Napoleon fell. He despaired of breaking through the naval defences of Great Britain. He saw no encouragement to resume the policy which had failed so hopelessly at Trafalgar. But was the supreme master of Europe reduced to helplessness by the nation of manufacturers, traders, and shopkeepers? The strength of England, he believed, lay in her export trade, and the nations of Europe formed her chief market. Could not the ruler of Europe exclude British ships from all the harbours of Europe, and would not this reduce Great Britain to starvation? There was something in this policy that was traditionally French. The Revolution in the early stages of the war had approved of the policy, but had been in no position to apply it.

The new policy was declared from Berlin in November 1806. No rhetoric could give such emphasis to the position of Napoleon as the fact that he sent out his decrees from the conquered capital of Frederick the Great. In the Berlin Decrees Great Britain was denounced for her breach of international law and the egotism of her commercial policy. Her own weapons were now to be used against her. The British Isles were declared to be in a state of blockade, and all commerce was prohibited between them and the lands over which Napoleon had power or influence. No British ships were to be allowed to enter the ports of France or her allies. Vessels that entered in spite of the order were liable to confiscation.

The British Government answered by the Orders in Council of January and November 1807. France in turn was charged with violating the usages of war. If Great Britain might not trade with Europe, neither should the neutral Powers. The French lands were placed under blockade. Napoleon by his military power had excluded Great Britain from trade with Europe. Great Britain by her navy now cut off French Europe from trade with the rest of the world. The new policy was no passing idea or empty threat. Napoleon held to it as a certain means of ruining Great Britain. All nations which came under his influence were forced to adopt it. The desire to extend it was a cause of other wars. In November and December 1807, when the Peace of Tilsit had secured the support of Russia and the armies of Napoleon had no rival, by the Decrees of Milan he reaffirmed and strengthened his declaration against all commerce between Europe and Great Britain.

Unquestionably Great Britain suffered severely from this so-called 'continental system.' There was much unemployment, many bankruptcies, and great suffering from the commercial situation thus created. But, though the European markets were of the utmost importance to Great Britain, the rest of the world was open to her.[1] The new machines and methods which had been introduced by the industrial revolution gave England a great advantage in production. The country suffered, but her sufferings rather hardened than weakened her determination to struggle on.

The inhabitants of France itself were in many ways prosperous during these years. The conquests of Napoleon opened up to their trade new and wide districts. The results of the social legislation of the Revolution were seen and felt in the flourishing condition of agriculture. When France began to suffer from the failure of the colonial products, which had been stopped by the policy of Britain, French science, supported and directed by the State, was able partly to provide a remedy. The price of sugar reached a prohibitive figure, but then the manufacture of beet sugar was developed and improved and became a lasting source of French wealth. Indigo was made, or a substitute for it. There were indeed some trades that found no such relief; but the worst results of Napoleon's 'continental system' were not to be found in France but

[1] Dr. Holland Rose has shown that, if Napoleon had stopped the corn supply to England from the Continent, he could probably have forced her to surrender, as she could not import food rapidly enough or in sufficient quantities from the New World (*Napoleonic Studies*, 'Britain's Food Supply in the Napoleonic War').

in the European states which had fallen under her control. This was all the more apparent when Napoleon, convinced that all colonial products that arrived in Europe were really smuggled in by the British, placed on them a high tariff, amounting usually to about half their value.

Holland, which was ruled by Napoleon's brother Louis as king, found her whole commercial life overthrown by the new arrangements. She complained and protested, but in vain. King Louis sympathised with his people and was doubtful of his brother's success, and in the end he abdicated his uneasy throne. His abdication won no relief for the country. Holland was formally annexed to the French Empire in July 1810. Similar motives produced the annexation of the north-west coast of Germany in December of the same year. This violent act was officially justified, on the ground that British commerce would 'continue to flow into the Continent—if the mouths of the Weser and Elbe were not closed against it for ever.' If there had ever been any chance that Central Europe would be reconciled to the dominion of Napoleon, it was destroyed by the 'continental system.' The rule of France had brought welcome social freedom and the humane provisions of the Civil Code; but for most of the population these advantages were quite outweighed by the high prices and semi-starvation which were produced by the economic war against England.

Let us turn to Germany and to Prussia and see what shape was taken by the forces that fermented there. The overthrow of Prussia was amazing, but not so remarkable as her recovery, which is among the heroic things of history, to be classed with the triumph of the Romans after Cannae, and of the French after Agincourt. The catastrophe of Jena did not at all mark a crumbling and decadent State. On the contrary, Germany was full of activity of all sorts, and the beginning of the century is in many respects, despite Jena, the age to which Germany looks back with most pride. And yet her military strength lay prone in the dust.

The cause of the catastrophe can now be clearly made out. Prussia was the very best example of the old type of government, which the French Revolution destroyed in France by its direct action, and elsewhere by its influence. Frederick the Great, with energy as great as Napoleon's, but without his imaginative genius, had created an exceedingly efficient machine of government, as entirely dependent on the King as the clerks in an office are on the head of the business; working for the welfare of the people, but never consulting them; not in its essential qualities different from the ideal of Louis XIV or of George III of England, though much superior in efficiency. The army reflected the same character. It was not in any way an embodiment of the spirit of the nation, but a weapon in the hands of the King to be used for such purposes as he might think good. The common soldiers were drawn from the serf-peasants; the officers were all necessarily of noble birth; the discipline was harsh and brutal. The army was proud of the high tradition of Frederick the Great; but the soldiers were not inspired by national spirit nor by a consciousness of personal interest in the well-being of the State. A system whereby 'the peasant was forced by brutal punishments to defend the country which starved him' was in harmony with many features of the eighteenth century, but the advent of the French Revolution and the circulation of its ideas made it intolerable in the nineteenth.

It is the glory of the Prussia of those days that men were found in high places who saw that radical change was necessary, and were strong enough to make it. The characteristic of all the changes was a desire to bring State and people into organic relation, and to give to the people a real interest in the success of the government. This ideal was by no means realised; but much was done, and henceforth France would be fought with her own weapons. Liberty, Equality, and Fraternity were not words that suited the German mind; but much of what France had meant by them passed into the life of Germany.

The military reforms may be taken first. These were the work of three remarkable men—Scharnhorst, Gneisenau, and Clausewitz. Scharnhorst was the great organiser of the new army; he threw into his task a religious fervour, and regarded his work as only possible through a moral regeneration of the people. Gneisenau was an idealist, who found in his military work the satisfaction of his highest aspirations. He found much to admire in the French Revolution; and, loyal though he was to the Prussian throne, he has something that is akin to the French Jacobins of 1793. Clausewitz was the great theorist of military tactics, who took much or most of what Napoleon had invented and adapted it to German conditions. He is reckoned the father of those ideas in tactics and strategy which carried Prussia to victory in 1814, 1866, and 1870. The main points of the military changes were these: the army became national; foreigners were excluded. The system of privilege was destroyed. The officers were no longer drawn exclusively from the nobles; service in the ranks was no longer a mark of serfdom. All citizens were called on for military service, and the officers were chosen on grounds of ability. A new spirit, a new standard of military honour, a new code of ethics, were also introduced with wonderful success into the army. It was claimed for the army that instead of being a school of vice it became a school of honour. Napoleon had, by definite provision, laid down that the Prussian army must not exceed 42,000 men. The military reformers, however, reduced the term of service; passed the men rapidly through the ranks; instituted a reserve force which was kept in touch with military discipline and drill; and thus, when at last the call for action came, there was a Prussian army ready and prepared for action vastly in excess of the limit prescribed by Napoleon.

The political and social reorganisation of Prussia is even more important. The King had little share in what was most important in this work. The name most closely associated with it is vom Stein, by birth

a citizen of one of the smallest of German states, who had transferred
his services to Prussia when the French flood effaced the old landmarks
of western Germany. Hardenberg, now Chancellor, aristocratic in bearing and appearance, slow in his decisions, but in the end a warm supporter of Stein and the anti-French party, also gave valuable assistance.
Along with these should be mentioned Queen Louise, who came to
be the symbol of Prussian and even of German national feeling. The
objects of this group were akin to those of the military reformers. They
wished to bring government and people into living relationship; to make
Prussia no longer the tyrant but the protector of the common man.
The independence of Germany from French control was their constant
but undeclared aim.

First, serfdom was abolished. 'After St. Martin's Day, 1810,' says the
edict of liberation, 'there are only free citizens in Prussia.' The peasant-
serfs of Prussia had been in a far worse condition than the peasants of
France. They now were placed in something like the position that had
been won for the French by the Revolution. They were freed from
forced labour and from the feudal jurisdiction of their lords. They
were no longer liable to degrading corporal punishments in the army.
More important still, the lands which they had cultivated for others
now became their own property, which they were free to sell. There
was danger in this last provision, for if the peasants sold their lands they
might become a landless proletariat and drift into the towns. The provisions that Stein made to avoid this were not altogether successful.
But the peasantry felt now that in fighting for their land they were
fighting for something in which they had a personal interest.

Stein turned next to the townsmen of Prussia, who had lived a separate life of their own, dominated by the decadent gilds and excluded
from service in the army. He acted upon the principle of free-trade.
The legal barriers between the towns of Prussia and the rest of the
country were broken down. Liberty had made at least an appearance
on Prussian soil; but the country was not favourable to the growth of
self-government. Hardenberg in his 'Testament' declared in favour of
'democratic principles in a monarchical state,' and Stein looked in the
same direction. But nothing was done except to make a beginning with
provincial assemblies.

These changes in organisation would not in the end have availed
much if they had not been supported by a corresponding movement in
the minds of men. Intellectually, Prussia was awake, as wideawake
as France had been before the Revolution. The rousing appeals to
the nation of Fichte and Schleiermacher, the patriotic poetry of writers
such as Arndt, were more vital to this generation than the cosmopolitan outlook of the giants of the classical age, Kant, Schiller or Goethe.
The League of Virtue (the *Tugendbund*) founded at Königsberg in
1808, strengthened the feelings of patriotism and idealism which
were required for the triumph of the national cause. Its working was

supported by F. L. Jahn's Gymnastic Society, which, often absurd in its manifestations and perhaps not so powerful in its influence on public opinion as has sometimes been represented, was nevertheless among the forces that stirred and quickened German opinion at this epoch.

One other and most characteristic feature of Prussian reorganisation must be noted. The importance of education for the strength and even for the military strength of the State was a Prussian belief before it was accepted elsewhere in Europe. The chief stages in the advance of her power have been marked by the founding of Universities. Now, when, in the hour of her deepest humiliation, she was daring to hope for liberation and victory, the University of Berlin was founded. Halle had hitherto been the chief University for the old Brandenburg lands, but Halle was now under Napoleonic influence, and its sessions had been for a time suspended. It was proposed to establish a new seat of learning at Berlin, and in spite of some opposition, chiefly on the ground that the life of a great capital was not suitable for study, the proposal was adopted. The beginnings of this institution, which has had such immense importance for European thought, were on a comparatively modest scale. But it attracted from the first men of outstanding distinction, and it was soon housed in a palace and received an adequate income from the State.

Prussia would clearly have to be reckoned with. Napoleon had at first approved of Stein's appointment to the Prussian service, and apparently believed Prussia to be incapable of recovery. Later he realised the meaning and the danger of the movement in Prussia, and insisted on the dismissal of Stein and the confiscation of his property. Stein passed into the service of the Czar and continued to work against Napoleon.

Long before Prussia was prepared to re-enter the war, Napoleon had to draw his sword against other and weaker Powers—against Spain and against Austria. And in these wars there is a quality which separates them from the earlier wars that the French Republic and Napoleon had waged. Napoleon has to fight now not merely against governments and official armies. The peoples themselves take a spontaneous part in them. We can hardly yet speak of the rise of a national spirit or of the sentiment of nationalism, but it is a preparation for that. The common man found that the doings of diplomatists, statesmen, and generals concerned him intimately. Nor was it only his economic interest that was affected. He found too that his country had some meaning for him; he became aware of a common tie that bound him to his fellow-countrymen; he became ready to resist the invader—in spite of material and social advantages that might be offered—not merely on the orders of a government, but on his own impulse. It was not until 1813 that the main French armies were fairly beaten by an organised military force, but they soon encountered in the valleys of Spain and the mountains of the Tyrol a popular resistance that strained their powers to the utmost.

The war with Spain is in every way most notable and interesting. That France should receive there her first decisive check on land was quite beyond the bounds of probability. Spain had indeed played a great part in the history of Europe. The stubborn valour of her infantry had been a proverb in the sixteenth and early seventeenth centuries. But for a century she had fallen behind in the race for power and wealth. She was the classical instance of a decadent State. The efforts of her Government to interfere in European affairs had, during the eighteenth century, been uniformly failures. There was no indication that the Government had improved in sagacity or honesty. The Spanish armies could not hope to make an effective resistance to France. Yet the first broad gleam of hope that Europe might be delivered from the dominion of Napoleonic France came from Spain.

We have seen the varying relations of Spain to France since the outbreak of the Revolution. The royal house was a branch of the Bourbon family of which the French kings had been the head. Spain had taken part with the First Coalition against the French Republic, but had withdrawn in 1795. Since then Spain had more and more been drawn into the orbit of France. After the rupture of the Peace of Amiens, Spain had provided France with financial and naval assistance, and had sent ships to the Battle of Trafalgar. Since then Napoleon had assumed a superiority over the royal family of Spain, which explains the next act in the drama. The royal house of Spain was almost a caricature of monarchy. It had fallen into corruption and inefficiency far beyond what had been shown by the Bourbons of France. The King, Charles IV, was of notorious incapacity. The driving force in the royal circle was Godoy—ambitious, avaricious, and notoriously the paramour of the Queen. This group was on the worst of terms with Ferdinand (the Prince of the Asturias) and his Neapolitan wife. Ferdinand was not in character or ability any improvement on his father, and his future career was to show to what depths of cowardice and treachery he could descend. But his hostility to his father and to Godoy was well known, and this sufficed to make him a sort of popular hero to whom the nation clung with pathetic and ill-repaid loyalty. The royal house of Spain showed no sign of patriotism or virtue, and the revolutionary storm was wanted to cleanse those Augean stables. The spirit of revolutionary France would find much that it could change with advantage in the country. Commerce was strangled by ancient restrictions. Aristocratic privilege was as great and as absurd as ever it had been in France. The intellectual condition of the country was torpid. The strongest conscious sentiment of the people was probably its devotion to the Church, and from the Church it derived much of its strength and cohesion in the great struggle which was soon to break out. But the Church was itself corrupt, unenlightened, and inhuman; it still cherished the ideals of the Inquisition, though there had been little persecution of late. The principles of the constitution of 1791 and of Napoleon's

Civil Code were much needed in the land, and there was a small but important section of the people ready to welcome them.

Napoleon believed that Spain would offer no greater resistance than Italy had done. What national devotion could there be to such a royal house which failed in every duty that specially belongs to monarchy; which was no longer the leader of the armies of Spain, or the representative of national unity, or the upholder of the cause of the people as a whole against the claims of a class? 'I shall write upon my banner the words *Liberty, Freedom from Superstition, the Destruction of the Nobility*, and I shall be received as I was in Italy, and all the classes that have national spirit will be on my side. I shall drag from their lethargy a people that once had generous instincts, and you will see that they will regard me as a liberator.' So Napoleon believed; and there were strong arguments in favour of this view. The explanation of Napoleon's failure and bitter disappointment in Spain is that he woke in the people of Spain the sentiment of nationality. Spain was not like Italy divided into separate states and under the rule of the foreigner. She had not to look to the past or to the distant future to find herself united. She was poor, ill-governed, of little importance among the Great Powers of Europe. But she was united in spite of the strong local feeling of the provinces, and she was intensely proud. She detested foreigners of any kind, and was determined not to submit to alien rule. The leaven of the French Revolution was working in the population of Spain, but even that turned against Napoleon. The Spaniards appealed in the name of liberty, equality, and fraternity against a tyrant who tried to impose a foreign yoke and to sow dissension among them.

Napoleon had every reason to despise the policy of the Spanish Government, and he made the natural mistake of confusing the Government with the nation, and thought that the conquest of the whole country would be easily and cheaply effected. The royal family could hardly have served Napoleon better if it had been their conscious object to betray Spain into the hands of France. As early as 1807 Prince Ferdinand had appealed to Napoleon to grant him his paternal protection and to open the eyes of 'my good and dearly loved parents.' The King and Queen, hearing of the appeal, had themselves requested the help of Napoleon to settle their family troubles. He felt that he held them in the hollow of his hand, and already dreamed of annexing the country. He forced Spain into a war against Portugal, the aim of which was to deprive the English of harbours, by means of which, in spite of the Berlin Decrees, their goods gained access to the markets of Europe. The campaign was successful, and aollwed Napoleon to introduce considerable bodies of French troops into the country, under the pretext of supporting the war against Portugal. He was thus almost in military possession of Spain, and he did not see how the presence of his armies was exasperating against him the sentiment of the country which at first had not been unfriendly. He waited for an opportunity to strike, and it came in 1808. The savage quarrels in the bosom of the royal family led to an open struggle. A crowd gathered at Aranjuez, where the royal party were staying, and attacked the residence of Godoy, the detestable agent of the King, in whom they saw rightly a chief cause of the humiliation of the country. The old King was frightened by the attitude of the people, and signed a paper abdicating the throne in favour of his son Ferdinand, who was acclaimed by the whole country as the man who should regenerate and free Spain. But the King, in a letter to the all-powerful Emperor of the French, repudiated his act of abdication and declared that it had been extorted from him by threats. Napoleon saw his opportunity and used it to the full. He induced Ferdinand to come to him at Bayonne by trickery and by force. Then the King and Queen and Godoy came thither too. Napoleon refused to recognise Ferdinand as king, and threatened him with prosecution for high treason. The old King Charles signed a treaty whereby he resigned all his rights to the throne of Spain to the Emperor of the French. Napoleon could claim that he had thus come legitimately into possession of the throne of Spain.

Napoleon was in the position of Louis XIV in 1700. Spain was in the power of France. 'The Pyrenees existed no longer.' Surely the whole Continent would now be at his feet, and the power of Great Britain would be at last brought low. But Spain was as great a disappointment to Napoleon as it had been to his royal predecessor.

His policy in Spain was his greatest blunder. Here, more than anywhere else—more even than in Russia—he misunderstood the problem with which he had to deal. He did not see—perhaps no one in Europe could see—how independent Spain was of its Government, how capable of spontaneous resistance, how difficult to subdue amidst its mountains and arid plains. Religion and national pride were the chief passions of the people, and both passions impelled them to an obstinate resistance to the French. There was no Government to speak on behalf of the whole of Spain, but the provincial and local life of Spain was vigorous, and provinces and cities spontaneously declared against the acceptance of Napoleon's rule. The little province of Asturias, with its half-million of inhabitants, declared formal war against him. Great Britain at once promised assistance and was quick to send it. Napoleon had no idea of the severity of the task that awaited him. 'If I thought it would cost me 80,000 men I would not attempt it, but it will not cost more than 12,000,' he said. It cost him half a million men and perhaps his crown!

It is plain from the course of this war how completely Napoleon and his enemies had changed their weapons and the causes for which they fought. He had struck into Italy in 1796 in the name of liberty; he had promised constitutional life in place of despotism; he had commanded a national army against armies of the old and really mercenary stamp. But it was Spain now that appealed to liberty and demanded a ruler of her own choice; and it was from Spain that the next most notable experiments in Constitution-making came.

Napoleon showed that he regarded the deposition of the royal family as irrevocable by calling his brother Joseph from the throne of Naples and making him King of Spain. It was despotism establishing despotism, and the constitutional arrangements which he promised were never brought into action. The resistance of Spain, on the other hand, was at first carried on by local committees (*juntas*). From these in 1808 a central and supreme committee was formed. In 1810 the Cortes—the Parliament of Spain—were convoked under popular pressure, with a complete and liberal electoral system, at Cadiz. They formed themselves into a Constituent Assembly and drew up a form of government after the pattern of the first constitution of the French Revolution. The sovereignty of the people, and the liberty of the individual and of the press, were declared. Torture was suppressed; the finances were reformed. The legislative power was placed in the hands of the Cortes, which were to consist—and in this they went back to the French example of 1791—of a single chamber elected by a complicated method, which was, however, founded on manhood suffrage. The executive was in the hands of a monarchy hereditary in the family of the still beloved Ferdinand. This constitution of 1812 became the watchword of the Liberals of the next generation. There was no other constitution in Europe which declared honestly for manhood suffrage and a single chamber. On one point only—and that a most characteristic one—was the constitution of 1812 behind the general demands of Europe: the Catholic faith was declared to be the only true one, and to be the permanent religion of Spain. No other form of worship was to be allowed in the country.

The sword had to decide between the opposing policies. Great Britain gave her help from the first; but, before Wellington had begun his career of stubborn resistance which led to so complete a victory, the Spaniards unaided had inflicted on Napoleon's armies their first serious defeat. This was the famous Battle of Baylen, July 1808. The French General, Dupont, had been sent from Madrid to occupy Seville, which was in the hands of the Nationalists. His early victories made him despise the military qualities of the Spanish. His soldiers had gained much plunder, which they dragged with them in a long array of waggons. He was cut off from reinforcements and from water by the forces of the enemy. Even so, in the judgment of military critics, he might have saved the situation if he had shown energy and courage. But he showed neither, and capitulated with his force of 20,000 men. Europe rang with the wonderful news that a General of Napoleon had laid down his arms before an army of the despised Spaniards. If Central Europe had taken up arms, Leipzig and Waterloo might have been anticipated.

The situation was so dangerous that Napoleon came and took over the command himself. He re-established the prestige of the French arms. Madrid was reoccupied. Joseph, who had fled after the Battle of Baylen, was replaced on the throne, and gained the nominal allegiance of the capital. Sir John Moore and the English army had advanced into the neighbourhood, but turned towards the coast when the presence of Napoleon was known, and with difficulty escaped to Corunna. If Napoleon could have stayed in Spain with the bulk of his army all might have gone well; but his vast Empire demanded his attention, and events on the Danube soon drained away a large part of his forces.

With smaller forces Napoleon's Generals—the chief were Soult and Ney—found the task a terrible one. 'It is a country,' said King Joseph, 'like no other; we can find in it neither a spy nor a courier to carry messages'; and Marbot's *Memoirs* show at what risk detachments of the French army lived among a savagely hostile population. The Spaniards showed little inclination for the more formal operations of war, and their unpunctuality and the looseness of their organisation strained Wellington's temper at times to breaking point. But they carried on irregular warfare with wonderful persistence and skill, and showed extraordinary endurance and fury in defence of their towns. The Siege of Saragossa is among the most heroic acts in the annals of Europe. The place seemed hardly defensible, but it was defended against the French armies by the citizens and soldiers, who held them at bay from June to August, when it was relieved. 'Flinty and indomitable,' Spain had often—from Roman times onwards—shown herself well adapted for irregular warfare. The help of the British was of the utmost possible value; the brunt of the more formal military operations fell upon them. But the resistance made by the Spanish themselves was greater than is sometimes recognised. Spain never showed, even in moments of depression or defeat, the least inclination to accept the Napoleonic system or Joseph as king. The Spanish War has been well called the cancer that drained away the strength of Napoleon. And the European situation demanded all his attention, and soon all his strength.

The defeat of Baylen and the rise in Spain of dangers and difficulties, to which no end could be seen, created a profound impression in Central Europe. There were some, both in Prussia and in Austria, who thought that the time had come for a general rising against the French power. The rising did not come, but Napoleon was not blind to the dangers that were just hidden from view. It was the fatality of his position that every victory seemed to add to his difficulties and brought with it the occasion of another war. Two main ideas dominated Napoleon's policy at this period: war *à outrance* against Great Britain and an intimate alliance with Russia. The two were closely associated in his mind. He believed still that the naval and commercial power of Britain could be destroyed by indirect attack. To convince the world of his unshaken power, and to prevent the development of any further movements against him in Germany, he arranged for an interview with the Czar Alexander at Erfurt. It was the spectacular zenith of his career. France made parade there, not only of her military strength, but also of her scientific, literary, artistic, and theatrical greatness. The Czar and the French Emperor appeared in public on terms of the closest intimacy. The princes and kings of the Confederation of the Rhine crowded to salute the great man from whom they had received their titles and powers. Many of the intellectual leaders of Germany consented to come. Among them was Goethe, to whom Napoleon and Alexander found time to pay a visit at Weimar. Both he and the veteran poet and novelist Wieland were decorated with the Legion of Honour The Erfurt conference was admirably organised, and was an occasion of impressive homage to the French conqueror.

There was much serious business done or attempted amidst all the banquets and festivals and theatrical performances, and here the success of Napoleon was not quite so great. Talleyrand was his chief agent; and Talleyrand, who perhaps had betrayed him at Tilsit, certainly betrayed him at Erfurt. He was convinced that his master's power was unstable and tried to secure protection, in the event of his fall, by revealing state secrets to Russia, and even to Austria. Napoleon had at first tried to dazzle the Czar by the prospect of a joint attack on the territories of the Sultan of Turkey and the partition of his lands. He now wanted the Czar to join with him in resisting all movements that might menace the French power in Central Europe, and here he could get nothing from the Czar that was definite or conclusive. The alliance between Napoleon and Alexander was, indeed, unnatural. The men and their countries were separated by an immense gulf. In spite of all the embraces and compliments of Erfurt the relations between the two men began to cool, and a tone of irritation and suspicion creeps into Napoleon's correspondence with the Czar and his representatives. The ground was everywhere uncertain under the feet of the French Emperor. Before the new forces that were entering the arena—forces of opinion, faith, and economic interest—he lost much of his old clearness of vision. He had no longer 'the sense of the possible.' He saw no remedy except in the use of military force, and the situation was becoming one beyond the reach of military remedies. He felt himself surrounded at home by tepid loyalty or actual treason. Talleyrand was not the only traitor. He was in close relations with Fouché, Napoleon's great Chief of Police, and when the news of the French disasters in Spain came, these two made some sort of arrangement for the succession if Napoleon fell. Napoleon knew enough of all this to exclude Talleyrand from his confidential service in the future. But it was difficult to find real devotion anywhere. His Marshals—loaded with benefits at his hand—were ready to desert. There was something like treason even among the members of his own family.

In this age, when resistance to France was taking the form of popular and national movements, it is strange to find Austria playing a leading part; for the Austrian Monarchy was the negation of nationalism, and was finally to be destroyed by the triumph of nationalism. The motive of the action of the Austrian Emperor was, however, not nationalistic. The Peace of Pressburg—signed with France after the Battle of Auster-litz—had reduced Austria to a position of impotence in Europe, and she felt herself still further threatened by the designs of Napoleon. There was at Vienna a movement of reconstruction which seemed a pale reflection of what was happening at Berlin. The army system was re-vised. The Archduke Charles and the Count of Stadion were the chief agents in this process. Even the Emperor and the Empress consented to make some appeal to the loyalty of their people. Negotiations were opened with Prussia and with Russia. Talleyrand furnished encourag-ing information.

Napoleon anticipated the action of Austria by declaring war. He spoke of the coming struggle as of little importance, and of Austria and her armies with contempt. 'I will box both her ears, and then she will thank me and ask what orders I have to give.' But his efforts to draw the Czar into a hearty co-operation failed. The Czar could not refuse to abide by the promise which he had given at Erfurt, but he let the Austrian leaders know that he would strike no hard blow.

The despised armies of Austria put up a resistance desperate beyond anything that Napoleon had yet encountered. It is true that the first part of the campaign in Bavaria went easily in favour of the French. The Austrians, though commanded by the Archduke Charles, who was later to show himself no unworthy opponent of Napoleon, were swept out of the country with heavy loss in what is known as 'the campaign of five days.' But it was different when Napoleon approached Vienna. His first effort to cross the Danube resulted in the stubborn and bloody Battle of Aspern, May 1809, and failed to achieve its purpose. The rumour spread like wildfire that it was another Battle of Baylen, and that this time the French had been defeated under the direction of Napoleon himself. But Napoleon studied the situation with the greatest care, extemporised boats and bridges, deceived the Austrians as to the point where he intended to cross, and passed the river in safety. Then followed the desperate Battle of Wagram, July 1809. It was a complete French victory, and has been thought by some to be the masterpiece of his tactical skill. But the slaughter was enormous on both sides. The enemy was more difficult to subdue after each victory. He was learning rapidly the methods of Napoleon himself. 'The brutes have learnt something,' said Napoleon when he saw the dispositions of the enemy at a later battle. In truth, the process of learning had already begun, and Napoleon was the one great schoolmaster of the soldiers of Europe. The French armies, too, had lost something of their old quality. They were no longer really French armies. Soldiers from the Confederation of the Rhine and from Italy were to be found in great numbers in the French ranks. They were efficient and courageous, but they lacked something of the spontaneity and dash that had distinguished the

Emperor's troops in his early campaigns. It was Napoleon now who used troops essentially mercenary, and he encountered a resistance which became more and more national. The Czar's alliance had not helped Napoleon at all; the Russian troops had abstained from real fighting.

The Austrians somewhat unexpectedly accepted a humiliating peace after the Battle of Wagram. Their aged statesman, Thugut, was consulted and advised surrender. 'Make peace at any price,' he is reported to have said. 'The existence of the Austrian Monarchy is at stake; the dissolution of the French Empire is not far off.' The Austrian Empire lost three million and a half of subjects; she had to reduce her army to 150,000 and to pay a considerable war indemnity. Most of what is now Croatia, Dalmatia and Slovenia were ceded to Napoleon under the title of 'the Illyrian Provinces.' The King of Saxony received the Duchy of Warsaw (Peace of Schoenbrunn, October 10, 1809). Austria's humiliation was as deep as that of Prussia; her revenge and her triumph would come at the same time.

Certain subordinate incidents illustrate the condition of Europe more clearly than the great battles. The Prussian Government would not move, but there were individual movements which showed how ready the country was for a war of liberation. Major Schill raised a regiment of hussars and, failing to win the support of the interior, threw himself into Stralsund, expecting help from England which never came. There were other movements of the same kind in Germany, but the terror of the French arms and the Battle of Wagram repressed all. The Tyrolese war was a more serious affair. The Tyrol was a part of the dominions of Austria which had been ceded to Bavaria. When the war came the Tyrolese rose on behalf of their old Hapsburg rulers. It was the Spanish war in miniature. The peasants were inspired by a love of independence and by religious hatred of the French. Chief among their leaders was Andreas Hofer, an innkeeper of remarkable powers of body and mind. Within their mountain fastnesses the Tyrolese proved extremely difficult to subdue, for it was a genuinely popular rising, and defeat in battle made little impression upon them. After Wagram, however, they were overwhelmed by numbers, and Andreas Hofer was captured and shot at Mantua. But the writing on the wall was beginning to be intelligible to many eyes in Europe.

CHAPTER VIII

THE CATASTROPHE OF NAPOLEON

THE military incidents at which we are now to glance form one of the most dramatic chapters in the military history of modern Europe. We must go to the career of Alexander the Great or of Hannibal for wars so full of personal, military, and national interest as those which saw the fall and the overthrow of Napoleon. But in accordance with the general purposes of this book the story of the fighting will be very lightly passed over. Our chief effort will be to gain some idea of the forces which were making for the overthrow of the great conqueror.

Napoleon did not deserve the title that was given to an early king of France; he was not 'well-served.' True, he had great servants both for peace and war in the earlier part of his career, and he showed himself jealous of the reputations of some of them. But as his career advanced, and every victory only increased the number of his enemies, many drew from his side and began to think of making terms with his opponents. We have already seen this in the careers of Talleyrand and Fouché, and the same tendency may be seen among his soldiers. One of the most determined of his later enemies was Bernadotte. He had been a soldier of the Republic and had not welcomed the rise of Napoleon to supreme power in the *coup d'état* of Brumaire; but he had accepted the new ruler of France and had served with distinction under him, and, though his conduct of campaigns had sometimes been sharply criticised, he had won wealth, glory, and title. After the Battle of Austerlitz he had been raised to the rank of prince. His destiny seemed closely linked to that of the Emperor.

A strange turn of fortune carried him to the throne of Sweden and made him the leader of the enemies of France. The Swedes had played a great part in the wars of Europe in the seventeenth and early eighteenth centuries. But they had overtaxed the resources of the nation, and the last quarter of a century had been full of domestic unrest. In 1789 there had been a sort of revolution which had reaffirmed the almost absolute authority of the Monarchy. But King Gustavus III was murdered in 1792, and the reign of his son, Gustavus IV, saw nothing but failure at home and abroad. In 1809 came another revolution: the King was deposed. His uncle reigned in his place as Charles XIII; he had no children, and a successor was chosen in the royal house of Denmark.

The condition of the country was wretched. It had been forced by Napoleon to take part in the 'continental system' and was thus deprived of much trade in the Baltic, which legitimately belonged to it, and incurred at the same time the hostility of Great Britain. Finland had been handed over to Russia shortly after the Treaty of Tilsit. Norway was, as it had been for many generations, attached to the Crown of Denmark. When therefore the heir, so recently chosen, died in 1810, the Diet hoped to make a choice that should secure for them commercial and perhaps territorial advantages. If they chose one of Napoleon's Marshals they hoped—in strange error—that the Emperor might be induced to allow the relaxation of the 'continental system' in their interest. In any case, they looked forward to winning the favour of the one great military Power in Europe. So Bernadotte was approached and accepted the throne, and ultimately reigned as King Charles John, though we shall continue to call him Bernadotte.

The choice was a veritable 'comedy of errors.' The 'continental system' was the central point of the policy of Napoleon and would under no circumstances be voluntarily withdrawn. He was uncertain of the fidelity of Bernadotte and saw his elevation to a throne with jealousy. Sweden was brought by the election, not into friendship with France, but into bitter conflict.

To return to France and Napoleon. There was little trace in him now of the former armed champion of the Revolution, of the old leader of the national armies of France against the 'bloody standards of tyranny.' His armies were cosmopolitan and all served of necessity. He ruled without more than the dim shadow of constitutional liberty at home. He paraded his friendship and admiration for the autocratic Czar. Further, after his last peace with Austria he had used his power to procure for himself an Austrian wife in place of Josephine, whom he had recently divorced—not for personal but for political reasons, hoping in a new marriage to find an heir to the Empire and the support of Austria for his schemes. So the unfortunate Marie Louise came from Vienna to Paris, bore the Emperor a son, and soon saw the collapse of his fortunes. He became by this marriage the nephew of Marie Antoinette, the guillotined Queen of France.

The situation in Europe changed, but never became more favourable to Napoleon's hopes. The only chance of the permanence of Napoleon's 'European settlement' would have been the winning over of European opinion to the acceptance of a system that brought with it the triumph of the principles of the French Revolution. But there was no sign of that. Public opinion grew more and more hostile. National sentiment grew stronger. The economic hardships and the burden of conscription alienated even those who were best disposed. The Spanish war still dragged on, and before Napoleon could turn to it with all his forces and energy a much greater danger came in the east.

The Russian alliance was the very foundation of his new policy and an integral part of his schemes against Great Britain; and now there came, instead of alliance with Russia, war. The relations of Napoleon and Alexander had never been really cordial—not even amidst the festivities of Erfurt. There was no principle of stability in the alliance, no common aim.[1] At bottom Napoleon merely wanted to use the Czar for his own purposes and to strengthen his own position in Europe. The Czar, naturally, had different views, and there were soon many causes of friction. During the last Austrian war the Czar had given no real help, when perhaps, if he had liked, he might have prevented the war. The Czar, too, showed no inclination to accept and co-operate in the blockade of Great Britain. On the contrary, it was known that British commerce was secretly admitted, while a high tariff was openly placed

---

[1] 'At bottom the great question is—who shall have Constantinople?' wrote Napoleon (May 31, 1808); and this was one of the reasons why he and Alexander could not agree.

on French goods coming into Russia. Nor were the grievances of the Czar against Napoleon fewer or smaller. His Austrian marriage seemed to show a tendency to look away from Russia to Austria for support. He had not considered the susceptibilities of Russia in more serious things. When, in 1810, he had annexed Holland and the north-west of Germany, in order to bar that entrance against English commerce, the Duchy of Oldenburg was one of the places occupied by the French Emperor. The heir to the duchy was the brother-in-law of the Czar, and the Czar was naturally offended. Nearer home there was a more serious question. Napoleon had formed most of the Polish territories which he had taken from Prussia and from Austria into the 'Duchy of Warsaw.' The Russian Government was always peculiarly sensitive to what happened in Poland. She had many millions of Poles among her own subjects, and the idea of independence might have an awkward effect on their imaginations. Napoleon had promised that the name of Poland should not reappear on the map; but the Duchy of Warsaw was Poland under a thin veil. The Czar was profoundly discontented with Napoleon's Polish policy. Of all the causes of conflict between the two the Polish question was probably the most important.

It was quite beyond the power of diplomacy or arbitration to prevent the collision. As irritation deepened into enmity both sides worked feverishly to find alliance and military support. Fear kept the centre of Europe in Napoleon's train, but no one could be ignorant that Austria and Prussia would fall from him in the hour of defeat. Russia made offers to the Poles and hoped to win them from the side of France, but they were the only people who regarded the prospect of another French victory with enthusiasm; it would bring, they hoped, an independent Polish kingdom. Russia had better fortune with the northern Powers. Bernadotte, the new ruler of Sweden, was won over by the promise that he should be allowed to annex Norway. He counted henceforth as the bitterest of Napoleon's enemies, and brought to the Allies a valuable knowledge of the character and methods of the French army. Great Britain made a treaty with Sweden and Russia, and as usual provided subsidies. The Czar had more valuable allies even than Sweden or Britain. The vast distances, the climate, the thin population, and the strong national feeling of Russia were enemies beyond the power of Napoleon to cope with.

At the end of June 1812 the Grand Army passed over the Niemen, in four main divisions, amounting in all to about 600,000 men, and the invasion of Russia began. It was a vast force, but not the largest ever gathered under a single command up to that time, and it has been immensely exceeded since then. The Russian commander, Barclay, had less than half the French force and he retreated before it. Napoleon marched as far as Vitebsk—about half of the 500 miles that separated the Niemen from Moscow—and had some thoughts of stopping there and trying to organise the vast district which had been abandoned to him. But there were dangers on all sides: he was lured on by the hope of settling all difficulties by a great victory and the surrender of the Czar. So he pushed on towards Moscow; disease, desertion, and the need of establishing garrisons in the country he passed through had already reduced his army dangerously. The Russians had now determined to fight. Kutusov had displaced Barclay. The Russian army stood at bay on the banks of the Borodino (September 1812). The murderous battle that followed was a victory for Napoleon in that the Russian army retreated and left the road to Moscow open to him; but his losses had amounted to 40,000, and the Russians had lost fewer. A little later he was at the gates of Moscow, expecting a formal surrender. None came, and he entered an empty and abandoned city. Napoleon took up his quarters in the Kremlin—the ancient palace of the Czars. It seemed the culmination of his career of triumph.

Napoleon knew how unreal the triumph was. No message came from St. Petersburg. A great fire broke out in Moscow—not accidentally—and consumed valuable provisions for men and horses. It would perhaps have been possible to remain in Moscow for the winter and to return to Europe when the spring had brought food and warmth. But that was dangerous in any case, and what would happen in Europe while Napoleon was away? It was clear that this was no war against armies and governments; it was the nation against which he had to fight. When the news came to Paris there was but one cry: 'It is another Spanish war!'

The retreat began on October 19. Napoleon hoped to force his way farther south and return by a route that would afford him provisions; but Kutusov blocked his way at Jaroslavetz and held it against the French attacks. Napoleon was forced back on to the route he had already swept clear of provisions on his march to Moscow. This sealed the destruction of the army. The Russian winter came on November 5. Already many thousands of soldiers had been lost by cold or disease or desertion. But the worst was yet to come. The Nieman was reached on December 13. Napoleon's losses are reckoned at 170,000 prisoners and 170,000 dead. That is all we can say of a tragedy almost without parallel in history.

Western Europe had listened with incredulous amazement to the news from Russia. But, as it became clear that Napoleon had suffered decisive defeat and crippling losses, there was a universal stirring which soon took the form of widespread resistance. The Russian armies, under the command of the Czar himself, entered Germany. He had with him Stein, the Prussian reformer, who had been driven from Prussia by the orders of Napoleon and now preached the duty of national resistance. Napoleon had by no means given up hope of recovering from his Russian disaster. He called on France for immense efforts in men and money. There was by no means universal readiness to obey. There were stirrings of revolt in La Vendée and in some other parts of the country. There were many stories of men who broke out their teeth or cut off their thumbs in order to avoid military service. But the great danger that threatened France, and the pride of the country in the military triumphs of Napoleon, worked wonders. In 1813 he had again half a million of men under his command. They were young and unequal to the veterans of the Grand Army; but both Ney and his master were loud in their praise of the courage and endurance of the young conscripts. Napoleon again dreamed of a peace enforced in Europe by complete victory. If he surrendered anything it would lead to the surrender of all. And victory would allow him to hold what he had and to regain what he had lost. He hoped by a show of strength to keep Prussia on his side. He believed himself secure of Austria through his marriage with Marie Louise and his understanding with Metternich, the crafty Chancellor who had ruled since 1810. He determined, therefore, to make no concessions—though large concessions might perhaps have kept Austria faithful to the French alliance —and to let the sword decide. He could not yet believe that the sword had broken in his hands. Yet he was himself not the old Napoleon: he had grown stout and was at times, and even at critical moments, overcome by fatigue. His power of will was as great as ever and his tactical and strategic skill is thought to have suffered no diminution. But he had lost much in elasticity of mind and had no longer his old quick sense of the realities of the situation.

Frederick William, the King of Prussia, was not so ready to rise as his people. He had had bitter experience of the weight of Napoleon's hand, and hesitated to challenge him again; but the country was full of enthusiasm. The League of Virtue (the *Tugendbund*) had won many adherents. The patriotic poems and songs of Arndt, Körner, and others did much to inflame the popular mind. There were, too, more serious forces in the background. The reforms of Stein had given new life to the body politic of Prussia and Scharnhorst's reform of the army gave her a force of 150,000 men.

The first movement in Prussia against the French came in spite of the King. Colonel Yorck was besieging the Russians in Riga as an ally of the French. When the news of the Russian catastrophe reached him, acting on his own responsibility, he refused to continue the siege against those whom he considered his allies, and made with them an agreement by which he declared his army to be neutral. Such neutrality did not really differ from hostility to the French. The King of Prussia was bound to repudiate his action, but he soon followed it. Eastern Prussia had risen spontaneously as the Russian troops advanced. The Provincial Assembly of Eastern Prussia was summoned, and put all its forces at the disposal of the enemies of Napoleon. It was impossible for the King of Prussia to delay any longer. In January 1813 he signed with the Czar the Treaty of Kalisch. The two sovereigns undertook not to make any separate peace, and the Czar promised that Prussia should recover its ancient boundaries, and that Germany should be free. A little later it was declared that if any princes or peoples in Germany did not join the Allies they should lose their independence when the settlement came, and that their territories should be at the disposal of the allies. Austria came in to the same side, but more slowly and with more duplicity. Metternich assured the French Ambassador that the alliance with his master corresponded to the permanent interests of the two countries. But all the time he was negotiating with Prussia, and ultimately joined the Convention of Breslau. Napoleon was driven back to the west of the Elbe; and Hamburg and Dresden, both situated on that river, were soon occupied by the army of liberation. Nor was it only his allies who were falling from Napoleon. His own Generals were, many of them, on the edge of desertion. Bernadotte commanded already in the ranks of the enemy. Murat and Jomini were soon to pass over to that side, and the Marshals who remained with him were often critical, negligent, and depressed.

And yet Napoleon gained victories which would have been reckoned great if it were not for the disasters which so soon followed them. He defeated the allied Russians and Prussians, first at Lützen and then at Bautzen. They were unquestionable victories, and threw the enemy into great depression, but they were won at a terrible cost to the victors. The orders of Napoleon, moreover, were no longer carried out by his subordinates with the old eager loyalty. There was little that resembled Austerlitz and Jena in these obstinate struggles. The defeated allies, moreover, retreated eastward and had soon re-formed their armies and were ready for a further struggle.

It was at this juncture, moreover, that Austria threw in her lot openly with the Allies. Metternich played his cards with the most perfect skill and lack of scruple. He proposed to Napoleon an armistice which should last from June 4 to July 28, 1813; this period was to be used to prepare the ground for a general peace congress. Napoleon accepted the proposal and signed the armistice.

Was peace possible? Were the two chief negotiators in earnest? With whom lies the responsibility for the failure? It is clear that the situation did not admit of a peaceful solution of the problems, and that neither party sincerely desired the cessation of the war. Metternich was aware of the growing enthusiasm of Germany and of the rapidly accumulating forces against Napoleon. Napoleon on his side still hoped for a settlement through victory, and knew that only victory could secure his power either in Europe or in France. He is reported to have said to Metternich: 'Sovereigns who are born on the throne can be beaten twenty times and still go back to their capitals. But I can't, because I am a parvenu.' It is a sentence which reveals a permanent feature of Napoleon's position, and explains much of his policy. In a conference with Napoleon which took place at Dresden, Metternich suggested the abandonment by France of nearly all her territories beyond the Rhine. The interview between the two men was a very stormy one, and

Napoleon talked at one time about going to Vienna again, at the head of his army, to settle the dispute. He consented, however, to prolong the armistice and to attend a Peace Congress at Prague. The Congress was never really constituted. Austria despatched an ultimatum. Napoleon disdained to reply to it, and Austria issued a declaration of war.

The Allies had nearly a million men under arms, and henceforth Napoleon was usually outnumbered. His enemies hoped to overwhelm him by a series of indecisive attacks and to defeat him in detail. Yet the campaign consisted of two great battles: one deserving to rank among his greatest victories; and the other his most serious, his one altogether irreparable defeat.

At Dresden he anticipated the attack of his enemies and gained a complete victory. Earlier in his career he would have followed it up with furious energy, and would perhaps have made it decisive of the campaign in Germany. But he seemed incapable of the continuous exertion which he had so often shown in his youth. His lieutenants, too, failed to support his plans. Five successive actions in which they were defeated almost neutralised the effects of the Battle of Dresden. Diplomacy gained important advantages against him. Metternich insisted on negotiations with the princes of the Confederation of the Rhine. They were offered a continuation of their powers and titles after the peace if they would join the Allies now. Stein deplored the offer as involving the sacrifice of all hopes of building up a united Germany at the peace. The offer was accepted by most. Bavaria came over to join the Allies. Saxony almost alone remained faithful to Napoleon.

Meanwhile Blücher and the Prussians had crossed the Elbe. Napoleon's position at Dresden was untenable. He fell back westward, and on October 16, 1813, began the Battle of Leipzig—'the battle of the Peoples,' as it is called. There was fighting for three days, and it was not all favourable to the Allies. The losses amounted to some 130,000 men, and of these about 50,000 were French. The broken fragments of the French army escaped by the one route that was left open. With what troops he had left Napoleon made for the Rhine. An army of 50,000 men, chiefly Bavarians, tried to stop him at Hanau, but was easily brushed aside. The French army reached the Rhine at the beginning of December, and the ravages of disease were almost as fatal to it as the German sword had been. The garrisons that had been left behind in Germany—about 190,000 men—soon surrendered. East of the Rhine Napoleon's power had disappeared. The French armies had almost been withdrawn from Spain. Wellington entered France victoriously from the south.

France had now to face the horrors of invasion, which she had inflicted on so many lands but had not herself known since 1793. She was weary of war. Her dreams of world victory were all dissipated. She was exhausted in men; her commerce was destroyed or languishing.

There had been during the last ten years singularly little political interest in the country. The movement of the armies had engrossed the attention of all men. But now, when the Emperor was coming back to France a beaten man, men's minds recurred to their old ideals. Some liberals dared to utter again the watchwords of the Revolution. The Royalists saw again a chance—after so many disappointments—of the return of the Bourbons. Louis XVIII, as all Royalists called the brother of Louis XVI, who had fought against the Revolution as the Comte de Provence, issued a proclamation urging the French to regard the invading allies as their friends and promising a diminution of taxes, a regard for acquired property, peace and pardon. The old nobility showed no hesitation about returning to France in the ranks of the invaders. The restoration of the Bourbons was openly advocated in France. Yet there was a good deal of enthusiasm still for the Emperor. He represented, at least to many, the cause of national defence. The Government was strong enough or popular enough to draw 350,000 soldiers from the country. Napoleon would not fall without a struggle.

The military genius of Napoleon as strategist was never shown more clearly than in the war for the soil of France. The invaders were perhaps taking things too easily, and assumed too readily that no further resistance was probable. It is quite possible, too, that the wisest and most patriotic course for Napoleon to pursue would have been to recognise the inevitability of defeat, and to have spared to France the sufferings, and to the Allies the exasperation, of a further campaign. But it is impossible not to admire the steady nerve, and the strength of will, which seemed at one time likely to turn defeat into victory. Twice over he defeated Blücher with heavy loss. The whole Allied army seemed for a time in real danger of destruction. They had lost confidence in the presence of the French and their great commander. An army with twice the numbers of the French refused battle. It might seem that the triumphs of Valmy were to be repeated on an immensely greater scale, and the Emperor was popular once more. The cruelties of the Prussian and Russian invaders made the task of defence all the more necessary in the eyes of the people, and the invading Allies encountered a genuinely popular resistance. The peasants in many districts, exasperated by the exactions and cruelties of the invaders, rose against them in a way which recalled the Vendean war. The coalition seemed really in danger of dissolution.

The diplomatists were active during these months as well as the soldiers. It is, however, very rare that a war in which the passions of the combatants have been violently roused can be settled by negotiation before a military decision has been reached. On two occasions there were negotiations with a view to a settlement. First, Metternich had interviewed a representative of Napoleon in November 1813. It was suggested that France should abandon all her conquests except Belgium and what lay within the limits of the Rhine and the Alps. There was probably little sincerity on either side, and as we have seen the war went on. Next, when Napoleon had shown how dangerous he could still be, a congress was held at Châtillon. Now it was proposed that Belgium should be abandoned and what France had won under the Revolution in the east and south. She was to return to her pre-revolutionary boundaries, and some hope was held out that Great Britain would restore some of the colonies which had been taken from her during the war. But all ended in smoke. The sword must decide.

In the final campaign Napoleon showed daring and hope. He gained some wonderful successes, and he was at times marvellously supported by his soldiers. But his whole position was undermined. His forces were exhausted, while the enemy could draw on an immense reservoir. His plans presupposed the resistance of Paris, and Paris was in no mood for resistance. When by a daring move Napoleon placed himself in the rear of the Allies, they determined at last that courage was safer than prudence and pushed on for Paris. The Emperor had foreseen the possibility of an attack on Paris, and he had sent orders for the Government to be moved to the Loire. But his orders in the hour of his weakness were no longer loyally obeyed. The Empress was sent away with the child, who, it was hoped, was to carry on the glories of the Empire, but Napoleon's brother Joseph remained in the city. A battle was fought outside of Paris, stubbornly contested, and entailing great loss of life. Then the city capitulated. Napoleon had some thought of continuing the war outside of Paris, but he saw the impossibility of his plan. His Marshals were weary of fighting, and showed less readiness to obey than many of the common soldiers. At last, on April 6, he signed his abdication. 'As the Allied Powers have declared that the Emperor Napoleon is the only obstacle to the re-establishment of peace in Europe the Emperor Napoleon, obedient to the oaths that he has sworn, declares that he renounces for himself and for his heirs the thrones of France and Italy, because there is no personal sacrifice, even that of life itself, which he is not ready to make in the interests of France.' He is thought to have attempted suicide. A fortnight later he bade a touching farewell to his Old Guard and retired to the island of Elba, where he was to be allowed to maintain the empty name and ceremony of Empire.

The fall of Napoleon's power settled some questions, but brought forward others that proved very difficult. Who was to rule in France, and by what right and in what manner? What was to be done with the vast European territories over which Napoleon had ruled or in which he had exercised a decisive influence? As the flood subsided many of the old landmarks reappeared, but some had been swept away for ever. There were many concurrent forces deciding these issues; but there were two dominating personalities. Among the Allies there was no one to rival in influence Alexander of Russia, a strange and baffling character. He was the object of endless adulation from Frenchmen and foreigners, and he oscillated between humanitarian and religious ideals on the one hand and egoistic and Russian aims on the other. And on the French side there was Talleyrand, who, after his strange career as Jacobin and imperialist, as trusted agent of Napoleon's schemes and traitor to Napoleon even while he served him, was now the one man who seemed to exercise a prevailing influence with the hesitating politicians of France. For the moment Castlereagh, Wellington, and the English were of less account than these two men.

A regency on behalf of Napoleon's infant son; the transference of the Crown to one of his Marshals—these schemes were suggested and considered. But in the end the restoration of the Bourbon dynasty in the person of Louis XVIII was decided on. It was a solution founded on a principle—the principle of legitimacy—and it won the assent of all the Allies. The Senate, the impotent body which was nearly all that remained of the Constitution of Brumaire, and contained some members who had voted for the execution of Louis XVI, under Talleyrand's guidance declared that 'the French people freely call to the throne Louis-Stanislas-Xavier de France, brother of the late king'; and they added to their invitation certain constitutional articles guaranteeing the principles of the Revolution. It was twenty-two years since the Bourbons had disappeared from the soil of France, and the number of those who really cherished their memory was small. France as a whole had no hand in the matter. Paris accepted a decision which was really dictated by the armies of the Allies, and the affair was settled. Louis XVIII soon returned to Paris, and his awkward reserve, his assumption of Divine Right, and his faint expressions of gratitude to those who had restored him to the throne, especially his coldness to the Czar, had a depressing effect. It is said that at his formal entry into Paris there were some of the troops who insisted on crying 'Vive l'Empereur!'

Louis XVIII, then, would reign—though already some were asking for how long—but by what right and within what frontiers? The first question was settled when Louis XVIII 'granted' a charter regulating the methods of government—that is to say, he insisted on his 'Divine Right' and gave to the people only such liberties as he thought well. The general settlement was adjourned to a congress which was to meet at once at Vienna; but before the plenipotentiaries met there it was agreed that France should have the frontiers of 1792—the frontiers, that is, which she possessed before the revolutionary wars had begun—with some small rectifications which were nearly all to her advantage. France was to be represented at Vienna. The Allies could not refuse to treat on terms of equality a king whom they had themselves established on the throne of France; but before the diplomatists met at Vienna they had procured from the French King a definite promise that he would accept all the decisions of the Allies.

The aims and intrigues and difficulties of the diplomatists of Vienna will be treated in the next chapter. They were working their way

5

through passionate rivalries, that at one time threatened war, to some sort of solution when the news of Napoleon's return to France fell like a bombshell upon the Assembly and threw everything into confusion. Napoleon had been encouraged to attempt his great adventure by the rumours of the dissensions of the Powers over the Saxon-Polish question. The news from France also made him think that his return would be welcome to many. The Government of Louis XVIII had hardly begun to function, but its general character was apparent. It was associated with the loss of the territories that Napoleon had conquered, and offended thus the pride of the French people. The *émigré* nobles were returning, and they clamoured for the restoration of their confiscated lands. The peasantry—always so important a force at the basis of the social fabric of France—believed themselves to be threatened in their possessions. Napoleon's soldiers too, whether still in the ranks of the army or dismissed from it, were bitterly discontented. Those who had been disbanded could in many cases find no employment. Dupont, whose surrender at Baylen had first shown that a Napoleonic army could be defeated, was made Minister of War, to the great irritation of the soldiers. There were thus mutterings of discontent, though there was nothing to indicate the miraculous success which awaited Napoleon on his arrival in France.

His banishment to Elba with an important title and a toy Court was an absurdity. It was impossible to keep him under supervision, and yet his position was one from which he inevitably wanted to escape. The income that had been promised to him was not paid, and its non-payment gave him the pretext that he needed. He slipped away from Elba and landed near Antibes on the south coast of France. He had no support of importance except his name and the memories of twenty years; but that proved more than sufficient. The new Government had struck no roots, and the Powers of Europe, who had defeated Napoleon, had not thought it necessary to provide for the support of the restored monarchy. The army deserted Louis XVIII almost *en masse*; the great majority of the people welcomed Napoleon. Ney, who had been sent out to resist him and had promised to bring him back to Paris 'in a cage,' came back as his supporter and general. The King and his brother and the emigrant nobility had once more to 'go on their travels.'

The iron dice of war fell, as we know, fatally for Napoleon, but it would be rash to assume from the event that he had no chance of success. He had a large and enthusiastic army, strengthened by the return of large numbers of prisoners from Russia. It had been clearly shown at the Congress of Vienna how strong were the antagonisms that underlay the official harmony of the Allies. If Napoleon had won a great victory he would probably have offered terms of studied moderation, and it is not impossible that they would have been accepted. But there were permanent features in the life of Europe which made the return of the days of Marengo and Austerlitz and Jena unthinkable. The nations of

Europe were awake. The Governments were nowhere the mere lifeless machines that they had been before the French Revolution. They had a large enthusiastic popular support. Europe was fighting France with her own weapons. And, further, the support that Napoleon received in France was by no means untroubled by hesitations and suspicions. As soon as the first moment of delirium was past there were few indeed who were willing to support the idea of Napoleon reigning as he had reigned in 1805. He was sensitive to the condition of public opinion. He issued a decree instituting two Chambers for legislation, one of which was to be popularly elected; the press was to be free; Ministers were to be responsible to the Chambers. Then, though the organisation of the military force was occupying all his attention, he submitted this new Constitution to a plebiscite. Only a million and a half of voters went to the poll, but the support of a large majority gave him the appearance of a constitutional position. Had he returned victoriously from Belgium the Constitution could hardly have lived unchanged. All turned on the decision of battle.

Napoleon was without an ally in Europe. Murat, King of Naples, had indeed raised an army and appealed for the support of Italian senti-ment, knowing that he would be expelled from the throne of Naples by the Congress of Vienna. But Napoleon believed that Murat's action was prejudicial to his own chances, and the Italian movement was soon suppressed. Napoleon started for the front on June 12. He aimed at striking against the British and the Prussian armies before they could effect a concentration of their forces. He gained a considerable though a partial success against the Prussians at Ligny. Blücher, the Prussian commander, promised Wellington that he would join him at Mont St. Jean, and it was in reliance on this promise that Wellington accepted the Battle of Waterloo on June 18. At the end of the day Napoleon was beaten beyond possibility of recovery. Paris capitulated on July 3. Napoleon surrendered on July 9 and was sent to St. Helena.

The dramatic episode of the Hundred Days' Campaign had altered the outlook in Europe, and materially for the worse. In 1814, the allies had been willing to maintain the view that they had been fighting against Napoleon, not against France, and they were prepared to give France fair if not generous terms, inflicting on her no war indemnity and insisting on no military occupation of her territory. At the Congress of Vienna, under the skilful management of Talleyrand, France had begun to assume the rôle of an equal among the Great Powers of Europe. There were many who would have liked to punish her more severely; but on the whole the absence of bitterness was remarkable. After Waterloo, the attitude of the Powers was different. The welcome that the country had given to Napoleon seemed to show that it identified itself with him. France had now to pay an indemnity of 700 million francs and to submit to a military occupation by 150,000 men under the command of Wellington. The art treasures which had been brought to Paris from all parts of Europe by Napoleon were, quite justly, restored.

It was not certain at first that Louis XVIII would be restored. The regency for Napoleon's baby son, or a prince of the House of Orleans, were suggested as alternatives. But Louis was decided on in the end. The past utterances of the Allies and the difficulties that would be caused by any other settlement made him inevitable. The question of the frontiers of France was hotly disputed. All Germany would have liked to annex something on the eastern frontier of France. Prussia was the spokesman of the nation in demanding the cession to Germany of Alsace and Lorraine. But both Russia and Great Britain opposed the mutilation of France. The Czar Alexander was the supreme figure in Europe for a time. He was moved to defend France by the sentiment of generosity which was powerful and genuine with him, and also by the feeling that a strong France was essential to Russia in the political combinations of Europe. Political and diplomatic considerations also moved Castlereagh and the British Government, though they, too, were by no means insensible to the appeal of justice. So, with small exceptions, the territory of France remained what it was before the Revolution began. The Germans were especially fierce against France and their demands were resisted with difficulty, but they were resisted. Alsace and Lorraine were not surrendered. The Pont de Jéna was not blown up. Their plundering of the provinces which they occupied was checked.

The declared intention of those who fought against France had been to resist the Revolution and its principles and to restore the old order which had been destroyed by Napoleon. It was assumed that the storm which had raged in Europe for nearly a quarter of a century would now pass off and the Continent would reassume its old life, aims, and methods. The diplomatists of 1814 and 1815 were in no mood to profit by the great opportunity afforded for social and political experiment and reconstruction. Liberty, equality, fraternity, democracy, progress, humanity, were words of dangerous associations. But it was soon seen that the forces identified with the French Revolution were not to be so easily controlled. The enthusiasms which they represented would, it was hoped, be suppressed and the Balance of Power restored, but despite the efforts of the statesmen of 1815 to restore the Old Europe, history dates the rise of a new Europe from these events.

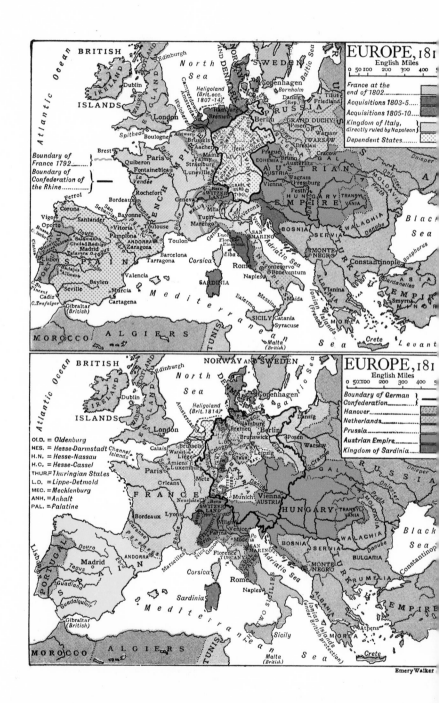

EmeryWalker

PART II

FROM INTERNATIONAL GOVERNMENT TO REVOLUTION, 1814–48

CHAPTER IX

THE FAILURE OF INTERNATIONAL GOVERNMENT
(1814–25)

The defeat of Napoleon was followed by a long period of peace among the Great Powers—a peace moreover that was only in part one of exhaustion. It opened with the attempt of the Great Powers of Europe to make a constructive agreement for peace, the greatest attempt ever made in the history of Europe to this date, an attempt of such importance that it may properly be regarded as beginning a new era of European relationships. The breakdown of this international experiment must not blind us to the magnitude of its results. There was no great war in Europe for a century and no major war until 1853; the territorial settlement remained the political basis of Europe for thirty years; the system of government by Congress, destroyed before the end of the first decade, left as a tradition behind it the practice of international conferences, inherited by the twentieth century from the nineteenth.

The explanation of the breakdown is to be found in a combination of factors. A policy of reaction was pursued in varying forms by most of the governments in Europe; in Austria under Metternich, in Prussia, saved from the worst excesses by the results of her earlier reforms, and in Russia, most conspicuously after Nicholas I succeeded Alexander in 1825. In comparison with these governments the Tory administration in England seemed dangerously liberal, and the breach which developed between Britain and her three allies in the time of Canning was no mere matter of diplomacy; beneath the divergencies of policy at the Conference tables lay a fundamental difference of outlook. Britain as the exponent of constitutional monarchy had adherents in France, in the Netherlands, in Greece, Portugal and Spain, and contesting parties in all these countries provided opportunities for diplomatic rivalry. Deeper still in the body politic of Europe were the great forces of nationalism and revolutionary discontent, breaking out from time to time to the surface. In Italy and Spain, in Greece, Poland and Belgium, revolution was active, although only in Greece and Belgium was it successful. In Germany and Austria it was latent, showing itself in incidents and agitation rather than in open war, until the Year of

Revolution gave a new turn to European development. The main responsibility for the failure of the attempt to bring a lasting peace by a combination of the Great Powers must be attributed first to those who acted as the High Priests of reaction, and in the second place to those who were led by their national and liberal fervours to seek redress by violence. Some responsibility must be given, too, to the successive statesmen of Britain who followed a policy which made impossible the maintenance of the unity of the Alliance.

The Four Great Powers, Austria, England, Prussia and Russia, had finally been brought into a great alliance by the Treaty of Chaumont (March 9, 1814).[1] By this agreement the Signatory Powers undertook to unite in an alliance for twenty years. They proposed first to over-throw Napoleon, next to prevent him or his dynasty from returning to France, lastly to guarantee the territorial settlement to be made by a concerted alliance for twenty years. Austria (Metternich) and Russia (Alexander) had quarrelled so much that they found agreement diffi-cult, and it was due to Castlereagh's influence that this union and agree-ment were brought about. Its effects were immediate. By the end of March the Allies had decided to restore the Bourbons to France and had occupied Paris. Napoleon abdicated for himself and his family in the first days of April, and the Allies sat down to mould the map of Europe anew, according to their hearts' desire.

Their task was not an easy one. The Bourbons had returned to France 'in the baggage of the Allies.' A cartoon represented Louis XVIII mounted on a horse beside a Cossack, and trampling on the body of a dead Frenchman. Louis XVIII was not popular, for he seemed to be degrading the glory which France had won under Napoleon, by shaking hands with the Allies. His acts were not prudent. He pro-claimed indeed a constitution, but he asserted, to some extent, the old theory of Divine Right, which Frenchmen had learnt to despise. His followers inaugurated a 'white terror' against the supporters of Napo-leon, whom they plundered or murdered. The army, the pride of France, was greatly reduced, many of its great leaders and more of its fine soldiers were dismissed. The Church, which so many Frenchmen had assailed, was re-established in something like its old bigotry and power. Worse than all this, Louis XVIII was asked by the Allies to consent to a reduction of the boundaries of France. The ideal of the Revolution and Napoleon was that France should realise the age-long dream of French diplomacy, that she should extend to her natural boundaries, and include Belgium and the left bank of the Rhine in her territory. That ideal had been achieved and France had held these territories for over twenty years. She was now to be called upon to surrender them.

The Allies lost no time in enforcing these sacrifices on France. By May 30 the First Treaty of Paris was signed. France was treated with as much consideration as was possible under the circumstances, but it was not a consideration which could satisfy patriotic Frenchmen. She was

[1] The date given on the document, March 1, 1814, is fictitious.

not disarmed, nor was she called upon to pay a war indemnity, nor to restore the masterpieces of art which she had removed from Italy or Germany. Her boundaries in Europe were not to be those of 1789 but of 1792, and she even received certain extensions beyond this line. Malta, which Napoleon had conquered, but which England had taken from him, remained British. Outside Europe her treatment was less generous. She retained all her trading stations and commercial privileges in India, but was compelled to dismantle all fortresses. She ceded to England Mauritius, a naval station on the way to India. But the Powers returned to her the rich island of Guadeloupe and most of her other possessions in the West Indies. Tobago and St. Lucia (which had great strategic importance) were ceded to England, and part of San Domingo to Spain. France retained her Fishery Rights in the St. Lawrence and off Newfoundland. Her military advantages in her colonies were, therefore, lessened, but her commercial wealth remained practically unimpaired. Yet the Allies could have deprived her of every colony she possessed.

In the published articles of the First Treaty of Paris, the Powers announced that they intended to restore Holland with increased territory; to form an independent German Federation; to recognise the independence of Switzerland; and to form a new Italy, composed of sovereign states, 'beyond the limits of those countries which are to revert to Austria.' This first sketch of the territorial arrangements of Vienna was defined in more detail in secret articles to the Treaty, which need not detain us here.

The Allies agreed to meet at a Congress at Vienna in the autumn to settle the rest of Europe (outside France) on an agreed basis. But they had reckoned without France. Redeemed, restored, forgiven, a monarchy again and akin to the old type of European states, France claimed a share in the discussions of Vienna. She was there to play for her own hand and to make mischief, and Talleyrand, her representative, was able greatly to trouble the waters. Russia and Prussia, on the one hand, quarrelled fiercely with Austria and England, on the other. Talleyrand held the balance and used it to the advantage of France. Finally, at the beginning of 1815, the differences at Vienna became so serious, that France, Austria and England formed a defensive alliance to resist the claims of Russia and Prussia.[1] This extreme step produced

---

[1] This extraordinary alliance was signed on January 3, 1815. Technically it was secret and not known either to Czar Alexander or to the King of Prussia. But its substance was certainly known to them at the time and produced a very marked effect immediately on their policy. The point, on which the Russo-Prussian group was opposed to the Anglo-Franco-Austrian group, was simple: Prussia desired to annex the whole of Saxony in exchange for the large amount of Polish territory she was surrendering to Russia, and Alexander 'backed up' Prussia to the limit. Metternich refused to allow Prussia so large an extension of territory contiguous to Austria, and Castlereagh (and ultimately Talleyrand) stood with him. The difference went right up to the brink of war and it was only when Alexander was convinced that the other group would fight that he gave way. Ultimately, Prussia secured only about half of

good results: Alexander gave way on some points, Prussia followed suit. All matters were really adjusted when the world was suddenly startled by the news that Napoleon had broken loose from Elba, that Louis XVIII was in flight, and that France had once again welcomed the Emperor, whose downfall the rest of Europe had decreed.

The return from Elba and the campaign of Waterloo have been well described as 'the most wonderful adventure in history.' It reads like a romance. Napoleon landed with a small force, bared his breast to Royalist soldiers who refused to fire on him, traversed half France without difficulty or bloodshed, and finally, late at night on March 20, was borne up the stairs of the Tuileries by a crowd frantic with enthusiasm. The greatest of living soldiers had achieved a bloodless conquest, and he now declared his intention of being a constitutional ruler at home, and of maintaining pacific relations with every Power abroad. Yet in a hundred days it was all over. Napoleon was only forty-six and he had still six years to live. But on the evening of June 18 he rode away both from Waterloo and from history.

Even had Napoleon won at Waterloo, he would probably have been crushed a little later by the Austro-Russian armies advancing from the east. And his defeat ended the matter. The French people showed no desire to cling to him after his disaster, and submitted once more to the return and the rule of the gouty and uninspiring Bourbon. Napoleon's adventure has only importance in that it brought further misfortunes on France. The terms imposed on France by Europe were sterner. She was now compelled to pay a war indemnity, to restore the works of art, to submit to being garrisoned by an Allied army until 1818. Her boundaries in Europe were further reduced from the line of 1792 to that of 1790, and certain places of strategic importance on the frontier were now taken from her.[1] Indeed, had it not been for the moderating counsels of Castlereagh and Wellington, she might have been compelled to cede Alsace and Lorraine.

Setting aside the more drastic terms imposed upon France, the Vienna settlement was not materially altered by the return from Elba. The Treaty of Vienna was actually signed on June 9, before the decisive day of Waterloo. Its provisions fell into several great groups. The first of these may be best indicated by describing it as the settlement of the Balance of Power. The principle was that each Great Power was to obtain the territory or its equivalent that it had held in 1805. Except in the case of Russia, this was fairly carried out. Russia negotiated with

Saxony. Talleyrand's part in the matter has been somewhat exaggerated. He did not create the difference between the Allies, which were fundamental, but he inflamed and exploited those difficulties to the advantage of France. Much, however, of what he gained for France was thrown away by Napoleon's intervention. *v.* C. K. Webster: *The Congress of Vienna, 1814–15*, pp. 106 *sqq.* (Bell, 1934).

[1] These stiffened terms were embodied in the Second Treaty of Paris, signed November 20, 1815. As will be seen below, the general settlement of Europe, made by the Treaty of Vienna, signed June 9, 1815, remained substantially unaltered.

the sword in her hand and obtained more than the other Allies liked. She got a large part of Poland, including Warsaw the capital, which she recovered from Prussia, and promised to form a national kingdom of Poland and to endow her with a constitution. In the opinion of both Castlereagh and Metternich this accession of power and population was too great, and upset the Balance of Power. Alarm was increased by the fact that Alexander maintained an army of nearly a million men, which was about twice the number that good judges thought necessary.

As regards Germany, the balancing of power was fairly carried out. Prussia complained that she got less than the 1805 standard, and this was true. But she had had a great deal of Polish territory in 1805, and she exchanged this for half of Saxony and for the Rhine Province, German in blood and speech. It is singular that Prussia at the time showed no special desire for this last acquisition, which made her ultimately the national champion of Germany against France.

Austria adjusted the balance against Prussia in Germany by preventing her from annexing all Saxony as she had desired. Further, Metternich erected Bavaria once more into a powerful state, on whose co-operation Austria could depend. Hanover, from its British connection, obtained a good accession of territory. The other smaller states of Germany were cut up and carved out to suit Austrian or Prussian convenience. Their own interests were hardly considered, but a good deal of common sense was shown in rounding off territories and in settling old-time differences, and the total number of German states included in the new Federation was reduced to thirty-nine. Austria retained, in effect, the headship of Germany, though Prussia was not far behind her in authority.

The fact is Austria did not aim at gains in Germany, but in Italy. She acquired Venetia and recovered Lombardy. All the other states in Italy were really satellites in her train. Piedmont acquired Genoa, and was helped by this acquisition to defend the North against France. The Papal States were restored, and Naples was again set up as a kingdom under a Bourbon. By a secret treaty, made (with Castlereagh's approval) between Metternich and the King of Naples, the latter promised not to grant a constitution without Austria's consent. Metternich's avowed object was to break up and dismember Italy, and he regarded a constitution as likely to lead to an agitation against his views. Hence his action. The Congress of Vienna endorsed and underlined Metternich's contention that Italy was 'a geographical expression.'

The next important phase of the settlement concerned Holland and Belgium. These were united into one kingdom, again with the idea of strengthening the resisting power of small states against France. Castlereagh further restored to the United Kingdom of the Netherlands the enormously rich Dutch colony of Java, and lent her two million pounds to fortify her frontier against France. This policy has been described as 'wise but unsuccessful.' It certainly was unsuccessful, for the Belgians hated the Dutch and separated from them in half a

5*

generation. But Castlereagh doubtless thought that his generous economic concessions would reconcile the two peoples.

Switzerland was recognised as independent and was guaranteed by all the Powers. Spain and Portugal recovered their old boundaries in Europe. Denmark was deprived of Norway, which was handed to Sweden. This settlement caused heartburnings, as Castlereagh had to threaten Norway with a blockade before she gave way. But, though this incident was an unpleasant one, it was not one for which practical diplomats will blame Castlereagh. At a critical moment, Sweden refused to join the coalition against Napoleon unless Norway was promised to her, and Castlereagh was compelled to pay the price.[1]

Certain other settlements were made by, or in consequence of, the Treaty of Vienna. The property claims of individuals who had suffered by the war were fairly met. The vexatious disputes as to diplomatic etiquette and precedence were finally settled. A doctrine as to international rivers was laid down, which was important for the future. The slave trade was declared inhuman and it was abolished by France, Spain, Holland, and Sweden, and promised to be abolished by Portugal. This great concession to humane ideas was almost solely due to Castlereagh, and to the British popular agitation behind him.

It has been customary to denounce the peacemakers of Vienna as reactionary and illiberal in the extreme. It is indeed true that they represented the old régime and were, to a large extent, untouched by the new ideas. But they represented the best and not the worst of the old régime, and their settlement averted any major war in Europe for forty years. According to their lights the settlement was a fair one. France was treated with leniency, and the adjustments of the Balance of Power and territory were carried out with the scrupulous nicety of a grocer weighing out his wares, or of a banker balancing his accounts. Russia alone gained more than her fair share, and this was because she had an undue proportion of armed force. The settlement disregarded national claims, forced 'unnatural unions' on Norway and Sweden, on Belgium and Holland. But in each case the ally and the stronger partner (Sweden and Holland) demanded it, and the Allies did not see their way to resist the demand. A more serious criticism was the disrespect paid to the views of smaller Powers. Though the settlement was supposed to be in favour of the old order and existing rights, the smaller states were ruthlessly sacrificed for the benefit of the larger. For this side of the activities of the peacemakers there is little excuse, and it is the gravest criticism of their actions.

The work of Vienna, interrupted by Napoleon, was completed by two treaties, signed at Paris on November 20, 1815. Of these, one, the Second Treaty of Paris, bound France to carry out the new arrange-

---

[1] An almost exact parallel is afforded by the secret Treaty of London (April 26, 1915) in which Italy obtained great concessions from France, England and Russia as the price of entering the war. Castlereagh's treaty was, however, discussed in the Commons before Norway was coerced.

ments imposed in consequence of the return of Napoleon, to submit to the frontiers of 1790, to pay an indemnity, and to return the works of art to foreign capitals. The second treaty was the Quadruple Alliance between the Four Great Powers. They bound themselves to maintain the arrangements of Chaumont, Vienna, and Paris by armed force for twenty years, both as regards the territorial boundaries now fixed and as regards the perpetual exclusion of Bonaparte and his dynasty from the throne of France. Finally, by Article VI, they agreed to 'renew their meetings at fixed periods' to discuss matters 'of common interest.' In the last article lay the germ of future international government.

The germ of its destruction lay in a solemn declaration by which Alexander sought to bind all monarchs together in a Christian union of charity, peace, and love, issued on September 26, 1815. It was to be signed by kings alone. The Regent of Great Britain was unable to sign it, though he sent a private letter to Alexander, expressing his sympathy with the sentiments. With this exception it was signed by every king in Europe and by the President of the Swiss Republic.[1] Its importance was, in a sense, fortuitous, for it came to be regarded by European liberals as a hateful compact of despots against the liberties of mankind. It was not that, nor had it any diplomatic or binding force. Charity and love are not capable of being defined in diplomatic terms, and no one except Alexander thought seriously of the Treaty. Castlereagh called it a 'piece of sublime mysticism and nonsense.' Metternich made profane jests about Christianity in connection with it. Neither regarded himself as in any way bound by it.[2]

[1] It was originally signed by the three rulers of Austria, Russia and Prussia. The Sultan was not asked to sign; Alexander thought at one time of asking the President of the United States to do so.

[2] Two quotations may here be profitably contrasted (E. Hertslet: *Map of Europe by Treaty* (1875), vol. I. pp. 318, 375):

Article II of the Holy Alliance Declaration, September 26, 1815	Article VI of the Quadruple Alliance of Paris, November 20, 1815
'In consequence, the sole principle of force, whether between the said Governments or between their Subjects, shall be that of doing each other reciprocal service, and of testifying by unalterable good will the mutual affection with which they ought to be animated, to consider themselves all as members of one and the same Christian nation; the three allied Princes looking on themselves as merely delegated by Providence to govern three branches of the One family, namely, Austria, Prussia, and Russia, thus confessing that the Christian world, of which they and their people form a part, has in reality no other Sovereign than Him to whom alone power really belongs,' etc.	'To facilitate and to secure the execution of the present Treaty, and to consolidate the connections which at the present moment so closely unite the Four Sovereigns for the happiness of the world, the High Contracting Parties have agreed to renew their Meetings at fixed periods, either under the immediate auspices of the Sovereigns themselves, or by their respective Ministers, for the purpose of consulting upon their common interests, and for the consideration of the measures which at each of these periods shall be considered the most salutary for the repose and prosperity of Nations, and for the maintenance of the Peace of Europe.'

Does one not see in the first quotation the warm, vague mysticism of Alexander, and in the second the cold practicability of Castlereagh?

The bond which Castlereagh and Metternich did recognise was that of the Quadruple Alliance. But they differed greatly about its interpretation. According to Castlereagh, England was bound to defend the territorial limits laid down at Vienna for twenty years. She was bound also to meet periodically in congresses with her Allies, but she was not bound to interfere in case of internal revolution in any country (other than an attempt to restore Napoleon). Metternich argued that the Quadruple Alliance did commit its members to armed interference to suppress internal revolution in any country, if the Congress thought it advisable. In the end these two views were bound to come into conflict.

International control worked well for a time. The chief statesmen of Europe knew one another personally, and they were all interested in seeing that France remained quiet and paid her debts. At the first ' periodic reunion' in 1818, at Aix-la-Chapelle, it was agreed that French conduct had been satisfactory, and that the allied armies should evacuate her soil at once. France was once more forgiven and restored and readmitted to the rank of a Great Power. She was admitted into a new quintuple combination (consisting of herself and the Four Great Powers), and invited to take part in any further periodic reunions. The Quadruple Alliance was, however, strictly maintained, for the Allies thought it might still be necessary to act against France.

Alexander now came forward, flourishing the Treaty of the Holy Alliance and demanding a general union of sovereigns against revolution. He wanted, among other things, to send an armed allied force to help the Spanish king to subdue his revolted colonies in America. Castlereagh strongly opposed this project and prevailed on the Congress to disclaim the use of force in any such attempt. Alexander pressed on with his doctrine of general intervention, but was again resisted by Castlereagh, who was now joined by Metternich. Eventually, the two contented Alexander by agreeing to a vague formula about moral solidarity, which meant very little to them but a good deal to him.

For two years longer the 'moral union' endured, and then in 1820 came a thunderclap. A military revolution broke out in Spain, which demanded the very democratic constitution of 1812. The king's life was in peril, and he eventually gave way to all demands. He adopted the wildly impracticable constitution and professed to be a complete and liberal constitutional monarch. Alexander was horrified at the news. He feared the army and he feared democracy, and both had been triumphant in Spain. If these movements spread elsewhere no monarch would be safe and the Christian union would be dissolved. He issued a circular saying that it was clearly the duty of other monarchs to assemble at once in Congress, to denounce the Spanish Constitution of 1812, and, if necessary, to send an allied army to repress it by force. All this, he claimed, had already been admitted by the Great Powers in the formula to which they had subscribed in the Holy Alliance and at Aix-la-Chapelle.

This extravagant extension of the obligations of Vienna obliged Castlereagh to declare himself. On May 5, 1820, he issued a lengthy State paper, which was the foundation of British foreign policy in the nineteenth century.[1] He said that England was committed only to preventing the return of Napoleon or his dynasty to France, and to maintaining the territorial arrangements of Vienna by armed force for twenty years. He regarded the Spanish revolution as an internal affair not dangerous to other countries, and he did not think England would be justified in sanctioning any attempt to suppress it by force. England, he explained to the diplomats of the Continent, owed her present dynasty and constitution to an internal revolution. She could not, therefore, deny to other countries the same right of changing their form of government. Moreover, the English Government could not act without the support of its Parliament and people. Neither had been informed that any obligations, other than those he had explained, had been contracted at Vienna. England would fulfil those obligations, but no others.

---

[1] Full text is, for the first time, printed in *Cambridge History of British Foreign Policy*, vol. II. pp. 623–633. Cp. also H. Temperley and L. Penson: *Foundations of British Foreign Policy*, pp. 48–63 (C. U. P. 1938). A few extracts are given here. 'It [the Alliance of the Great Powers] was an Union for the re-conquest and liberation of a great proportion of the Continent of Europe from the military dominion of France; and having subdued the Conqueror, it took the State of Possession, as established by the Peace, under the protection of the Alliance.—It never was, however, intended as an Union for the Government of the World, or for the Superintendence of the Internal Affairs of other States.

'It provided specifically against an infraction on the part of France of the state of possession then created: It provided against the Return of the Usurper [Napoleon] or any of his Family to the throne: It further designated the Revolutionary Power which had convulsed France and desolated Europe, as an object of it's constant solicitude, but it was the Revolutionary power more particularly in its Military Character actual and existent within France against which it intended to take Precautions, rather than against the Democratic Principles, then as now, but too generally spread throughout Europe. . . .

'. . . Nothing could be more injurious to the Continental Powers than to have their affairs made matter of daily Discussion in our Parliament, which nevertheless must be the consequence of Their precipitately mixing themselves in the affairs of other States, if We should consent to proceed pari passu with them in such interferences. . . .

'. . . The fact is that we do not, and cannot feel alike upon all subjects. Our Position, our Institutions, the Habits of thinking, and the prejudice of our People, render us essentially different. . . .

'. . . No Country having a Representative System of Gov[ernmen]t could act upon it [the principle of one State interfering by force in the internal affairs of another], — and the sooner such a Doctrine shall be distinctly abjured as forming in any Degree the Basis of our Alliance, the better. . . .

'. . . We [England] shall be found in our Place when actual danger menaces the [territorial] System of Europe; but this Country cannot, and will not, act upon abstract and speculative Principles of Precaution. . . .' In one word, as Castlereagh writes, keep the Alliance 'within its *commonsense* limits.' [His own italics.]

At first the Continental diplomats thought that England was not in earnest. Moreover, further democratic revolutions broke out in Naples, Piedmont and Portugal. The 'Constitution of 1812' was demanded in each case. Metternich was affected by the first two, and now accepted the idea of a Congress. Castlereagh was still reluctant to attend one, and so sent only subordinate officials to represent England.

The Congress met towards the end of 1820 at Troppau. Alexander drove furiously and induced Metternich and Prussia to concur in a circular, which asserted that the Three Powers would never recognise the right of a people to circumscribe the power of their kings. The three monarchs of Eastern Europe threatened, in fact, to make war on revolution, in the interests of kings, wherever it raised its head. Castlereagh, as soon as these sentiments became known, published a despatch (January 1821), in which he repeated the sentiments of May 5, 1820. In Parliament he declared that the Troppau Circular was 'destitute of common sense.'

The breach between the Allies was now widening. But Alexander went on. He issued further circulars full of 'high-flying sentiments.' He commissioned Metternich, as the instrument of the Alliance, to suppress revolution and constitutions in Naples and Piedmont. The Austrian armies moved into Italy in March 1821, destroyed the constitutions of Piedmont and Naples, and set up the Kings once more upon their old thrones. Castlereagh openly declined to have anything to do with such proceedings.

Most people would now have said that the period of international government was at an end; but this was not yet the case. In March 1821 a revolt broke out in Greece against the Turks. It was not really a democratic revolt or a demand for a constitution at all; it was a national revolt, a movement of Greek Christians to overthrow an abominable alien tyrant. Metternich, however, recognised no difference between Sultan Mahmud of Turkey and King Ferdinand of Naples or of Spain. The cause of monarchy was, he thought, equally endangered, the support of the moral union equally necessary; and this view might be used to counter the possibility that Alexander would declare war against the Turk at once in the interests of his co-religionists in Greece. To avert this peril was an evident necessity. Metternich and Castlereagh met one another at Hanover towards the end of 1821, patched over their difficulties and agreed to summon one more Congress, where they hoped to prevent Alexander from taking any active measures against Turkey.

The Congress was summoned for the autumn of 1822, but, before it met, two events happened. The disturbances in Spain became so serious in July that France began to talk of interference there; and, on August 3, Castlereagh, whose mind had given way, took his own life. In his later years Castlereagh had shown some objections to the Congress System; he was succeeded by Canning, who destroyed it.

The Congress at Verona was soon occupied with Spain rather than with Greece, for at the beginning of the meeting France asked the Alliance if it would support her in the invasion of Spain. Canning, who regarded Congresses with suspicion, sent the instruction that, if there was a determined project to interfere by force or by menace, then, *come what may*, England would not be a party. This instruction was communicated by Wellington to the Congress on October 30, 1822. It was a bombshell and prevented the Alliance as a whole from acting by armed force in Spain, though France took separate action.[1]

Canning's attitude in 1822 had damaged the 'moral solidarity' of Europe, and injured the Congress System. But the system was not yet extinguished. In December 1823 the King of Spain, now restored to his throne, summoned the Allies to a Congress on Spanish America. To the astonishment of Europe, Canning flatly declined to send an English representative (January 30, 1824). The result was that the attempted Congress was a failure. Later, in 1824, Alexander attempted to call a Congress over the question of Turkey and Greece. Canning finally refused to attend this, on behalf of England, in November 1824. The other Four Great Powers, however, met at St. Petersburg in January 1825, although they broke up in May on very bad terms and without having decided anything. To all intents and purposes this was the end of the Congress System.

Canning's objections to this project of international government may be stated as follows. Congresses, he said, were all very well to settle a Treaty. But a sytem of 'periodic reunions' of Powers was highly dangerous. In the first place, the people of England did not like their delegate, who represented a parliamentary state, to commune in secret with despotic powers. England, too, was liable to be outvoted. In the second place, the Congress System tended to establish the system of general intervention by force in the internal affairs of different countries, a system which England, by the very nature of its government, was bound to oppose. In the third place, small powers were not represented and their rights were apt to be disregarded or overridden. Canning would have had no objection to a Congress, limited to a policy of 'moral solidarity,' consulting the wishes of small Powers, and disclaiming the use of force. But the Congress System, as it had developed by 1822, did none of these things, and Canning thought it better to oppose it altogether. And in this opposition he was entirely successful. From 1825 onwards the Congress System was discredited; and the policy for Europe was defined by Canning as 'Every nation for itself, and God for us all!'

It is not fair, however, to dismiss this first serious experiment in international government without pointing out some of its merits. The idea of personal conference and mutual confidence between rulers was excellent. Castlereagh was sincere in promoting the reunions, and so

---

[1] France eventually invaded Spain on her own responsibility in April 1823, restored King Ferdinand, and abolished the Spanish Constitution.

was Metternich, up to a point. But Alexander went too far and too fast for both. After 1820 the Congress System became in effect a trade-union of Kings for suppressing the liberties of peoples. To the continuance of that system, parliamentary England could not consent and parliamentary France only shared in it with reluctance. The smaller Powers, who did not share in it at all, were naturally opposed to it. In the thirties there were European Congresses again which did much good. But, though the Great Powers still took the lead, there was no collective attempt to revive the doctrines of absolutism, to condemn revolution as such, or to proclaim a general policy of intervention by force. Parliamentary England and parliamentary France were, therefore, able to enter freely into conference with the three despotic monarchies of East Europe. The Congress which settled the independence of Belgium is a good example of how Great Powers can meet without embarrassment and effect lasting good, because each respected the institutions and difficulties of the other.

It is worth while comparing the period of Congressional Government with the second great attempt to create an international organisation, that which gave birth to the League of Nations in 1919. The Holy Alliance Declaration had really nothing to do with the Treaty of Vienna, while the Covenant of the League was a vital part, indeed obviously the most vital part, of the Treaty of Versailles. Congressional Government failed because it attempted first to promote, and then to enforce, the monarchical principle upon the different states of Europe. In the League there were monarchies, despotic and constitutional, and republics, and semi-sovereign communities. Members were not, as in the Holy Alliance, 'members of one and the same Christian nation'; they were members of a League of Nations, Buddhist, Mussulman and Christian. Congressional Government was attacked by Canning because it infringed the rights of small states; on the Council of the League of Nations small states could outvote the Great Powers, while any small Power could express its views in the Assembly. The Congress system died because despotism was not reconcilable with the opposed system of parliamentary freedom; the League of Nations survived until it was destroyed in a world at war. Both were dangerously weakened by the fact that they were never universal; in neither case did the Powers learn the secret of reconciling national interests with the common good. It is too soon yet to judge whether the secret has been found by the makers of the third great experiment in international organisation.

CHAPTER X

AUTOCRACY, CONSTITUTIONALISM AND REVOLUTION
(1815–48)

THE Germanic Federation, established by the Powers in 1815, was intended to hand over Germany to the management of Austria and Prussia. Metternich quickly assumed the lead. His aims, though concealed with much art beneath a cloud of pompous phrases, were simply and brutally realistic. He believed that the one necessity was to crush Liberalism, Constitutionalism and Parliamentarism in Germany. Prussia was militaristic at any rate (Canning called her 'a downright grenadier, with no politics but the drumhead and cat-o'-nine-tails'). So long, therefore, as Austria pursued this reactionary policy, Prussia would be obliged to follow in her wake. Metternich trusted to win her gratitude and support by discouraging the feeble constitutional experiments made by the rulers of Bavaria, Würtemberg, Saxe-Weimar, etc. He was to prove completely successful.

The Congress of German Powers, which met at Carlsbad in 1819, endorsed the decrees of Metternich. Regulations for controlling the press, for intimidating the universities and for curbing the full expression of opinion throughout Germany, were adopted with unanimity. Metternich thus became possessed of a powerful police instrument, which he used without mercy. For a time he was quite successful. During 1820–21 the revolutions in other parts of Europe did not affect Germany, where Metternich's iron rod kept Liberals in awe. The revolutionary wave of 1830 caused some slight disturbances in German states; it would have caused more but for Metternich. But, from that time forward, his power declined. He had nothing to offer young Germany but repression, intimidation, and a police régime. His rule was barren and sterile and unimaginative. It was impossible for the rising tide in Germany to be bound within this narrow dyke. Hence, in 1848 the wave, which for a moment overthrew all old institutions in Germany, had gathered force from the repression itself. *Après moi le déluge* was repeated when Metternich and Old Austria vanished together in 1848. As a negative force Metternich's system in Germany had been admirable, but no such system could endure for ever. A repressive rule, which is neither intelligent nor efficient, might have been imposed for an indefinite time on Russia. It was Metternich's fate to discover that it could not be imposed upon 'solitary, deep-thinking Germany.' With him the whole worm-eaten mouldy structure collapsed, and the new structure which was later to be built by Bismarck was wholly different in character.

Old Austria really did vanish in 1848, because it was feudal, archaic, despotic and despised. Old Prussia did not vanish then because, in fact, it was not Old Prussia but a new one born in the bitterness and humiliation of Napoleon's colossal triumph at Jena. The reform of the Prussian State between 1806 and 1848 witnessed a transformation of a mediaeval state into a modern one remarkable for efficiency and intelligence. The disaster to Prussia was so great that even Conservatives recognised that reform was necessary; the national humiliation was so complete that every class was ready to make sacrifices for the sake of improvement. Under Frederick the Great, Prussia was a state with a feudal class of nobles acting as bureaucrats or officers, a smallish class of burghers who created wealth, and a mass of serfs who acted as food for powder or for labour. In 1848 Prussia had only free citizens, better educated, better disciplined, more enterprising and efficient than any in Germany.

The first necessity after Jena was the reform of the army. This was placed in the hands of Scharnhorst.[1] He instituted conscription and the short-service system and trained a large force equal in bravery, in ability, and in *moral* to any in Europe. The sword which he had forged was wielded by Blücher with effect in the campaigns of 1813, 1814, and 1815. After that, cool judges could have seen that the Prussian army was restored to more than its old state of efficiency. And in Prussia then, as always, the army was the most important factor in state-development. Bismarck used to explain his successes by saying that, after all, he had always the army. And, but for Jena and Scharnhorst, the machine could not have been perfected for the use of Moltke by the hand of Roon.

For a time the great Stein was in charge of the internal reforms. He started by abolishing serfdom and by promoting education. He thereby made room for the development of the modern man. Experience has shown that serfs are of little more economic or political or even military use in a modern state than negro slaves. To free a man and to educate him is to make him more profitable to the State, and it by no means follows that these processes lead to revolution or to disorganisation. Much depends on the previous history and the previous habit of mind of the people in question. The Prussians had lived obediently under Frederick and under his feeble successors, unaware of their present degradation and future calamities. Before they had time to recover from the latter, a revolution was initiated by the King. It was followed in seven years by brilliant military successes and fresh acquisitions of territory. The people of Prussia settled down contentedly again. A revolution such as this must be a good thing, especially as it was made by the King. Until 1914 revolutions in Prussia 'were always made by the Kings.'

Thus, though there was a very great change in the State in every direction, there was no change in the organ which had always ruled and made changes. The King indeed had not made them, he had allowed his ministers to do so, but the mass of Prussians did not understand that. The bureaucracy, at once efficient and pure, reformed the finances,

[1] These changes are treated in more detail in Chapter VII.

organised the municipalities, governed the State, with increasing skill. Finally, it set in motion an agency which was to influence all Germany in the end, by subtly interweaving itself with every activity of commercial enterprise.

In 1818 Prussia began to work for the Zollverein or Customs Union.[1] She began in a small way by negotiating customs agreements with a few states. She pursued her advantage cautiously, cleverly, relentlessly. She manipulated her tariffs so that she benefited states within the Zollverein and injured those without. Her methods were those of the manager of a trust, squeezing out smaller competitors by every means fair and foul, and by the use of superior capital and brains. When he has done this he is ready to meet and crush his big rivals. It marks the supineness of Austria that Metternich was irritating the smaller states by organising police raids and intimidating their editors and professors, while the Prussians were bargaining with their business men. Metternich, who was indeed no economist, awoke to the situation too late. In 1834 he sought to organise resistance to the Zollverein. But the time had gone by for resistance. Bavaria and Saxony joined the Union in this year, and practically all Germany was in it by 1844, except Austria, Hanover, Oldenburg, Mecklenburg, and the three Hansa towns. The members were fettered and attached to Prussia by the silken meshes of an economic net, which had enveloped them before they were aware of it. The net only grew stronger and the ties only became closer, as the years went on. With every state added it became more and more difficult for old states to retire, or independent states to resist. In 1848 Prussia had already economic supremacy in Germany, and this was the forerunner, and in part the cause, of her future military and political supremacy.

That there were some defects in Prussian policy before 1848 is evident, for otherwise she would not have found disaster and undergone humiliation at that time. The fact is that her ideas, though in the main clear, were not always consistently pursued. Frederick William III (died 1840) was a weak man, but had wisely left everything to his advisers. Frederick William IV (1840–61) was a brilliant artistic romanticist; his mind eventually failed, but, before that event occurred, his restless meddling had greatly injured the unity and direction of Prussian policy. The treatment of the Poles in Prussia was not handled with ability. Sometimes they were cajoled, sometimes they were awed. And though the Poles might have been conciliated by the one process or intimidated by the other, they were too intelligent a people not to despise and to counterwork a Government which could not make up its mind to be either benevolent or harsh.

[1] Of course, a Customs Union was a paramount necessity for Prussia. Austria's territory was relatively remote and self-contained. Prussia's territory corresponded to no true economic unity and touched the borders of a dozen states. Hence a uniform German tariff was enormously to Prussia's advantage.

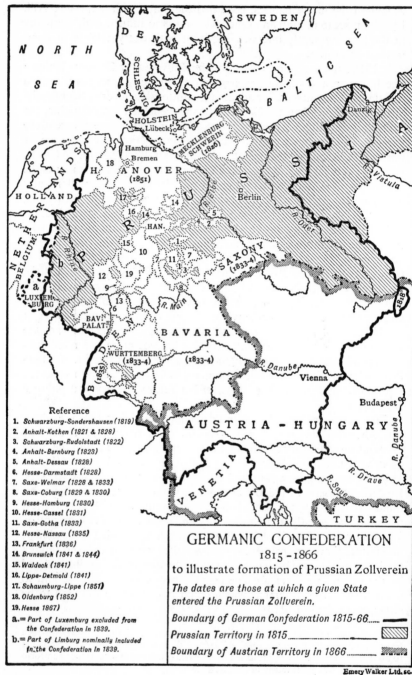

Reference

1. Schwarzburg-Sondershausen (1819)
2. Anhalt-Kothen (1821 & 1828)
3. Schwarzburg-Rudolstadt (1822)
4. Anhalt-Bernburg (1823)
5. Anhalt-Dessau (1828)
6. Hesse-Darmstadt (1828)
7. Saxe-Weimar (1828 & 1833)
8. Saxe-Coburg (1829 & 1830)
9. Hesse-Homburg (1830)
10. Hesse-Cassel (1831)
11. Saxe-Gotha (1833)
12. Hesse-Nassau (1835)
13. Frankfurt (1836)
14. Brunswick (1841 & 1844)
15. Waldeck (1841)
16. Lippe-Detmold (1841)
17. Schaumburg-Lippe (1851)
18. Oldenburg (1852)
19. Hesse 1867)

a.= Part of Luxemburg excluded from
     the Confederation in 1839.
b.= Part of Limburg nominally included
     in the Confederation in 1839.

GERMANIC CONFEDERATION
1815 – 1866
to illustrate formation of Prussian Zollverein

The dates are those at which a given State
entered the Prussian Zollverein.

Boundary of German Confederation 1815-66 ......
Prussian Territory in 1815 ....
Boundary of Austrian Territory in 1866 ....

Emery Walker Ltd, sc.

An even more serious question was the attitude towards **Parliament** and a constitution.[1] Hardenberg, one of the great reformers after Jena, and long the head of the Prussian Ministry, was in favour of both, as well as of a reasonable liberty of opinion and of speech. But his own infirmities, and opposition from other bureaucrats, hindered the realisation of the design. The strongest current in the bureaucracy was in favour of intelligent absolutism, governing through experts, with no regard to representative government or to assemblies or to the press. But this view Frederick William IV would not accept.

Frederick William IV believed not in modern Parliaments but in a system of mediaeval estates, in little provincial diets, or else in assemblies of different classes, burghers, nobles, etc. He made all sorts of experiments in these directions. He summoned one form of estate after another, and addressed them with fiery eloquence. But he soon became indignant when they showed any desire to assert their independence, or to approximate to the powers of a modern legislature. The whole policy was anomalous and bewildering. The King did just enough to awaken parliamentary ideas among his subjects, and yet not enough to give them any satisfaction. He admitted that something was necessary, or that something should be created, but he created nothing that was coherent or intelligible. This attitude was just the one to arouse discontent and to encourage aspiration. His sentimental appeals to the loyalty of the people, and his strange inability to realise their desires, account for much of the confusion and turbulence in Prussia during 1848–49. The policy of the bureaucracy, that of a single-minded, efficient civil service, doing everything for, and nothing by, the people, supported by an army that was blindly obedient, was at least consistent. Had that been the attitude of Frederick William in 1848, there might have been bloodshed; there would not have been confusion or disillusionment. As it turned out, the monarchy incurred the blame for all three. But it was the bureaucracy and the army which enabled the King to outride the storm.

In 1814 France began the experiment of a Constitutional Monarchy. Alexander had insisted that the Bourbons should not return till a charter was granted and the constitutional experiment tried. Louis XVIII consented to the change but tried to retain as much power as he could. He was wiser than his Ministers, but incurably indolent. Hence the policy of his Clerical and Absolutist Ministers (usually called the Ultras) tended to prevail. They showed unwisdom in all directions. They cut down the army, they gagged or bribed or intimidated the press, they made all

---

[1] Parliament and a constitution were not quite the same thing in Germany. Thus Frederick William IV's experiments with his estates might be termed parliamentary, but they were not constitutional.

sorts of mistakes in detail. They abolished the tricolour. After Napoleon's defeat at Waterloo they shot Marshal Ney. Frenchmen were
indignant that a man who was an heroic soldier but no politician should
have been condemned by dubious methods and shot under circumstances of peculiar atrocity. It was openly said (and with some truth)
that he was executed at the dictation of the Allies. Some have said that
the Bourbons owed their fall to the execution of 'the bravest of the
brave.'

Their domestic measures were singularly unfortunate. The restoration of property to *émigrés*, the endowment of the Church property,
suggested to the common man that the Bourbons meant to take from
the peasant his land and upset the Revolution. Despite every effort the
opposition in Parliament increased. In 1823 the Government took a
bold plunge and went to war with Spain, which had forced a Bourbon
king to accept a democratic constitution. The enterprise was brilliantly
successful, the king was freed and the constitution abolished. The Duc
d'Angoulême, who had commanded the forces, returned to Paris with
applause; but every one knew that he was without experience and that
the Marshal of Napoleon, who had accompanied him, had won the
laurels which he wore. These tinsel glories only awakened the anger or
contempt of the veterans of Napoleon.

Louis XVIII died in 1824, and the last restraint of wisdom was removed. Charles X began well by announcing his attachment to parliamentary institutions and by appealing to the French love of ceremonial. But he soon became unpopular. He was ultra-reactionary and
clerical to the core. France became bored, and the boredom of the
people is dangerous to the rulers of France. In 1827 the opposition in
Parliament got worse; the National Guard could not be trusted, and
had to be disbanded; finally Villèle, who had been Premier since 1822,
was dismissed. He was succeeded, after an interval, by Polignac, an
intriguing diplomat wholly unfitted for the post. He was Chauvinist,
which was bad; ultra-clerical, which was worse; and an enemy of Parliament, which was fatal. He seems to have believed that a 'spirited foreign
policy' would reconcile France to the loss of such liberties as she possessed. He planned an invasion of Belgium (which would certainly have
meant war with England), and at the same time he plotted to overthrow the Parliament and Constitution of France. Public opinion was
thoroughly aroused and hostile. Finally, this gingerbread conspirator
induced the King to issue decrees suppressing the Parliament, and
gagging the press.

The best that can be said for Polignac is that he was wholly ignorant
of the forces of public opinion in France. The revolution which occurred
was due largely to Lafayette and to Talleyrand, two men who were not
often found in agreement, and their agreement on this occasion is
suggestive. Their plan was a Constitutional Monarchy of the English
type, with Louis Philippe (the Orleanist Bourbon) as a good solid

bourgeois and constitutional king. With comparatively little difficulty
the public was persuaded to try the experiment, and to accept Louis
Philippe as their ruler. The choice was not a bad one, and the event
impressed Europe a good deal. A revolution in France had been bloodless, and it had set up a solid constitutional monarchy. It seemed to
hail the approach of the millennium, when all nations would be endowed with parliaments and carry Magna Carta written on their hearts.
It was really thought that democracy had been tamed.

Louis Philippe had many qualifications for his task. He was shrewd
though not scrupulous, and fully conscious that he must never forget
his rôle of constitutional king. He was tolerant in religious matters,
whereas his predecessors had been bigoted. He took pains to divest
himself of any character of Divine Right. He sent his sons to the
ordinary schools, he walked about the streets with an umbrella under
his arm, he lived in the Tuileries and appeared readily to bow from the
balcony when there was any applause in the streets. He was anxious to
represent himself as the heir of all the historic tendencies of France. As
a Bourbon he claimed to embody the historic past, as the son of Egalité
and the soldier of Jemmappes he claimed to have shared in the glories of
the Revolution. He restored the tricolour and the National Guard. He
did not even refuse to recognise Napoleon. During his reign, the body
of the great Conqueror was brought from St. Helena by a son of the
royal house and laid in the most magnificent of resting places at the
Invalides. He filled the Palace of Versailles with pictures of all the
battles of French history and solemnly dedicated it 'to all the glories of
France.'

At first sight it is difficult to see how any ruler could have done more
to conciliate his subjects. He did much, but he did not do enough. It
may be that the Revolution or Napoleon had drawn too deep a trench
between Bourbonist France and the France which succeeded it. Now
there were no Declarations of Liberty and Equality, no colossal victories over kings, no dazzling or splendid personalities. At any rate
the Bourbons had been hopelessly discredited, and Louis Philippe could
not deny that he was a Bourbon. His aim was peace and commerce,
and these had no brilliance, none of that *éclat* so dear to French minds.
Perhaps the Revolution of 1848 would not have been caused by the
ennui of France, though Lamartine has written that it was. There was
something deeper than the resentment of Paris at the tedium of his rule.
Parliament was an assembly of business men and bourgeois, it was
manipulated by bribery and by tricks, and in this manipulation Louis
Philippe had a full share. A king who excelled in shuffling the parliamentary cards, and was suspected of marking them, could not be the
ideal of France.

Louis Philippe's reign was unfortunate in result and in France, but it
was not without benefits in Europe. At the very outset he lent great aid
to the cause of constitutionalism and to peace. Neither was wholly to

his own advantage. Polignac had actually planned to seize part of Belgium by force; Louis Philippe would certainly have liked to establish his younger son on the Belgian throne, and, thereby, to promote French influence and control in a neighbouring land. But it was very awkward for a professed constitutional king and an avowed lover of peace to engage in war.

As a direct result of the July Revolution in France, the long-rumbling revolution in Belgium broke out in August. The Dutch were hated by the Belgians and the movement was essentially one for national independence. A Belgian Deputation laid their grievances before the Dutch King at the Hague. At first they demanded only an administrative separation from Holland, and were ready to accept the Prince of Orange as a Viceroy. The King insisted, before complying with these demands, that Dutch troops should occupy Brussels, and their entry into the Belgian capital produced three days of street fighting (end of September 1830). At the end of that time they were expelled. All Belgium now rose, and the Dutch troops were confined within the walls of Antwerp and Maestricht. A provisional Government was appointed, a National Convention summoned, and it was proclaimed that 'the Belgian Provinces, detached by force from Holland, shall form an independent State.'

The Dutch King now took the judicious step of appealing to the Five Great Powers to intervene, on the ground that the territorial settlement of Vienna was threatened. He was right. The Quadruple Alliance had guaranteed to maintain by force the territorial limits imposed at Vienna for twenty years. France had agreed to these limits, and, if Louis Philippe broke this agreement, the four other Great Powers had the right to make war upon him. Louis Philippe's position was, therefore, peculiarly delicate. Many Frenchmen wanted to annex Belgium or part of it, and he was still insecure on the throne. If he surrendered to the patriots of France, he risked war with Europe; if he surrendered to Europe, he risked dethronement in France.

The position for the four Allies was difficult too. The first breach was thus threatened in the fabric of Vienna. Were they to permit it or not? Fortunately the three great despotic monarchies of the East were not prepared to act at once in the matter. It was England that was most concerned, and in November 1830, before negotiations had got very far, the agitations in England over the Great Reform Bill produced a change of government, and Palmerston came into the Foreign Office. His arrival was providential, since he was the right man for the situation. He was quite resolved not to let France gain any influence over Belgium, but he was not equally resolved to maintain the settlements of Vienna. After all, treaties had to come to an end sometime, and he did not think highly of this particular arrangement at Vienna. Being a disciple of Canning, he sympathised with nationality and, provided Belgium could be formed into a nation, he thought that she could be turned into a good bulwark against France. He had the sense to see that a reluctant Belgium, attached to Holland, would invite French attacks, while a free Belgium would be more likely to repel them. He was, moreover, not unwilling to consider the posssibility of a self-governing Belgium under a separate Dutch ruler.

The Belgian National Congress met at Brussels on November 10, 1830. Feeling was in favour of France, and, but for the fear of England, a French prince would probably have been proposed for the throne. As it was, the Congress declared the House of Orange deposed, the throne vacant, and the future form of government a limited and hereditary monarchy. The Five Powers now intimated to the Belgian Congress that they should maintain the House of Orange, and that, if they did not, Allied armies might occupy the country. The Belgian Congress haughtily refused to yield. Most fortunately for them a revolution broke out in Poland at the end of November. This attracted the direct attention of the Czar, and indirectly concerned both Austria and Prussia, whose Polish subjects were in sympathy with the rising. Hence the attention of the three Eastern Powers was drawn elsewhere, and Palmerston was left to face Louis Philippe.

Talleyrand was sent by Louis Philippe to England to see if he could not secure advantages from Palmerston. The veteran diplomat, however, found his match. He had the worst cards, and Palmerston was not afraid of playing his trumps. Talleyrand first demanded Luxemburg, and next Philippeville and Marienburg for France. Palmerston showed no sign of yielding, so that Talleyrand was compelled to collapse. The solution, which saved the face of France, was to announce the perpetual neutrality of Belgium and to guarantee it by the word of the Five Powers. This decision was announced in January 1831. The French Government blustered and talked of disavowing Talleyrand, but eventually accepted the terms, as did the King of Holland. The Belgian Congress refused to do so, and the proposal for a French prince remained a possibility. On February 3 they chose the second son of Louis Philippe, the Duc de Nemours, as their king. The Five Powers now sent Belgium an ultimatum, embodying their demand for neutrality and thus excluding the Duc de Nemours. This expired on June 1. On June 4 the Congress gave way, revoked its previous decision and elected Leopold as their king.

Leopold of Saxe-Coburg-Gotha had been the husband of Princess Charlotte, and after her death he had continued to reside in England. He was a liberal in principle, and a most able, prudent, and sagacious man. By infinite tact and patience Leopold succeeded in working out a settlement, known as the Eighteen Articles, which he persuaded the Five Great Powers to accept. After much trouble the Belgian Congress also accepted them, but the King of Holland refused to do so. He sent his troops again into Belgium in August, and Louis Philippe promptly replied by marching in French troops who occupied Brussels.

The settlement seemed as far off, and the French danger as great, as ever.

Palmerston, however, now again took a strong line. The Polish revolution was over, and the Czar and the King of Prussia both offered to send troops to expel the French. Palmerston bluntly told France that she must evacuate Belgium 'in a few days,' and in September France consented to do so. The settlement was really arrived at in the Five-Power Treaty with Belgium of November 15, 1831. But infinite difficulties and delays appeared. The three Great Eastern Powers were unwilling to ratify the treaty, and the Dutch King refused to accept it or evacuate Antwerp. Eventually, a French army and a Franco-British fleet operated against him and expelled the Dutch finally from Belgium (1832–3). It took six years more before a definitive treaty satisfying all parties was signed by the Five Great Powers (April 19, 1839). This treaty, which finally established the independence of Belgium, is the famous 'scrap of paper' torn up by Germany when she invaded Belgium in 1914.

It has been right to dwell at some length on this Belgian incident for two reasons. It illustrates the difficulties of Louis Philippe, anxious for peace yet afraid of his Chauvinists, and compelled to shuffle and balance between Europe and France. More important than all this, it exhibits a breach made in the Treaty of Vienna in the name of national independence. It marks the triumph of parliamentarism and constitutionalism, alike in France, Belgium, and England. For Belgium the results were entirely good. She obtained an ideal constitutional king and was able to draw up a constitution remarkable for its liberality and breadth. Behind the guarantee she built up her national life and characteristics, her art, her literature, her patriotism, her individuality. It is doubtful whether Belgium was a nation in 1830; it is certain that she was eighty years later. And she owed her life to Palmerston and her marvellous development to her sagacious ruler.

In the matter of Belgium, Palmerston achieved decisive success in promulgating the cause of limited and constitutional monarchy throughout Europe. That was because the Belgians were fitted by nature to be free and orderly, ready to obey the law and to enjoy the gift of liberty. For a precisely opposite reason he was to fail in bringing the lessons of liberty to Portugal and to Spain. And, in the result, he was involved in disagreeable controversy with Louis Philippe. The situation was simple, though the details are complex. During the early thirties, Portugal and Spain, were both ruled by child-queens whose advisers professed to be constitutional, and opposed by Absolutist pretenders who raised rebellions against them. Palmerston sided with the constitutionalists in each case, and finally offered an alliance to both Portuguese and Spanish Queens to expel their pretenders. It was accepted, and being joined also by France (April 22, 1834), was known as the Quadruple Alliance. The Portuguese Pretender was easily expelled

(1834), but it needed some years to get rid of Don Carlos in Spain (1839). Palmerston had hoped by this arrangement to erect a constitutional *bloc* in West Europe, which would balance the three despotic monarchies in the East. He thought that England would keep the lead, and that Portugal and Spain could be used to persuade France to follow. Nothing of the sort happened. Portugal and Spain were no more important as constitutional states than as despotic monarchies. They might, with perfect safety, have been left to conclude their sordid and futile quarrels without help from outside. They proved no aid to either England or France; on the contrary, the Spanish question involved both countries in a serious quarrel, which contributed to the overthrow of Louis Philippe.

The Louis Philippe period, despite several serious incidents, was marked, during most of its time, by increasing co-operation between England and France. Royal visits took place and a species of *entente cordiale* was established which seemed complete by 1845. It was not only a memorable epoch in the history of the two countries, but an immense support to Louis Philippe in France. The rupture, which took place in 1846 over Spain, was, therefore, doubly unfortunate. It turned on the question of the marriage of the young Queen Isabella and her sister. Louis Philippe finally brought it about that Francis, Duke of Cadiz should marry the Queen, and her sister should marry the Duc de Montpensier. These arrangements, celebrated on October 10, 1846, concealed a mean trick. The French Government had promised the British that the Queen's sister should not marry a French prince until Isabella *was married and had had children*. The marriages were now simultaneous, and the Duke of Cadiz *was incapable of having children*.[1] It is clear that Louis Philippe thought that he had secured the reversion of the Spanish throne to his son, though he himself regretted the trick.

Palmerston's wrath was great. He protested violently against the 'indirect influence' and 'illegitimate methods' of France with regard to Spain. War did not follow, but hostility did. Louis Philippe had lost his best friend in Europe, and ruined the *entente cordiale*. He had no more to hope from England, and the continuance of his throne and dynasty depended henceforth upon France and upon himself.

Even so late as 1846 many people thought that France had at last learnt England's ways and was modelling herself on her Parliament and Constitution. They little knew France who said that. From all sides came mutterings of the storm. The French papers were scathing in their comments on the trickery shown both in the home and in the

---

[1] The children Isabella eventually bore were apparently those of someone not her husband. The Duc de Montpensier was the son of Louis Philippe. The view here given is that of Palmerston, *v.* Public Record Office, F.O. 96/21, minute of September 30, 1846, and that of August 22, 1847, which recommends 'an annulment of the Queen's marriage, and the choice of another and more suitable Consort for her'; cp. C. A. Fyffe; *Modern Europe* (1924), vol. II. p. 182; *Cambridge Modern History*, vol. XI. p. 555.

foreign policy of the Governmnet. The transport of the body of Napoleon to the Invalides revived Bonapartism and Napoleon-worship in all its fervour. While Thiers was writing lyrical raptures about imperialism, Lamartine revived the sentimental enthusiasm for a republic by the eloquence of his 'History of the Girondins.' [1] Louis Philippe and Guizot, his Foreign Minister, saw well enough that France wanted something. But the small remedies and concessions they were prepared to offer were taken as signs of weakness by their opponents.

The Orleans Monarchy was based on a definite theory. It had rejected Divine Right and established the reign of 'pure reason.' It had thrown over the Catholic party and the Bourbon Legitimists, but it had made no effort to come to terms with the revolutionists or the democrats. It attempted to establish the rule of the bourgeois, the middle class, as a 'golden mean' between Ultraism and Republicanism. Citizens who paid 500 francs in taxes were eligible for election as deputies to Parliament; those who paid 200 francs were eligible as voters. No one else had any rights whatever. But the poorer bourgeois had an important privilege. They formed the National Guard, a body which performed (inefficiently and irregularly) the functions of gendarmes and of soldiers. They thus possessed considerable power. But they were expected blindly to obey the dictates of the Parliament and of the wealthier bourgeois. They became restless and showed lack of discipline on parade. The King was obliged to discontinue reviewing them because they uttered hostile cries when they saw him. In Parliament, through what was termed the 'fatal dexterity' of Guizot in manipulating the instruments of corruption, Louis Philippe was secure. There was, indeed, a formidable opposition led by Thiers, but this opposition in itself would not have been disastrous, for Thiers wished to return to power and his methods were, on the whole, constitutional. But there was much angry talk both in the Parliament and the Press and on the public platform which fanned and excited the wilder revolutionary elements without.

The situation at the end of 1847, therefore, was that Louis Philippe had a majority but also a formidable opposition in Parliament, and that the poorer bourgeois in the National Guard were discontented and uncertain. Outside, the agitation both of the Right and of the Left was extreme. The Ultra-Right demanded the Legitimist Bourbons, the White Flag and Catholic education in the schools. The Left was moved by two strong currents. Lamartine was proclaiming the glories of the old Republic, free, conquering, and enlightened. Louis Blanc led a party which added the propaganda of socialism to the already formidable elements of democratic unrest. To the rights of man, to universal suffrage and political equality, he added national workshops, a social

---

[1] Published 1847. Dr. Gooch, *History and Historians* (1913), p. 228, goes so far as to say of it: 'The most worthless and the most eloquent of books had done its work. The Constitutional Monarchy had been succeeded by the Second Empire.'

policy and a class warfare. What made these attacks from all quarters so effective against Louis Philippe was that all the different elements of opposition agreed on two points. Whatever the merits of Louis Philippe, his home policy was sordid and corrupt, and his foreign policy had ended by provoking the hostility of England. Louis Philippe had counted on England to raise him from the condition of a parvenu monarch by acting as 'sponsor' for him in the Courts of Europe. This policy, at one time successful, had now totally failed. The bourgeois monarchy had no longer a *raison d'être*. It had no longer a consistent or intelligible policy. Nothing shows this fact more clearly than that Catholics and Republicans began to approach one another, to concert an attack on the Government.

Guizot, in an unwise speech at the beginning of 1848, denounced the 'blind and hostile passions' which aimed at destroying existing institutions. The opposition, Catholic as well as Republican, decided to hold a great banquet in Paris as a protest against Guizot's utterance. The Government threatened to prohibit the banquet, which had been fixed for February 22, 1848. This firm attitude for a moment dismayed the ill-assorted coalition of Catholic Ultras, Democratic Republicans, and of Socialists. But, on the night of February 21–22, the Paris mob intervened, and the result was the fall of Constitutional Monarchy in France (February 25), and the flight of the King and his family to England.

It was the destiny of Louis Philippe to prove that France had no love for Constitutional Monarchy of the English type. Balances of power, limitations of democracy, compromises of ideal, were not favoured in France then or now. She liked least of all Louis Philippe's compromise, which was not the rule of a religious idea as under Legitimist Bourbons, nor of a strong man like Napoleon, nor of a democracy like the Republic of 1793. And so, in 1848, France overthrew Louis Philippe and once more tried first the Republican, and then the Napoleonic, experiment.

During this period Belgium successfully established constitutionalism, and France made a prolonged experiment in the same direction, which was feebly imitated by Portugal and by Spain. Elsewhere the resentment of two nations against alien rule fanned hotter passions and led direct to revolution. These two nations had each been partitioned and divided by several powers. Poland was split into three parts, Italy into seven.

When Alexander obtained the larger part of Poland in 1815 he gave it a constitution and declared his intention of governing it as a National Kingdom. He was sincere in his aim and was supported for a time by many patriotic Poles, notably by the noble Czartoryski. But the Russian oil and the Polish vinegar declined to mix. The Poles, the subjected race, felt themselves superior in everything but force. They had a Latin culture to set against a quasi-Greek one; a glorious history to set against a chronicle of bloodshed; a tradition of aristocratic equality to set against one of slavish subservience to the ruler; a spirit of chivalry and liberty to set against one of despotism and tyranny. It made little difference that Alexander granted them a liberal and progressive constitution. A gift from a Russian ruler, however gracious, was an object of suspicion to most patriotic Poles. Moreover, Alexander, benign and gentle as he seemed, set over them as commander-in-chief his brother, the Grand Duke Constantine, a foolish tyrant, who dominated the weak Viceroy. The first Diet opened in 1818, but a severe press-censorship was established in 1819. Though the Diet met again in 1820, Alexander soon dismissed it, and did not summon another for five years.

Secret societies had begun to grow, and Alexander, on opening the third Diet in 1825, so restricted its powers as practically to suppress the constitution. As Byron said he

'had no objection to true liberty,
Except that it would make the nations free.'

When Alexander died at the end of 1825 a conspiracy broke out against his successor in which Poles were involved. The young Czar Nicholas was an autocrat. He was deeply incensed by the attitude of Poland, and although it was probably at this time that he resolved to suppress such liberties as remained to Poland, he concealed his purpose for some years. After five years he summoned the fourth and (as it proved) the last Diet. The session was short, and suspicion was evident on both sides. The French Revolution, which burst out in July 1830, greatly excited the Poles, and secret societies developed even among the officers of the army. The preparations which Nicholas now made to suppress revolution in France and in Belgium provoked a rising in Poland. On November 29 an insurrection took place at Warsaw. The Grand Duke Constantine lost his nerve, withdrew the Russian troops from the capital and left the kingdom. An interim government was formed by the end of the year, which was pro-national and anti-Russian.

The Poles showed great indecision. Their army numbered over 50,000 men and the Czar was caught unprepared; but they wasted time in futile negotiation. At the same time they made the breach inevitable by deposing the Czar (January 1831). The Russians, who had now concentrated their troops, entered the kingdom in February in overwhelming numbers. The first battles were indecisive, and the Poles held their own till May. But the end was only delayed till September. The Russians then entered Warsaw and destroyed the constitutional kingdom and liberties of Poland at a blow. For a quarter of a century an iron rule was imposed upon her. She lost all separate and organic life, and was governed purely by the sword of Russia.

The chivalrous character of the Poles, their revolutionary zeal and their gallant resistance awakened great sympathy in Europe. France and England both remonstrated with Russia, but Russia was in no mood to listen to academic protests. Nothing availed to hinder her purpose of blotting out the separate existence of Poland. It is important to note that some sort of constitutional government had been tried by Russia, and that its failure was partly due to Poland herself. But the national feeling was alike too intense to permit co-operation with Russia and too strong to be subdued even by the harsh and brutal measures of repression which were applied. Poland was helpless and disarmed, but her spirit remained unconquerable. Moreover, though separated into three parts, Poland preserved her ideal of national unity. She remained, wrote Maitland, 'three undigested fragments in three stomachs.' And the Poles under Austrian, and even at times under Prussian, rule, had some chance of expressing their nationality. The annexation of Cracow by Austria in 1846 proved a real aid to a Polish resurrection. For Austria allowed the Poles of Galicia something like 'home rule,' and under her mild sway the national feeling developed. Cracow became the centre of Polish culture, art, literature, and national propaganda. And the nucleus of national aspiration formed there was eventually to expand over all Poland.

Napoleon's rule had brought benefits to Italy. The Northern area was well governed and judicious appeals had been made to national feeling. The kingdom of Naples fell to the vigorous and dashing Murat, who finally conceived the bold scheme of uniting all Italy under his rule. During 1814 and 1815, Murat put his plan into practice, and finally proclaimed the Union of Italy. He was defeated, and eventually shot, but the ideal he had proclaimed did not die. Indeed, Murat, though a Frenchman, is still revered by Italians as the earliest modern champion of her union and independence.

Nothing could seem more hopeless than the state of Italy in 1815. Ferdinand, the Bourbon King restored to Naples, was a brutal and treacherous tyrant who was under the thumb of Metternich. The Pope recovered Central Italy and governed it in a mediaeval and intolerant spirit. Metternich not only obtained all Lombardy and Venetia for Austria, but dominated the lesser princes of the North. Only Piedmont, the land of priests and soldiers, was relatively strong, but few as yet saw in her the regenerator of Italy. Her King was still a despot, and thus suspect to all liberals.

Secret societies (chief among them that of the Carbonari) were formed everywhere to work for the union of Italy. In 1820 revolution broke out in Naples, and Ferdinand swore to a democratic constitution. It was followed by a rising in Piedmont (1821), where the heir to the throne (afterwards Charles Albert) aided it with his sympathy. It was almost immediately suppressed and an Austrian Army soon made an end of the Constitution of Naples. Brutal repression reigned everywhere. Men were 'proscribed,' wrote Byron, 'for having dreamt of liberty.' The conspirators, who fled from Piedmont, met the young Mazzini at Genoa. Their grief and their devotion touched him. 'For the first time on that day,' wrote he, 'there was vaguely presented to my mind, I will not say the thought of country and of liberty, but the thought that it was possible, and therefore a duty, to fight for the freedom of one's country.' This vague idea in the mind of a young man ripened into the splendid Mazzinian vision of an Italy, 'free and united from Alps to Ocean,' a dream which was to come true in forty years.

After these experiments it seemed useless to contend by arms against the despots. Revolution burrowed underground, secret societies, covert propaganda, worked everywhere. The revolutions of 1830 provoked a few outbursts in Italy, and fanned the flames. Next year Mazzini founded at Marseilles the society of 'Young Italy.' In two years it numbered 60,000 members. 'Ideas,' he said, 'grow quickly when watered by the blood of martyrs.' And the blood was not wanting. In 1844 the brothers Bandiera deserted from the Austrian Navy and went to head a revolt in Calabria. They and their followers were quickly surrounded by the troops of Ferdinand of Naples and captured. Nine of them were shot by his soldiers, while the cry 'Long live Italy!' still echoed on their lips. The martyrdom was a symbolic one, for the victims came from all parts of Italy. The Bandiera brothers were Venetians; others who suffered with them came from the Romagna, from Modena and from Perugia. If Italians could not live, they could at least die, together.

Three events, which occurred just before 1848, lent great strength to the surprising movement in favour of national unity which then electrified all Italy. Charles Albert succeeded to the throne of Piedmont in 1831. He had been discredited by the failure of the constitutional movement in 1821; he was clerical and therefore suspected of being antinational; and his early measures were repressive. But, though timid and hesitating, he was sincere. Those about him gradually recognised that he had the cause of Italy at heart, and dreamed that one day she might be free. The cause of Moderate Reform was preached by Gioberti. Charles Albert indicated some sympathy with him in private, and began to be recognised as a possible leader for the future. In one respect he had an advantage. Every other lay ruler of Italy was odious or ridiculous. Ferdinand II of Naples was a coarse, indifferent, and vulgar despot; Modena was ruled by a selfish tyrant, Lucca by a gloomy madman, Parma by the widow of Napoleon who governed through her lover. In comparison with such a quartet Charles Albert was a hero of freedom and of light, and a possible saviour of Italy.

Meanwhile 'Young Italy' gained ground. Their propaganda convinced many that active and violent revolution was the only way to save Italy. They were deadly enemies of the Moderate Reformers, and the severe repression of Metternich won them many followers. Browning's account of Italy represents the feeling of the common people. He tells us how his maid-servant rejoiced that Ferdinand of Naples had been wounded by conspirators, and hoped that 'they had not caught the felons.' And he makes the Italian in England say:

> 'However, if I pleased to spend
> Real wishes on myself—say three—
> I know at least what one should be.
> I would grasp Metternich until
> I felt his red, wet throat distil
> In blood through these two hands.'

The Italian genius for intrigue, the desire for vengeance was stimulated into furious hatred by the brutal oppressions of Ferdinand and of Metternich. This feeling needed only an opportunity, an outlet, to burst forth in blood and flame.

The two currents, flowing towards national unity, that of Moderate Reform and of Revolution, were stimulated by a third from an unexpected source. For the first, and almost the only, time in Italy's history, a Pope proved a Liberal, a nationalist and a patriot. In 1846 a new Pope (Pius IX) was elected. He is said to have imbibed patriotism from the Carbonari in his youth. It is certain that when a Cardinal at Imola in 1840, he openly expressed his disgust at Austrian police methods, sentences, imprisonments, exiles and executions. In principle he belonged to the party of Moderate Reform, but he was rather an easy, amiable man than a serious leader. But the great position which he held, and the first measures which he took, not only concentrated attention upon him, but gave an extraordinary impulse to national aspirations. One of his first measures was to proclaim an amnesty in the Papal States, and to pardon all political offenders and suspects. The effect of this step was quite indescribable. By one act he became famous, and the appearance of a liberty-loving Pope was hailed as a miracle from heaven. Metternich was astounded. 'We were prepared for everything,' he said, 'but a Liberal Pope. Now we have got one there is no answering for anything.' The 'Revolution,' wrote a keen observer to Carlo Alberto, 'wants no making. It is made already.' Metternich began to contemplate the use of force in 1847, and the inevitable revolution began early in 1848. Charles Albert granted a constitution on February 8, and on February 10 Pius IX published his allocution which contained the famous phrase 'God bless Italy!' The next day he used the same words in addressing the crowd from the balcony of the Quirinal, and evoked the most frantic enthusiasm. With a Liberal Pope at Rome and a constitutional king at Turin, Italy was already revolution-ripe. Mazzini, for a moment obscured, was soon to be in the

6

forefront, and Garibaldi was already at hand to command the army of 'Young Italy.'

The period 1815–48 opens with an attempt by the diplomats of Europe to bridle the forces unloosed by the revolution and by Napoleon. The settlements of Vienna were made to adjust the territorial ambitions of Great Powers, not to satisfy the claims of nationalities. But, so far as the Great Powers were concerned, the territorial settlement was successful and kept Europe out of wars on the grand scale for forty years. The more ambitious experiment in international or congressional government, which lasted from 1815 to 1825, ended in disaster. It turned into a 'Trade Union of Kings' with a mutual insurance policy, and failed to take account of the needs and desires of a strongly popular and parliamentary government like that of England. Canning rendered a service not only to England, but to Europe, in ending this hazardous experiment.

The Metternich policy, both in Austria and in Germany, was a similar attempt, which failed for similar reasons. Metternich aimed at imposing a uniform system of repression on a series of peoples or states, which objected to being denied the aspirations of race or of liberty. The peoples of Austria-Hungary and the states of Germany struggled against the Metternichian strait-waistcoat and burst it asunder in 1848. And the success of this revolution was permanent. Neither the Germany nor the Austria which Metternich had known was restored after the convulsions of 1848.

In Prussia, on the other hand, a series of able men anticipated liberalism and revolution by a wise and intelligent policy of education and reform, and by imposing on the State a system of military discipline, which proved the strongest security of law and order. The system was suited to the people, who valued intelligence and strong government, and recognised their own political incapacity. Hence the waves of 1848, which turned Metternich's castles into sand heaps, broke fiercely but vainly upon the solid rock of the Prussian State.

England, under Canning and Palmerston, pursued a policy of adroit opportunism, of judicious sympathy with national aspirations, and finally of an outspoken advocacy of parliamentary and constitutional government. They succeeded in doing something in Portugal and Spain, in freeing Greece, and in creating Belgium. And their gospel proved the salvation of kings in 1848. It was they who had 'made the world safe for constitutional monarchy,' but for constitutional monarchy alone.

Louis Philippe might not indeed have agreed with this view. For he had tried to be a constitutional monarch and was the first to fall in 1848. But the system which he applied was unsuited to the French nation. It took no account of equality and the rights of man, which were the most enduring legacies of the Revolution of 1789. It had nothing of the splendour and enlightenment of the Napoleonic régime. A government based on a narrow franchise, dull and not brilliant, pacific and not military, oligarchic and not democratic, was bound to fail. France might be ruled by an emperor and by plebiscites, or by universal suffrage and a republic. It could not be ruled by a bad compromise between any two. In Belgium or in Piedmont or in England, the masses were content at this time to accept the rule of the middle class; in France they were not. So constitutional monarchy succeeded in other lands just for the reason that it failed in France. While it averted or tranquillised revolution elsewhere, it produced or enforced it in France.

Poland and Italy differed both from revolutionary France and from the constitutional countries, for they showed themselves more ardent for national independence than for democracy, and more ardent for democracy than for constitutionalism. Their hatred of the foreigner made them plunge into revolutionary courses, and too soon for success to be achieved. The failure of Poland was evident in 1831, that of Italy in 1849. But the strength and force of their effort, the enthusiasm evoked by their heroism and devotion, did not perish altogether. Italy had made a revolution, but at the same time she had made a nation; and the failure of the one caused the success of the other. Italy was to succeed in 1860, Poland to fail again in 1863. But, though it took much longer, Poland won her national independence by self-sacrifice as truly and surely as Italy had done.

Looking, however, actually at the results we may say that autocracy and revolution fared badly, and constitutionalism well, during this period. The autocratic powers, by trying to repress and not to moderate or assimilate the expansive force of the new ideas, produced the explosion of 1848. And it was then that the advantages of constitutionalism were seen. The world was not 'revolution-ripe' in 1848, but it was 'made safe' for limited monarchy. Everywhere—except in France —the results of that upheaval tended in favour of Palmerstonian liberalism and of constitutional monarchy.

PART III

FRENCH, GERMAN, AND RUSSIAN IMPERIALISM

CHAPTER XI

THE FRENCH REVOLUTION OF 1848 AND THE ESTABLISH-MENT OF THE EMPIRE

THE French Revolution of 1848 was the work of Paris alone, and of only a small part of the population of Paris. There had been agitation in the provinces against the narrow character of the franchise, but in the movement which sent the Orleanist monarchy 'on its travels' the provinces had taken no part. It can hardly be doubted that the great majority of Frenchmen were opposed to what happened.

Louis Philippe had hoped that his dynasty might be continued in the person of his grandson, under the regency of the Duchess of Orleans. But the Chamber was in no mood to adopt that solution, and the Paris crowd soon invaded its precincts. The session was closed, but the members who remained behind, supported by the crowd, acclaimed as a provisional government a list of names which were suggested to them by Lamartine. The list had already been drawn up by the *National* newspaper; this revolution in Paris marks the very zenith of the direct political influence of newspapers. The list contained seven names; all were well-known reformers and republicans. The most notable among them were Lamartine, Ledru-Rollin, and Garnier-Pagès. But while this was going on in the Assembly hall another government had been drawn up in the offices of the *Réforme*, a paper of strong socialist opinions. The men on the *National* list were on this too, but it also contained some other names, especially that of Louis Blanc, the one great representative of socialism to his generation. The two were merged together, and thus was formed the 'Provisional Government.' They owed their powers entirely to revolution and had no constitutional standing.

From the first there were sharp divisions among them. The socialist section had been accepted very unwillingly by the moderate middle-class republicans, of whom Lamartine was the eloquent spokesman, and who were contented with a republic and an extended suffrage. They regarded Louis Blanc almost as an enemy, and were far from ready to give loyal support to his schemes. Certain important steps were taken immediately. Universal suffrage was declared. The new electors, over nine million in number, were at an early date to elect an Assembly which was to settle the constitution. The National Guard, which had long been restricted to the middle class and regarded as primarily a safeguard for property, was declared to be thrown open to all citizens. Louis Blanc had also, in appearance at least, gained a great victory for his favourite idea. He had declared to a body of petitioners that the Government undertook to guarantee to all Frenchmen sufficient work to support life, and a decree at once declared the establishment of 'National Workshops.' This last was a decision of the utmost importance for the future of the Republic.

The course of a revolution, when once it has broken out, inevitably follows the impulse of the ideas of the time. Paris before 1848, and to a smaller extent France, had been full of political and social speculation. The chief influence came from Saint-Simon, who had died in 1825. This strange man and powerful thinker had thrown out a great mass of ideas, partly scientific and partly Utopian. His proposals rested on a general view of human history. Critical and constructive epochs had, he believed, alternated, and the French Revolution of 1789 had marked the end of the last epoch of criticism and destruction. The task before the world, and especially before France, was to build up a new order. The chief aim of that order was to procure a better life for the industrial classes. It was to be carried out under the direction of a new religion, which was vaguely theistic in character, but which was to possess an elaborate organisation of savants and priests. Social industry was to take the place of private enterprise, but the new order was to be substituted for the old without violence or confiscation. Many of the details of his schemes, as of his life, lend themselves to ridicule; but he exercised a great influence on thinkers and politicians of the next generation. Fourier also attracted much attention from his contemporaries, but has had little influence on subsequent thought. He belongs indeed to the pre-revolutionary epoch when men believed that nature was altogether good and that evil was the result of human control and interference. He believed that if men were left to organise themselves freely they would fall into 'natural' groups, with special aptitudes and likings for different occupations, and thus the necessary work of the world would be performed freely, joyfully, and efficiently.

More immediately important than either of these views, but closely connected with those of Saint-Simon, was the socialist movement, which for the first time during the Revolution of 1848 becomes a great force among the peoples of Europe. Its meaning has changed much since then, especially through the influence of Karl Marx. Its chief exponent for France at this epoch was Louis Blanc, an immensely voluminous writer on political and economic subjects. He had written with passion of the condition of the industrial classes in Paris and elsewhere, and he called upon the State to make the remedying of their condition its chief concern. His own schemes were many, and are characterised by a good deal of vagueness and sentimentalism. In his view the history of mankind revealed three stages: first, a stage of

authority in politics and religion; then, a period of individualism represented by the Protestant revolution and by such writers as Montaigne;
then, lastly, there would come a period of association and fraternity.
There had been strivings after this in all periods, but it had culminated
in the great French Revolution, with its immortal formula 'Liberty,
Equality, and Fraternity.' The task before mankind now was to organise
life on a basis of association and fraternity. He was sure of victory, for
he believed in the essential goodness of human nature, and he believed
that the transformation to the final stage would come easily and without
bloodshed. 'All that is necessary is to provide workmen with money,
form a co-operative workshop, and success will come inevitably.'
There was thus something Utopian in his outlook; but his scheme was
a wide and general one and he had his plans for every part of life and
government. Public opinion had seized on one point only, and had
misrepresented that—the right to work. 'We will work and live or we
will fight and die' was the watchword of those who thought themselves
Louis Blanc's followers. We have seen how he was carried into the
Provisional Government by popular support, and how he had declared
that work would be provided for all. The majority of his colleagues disliked his ideas, but an attempt would have to be made to put them into
practice. Many of Louis Blanc's colleagues hoped that the scheme
would fail, and did their best to make it fail. He proposed also the
formation of a Ministry of 'Progress.' This very vague title did not
commend itself to the Provisional Government, and they established
instead a 'Government Commission for Workmen,' which was to consider all questions relative to their welfare.

Was the failure of the National Workshops due to some intrinsic
fault in the scheme, or was it caused by the lukewarm support or actual
disloyalty of Blanc's colleagues? Modern socialists have with one accord declared against the idea of providing work for the unemployed,
unless it can be made really useful and remunerative. The failure of
Louis Blanc's scheme is at any rate certain. The promise of constant
work at a fair wage drew to the workshops all the casual labour of
Paris, and soon great numbers from the provinces as well. In two
months the numbers of those who drew a wage—we cannot say who
worked—rose from 25,000 to 66,000. Then only two days' work was
provided each week; on the other days the unemployed received a dole
(called *un salaire d'inactivité*) of one franc per day. The scheme had
taken a turn quite different from what Louis Blanc had imagined; he
had hoped to provide genuine and productive work in ordinary workshops by means of State subvention. On every ground, economic or
moral, the actual scheme adopted was a failure.

The National or Constituent Assembly, elected by manhood suffrage
to draw up a constitution, came together on May 4. Every effort had
been employed to produce a republican majority, and of the 900 members there were hardly any open monarchists. But the great majority

of the members were unknown, and they showed their attitude to the social question, which interested Paris so deeply, when they established an executive Government consisting of Arago, Garnier-Pagès, Lamartine, and Ledru-Rollin; but without Louis Blanc. Paris and France were not in accord on great questions of policy. It is the beginning of that opposition between the country and the capital which is one of the prominent features and factors of French political life for the next twenty-five years.

Paris was angry with the Government for its reactionary tone; angry with it too for its refusal to lend help to the Poles in their resistance to Russia. A great popular demonstration invaded the Assembly, and tried to dissolve the Government and substitute another with Louis Blanc at its head. But the attempt failed; the hall was cleared by the National Guard; Louis Blanc retired into exile. The victorious Assembly then turned to the workshops, in which they saw the great support of the socialist opposition. An inquiry was held, and the workshops were declared closed on June 22. A mass of misery was thrown on the streets of Paris without resource or hope. But the socialist party had its organisation, its clubs, and its newspapers, and it took up the challenge. Barricades were drawn across the narrow and tortuous streets of Paris. The Assembly was declared dissolved and the workshops re-established. It was civil war, for much the same motives and of much the same kind as that which was to desolate the capital in the days of the Commune of 1871.

General Cavaignac was given sole power, and he carried war into the enemy's camp with great vigour. There were four days of desperate fighting, during which each side charged the other with treason and massacre. On June 26 the Assembly was again master of the city. But this terrible incident left behind bitter hatreds and suspicions, and made the task of finding some basis of national unity far harder during the following years. The middle and propertied classes had been much frightened, and demanded a Government strong enough to save them from further danger of insurrection.

The Assembly could now go on with its work of constitution-making. There were some points on which there was no doubt. They began with a vague Declaration of Rights in the traditional French manner. They accepted universal, or rather manhood, suffrage. They gave the legislative power to a single Assembly of 750 representatives. The future of France was closely bound up with their decision as to the form of the executive. Monarchy and Empire were not considered. France was to be a Republic and was to have a President. But what sort of President? A figure-head or a real ruler? A President after the fashion of the President of the United States, who is the real head of the executive Government, or a powerless official such as the President of the Swiss Confederation? It was really a difficult problem. The decision that was taken proved fatal to the existence of the Republic, but it is not certain that it was not under most circumstances the wisest course. The legislators were influenced by two main considerations. First, they held, as Frenchmen had for long held—being led to that conclusion by the teaching of Montesquieu among others—that the executive should be separate from the legislative, and that therefore the executive should not proceed from the legislative and depend upon it; and, secondly, they stood for the sovereignty of the people. Why, therefore, should not the people appoint the executive head of the State as well as the legislators? Was it not as important that he who carried on the work of the State should do so in the interest of the people as that the laws should be made by men who were appointed by popular election? By a large majority the Assembly declared that the President should be elected by manhood suffrage, should hold office for four years, and should not be re-eligible. Some have held that constitutional forms are not of real importance, and that 'whate'er is best administered is best.' A clearer refutation of this view could hardly be found than this. The decision of the Assembly led swiftly to the Second Empire, to a period when the military glory of France seemed restored, and then to Sedan and the Commune. The history of Europe still bears the traces of that vote of the Assembly.

Louis Bonaparte, the son of the King of Holland and nephew of the great Napoleon, was the eldest representative of the Napoleonic family. The world had heard a good deal of him already. He had lived in Switzerland, in Italy, in England, and in America. He had mixed with revolutionists in Italy, and had moved in the higher ranks of society in London. He had always taken himself seriously and believed himself reserved for a high destiny. In 1836 he had struck into France from Strasburg and had raised the imperial flag, but the attempt had ended in a fiasco, and he had been captured and sent to America. Then, in 1840, when the bones of his uncle were being brought to their stately resting-place in Paris, he had tried again. He had landed at Boulogne with much dramatic preparation, and again had come to swift ruin. This time he was sent to the fortress of Ham on the northern frontier of France, and there was kept for some time in very easy confinement. He saw friends, wrote much, and finally escaped without much difficulty. The fall of the House of Orleans allowed him to return to Paris, and he was elected to the Assembly.

What had he in his favour? He had ideas, but they were as yet hardly known. He had not a striking presence, but he had great tact and pleasant manners and the power of keeping silence impressively. But, above all, he was a Napoleon. France had forgotten the suffering and the humiliation that Napoleon had brought upon her. She remembered only the glory, the victories, the prestige of France. Thiers had recently written about him in volumes that were widely read. Though not wholly composed in the spirit of hero-worship, they had fired the imagination of France. The successes, such as they were, of the

6*

Orleanist régime seemed drab in comparison. But Napoleon seemed to offer France something beside glory. He seemed to offer security and stability under a strong Government. The days of the barricades had left a deep impression on the mind of France. They wanted a ruler with a strong hand and will, who would prevent that horror from reappearing. The popularity of Louis Bonaparte had already been shown during the elections to the Assembly. When he became a candidate for the Presidency the country was swept by a fire of enthusiasm that destroyed the chances of every other candidate. Cavaignac, who had suppressed the rising, received a million and a half of votes; Ledru-Rollin, the faithful radical, some 370,000; Lamartine, who at one time had seemed to sway Paris by his eloquence, had only 17,000 supporters. Louis Napoleon had five and a half million of votes. He assumed the office of President in December 1848 and took the oath: 'I shall regard as enemies of the fatherland all those who attempt by illegal means to change what France has established.'

The new President was no ordinary man. He was a man of ideas, and he dreamed dreams, some of which have become realities. The Suez and the Panama canals were foreseen by him, and he contributed to the ultimate completion of both. He had none of the temperament of a soldier, but he had written suggestively on the use of artillery. He regarded European diplomacy with a comprehensive imagination, which allowed him sometimes to anticipate the future. He had clear and interesting ideas on politics. It seemed to him that the time of Parliaments was passing, and that they could not again play the all-important part that had been played by the English Parliament in the past. They belonged to a time before means of communication were fully developed. Now, the executive Government could come into direct touch with the people and need no longer rely on a great Assembly to such an extent as formerly. In his view there were two essentials in the life of the State: manhood suffrage and a Government resting directly on it. That he was a Napoleon was at once the cause of his triumph and the fatality of his whole career. It pushed him on irresistibly towards military adventure, and in war he showed no talents, and through war he came to his catastrophic fall.

It was no easy post that the President of the Republic had accepted. He had difficulties at once with the Constituent Assembly, which differed from him in foreign policy, especially with regard to Italy, and seemed to desire to prolong its sessions unduly. The position was hardly easier when the Constituent gave way in 1849 to the Legislative Assembly, elected under the new constitution. The moderate republicans of the Constituent had sunk to an insignificant handful. There was a larger group—some 180—of revolutionary republicans who still cherished the ideals that seemed to have been suppressed in the days of the barricades. Much the largest party was 'the party of order,' Catholics and monarchists who saw in the 'extreme left' the great danger to their ideals and to France. Louis Bonaparte was personally popular in the country, but there was hardly a sign of a Bonapartist party in the Legislature.

Fear of revolution was the dominant passion of the Assembly. Yet the danger does not seem really to have been great. An armed demonstration against the Italian policy of the President led by Ledru-Rollin was beaten down with the greatest ease. A number of members were expelled from the Assembly. But men of the same opinions were sent by the constituencies to take their places. The Assembly in alarm determined to purge (*épurer*) the suffrage. Universal suffrage was the very base of the constitution and it was not attacked in name; but conditions were attached to its exercise—especially three years' residence in one place—which reduced the number of voters on the register by about three million. Those excluded belonged very largely to the shifting industrial population of the great towns.

The 'red peril' was thus banished. But the result was that the tension between the Assembly and the President became much greater. They had accepted him as an ally against revolution, and now that danger seemed removed. The majority were monarchists, and he could not be anything but hostile to their aims. The monarchists were themselves divided: some—the legitimists—desiring the restoration of the Bourbons in the person of the Count de Chambord, who for them was King Henry V; while others looked to some member of the Orleanist house. This far-reaching difference now led to the establishment of the Empire, as it later led to the Third Republic.

It must be admitted that Louis Bonaparte displayed none of the fairness and openness that should characterise the head of a state. His attitude towards the grave situation was that of an adventurer and a conspirator; not that of a President or a patriot. He saw the chance of seizing an imperial crown, and all other considerations were swept aside by the consuming passion of ambition. And yet it is not difficult to make out a case for his policy. The days of the barricades were near. France still feared the recurrence of the 'red peril.' The bitter hostility of the parties threatened the very existence of the Republic. The demagogic conspiracy of which the President spoke in one of his addresses was a reality, and the monarchists were inevitably enemies of the constitution. He was personally popular, as the plebiscite was soon to show. Parliamentary institutions had struck no deep roots in the country. France needed a strong hand to maintain order until the people had really made up their minds as to the form of government they desired. The situation has many clear points of resemblance with that which Napoleon I had dealt with in the days of Brumaire (1799). His nephew had the thoughts of his uncle's career constantly before him; and like his uncle he thought much of France, but more of himself and the personal position which the crisis would enable him to win.

His four years' tenure of office would soon be at an end. Was he to obey the law and sink into the obscurity and comparative poverty of private life? He was determined to secure a prolongation of his power, and he hoped—as Napoleon I had hoped at the Revolution of Brumaire —to secure his aims by constitutional means. The constitution allowed an alteration of its articles if three-quarters of the Assembly voted in favour of revision. In July 1851 the proposal was made that the President should be allowed a second term of office: 446 voted for it and 270 against it. That was not the required three-quarters majority. It would be necessary for him, as it had been for his great-uncle, to draw the sword. He would appear as the champion of the people and of order. He had not protested against the Bill that had limited the franchise when it was passed, but now he demanded its repeal in the name of the sovereignty of the people. The Assembly refused, and gave him the chance of posing as the champion of outraged democracy. His schemes had been penetrated by many. Saint-Arnaud, his most trusted confederate, had been brought home from Algiers and given the command of the home army. In January 1851 Thiers had said: 'The Empire is already in existence.'

His plan was to dissolve the Assembly and to appeal directly to the people to vote a new constitution which should give him large personal powers. On December 2, 1851, the blow was struck. In the night the walls were placarded with a proclamation to the French people. The Assembly was declared dissolved; a new constitution was to be submitted in outline to the vote of the whole people. If they did not support him he would retire. 'But if you think that the cause of which my name is the symbol—that is, France regenerated by the Revolution and organised by the Empire—is also yours, proclaim it to the world by granting me the powers that I ask for.' The Palais Bourbon—the hall of the Assembly—was occupied. Several prominent members were arrested: Thiers, Cavaignac, and Changarnier among them. So far there had been no bloodshed. Perhaps there need have been none. But there came a rising in the streets of Paris; 'the barricades' again on a small scale. It was beaten down easily, and perhaps a conflict might have been avoided altogether. The bloodshed of those days was never forgotten, and Victor Hugo put his eloquent pen at the service of the enemies of the future Emperor, and branded him as the criminal who had shed innocent blood in order to overthrow a constitution which he had sworn to defend. There were some 800 victims, and a greater number were subsequently deported to Cayenne and Algeria.

The new constitution was soon placed before the voters. The President was to hold office for ten years and was to nominate all the Ministers. There was to be a Council of State—nominated, of course, by the President—which was to prepare the laws. A legislative Assembly elected by universal suffrage was to vote on the laws and the budget. Lastly, there was to be a nominated Senate which was to 'guard the fundamental pact and the public liberties.' Much in all this was very vague; but it was clear that all the reality of power would rest with the President, and that the Assembly would have at most a power of veto on such measures as were submitted to it. A few days later all the voters of France were called to vote 'Yes' or 'No' on the following resolution: 'The people desires the maintenance of the authority of Napoleon Bonaparte, and delegates to him the necessary powers to establish a constitution on the basis proposed in his proclamation of December 2.' Every effort was made by the Government to secure a favourable verdict, and the means employed were often unfair. Yet when every deduction has been made, the answer showed an overwhelming encouragement to the President in his new task. There were 7,439,000 who voted Yes, and only 640,000 Noes.[1]

Louis Bonaparte became President on those terms on December 21, 1851. In less than a year he exchanged the Presidential for an Imperial title. Again there was much intrigue and corruption used to bring about the result; but again we cannot doubt that there was much real popular enthusiasm for the restoration of the glorious title of Empire. It was one of the things always remembered against him that he said at Bordeaux: 'It seems that France is inclined to return to the Empire; well, the Empire means Peace.' The proposal that the hereditary Empire should be conferred on him came from the obsequious Senate. It was submitted to a plebiscite, and 7,824,000 were returned as saying 'Yes', while only 253,000 said 'No'! Napoleon reigned at once as the Emperor Napoleon III; for to all true imperialists Napoleon's son, the Duke of Reichstadt, who had died in 1832, was Napoleon II, though he had died uncrowned.

The new Empire that thus came into being was in theory the ideal of paternal monarchy. It contained all that was best in the principles of the great Revolution, and all that was most efficient in the organisation of the first Napoleon. In his proclamation after his election as President, Napoleon had said that 'he had searched the past for the best examples to follow; that he preferred the principles of genius to the specious doctrines of men of abstract ideas'; and that, as France for the last fifty years owed her progress to the administrative organisation of the Consulate of Napoleon, he had thought it best to adopt also the political institutions of the Consulate. The Emperor was to be in constant and close touch with his people; he was to be their true representative and to interpret their will, securing liberty, relieving poverty, putting at the disposal of the nation the best intelligence of the nation in his Council of State, and avoiding always the dangers and delays of party strife. He found, as we have said, his ideal in the Consulate of Napoleon. He might have found some resemblance to his dream in

---

[1] F. A. Simpson: *Louis Napoleon and the Recovery of France* (2nd ed., 1930), p. 162, says that the authenticity of the figures is now generally admitted, and that official pressure did not create but merely exaggerated Louis Napoleon's majority. Incidentally (pp. 163–76) he makes out a strong case for the *coup d'état*.

the English monarchy under the Tudors and in the Utopia of Boling-broke's Patriot King.

The reality was something different. The love of France and of the French people was doubtless a very real sentiment with Napoleon III; but the possession of personal power was the first necessity for the realisation of his aims both personal and public, and he showed no scruple and much ingenuity in the methods which he adopted to secure his personal power.

France had a legislative Assembly elected by manhood suffrage. It is of the essence of such assemblies that they try to extend their powers and are jealous of all interference. Napoleon saw in this Assembly his most serious rival, and was determined to control it. First by con-trolling the elections. Universal suffrage was maintained, but all who were convicted for a political offence lost the vote; this was interpreted so widely that membership of an obnoxious club lost a man his vote, and the Government could remove from the electoral roll most of its known opponents. Then the arrangement of the constituencies was at the will of the Government, and it used this power to swamp the radical towns in the conservative country, the town being rarely allowed to vote as a whole, but broken up and its parts arranged as constituencies with the surrounding country districts. The Government, too, put before the electors 'official candidates,' and used all its influence to secure their election. The prefects who ruled provincial France, and the mayors of the towns, who were all of them appointed by the Government, used all their powers to secure the return of men favour-able to the Empire. Sometimes it seems the votes when given were tampered with.

When the Assembly had been elected it was regarded with the utmost jealousy. It could not initiate measures. It could not amend the budget. It voted secretly. If it passed any offensive measure it could be thrown out by the obsequious conservative Senate as being in conflict with the vague 'fundamental pact.' It is strange that an Assembly so elected and so controlled could at times make itself disagreeable to the Govern-ment.

Napoleon realised too that there was another and more intangible enemy: a public opinion influenced or dominated by men of literature, by those in charge of education, and by journalists. It was impossible to control literature. He found writers to support his régime; but, in exile, Louis Blanc and Victor Hugo and many others never ceased to attack him in books and pamphlets of all kinds. The pen of Victor Hugo was an enemy whose attacks never ceased or slackened, and for nearly all the period of the Empire his was the most powerful voice among the writers of Europe. Education, on the other hand, could be and was controlled by the Minister of Public Instruction acting in the interests of the Government. The professors of the University were brought under the direct control of the Minister; they were ordered to dress neatly and not to let their beards grow 'that the last traces of anarchy may disappear.' In the normal schools—where teachers were trained—no history or philosophy was to be taught. Private schools, especially those in the hands of the clergy, were encouraged. All were carefully watched in the interest of the Government. Newspapers were rigorously supervised and controlled. None could be started without permission from the Government. There was a heavy stamp duty. For writing contrary to the wishes of the Government, journals could be easily suspended or suppressed. The printing of books was hardly freer. The right of association and of public meeting was so closely limited as almost to be destroyed.

What did France think of all this? Napoleon never won the great towns to his side. Paris, in spite of all he did for the buildings and the trade of the city, was always his bitter opponent. The country districts were, however, always friendly, and the plebiscites, which supported his different appeals, cannot be interpreted except as signs of this approval. Some eminent historians have thought that if he could have maintained peace he might have made his régime durable; but the history of France does not encourage us to think that a régime could last long, if it did not satisfy the desire for glory, neglected liberty, and denied freedom of thought.

The road of conspiracy and adventure by which Napoleon had made his way to the Empire fatally limited his choice of agents. Republicans such as Cavaignac, Orleanists such as Thiers, would not take service under him, and there were many others on whose loyalty he could not rely. He was forced to accept the services of men who were to a greater or smaller extent his fellow-conspirators. His most trusted supporters and agents were Persigny, Walewski, Morny, and Saint-Arnaud. As an adventurer, too, he could not procure the alliance of one of the reigning families of Europe. Napoleon's marriage to Marie Louise was a warning here. Yet a marriage was necessary to complete the imperial establishment. In January 1853 he married Eugénie de Montijo, Countess of Teba, a beautiful Spaniard with some Scottish blood in her veins. Her presence added great charm to the life of the Court, and she played her part with wonderful success. It was policy as well as inclination which made Napoleon inaugurate a series of balls and receptions. It was not only the Court but Paris also which plunged into a round of gaiety that soon made the city, what it had not previously been, the great centre for the pleasure-seekers of Europe. The city was rebuilt under the direction of the Prefect Haussmann. Its narrow streets gave way to wide thoroughfares, and the health and amenities of the city were much improved. Incidentally, too, the new arrangement of the streets made it much more difficult for a revolution to turn them into fortresses by means of barricades.

The restoration of order and of religion was accomplished. Paris was gay and splendid. The majority of the inhabitants of France were certainly contented. But Napoleon had also promised that the Empire should bring peace. In a little over two and a half years from the *coup d'état* he was engaged in a great European war.

CHAPTER XII

THE REVOLUTION OF 1848–49 IN GERMANY, IN THE AUSTRIAN EMPIRE, AND IN HUNGARY

METTERNICH had said that Austria was suffering from a mortal disease in October 1847. It was so, and the disease had been accelerated by his own policy. Not only in Austria but in Germany and in Europe as a whole, a policy of pure repression, anti-national and anti-liberal, ended, as it was bound to end, in inanition. The old fabric both in Germany and in Austria was like a piece of furniture, of which the outside was still imposing though the interior was corroded by insects. All that was needed to show the total rottenness of the inside was a bold stroke upon the outside. When that came the structure collapsed, and completely. The Germany and Austria of the Metternichian régime went away for ever. The reaction of 1849 could not return to the past: it could only improvise for the future.

The spark which set Germany and Austria alight came from France, and the flame was fanned by the revolutionary breeze from Italy. Indeed, revolution might have triumphed throughout Germany and Austria had the French Republic lent positive aid to the struggling liberalism of Germany and had the King of Sardinia successfully crushed the Austrians in Italy. Unaided as they were, the inexperienced revolutionaries in Germany, in Austria, and in Hungary were ultimately subdued by the reactionaries.

The character of the revolution assumed different forms in the various parts of Central Europe. In Germany the movement was based on a strong desire for national unity linked to a strong belief that liberalism (*i.e.* representative governments and constitutions) would achieve this end. These impulses united professors and students, who dreamed of unity, to the workers who wished for the suffrage and to peasants who wished to abolish feudal rights. In the German part of Austria the movement was similar, but the population, as a whole, was liberal rather than national in its outlook. In Hungary and the non-German parts of the Austrian Empire the impulse, though sometimes liberal on the surface, was in essence always national. A wholly different set of forces was there put in motion. The Czechs of Bohemia, sturdy patriots from the days of Huss, fought fiercely for their rights against the hated Austrian. The Magyars, proud of an old constitution and a parliament, struggled to free themselves altogether from Austrian

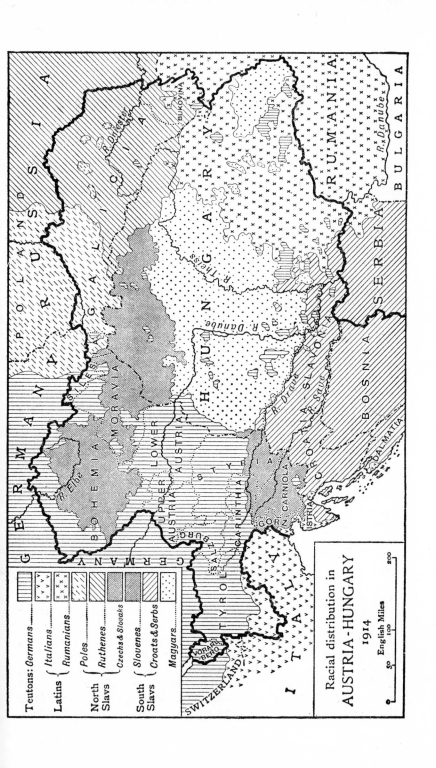

Racial distribution in
AUSTRIA-HUNGARY
1914
English Miles

Teutons: Germans
Latins { Italians
       { Rumanians
North { Poles
Slavs { Ruthenes
       { Czechs & Slovaks
South { Slovenes
Slavs { Croats & Serbs
       Magyars

rule, but they struggled equally to place under their own racial domination a mass of Slavs and Rumans, who formed more than half of their population, and were fiercely insistent on their own rights. The paradox therefore emerged in Hungary that Serbs, Croats, and Rumans ultimately fought for Austria against Hungary to secure their national rights. And, greater paradox still, the Czar of Russia came to their assistance. Thus Austria was saved partly by the division of her enemies, partly by aid from outside. And the recovery of Austria brought with it the success of reaction in Germany. The course of events was indeed exceedingly dramatic. In March 1848 every throne in Central Europe was tottering and revolution was everywhere triumphant. Before the end of the year the prospects of revolution were dark, and in 1849 reaction again prevailed everywhere.

Liberals and revolutionaries had long been of opinion that Germany stood in need of three things. She needed freedom of opinion and of the press; a parliamentary government; and a strong national (or Federal) constitution instead of the feeble, worm-eaten, ramshackle structure of the *Bund* (Confederation). The February revolution in France gave Germany the chance to realise her dreams. In March 1848 a marvellous transformation scene was displayed in Germany. Every king, duke, or princelet either swore to a liberal constitution or appointed a liberal ministry. Kings shook hands with the leaders of revolution; their soldiers fraternised everywhere with the mob; professors appeared as prime ministers, and students, artisans, and shopkeepers sat as deputies in newly summoned popular legislatures. There was almost no resistance, and consequently almost no bloodshed, and no violent deposition of reigning sovereigns. On March 16, 1848, indeed, the King of Bavaria abdicated in favour of his son, but this step was due to special causes and formed an exception to the general rule. Two points are to be specially noted. Würtemberg and Hanover, though adopting liberal principles, opposed the idea of German national unity. In other parts the idea of unity was dominant, and by a movement originating in Hesse-Darmstadt and Baden arrangements were made to summon a National German Parliament. To ensure its meeting, a self-constituted preliminary Parliament (*Vorparlament*) met before the end of March.

The success of the revolution was, however, assured, not by what happened in Germany, but by what happened in Austria. There the reins of power were feebly held. The Emperor was semi-imbecile. Metternich was aged, the counsellors were timid and ignorant, no one was ready to lead or to make generous concessions. Hesitation and timidity marked the imperial attitude during the first fortnight in March, and, before it ended, the struggle was over. Students and professors led a demonstration to the Emperor on March 12, and on the 13th a conflict arose between the mob and the troops, in which the latter ended by going over to the revolution. Metternich resigned that night and fled the country, exclaiming, so they say, that a deluge would follow him.

The flight of Metternich was of immense typical significance. It marked the era of the revolution's glory. The strongest symbol of reaction had fallen at the first touch of the revolution's hand. A man, who for thirty years had gagged the press, cowed or destroyed the parliaments, and imprisoned the revolutionaries of Central Europe, was hunted from his capital and the Continent amid the scorn and execration of the world. The fall and flight of Metternich meant that a tide was sweeping over Europe, and that kings were running before it in terror.

On March 15 the Emperor issued an Edict at Vienna, which promised a liberal constitution, freedom of the press, and a Parliament (*Reichstag*). A National Guard (the symbol of the power of the bourgeoisie) was also to be established. This showed that revolution had prevailed even in the arch-capital of reaction. The day before (the 14th), the revolution had triumphed at Budapest, and the Hungarians demanded that, in accordance with their old constitution, the Ministers should become responsible to the majority in the Lower House. This demand was granted (March 17) by the Emperor in his capacity of King of Hungary. On the 15th, the revolution at Budapest had also demanded freedom of the press and the establishment of a National Guard, and these demands were ultimately also conceded, together with an admission of the autonomy of Hungary. What had in fact happened in Budapest was quite different from what had happened in Vienna. In the latter capital a liberal and popular movement had prevailed, but in Budapest an intensely anti-German and anti-Hapsburg national Hungarian Government had taken charge.

The Hapsburgs had bent their stiff necks to the yoke at Vienna and Budapest; and the triumph of revolution was completed by the capitulation of the Hohenzollern King at Berlin (March 19). Frederick William IV had conceded a representative constitution and freedom of the press (March 18), but the news of this had been followed by a conflict of the mob with the soldiers in Berlin. In this case the troops might have stood firm had not Frederick William IV, who was in a sort of religious dementia, withdrawn his troops on March 19 and left his palace wholly unprotected. The King opened his arsenal and supplied the mob with arms, and saluted a procession which carried before him the bodies of civilians slain by his own soldiers. On the 21st the King, who had appointed a Liberal Ministry, issued a proclamation that Prussia was merged in Germany. He rode round the capital under a black, red, and gold standard (the Pan-German colours),[1] stopping on the way to address students and speak to the people. The next day his heir, the Prince of Prussia, who was hated as a reactionary, was smuggled out of the capital and fled to England. The Prince (who was to be William I) shared with Bismarck the honour of being the most unpopular man in that Germany which they were in twenty years to unite and to rule with brilliant and popular success.

[1] These were adopted by the German Republic in 1919.

On March 31 the *Vorparlament* had met at Frankfort to prepare the way for the National German Assembly. Though sufficiently representative otherwise, it had only two delegates from Austria. It was not a very wise body and was rent by all kinds of dissensions; but it was supported by public opinion and was able to disregard altogether the Diet of the old Confederation (*Bund*). The *Bund* had drawn up a new and fairly conservative constitution of its own, and this, with some alterations, the *Vorparlament* adopted. They arranged for direct elections to a single chamber, and avoided any concession to republicanism. On these terms the National Assembly (or National Parliament) was ultimately elected, and actually met in the middle of May.

The National Parliament consisted chiefly of the middle class, the bourgeoisie, the patriotic class; the landed interest and 'big business' were inadequately represented, and labour hardly at all. The Assembly was deeply influenced by the professors, lawyers, and literary men who sat in it. After a preliminary struggle the Austrian interest won a victory over the Prussian, and the Archduke John, a liberal and popular Hapsburg, was appointed *Reichsverweser* (Imperial Vicar). An executive which ignored the separate governments had thus been created, and an Austrian and a prince was at its head. This policy ignored alike the prejudices of conservatives who favoured separate governments and of radicals who objected to a prince. But neither Governments nor the radicals were strong enough to protest at the moment.

Almost the first act of the Assembly produced a humiliating rebuff. The *Vorparlament* had tried to liberate Schleswig-Holstein from Danish rule. Prussia, which had sent troops to occupy these two Duchies, had been defeated by the Danes, and a truce favourable to Denmark concluded. This truce the Assembly, after suffering much humiliation, was compelled to accept. When this became known, the members of the Assembly were hustled and intimidated by the mob at Frankfort. Order was finally restored (September 18) by the arrival of Prussian and Austrian troops, but not before two blameless and popular deputies had been murdered. Thus, even in the autumn of 1848, it seemed clear that the revolutionary element was getting out of hand and that the historic Governments alone could keep order.

We must now see how far the Governments at Vienna and Berlin had been able to settle their own affairs by September 1848. The Austrian Germans as a whole showed very little interest in the rest of Germany. They were occupied with their own affairs and with other parts of the Hapsburg territory. The Hungarians under the lead of Kossuth went far on the way to separation, abolishing feudalism and giving the land to the peasantry. At the same time he made it quite clear that the Hungarians (Magyars) would give no racial privileges to the Serbs, Croats, or Rumans within their kingdom. Thus, at the very moment that Austrian authority was crumbling at Vienna, Kossuth, by his own folly, was finding allies for it and against himself among the non-Magyar subjects of the Hungarian Crown.

A liberal constitution was published in Vienna on April 25. The Emperor was quite helpless, he could not trust his troops in the capital, and on May 15 he was forced into more liberal concessions by a mob of students, with whom the National Guard did not interfere. In consequence the Emperor fled secretly to Innsbruck (May 17). The flight of the Emperor from his capital showed that the conditions now approached anarchy, and the immediate result was to unloose further nationalistic aspirations. On June 13 the Czechs rose in Prague. But, after some weakness on the part of Windischgrätz, the Austrian commander, the Czech revolutionaries were bombarded in their capital and forced to surrender (June 17). Windischgrätz thus achieved the first victory of reaction in Austria, or indeed in Europe, and all the supporters of the old régime again raised their heads. This first success was soon followed by the news that Radetzsky had beaten the Sardinians in Italy (July 25) and reoccupied Milan (August 6). Thus the generals were gaining victories and the *moral* of their troops was being strengthened. The fact that further reaction was expected was clearly shown when the Emperor returned to Vienna (August 12).

The Court returned to Vienna just at the moment that a conflict with Hungary had become inevitable. This conflict was due largely to two men—to Kossuth, the revolutionary leader of Hungary, and to Jellačić, the artful Ban or Governor of Croatia. Kossuth had been working steadily for the independence of Hungary and had been openly arming to crush the rebellious Serbs and Croats. Jellačić, appointed Ban of Croatia in June, had used his power to forward the Croat National Movement and to stir up both Serbs and Croats against Hungary. Jellačić, at once an adroit intriguer and a bold gambler, played his cards well. He was suspended from his office, but he visited the Emperor at Innsbruck, pointed out to him the advantage of conciliating the Slavs, and was finally restored to power (September 4). He lost no time and, summoning both Croats and Serbs to his aid, he crossed the Drave and invaded Hungary with an army (September 17). His military venture was not successful, but it had one important effect. Crossing the Drave was 'Crossing the Rubicon,' not only for Jellačić, but for the Austrian Court. The Hapsburg was now irrevocably committed to war against Hungary, and an actual declaration of war was issued by the Austrian Government on October 3.

One hope, however, remained. The revolutionary leaders at Vienna might coerce the Government and join hands with those at Budapest to make the revolution triumph in both capitals. Kossuth promised to send Hungarian forces to the aid of his brother revolutionaries in Vienna. Demonstrations against war with Hungary took place in Vienna in September and culminated in riots, in the murder of the Austrian Minister of War, in the erection of barricades, and in a second flight of the Emperor (October 7). But this time the Austrian Government was to be saved by its generals. On October 13 Jellačić and his army were close to Vienna, and on the 17th Windischgrätz and a still larger force appeared from the direction of Prague. Windischgrätz decided to offer no terms and refused to negotiate with rebels. He simply demanded disarmament and unconditional surrender. There was a chance that the Hungarian forces might liberate their brother revolutionaries, for they were nearing Vienna; but on October 30 they were defeated by Jellačić within sight of the capital, and all hope was gone. This ended the resistance of the city, and Windischgrätz entered it as a conqueror the next day. Like Jellačić he had often acted without, or in defiance of, the orders of the Court and had saved the dynasty despite itself.

So far as Austria was concerned the revolution ended with the fall of Vienna. Windischgrätz appointed his brother-in-law, Prince Felix Schwarzenberg, as Chief Minister, a man of iron will and great ability, who governed as an autocrat and coolly disregarded the revolutionary Ministry and the Austrian Reichstag. On December 2 the incapable Emperor abdicated in favour of his eighteen-year-old nephew, Francis Joseph. Schwarzenberg remained the real ruler of Austria with the programme of an indivisible Austrian Monarchy, ruled by a bureaucracy. He disdained the new constitution and contemptuously superseded it, and dissolved the Austrian Reichstag in the early days of March 1849.

Liberalism had been scotched in Prussia in November 1848, about a fortnight after it had been suppressed in Austria. Frederick William had long vacillated between unworthy deference to mob violence and absurd insistence on his Divine Right. At length, however, he made up his mind, and summoned Count Brandenburg and Otto von Manteuffel to his councils (November 1). They acted quickly, and announced (November 9) that the new Liberal Assembly would be transferred from Berlin to Brandenburg. Troops entered the capital on the 10th and rendered all further resistance hopeless. As the Assembly refused to vote taxes or to go to Brandenburg, it was dissolved on December 5. The Potsdam grenadiers had again done their duty and made the Hohenzollern King once more. The two greatest German Powers had thus again asserted their authority in their own capitals. Experience had shown that the strong hand availed and that the troops could be trusted. Prussia was entirely able to keep order. Austria, now secure in its own hereditary provinces, still had to suppress revolution in Hungary and in Italy.

While the end of 1848 portended the victory of reaction in Germany and Austria, it was still possible for the revolution to be successful elsewhere. In Italy the cause of national unity was not yet hopeless, and Hungary was to amaze the world by her vitality. Her resistance was even more remarkable than appears at first sight. For Hungary had not only to improvise an army and to fight regulars superior in numbers, equipment, and organisation, but she had also to meet irregular levies of Serbs, Rumans, and Slovaks within her own demesne. Even so, it is doubtful if Austria would have prevailed had not she summoned to her aid the armies of Russia. Hungary was fortunate in possessing a governing class of conspicuous political gifts, but she owed most to the enthusiasm aroused by Kossuth and to the great military ability displayed by Görgei, the most prominent of the Hungarian commanders. Unfortunately, Kossuth was as militarily ignorant as Görgei was politically inept, and the two men were always at variance. Owing to these jealousies and discords it was not until March 1849 that Görgei really obtained control of the Hungarian army.

During the winter of 1848–49 Hungary owed its safety to the slowness with which Windischgrätz moved. He was influenced partly by political considerations, but was, in general, cautious to the verge of cowardice. He held Budapest as well as Vienna, but made little attempt to harass his opponents, and least of all to pursue Görgei into the mountainous districts in which he was reorganising his army. Early in April Görgei moved swiftly upon him, caught him unprepared at Isaszeg (April 6, 1849) and defeated him heavily. Görgei followed up this success by relieving Komárom, the strongest fortress of Hungary, forcing one Austrian army back on Vienna, and another under Jellačić back on Zagreb. The military success was startling. Görgei had dispersed and divided the Austrian armies, and his recovery of Budapest was only a question of time.

The changes in the situation were marked by three signs. The Austrian Government recalled Windischgrätz from command in the field; they appealed to Russia for help; and drove Kossuth into open rebellion. The latter, holding his Parliament at Debreczen, felt strong enough to depose the Hapsburg (April 14), to declare the Monarchy suspended, to proclaim himself governor, and to issue a Hungarian declaration of independence.[1] So strong was Hungary's position that even the utter defeat of the King of Sardinia at Novara (March 23) did not shake her. Kossuth even urged Görgei to advance on Vienna, though Görgei for military reasons declined to undertake this hazardous measure. Early in May he moved on Budapest and, after some weeks, captured the place. On June 6 Kossuth triumphantly entered Budapest, and for a few weeks enjoyed the glittering semblance of power. In reality his position was precarious. Görgei well knew his military weakness, due both to inferior numbers and to paucity of supplies. But there were grave political weaknesses as well. Görgei and the army believed in constitutional monarchy, Kossuth in sentimental revolution. The magnates and the wealthier classes were alarmed at the revolutionary excesses of Kossuth, and the revolutionary paper currency was dropping in value every day. Görgei was probably right in thinking that only a military dictatorship could save the country. But, though h‹ was the

---

[1] This was erroneously dated the 19th March.

only possible candidate, he was not endowed with any political insight, and Kossuth was determined to retain the whole civil power as long as he could. So there were delays over this most vital matter until the step, when taken, was too late to save the situation.

In point of fact the issue was already decided. On May 1 it was known that the Czar of Russia had answered Austria's call for aid, and was about to send a fully equipped and independent army into Hungary under Field-Marshal Paskiévič. This intervention was ultimately to be decisive. The motives of the Czar have been much debated, but they seem, in reality, to have been simple. Numbers of Poles had fought in the Hungarian army, and several of them had been eminent as generals at the head of it. In March, Russian troops had entered Transylvania and been expelled by the Hungarian forces, and a Hungarian division had been stationed near the Galician frontier expressly to encourage the Poles to revolt against Austria. The Czar was particularly sensitive about the Poles, and considered that all sovereigns ought to unite against revolutionaries. He intervened partly to suppress the Polish revolt in the bud, partly to aid the Divine Right of a brother ruler against revolutionaries. Both objects were congenial to Nicholas, and both were to be attained. The two sovereigns met at Warsaw on May 21 and there settled upon the plan of campaign.[1]

Hungary was to be invaded from three sides—by Haynau, the new Austrian commander, from Vienna, by Jellačić from Zagreb, and by Paskiévič, who was to cross the Carpathians and take the Hungarians in the rear. Görgei was in a bad position, hopelessly outnumbered and hampered by the political necessity of defending Komárom and Budapest. By July 14 Jellačić, though he had met with reverses, contrived to join hands with Haynau, and on the 18th the combined Austrian army entered Budapest. Operations were then transferred to the Theiss (Tisza). Görgei skilfully avoided contact with the Russians of Paskiévič, but Haynau caught up with the southern Hungarian army and utterly routed it at Temesvár (August 9).

Görgei had anticipated defeat, and informed Kossuth at Arad on August 10 that he would surrender if Haynau were victorious at Temesvár. Kossuth dramatically answered that, in such case, he would commit suicide. On the 11th the news of the Temesvár disaster arrived. Thereupon Görgei prepared to surrender and asked Kossuth to abdicate, in order to relieve the political head of responsibility for surrender. There is much mystery about these negotiations and Kossuth subsequently asserted that Görgei had been ordered to insist on the autonomy of Hungary and accused him of deliberately betraying her to the enemy.

---

[1] Nicholas, after he had quarrelled with Austria in 1854, asked her ambassador whether he knew who had been the two stupidest Kings of Poland. He answered his own question thus: 'The first was King John Sobieski, who liberated Vienna (1683) from the siege laid by the Turks, the second am I. For both of us . . . saved the House of Habsburg.' J. Redlich: *Emperor Francis Joseph of Austria* (1929), p. 156

The charge is absurd, and was probably put forward merely as a popular explanation of Hungarian disaster. For Kossuth knew quite as well as Görgei that resistance was impossible.[1] Even if Görgei had demanded the autonomy of Hungary, neither Haynau nor Paskiévić would have admitted any terms but those of unconditional surrender on a military basis. On August 13 Görgei therefore led over 23,000 troops to the Russians at Világos and laid down his arms. He was the most remarkable of revolutionary soldiers produced by the upheavals of 1848.

'Hungary lies at the feet of Your Majesty,' wrote the triumphant Paskiévić to the Czar. But, in fact, Görgei's army and the settlement of Hungary were both handed over to Haynau. That worthy proceeded to punish the rebels. Owing to the intervention of the Czar, Görgei's own life was spared, but thirteen of his generals ('The martyrs of Arad') were shot or hanged, and nearly 400 officers were imprisoned. Batthyány, who had been Prime Minister of Hungary, and over a hundred politicians were executed. Kossuth himself, Count Julius Andrássy, and seventy-four others were hanged in effigy. Cruelties of all kinds took place, and the atrocities of Slav and Ruman guerrillas passed wholly unpunished. Haynau's ruthless rule earned for him the nickname of 'Hyena' and brought him a severe punishment at the generous hands of the draymen of Messrs. Barclay and Perkins when he visited England some years later. There can be little question that undue severity was shown, and it is instructive to compare the leniency shown towards the Confederate politicians and generals by the victorious North in the American Civil War with the brutality of Austrian methods in Hungary and Italy in 1849.

Kossuth had not committed suicide when surrender came, as he said he would. On August 17 he buried the Hungarian crown near the border town of Orsova and fled to Turkey from Hungary, which he never saw again. He became an eloquent voice in the wilderness, displaying both in England and in the United States that marvellous gift of exciting human emotion which had made him the first man in Hungary. He lived for nearly fifty years and remained irreconcilably anti-Hapsburg. In 1902 his bones were brought back to rest in his own land amid scenes of emotion such as Hungary had never witnessed. He had indeed exercised a volcanic and incalculable power. For conservative forces had been strong in Hungary, and without Kossuth there would have been no revolution.

The course of revolution was fairly run by the summer of 1849. For,

---

[1] Kossuth made the charge of treachery in a moment of great excitement when fleeing from Hungary. He never repudiated it, but it is no longer sustained by serious writers. The main charge is that Kossuth stipulated that, in case of surrender, the autonomy of Hungary should be reserved. Even if this is true (which it probably is not), Kossuth was insisting on a condition which Görgei could not have possibly obtained.—Cp. Sir A. W. Ward in *Cambridge Modern History*, vol. XI. pp. 212-14.

though there remained much unrest, there was no longer any doubt that the constituted authorities would ultimately prevail over the revolutionaries. The revolution had been like a wave or like a charge of cavalry, sweeping over a vast surface resistlessly for a moment, but unable to hold for long the ground thus gained. It had been beaten back everywhere by material force and the Kings had returned to their capitals as soon as the soldiers had returned to their obedience. The first blow to revolution was the capture of Prague on June 17; the second the fall of Vienna at the end of October; the third the reassertion of the King of Prussia's authority in Berlin in November. The last and most stubborn resistance, that of the Hungarians, where national patriotism stimulated revolution, was only ended by calling in a foreign and a Russian army. In every case revolution had begun without bloodshed; in every case reaction triumphed by violence and by militarism. Sentimental liberalism, rose-water revolutions, even national uprisings, had failed before the iron hand and naked force of authority. What was now to be seen was whether the revolutions had been altogether in vain, and whether reaction could be permanent.

CHAPTER XIII

REACTION IN GERMANY, AUSTRIA, AND HUNGARY, 1849–60

THE year 1849 opened in singular obscurity. Prussia had restored her kingly power, Austria had restored order in her German provinces: so the two greatest states in Germany were again in existence. But the German National Parliament remained with a Central Executive and *Reichsverweser*,[1] as the living symbol of German unity, as the body which might hope still to realise the dreams of so many and to make Germany no longer a name but a nation. There were too many of the smaller states committed to its policy, there was too much public opinion still in its favour, for it to be flouted altogether or at once. It was therefore in a position to force, and did force, upon Austria a great decision as to the future. After long debate the members of the National Assembly had decided not to exclude Austria from the proposed Federation (or Empire, as it was often called), but they equally declined to include any non-German part of Austria in the new German union. So they offered Austria a place in the new German Empire, but stipulated that her non-German parts (Hungary, etc.) should stand aside. Schwarzenberg replied to this offer on December 13, 1848, by saying that Austria and all its parts would, in future, be one single, organic

---

[1] Imperial Vicar.

centralised state, and, as such, must enter the Confederation (*Bund*). He rejected the new German Empire altogether, and proposed to revive the old *Bund* with a stronger executive.

His reply gave Prussia a great chance for obtaining the leadership in Germany. For the National Assembly, affronted by the Schwarzenberg proposal, turned to Prussia for sympathy and aid. After further insults from Schwarzenberg, the National Assembly completed their constitution and chose the King of Prussia as German Emperor (March 27–8, 1849). Had Frederick William been a great ruler, as he admitted he was not, Prussia might have obtained the leadership of Germany. After much hesitation Frederick William refused the offered crown (April 3),[1] and so threw away the prize which his successor was one day to enjoy.

The refusal of the King of Prussia was a great blow. But the popular support and the serious differences between Austria and Prussia still permitted the possibility of a united Germany, for twenty-eight states had solemnly signified their assent to the resolutions of the National Assembly which established the new constitution and the German Emperor (April 4). The day after this assent was signified Austria withdrew her representatives from Frankfort. The National Assembly replied by reaffirming the constitution. Then, on May 4, Prussia denied the authority of the Assembly and withdrew her deputies. This step was decisive. The shadow of an Assembly continued to exist, transferred from Frankfort to Stuttgart. But, on September 30, 1849, Austria and Prussia took over the functions of the Central German Power, and thus ended the power, if not the existence, of the Frankfort Assembly. And the constitution fell with it. It was not at all like the German constitution which was produced by the German victories of 1870; but in many respects it was not unlike that one which was produced by the German defeats of 1918. It contained the same assertion of the rights of the Empire against those of the states; it had a strong popular element in the Upper House; it made a real attempt to introduce popular representation; and it sought to establish personal liberty as the fundamental right of a German citizen.

In April and May 1849 revolutions or military mutinies occurred at Baden, in the Rhenish Palatinate (part of Bavaria), and in Saxony. Prussian troops were at once sent to restore order in Saxony, and were also used to suppress some fresh but not dangerous disorders in Prussia herself. Prussian forces also moved into Baden, into the Bavarian Palatinate, and into Würtemberg. As Prussia was at the same time pursuing a policy of friendship towards some other minor states, Austria became highly suspicious. If Prussia could restore order in states, she was likely to control them, and, if she controlled many of them, Austria would no longer be the first Power in Germany. Schwarzenberg was quite ruthless and quite determined. He meant to restore the old *Bund*,

[1] It would be more correct to say he adjourned the question *sine die*.

to reassert the Austrian hegemony in Germany, and to brush aside all other schemes as idle. And he could not do this without a spectacular humiliation of Prussia.

Late in 1850, disturbances in Hesse-Cassel put a match to the powder magazine. Schwarzenberg was not going to have Prussia gaining any more prestige by a restoration of order there. He determined that Austria should play that part, and prepared to move on Hesse-Cassel with an Austrian army of 200,000 men (reinforced by contingents from Bavaria and Würtemberg). Prussia mobilised in reply, and a collision actually took place between Prussian and Bavarian troops. But, as always happened at a crisis, Frederick William tottered and gave way. At Olmütz the iron Schwarzenberg dictated to Prussia a settlement of the Hesse affair, which left all the honours in the hands of Austria, while making some feeble attempt to save Prussia's face in public (November 28, 1850). Before the end of the year Schwarzenberg carried the restoration of the old Confederation (*Bund*) intact, of course with Austria at the head of it as of old. To all appearance Austria was stronger than ever, and reaction in his person was dominant and supreme.

The pitiable humiliation of Olmütz marked the lowest point of Prussia's timidity and surrender. Schwarzenberg seemed a greater Metternich, and Prussia appeared to be brought as low in the dust as after Jena. And there was a further degradation now. When Prussia had been vanquished by Napoleon she had at least been true to the idea of German unity. Now she had begun by promising to champion that cause, had betrayed those who supported it, and acquiesced in the haughty demands of Austria. Germany seemed as feeble, as disunited, as nerveless as ever. Prussia had had the chance of being the first Power in Germany, and her King that of wearing an Imperial crown. All she had done was to rivet still tighter the chains which bound Germany at the feet of Schwarzenberg. The 'humiliation of Olmütz' seemed to put the union of Germany at a more distant date than ever, and permanently to disqualify Prussia as its champion.

This way of looking at things was in reality very fallacious. Schwarzenberg's strong will and ruthless energy had indeed enabled him to achieve diplomatic victories without and order within. But the plan for the future settlement of the Hapsburg dominions was doomed to failure from the start. Schwarzenberg was right to try something new, but what he actually tried had already been condemned by experience. His idea, in brief, was to treat all Austria-Hungary as a mass of molten metal—to run it out in one mould, and to stamp it with one die—to make it speak one language, have one law and one Government, and obey one master. It was to be unified, centralised, and bureaucratised. The scheme ran counter to the nature of things, and had already been attempted in vain by Joseph II under far more favourable circumstances. Even if the lessons of history could have been dismissed and the aspirations of a dozen races[1] could have been trodden out, there was no possibility of the plan succeeding unless there were at least twenty years of uninterrupted peace. And, within eighteen years, Austria met two crushing defeats at the hands of a conqueror. The second of those conquerors was Prussia, which, in a campaign of six weeks, reversed the verdict of Olmütz.

As a matter of fact, Schwarzenberg had it in his power to conciliate different races in Austria, and to reduce the Magyars to impotence in the Kingdom of Hungary. His best plan would probably have been to extend a system of thorough devolution of self-government to different races.[2] By this means he could have confined the five million Magyars within the territory they inhabited, and separated from their body politic five million Slavs and two million Rumans. Valuable economic resources and strong alien populations would have been cut off from Hungary and would then have been at the disposal of the Hapsburgs. Schwarzenberg's determination to crush Magyars and Slavs alike beneath a common yoke was recognised by the former as a great blunder. 'What is given to us,' sneered the Magyars, 'as a punishment, is given to you [the Slavs] as a reward.' A golden opportunity of fashioning the Austrian state anew on the basis of liberal and moderate self-government was thus lost. The course Schwarzenberg took led not only to disaster abroad, but to the *Ausgleich* (1867) within; it involved ultimately a dual system (Austria-Hungary) in which the Magyars became in reality the more powerful element, a result which a judicious policy could easily have averted.

Throughout the decade 1849–60 the centralising measures, initiated by Schwarzenberg and continued by Bach, worked steadily for the destruction of the Hapsburg monarchy. Nationalistic tendencies, everywhere repressed in 1849, were in fact restored and revived by the excesses of reaction. In Austrian Italy the hatred of the Hapsburg burnt strongest, but it flamed hardly less fiercely among Magyars and Czechs. When Austrian armies were in the field in 1859 and in 1866 neither Slavs nor Magyars showed any readiness to fight for the Hapsburg. And it could only have been a very stupid policy which brought Magyars and Slavs into agreement.

Austria then was doomed when she adopted a centralising policy at home, for that was certain in the end to lead to disasters abroad. Also, a close observer would have noted that, despite the brilliant triumph of Olmütz, Austrian policy had met with virtual defeat even in Germany. Prussia had indeed been momentarily humiliated, but Austria had been

---

[1] In addition to Germans, there were seven Slav races, Czechs, Poles, Ruthenes, Croats, Serbs, Slovaks, Slovenes; three Latin, Ruman, Ladin, and Italian; two Ugrian, Magyar and Szekler.

[2] It is exceedingly interesting that this plan is substantially that which Franz Ferdinand is known to have adopted in 1914. He was convinced that the way for the Hapsburg Empire to continue to exist was to upset the dual system and to make all nations equal under the House of Austria.

unable to realise the wider programme of Schwarzenberg. She had not obtained inclusion of her whole territory as a unified state in the *Bund* as he had wished. She had failed also to break up the Prussian Zoll-verein, or to substitute for it a more general customs union in which she was included. So, though temporarily triumphant, Austria's position was really dangerous and unstable.

It may be well at this point to sum up the results of 1848–49. An un-paralleled outpouring of human emotions had deluged Central Europe. And, though the tide appeared to ebb, its marks were everywhere, and were often ineffaceable. A heavy blow was struck in Germany, in Austria, and in Hungary at the servitude of the peasant, and free land became the rule for him. So, even the revival of political tyranny in its acutest form was accompanied by a large measure of economic freedom for the peasants all over Central Europe.

The liberalism, so much in evidence everywhere, had been primarily a bourgeois movement. It was of the sentimental and romantic order. Its leaders were generally men without political experience or organisa-tion, and the movement appeared to have been crushed by the heavy-handed policemanship of Berlin and Vienna. In some cases this con-clusion was true; political activity never again endangered the existing régime either in Vienna or in Germany until 1914. But all the German rulers were compelled to grant or to liberalise constitutions, and these instruments led to some restraint on the power of rulers and to the growth of a real parliamentary life in states like Baden and Bavaria. Even Prussia was compelled to grant a constitution which, as Bismarck found later, was sometimes embarrassing to its ruler.[1] Though most German sovereigns still held personally to the idea of Divine Right, the result of 1848 was to emancipate their subjects from that superstition. Henceforward more national tests were applied, and allegiance was given to rulers in proportion as they were able, or strong, or successful. The triumph of Bismarckian absolutism in Prussia was not due to mysticism and reverence for the crown, but to respect for its intelligence, its power, and its wisdom.

Nationalism, though less in evidence than liberalism in 1848, was actually more successful in outriding the storm. The sense of German national unity was checked, but in no sense destroyed, by the reaction after 1848. There had been a German Parliament and executive; most men felt that they would see both again. Yet the internal weaknesses and alien populations of Austria made it difficult to suppose that she would ever lead the way in that direction. To a keen observer, indeed, the peril of Austria lay in her repression of nationalistic tendencies in

---

[1] Frederick William left a secret injunction, to be read to each of his successors, praying them to destroy the constitution. This injunction was itself destroyed by order of Kaiser William II, King of Prussia. It would not have been written and, if written, would not have been destroyed if the Prussian Constitution in no way embar-rassed its rulers.

her own lands. Palmerston held the view in 1848 that her Italian possessions were a weakness of which she would be well rid, and that Hungary could be conciliated by liberal self-government. He was right in both respects, but, had he the knowledge we have to-day, he could have gone further. He might have pointed out that the Czechs would never be satisfied until their national aspirations were fulfilled, and that even obscure races, like the Slovenes, the Croats, and the Serbs, needed to be conciliated by Austria, if she was to survive. Certainly no one would have dreamed in 1848 that the Hapsburgs would have to fight Serbia in 1914, because the aspirations of Yugo-Slavs were incompatible with the existence of Austria. But the nationalistic leaven set to work in 1848 was to leaven the whole of Central Europe, and ultimately to produce a ferment which only a universal war could allay.

Could any man have seen in 1849 that Prussia would be the champion of German unity twenty years later? Perhaps not, but there were, none the less, some interesting signs to be noted. Prussia still held half Germany in the tightening meshes of her Zollverein. The people and the soldiers of Prussia, though affected by the ferment of revolution, had not actually or actively shown detestation of their sovereign. The King, the army, and the people still formed that organic whole, the Prussian State. A constitution had been granted which to some degree met the needs of the times, and Prussia's King had not disgraced himself, as had Austria's Emperor, by revoking this constitution and by breaking his word. Nothing was to be hoped from Austria, but something good might yet come out of Prussia, when strong men and bold leaders stood on her quarter-deck.

Had Frederick William studied past history he might have remembered that there was a decade in Germany's history when a haughty Austria by her prestige or by her diplomacy had imposed on the world and put a feeble Prussian ruler to shame. When that period ended a strong man grasped power in Prussia and smote Austria down into the dust. History was about to repeat itself. The King knew that the name of the man who began the first era of Prussia's glory was Frederick; he did not know that the name of the man who was to begin the second was William.

CHAPTER XIV

REVOLUTIONARY MOVEMENTS IN ITALY

WE have already seen that there was a fermentation of opinion in Italy very dangerous to all the governments established there. National sentiment and the feeling that Italy, which had once been the great home of centralisation, should achieve unity and centralisation again, had taken possession of the minds of a large part of the educated classes and had vaguely permeated also the rest of the population. Balbo, in his history of Italy, had shown how the land had been enslaved to the barbarian, and had held up the hope of liberation. Gioberti, in his remarkable book, *Del Primato morale e civile degli Italiani* (1843), had pointed to the Papacy as the power which should reorganise and unite the different states of Italy and give the Italians the leadership of Europe; and Mazzini had preached nationalism in alliance with democracy in a manner which made him feared as a revolutionary force, dangerous to the constitution of society as well as to the established governments. There was, however, no sign of any great change. Metternich ruled in Italy as completely as in Vienna, and there seemed little likelihood that the country would cease to be that 'geographical expression' which he had called it in 1815. Yet the first step in the movement of revolution which was to shake nearly every throne in Europe came from this land of despotism, and from the part of it which seemed most wedded to the ideas of the past—the Papacy itself.

In June 1846 Cardinal Mastai-Ferretti was elected Pope, and took the title of Pius the Ninth. Though at the time of his election he was little known outside a restricted circle, he became for the next two years the most prominent of European leaders and the centre of the hopes of the liberals of Europe. He was eulogised as few statesmen in modern times have ever been eulogised. Then there came disappointment and reaction; and he was regarded as an arch-traitor and the enemy of the progress of mankind. The man himself was simple and well-intentioned. His love of Italy and his dislike of the Austrian dominion were perfectly genuine. 'I stand for Italy and belong to Italy,' he said. He had imbibed from Gioberti's book the idea of a Pope as the champion and liberator of the country, and he was flattered by the belief that it was for him to carry out the great task. But he also too truly said that he knew nothing of politics, and he had no conception of all the courage and energy and wisdom that would be required before the liberation of Italy could be accomplished. He knew nothing of the dangers which surrounded him. With the best intentions he struck a match to light a candle, and discovered to his horror that he was in a powder magazine. No wonder if in terror he tried to withdraw from the work which he had initiated. But he had two years of enthusiasm, hope, and immense popularity. The first act of his reign was to issue an amnesty for the exiles and for political prisoners, and this was taken—in the prevailing excitement of men's minds—as a sign that he was the destined liberator, and the man who would introduce into the Papal States 'gas, railways, and a constitution.' Crowds gathered spontaneously to acclaim him: he was declared to be 'the prophet not only of his own people but of the whole world.' He was intoxicated by this outburst of popularity and believed that it meant more than it did. The French Ambassador saw a danger that he might think it possible to 'sleep on this popularity as on a bed of roses.'

His first measures did not go far, but they were all in the desired direction. After the amnesty came a modification of the censorship of the press. The entirely authoritative and ecclesiastical character of the Government was modified. A Council of State was established in April 1847, chosen by the Pope from the names submitted to him by the governors of the provinces. A Council of Ministers was appointed in June to discuss, but not to control, the action of the Papal Government. The Jews were released from their Ghetto at Rome. Men believed that there was much more behind these moderate changes, and that they were carried out by the will of the Pope alone, in opposition to his reactionary surroundings.

All Italy caught fire from these events in Rome. Metternich was much alarmed. He had foreseen everything, he said, except a liberal Pope. Liberalism—for that name at this epoch was applied even to violent revolutionary opinions—raised its head all over Italy; in Sicily, in Naples, in Tuscany, in Parma, in Milan, in Venice, and even in Savoy. Everywhere it was the mark of a liberal to applaud the Pope, and in some states it was forbidden to cheer the name of Pius IX under heavy penalties. But all this enthusiasm and this hope of an early victory for liberal nationalism rested on illusion. The changes that had been introduced in Rome were far from revolutionary. The Pope was essentially conservative ('no Pope could be a liberal'); and his task would have been impossible of solution even to a much more powerful intellect and will. It is clear that in the long run nothing would satisfy the logical demands of Italian nationalism short of the abdication of the Papacy from its temporal power; and Pius could not even contemplate that. When he ceased to be carried along by the tide of popularity he turned again to the Austrian power to rescue and support him.

It will be well to follow Pius to the end of his liberal phase, though before that came to an end important movements had begun in other parts of Italy; these had a decisive influence on events in Rome, which soon ceased to occupy the centre of the Italian stage. Some progress was made with the promised reforms. A municipal council was established for Rome. Some of the public buildings of Rome were put in its power, and the famous letters S.P.Q.R. were again to be seen on the walls of Rome. The enthusiastic demonstrations which welcomed these acts showed no diminution in the popularity of the Pope. Even the men of extreme views were in some instances swept away by it, and Mazzini wrote a public letter expressing approval of what the Pope had done, 'because it will shorten the way, and spare us dangers, bloodshed, and disasters, and because Italy will be at one stroke placed at the head of European progress.' The Pope used language which might have warned men that he was not willing to go all the way that the revolutionaries desired, for in a public speech he spoke of his determination to maintain the rights of the Sacred College of Cardinals and warned his hearers against dreaming of a Utopia incompatible with the

7

sovereignty of the Pope. In truth the Pope was growing seriously alarmed by the consequences of his action, as seen in the revolutions that were breaking out in all parts of Italy. He began to withdraw himself from public applause and to dream of reaction.

Yet for a short time the progress of the liberal movement in Rome continued. The revolutions that were happening elsewhere—in Naples, in Milan, in France—which frightened the Pope so much, made it impossible for him to stop. It was fear now, not enthusiasm, that drove him on. He appointed a Ministry consisting mainly of laymen, and then hastily, in March 1848, promulgated a constitution. It was warmly but uncritically welcomed, for it maintained the Sacred College of Cardinals as a dominant part of the political constitution, and declared that no law could be accepted which conflicted with the canons or customs of the Church. But it was a constitution with two chambers, and 'constitution' was almost a magical word at this epoch.

The rest of the history of the Pope's constitutional schemes depends directly on the war against Austria waged by northern Italy, to which we must turn in a moment. The Pope declared against any idea of participating in the struggle, and lost at once the support of the nationalists everywhere.[1] He still hoped to work the constitution that he had promulgated, but the fiercer spirits were rapidly gaining the upper hand in Rome. The Pope's chief Minister was Rossi, who sympathised with many phases of liberalism. In November 1848, as he went to the Assembly of Deputies, he was assassinated, probably by the anarchical section of the revolutionaries. Rome was in turmoil and the Pope, now terribly alarmed, abandoned all ideas of working with the constitution in a liberal spirit. Fearing that he might be forced to further concessions, he left Rome and took refuge at Gaeta in Neapolitan territory. Through weakness rather than through cowardice he had refused the part that the liberals pressed upon him. He had no further influence on the contest for Italian liberty and unity; nor was Rome any longer the centre of the struggle.

Italy was well prepared for the spread of the revolutionary movement. The secret societies of Young Italy had enrolled many members throughout the country, and the middle classes generally were almost unanimous in support of Italian national unity. Thus, when the opportunity came, the movement was almost universal and really spontaneous. That the first signal should have been given from Rome and by the Pope was the most amazing thing about the movement. But it was not much less remarkable that the next decisive step came from Ferdinand, the King of Naples and Sicily. In no part of Italy was misgovernment greater; nowhere was the population more uneducated; no ruler was less open to the appeal of nationality and constitutionalism than Ferdinand,

---

[1] The Pope issued an Allocution on 29th April that he disavowed all participation in a war against Austria, but that his troops would defend the integrity of the Roman State. At that moment the Papal forces were in Venetia.

who, in spite of some good humour and bonhomie, had the traditional hatred of his Bourbon house for all popular movements, and felt himself a foreigner in the land. His concession was due to one motive only —fear. There had been mutterings of discontent, and the name of Pius IX was in Naples, as everywhere, the excuse for a demand for more liberal methods of government, and Ferdinand had made some concessions more apparent than real. Then, in January 1848, a manifesto was issued in Palermo demanding 'reforms in agreement with the progress of the age and in accordance with the wishes of Europe, Italy, and France.' The insurrection was announced for January 12, and it actually broke out on that day. For fifteen days Palermo was held by a force which numbered in its ranks all classes of society, including the aristocracy. The half-mutinous troops of the Government were successfully resisted, and in the end were forced to abandon the city. Encouraged by this success, the rebellion soon spread over the whole island. The fighting had never been fierce; the royal troops had lost only some 500 killed and wounded.

The news from Palermo alarmed Ferdinand beyond what seemed necessary, but he was aware of the slight hold that his Government had on the population, and he had little courage or initiative. He yielded to the danger without dignity and without deceiving anyone as to his motives. He issued an amnesty to political prisoners and then actually sanctioned a constitution. It was so transitory that it does not deserve to be examined; we may only note that it did not include religious toleration. It sufficed, however, to make of him a rival in popularity to Pope Pius IX; and it had an immediate effect on the other Governments of the peninsula. When the despised south had entered on the road of reform, the north could hardly lag behind.

It had a direct effect in inducing the Pope to grant the constitution for the Papal States which we have already noticed. It excited the nationalists of Tuscany to action. The Government of the Grand Duke Leopold II was not one of the most oppressive in Italy, and journalism there was already influential. The Grand Duke made small concessions at first, but these were far from contenting the population of Florence, Leghorn, and the other towns of Tuscany; and, in February 1848, he issued a constitution on the model of the Neapolitan one.

What happened in Tuscany was not of much importance, for she could rarely pursue a really independent policy. The future of Italy turned mainly on one point: could the power of Austria be shaken in the north of the peninsula? The fate of Italy, therefore, was decided in Piedmont (the real basis of the kingdom of Sardinia), and in Lombardy, where Austria maintained an authority which the inhabitants never ceased to regard as foreign and oppressive. Sardinia was the least Italian of all the Italian States. Its King, Charles Albert, preferred to speak French instead of Italian, and its population had very incomplete racial affinities with the peoples of the south. The House of Savoy, which held the crown of the Sardinian kingdom, stood to Italy very closely in the relation in which the House of Hohenzollern in Prussia stood to Germany. Half non-Italian though it was, its population was far more military than any other within the borders of Italy, and its royal family was energetic and ambitious. It was military strength, good statesmanship and a certain honesty which allowed the House of Savoy to be recognised as the representative of the national aspirations of Italy; much the same qualities produced an analogous result for the Hohenzollerns in Germany. The King, Charles Albert, was already favourably known for his decided opposition to the House of Austria. He had declared his hope that all Italy would join to expel the foreigner: he was brave, with a real touch of heroism in his character; but his policy was so hesitating that he was called *Re tentenna*; his policy was declared to be the policy of see-saw; and he is generally known to history as 'the Hamlet of Savoy.' The explanation of his hesitations and changes is to be found partly in his temperament; partly in his strong devotion to the Catholic Church; but above all in the fact that he distrusted liberalism as endangering the unity and energy of the State. He would have liked to have driven out the Austrians from Italy without conceding political liberty to the people, and he would have wished to reign over a United Italy as a strong if not an absolute monarch. Only gradually did he see that political liberty was an essential condition of national victory.

The eyes of Italian patriots were already fixed on Charles Albert. His declarations in favour of a united Italy had been outspoken. Journalism was freer in Turin than elsewhere in Italy, and patriots driven from their own states found an asylum there. Foremost among the writers in the journals was the Count Cavour, destined to so great a share in the emancipation of Italy. He was editor of the *Risorgimento*, and it was he who, at a meeting of editors to consider the situation, urged them frankly to demand a constitution; all other reforms which they desired, he said, would either flow from this or were contained in it. Their opinion was forwarded to the King, but received no answer. But Charles Albert had to choose between a determined resistance to, or a frank acceptance of, the wishes of his people. The first would have meant civil war and union with the hated Austrian power. He chose the second, not half-heartedly as Ferdinand and Leopold had done, but with a thoroughly honest purpose. In February 1848 he issued an edict announcing the early grant of a constitution, which followed a few days later. It led him to war, to disaster, to exile, and to death; but it led his son to the throne of a United Italy. It established a limited and parliamentary monarchy, on the model of the English Constitution. It served not only for the kingdom of Sardinia, but for the kingdom of Italy, which was soon to come into being; and with slight changes it was the constitution of Italy till Mussolini came.

Not only Italy, but all Europe was ablaze with revolution now. In

February 1848 the monarchy of Louis Philippe fell in France. And in March Prince Metternich fled from hostile demonstrations in Vienna. He had ruled Austria and, through Austria, Italy for so long that his fall, which proved final, was bound to have the most important consequences. Popular demonstrations broke out in Milan at once. Students, workmen, journalists and tradesmen surrounded the castle with hostile intentions. The Viceroy was away from Milan. His deputy made concessions, but they were far from satisfying the demands of the insurgents. The revolt assumed definite form and organisation, and after five days of hard fighting the Austrian troops were driven off and the patriots were left in possession of the great city. About the same time the Governments (which were really Austrian) were driven from Parma and Modena. More important was the rising of Venice against her Austrian masters. The patriotic leader, Daniel Manin, was released from prison, and he at once assumed the leadership of the movement. A civic guard was organised and the Austrian garrison found itself hopelessly outnumbered. The governor determined to withdraw his men from the city, and their departure was greeted with cheers for Saint Mark, Italy, and Pius IX. The Pope's name would soon cease to be associated with the national hopes!

War was inevitable, for Austria would certainly not accept as final her humiliating surrender to the despised Italians. Nor could Milan, Venice, and Lombardy by themselves hope to resist the reinforced armies of Austria. All turned on Charles Albert and the kingdom of Sardinia. He had less hesitation about making war than about granting a constitution. On March 23 he issued a proclamation to the peoples of Lombardy and Venice declaring that his people sympathised with the heroic struggles of their neighbours against their oppressors, and that they were coming to give them that assistance which a brother expects from a brother, and a friend from a friend. He declared that they trusted in the help of God 'who had given Pius IX to Italy to show her the way to help herself,' and he unfurled the tricolour banner of a United Italy. The Sardinian army, mainly consisting of Piedmontese soldiers, at once crossed the Ticino. The sword must now decide the fate of Italy; and the sword of Austria proved the heavier and the sharper.

The war was a great disappointment to the patriots. In truth they had little to which they could trust except the genuine enthusiasm and devotion which actuated most of those who fought in the Italian ranks. Outside Piedmont there was little organisation, and the help that came from the states of the centre and the south was of little consequence. Charles Albert's heart was in the struggle, as he clearly showed when disaster came, and his physical courage was beyond reproach, but he had little military skill and he found no generals to distinguish themselves in the war. The Austrians—in spite of the troubles that were shaking the State at home—were more favourably situated. Though forced to retire before the first attack of the Italians, they held in the famous quadrilateral (Verona, Peschiera, Legnago and Mantua) places of great strength which gave to the Austrian army a sure road by which it could maintain its connections with Austria and receive reinforcements. In Radetzky, though he was over eighty years of age, they had a commander whose energy and skill were recognised by his bitterest opponents,[1] and the general discipline and skill of the Austrian armies were far above those of their opponents. Only the complete collapse of the Austrian power north of the Alps could probably have saved the Italians from complete defeat.

There was no real union among the Italian states. There was strong local feeling in Milan, in Venice, in the duchies of the centre, and above all in Naples and Sicily. Until the fortunes of the war threatened to turn against them they were for the most part unwilling to subordinate themselves to the kingdom of Sardinia, and still more to incorporate themselves with it. There was friction between Milan and Venice, and in all the states there was strife between the republicans and the royalists. Mazzini came to Milan, and hoped to turn the movement in a republican direction; for the republic was to him a matter of religion and almost untouched by considerations of prudence. Beneath the surface there were anarchical groups working equally against both Mazzini and the royalists. There was talk of an Italian league, but it was never a favourite idea with Charles Albert, and it came to nothing. Towards the end of the war several states—Piacenza, Parma, Modena, Milan and Venice—voted for incorporation with Sardinia; but the movement was too late to be effective, though it prepared the way for the subsequent action of all Italian states ten years later.

The Austrians had already been driven out of Milan. They withdrew still further to the east. The Italian troops showed at times great courage and could claim victories. Their greatest was the capture of the important fortress of Peschiera. But when Radetzky was ready for the counter-attack the end soon came. On July 25, 1848, the Italians were heavily defeated on the twice fatal field of Custozza. Charles Albert was driven back on Milan. The Milanese were of course angry at the failure of their hopes. The friction with the Piedmontese was increased by defeat, and Charles Albert was even accused of having betrayed the national cause. The way in which the patriots threw mud at one another in the hour of crisis is not a pleasant story for the modern historians of Italy. The Austrians entered Milan again. Charles Albert and the Sardinian army were allowed to withdraw beyond the frontier. Mazzini declared that the royal war was over and the people's war must now begin, and he raised a banner with his favourite device 'God and the People.' Garibaldi withdrew to the mountains and

---

[1] The famous phrase 'In Ihrem Lager liegt Oesterreich' (All Austria is in your camp), applied to Radetzky, shows alike the desperate situation of Austria and her dependence on military success.

dreamed of continuing a guerrilla war. But to most men it was obvious
that all prospect of successful resistance was over.

It remains to consider briefly the behaviour of the rulers of the
various Italian states during this time of hope and confusion; for in
their behaviour is to be found the explanation of the fact that when at
last the Italian victory was won Italian unity was secured not by any
scheme of federation, such as was adopted in Germany—where the
local differences in language, race, and character were not nearly so
great as in Italy—but by the incorporation of the whole of Italy in the
kingdom of Sardinia. No ruler of Italy, with the single exception of
Charles Albert, showed any real devotion to the national cause; and the
national cause, therefore, when it triumphed could make no use of any
other of them.

We have already traced the fortunes of Pius IX as far as his flight to
Gaeta. His name disappeared from the hatbands, the standards, and
the battle-cries of Italian soldiers henceforth. The King of Naples had
never had any of the real belief which animated Pius IX in the cause of
Italy and constitutionalism, and took the first opportunity of joining
the cause of reaction. The national movement threatened indeed his
dominions with disruption, for Sicily showed no inclination to be satisfied with equal rights in the constitution of Naples. The inhabitants
had thrown down the statues of the Bourbon kings and had declared
that Sicily was henceforward an independent State. The rebellion mas-
tered the whole island, and the crown was offered to the second son of
Charles Albert, who, however, thought it wise to refuse it. Ferdinand's
acceptance of the constitution had from the first been hypocritical, and
the denunciation of the war by the Pope induced him to throw away all
pretence. He declared indeed at first that it was his 'firm and immutable
will' to maintain the constitution, but he withdrew the troops that he
had sent to the help of the national cause in the north of Italy. Then,
disorders in Naples, which were easily suppressed, gave him an excuse
for dismissing his Parliament and in fact withdrawing the constitution.
Sicily was now invaded. Messina was taken and cruelly punished. The
intervention of the French and English fleets stopped further military
operations; but it was clear that the old régime would be restored in
both parts of the Neapolitan monarchy.

Leopold, the Grand Duke of Tuscany, was not of such base metal as
Ferdinand of Naples, and we have seen how easily the constitution had
been established in Tuscany. The Parliament was organised; a popular
Ministry was appointed. The Grand Duke even declared his approval
of the idea which seemed to many, including Mazzini, to offer some
chance of Italian liberty and unity, when the arms of Sardinia had been
broken in the campaign which ended at Custozza. This was to call a
Constituent Assembly consisting of representatives of the different
Italian states, which should settle the conditions of union and a federal
government for Italy. The scheme failed, and was bound to fail because

Sardinia, which even in defeat was the most powerful of Italian states, would have none of it. Soon afterwards it was denounced by the Pope. The opposition of the Pope was the cause or the excuse for Leopold to abandon not only the idea of 'the Constituent Assembly,' but also the national cause as a whole. He went first to Siena and then escaped to Gaeta and joined the Pope in the territory of the King of Naples. There was therefore, ten years later, no place for the Grand Duke of Tuscany in the free Italy that was then established. The smaller dukes played no better part, and Modena and Parma readily accepted the rule of Austria which they had for the moment thrown off.

The behaviour of Sardinia was very different, and she had her reward. The truce which had been signed after the Austrian occupation of Milan was no settlement of the problem of the future of Italy. The Parliament at Turin demanded the renewal of the war and Genoa threatened a republic if the Austrian terms were accepted. Charles Albert therefore led out again the discouraged troops to face their victorious opponents. At Novara (on March 23, 1849) the Piedmontese army (for the Sardinian army had its main support in Piedmontese soldiers) was completely defeated, with some suspicion of treason among the commanders. Charles Albert declared that he had sacrificed everything for the cause of Italy; that he had not been able to find death on the battlefield; and that as he was now the chief obstacle to peace he would resign the crown. His son Victor Emmanuel became king; Charles Albert retired to Portugal and died there a few months later.

Victor Emmanuel could not foresee that fate had in store for him the glorious throne of a United Italy. But in the first days of his reign he did much to secure it. He was urged, in the negotiations which followed the battle of Novara, to abandon the constitution and better terms were offered him if he would consent; but he steadily refused. In his first proclamation to the people he pointed to the enemies, both internal and external, which threatened the constitution; but declared himself its determined defender. Alone among the princes of Italy he nailed the flag of liberty to his mast.

The Revolution now only held its own at two points on Italian soil: at Rome and Venice. These two romantic chapters of Italian history must be very briefly summarised. The flight of the Pope had left the Eternal City in great confusion. The Pope in vain tried to rule from his place of exile. The extremer spirits of the nationalist movement came to Rome, and among them Mazzini. A revolutionary republic was set up and the government was placed in the hands of a triumvirate (consisting of Mazzini, Saffi and Armellini); but in fact it was Mazzini who directed the whole policy of the republic. Garibaldi—already the chosen hero of Italy—came and placed his sword at the disposal of the triumvirate. Together Mazzini and Garibaldi challenged the power of Austria and of the Papacy in the name of God and the People.

The contest was in any case a hopeless one, for the republic would soon have been crushed between the forces of Naples and of Austria. But another Power entered the arena and decided the issue. France was still a republic and its president was Bonaparte, soon to be Napoleon III, who knew something of Italian revolutions and had some sympathy with them. He needed, however, the support of the clergy, and he feared the establishment of the power of Austria in Rome. He decided, therefore, to interfere, and he despatched a French army to Civita Vecchia to overthrow the republic and restore the government of the Pope. Oudinot, the French commander, underrated at first the power of Garibaldi, and was sharply checked on his first advance. But then reinforcements were brought up. The Neapolitans gave some assistance to the foreign invader. On June 30 the city fell into the hands of the French. Garibaldi decided to withdraw into the mountains before the French entered, and appealed for volunteers to follow him. 'I offer neither pay nor quarters nor provisions; I offer hunger, thirst, forced marches, battles and death. Let him who loves his country in his heart and not with his lips only follow me.' A number of volunteers responded to the heroic challenge. They were pursued and dispersed, and Garibaldi only escaped at last after much suffering; but many of those who went out of Rome with him lived to play a part in the triumph of ten years later.

Venice had shaken off the lethargy of centuries to take a part in the national movement. We have seen how the news of the revolution at Milan had stirred her to a similar movement. Manin proved a great leader. Venice declared herself an independent republic and co-operated with the movement in Milan. Later, when fortune was turning against the national cause, the Venetians consented to a close union with Milan and Piedmont under the leadership of Charles Albert. But, as we have seen, the Austrian arms pressed on to victory. Even after Custozza and Novara, however, the Venetians fought on. But Venice was no longer the impregnable city that she had been in the days before long-distance artillery had been invented. The Austrians bombarded the city and did great damage. Cholera came to intensify the sufferings of the population. At last, on August 24, Manin recognised that further resistance was impossible. He retired into exile and the city passed again into the power of the Austrians.

So ended in entire failure the first attempt of Italy to win unity and liberty. What enthusiasm and a few great leaders could do had been nobly done. But discipline and unity in leadership and in organisation had been notably and fatally absent. Italy, moreover, had found no help from any outside power. Charles Albert had proudly declared that Italy could save herself (*Italia farà da se*). Count Cavour, the soberest and wisest brain among the statesmen of Italy, was among his supporters. He doubted Italy's power of settling her own fate without foreign help. He saw that the sword of France must if possible be thrown into the scale against the sword of Austria, and it was the constant effort of his statecraft to bring about that result.

7•

CHAPTER XV

THE EASTERN QUESTION AND THE CRIMEAN WAR

SECTION I.—THE NEAR EASTERN QUESTION, 1804–53

AT the end of the eighteenth century the Near Eastern question assumed its modern form. Three factors determined it: the growing weakness of the Turk at Constantinople, the rise of small, vigorous Christian nationalities in the Balkan peninsula, and the effect of both on the policy of the Great Powers. Between the years 1788 and 1791 Austria and Russia attacked Turkey in concert, and Russia, asserting that she was the protector of Christians in the Turkish Empire, advanced as far as the port of Oczakov on the Black Sea. The younger Pitt, speaking for England, denounced the danger of the Russian advance and the menace to Turkey's integrity. Parliament did not support him over this incident, but he had set the fashion for his successors; for almost ninety years to come they followed a pro-Turkish and anti-Russian policy. Austria, too, showed a moderate attitude to Turkey in 1791. She returned nearly all her conquests to Turkey and henceforth sought to protect her. For, by 1791, both England and Austria had recognised that Turkey was a menace, not because of her strength, but because of her weakness.

At the dawn of the nineteenth century, then, Russia began to creep south down the Black Sea coast, her eyes always on Constantinople as an ultimate goal. Austria couched on Russia's flank, a suspicious hound threatening to spring when Russia was once engaged with Turkey. England watched from afar, resolved to protect the commerce of the East Mediterranean and to defend Constantinople itself against attack. The disturbances always began by the attempts of small Balkan nationalities to assert their independence of Turkey, and the Great Powers then interfered to regulate or to improve their status. The Turkish attitude was always the same. For Christian subjects (*rayahs* as they were called) to rebel was an unspeakable presumption. Sometimes the Turk tried to anticipate such plans by massacre, and his massacres increased as his power grew weaker. At other times the Turk, though forced to grant some status or privileges to Christian individuals or races, attempted to evade or delay the execution of the provisions. Reform or concession was never granted to a Turkish subject except under pressure of the Great Powers. If granted in theory it was always, as far as possible, withdrawn in practice. Much ingenuity was shown in setting the Great Powers by the ears. The three several elements of the problem then are, first, an Oriental Government established in Europe, misgoverning millions of Christians, and slowly disintegrating in power. Next, there is a collection of Great Powers, of which Russia alone generally seeks to accelerate Turkish disintegration.

Last, a collection of small subject Christian nationalities all gradually organising, educating and strengthening themselves to throw off the Turkish yoke. This situation produced, during the nineteenth century, endless rebellions of subjects against the Sultan, three Russo-Turkish wars, and two wars in which France and England, as well as Russia, took a part for or against Turkey. Of these subject nationalities the Rumanians inhabited the provinces of Moldavia and Wallachia (modern Rumania).[1] They had always been ruled as separate principalities with native governors and a quasi-independent status. The chief racial areas, inhabited respectively by Serbs, Bulgars and Greeks, correspond roughly to the boundaries of their respective territories in 1913. Serbia and Greece were more dependent on Constantinople than Moldavia and Wallachia, but no large Turkish population lived in either. Both the district and population of Bulgaria adjoined Constantinople, and hence the emancipation of Bulgaria lagged behind that of Serbia or Greece.

It was the Serbs, and not the Greeks, who struck the first blow for Balkan freedom. The revolt began in 1804 under Kara (Black) George, the ancestor of the Karageorgević dynasty of Serbia. It was a story of heroic fights and bloody massacres on both sides. But after eight years Kara George maintained his position, and in the Russo-Turkish Treaty of 1812 obtained a promise of autonomy. He was defeated in 1813, and fled the country. Then in 1815 his rival, enemy and ultimate murderer, Miloš Obrenović, raised another revolt. He was successful in asserting the *de facto* independence of Serbia at once and, after many and very tedious delays, secured a constitution and the recognition of himself as Prince of Serbia.[2]

The obscure struggle of peasant heroes against Turkish armies thrice their size attracted little attention in Europe. But all the Great Powers became stirred when the Greeks rebelled in 1820. Russia was excited by the execution of the Patriarch of Constantinople and by massacres of Greek Christians, and it was feared that she would at once attack Turkey. Austria and England at once took measures to avert this danger. For some years Canning and Metternich were in agreement in principle. The struggle between Turkey and her Greek rebels was nobody else's affair. The duty of the Great Powers was to 'hold the ring' and to permit none of their number to use force. For, if Russia tried to settle the quarrel by war, Canning believed she would 'gobble Greece at one mouthful and Turkey at the next!' This situation lasted from 1820 till the end of 1825. Then a striking change occurred. The Sultan appealed for aid to Mehemet Ali, Pasha of Egypt, and Mehemet

---

[1] Rumania, as constituted in 1913, included Moldavia and Wallachia and part of the Dobruja, about 7–8 millions in all. After the war of 1914–18 she doubled her population and added Bessarabia, the Bukovina, Transylvania and part of Hungary.

[2] In substance, though the treaty took years to execute, Miloš was assured of this by 1829.

sent his son Ibrahim and a disciplined army to the Morea. His success was so great that Russia declared she must intervene to save the Greeks from extinction.

Canning decided that the only way of averting war was for England to act with Russia in putting pressure on Turkey. Austria declined to do this and stood aloof. England and Russia signed an agreement to this effect on April 4, 1826. Turkey was to be urged to make an armistice with the Greeks and to grant to them a measure of 'Home Rule.' But even so, force was not actually proposed, and it was not until July 6, 1827 (and after France had joined as a third party), that the Allies signed a definite treaty to employ force towards Turkey, in case of her refusal to listen to the Allies' proposal to accept an armistice and give autonomy to Greece. This led, just after Canning's death (August 12, 1827), to the Battle of Navarino. There, the joint British, French, and Russian squadrons destroyed the Turkish and Egyptian fleets. This great catastrophe to Turkey rendered not only the autonomy, but the independence, of Greece inevitable, though the death of Canning probably made a great difference to the form it assumed.

Early in 1828 Russia took exactly the step which Canning had tried to prevent, and declared war upon Turkey direct and alone.[1] But, though English and French remonstrances were little heeded by Czar Nicholas, it does not seem that at this time he intended the destruction of the Turkish Empire, or even the immediate annexation of large parts of it.

After preliminary reverses the Russian army reached Adrianople in the summer of 1829. Diebitsch, the commanding general, despite the smallness and demoralisation of his army, assumed the airs of a conqueror and summoned the Turks to make peace. The Sultan was cowed and the Treaty of Adrianople was promptly signed (September 14, 1829). Territory was indeed acquired in Asia at Turkey's expense, which resulted in an advance in the Caucasus area. But nothing similar was acquired, or attempted to be acquired, in Europe. Russia's boundary with Turkey was still the river Pruth, far to the north of Moldavia. Her policy in Europe was not annexation but peaceful penetration.

France and England were very much afraid that Greece would become a vassal state dependent on Russia. Wellington, therefore, proposed to divide her into two halves so as to make her as small and weak as possible. Aberdeen even went further, and proposed to 'trisect' her. Happily Wellington and Aberdeen were turned out, and wiser counsels

---

[1] As is well known, the Allies had maintained that the battle of Navarino was 'an untoward event' and England refused throughout to consider herself at war with Turkey. So did France, though she took the strong step in 1828 of sending troops to compel the evacuation of the Morea. The fact is that the Treaty of London of July 6, 1827, was Canning's work, and not approved by his successor Wellington or by France.

prevailed under Palmerston and Grey. The boundaries of Greece were enlarged to include Arta and Volo; she was declared independent, and guaranteed a loan and a monarchy (1832). The recognition by Russia, France and England of her independence, to which Russia consented with extreme reluctance, was an important landmark in Balkan history. The experience of the later nineteenth century showed that Balkan states which became independent were zealous to remain so. They regarded their own interests first, and those did not usually coincide with Russia's or with those of any other Great Power. To recognise a Balkan state as independent of Turkey was really a way of helping her to become independent of Russia. And Greece got rid of Russian influence at once. In the Principalities Russia was by no means successful in asserting her influence; the Rumanians already cherished, and for long maintained, a bitter hatred of Russia. In Serbia the reigning Prince (Miloš Obrenović) managed to use Russia as a catspaw in his frequent bickerings with the Turks.

In relation to Turkey herself the experience of Russia was wholly different. For her the Czar Nicholas soon won what seemed to be a great and startling triumph. The policy of Russia after 1829 was, for at least ten years, a singular reversal of her traditional aim to press on to Constantinople, annexing as much territory as possible on the way. A committee of Russian statesmen was appointed by Czar Nicholas in 1829 to examine the results of the probable break-up of the Turkish Empire. They reported, contrary to Russian traditional policy, that it was desirable to preserve the integrity of the Turkish Empire. If Turkey dissolved further, they said, with a good deal of prophetic insight, strong small Balkan states would be formed, and Russia would prove unable to influence them. On the other hand, she already had treaty rights and influence in Turkey as it was, which she could increase by economic control and peaceful penetration. If Russia was to seek territory it should be in the direction of Armenia or Baghdad, not Constantinople. Nicholas grumbled but accepted the report, and his policy was for ten years the *status quo* and the integrity of Turkey.

Nicholas communicated his ideas to Austria, and obtained Metternich's support for a decade. But he was too proud to explain his policy to England, and Palmerston continued to oppose Russia and to believe that she intended to annex Constantinople and to seize the Dardanelles. 'Pam' might have divined the truth when he saw Austria so friendly with Russia, but he did not.[1]

It was, in fact, not Russia but France which was active in a policy of dismembering Turkey during the period 1830–41. This is the time when she secured Algiers; it is the period also when she favoured the revolt of Egypt against Turkey, and sought by this means to secure

---

[1] Palmerston believed, quite wrongly, that the Convention of Münchengrätz (September 18, 1833) was, in fact, a partition of Turkey by Austria and Russia. Secrecy again was harmful to the despotic Powers.

help for her own Mediterranean schemes. England, on the other hand, was as anxious as ever to preserve the Turkish Empire, and therefore naturally opposed the French scheme.

The real trouble lay in Egypt. There, Mehemet Ali, the bold and ambitious Pasha, had long been in only nominal subordination to the Sultan, but had sent troops to assist the Sultan in subduing Greece. He had already become Pasha of Crete, and hoped to add the pashaliks of Syria and Damascus to that of Egypt. The Sultan showed himself jealous and suspicious, and listened to advisers who were the personal enemies of Mehemet. That bold Pasha thought himself, and perhaps actually was, in danger, and decided to avert any possible design to expel him from Egypt by attacking the Sultan and seizing Damascus and Syria. So Mehemet Ali called on his warlike son Ibrahim, and instructed him to start a 'preventive war' against the Sultan.

In November 1831 Ibrahim invaded Palestine by sea and land with a small but well-disciplined army. His march was as successful as Allenby's in 1918. Jaffa, Gaza, and Jerusalem fell in rapid succession; he was delayed, like Napoleon, at Acre, but ultimately captured the city (May 1832). Damascus fell in June, Aleppo in July, and Ibrahim actually crossed the Taurus mountain range, winning another victory in the Beylan Pass, before the end of the month. He was equally successful in diplomacy, posing as a liberal and a loyal subject of the Sultan at the same time. In December 1832 Sultan Mahmud sent his last army against Ibrahim. That great warrior utterly routed it at Koniah. The Sultan was thus at the mercy of his victorious and rebellious vassal.

The Sultan had already been imploring England for aid, but for once Palmerston was unwilling to bring England to the aid of Turkey, a policy at once very bold and very dangerous.[1] At the moment of the disaster of Koniah a Russian mission arrived at Constantinople and the Sultan, in despair, turned to the hereditary enemy for help. 'A drowning man,' said one of his advisers, 'clings to a serpent (for aid)'; and the Sultan clung to Russia. The Czar, like the Sultan, hated 'rebels,' and a bargain was ultimately struck. In February 1833 the 'drowning man' formally demanded assistance from 'the serpent.' On February 20 a Russian naval squadron anchored off Constantinople, the only time one ever appeared there with Turkish consent. In April six thousand Russian troops landed on the Asiatic shore opposite Constantinople. The Sultan was thus safe, and meanwhile France and England both put pressure on Turkey to make concessions to Mehemet Ali. As a result, by the end of April 1833, the Sultan ceded to him Palestine, Syria, Aleppo, Damascus, with permission to occupy the seaports of Adana, and Ibrahim withdrew to Syria. The crisis seemed ended.

[1] Stratford Canning, England's Ambassador at Constantinople, dissented from 'Pam's' view and advocated at this time, in substance, the policy 'Pam' adopted in 1841.

The Russian troops also began to withdraw from Asia, but, before they did so, the Turkish Sultan was made to sign a secret treaty with Russia. The Treaty of Unkiar Skelessi (July 8, 1833) was in reality an offensive and defensive alliance between the two Powers. By a secret article, which only gradually leaked out, Russia waived her rights for Turkish military aid, and Turkey agreed in return to close the Dardanelles to all warships *au besoin* (and *au besoin* meant at the demand of Russia). Had this treaty ever become operative Turkey would have been, in every sense, a vassal of Russia. Nicholas seemed to have the practical, if unavowed, control of the Straits, of Constantinople, and of the Sultan.[1] But the victory was too complete, the obstacles too great. The entry of Russia's warships into the Straits would have meant war with England, and France had strong reasons for supporting Egypt against Turkey. Palmerston was all for the integrity of the Turk as against Egypt, and therefore high in favour with the Sultan. If he was able to avert the Egyptian danger, the Sultan would lean in future on England and not on Russia. His dependence on the latter Power was veiled, so he need not be embarrassed when evading the obligations of Unkiar Skelessi.

Sultan Mahmud was prepared to be just as treacherous towards Egypt as he intended to be to Russia. And he had a chance of success against Ibrahim, for that professed liberal had speedily alienated his Syrian subjects by his tyranny. Sultan Mahmud realised that, if his generals struck Ibrahim on the flank, the Syrians might rise against him. The Sultan undoubtedly gave the provocation, for in April 1839 he sent a Turkish army to Bir on the Euphrates and made it cross from the left to the right bank, thus enabling it to strike at Ibrahim's communications between Palestine and the Adana ports. The Great Powers at once got alarmed, and it was agreed to send a joint Franco-British squadron to the Bosphorus, in case the Russians entered Turkey. It was too late: the last act of the dying Sultan was to tell his general to attack Ibrahim. The Turks moved against Ibrahim early in June. Three severe blows followed in relentless succession. On the 24th Ibrahim utterly routed the Turks at Nezib, capturing 15,000 prisoners and all their guns and stores. On July 1 old Mahmud died, and was succeeded by Abdul Mejid, an ignorant boy of sixteen. Immediately afterwards the Ottoman fleet sailed off to Alexandria and surrendered to Mehemet Ali, alleging as a pretext that Constantinople was sold to the Russians. Mehemet Ali, proud of the triumphs of his son and of Egyptian arms, was intoxicated, and thought he could retain his prizes and his power. But he had gravely miscalculated. Turkey, or even Europe, he might defy, but there was one person he could not defy, and that was Palmerston.

---

[1] The meaning of this secret article is still disputed. But it is noticeable that the Strait of the Dardanelles is at the western end of the Sea of Marmora and that the article makes no reference to the strait at the eastern end, *i.e.* the Bosphorus.

If Palmerston had hesitated in 1832, he acted at once in 1839. The boy-Sultan alternated between bombast and panic, France was secretly supporting Egypt, Nicholas was playing his own game, Austria was timid and doubtful. But Palmerston had two assets: his own resolution and British sea power. A British blockade of Alexandria at once began, though the French refused to co-operate. Palmerston replied by proposing a Conference of the Great Powers at Vienna. Negotiations dragged on, Russia intervened, and France procrastinated. Palmerston drove on the European team with the fury of Jehu, and Egypt and France were crushed beneath his wheels.

What happened was this. Finding reason to suspect France of favouring Egypt, 'Pam' got a Convention signed in London on July 15, 1840, with Austria, Prussia, and Russia. The terms were that Mehemet Ali was to become hereditary Pasha of Egypt and Pasha of Acre for life. If he did not evacuate all other conquests and accept these terms within ten days, he was henceforth to be confined to Egypt alone.[1] There were two difficulties in this Convention. It was signed without France and force would be necessary to make it effective against Mehemet Ali. 'Pam' soon showed that he was equal to both emergencies and was prepared, in cheerful and characteristic fashion, to 'call' both 'bluffs.'

Guizot, to whom 'Pam' communicated the news of the Convention, told him that the exclusion of France was 'a mortal affront.' Thiers, the Prime Minister, declared that the good relations with England were shattered, and pushed on military preparations; the whole French press screamed with rage. Palmerston never had believed that France would make war on him, and in this case he was right in his belief. The wrath of France evaporated soon after the fiery words had been uttered. Brave old Soult, who became French Prime Minister in October, knew that war with England would risk the dynasty. Meanwhile, 'Pam' secured a great triumph over his other opponent.

Mehemet Ali allowed the ten days prescribed in the terms of the Great Powers to pass without any formal notice, but a British and Austrian squadron appeared off Beirut and demanded the Egyptian evacuation of Syria (August 11). On September 9 Admiral Stopford bombarded the town and landed a Turkish force. On October 9 he captured Beirut. Syria at once rose in revolt against Ibrahim, and the British squadron moved on to Acre. That city had defied the Crusaders for two years, Ibrahim for six months, and Napoleon for two. On November 3 Admiral Stopford destroyed it in three hours! For the second time a British Admiral had made Ibrahim miss his destiny.[2]

Ibrahim knew well enough the value of sea power and the danger to his communications, and prepared hastily to evacuate Syria. Egypt

---

[1] Austria, as well as Great Britain, definitely promised to give naval aid to Turkey (Art. 2) if Mehemet Ali refused the terms.

[2] Sir E. Codrington, by destroying the Turkish and Egyptian fleet at Navarino, prevented Ibrahim from conquering Greece in 1827.

itself was now in danger. The boy-Sultan had plucked up courage to depose Mehemet Ali.[1] That worthy received the news with calmness. This, he said, was his fourth deposition. He hoped to get over it as well as he had done the other three, with the help of God and the Prophet! But he changed his tone when Admiral Napier appeared before Alexandria and threatened to address him with the iron lips of cannon. He capitulated at once, and signed a Convention (November 27) promising to submit and to evacuate Syria, provided that he was guaranteed as the hereditary Pasha of Egypt. The Sultan and the Great Powers demurred to this conclusion. But 'Pam' had his way, and triumphed over all opponents. Mehemet Ali survived his fourth deposition, but was confined in future to Egypt. The solution was a permanent one. Men began to see what they had previously forgotten, that the conquests of one Eastern potentate over the other, of Amurath over Amurath, are essentially fleeting. The Syrians, who had welcomed Ibrahim as a deliverer, revolted against him as a tyrant. Mehemet Ali had once threatened Constantinople: neither he nor his son ever again even threatened Palestine. Egypt, which Mehemet Ali and Ibrahim had made greater than Turkey, actually became weaker than it in the space of fourteen years. Deprived of its leaders, overburdened with debt, and distracted by internal disputes, it was the feeblest of the provinces of the Turkish Empire in 1854. France, which had aimed at giving Syria to Egypt or to herself, was discredited, and Palmerston earned the undying gratitude of the Sultan.

The triumph of 'Pam' was completed by the signing of a Convention on July 13, 1841, whereby the Great Powers and the Sultan pledged themselves not to permit 'vessels of war belonging to foreign powers' to enter the Dardanelles and the Bosphorus. Russia still believed that the principles of the Treaty of Unkiar Skelessi could be maintained, and was inclined to be quite friendly to England, whom she regarded as a dupe. In fact, the Czar was wholly mistaken. The Sultan regarded him as an interested bully, to whose menaces he had been compelled to submit while in danger, but against whom he could now invoke the disinterested England. Quite unaware of all this Nicholas sought a *rapprochement* with England, and an understanding as to the future, in the famous conversation he had with Lord Aberdeen in 1844.[2] There is no doubt about what he said. Czar Nicholas expressed the view that the Turk was 'a dying man,' that his Empire was disintegrating, and that it was well to make provision beforehand. He meant to have Constantinople and, in return, England was to have Egypt or Crete as

---

[1] This was a distinct blunder and contrary to the terms of the Allied Convention of July 15, 1840.

[2] In 1841 the Whigs (and 'Pam') went out and were succeeded by Peel, with Aberdeen as Foreign Secretary. The conversation of 1844 is in Stockmar, *Memoirs*, vol. II. pp. 106 *sqq*., and Martin's *Prince Consort*, vol. I. p. 215; cp. H. Temperley: *England and the Near East: The Crimea*, pp. 253–7 (Longmans, 1936).

well if she liked.   That, said Nicholas, would show that he was ready
to observe the Balance of Power and to give a fair compensation
to England.   The proposition was much misrepresented during the
Crimean War, when Czar Nicholas figured in the Jingo Press as 'a giant
liar,' and England as a Crusader protecting the right.   But it is singular
to note that this wise and statesmanlike suggestion of Nicholas was
actually adopted in 1915.   Sir Edward Grey then agreed to Russia
having Constantinople, and his reason is obvious.   Cyprus and Egypt
had already been declared British possessions and the Suez Canal route
to India was in our hands.   There was, therefore, no reason why we
should not favour Russia's claims on Constantinople.   As we were
offered equally efficient safeguards in 1844 it seems to follow that
England might have agreed to this proposition then.

The reason England did not had already been brusquely and brutally
expressed by 'Pam' in 1839.   'All that we hear every day of the week
about the decay of the Turkish Empire, and its being a dead body or a
sapless trunk, and so forth, is pure and unadulterated nonsense.'[1]   No
compromise was possible when the Czar said the Turk was 'a dying
man' and 'Pam' answered 'Nonsense!'   Therein lay the germ of the
Crimean War.

SECTION II.—THE CRIMEAN WAR

THE Crimean War occupies a peculiar place in the history of Europe in
the nineteenth century.   The military methods resemble rather those of
the Napoleonic age than of the period soon to be opened by Moltke
and the military system of Prussia.   Steam vessels were used, but their
full importance was not appreciated.   The telegraph had been brought
to Vienna, but Constantinople and the Crimea were still beyond its
reach.   All that concerned the feeding and the sanitation of the armies
was almost mediaeval in character.   It was the last war on a large scale
to be fought without the help of the modern resources of science.   And
if its methods and instruments are strange to the modern student, its
aims and its diplomacy seem still more so.   Ecclesiastical questions that
might belong to the time of the Crusades play a part in the causes of
the war.   The victors in the struggle gained little if anything from it.
The integrity of Turkey was in fact not maintained.   The advance of
Russia was not permanently checked.   In the Great War of 1914 France
and Britain spent many thousands of lives and many millions of money
in the effort to undo some of the consequences of their victory in the
Crimean War, which had been won with so much loss of blood and
treasure.   Yet the war is in many ways very interesting.   It provides us
especially with a singularly instructive illustration of the way in which
wars are brought about, and the procedure of some of the actors in

---

[1] P. Guedalla: *Palmerston* (1926), pp. 212–13.

the story is seen without the concealment and the allegation of false motives behind which diplomatists have usually liked to work.

There were for this war, as for all wars, many converging causes. But of all these causes the condition of the Balkan peninsula was the most important. The Turkish power extended over the whole of it with the exception of the free kingdom of Greece. Few even among European diplomatists of that epoch had any clear idea of the network of races and religions and languages that filled up the peninsula. The Turkish rule was not intentionally cruel, nor actually so except when its authority was dangerously challenged, or, which was not always the same thing, thought by the Turks to be so challenged. It was everywhere little more than a garrison of occupation—maintaining, not very effectively, a sort of order, raising taxes, and for the rest letting the subject populations go their own way and follow their own ideas in social life and religion. But without question the Turkish power was growing weaker, less effective militarily, and more corrupt. It was little influenced by the progress of science and industry which had so changed the character of Western Europe, and for political liberty and the participation of the people in the administration of the government it had a deep-seated aversion. As Turkey grew weaker, and partly because it grew weaker, the subject nationalities and religions grew more self-conscious. The Greeks had already broken away and established an independent power. Their example produced inevitably stirrings among the other races. Beyond the Danube, in the Principalities of Moldavia and Wallachia, there was, in accordance with recent treaties, a large measure of self-government, and the people—not yet known as Rumanians—were eager for more. The Serbians were conscious of their great past and dissatisfied with the considerable amount of self-government which they had already won. The Montenegrins still maintained their practical independence behind their mountain fortresses. The Bulgarians, Albanians, and Macedonians were as yet hardly conscious of any separate existence, but their lands were full of disturbances resulting from a sense of the differences which separated them from their rulers. Religion was a potent element of the ferment of the country. There were many Mohammedans among the conquered peoples; but the Orthodox or Greek form of Christianity persisted among most, and of the Orthodox Church the Russian Czar was the admitted head. Religion in the Balkans was always apt to assume a strong political character, as has so often been the case in countries where open political action has been impossible.

The position in the Balkans was obviously unstable. A revolution might at any time occur in one of its districts which would seriously upset the Balance of Power; and the Great Powers to the north of the Danube watched events with anxiety in which ambition and fear both played a part. The Empire of Austria owed its origin to the necessity of barring the way against an invader from the lower course of the Danube, and its whole life was closely bound up with resistance to the Turkish power. Fear of the Turkish power had indeed now passed away; but that fear had been followed by another—the fear of the power which might take Turkey's place in the Balkan peninsula. Austria desired influence, if not territory, there for herself, and she feared the designs and ambitions of Russia. Of the nature of these ambitions there could hardly be any doubt. Russia was the great Slav state, and the majority of the population of the Balkans spoke Slavonic tongues. Even the Bulgarians, though not wholly Slavonic, had adopted a Slavonic language. Moreover, Russia, as we have already said, had religious grounds for interference on behalf of the members of the Orthodox Church. She claimed also that she possessed treaty rights of interference as well; and it was a constant matter of dispute as to how far these rights extended. In the Treaty of Kutchuk Kainarji, which was drawn up in 1774 between Russia and Turkey, there were two clauses which bear upon the controversy. By one article (14) Russia was allowed to build a Christian Church in Galata—a part of Constantinople —and to keep it always under her protection. By another article (7) Turkey promised to protect the Christian Church and religion within her dominions and to allow the Russian Ambassadors to make representations on behalf of the Church in Galata. On the ground of these articles the Russians claimed a right to represent and protect the Christian communities of the Balkans. This would have meant a perpetual danger of interference (think what it would have meant if the French had had the right in the eighteenth century to 'protect' the Catholics of Ireland), and the right claimed by Russia had never been admitted by Turkey.[1]

There was nothing necessarily evil or mean in Russia's ambitions. It doubtless seemed to the Czar a religious and national duty to do his best for those who belonged to the same religious communion and spoke the same tongue with his own Russian people. There could at any rate be no doubt about them. In January 1853 the Czar Nicholas had had a conversation with the English Ambassador which became famous. The Czar was an old friend of Lord Aberdeen, the English Prime Minister, and was on very friendly terms with Sir Hamilton Seymour. In this conversation, which had at once been reported to London and was published when the Crimean War broke out, the Czar spoke of Turkey as a country that 'seemed to be falling to pieces.' The Turk was, he said, 'a very sick man' who might suddenly die on their hands. It was very important to make up their minds as to what should

---

[1] But the other Great Powers (e.g. Austria-Hungary and Great Britain) had long admitted Russia had *some* right in the matter. In 1823 Metternich admitted this, and Canning stated that Russia had a special right of friendly advice on behalf of Christians in Turkey in peace time. He qualified this by saying he doubted whether this 'right extended to interference on behalf of subjects of the Party who had thrown off their allegiance.' *v.* H. Temperley: *The Foreign Policy of Canning* (1925), p. 325.

be done with his territories before that event occurred. England and Russia between them could settle it without war. Then he hinted pretty plainly at the settlement that he desired. The Balkan states were to be independent under Russian protection. Russia was to occupy Constantinople but not to annex it. Great Britain was to lay hands on Egypt. It was a partition of Turkish territories that he suggested between Great Britain and Russia, with France left out of the deal.[1] Great Britain showed no inclination to fall in with this scheme. The maintenance of the integrity of Turkey was the traditional British policy and there was no desire to alter it. The conversation created a deep distrust of the designs of Russia, perhaps unjustly.

Then arose the question of the Holy Places. This was in itself a serious matter, or rather the passions which it aroused were serious. It concerned the management of the places of pilgrimage at Jerusalem and especially the Church of the Nativity at Bethlehem. The Turkish Government kept order between the rival claims of the Latins or Roman Catholics and the Orthodox or Greek and Russian Christians. The French Government had a traditional right—running back to the times of the Crusades—to be considered the protector of the Christians in the East, but since the development of the power of Russia the Czars had begun to put forward their own claims. Genuine religious feeling came to strengthen national rivalry and political ambition, and furious passions were aroused by the question of the custody of the keys of the church at Bethlehem and the placing of a star in the grotto of the Sacred Manger.

Yet the world was hardly so mad as to be driven to war by these questions alone. The situation became grave only when the Czar sent to Constantinople Prince Menschikov—one of the most prominent figures at the Russian Court—to demand not merely concessions on these points, but also the recognition of the Russian claim to be accepted as the protector of the Christians of the Balkan peninsula. The chief part on the other side was played by Lord Stratford de Redcliffe (this title had been conferred on Stratford Canning in 1852). He feared and disliked Russia, and though he saw the weak points of Turkey very clearly, he was nevertheless determined to uphold her integrity and independence even at the risk of war. He took much responsibility upon himself. Communication with London took a long time, for the telegraph had not yet been brought to Constantinople. He persuaded the Sultan to make concessions on the comparatively trivial question of the 'Holy Places,' but to stand firm against the recognition of the

---

[1] The Czar was in fact only repeating a conversation he had had with Aberdeen at Windsor in 1844 (pp. 209–10 and notes)—and seems to have thought the latter agreed with him. The text of this conversation is in Stockmar's *Memoirs*, vol. II. p. 106, and Martin's *Prince Consort*, vol. I. p. 215. The transaction was communicated to each succeeding Foreign Secretary up till 1853, but none of them explicitly accepted it, nor did any Cabinet endorse it. Derby certainly rejected it for his government. *v.* H. Temperley: *England and the Near East*, pp. 253–7.

Russian protectorate of the Balkan Christians, which would inevitably lead to loss of independence. In May 1853 Menschikov left Constantinople in protest against this decision, and it was clear that war was dangerously threatening. The view that wars are always fought for economic interests finds little support in the origins of the Crimean War. National ambition, rivalry and fear are the motives which impelled the nations to what proved a severe struggle.

The withdrawal of Menschikov from Constantinople was a serious step; and the war that threatened all but came when a Russian army in July 1853 crossed the Pruth and occupied Moldavia and Wallachia. The action of Russia could be represented as falling short of actual war, for she had certain treaty rights in the Principalities; and diplomacy made a last attempt to avoid the outbreak of hostilities. Austria regarded the course of affairs with great interest, for the contest was close to her frontiers, and on lands in which she had ambitions if not claims. A conference was called at Vienna and a declaration was drawn up which aimed at protecting the Christian population of the Balkans without admitting the right of Russia to interfere. There was hope for a moment that peace might be preserved. Turkey refused to accept the declaration in its simple form; Russia accepted but gave a dangerous interpretation of it. Passion was growing hot in both countries, and on October 4, 1853, Turkey declared war against Russia. Lord Stratford de Redcliffe had perhaps tried to restrain her at the last moment.[1]

Who would be the combatants? The nations of Europe would not allow the war to be fought out as a duel between Turkey and Russia, for the interests involved were too great. Austria watched the contest with close attention; seemed again and again on the point of interfering, but never interfered. Prussia was sore, but she had lost confidence in herself through her failures during the revolutionary period. Some of her statesmen, including the rising Bismarck, saw in a situation which occupied the forces of Russia and the attention of Austria an opportunity for Prussia to play an important and decisive part. But the Prussian King was immovably disinclined to adventure, and Prussian influence was hardly perceptible during the course of the war. The actual combatants came from a further distance. Support of Turkey and jealousy of Russia were traditional in the foreign policy of England. The spread of Russian power into the Mediterranean would, it was thought, threaten Egypt and the road to India. The war fever developed under the influence of Palmerston and the press. In France under the régime of the new Empire public opinion played a much less important part. All rested with Napoleon III, and he had declared in words never to be forgotten that 'The Empire means peace.' Strong forces, however,

---

[1] Stratford's conduct is a source of much dispute. Aberdeen complained of his 'dishonesty,' and it has been asserted that, while formally trying to restrain the Sultan, he was secretly urging him on to war. It is not certain that all of his secret papers are extant, but the reluctance of Stratford to order up the fleet is in his favour.

pushed him into war; the desire to maintain the prestige of France in the East, his dependence on the Catholic and Clerical party in France, above all the need which he instinctively felt to give the country what it expected from a Napoleon—glory and victory. At the end of October 1853 the joint French and English fleets passed the Dardanelles to give their moral support to Turkey. While they were in the neighbourhood of Constantinople a Russian fleet attacked and destroyed a Turkish squadron near Sinope. This quite natural act of war seemed an insult to the two great Western Powers; and open war came on apace. It was declared by France and Britain in March 1854. It marked a great change in European politics when English and French soldiers appeared as allies and comrades on the battlefield (it was said with some exaggeration that it was the first time since the Crusades), and it may be said to mark the beginning of the *entente* which became fully established in the early twentieth century.

The Russians were in 'the Principalities.'[1] The first object of the Allies was to drive them out. This was soon accomplished—too soon to allow it to seem a great triumph and a reason for ending the war. The Russians had laid siege to Silistria, through which they thought to pass to a crossing of the Balkans and to a march on Constantinople. But the defence of the place was unexpectedly stubborn. The attitude of Austria, while Russia remained on the Danube, was menacing. The siege was abandoned and the Russians withdrew altogether from the Principalities, into which Austria sent a garrison, which was to hold them until the peace, when they were to be handed over to Turkey. If it had not been for the passions that had been aroused by the war peace might perhaps have come. But it would have seemed a tame ending to such great preparations. After an interchange of communications with Austria, Four Points were agreed on as summarising the programme of the war: (1) the abolition of the Russian Protectorate of the Danubian provinces; (2) the freedom of the navigation of the Danube; (3) the complete introduction of Turkey into 'the European equilibrium'; (4) the renunciation by Russia of her exclusive patronage of the Balkan Christians.

The war then must go on, but in what theatre? As often before, it proved difficult to discover a really vulnerable point in the wide territories of this loosely organised state. Cholera had already shown itself with appalling deadliness in the ranks of the Allies, and the French and English armies were in many ways unprepared for a great enterprise. But, on the insistence of the home authorities, it was determined to attack the Russian naval station of Sebastopol. It was believed that the task would be an easy one. The naval power of the Allies could be brought

---

[1] Roughly what was Rumania in 1913, forming the two provinces of Moldavia and Wallachia. Each was ruled by a native, but elected, Prince or Hospodar, under Turkish control. They had been several times militarily occupied by Russia since the beginning of the nineteenth century.

into use, and it would lead to the destruction of the Russian preponderance in the Black Sea, which was one of the declared objects of the war.

In September of the year 1854 the Allies—Turks, French and English—landed at Eupatoria to the north of Sebastopol. Marshal Saint-Arnaud and Lord Raglan then began their march on to the city itself. On September 20 they met the Russian commander, Menschikov, posted on the northern side of the river Alma. After hard fighting, in which the rapid dash of the French *zouaves* contrasted with the more deliberate methods of the English, the Russians were completely defeated, and the road to Sebastopol was open. The Allies probably made here the greatest of the many mistakes during the campaign. They did not attack the city at once, though the Russian commander, Todleben, held that such an attack could not have been resisted; and they made no attempt to establish any blockade on the north side of the river on which Sebastopol stands. Instead, they undertook a long and difficult march round to the south of the city and established their camp there. The interval thus allowed was brilliantly used by Todleben to throw up the fortifications which held the besiegers at bay from September 1854 to September 1855.

The great siege had some peculiar features. It was never a blockade. No serious attempt was made to cut off the city from communication with Russia. Stores and reinforcements were often attacked, but all through the siege men and supplies were thrown into Sebastopol after a long journey from Russia. Prince Menschikov commanded a considerable army in the hilly region to the east of the city, and from thence he constantly threatened the besieging armies and sometimes attacked them and inflicted serious loss. The plan of the Allies was to capture Sebastopol not by starvation but by bombardment and direct assault. The supremacy of the Allied navies was the very basis on which the whole siege depended; but the direct action of the navy was small. Neither in the Baltic nor in the Black Sea were the navies of the Allies able to inflict on the Russians really serious loss. The Russian fleet was sunk in the mouth of Sebastopol harbour. The Allied fleets could not enter and their guns could not reach the city from the outside. The Allies pounded with their artillery Todleben's fortifications from the south and then attacked the shattered fortresses. Menschikov watched and attempted to interrupt the siege from the outside. The one all-important question was whether the Allies could force their way in or not.

Their military superiority was unquestionable. When Menschikov on October 25 endeavoured to break the communications with their naval base at Balaclava he was driven off, though important redoubts fell into his hands and a new road had to be adopted and built. When on November 5 he attacked the English at Inkerman he was in the end driven off by the English and their French Allies. On August 16, 1855, he attacked the French and the Sardinians (we shall see shortly how they came to enter the war), and was again driven off after heavy fighting. But these attacks had not been by any means without their result. They had seriously embarrassed, and sometimes postponed, the attack on the city.

The attack encountered difficulties of various kinds. No great soldier appeared on the side of the Allies. Lord Raglan commanded the English forces until his death in June 1855. He had fought at Waterloo and was perhaps too old for the novel circumstances of the war. He was succeeded by General Simpson, who had not won so good a reputation as his predecessor. The French were at first commanded by Saint-Arnaud, who had played an important part in the *coup d'état*. When cholera had carried him off in September 1854 he was succeeded first by Canrobert and then by Pélissier. The difficulties of the command were increased by occasional divergence of aim between the French and English; but none of the Allied commanders showed originality or genius. Todleben, the Russian engineer of German origin, is the one soldier on either side who won for himself high admiration. The others had to struggle against enemies that seemed at one time more difficult to overcome than the Russians—namely, against disease and the climate. Cholera had shown itself in the early stages of the war and had been alleged as a reason against going to the Crimea at all. It attacked the camps before Sebastopol with terrible fury, and was hardly less fatal in the base camps and the hospitals. The way in which the dread enemy was attacked and subdued by Miss Florence Nightingale is among the heroic chapters of English history. The ravages of the disease reduced the numbers of the attacking force to a dangerous extent and weakened the *moral* of the troops that were not touched by it. Then there was the winter—the Russian winter—against which no precautions had been taken. Even the Great War produced no picture of misery more depressing than what was afforded by the cholera-haunted, frozen trenches and miserable tents on the heights before Sebastopol. It seemed at one time as though the siege might be made impossible by the double curse of cold and cholera. The English effectives were at one time reduced to 11,000. The Russians suffered as great or greater hardships. Their courage and endurance won the ungrudging admiration of their enemies.

Amidst all these difficulties the approaches to Sebastopol were made far more slowly than had been expected. There was a heavy bombardment from the 17th to the 30th October 1854; but the hold of the Russians was not shaken, and then for the first time it became plain that the armies 'were there for the winter.'

During the winter, diplomacy was active and eager to bring more Allies into the field against Russia. Austria would yield to no inducements. A conference was held at Vienna which lasted from March till May 1855. The Russian Czar Nicholas had died during the course of the siege and had been succeeded by Alexander II, who sent a representative to Vienna. The 'Four Points' were accepted by Russia as a basis of negotiation. It appeared at one time as if peace might really come. But when war has once begun diplomacy has rarely availed to bring hostilities to an end before some decisive blow has been struck, and so it proved here. Austria judged that the Russian concessions were sufficient, and refused to join in the war. France, Britain and Turkey determined to struggle on. They found an ally in a strange quarter. Cavour was at this time Minister of the strangely named Kingdom of Sardinia. The Italian lands contained in that kingdom had no direct interest in the Crimean struggle; but Cavour had his mind fixed on a more distant goal. He wished to see his king at the head of a United Italy. To send Sardinian troops to the Crimea would vindicate the claim of Sardinia to rank with the Great Powers; would set up a claim to the support of France, and give the representative of Sardinia a place at the Conference table when the terms of peace were settled. So 15,000 Italian troops landed in the Crimea.

Soon after the winter had relaxed its hold the attack on the fortresses was renewed. Some successes were gained, though the joint attack arranged for the anniversary of the Battle of Waterloo (June 18) was a costly failure. The death of Lord Raglan and the attack on the Allied lines which resulted in the battle of the Černaya postponed the final attack. On September 5 there was a heavy bombardment (during the Great War it would not have been called heavy!) for three days. The attack was launched on the 8th. The English failed in the attack on the fortress of the Redan; but the French under MacMahon seized the Malakov and could not be driven out, and the Malakov commanded the city. The Russian army marched out and joined the forces of Menschikov. The Allies marched in and possessed themselves of the forts and the harbour, of a vast quantity of guns, and of hospitals where were heaped under horrifying conditions a mass of wounded and sick Russian soldiers who could not be removed (September 8, 1855).

There was nothing necessarily in the loss of Sebastopol to bring the war to an end. The war went on indeed for some little time yet; and the Russians ended with a success when they captured the fortress of Kars in Asia Minor from the Turks and the English officers who commanded them. But the losses of Russia and her financial exhaustion made peace most desirable.[1] The new Czar was anxious to give his country peace, and through the mediation of Austria a conference was called at Paris.

The relations between Great Britain and France had stood the strain of the war very well. There had been differences of opinion as to the

---

[1] It is an interesting contrast to the Great War of 1914 that the Russian Government went on paying British bondholders their interest on the Russian Debt throughout the war. The attempt of Hungary to pay interest in 1915 to British bondholders was prohibited by the British Government on the ground that it was 'trading with the enemy.'

conduct of operations, and some criticism of policy, but nothing serious. At the Peace Congress in Paris, however, the French Emperor seemed to be cooling in his relations with England, and to be turning towards his late enemies the Russians with sympathy and admiration. The value of a Russian alliance to France was presenting itself to his mind. The Congress sat for nearly eight weeks.

We may look first—though quite out of chronological order—at some points not directly connected with the Eastern Question. On the proposal of Lord Clarendon, the Powers expressed a 'wish' that before having recourse to arms States 'should have recourse to the good offices of a friendly Power.' A very hesitating and quite fruitless approach to the greatest of European problems! It deserves notice as being one of the signs that the problem of international organisation and the wisdom of arbitration to prevent war was forcing itself on the attention of Europe.

Then came the great Declaration respecting Maritime Law and the management of a naval war, whereby Great Britain at last consented to conditions which she had long resisted. The points are highly technical. Privateering was abolished. Enemy goods could not henceforth be seized on a neutral vessel unless they came under the category of 'contraband of war.' Neutral goods carried by an enemy could not henceforth be seized. Blockades 'to be binding must be effective'; such a general blockade as was declared by Britain against Napoleon could no longer be used. It was an honourable attempt to regulate and humanise naval warfare. But 'contraband of war' proved an elastic term, and the Wars of 1914 and 1939 have made the world sceptical about the possibility of humanising what is essentially inhuman.

The real business of the Conference was to decide the future of Turkey, and (what was the same thing from another point of view) to check the advance of Russia. Here much was achieved, although the sum of the achievement did not amount to a final settlement. The Black Sea was neutralised: no 'flag of war' could appear in it; no military or naval establishment could be made in it; the Straits were closed to foreign warships. The independence of Turkey was affirmed: no Power had the right to interfere between the Sultan and his subjects; the privileges of Moldavia, Wallachia, and Serbia were guaranteed, but always under the suzerainty of Turkey; 'the generous intentions' of the Sultan towards his subjects 'without distinction of religion or of race' were recognised, as was the 'high value' of the proposals he had made in a recent Firman.

So the war was ended, and Turkey was saved from the destruction which unquestionably had menaced her. Henceforth there was to be (if diplomacy and treaties availed to produce it) a Turkey, united, independent, tolerant, progressive; a Turkey that would rapidly come into line with the constitutional life of the West, that would abandon massacre and corruption, and become an equal member of the comity of nations.[1] Let us look into the next few years and see the results of all these schemes.

The hopes of Turkish reforms were all disappointed. The Turks did not believe in them, and in the mass of the population there was an entire absence of the mutual considerations and self-restraint which alone make free institutions workable. Religious equality struck at the basis on which Mohammedan life had rested since the time of Mohammed. Among the reforms promised was equal admissibility to military service. But most of the Christian populations disliked military service and preferred to pay a tax, and the Turks infinitely preferred their money to their service.[2] It was declared a few years later that the only result of the promise of reforms was the creation of a few more officials. Protests and complaints produced only expressions of good will and promises of inquiry. In 1861 Abdul Aziz succeeded to the Turkish throne. He promised many reforms. He would reduce expenses; suppress corruption; have only one wife. But little, if anything, was done; a harem of 900 wives was soon re-established with a correspondingly large court expenditure. Lord Stratford de Redcliffe had said 'Turkey cannot float; she must either sink or swim,' but the Sultan seemed of the opposite opinion.

While Turkey floated on to destruction, the subject nationalities were showing a stirring vigour which was often uncomfortable to their subjects and neighbours as well as to their rulers. Greece had enjoyed twenty years and more of 'liberty,' but she had disappointed many of the hopes that had been founded on her. Many things were against her. Her territories were small; her frontiers were dangerous; her past and her position as representative of all those who called themselves Greeks, attracted her towards dangerous ambitions. Her King, Otto, was most sincerely devoted to the well-being of the country, but he failed to win the loyal support of the nation. During the Crimean War the general opinion of Greece was favourable to the Russians rather than the Allies, and Otto became unpopular for refusing to take part in some wild escapade for an insurrection in Turkish territory. In 1862 a revolution broke out, and though the first movements were suppressed Otto found it necessary to abdicate. The next King, George, was of Danish blood, and Great Britain made the prospects of his reign brighter by ceding the Ionian Islands to Greece. Yet the task of the new King was exceedingly difficult. The armies were in an almost constant condition of mutiny; there was no stability in the political life of the country; and

---

[1] The admission of Turkey into the 'comity of nations' was a new and unprecedented action. It was clearly due to the desire of France, Great Britain and Austria to emancipate Turkey from the religious control or interference of Russia [v. p. 212, n. 1]. Yet, in fact, the Powers as a whole found it necessary to make elaborate provisions for the protection of their own national interests within the Turkish Empire.

[2] In 1869 recruiting was again openly restricted in the Turkish Empire to Moslems.

the popular sentiment was always profoundly stirred by the news of resistance to the Sultan in different parts of his dominions. It is to these that we must now turn.

In the north-west—in Serbia and in Montenegro—the native population made considerable advances towards independence. The right of Serbia to self-government under the suzerainty of Turkey had been guaranteed by the Treaty of Paris, and there were Turkish garrisons in the forts at Belgrade and elsewhere and a certain number of Turks living under the protection of the forts. But the Serbians were determined to increase the liberties which they had already won. They were for the most part a vigorous peasant population, living largely by the breeding and sale of pigs, and they formed a military material capable of all acts of daring and heroism. Their effectiveness was weakened by their sharp local feuds, their readiness to prosecute family quarrels in the spirit of a vendetta, and the rivalry of two families for the headship of the State. These were the Obrenović and the Karageorgević, something of whose fortunes has already been told. Alexander Karageorgević was ruling Serbia at the time of the Crimean War, and he seemed to many of his people to have played a tame game, when circumstances would have allowed him to play a bold one. He had also great difficulties with his people as to the introduction of forms of constitutional liberty. In 1859 the situation became impossible for him and he abdicated; and the Skupshtina—the very turbulent Parliament of Serbia—asked Miloš Obrenović, who had been driven from the throne twenty years before, to return. He came with the approval of Turkey, but he showed his independence of Turkey by declaring his authority to be hereditary, against the will of the Sultan, and when he died in 1860 he was succeeded by his son Michael. There have been more heroic and romantic figures on the Serbian throne, but none more successful. He organised the Government and the army, and gave to Serbia the appearance of a civilised European State. Much was done for the culture and the education of the Serbians. The language was purified; the legends were carefully collected and became a great source of pride and patriotic inspiration to the people. But for our purposes it is more important to notice that his people made a great advance towards independence by securing the withdrawal of the Turkish garrisons. The murder of individual Serbians by Turkish soldiers and the bombardment of the town of Belgrade by the Turks in the citadel brought the matter to a head. Michael was supported by the Great Powers, and in the end all the Turkish troops were withdrawn, and nothing was left of the Turkish power in Serbia except the stipulation that the Turkish flag should fly by the side of the Serbian on the ramparts of Belgrade. It would clearly not be long before a further step was taken. Some diplomatists thought it might be incorporation with Austria or with Russia; but the Serbs themselves were in no mood to exchange one suzerainty for another.

The Principality of Montenegro was inhabited by a people closely akin in race and language to the Serbians. The little mountain state had always maintained its independence of Turkey, though the Turks had never admitted that independence as a right. In 1858 the Turks endeavoured to force their claims on the Montenegrins, but they were defeated among the mountains at Grahovo with immense loss, in a battle that deserves to rank along with Marathon and Morgarten as one of the most heroic deeds of men defending their freedom against the invasion of a tyrant. But the Turkish danger remained, and Michael of Serbia was aiming at some closer union between Serbia and Montenegro when he was assassinated in 1868. Michael was a man both of ability and ambition, and his plans extended beyond Montenegro and Serbia to the formation of a sort of Balkan League against Turkey. He had a secret treaty with the representatives of the downtrodden Bulgarian subjects of the Turk, and close diplomatic relations with Rumania and Greece. So much can be said with certainty and more can be inferred, but the death of Michael brought these far-reaching plans to nought.

In Serbia and Montenegro the Turkish power ebbed, as it ebbed everywhere, now slowly, now rapidly, down to the time of the Great War. The rule of Turkey was even weaker in 'the Principalities' than in Serbia and Montenegro, and it suffered an equally obvious rebuff. By the Treaty of Paris the protectorate of the two principalities—with some intentional emphasis on the word 'two'—had been transferred from Turkey to the Great Powers collectively. The object of the diplomatists was that the principalities should be kept separate and therefore weak, and that they should not challenge the suzerainty of Turkey. But the sense of nationality was strong in this strange Ruman people despite its varied composition and its marked social cleavage. Town was in sharp contrast with country; the native Rumanians with the large minority of Jews. But all spoke the Latin tongue which had been so strangely preserved during the Middle Ages; all were proud of their Latin civilisation, and thought of themselves as the representatives of Western culture amidst Slavonic barbarism, following as far as they could the fashions of Paris in social and political ideas. By the Treaty of Paris there were to be two States with separate constitutions, and the Sultan refused the demand of Moldavia and Wallachia that they should be allowed to unite under the name of Rumania. The utmost concession that could be won was that they should be known as the 'United Principalities' and that affairs which concerned them both should be regulated by a joint Commission. But the Rumanians adroitly won their way against the wishes of Turkey and of Europe. Each principality had to choose its head or 'hospodar.' They both chose the same man, a Moldavian nobleman, who took the title of 'Alexander the First, Prince of Rumania.' He declared that the Rumanian nation was founded, and united the two Parliaments. Europe had other problems to attend to, and the accomplished fact was accepted. Bucharest became the capital of united Rumania. The new ruler proved one of the most remarkable of Balkan rulers. He watched events in the West, and especially in France, very closely, and his policy was clearly founded on that of Napoleon III, and the methods by which he carried it through had some likeness to the *coup d'état*. Three great measures are associated with his name. He found a large proportion of the land of Rumania in possession of the monasteries. By a series of measures he transferred nearly the whole of these lands to secular uses, and at the same time gave to Rumania a large measure of religious independence. Then came his measures connected with land tenure. The Parliament resisted his first suggestions. He expelled the members by force and asked the people to choose by plebiscite between him and the Parliament. They supported him by the suspiciously large majority of 682,000 against 1000. Then he created a vast system of peasant proprietorships, and at the same time freed the peasants from the 'feudal' burdens which they had hitherto paid. It was the work of the French Revolution carried out without bloodshed. His last law established free and compulsory education. Modern Rumania still rests on the foundation which he laid.

But the towns disliked what seemed his devotion to agricultural interests. The nobility were bitterly angry at the destruction of their privileges. The clergy regarded his high-handed treatment of ecclesiastical questions as sacrilege. A revolution was plotted against him—they are made with a facility in the Balkans hardly to be paralleled elsewhere—and finding himself deserted by his troops he abdicated. The conspirators looked round for a foreign prince, and found one in Prince Charles of Hohenzollern-Sigmaringen. He belonged to the family of the King of Prussia, but he was also related to Napoleon III and was supported by him.[1] On the advice of Bismarck he accepted the offer, and it was announced that in the plebiscite 685,000 had voted for him and only 224 against him. The presence of a Hohenzollern on the throne of Rumania was important during the war of 1866, and it may be well to say here that it was his brother Leopold who figured so prominently in the events which led to the Franco-Prussian War of 1870. We need not follow Balkan events any further, but it is clear that there was little probability of Turkey becoming again the accepted suzerain of the Peninsula in any real sense. One district after another detached itself from the rule of the Turk; and their example proved infectious to other races and districts outside of the Balkan Peninsula.

[1] Alexander I (Cuza) was deposed in February 1866, and Charles elected in May.

CHAPTER XVI

THE *RISORGIMENTO* AND THE UNION OF ITALY

NAPOLEON III's claim that the Empire meant peace was soon submitted to another test. And again the ideas and personal interests of the Emperor were largely responsible for hostilities which took French armies once more to the well-known battle-ground of North Italy. The new war was in many ways a great contrast to the Crimean War. It was settled by two important battles, and produced nothing like the long agonies of the trench war round Sebastopol. It was, moreover, the first war clearly fought for that principle of nationality which was the one great and novel feature of the international difficulties of the nineteenth century. Nationality was the enthusiasm, almost the superstition, of the time. It was on the one hand the completion of the process that had been going on ever since the Reformation. As all agencies of human unity fell into the background or were destroyed—the Empire had disappeared, the Church had lost its old political influence—the State had become the all-important unit of organisation. It recognised no superior and admitted no control. But the more important and powerful the State became the more important was it to consider on what basis the power of the State rested. The movement towards constitutionalism which had been led by England was more than two hundred years old and had achieved great victories. It was widely claimed and often granted that the State should be identified with the people and that Government and people should be in active partnership. Now another question arose behind that. Who were the people that should form a state? Was any collection of individuals equally well adapted for state life? Men awoke with a new clearness and self-consciousness to the sense of nationality. This new sense appeared most strongly not among those nations which had already won a large measure of national independence and unity, not among the French or the English or the Spaniards; but among those who were still without a national state, and who, as a result of historical development, found themselves mixed up with other nationalities in the same state.

National feeling had shown itself strong though often vague in the Balkan Peninsula. It was a religious passion with large numbers of Poles. It had had much to do with the failure of the union of Holland and Belgium. But the two countries where it produced the most striking political and military results were Germany and Italy. Germany since the Middle Ages had been divided and subdivided, and her vague constitution, which embraced Czechs, some Poles, and other non-German elements, gave no satisfaction to the national desire for unity. The case of Italy was even worse. She had won a large measure of national unity under Napoleon and had not forgotten the experience. But since 1815

SWITZERLAND

A U S T R I A

TYROL

FRANCE (to France 1860)

Trent

LOMBARDY
(1859)

Magenta

Milan

Peschiera

Solferino

Mantua

Turin

PIEDMONT

VENETIA
(1866)

Trieste

Verona

Custozza

Legnano

Venice

Fiume

R. Po

PARMA
(1860)

MODENA
(1860)

R. Po

ROMAGNA
(1860)

Ravenna

REP. OF
SAN MARINO

BOSNIA
(Turkish
till 1908)

ADRIATIC

Genoa

Monaco

Nice

LUCCA (1860)
(to Tuscany 1847)

Pisa

Leghorn

Florence

R. Tiber

MARCHES
(1860)

Ancona

Castelfidardo

SEA

CORSICA
(to France)

Elba

TUSCANY
(1860)

UMBRIA
(1860)

PAPAL STATES

Rome
(1870)

Pontecorvo (Papal)

Benevento
(Papal)

SARDINIA

Naples

Castellammare

N A P L E S

T W O
S I C I L I E S

(1860)

M E D I T E R R A N E A N

Messina

Palermo

Aspromonte

Marsala

Calatafimi

SICILY

Catania

Syracuse

T H E

S E A

Malta
(British)

The Unification of
ITALY
English Miles

Emery Walker Ltd. sc.

ustrian territory in 1859	
ingdom of Sardinia, 1815-1859	
oundary after 1870	
cquisitions after the Great War	

he dates (1860) are those of the union of the
arious States with the Kingdom of Sardinia,
orming together the Kingdom of Italy.

she had been declared to be a mere 'geographical expression' and had passed again under the control of the Austrian Emperors. We have already seen that her efforts in 1848 had ended in failure or apparently so. But failure had not stifled the sense of nationality. It had rather quickened it. There were indeed wide differences of race and temperament in the peninsula. The Lombard and the Sicilian were separated from one another by a wide difference of language and of historic development. But nationality, it is now clear to us, is rather a question of feeling than of objective fact. And the past greatness of the peoples of Italy, the dim memories of the Roman Empire, the poems of Dante, the art and science of the Renaissance, all served to keep alive the feeling that the Italians were a single and a great people. Whatever contributed to the patriotic pride of the Italians strengthened their desire to be a state to themselves. But more important than any other influence on the Italian mind was the work of Mazzini. To him and to his followers the claim of Italian nationality was not a matter of analysis and reason, but of passionate and almost religious belief. Italy united, free, democratic and republican was the one absorbing passion of his life; an ideal to be pursued at all costs and by all means. He held by each element of his programme. It was as important to him that Italy should be democratic and republican as that it should be united and free. He could not bring himself to accept the gift of unity and freedom at the hand of the Emperor or of the King of Sardinia. We must add that he was able to look beyond nationality, and dreamed of the free nations of Europe voluntarily organising themselves into a greater association for peaceful co-operation.

These or any other dreams that had Italian unity as their goal seemed very distant in the middle of the century. Austria ruled again stubbornly, stupidly, and often with a cruelty that was born of fear. Her rule was not confined to her own territories in the Lombard plain. The duchies of the centre were under her influence; the Papacy looked to Austria rather than to France to find real sympathy; and the King of Naples had shown his dependence on Vienna. Conciliation of the subject population would have been in any case difficult; but no serious efforts were made. In 1857 the younger brother of the Emperor Francis Joseph—Maximilian, later to play so tragic a part in Mexico—was appointed to take charge of Lombardy. He was genuinely liberal in his sympathies. He made a real attempt at the reform of the administration, but his conciliatory action was soon repudiated. The financial and military pressure on Venetia and the Milanese became heavier than before.

Free and United Italy was born of the Kingdom of Sardinia. The origin of this strangely named state lay in the mountains of Savoy; its real strength in the upper valleys of the Po and in Piedmont. It was a state only in part Italian, and had in the past pursued a narrow dynastic policy. Until the revolutions of 1848 there was nothing in the history of the state or the royal family to mark it out as the standard-bearer of Italian liberty and unity; but in 1848 it had laid the foundations of its future greatness by joining with Milan in resistance to Austria, and above all by granting to its own people a really liberal constitution. When Victor Emmanuel succeeded Charles Albert great efforts were made to induce him to withdraw the constitution and rule as an absolute ruler. 'I will hold the tricolour high and firm' he had answered, and it was that determination which gave him the crown of United Italy. He had taken his stand for Italy and for freedom; he had dissociated himself from Austria and all her ideals. And he had his reward.

His name will always be closely associated with that of Cavour, who began his 'Great Ministry' in the year 1852. Count Cavour was the son of a Piedmontese nobleman devoted to absolutist ideals, and was intended for the army. But the young man at an early date had adopted advanced liberal opinions and had left the army. He had travelled widely and had studied the political life of France and of England with particular care. He had gambled and he had lost much of his inheritance. For a time he had seemed inclined to throw up all ideas of a political career and to devote himself to the cultivation of his father's estates. But then the call to political service had come again. As a member of the Sardinian Parliament he had shown wide knowledge of the politics of Europe, and great hopefulness for the future of Piedmont and of Italy. He declared that it was the mission of the Sardinian State to 'gather to herself all the living forces of Italy and lead our mother country to those high destinies whereunto she is called.' He pointed with approval to the concessions made by the statesmen of England to the demands of the people, and urged confidence in the people as the safest policy. Before Cavour was in office measures had been taken against the legal and financial privileges of the Church in Piedmont. He held subordinate office in 1850 and was Prime Minister in 1852. One of his first measures had been the dissolution of the monasteries. He had made himself known as a liberal in the sense in which the word was then used, and his liberalism was genuine; but it was the cause of Italian nationalism that claimed all his devotion. His goal was the same as Mazzini's, the same as that of most great Italians for a long time past —Italy free and united. But what distinguished the policy of Cavour was its sense of reality,[1] its understanding of the practical difficulties of the problem. He did not believe that Italy could win her goal single-handed or by enthusiasm alone. He looked round for allies and employed all the methods of a skilful and unscrupulous diplomacy. He incurred by the methods which he was willing to employ the violent

---

[1] Realism was the note of his whole policy. He was thoroughly in sympathy with English ideas of finance and administration as practised in the age of Sir Robert Peel. His programme of internal reform, with its great financial and administratvie improvements, should not be obscured by the greater renown of his foreign policy.

hostility of Mazzini. Mazzini did not believe even in Cavour's honesty. He called him the 'ministerial liberator who taught his master how to prevent the union of Italy.' He disbelieved in the practicability of his schemes, and even if they were practicable they seemed a substitution of materialism for idealism and religion, treason for democracy, and a dragging down of the whole movement to a lower plane. Success when it came did not conciliate him. He had dreamed of a new earth and Cavour only gave him a rearrangement of the old one.

The Crimean War had provided Cavour with the opportunity for one of his skilful diplomatic strokes. Italy indeed had no interests in the issues between Russia and the Allies. But the enemies of Russia were much in need of help and support. Sardinia, if she came in, would appear as one of the important Powers of Europe; she would claim a seat at the Congress which settled terms of peace and which would perhaps rearrange the map of Europe. So the Sardinian soldiers went to the Crimea, fought at the battle of the Černaya with distinguished success, and showed that the failure of the Italian arms at the Battle of Novara did not spring from any incapacity of Italians for military effort. 'Out of this mud' (the mud of the Sebastopol trenches), said a Piedmontese soldier, 'Italy will be made'; and the words expressed the essential aim of Cavour. At the Paris Congress he got the opportunity he wanted of ventilating the grievances of Italy. He was warmly supported by Clarendon, the English Foreign Minister, and the Conference listened to a formal statement of the misgovernment of Italy both in the south and the north and of the international dangers which sprang from it. Sardinia now was a recognised part of the diplomatic web of Europe. It was the life task of the subtle mind of Cavour to rearrange that web so as to admit a free and United Italy.

'*Italia farà da sè*' (Italy will act by herself) had been the proud boast of an earlier period. It was Cavour's clear opinion that Italy acting by herself would not be able to reach the desired goal. And it was his chief effort to win for Italy in her struggle the alliance of France. Napoleon III in his youth had known something of the revolutionary movement in Italy. Real sympathy with the doctrine of nationality, which he sincerely preached, drew him to the side of Cavour. But it needed all Cavour's astuteness and strength to turn his vague sentiment into action and to prevent him from turning back when the dangers of the enterprise made themselves felt.

In January 1858, as Napoleon and the Empress were going to the opera, bombs were thrown at them. The imperial party escaped, but there were many killed and wounded. Several Italians were arrested, and the chief agent in the plot was discovered to be an Italian, Orsini. He had at one time been in close touch with Mazzini, though no sympathy with his attempt at assassination could be brought home to Mazzini. Orsini declared that what he had done had sprung from his belief that Napoleon had betrayed the cause of Italy. From his prison he wrote two letters to Napoleon appealing to him to free Italy, and on the scaffold of the guillotine his last cry was 'Long live Italy!' The effect of these events was—strangely—not to drive Napoleon from the cause of Italy, but to draw him nearer to it. He took what was the really decisive step in June 1858.

Napoleon liked to keep the conduct of foreign affairs largely in his own hands and sometimes to act without the knowledge of his own responsible Ministers. He sent a message to Cavour through a private source that he was going to spend the summer in Plombières, and that he would be glad to see Cavour there. Cavour realised what great issues underlay this simple-looking invitation. 'The drama,' he wrote to a friend, 'approaches its crisis.' He met the Emperor on July 21–2, and had a long discussion with him, first in his residence and then in a long drive round the town while Napoleon himself held the reins. The aim of the two conspirators (for they were that, however ideal their aims) was war. France promised to support Sardinia in a war with Austria on condition that Cavour provided a pretext, which would justify France's action in the eyes of Europe. The Austrians were to be driven out of Italy. The north was to form a kingdom of Italy under Victor Emmanuel; then all Italy was to be united in a federal bond under the presidency of the Pope. This, Cavour well knew could only be won by the sword of France and Napoleon. And what pay would he require? There can be no doubt that he would be glad to serve a cause in which he sincerely believed. The prestige which he would win and the consequent strengthening of his throne would be of the utmost value to him. But he demanded also tangible reward. Savoy and Nice were to be ceded to France—Savoy the cradle of the royal house and of the Sardinian State, Nice the birthplace of Garibaldi—and Victor Emmanuel was to consent to the marriage of his sixteen-year-old daughter to Napoleon's cousin, Prince Napoleon. The future was to show how unwise it was in Napoleon to insist on these or any terms. The catastrophe of 1870 might perhaps have been avoided if Napoleon had not alienated the sympathies of the Italians to whose freedom he contributed so much. But it must be remembered that he had to justify his action to the French as well as to the Italians.

Cavour had got the promise of the war he so passionately desired. It was his business now to bring about the war in such a way that it should seem to be an aggressive action on the part of Austria; and in the pursuit of this end he had often to complain of his imperial fellow-conspirator. With Napoleon the cold fit was always apt to follow the hot. Up to the end of the year 1858 all went well for his plans; in December of that year the secret Treaty between France and Sardinia was drawn up. It was called a defensive alliance. In case of war France was to provide 200,000 men and Austria was to be driven out of Italy. Cavour was confident. 'We have Austria in a cleft stick,' he wrote, 'and she cannot get out of it without firing the cannon.' The people of northern

Italy were excited. They cheered Victor Emmanuel and the Kingdom of Italy, and cried 'Long live the war!'

Yet during the following months there were times when it seemed as though the war might slip through Cavour's fingers after all. Napoleon had told the Austrian Ambassador on New Year's Day that he regretted 'that his relations to the Austrian Empire were not so good as they had formerly been.' A pamphlet had been issued with his approval on 'Napoleon and Italy,' preaching anew the doctrine of Nationality and pointing out that it was applicable to Germany as well as to Italy. But there seemed little eagerness for the war in France, except perhaps in the army itself. Great Britain, and to a lesser extent Russia, urged the possibility of settling the Italian trouble by means of a European Congress. That was also one of Napoleon's 'ideas' and he could not refuse to consider it. His will was so unstable that Cavour was in despair. Peace seemed for a moment certain. 'Nothing remains for me but to put a bullet through my head,' he said. Then came an incident never quite fully explained. Perhaps Austria was weary of the long delays; perhaps she was encouraged by addresses of loyalty from various parts of her dominions. She despatched to Turin an ultimatum demanding disarmament 'within three days,' and sent her troops into Piedmont on April 19, 1859. No military adventurer or despot has ever welcomed war with greater ardour than was shown by Cavour at this moment, and yet Cavour was a civilian, a parliamentary statesman, and his whole power rested on popular support and democracy. 'The die is cast and history is made,' he cried. The Austrian Emperor declared he was fighting for 'the rights of all peoples and states and for the most sacred blessings of mankind.' But the general feeling was that it was he who had broken the peace. Victor Emmanuel was declared Dictator by the Piedmontese Parliament, and the war began.

The Italian War interested nearly every Great Power in Europe, and there was much talk of intervention. Men asked with anxiety, what would Great Britain do, what would Russia do? But the action of Germany and of Prussia was really the most critical question. Austria, despite her mixed population, counted primarily as a German Power, and she was at the head of the Germanic Confederation. Prussia, despite her grievances against Austria, would not see unmoved the defeat of the Austrian armies by French and Italian forces. The federal army and the Prussian armies were both put on a war footing. Austrian diplomacy could not induce them to go further at first; but the thought of German or Prussian intervention was always in the mind of Napoleon III and was a chief influence on his actions.

The Austrian armies, however, had to bear the attack of their enemies without allies. The soldiers showed themselves brave, and one general, Benedek, gained a high reputation from his management of the campaign. But the different national elements in his army had no interest in the issue of the campaign and the higher ranks were confined to the nobles. The French armies were later than was expected in entering Italy, but the situation there was highly favourable to the national cause. There were spontaneous risings all over the north of Italy. There were risings in Modenese territory. Parma expelled its ruler. In Tuscany and in its capital, Florence, there were movements of the utmost importance. The Lorraine house, which had succeeded to the Medicis in the eighteenth century, had not struck deep roots. There were great popular meetings in Florence which cheered for 'war, independence and Victor Emmanuel.' The King of Sardinia was asked to undertake the military dictatorship of Tuscany. Yet we may see here the first hint of those difficulties which later ruined the popularity of Napoleon III in the eyes of the Italians. Perhaps he was misunderstood; but the suspicion arose that he was not anxious to see Tuscany absorbed in the Kingdom of Sardinia; that he had other designs for the country; and that he hoped to see Prince Jerome succeeding in some way to the Duchy. The enthusiasm for the national cause spread further south, as soon as the Allies had won their first victories. In the Romagna and the Legations the Papal troops were driven out; the popular cry was for union with Italy and Victor Emmanuel. There was no hope now that Pius IX would join the national cause, but there was an effort made to bring in Naples, or, to call it by its proper title, the 'Two Sicilies.' There Ferdinand II had just died and had been succeeded by his son Francis II. The attempt to win him over failed entirely. There was some sympathy among his Ministers and in the population; but the young King, who was married to the sister of the Austrian Empress, held by his father's policy.

Napoleon III had consulted Jomini—a General of the great Napoleon —as to his plan of campaign; but his schemes were far from settled when he arrived, and he is not judged to have shown any conspicuous talent in his management of the campaign. The Austrians were equally undecided. Their troops came in slowly. Count Gyulai held the supreme command and was thought to have owed his promotion over the heads of abler men to Court influences. On the Italian side public attention was chiefly given to the 'Hunters of the Alps'—a fine body of irregular troops collected from the most enthusiastic elements of the patriots of Italy and commanded by Garibaldi, who already was regarded by public opinion as the incarnation of the romance of the daring and the poetry of the national cause. Napoleon had no love for him, and per- haps might have made fuller use of his great talents. As the allied forces advanced into the Milanese territory Garibaldi acted on the left flank among the foothills of the Alps. But the brunt of the fighting fell on the French troops, and, without disparaging the great courage and de- votion of the Italian army, it is plain that it would have gone hard with the national cause if it had not had the support of the armies of France. Perhaps the Austrians would have been wiser if they had followed the suggestion of standing on the defensive under cover of the fortresses of the 'Quadrilateral.' But they decided to defend the Milanese, and the issue was decided in two great battles. On June 4 was fought the Battle of Magenta, and after heavy fighting, which fell almost entirely on the French, the Austrians were defeated. They were defeated, but not broken, and retreated towards the 'Quadrilateral.' Bolder counsels, however, prevailed; and a greater battle than Magenta was fought at Solferino, just to the south of Lake Garda, on June 24. It was a long-drawn-out and murderous encounter. In the centre and on the right the French and Italians gained a complete victory. The Austrians held their own under Benedek on their right with obstinate courage and only withdrew when the battle had been lost in other parts of the field. The losses on both sides reached many thousands, and the impression of horror was very much increased by the reports of the insufficiency of the medical services. The idea of the Red Cross organisation sprang from the impression produced by the spectacle of the battle.

The Battle of Solferino was a very heavy defeat for Austria, but it was not so overwhelming a blow as to appear decisive of the whole campaign. Yet through the action of Napoleon III the whole campaign ended here. What were his motives?

The war had been a great triumph for him. The year 1860 marks the very zenith of his power and reputation in Europe. He was credited by many with extraordinary diplomatic subtlety and was thought likely to establish a power in Europe as great as that of the first Napoleon. In the Crimean War he had turned back the power of Russia and re-established Turkey. Now he had crushed Austria and called a free Italy into being. When he entered Milan after the Battle of Magenta he was welcomed with an adoring rapture such as has fallen to the lot of few conquerors. 'Our liberator, our saviour, our benefactor,' the enthusiastic crowd called him. His way was strewn with flowers by the women of Milan. His words raised this enthusiasm still higher. He would do nothing, he said, 'to force his will on the people of Italy.' 'Use the good fortune that presents itself to you. Your dream of independence will be realised if you show yourself worthy of it. Unite in one great effort for the liberation of the country.'

Napoleon had snuffed up all this incense with unconcealed delight. And yet soon the enthusiasm of the Italians gave way to suspicion and their gratitude turned to resentment. Napoleon was always an adventurer and a dreamer. The 'sense of the possible,' that most necessary gift of the statesman, was not his. His imagination conjured up splendid scenes and glorious triumphs, but never showed him a firm road to his goal. We may see him, his whole life through, starting and turning back; desiring the end but frightened of the inevitable means.

Amidst the glories of the Italian campaign there was much to alarm him. Glory had to be paid for. The slaughter and the torture of the Solferino battlefield had profoundly impressed his imagination. The Italians, too, showed themselves by no means so malleable as he had hoped. Whatever schemes he had for the future of Tuscany broke down before the determination of the Tuscans to be masters of their own destiny. Moreover, despite his name, he was no soldier. His powers lay in another direction—in unexpected diplomatic combinations and in his power of appeal to the imagination of men. There were good reasons for desiring to be done with the war. But there was a more powerful one in the storm that now clearly threatened from the side of Germany. Prussia had her own bitter quarrel with Austria, but she could not see with pleasure the humiliation of a German power by France and Italy. Her army had already been placed on a war footing; she now prepared her whole forces and proposed that she should be given the command of the German army. She proposed to Great Britain and to Russia that they should join with her in an offer of mediation to the combatants. It was clear that the French forces might soon be wanted to protect the Rhine frontier.

Napoleon determined to bring the war to an end; and in pursuit of this end he acted—as he was accustomed to do—rather as a conspirator than a statesman. Everyone expected a renewal of the fighting, when Napoleon despatched General Fleury on a private mission to the headquarters of Francis Joseph, the Austrian Emperor, suggesting an armistice with a view to peace. The Austrian ruler was quite ready to receive the overtures. The defeats that his army had suffered were serious, but they were not the only ground. Hungary was threatening revolt and troops were wanted to suppress it. The prospect of Prussian intervention by no means suited Austrian diplomacy, for it would be accompanied by concessions to Prussia in Germany, which Francis Joseph was by no means willing to make. So he met Napoleon at Villafranca, and soon arranged the preliminaries of peace.[1] Lombardy was to be handed over to Napoleon, who would then transfer it to Victor Emmanuel. Both France and Austria would then support the formation of an Italian federation under the titular presidency of the Pope. Venice was to remain with Austria, but was to form part of the Italian Confederation. The rulers of Modena, Parma and Tuscany were to return. The Pope was to be urged to introduce reforms into his state. A meeting of the representatives of all the states concerned was to be held to ratify and develop these suggestions.

We know that this was the beginning of Italian independence and unity; and that the completion of the structure came with great rapidity. But to many Italians, and above all to Cavour, it seemed treason to the cause, the ruin of their hopes, the very negation of the liberty and unity that they aimed at. Cavour was full of despair. 'Nothing can come of this peace,' he said. 'I will turn conspirator and revolutionary, but this treaty shall not be carried out.' After a violent scene with his King he

---

[1] An armistice was signed July 8, and the preliminaries at Villafranca July 11, Sardinia not being consulted.

8*

resigned his post as Prime Minister. But soon hope dawned on him again; for events in the centre of Italy took a surprising turn.

In Tuscany, Modena, Parma and the Romagna the inhabitants were in no mood to allow the two Emperors to hand them back to their old rulers. The fame of Cavour, Garibaldi and Mazzini have obscured that of other Italian patriots who deserved well of the cause. Farini, Cavour's close friend, kept the national standard flying in Modena and in Parma. Ricasoli in Tuscany played an even more decisive part. A representative Assembly in Florence declared unanimously 'that Tuscany desired to become a part of a strong Italy under the constitutional rule of Victor Emmanuel' (August 1859). Victor Emmanuel expressed his sympathy, and praised 'the wonderful example of moderation and unity' given by Tuscany, and said that he would represent the claims of Tuscany in the coming Congress. Parma and Modena and Bologna demanded, equally strongly, union with the kingdom of Victor Emmanuel. He could at first only express sympathy, and a proposal to appoint a prince of the House of Savoy Regent over the central Italian lands was defeated by the opposition of Napoleon.

The projects of the Villafranca preliminaries proved to be very difficult to carry out. The representatives of France, Austria and Sardinia met together at Zurich. Lombardy was annexed to Sardinia, but the Pope showed not the least inclination to play his part in the formation of an Italian Confederation, and the central Italian states remained restless and dangerous. It was proposed to refer the settlement of these questions to a further Congress, which should consist of the signatories of the Peace of Vienna and should meet at Paris. But the Congress never came together. The Pope would have none of it, for a pamphlet, issued in France with the approval of the Emperor, had declared that the territories of the Papacy were to be reduced to a minimum. Austria was equally hostile; the idea of the Congress had to be abandoned.

Cavour had not remained out of office long. He was Prime Minister again in January 1860, and before that he had exercised a great influence on the course of affairs. He aimed at the settlement of the central Italian question by direct secret negotiation with Napoleon. It will be remembered that Napoleon had originally claimed Savoy and Nice as the price of his alliance with Sardinia. He had not claimed his payment, because he had not fulfilled his part of the contract. But now if the central duchies went to Victor Emmanuel he might claim it. The cession of Savoy and Nice was a terrible blow to Italian feeling, but Cavour determined that it must be done. Napoleon's favourite method of a plebiscite was to be employed both in the case of Italy and of France. An enormous majority in Tuscany and an almost unanimous vote in the other lands declared for union with the kingdom of Victor Emmanuel. The official name of the kingdom was still Sardinia, but it was generally known as Italy and was determined to deserve the name. Then came the voting in Savoy and Nice. The victory of annexation was suspiciously complete. Savoy by 130,538 votes to 235, Nice by 24,448 to 160, declared for union with the Empire of France. Napoleon's triumph seemed for the moment greater than Cavour's. But he had lost the gratitude of the Italians; they felt that he had been paid, and well paid, for the services which he had rendered. The whole movement for incorporation in a United Italy (for Sardinia was clearly but a first stage to Italy) had been carried out in the central provinces with calm, self-restraint, and dignity, in spite of the passionate enthusiasm that had been everywhere manifested. The political temper of the ancient Roman Republic seemed born again in the new Italy that Victor Emmanuel and Cavour had created.

This wonderful series of events had won for a United Italy a firm basis in the north and centre of the peninsula. But hardly more than half of the whole peninsula had been won. There remained Venice, Rome, and the kingdom of Naples to be added to the territories of free Italy before the long-dreamed-of national unity would be accomplished. Pope Pius IX had now no vestige of his old liberalism. He summed up liberalism, nationalism and democracy as 'the revolution,' and regarded it as a danger to Catholicism comparable to Islam in the Middle Ages; but the population of the Papal States was restless, and a large proportion of it sympathised with the ideas that had triumphed in the north. At Naples Francis II (as already mentioned) had succeeded in 1859. He was not a cruel tyrant, nor quite without sympathy with new ideas, but he inherited a task that was probably beyond the powers of any ruler to accomplish. It is particularly difficult to appreciate the condition of the Neapolitan and Sicilian kingdom; the popular temperament was divided from that of northern Europe by such great differences. The mass of the people was uneducated and illiterate, and took little interest in the political revolution which swept over the country. The power of the Church was very great, and the people were sincerely though not intellectually attached to its observances and beliefs. The secret societies—especially the famous Camorra—were a constant source of danger, impeding the establishment of a law-abiding society. One of the King's chief Ministers was in close touch with the Camorra, and his accession to the side of the invaders was a decisive factor in the struggle. But there was a section of the population as full of enthusiasm for Italian liberty as any that could be found in Lombardy or Tuscany. It was, however, for some time very doubtful what interpretation the Sicilians would wish to give to liberty and unity. It was not at all certain that they would be willing to merge the independence of Naples and Sicily in the Kingdom of Sardinia, even if it assumed the name of Italy, and there was a strong party that desired some form of autonomy.

Conspiracy and insurrection were almost continuous in the southern kingdom, and were powerfully stimulated by the success of the patriots in the north. King Francis was aware of his danger and considered

whether it might not be possible to adopt reforms which would satisfy
the national sentiment of his people. But before anything serious had
been done Garibaldi had landed in Sicily, and the greatest and most
successful adventure of nineteenth-century Europe had begun. For
anything like it we have to go back to the adventures of Robert Guis-
card, the Norman, in much the same lands, or the expedition of Cortes
to Mexico in the beginning of the sixteenth century. It is an amazing
story of heroism and of intrigue. Garibaldi held the eyes of all Europe
and he holds the attention of all who read the history of the period.
His courage and his skill as a leader of irregular forces; his sublime
enthusiasm for the cause of Italy; the simplicity and nobility of his
character—these are as clearly written on the events of those years as
his political incapacity and his ignorance of many of the forces which
dominated the European world at that time. In loose association with
him was Mazzini, who saw a chance in these southern movements to
establish a free and United Italy on a different basis from that constitutional and monarchical one which had triumphed in the north. He
hoped to see the banner of 'God and the People' raised against that of
Italy and Victor Emmanuel, and to establish at least the beginnings of a
republican régime in the south. When the triumph of Italian unity
came it was in a form so different from what Mazzini desired that he
declared 'I shall have no more joy in Italy; the country with its contempt for all ideals has killed the soul within me.' Garibaldi's bright
sword attracted all men's attention, and they hardly noted at the time
the all-importance of the action of Cavour and the Government of the
Kingdom of Sardinia (for such was still its official title). Yet the
annexation of Naples and Sicily depended as much on Cavour as on
Garibaldi. He knew of it before it took place; he told Garibaldi that
'when it is a question of undertakings of that kind, however bold they
may be, Count Cavour will be second to none.' Cavour never worked
easily with Garibaldi and was thoroughly distrusted and even hated by
him; but his support was necessary at every turn of the great drama.
The support was given courageously and quite unscrupulously. Never
did diplomacy employ with more skill the *double entendre*, the half-
truth, and even the lie direct. The union of Italy of which Dante had
dreamed was accomplished; but it was carried through, especially in its
last phase, in the spirit of Machiavelli.[1]

On May 5, 1860, Garibaldi left the Port of Genoa with two vessels
and 1136 volunteers, to whom were distributed on the passage the
famous red shirts which came quite accidentally to be so famous in
Europe. They landed at Marsala on the 11th. The little band was of
course utterly unequal to the defeat of the royal garrisons of Sicily. All

---

[1] In 1870 the Spanish statesman Castelar congratulated Rattazzi, Cavour's
successor, on having accomplished the Union of Italy, which 'Savonarola could not
achieve by giving himself to God, nor Machiavelli by giving himself to the Devil.'
Cavour made the best of both worlds.

depended on the impression which Garibaldi could produce on the imagination of the Sicilians, and for that purpose prudence was useless and reckless courage the highest wisdom. This was the quality which Garibaldi possessed in full measure. He advanced on Palermo, the chief military seat of the Government of Naples. The skill of his leadership, the courage of his troops, the support of the Sicilians and the miserable weakness of Lanza, the commander of the garrison at Palermo, along with some amazing good fortune, account for the wonderful victory won outside of Palermo and the subsequent capture of the city itself. This first triumph decided the issue of the campaign in Sicily, and soon King Francis had no supporters in Sicily outside the fortress of Messina. But now Garibaldi determined on an even bolder stroke. The events in Sicily had set in motion similar movements in Naples, and the nationalists appealed to Garibaldi for help. Victor Emmanuel forbade him to pass the Straits, and at the same time suggested to him the language in which he should refuse. He landed at the extreme south of Italy and marched on Naples through country excellently adapted for resistance, but there was no resistance. King Francis was betrayed by many of his Ministers and soldiers and loyally served by hardly any. The King left Naples for Gaeta on September 6 and Garibaldi entered the next day. The enthusiasm of the people was almost delirious. The triumph of the red-shirted Liberator was amazing, and it was borne with great modesty and simplicity.

The end of the story was a great contrast to the beginning. The diplomatist took the place of the soldier; and the story can no longer be told as a simple heroic epic.

Cavour had seen with mingled delight and alarm what had happened in Sicily and Naples. He was delighted that the throne of the Bourbon King was overthrown, but he was anxious to know what was to take its place. Garibaldi had always declared that he was acting in the name of Italy and Victor Emmanuel; but it was by no means certain what practical meaning he was prepared to give to that watchword. He had refused simply to declare Sicily annexed to the Kingdom of Sardinia, and was probably justified by military considerations. The future was still quite uncertain. Mazzini and his followers were working for a republic. There was a strong party who wanted to give to Naples and Sicily some separate and independent standing in a free and United Italy. The recovery of the supporters of the Bourbon monarchy could not be quite ruled out of the possible events of the future, for King Francis was holding out at Gaeta, and the inevitable disappointment with the results of liberty was bringing him some support. It seemed to Cavour that the time had fully come for his royal master to take an open part in a drama in which he had all along been a most important though concealed influence. He had no confidence in the intellectual capacity of Garibaldi to deal with the situation.

He saw, too, an opportunity of not only completing the settlement of

Naples but also of adding to the territories of Italy some part at least of the long-coveted Papal lands.

Pius IX knew of the impending danger. There were stirrings of revolution in the Marches and in Umbria. The Papal Government had entirely failed to win the support of the population since the events of 1849. The Papal army had, however, been considerably increased and improved. It consisted of men drawn from various countries, and especially from France, Ireland, and Belgium, and was under the command of General Lamoricière, a soldier who had seen distinguished service in the French army. The Papal Government was recognised as a part of the State system of Europe, and it was difficult to find an excuse for attacking it. Cavour declared in a despatch to Pius IX that the King of Sardinia felt himself bound 'in the cause of humanity' to prevent the Papal troops from suppressing with violence the popular movements in Umbria! ('If we did for ourselves,' said Cavour on another occasion, 'what we do for our country, what rascals we should be!') On this pretext the Italian army entered the Papal States and defeated the Papal army at Castelfidardo, after a struggle which reflected credit on the force of General Lamoricière. The forces of Victor Emmanuel then pushed on into Neapolitan territory and took over the authority which had been hitherto exercised by Garibaldi as Dictator. Garibaldi at first declared that he had no confidence in Cavour and that he would not declare annexation to the kingdom of Victor Emmanuel until Rome had been conquered. There seemed some danger of a collision between the red-shirts and the regulars; but the danger passed. King Francis was forced to abandon Gaeta and retired to Rome. Garibaldi met the King, and was warmly thanked by him for what he had done. He refused, however, all rewards with almost unexampled unselfishness, and retired to his island home in Caprera. Plebiscites were taken in Naples, in Sicily, and in the newly conquered Papal territories. By the usual overwhelming majorities the population declared for immediate annexation to 'the constitutional monarchy of Victor Emmanuel.'

The first Italian Parliament met in Turin in February 1861. In March a new constitutional decree containing a single article was promulgated: 'Victor Emmanuel II assumes for himself and his successors the title of King of Italy.' The most cherished dream of European liberalism had come true. We shall see later how in 1866 Venice and in 1870 Rome were joined to the territories of Italy.[1]

---

[1] *v. infra*, pp. 245, 246 n., 260–61, 281 n.

CHAPTER XVII

THE DEVELOPMENT OF THE FRENCH EMPIRE

In speaking of the Crimean War and of Italian events it has been necessary to say a good deal of Napoleon III and of his foreign policy. Here we shall attempt to trace the development of the internal history of France as far as 1866.

Napoleon III was an adventurer who had seized power by violence and in breach of the constitution to which he had sworn loyalty. The memory of the *coup d'état* clung to him always 'like the iron weight attached to the leg of a convict.' But his régime during its early years was supported by large and strong elements in French society. The agricultural population gave him its constant support right down to the time of his fall. The moneyed classes—industry, commerce, and the stock exchange—saw in him their defence against socialism and the red terror. The Catholic party—a strong element in French life—regarded him at first with decided favour. His experiment in government thus started with good auspices. Had it been permanently successful it would have had a great effect on political opinion in Europe and on the development of political forms.

The Emperor could rely on few loyal supporters. There were his fellow-conspirators of the *coup d'état*: Morny, Persigny, Walewski and a few others. But he was an upstart, and with difficulty was accepted as the real representative of the Napoleonic tradition. He could count on very little spontaneous loyalty. Successes of a striking character would be necessary to him. Despite his claim that the 'Empire means Peace' he was constantly pushed by his name and the Napoleonic tradition into a policy of demonstration and adventure. France would forgive him much or all if he gave her glory and prosperity; but failure of any sort would be fatal to him.

Of the members of the family of the great Napoleon he was in touch only with the ex-King Jerome and his two children, Mathilde and a son called Jerome. But from this group Napoleon III could hope for little help. The younger Jerome posed as a democrat and as an anti-clerical, and was a continual source of trouble to the Emperor. Napoleon III had been given the right to appoint his own successor, but he looked to a marriage and the birth of an heir to strengthen his position and to assure its continuance. He had some thoughts of connecting himself by marriage with one or other of the royal houses of Europe, but he found that he would not be welcomed as a son-in-law, while the stability of his throne was distrusted. It has been already related how he finally married in 1853 Eugénie de Montijo, a beautiful Spanish lady, of noble but not of princely birth. She behaved in the exalted position to which she was so unexpectedly raised with grace and dignity. She did not forget her own country, but she identified herself thoroughly with France. She was a strong Catholic and a decided opponent of liberal views, and when a son—the Prince Imperial—was born to her she looked at the policy of France largely in its bearing on her son's destiny; but her evil influence on the fate of the Empire, except perhaps in 1870, has been much exaggerated. The fate of Louis XVI and of Marie Antoinette were constantly in her mind and had their influence on her actions.

There was at first very little formal opposition. The proscriptions which had followed the *coup d'état* had shown the danger of opposition. The Assembly was powerless; the press was closely watched and quickly suppressed if it ventured to criticise the new régime. But the calm would not last long, and the Emperor was well aware of the forces of opposition hidden just under the surface. There were the royalists in their two groups: the legitimists who upheld the old Bourbons; and the Orleanists who desired the return of the family that had been driven off by the Revolution of 1848. The Comte de Chambord was the representative of the older line. He was a rigid and perfectly honest man to whom monarchy was a part of religion, who had no personal desire for a throne and would not attempt to win it by compromise or concession. He lived at Frohsdorf in Austria, and his party was for the present nearly negligible. The Orleanists had a much stronger following both in France and outside of it; and the princes of this house declared themselves in sympathy with much of the liberal thought of the time. The republican opposition was the really dangerous force. It could not show itself in the Assembly and could make little figure in the press; but it had the support of the populations of the great towns and especially of Paris. Napoleon's greatest failure was with the cities of France. All his efforts failed to win them to his side or even to abate their hostility. The intellectual leaders of France were also for the most part in opposition. The novelist and historian, Prosper Mérimée, and the historian Duruy supported the Emperor; Lamartine did not oppose him; but they were a feeble force to oppose to the names ranged against him—Thiers, Michelet, Louis Blanc, Renan, Georges Sand, and above all Victor Hugo. Victor Hugo refused to take advantage of the act of amnesty, and from his exile in the Channel Islands or in Belgium attacked Napoleon in writings which were of European importance.

In the general election of 1857 the imperial system worked successfully. The result of the Crimean War doubtless made the Napoleonic régime really popular with many, and in any case the scales were weighted so heavily against all opponents that it is difficult to see how the opposition came to send any representatives at all to the Assembly. A group of five—of which the chief names are Ollivier, Jules Favre, and Darimon—represented the opposition and did their best to criticise the measures of the Government.

His Italian policy struck the first serious blow against Napoleon's position; for it bitterly offended the clericals, who had hitherto supported him with enthusiasm. These now saw the hated House of Savoy raised by the support of France to a position which soon led it to the Italian throne. When the Pope's troops were defeated at Castelfidardo, and when his territories were reduced to an extent insufficient to support his power, it was Napoleon III almost as much as Cavour who was responsible for this. The clerical press—the chief paper was *L'Univers*—became as bitter as the republicans in its opposition to the policy of the Emperor. From the clericals Napoleon never again received wholehearted support. But, if Napoleon's Italian policy had lost him the support of the clericals, it had not won him the support either of the national party in Italy or of the liberals at home. We have seen that the Italians charged him with having deserted them and with breaking the word which he had given to Cavour at Plombières. The French liberals, on the other hand, did not forgive him for still upholding the power of the Pope, and their opposition was all the greater when, in 1862, Garibaldi was repulsed and captured at Aspromonte, in his effort to reach the Papal States and rally them to the national cause.

The moneyed classes were also alienated and, more than all, the manufacturing class. The Free Trade movement had triumphed in England, and Napoleon had much sympathy with its economic conclusions and its social aims. In 1860 Cobden went to Paris to discuss with him the wisdom of a commercial treaty which should lower the tariffs on English goods coming into France. Cobden thought highly of the Emperor's 'straightforwardness and fairness' and believed him to be genuinely interested in relieving the condition of the poor. Napoleon determined on the treaty without considering French opinion, and Cobden believed that the people of France were overwhelmingly against the project. Napoleon hoped by this measure to establish more friendly relations with Great Britain, to whose alliance he always attached the greatest importance. He did not succeed in that object, and he alienated the moneyed classes, who had given him hitherto their warm support as their defender against the forces of disorder.

Here too we will note, though a little out of chronological order, his great Mexican adventure, which contributed so much to the failure of his system of government. There is no incident more characteristic of the man and his methods; of his brilliant but uncontrolled imagination; of his way of confusing fancy and fact; of his habit of taking up a project with enthusiasm and then dropping it with disgust, when the first difficulties showed themselves.

Mexico was plunged in great disorder. Since her independence had been achieved in 1823 she had found little stable government, but early in 1861 Juárez had made himself President. Mexico owed money to creditors of many nationalities, but especially to the French, Spanish, and English. When President Juárez in 1861 suspended the payment of interest for two years the creditors appealed to their Governments for help.

The situation so far was simple, but Napoleon's imagination saw great possibilities behind it. The United States of America were torn by their great civil war, and foreign observers believed that the resistance of the Southern States would not be overcome. The Monroe doctrine, therefore—which excluded European Powers from any further acquisitions in America—could not now be upheld.[1] It might be possible to establish in Mexico a state under the control of some European Power, which would act as a bulwark against the Anglo-Saxons, 'this aggressive people which, if it be not stopped, will cover all America and then the whole world.' Even if this state were not in French hands it might be used to win valuable alliances for France. A new chapter in the history of the world might open!

A joint French, Spanish, and British expedition sailed for Vera Cruz, hoping to exercise pressure which would produce the payment of the required interest on the Mexican debt. But it turned out that it would be necessary to enter the country, and then, on different grounds, Great Britain and Spain withdrew, leaving France to go on alone, as her ruler was quite willing to do. The task, however, proved more difficult than was expected. Puebla offered a successful resistance to the invader, and the city of Mexico was only reached in the summer of 1863.

Napoleon now had the brilliant idea of offering the throne of the Mexican 'Empire'—for such was to be the title of the new state—to Maximilian, the brother of the Austrian Emperor, Francis Joseph. Maximilian was a traveller and a scientist of distinction and was believed to hold liberal views on politics. Among other great results, which were hoped for from this move, were the friendship and perhaps the alliance of Austria. Maximilian accepted the offer after some delay and against the advice of Francis Joseph and of Great Britain. He was supported by the French General, Forey, and an army of 23,000 men. He was received with an appearance of enthusiasm in the city of Mexico.

But then this gorgeous 'palace in the air' dissolved quickly and tragically. Maximilian's supporters were divided and his opponents were determined. The North was now clearly gaining the upper hand in the American Civil War, and refused to recognise the new régime in Mexico, which contradicted the principles of the Monroe doctrine. Napoleon too, in characteristic fashion, was as weary of the project as he had once been enthusiastic, for it was bringing constant disappointment and expense. Forey's place had been taken by Bazaine—destined later to so sinister a fame—and Napoleon determined to withdraw the French forces and leave Maximilian, hoping that he would see the wisdom of retiring (February 1867). Maximilian refused, and struggled a little longer courageously against his enemies. The end came in June

[1] cp. Dexter Perkins: *The Monroe Doctrine, 1826–67*, pp. 318 *sqq*. (Baltimore, 1933).

1867, when he was forced to surrender to the native forces at Queretaro, and was shot in the courtyard of that town. The blow to Napoleon's prestige was irreparable.

This narrative has anticipated by several years the course of events in France. Napoleon had seen with alarm the tide of opposition rising against him. As far back as 1860 he had tried to conciliate opinion by modifying the absolute character of his rule. The press was watched a little less severely. The Senate and the Legislative Assembly were allowed to discuss the policy of the Government once in the year. Ministers 'without portfolio'—that is, without definite administrative tasks—were given a seat in the Assembly in order to explain and defend the policy of the Government. The debates in the Assembly might henceforth be freely reported and published. These concessions naturally encouraged without conciliating the opposition, which did not cease to demand a free constitution after the English pattern, with Ministers responsible not to the Emperor but to the Assembly, and to attack the financial administration of the Empire.

The elections of 1863 afforded an important trial of strength. The Government tried in every way to control them. Persigny undertook to procure a good majority for the Emperor, and set all the usual machinery to work. Yet the result was disappointing. The Government had indeed a large majority; but the opposition had grown from five to thirty-five. All the efforts of Persigny had not availed to induce the city of Paris to return one supporter of the Government. There was a frankly republican group of seventeen, with such leaders as Berryer, Jules Simon, Favre and, above all, Thiers, who again entered the parliamentary arena. The total number of votes thrown against the Government amounted to two millions. The writing on the wall was plain to the eyes of Europe.

Two prominent members made noteworthy approaches to Napoleon. Thiers was the greatest and most observed statesman in France. In a much-quoted speech he demanded for France what he called the 'necessary liberties'—the constitutional liberties enjoyed at this time by Englishmen—and he declared that, if these were granted, he would support the Empire though he would never take service under it. The action of Emile Ollivier was of even more immediate importance. He was by tradition attached to the Liberal party. His father had suffered exile for his opinions, and he had been one of the most eloquent of those 'Five' who for some time had been the sole representatives of opposition in the Assembly. But he was essentially moderate and conservative in his temper, and when Napoleon brought forward a proposal for legalising certain 'coalitions' of workmen—contrary to the tradition of France since the great Revolution—Ollivier determined to assist him. He did not hold, he said, by the maxim 'All or nothing,' which he considered a dangerous one. He was content to take a little every day.

It was with this modified constitution, still strongly centralised and still authoritative, but showing some traces of a liberal tendency, that France faced the difficulties of the Danish and Austro-Prussian Wars.[1] And it was this constitution that had to bear the strain of the Mexican fiasco and tragedy. We shall look later on at the diplomacy of France during and after the triumph of Prussia in her contest with Austria. We are concerned with the development of the French Constitution down to the eve of the catastrophe of the Empire—that is, to the Franco-Prussian War.

Napoleon affected to make light of the astounding triumphs of Prussia. In an official *communiqué* he expounded his doctrine of nationality, but he also stated that France would increase her armaments and would see to it that Germany remained divided in the future. The first proposition was contradicted by the second, and the third revealed either the insecurity or the warlike spirit of France. But French feeling refused to be comforted. Thiers declared that Sadowa was a great defeat, as serious for France as the Battle of Pavia had been nearly three and a half centuries before. Many were undoubtedly found to agree with him.

The victory of the Prussian national army produced many heart-searchings in France. It has been customary to compare it with the French system, which was based on conscription (the casting of lots, that is, among all who were eligible and the entire exemption from all military burdens of those on whom the lot did not fall) and then on strict professional training for seven years; and to maintain that the Prussians were mere amateurs compared with the French soldiers and that they would prove on the field of battle little more than 'improved national guards.' But Sadowa had changed all that! It was patent to all that the French army must be increased and the French system altered. Some, among whom the chief was Trochu (afterwards commander of Paris in the great siege of 1870), were anxious to adopt the Prussian system of universal military service; but French opinion was not ready for that. In the end, the term of service was lengthened and a new reserve—the 'garde mobile'—was planned. But these changes were not fully introduced when the storm of 1870 broke over France.

The political system was more thoroughly reconstructed. There was urgent need to do something. The press used the greater freedom which it had been granted to attack Napoleon with the utmost bitterness. Henri Rochefort displayed in *La Lanterne* all his unscrupulous wit and Delescluze was hardly less bitter than Marat had been. Gambetta revealed his extraordinary powers as orator and agitator in his defence of Delescluze when prosecuted by the Government. The ideas and passions of the Paris Commune were fermenting just below the surface. In 1869 Napoleon had withdrawn some of the measures by which he had hitherto tried to control the elections. The rural districts

[1] *v. infra*, pp. 252 *sqq.*

stood firm in his support, but some of his bitterest opponents were elected in the great cities. His supporters had a large majority in the Chamber, but three million votes had been recorded against him. The foundations of his system were slipping away.

He determined to take a bold step and initiate an entirely new system which he announced in opening the session of the new Assembly. A large step was taken towards that English parliamentary system which Napoleon had at one time regarded as outworn. The Chamber was to be allowed to legislate freely and to control the budget in all its details. Members of the legislature might be Ministers. The English Cabinet system, resting on the support of a majority in the House, seemed on the point of adoption. The functions of the Senate were to be closely assimilated to those of the House of Lords. A clause was added which might mean little or much: the Emperor reserved to himself the pre-rogatives which the people had conferred upon him and which were essential for the preservation of order and of society. In January 1870 Emile Ollivier, once so ardent a liberal, was asked to form a Ministry. He induced Napoleon to submit his new system to a popular vote as he had submitted his earlier proposals. All the electors of France were called on to vote 'Yes' or 'No' to a declaration that they approved the liberal reforms introduced into the constitution by the Emperor with the assistance of the chief constitutional bodies in the State. Ollivier regarded the result with the greatest satisfaction. True, the great cities abated nothing of their determined opposition. In Paris 184,000 voted 'No' and only 138,000 'Yes.' Lyons, Marseilles, Toulouse were all against the Government, but in France generally 7,358,000 approved and only 1,571,000 disapproved. The abstentions were more numerous than the votes of dissent, but on the whole Ollivier was justified in re-garding the result as a great triumph for what was now called the 'Liberal Empire.' If there had been a few years of peace and calm it is at least possible that the new system might have led France peacefully into constitutional parliamentary life, with or without a Napoleon at the head of the State. But, before France got to understand the new system or how to work it, came the deluge!

We must pass soon to an examination of the position in Central Europe, which is the background of the Franco-Prussian War, but first we will glance at the relations between Napoleon and Italy, which are an important side-stream to the main current. Napoleon was destined, it seemed, never to derive any advantage for himself or France from all his Italian policy, well meaning though it had been and often of great advantage to Italy. By the Convention of September 1864, Napoleon had promised that the French garrison should evacuate Rome, and the King of Italy had given an assurance that Florence and not Rome should be adopted as the capital of the new Italian State. The French troops actually left in December 1866; and at once a movement started, with the connivance of Garibaldi, for the invasion and conquest of

Rome. Clearly the Papal *zouaves* were quite unequal to the emergency. The French garrison was still at Marseilles. It was re-embarked, and reached Italy in time to join the Papal troops and defeat the Garibaldians at Mentana. The Italian liberals denounced Napoleon more bitterly than ever. De Failly, the general in command, reported that the new French rifle, the chassepot, 'had done wonders,' and something specially brutal was found in this remark. France in her hour of need would not find the Italian kingdom which she had done so much to create ready to help her.[1]

The last months of the Empire were much occupied with a new Roman question. The Pope had summoned a new Ecumenical Council for 1869. He had already declared his opposition to modern liberal and democratic ideas in no doubtful terms. It was certain that the new council would issue decrees that would offend liberal opinion, whether in Italy or elsewhere, and many held that France should use the influence of her exceptional position to prevent the council from assembling. But Ollivier overruled these views, and the Assembly met. Just at the moment when the relations between France and Germany were leading to the great war the Ecumenical Council was debating the question of papal infallibility, and the war had already begun when, on July 18, 1870, the council declared that the Pope was infallible 'when in the exercise of his mission as supreme teacher of all Christians he defines by his apostolic authority that which should be held by the Universal Church in the matter of faith or morals.'

CHAPTER XVIII

GERMANY TO THE SEVEN WEEKS' WAR (1848–1866)

THE Revolutions of 1848 and 1849 had been a great disappointment to all 'liberals' in Germany and Europe. Nothing of what liberalism desired had been won. Austria still ruled over her variegated populations with despotic sway. In Germany no approximation had been made to national unity nor to a government based on the consent of the people. A large measure of German unity was destined to come in little more than twenty years, but the political ideals of liberalism were doomed to wait much longer before they realised any real triumph on German soil.

[1] On December 4, 1867, M. Rouher, when interpellated in the Assembly, declared for the Government that they would *never* (jamais) permit Italian occupation of Rome. As Bismarck did not take this line, the French parliamentary utterance inclined Italy to Prussia rather than to France, and prevented her paying any real heed to the negotiations for a Franco-Austro-Italian alliance, which Napoleon pursued from 1868 onwards.

In Austria the régime was thoroughly despotic, of the kind that all continental governments seemed inclined to when they were not frightened into concessions. What the Revolutions had won was soon abolished. The jury was withdrawn; the Ministers were made once more directly dependent on the Emperor; flogging was reintroduced into the administration of the law and given even wider extension. Distrust of the people was universal in Government circles.

No change in principle was made until the Italian war of 1859, but then the character of the Government was completely altered. A military form of government is inevitably shaken by military failure. Some constitutional change was inevitable, but there was no country where the problems of constitution-making were so difficult as in Austria, with its many competing races, its conflict of religions and languages, its long tradition of military rule. A permanent trouble was to be found in Hungary, which refused to its own subject races the national existence which it claimed for itself. Should the new constitution be centralised and unitary, or federal and national? Both courses found their supporters, and it was doubtful which raised the most difficulties. In October 1860 the Emperor issued what is known as the October Diploma, establishing by royal decree what was intended to be a liberal constitution. There was to be an imperial council (*Reichsrat*), with some elective members, which would deal with all questions which concerned the whole Empire; there were to be local parliaments (*Landtage*), which would handle purely local matters. It was a great experiment in Home Rule. The Hungarians were to be appeased by the recognition of their tongue—the Magyar language—as official. In the following year (1861) further concessions were made. A more truly representative system was now to be introduced. It was all doomed to early extinction, or else it would be interesting to examine some of its proposals; a few points only are worth mentioning. The German element welcomed the new system; especially that part of it which allowed a much freer press. (It was at this time that the era of newspapers began for Austria). The non-German elements in the state nowhere gave the new constitution a hearty welcome, and the Magyars were on the whole opposed and refused co-operation. Still there was hope that in time the constitution would work. Then came the war of 1866, and Austria had to turn for a time from experiments in government to the task of defence.

The driving force in Central Europe was not to be found in Austria, but in Prussia and Germany; and it is to Prussia that we must turn with more careful attention. The Prussian system was much more competent but not more liberal than that of Austria. When in 1850 a lunatic shot at the King this was made an excuse for a further sharpening of the repressive system. The action of the jury system was still further restricted. Newspapers were closely supervised, and the Government exercised direct control over a great number. It is remembered that Froebel's *Kindergarten* was suppressed on the suspicion that it had some political object. Prussia, it was openly declared, was not a constitutional state but a state of officials and soldiers. It seemed for a time as if the Zollverein would disappear amidst the waves of reaction. The southern states were inclined to union with Austria, and Prussia would not hear of any commercial union with her great rival in Germany. Here, however, the danger passed. The Zollverein was enlarged by the inclusion of Hanover, and was renewed again in 1853 for twelve years.

One institution dear to the German revolutionaries and destined later to arouse the liveliest hopes in the German mind did not survive the reaction. A German fleet had been one of the creations of the short-lived German revolution. A fleet came into being and lay in Bremerhaven; a symbol, so it seemed to many, of a new opening for German energies. With the failure of the nationalist movement in the revolution, the enthusiasm for a German fleet died down. The federal Diet declared the dissolution of the fleet, and it was sold by auction.

In 1858 the intelligence of the Prussian King was definitely obscured, and his brother William succeeded, first as Regent in 1858, and then as King on his brother's death in 1861. Some had imagined that he was less reactionary than his predecessor. He was indeed more direct, clear-sighted, and capable; but he was as little of a liberal as could be found. He spoke in the true Hohenzollern tone at his coronation. 'I am the first King to mount the throne since it has been supported by modern institutions; but I do not forget that the crown has come to me from God alone and that I have received it from His hands.'[1] He had some sympathy with German aspirations towards national unity, and the 'National Association,' with its motto drawn from Schiller, 'Be united, united!' met with no opposition from him. But he had no love for or belief in liberal institutions. He was a true successor of Frederick the Great, though of a much more genial nature. His real enthusiasm was for the army. He looked at all problems with the eyes of a soldier, and his support of the army soon brought him into conflict with the representatives of the state.

There was reason to think that Prussia required a stronger army. The humiliation of Olmütz was fresh in men's minds; the history of Prussia was predominantly military, and there could be no thought of changing the character of the state. The King was assisted at this juncture by one of the makers of modern Prussia—the War Minister, Roon. This true organiser of victory had a religious belief in the destiny of Prussia and of Germany, and a deep conviction that the Prussian army was the instrument through which Prussia must accomplish her destiny. The army represented to him not only force, but morals and religion. The Assembly had shown a desire to decrease the extent of the military preparations of Prussia by reducing the term of service from three years to

---

[1] He was one of the few Prussian Kings who were crowned and, characteristically, he crowned himself.

two. Roon's proposal ran directly counter to all this. The period of service was to be three years; and then there was to be a period of four years spent with the reserve. There were changes in military organisation too, and the needle-gun was to be introduced. The Assembly did not definitely reject all this, but clearly meant to criticise and amend.

Then came the general elections of 1861, which gave a great majority to the party of progress. They demanded all manner of liberal reforms which would have started Prussia on a course of development the opposite of what Roon desired: the extension of the jury system; reform of the Upper House; education freed from all clerical influence; responsible Ministers; above all, the reduction of the term of military service to two years. The challenge of the Long Parliament to Charles I was not more direct. All possibility of misconception was cast aside when Roon, in September 1862, called on the Assembly to vote the war proposals *en bloc* and the Assembly refused by 308 votes to 11. The representatives of the nation had answered the royal challenge with an almost unanimous No! English and French history would seem to show that the King must yield and that some sort of constitutional life, to be won perhaps by revolution, was in store for Germany. Her destiny was just the opposite.

Neither Roon nor his master thought of yielding, though the idea of abdication passed seriously through William's mind. But while he was King he was determined not to abandon measures on which it seemed to him that the existence of the state might depend. Roon talked of a *coup d'état* and of carrying on the Government by the forcible collection of the taxes which the Assembly had refused to vote. But another idea had been revolving in his mind. He had for some time known and admired the ideas and character of Bismarck. He now felt that he was the one man who might pilot Prussia through the great storm that threatened. He induced the King to get rid of his present Ministry, (whose nominal head was Prince Adolph Hohenlohe), and to entrust the Government into Bismarck's hands. Bismarck was at this time Prussian diplomatic representative at Paris, where he had just arrived. The King instructed Roon to summon him. Two telegrams were sent. The second added 'Danger in delay.' Bismarck came at once to Berlin and saw the King. He promised to support the reorganisation of the army, and the promise of his assistance dispelled from the King's mind all thought of abdication. The new President declared on his side unyielding opposition to parliamentary claims. 'I will rather perish with the King than forsake your Majesty in the contest with parliamentary government.' Thus the lists were prepared for an all-important combat.

Bismarck and the King won. Parliamentary ideals were defeated and discredited. Germany entered on that road which led her through amazing triumphs in the battlefield and the council chamber to the ruin that has resulted from two disastrous Great Wars. To understand the issue of the vitally important internal conflict of 1862 we must note that

Bismarck did not attack the whole of the popular programme. On the contrary he carried to victory one-half of it, and that perhaps the half most passionately desired. For the national movement strove not only for constitutional government, but also for national unity. Bismarck induced Germany to forgo the first by giving her the second in full measure, and coupling it with the intoxicating draught of military glory.

Bismarck was a well-known man in governmental circles when he received the appointment of President of the Ministry. He had represented Prussia at the Frankfort Diet when a strong man was wanted who would not give way to the Austrian assumptions of superiority over all other German states; and stories, perhaps half legendary, were told of his coolness and success in that capacity. He had seen with bitter regret the capitulation of the monarchy in the days of the 1848 rising, and had told the King in a private letter that he could rely on the army and that the popular forces were not as strong as they seemed to be. The generations that succeeded him in Germany looked upon him as the great heroic representative of the nation in the world of action. But in some important points he is by no means characteristic. In the first place his views and impulses rested on a basis of deeply-felt religious conviction. 'If I were not a Christian I should be a republican,' he is reported to have said. And in the next place he owed little or nothing to the academic training to which modern Germany owed so much. He had been at the University of Göttingen, but did not regret his neglect of the studies there. He spoke strongly of the cramping effect of university education and its tendency to check originality. His outlook on European politics was always Prussian rather than German. 'Prussians we are and Prussians we will remain,' he said. German unity was for him an extension of Prussian power. There was hardly a trace in him of the 'good European' that Talleyrand had looked for in vain at the Congress of Vienna. Outside of Court and Government circles he was little known. There were some who thought him a liberal and dangerously inclined to a French alliance. Yet he declared himself at once ready to fight constitutional ideas. When the King alluded to the parallel with English history and the fate of Charles I, which was much in men's minds, he did not shrink from it. 'I would fall like Lord Strafford; and your Majesty, not as Louis XVI, but as Charles I. He is a quite respectable historical figure.' [1]

A difficult question soon came up for solution. Austria made herself the spokesman of German liberalism, and invited Prussia to send delegates to Frankfort to discuss a scheme for a German federal union. The proposals were interesting. There was to be a 'directory' consisting of the representatives of six states, and Prussia, Austria and Bavaria

[1] Even in later life when advising William II, Bismarck told him that a King of Prussia ought to die sword in hand rather than submit to the demands of the democracy.

were always to be of the number. There was to be a federal council and a federal assembly. The King, always anxious to work with Austria, was for accepting the invitation, and if we look at the issue from a 'European' point of view we can hardly doubt that he was right. But the new constitution would curb the action of Prussia, and Bismarck refused compliance. His will was usually stronger than his master's, and after a long struggle, which left both of them exhausted, the King agreed to abstain. The refusal of Prussia to co-operate brought down the whole proposal. The rivalry of Prussia and Austria for the leadership of Germany was a patent fact, and many saw that the sword must in the end decide.

Next came the Polish question. The country had not resigned itself to the measures of repression that had been undertaken after the rising of 1848. Dreams of national independence had never ceased to haunt the minds of the enlightened classes among the Poles. They saw their own past through a haze of romance and regret, and thought that whatever had been Poland in the sixteenth century should be Poland again. There was much that was well-intentioned in the treatment of Poland by Czar Alexander II. He desired to emancipate the serfs and to establish a peasantry that should recognise its debt to Russia and re-pay it by loyalty to the Russian connection. Unfortunately, he joined to these measures some that directly attacked the middle and upper classes of Poland; and, especially, he enforced his military levy against them. While the peasants were to be left upon their lands, the classes associated with the national movement were to be swept into the Russian army. There followed a Polish insurrection, which gained some success at first and advanced beyond the boundaries of Poland on to territories which were thoroughly Russian. But the victory of Russia was certain unless Europe interfered.

European interference did not seem impossible; for Poland was a word that inflamed the imagination of all 'liberals' of that age. There was great excitement in Paris and the feeling of England was decidedly in favour of Poland. Had Prussia shown any inclination to co-operate with the Western Powers Russia would have been faced with the prospect of a very dangerous coalition. But Bismarck was wholly against any support of rebels. He had a strong feeling that the friendship of Russia would be a necessity for Prussia in the contests which awaited her. He paid no attention to the protests of German liberals and the Prussian Assembly, nor even to the representations of the Prussian Crown Prince. He assured the Czar of Prussian sympathy and Prussian support, and the Polish revolt was beaten down. The understanding with Russia that was thus established was one of the pillars of Prussian policy while Bismarck remained in charge of it; and the Czar did not show himself ungrateful for what Bismarck had done.

The Prussian Parliament stormed and threatened. German liberal opinion regarded Bismarck as the great enemy. It was difficult to see how he could carry his policy through to victory in the face of general Prussian opposition. He was saved by the Schleswig-Holstein question, which led up to two wars.

The Schleswig-Holstein question has become a byword for obscurity. It is like some intricate trial at law where the opinion of the onlooker changes with the addresses of the different advocates. Denmark was an ancient and honoured monarchy connected with many of the greatest royal families of Europe. Her population was for industry, intelligence, and character on a level with the most advanced populations of Europe. Her southern frontier had, however, for long presented difficulties which had of late years become more acute. There lay the two provinces of Schleswig and Holstein, which were admittedly no part of Denmark but which had been for long attached to the crown of Denmark. Schleswig was predominantly Danish in character and had been given a separate Diet of her own. Holstein was very largely German. It had formed part of the Holy Roman Empire of which Germans were beginning to think now with romantic regret, and it had been recognised as a member of the Germanic Confederation by the Treaty of Vienna. It was separate from Schleswig, but had a common Ministry with it. As the strong sense of German nationality developed in Germany the hope grew that some means might be found to incorporate *both* the Duchies in the German State. The troubles of 1848 have already been touched on. The effort of the Duchies to break away from Denmark had been crushed and the whole Danish question had been, it was hoped, settled by the Treaty of London in 1852. This treaty laid down first that the present childless King of Denmark should be succeeded by the husband of his niece, Christian, Prince of Glücksburg, in all his dominions, and that these dominions included the two Duchies. Another clause declared that the relation of Holstein to the Germanic Confederation was in no way altered by the treaty. The Great Powers— France, Prussia, Austria, Russia, Great Britain—signed the treaty, but it was not accepted by the Diet of Frankfort, the organ of the Germanic Confederation, nor by Frederick of Augustenburg, the rival claimant to the Danish throne. But the Diet was not taken seriously, and a personal claimant was not likely to throw Europe into war, if the signatories to the treaty stood firm.

The new King of Denmark, Christian IX, succeeded in 1863, and one of his first acts was to ratify an arrangement already made by his predecessor for the issue of a new Constitution, unifying his dominions and thus disregarding the traditional autonomy of the Duchies. The fact that Holstein was a member of the Germanic Confederation was one of the reasons for the disastrous results of this measure. It provided the necessary *casus belli* to a Germany which was peculiarly sensitive to what happened in the Duchies. So Frederick of Augustenburg claimed the monarchy of Denmark and his claims were supported by the Diet at Frankfort.

Apart then from the immediate occasion for the war the position was simple. There was a disputed claim to the Danish throne; and there was a dispute between Denmark and the Germanic Confederation as to the Duchies. In the issue Denmark lost, but the Confederation did not gain. The gains went by an ironic stroke of fate to Prussia and to Austria, both of which Powers had signed the Treaty of London and had recognised the right of Prince Christian to the succession to the Duchies. Yet the explanation of this strange turn is not hard to find. When weaker powers quarrel it is often the strong that profit. The decisive factor in the confusion that so puzzled Europe was the strength of Prussia and the determination and skill of Bismarck.

On the death of the Danish King, Frederick of Augustenburg, as we have said, protested against the succession of Prince Christian and claimed the throne. The German Diet considered the matter and decided to support him. The Diet had never accepted the Treaty of London and its hands were quite free. 'Federal execution' was ordered—that is, the Diet determined to support its decision by the weak forces which were at its disposal. Denmark could perhaps have held its ground against them. But mightier combatants entered the arena. Prussia and Austria could not see with equanimity these great decisions left in the hands of the smaller Powers. Their jealousy did not allow them to act separately. Bismarck made a hasty alliance with Austria; and then Prussia and Austria declared themselves the executants of the will of the Diet. They had signed the Treaty of London, but they had not guaranteed it. They held themselves free to act according to what they conceived to be their interests in the new situation that had arisen. So the federal army was withdrawn and a joint Austrian and Prussian army entered the territory of Denmark.

Europe saw the step with alarm and with general sympathy for the small Power that was attacked by two large ones. The two invaders would hardly have persisted in their action in face of any general European protest. But Europe did not exist except as a geographical and cultural unit. The idea of the European Concert which had grown up in the earlier nineteenth century had become ineffective, except, and this only to a limited extent, in relation to Turkey. The ideas of the twentieth century, expressed first in the League of Nations and then in the United Nations, were not yet born. Nor was there any power or group of powers ready to interfere. Norway and Sweden looked on with sympathy, but much to Ibsen's indignation took no action. Palmerston used words which seemed to imply that Great Britain would not regard the invasion of Denmark with equanimity; but he did not go beyond words. When the time came he was supported neither by the Opposition nor the Queen, and the majority of his Cabinet turned against him. He had crossed swords with a stronger antagonist than himself, and his prestige failed as Bismarck's grew. Napoleon III had the difficult Mexican affair on his hands and was not at this moment on good terms with Great Britain. Moreover, he had made himself the champion of the principle of nationality, and the action of the German Powers was defended as being a movement towards German national unity. What he had done and said in the case of Italy made it difficult for him to resist Prussia and Austria in Germany. There remained Russia, but Bismarck had secured the neutrality of Russia by his action in the Polish rising.

So the war went on to a rapid and certain end. The Austrian troops were supposed to have shown greater skill than the Prussians. When the Danish defeat was certain a conference was called in London; but the victors' terms were too hard to allow of settlement. The war continued. The Danish government was driven from the mainland, and had to accept the terms that the victorious enemy dictated. The terms were surprising. Prussia and Austria had been acting as executants for the German Federation and apparently for Frederick of Augustenburg. But their clients got nothing, and they took all for themselves. The interests of Europe and the rules of international right were openly flouted. In the Treaty of Peace which was hurried through by Bismarck, who always feared above all things the interference of a European Congress, it was declared that the King of Denmark 'renounces all his rights over the Duchies of Schleswig, Holstein, and Lauenburg in favour of their Majesties the King of Prussia and the Emperor of Austria.' [1] The Germanic Confederation was completely ignored. The bungling efforts of England and France to interfere in the settlement were swept aside. The Duke of Augustenburg, in whose behalf Prussia and Austria had seemed to interfere, was treated with complete cynicism. An inquiry was held in Berlin as to the legal position of the Danish succession. It was declared that Christian IX was the only rightful heir both to the Danish crown and to the Duchies. He had therefore full right to cede them in the treaty. Thus Austria and Prussia had to render account to no one for their occupation of the Duchies.

In these tangled events lie the beginnings of that condition of things in Europe which led at once to two major European wars and then forty years later to the first World War. 'England failed France and France failed England and both failed Europe. The triumph lay with Bismarck alone. He had laid his hand on the heart of France and detected its weakened movement. He had calculated the inertia

---

[1] Treaty of Vienna, Art. 3, of 30 October, 1864, between Austria, Prussia, and Denmark. The Convention of Gastein, 14 August, 1865, gave Schleswig to Prussia and Holstein to Austria, but only to administer. The Treaty of Prague, 23 August, 1866, by Article 5 transferred all Austrian rights to Prussia but arranged for a plebiscite in North Schleswig to decide whether the area should be returned to Denmark. Bismarck kept deferring the holding of this plebiscite, and nothing was done till 1919. Then Articles 109–114 of the Treaty of Versailles provided for this plebiscite. It was held and the northern area of Schleswig declared in favour of, and was returned to, Denmark.

of England. He held Russia by the memories of the Polish question.'

Schleswig and Holstein thus lay helplessly in the hands of Austria and Prussia. The two partners had from the first regarded each other with suspicion and hostility. The joint occupation of the Duchies had in it no principle of permanence, and in less than two years it led to a greater war between Prussia and Austria. The condition of Europe was restless and there were several questions out of which war might have come. But the driving force to war was without much doubt the ambition and power of Prussia and of her strong Minister. Germany dominated and united by Prussia—that was the dream that never ceased to occupy Bismarck's imagination; and the traditions and claims of Austria lay right across the road to its realisation.

The next question which contributed to the fulfilment of Bismarck's plans arose at the other end of the central block of European territory. South of the Alps the Italian Government, in spite of the many difficulties which it found in the management of its recently acquired territories was anxious for more. Rome was the city and land most desired, but the road to Rome was decisively blocked by the action of France. In September 1864 Italy had signed a convention with France by which she had promised not to attack Rome and to adopt Florence as her capital, and on these conditions France promised to withdraw her garrison from Rome. But, if Rome was forbidden, Venice was not. True, Venice was in many ways separate, both in history and character, from the rest of Italy; but she desired incorporation with Italy, and Italy felt herself manifestly incomplete while Venice remained under Hapsburg rule. Bismarck, conscious of the coming struggle with Austria, made overtures to Italy, and after some difficulty made an agreement: that in the event of an Austrian war both Prussia and Italy were to throw all their forces into the contest; and that Prussia was not to make peace until the possession of Venice was secured to Italy. But what of France? She might exercise a decisive influence, and Napoleon III still aspired to be the arbiter of peace and war in Europe. In October 1865 Bismarck paid a famous visit to him at Biarritz, and there, amidst much apparent light-hearted gaiety, he managed to secure the good will of France. Napoleon lived in a world of dreams. 'Prussia and France are the two nations of Europe whose interests are most nearly identical,' he said; and yet Sedan was less than five years off!

It seemed at one time that war would have come in 1865, for the partnership in the Duchies led to many difficult problems. But in August the Convention of Gastein 'plastered over the cracks' and the partners divided their spoil. Prussia was to administer Schleswig, the more northerly Duchy, and Austria Holstein, the more thoroughly German. The situation was difficult, but with a strong desire for peace it was not incapable of a pacific solution.

The political situation in Prussia contributed something to the un-likelihood of a policy of peace. The liberal opposition had not ceased to oppose Bismarck and all his works, though there was some satisfaction to be gained from the Danish settlement—for the two Duchies would henceforth be in German hands. But in February 1866 a vote of censure on the Government was proposed because it had prosecuted certain members of the Assembly. The never-failing memory of Charles and the Long Parliament was invoked again; and the vote of censure was passed by 263 votes to 35. Bismarck thereupon prorogued and then dismissed the Assembly. Paradoxically, political unrest at home strengthened rather than diminished the determination of Bismarck.

The rupture with Austria came over the supposed favour shown by Austria to the claims of Frederick of Augustenburg. In the adminis-tration of the two provinces Prussia and Austria had pursued widely different policies. The Austrian representative had done his utmost to conciliate the people of Holstein and had spoken of the claims of Frederick of Augustenburg as still valid. Prussia, on the contrary, had ruled with a strong hand, and had taken no account of the feelings or wishes of the people. When, therefore, a meeting was held in Altona— in the neighbourhood of Hamburg and in the territory controlled by Austria—in favour of the claims of Augustenburg this was regarded by Prussia as an unfriendly act, and as a sufficient excuse for the war, which had been foreseen and desired for some time by the leaders of Prussian policy. For there can be no doubt on this point. It is true that no war springs from a single cause or from the action of one man. There are always many contributing and supporting causes. But it is certain that in 1865 Bismarck, Moltke and Roon desired a war with Austria and believed it necessary in the interests of Prussia and of the German policy, which was identified with Prussia. The domestic difficulty too, and the violent resistance of the Parliamentary opposition, could only, it seemed, be met in this way. Moltke said later that 'it was a war which was foreseen long before, which was prepared with deliberation and recognised as necessary by the Cabinet, not in order to obtain territorial aggrandisement but in order to secure the establishment of Prussian hegemony in Germany.' Bismarck, too, realised clearly that his own personal position depended on the issue of the contest. 'Had I failed,' he said, 'the old women would have swept me with a curse with their besoms into the gutter.'

The fate of Schleswig and of Holstein was of great importance; but it soon fell into the background. A war between two great military Powers was clearly threatening; and the statesmen of Europe considered with feverish anxiety the problems that arose from the situation. The Powers not directly concerned abounded in well-meant schemes for avoiding the contest, and at the same time planned how to win for them-selves some gain in territory or prestige, if the war really came about. The atmosphere was one of rivalry, suspicion, and above all of fear, which made all peace efforts very difficult. The German Diet at Frankfort had some claim to be regarded as an umpire in the dispute, but neither Prussia nor Austria was inclined to accept interference from this quarter. So, in a fashion that Europe had so often seen, and was to see again, Europe staggered forward to war through a maze of proposals and counter-proposals, of projects of disarmament, and suggestions of settlement by congress. Bismarck never wavered in his belief that the sword alone could cut the Gordian knot, and in his desire to bring about that solution. King William only gradually yielded to his Minister's strong will.

Amidst all the uncertainty one thing was clear. Whatever happened Italy would gain Venice. Prussia had promised not to make peace except on that condition, and Austria, anxious above all things to win the neutrality, or if possible the support, of France, declared herself willing to surrender Venice, even if the war went in her favour in Italy and Germany. A scruple of military honour kept her from handing over the territory at once to Italy and so preventing her from taking any part in the coming war.

It was the French Emperor who seemed to hold the balance in his hands, and the negotiations between him and Austria, Prussia and Italy were unceasing. The action of France, despite Bismarck's famous interview with Napoleon at Biarritz, was quite uncertain up to the last. The Emperor was ill of the disease which, it seems, diminished his energy and his will power from this time until his death. In marked contrast with Bismarck he saw nothing clearly, was not sure of his own wishes, and lived in a world of cloudy and half-realised schemes. He would like to show France as the guardian of the peace of Europe; he would like to do something for the cause of nationality that he had so often preached; he would like to help Italy on the road to unity; above all, if there was to be a war, he would like to gain something for France, if possible, on the Rhine frontier. He believed that the forces of Prussia and Austria were about equally matched; that the war would be a long and indecisive one; and that in the end the sword of France would be thrown into the scale to decide the issue. Just before the outbreak of war he was moving decisively to the side of Austria. In June 1866 he signed an agreement whereby France promised her own neutrality and that she would use her best efforts to keep Italy neutral; while Austria promised to hand over Venice to Italy at the end of the war whatever its course, and to take France into her confidence with regard to any alterations in the German Constitution or in the Balance of Power among its members.

The Frankfort Diet was the scene of the last diplomatic struggles. The sympathy of the smaller German Powers had been alienated from both Austria and Prussia by the Gastein Convention. But they exercised little influence on the course of events. The decision, as Treitschke saw with delight, had passed from ideas and votes to power; and the Danish

9

war had shown how small was the power in the hands of the Diet. Prussia had for some time played with the idea of a reform of the constitution of Germany. Now, in June 1866, she brought forward a definite proposal that the present Diet should be dissolved and the constitution abolished; that a new National Assembly should be elected to decide on a national constitution; and that Austria and the Austrian lands should have no share in this constitution. Austria answered by declaring that Prussia had broken the Treaty of Vienna and the Gastein Convention, and called for the mobilisation of the federal army against her. Nine votes supported the Austrian proposal, while six were given against it. Bavaria, Saxony, Hanover, and Baden were among the supporters of Austria. The Prussian representative, Savigny, solemnly protested against the action of Austria as unconstitutional; once more declared the existing constitution at an end and that Prussia was ready to co-operate in the formation of a new one. But all this was idle talk until a military decision had been reached. That came with a rapidity and a decisiveness altogether unexpected.

CHAPTER XIX

THE DEFEAT OF AUSTRIA AND THE COMING OF THE FRANCO-GERMAN WAR

EUROPE looked on with amazement at the struggle between Prussia and Austria. The general opinion was that Austria had the better chance. The Prussian military system was untried; her short-service soldiers, it was thought, would prove to be little more than a 'national guard' against the Austrian troops with their long military training and traditions. Napoleon III hoped that an evenly balanced struggle would give him an opportunity of intervention and allow him to appear again as the bringer of victory and peace.

The actual spectacle afforded by the war was something very different. The Prussian machine worked with fatal precision. The needle-gun was a better weapon than the French chassepot. Moltke's strategy has been criticised, and it is certain that at times the struggle seemed equally balanced and that a small weight thrown into the other scale might have brought about a different issue. But if there was luck it was all on the side of Prussia. Moltke triumphed without encountering so much as a serious check. The campaign was conducted in what came to be regarded as the classical Prussian style. There was no delay in beginning. Everything was ready. Prussia took the offensive from the very beginning, and the issue was decided after three weeks of fighting.

The final scene in the German Diet produced war on June 14. Prussia had to deal with two enemy forces. There was the Austrian army in

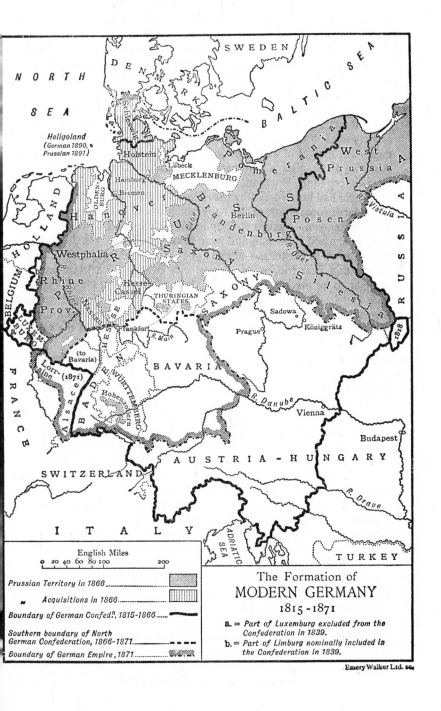

NORTH SEA

SWEDEN

DENMARK

BALTIC SEA

Heligoland
(German 1890,
Prussian 1891)

Schleswig

Holstein

Lübeck

MECKLENBURG

Pomerania

West Prussia

Hamburg

Bremen

OLDENBURG

Hanover

Brandenburg

Berlin

Posen

R. Vistula

HOLLAND

PRUSSIA

Elbe

S.

Silesia

R. Oder

Westphalia

Saxony

Rhine

Hesse Cassel

THURINGIAN STATES

SAXONY

Sadowa

Königgrätz

BELGIUM

Prov.

Nassau

Frankfort

R. Main

Prague

LUXEMBURG

(to Bavaria)

BAVARIA

FRANCE

Lorraine (1871)

HESSE

WÜRTTEMBERG

Hohenzollern

BADEN

Alsace

R. Danube

Vienna

Budapest

AUSTRIA - HUNGARY

SWITZERLAND

ITALY

ADRIATIC SEA

R. Drave

TURKEY

Emery Walker Ltd. sc.

English Miles

0   20 40 60 80 100   200

Prussian Territory in 1866..............

Acquisitions in 1866.............

Boundary of German Confed.ⁿ 1815-1866.....

Southern boundary of North
German Confederation, 1866-1871.............

Boundary of German Empire, 1871.................

The Formation of
MODERN GERMANY
1815-1871

a. = Part of Luxemburg excluded from the
Confederation in 1839.

b. = Part of Limburg nominally included in
the Confederation in 1839.

Bohemia, and there was the Hanoverian army whose aim was to join with the Bavarians and south Germans. On June 28—just a fortnight after the declaration of hostilities—the Hanoverian army was caught and crushed at Langensalza. Five days later, on July 3, the Austrian army was encountered by Moltke on the battlefield which English historians usually call Sadowa and German historians Königgrätz. The Austrians under Benedek fought skilfully and stubbornly, and there were moments when Bismarck watched Moltke's face with great anxiety to see if he could read there any indication of the fortunes of the day. The arrival of the Prussian Crown Prince on the right of the Austrian army, after a famous march, decided the fate of the day and gave victory to the Prussians.

Austria had been forced by the alliance of Italy with Prussia to maintain a large force south of the Alps which would have been of priceless value at Sadowa. Against Archduke Albrecht in the Lombard plain the Italians showed little skill and were heavily defeated. On July 24 they were crushed at Custozza—already once fatal to Italian patriotic hopes. The Italian fleet too, whose superiority over the Austrian fleet was thought to be certain, was heavily defeated at the Battle of Lissa. If Italy had stood alone the work of 1859 might have been undone. But Bismarck had promised that he would make no peace which did not give Venice to Italy, and the victory of Sadowa completed the work of Magenta and Solferino.

It was not certain that the war would end after Sadowa. The defeats of the Italians and the military aspirations of Moltke and the King of Prussia pointed rather to a continuation of the fighting and a march on to Vienna. That the fighting came to an end, and that negotiations for peace were undertaken after the Prussian armies had advanced a little further towards their goal, was almost entirely the work of Bismarck. He never showed himself a greater master of diplomacy than during the four years between 1866 and 1870; and it is not merely diplomatic skill that he exhibited but also real statesmanship. The unity of Germany under Prussia was the idea always uppermost in his thoughts. That could not be secured by military success against armies that were mainly German. The conciliation of the South Germans was essential, and Austria must be so treated that she would not regard Prussia with a hatred that would efface all other considerations. There was also another fear in Bismarck's mind—the interference of the French Emperor. True, the struggle was far removed from the even balance that Napoleon had hoped for; but he was anxious to be accepted as mediator, and sent Benedetti, the French Ambassador, to the Prussian headquarters at Nikolsburg. Bismarck has told us in a chapter of exceptional interest in his *Reflections and Reminiscences* what were his reasons for insisting on peace.[1] The centre of his thought was 'We must finish off rapidly, before France has time to bring diplomatic action to bear on

[1] Chapter xx. [Eng. translation] 1898.

Austria.' So he forced the King, sorely against his inclination, to forgo the march on Vienna and to content himself with terms which had seemed at first entirely inadequate.

The Treaty of Prague was signed on August 23, 1866. Venice with the adjacent territory went to Italy. Austria handed it over to Napoleon, who was gratified by this opportunity of playing some part in the great drama, and Napoleon gave it to Italy. The procedure bitterly hurt Italian pride, and is one more instance of Napoleon's failure to win Italian support by all that he did for Italy. Article 4 declared that Austria would no longer claim any share in the organisation of Germany. A North German Confederation was to be formed; and also an association 'with an independent international existence' of the states of Southern Germany. Schleswig and Holstein were to go to Prussia, though a clause, never acted on, declared that part of Schleswig was to return to Denmark if it expressed its wish by plebiscite to do so. The soldiers came back in triumph to Berlin. Moltke had shown his genius as a soldier, and King William a certain greatness of character; but the master mind had been Bismarck's throughout.

The feeling of Europe about these great happenings naturally varied from country to country. In Great Britain there was general satisfaction. Lord Stanley, the Foreign Minister, added words that the future was to emphasise: 'Egypt, Constantinople, Belgium—if you attach any value to the maintenance of peace with us avoid these three questions.' In France, on the contrary, the triumph of Prussia was felt to be a great disaster. The supremacy of France in Europe disappeared at Sadowa. 'It is France that was beaten at Sadowa,' said Marshal Randon. 'What has happened,' said Thiers, 'is for France the greatest disaster that she has suffered for four hundred years'—since the end, that is, of the Hundred Years' War. Napoleon III no doubt felt the deepest chagrin at the triumph of Prussia; but he tried to cover it by declaring that it was a victory for the doctrine of nationality which he had always so eagerly championed. He added somewhat inconsistently that Germany was divided into three independent parts and each part was smaller than France, and declared openly that France would prevent any further union of these sections and reorganise her military system. He hoped, too, to gain for France some compensation for the great increase in the power of Prussia in accordance with the idea of the Balance of Power. He was already so ill that much of the French diplomacy had to be carried on by his Ministers. Its course shows the extraordinary superiority of Bismarck in all departments of the game. He knew what he wanted and had made up his mind how it was to be got. In force and in finesse, in honesty and in duplicity, he was the assured master of the French diplomatists whom he encountered, and who were made to appear as amateurs fighting against a master of fence.

First, before peace was concluded between Prussia and Austria, Napoleon put forward through his Ambassador in Prussia, Benedetti, the idea that France might be induced to accept the annexations which Prussia proposed for herself in Germany on condition that France should advance her frontier up to the Rhine and even lay hands on Mainz. This would have meant the French annexation of territories that were thoroughly German in origin and character. Part of them, moreover, belonged to Bavaria, the leader of the South Germans, whose favour France was particularly anxious to win. Bismarck was careful not to show at first all the hostility which he felt to these proposals. He induced Benedetti to make a formal statement of the French claims. No sooner were they made than they were decisively rejected. The King of Prussia declared that under no circumstances would he abandon a single German village; he would rather risk another war. The French Emperor had to withdraw his proposals, for he was not prepared to enforce them by arms. It was a humiliating check for French diplomacy, and it did not end there. Bismarck communicated the French proposals to the correspondent of a French newspaper, *Le Siècle*, and they became known to all the world. The Southern Germans were thus taught to see in Napoleon a false friend and in Prussia the champion of German integrity, even of the integrity of those states against whom she was fighting.[1] Nor could Napoleon's action this time be justified by his favourite doctrine of nationality.

France had failed to get compensation on the eastern frontier; might she have better luck on the north? Bismarck had warned her off from German territory; would he be as strict a guardian of the lands of Belgium? To advance her frontier farther to the north had been for centuries the dream of the statesmen of France. Much of Belgium spoke French. The state was a comparatively recent creation of European diplomacy. Bismarck had used words which seemed to imply that he would not regard French occupation of Belgium as necessarily hostile to Prussia. Benedetti was instructed to bring this new idea before the Prussian Government. There is much obscurity and conflict of evidence over the incident and its details. Even its date is far from certain, but is believed to be August. But it is certain that Benedetti made his proposals piecemeal, and at last submitted to Bismarck in writing a suggestion that Prussia should help France if she invaded Belgium and protect her against foreign interference. But the situation in Europe was constantly becoming more favourable to Prussia and French help of less importance. Bismarck rejected the idea of a French advance in Belgium as decisively as he had rejected compensation on the Rhine frontier. He kept Benedetti's draft proposal by him and used it three years later

---

[1] The Prussian treaties with the various Southern States of Germany were signed at this time, i.e. *before* the Peace of Prague. In that treaty Article 4 provided that the new North German Confederation should be 'north of the line of the [river] Main.' The treaties with the Southern States provided for the extension of Prussian influence south of that river. Thus, to use a paradox, Art. 4 of the Prague Treaty was violated before it was signed.

with decisive effect at a critical moment. For when in 1870 the war had broken out between France and Germany and there was fear that English opinion might veer to the side of France he gave the document to the correspondent of *The Times*. When it was published English readers saw that the French Emperor had actually proposed to violate the neutrality of those Belgian lands whose independence had always seemed so necessary to English interests; and a revulsion of feeling followed in favour of Germany.

The Rhine frontier was forbidden; Belgium was forbidden. But what of Luxemburg? It would be a great triumph to annex that tiny state, and perhaps it might be done without incurring the opposition of the great statesman of Prussia. The Grand Duchy of Luxemburg was indeed a strange bundle of contradictions. It was recognised as an independent state, and the King of Holland was the hereditary Grand Duke. But it was also a member of the German Confederation and of the Zollverein, and ever since 1815 a Prussian garrison had held its strong fortress as a protection against a French attack upon Germany.

The French Foreign Minister, De Moustier, undertook the delicate negotiation. The King of Holland was in financial difficulties and derived no real advantage from his nominal rule over this French-speaking population of 200,000. A sum was offered him by way of indemnity. He demanded more; Napoleon demurred, but eventually gave way. The proposal might have gone through; and Prussia and Europe would have been presented with an accomplished fact if Napoleon had not haggled about the terms, and if the King of Holland had not thought it necessary to inform the Powers, who had signed the guarantee of the neutrality of Luxemburg in 1839, of what was proposed. Prussia was among these, and thus the affair, which was already known to Bismarck in his private capacity, came before the official Government of Prussia. German national sentiment, immensely inflamed and strengthened by the victory over Austria, now blazed out against this proposal to cede what might be regarded as German territory to the great rival. Prussia refused her consent to the proposed arrangement and the affair fell to the ground. It seemed as though it might easily have led to war, which a large party in Germany and the Prussian war-chiefs would have welcomed. Conciliatory voices, however, made themselves heard. Queen Victoria wrote to the Prussian King. Russia also used her influence in favour of peace. Bismarck himself was not for war. So a settlement was made in Luxemburg; only the Prussian garrison, which had clearly now lost all justification, was withdrawn. But war had seemed near. 'Nothing could have been more welcome than war,' said Moltke, 'and after all it must come.' Both German and French feeling had become embittered and hostile.

While France was thus making embarrassed and unsuccessful efforts to recover her position and prestige in Europe, Prussia advanced from strength to strength and was building the road along which in four years from the Battle of Sadowa she would advance to unity in **Germany** and supremacy in Europe.

The Peace of Prague had spoken of a federal constitution for North Germany. Prussia was absolute master there. Hanover had to pay for her alliance with Austria and the southern states of Germany in the late war by the loss of her independence and the annexation of her territories to Prussia. The other states of North Germany, such as Oldenburg, and the Mecklenburgs, Brunswick, Anhalt, Coburg-Gotha and Detmold, were powerless to resist in the least detail the will of Prussia. If Bismarck had wished to annex them all there could have been no effective resistance, and some advised that a centralised German state and not a federal league should be the form of the new Germany. This would, however, have conflicted with the words of the Treaty of Prague, and the supremacy of Prussia was so great that no real rivalry could be feared. It would also have made more difficult that union of Northern and Southern Germany on which Bismarck's hopes were set.

There was much speculation as to the form which the new constitution would take. Many brains were at work on it, but the decisive influence was with Bismarck. The result was something new in the constitutional history of Europe, a federal state of a kind which had in reality no precedent in Europe. Certain objects were clearly kept in sight throughout. There was to be a new State, and not merely a union or league of states already in existence, and in this new State Prussia must be supreme. The executive Government must depend on the King, not on the fluctuating majorities of an Assembly. Above all, if the southern states wished at any time to join their brethren of the north there must be no constitutional difficulty in the way. The work was accomplished rapidly and a constitution was adopted in July 1867, which made possible the fulfilment of all Bismarck's aims.

The King of Prussia was hereditary head of the Confederation. He appointed its officials and controlled them through the Chancellor. The Chancellor was not a Prime Minister dependent on the support of an Assembly, nor the technical equal of the Ministers over whom he presided. He depended wholly upon the King. The Ministers were his subordinates, not his colleagues. It was as inevitable that the first Chancellor should be Bismarck as that the first President of the Confederation should be King William of Prussia.

The Council of the Confederation (*Bundesrat*) consisted of the representatives of the different states of the Confederation. They represented the Governments, not the peoples of the various states. The number of votes possessed by each was determined by the constitution. Prussia had seventeen. No other state had more than four. Through it Prussia controlled the policy and the constitution of North Germany.

The other Council, the Diet of the Confederation, was 'elected by universal and direct election with secret votes.' Yet the appearance of democracy was belied in the working of the constitution. It will be more convenient to trace the story when this constitution became merged in that of the German Empire in 1871.[1]

When the constitution began to work it was soon seen that Bismarck had gained another important victory. The Battle of Sadowa had overthrown not only the Austrians but the opposition to Bismarck's policy in Prussia and the German states of the north. In place of liberty he gave them military glory and the admiration of Europe. Whatever was illegal in his action was covered by an indemnity. More and more, Bismarck became the national hero of Germany, and the opposition to him was soon reduced to trivial proportions.

Another victory awaited him. The states of the south had fought against Prussia in alliance with the Austrians, and it was the hope of French statesmen that their hostility would be intensified by defeat, and that they might be counted on as a permanently hostile force on the flank of Prussia. But the opposite happened. They were drawn towards Prussia by their common German nationality, by their association in the Zollverein, by Bismarck's championship of their interests against France, which we have already noted, and by admiration for the military glory which Prussia had given to the German name. The south would not be strong if it stood alone. Bismarck knew how to make the change of face easy to them. He found assistance from some of their statesmen, especially from Varnbüler of Würtemberg. Offensive and defensive treaties were signed between Prussia and the individual states of the south. This meant that in the next war Germany would present a united military front.

The chief interest of these years is to see the forces gathering which produced the great collision between France and Germany in 1870. But first we must turn to Austria and see the enormous change that was passing over the character and organisation of that state.

All the efforts to reform the constitution of the Hapsburg Dominions had failed to establish any stability in the state. Two powerful nationalities—the German and the Magyar (Hungarian)—faced one another, and behind them or under them were ranged nearly a dozen others. The efforts to submit all the divisions of the state to a central parliament had proved unacceptable in whatever form it had been presented. Before the war with Prussia in 1866 the Emperor was already negotiating for reconciliation with the Magyars and for the settlement of the state on a new basis. The crushing blow of Sadowa quickened the process. If the war had been prolonged the Prussians would have had assistance from the discontented elements of the state and especially from the Magyars. The 'House of Austria' could have no future unless it succeeded in establishing an equal understanding with Hungary, and it is to the credit of the Emperor Francis Joseph that he recognised this. His new aims were admirably served by two capable men. He summoned to his councils Count Beust, who had hitherto been in the service

---

[1] *v. infra*, pp. 278–9.

of the King of Saxony, and was a stranger to the passions or resent-
ments that made any solution of the Austrian problem so difficult.
The claims of Hungary were presented firmly but temperately and without any trace of revolutionary passion by Francis Deák.[1] Both these
men had to struggle against violent counsels among their own followers.
The settlement was made easier by the fact that the Hungarians ruled
over a number of subject nationalities—Rumanians, Serbs, Croats,
Slovaks—and were anxious not to give them any opportunity for protest and revolution. So in 1867 a settlement was reached—the *Ausgleich*
—by which a complete equality or dualism was established between the
two component states, dominated respectively by the Germans and the
Hungarians so far as internal affairs were concerned.

Francis Joseph was now, for the first time, formally crowned King
of Hungary. His dominions were separated into two parts, divided by
the little river Leitha, an unimportant affluent of the Danube; and each
part had a Government and administration of its own—the one sitting
at Pesth, the other at Vienna—charged with all domestic concerns
(which were widely interpreted). In Austria Francis Joseph was Emperor and in Hungary he was King. It was made a legal and punishable
offence to speak in public in Hungary of Francis Joseph as Emperor.
In addition to these two Governments there was a third, dealing with
war and foreign affairs and the finances affecting the two, and acting
for both the states. The third Government, which was stronger than
Austria or Hungary, was known as the Common Monarchy.

The dualistic system was a piece of wise and conciliatory statesmanship, and it gave to Austria-Hungary nearly half a century of comparative quiet and stability. But in essence it established two national
tyrannies in place of one. The national aspirations which had been
aroused among the Czechs, Slovaks, Poles, Rumanians, Croats, and
Serbs were not in the least satisfied by the new arrangement, nor were
they conciliated by the apparently liberal and democratic principles of
the new constitution. Bohemia claimed equality with Hungary and used
the fifth centenary of the birth of Huss to proclaim her rights. There was
discontent and disorder among the Czechs and Ruthenians. These
movements were directed against the German majority of the Cis-
Leithan state (for so it was sometimes called); but the Magyars in
Trans-Leitha had their own difficulties. Croats, Serbs, and Rumanians
showed themselves galled by the Magyar yoke, and their discontent was
a continuous menace to the dual state, until the Great War of 1914

---

[1] There were two schools of political thought in Hungary: that of Kossuth
which ended in revolution and in a demand for the dethronement of the Hapsburg;
and that of Széchenyi, who was a constructive Conservative and who had even played
with the idea of a 'Combined Monarchy.' Deák represented the school of Széchenyi
and adopted a moderate constitutionalism, avowedly based on the English model.
He told Francis Joseph that he asked for no more after Sadowa than before, a truly
constitutional position.

came and threw a fierce light on all the national animosities that fermented within Austria-Hungary before they destroyed that Empire-Kingdom.

In 1867 the position in Central Europe was this. The North German Confederation dominated Germany north of the River Main. South Germany was a group of independent states. The Common Monarchy established by the *Ausgleich* brought together Austria and Hungary in greater harmony then ever before, and seemed likely to provide a counterpoise to the strength of the Prussianised north. Italy was independent but not yet completely united, for Rome, the traditional capital, was outside the Italian Kingdom. The position was, however, far from stable. In all sections there were elements of instability which looked forward to future change. The opportunity came with the Franco-Prussian War, and this arose over the problem of Spain.

Spain had been the chief representative of 'liberalism' in the early part of the century, and the Spanish Constitution of 1812 had been the rallying-cry of liberals in many parts of Europe. But constitutional government did not work easily or well in the Spanish peninsula. The change of Ministries and the succession of Parliaments (*Cortes*) seem to float on the surface of the state. A revolutionary movement in sympathy with the socialism and even the anarchy of French and German thinkers was to be found under the surface. But among the politicians, though there were political parties, personal rivalries and ambitions were the chief moving force. The army and the Church were often more powerful than the Government. Every Government in turn established a military dictatorship; and until the end of the century it proved impossible to establish religious liberty, except in name, in face of the strong resistance of the Catholic Church and the dislike of the people for all religious variations.

Queen Isabella had been declared of age in 1843, but for ten years after this—even after the Queen had married her cousin Francis—power still lay in the hands of the Queen-Mother, Christina. The chief features of the Government were its strong Catholicism and its resistance to all reforms. A revolution—supported by the army, as is nearly always the case with Spanish revolutions—came in 1854. It was supported by practically all the politicians, whose names fill the troubled parliamentary history of the next fifteen years—chief among them Narvaez, Espartero, O'Donnell. The Queen-Mother, Christina, was driven into exile: a more liberal era seemed to have begun.

The change in the character of the Government was really not great. A large part of the responsibility for the troubles of Spain during the following years must be put down to Queen Isabella herself. She was superstitious rather than religious; her private life was never free from gross scandals; of real patriotism or of political insight she showed no sign. In her Ministries she rang the changes between Narvaez, conservative and autocratic, and O'Donnell, leader of the 'Liberal Union,' who found it impossible to govern with the Queen and who therefore inclined to a change of ruler. Another striking figure in the politics of the time was Prim, who had gained some military reputation in the Moroccan war and was decidedly of the opinion that Queen Isabella must go. O'Donnell died in 1867; Narvaez in 1868. An attempt of the Government to arrest and exile the generals of the opposition, especially of the 'Liberal Union,' led to an outbreak. Navy and army declared against the Queen. She neither deserved nor found any effective support. She fled from the country (September 30, 1868) and her reign was declared at an end.

There was a republican party in Spain, but it was thought best not to challenge European opinion by declaring for a republic. It was decided that there should be a constitutional monarchy. But where was the monarch to be found? The Spanish throne was an uneasy seat and proved no attraction to the princes of Europe. Seven candidates were considered or approached. Finally in June 1870 it was believed that a solution had been found and that Prince Leopold of Hohenzollern-Sigmaringen had been induced to accept the crown. It was this candidature which provided the occasion for the Franco-German War. Prince Leopold, indeed, withdrew his candidature when he found how great a storm it was causing, but the War opened nevertheless on July 15. The hunt for a king began again, but although in November 1870 Prim induced the Duke of Aosta, son of the King of Italy, to accept the throne, after a disturbed reign of only two years he refused to continue any longer in an impossible position and abdicated. There followed a short experiment in a republican constitution, and then the old line was restored in the person of Alfonso, son of Isabella. Under him Spain came nearer to constitutional stability.

At midsummer of the year 1870 the international situation seemed particularly calm. Lord Granville was told when he took over the post of Foreign Secretary on the death of Lord Clarendon that the international horizon showed no signs of coming storm. In France Emile Ollivier was head of the Government, and he was devoted to peace and resolved to pick no quarrel with Germany; and yet war was declared against Germany on July 15. The causes of this sudden change are still matters of hot discussion. Both German and French historians have sincerely held that it was a war engineered by their enemies, and that they themselves were entirely innocent of evil intentions or of provocative conduct. In German eyes, Napoleon III is the villain of the piece, conscious of a tottering throne and anxious to re-establish it by victory against the national enemy. The French see in all the hand of Bismarck, forcing on France a war that she did not want, in order that he might complete the fabric of German national unity. Behind the mass of details, however, used in the arguments on both sides, certain facts remain incontestable. The tension between the two countries was undoubtedly great. German ambition and French jealousy and fear were driving forces of unquestioned importance. The international system of Europe afforded no means of settling peacefully the manifold difficulties which arose from the rivalry of two Great Powers. A French statesman had compared France and Germany to two locomotives running in opposite directions on a single line of rails and had maintained that a collision was inevitable.

The question of the Spanish throne brought the rivalry to a head. There is now no doubt that Leopold of Hohenzollern-Sigmaringen's candidature had been suggested with the approval and support of Bismarck. It had been debated at an informal meeting in Berlin held under the presidency of the King of Prussia and in the presence of Bismarck, Moltke, and Roon, but it was then rejected. It was revived subsequently and secretly by Bismarck and Prim, without the knowledge of King William. Prince Leopold was a distant relation of the Prussian King and a Catholic. His brother had recently become Prince of Rumania. His accession to the Spanish throne would be a great gain to Prussia both politically and commercially. It was feared by France for the same reasons. The French saw the re-creation of the Empire of Charles V against which France had fought for two centuries. When, therefore, De Gramont, the French Minister of Foreign Affairs, received a telegram from Berlin announcing the acceptance of the crown by Leopold, he determined to resist with all his power, and from the first he said that if Prussia insisted on the candidature it would mean war. He tried first to protest through the ordinary diplomatic channels in Berlin, but Bismarck was away and there was no one who could give serious attention to the French claims. It was denied that it was anything but a family matter for the Hohenzollerns, and falsely asserted that the Prussian Government knew nothing of it.[1] De Gramont determined to bring the matter before the French Assembly. He feared that Leopold might have been accepted by the Spanish *Cortes* before the French protest was heard, and that then France would seem to be insulting Spain. He read on July 6 a short speech, which had been approved by the council of Ministers. In grave language he made it plain that if the candidature was not withdrawn France would regard it as a cause for war. Ollivier followed with equally weighty words. 'The Government desires peace; it desires peace passionately; but it must be an honourable peace.'

The war cloud was very threatening, but for a time it seemed as if it would pass. Agencies were set to work from at least four sides to

[1] *E.g.*, by Von Thile, Bismarck's under-secretary, who had been present at the meeting alluded to above!

induce Prince Leopold to withdraw his candidature, and on July 12 there came the welcome news that he had consented to do so. Prussia seemed to retreat before the threatening attitude of France. Thiers said that Sadowa was avenged. Guizot said it was the greatest diplomatic triumph he ever remembered.

Then came the suicidal mistake. At a council held at Saint Cloud, at which the Prime Minister, Emile Ollivier, was not present (so far was France from really constitutional government!), it was decided not to leave the matter where it was but to demand guarantees against renewal of the candidature. Benedetti, the French Ambassador at Berlin, was instructed to demand directly from the King of Prussia, first that he should associate himself with the resignation, and secondly that he should promise not to support the candidature of the Hohenzollern prince if it were raised again. Benedetti presented these demands at Ems on July 13. The King received him courteously, but declared the demands to be inadmissible. In the afternoon he received official news of Leopold's resignation and sent to Benedetti to say that he regarded the affair as ended. Peace once more seemed possible.

It was the action of Bismarck which brought war out of an apparent settlement. He believed war to be inevitable sooner or later, and necessary in the interests of Prussia and Germany. But he did not want war unless and until it would appear in public that France was the aggressor. He was discontented with the King's conduct of the French negotiations. He had made up his mind to resign as a protest, and met his two great colleagues, Moltke and Roon, at dinner in Berlin on July 13 and acquainted them with his resolution. While he was at dinner there came a telegram from the King saying that Benedetti had presented demands that were impossible of acceptance; that in the afternoon he had heard officially that Prince Leopold's candidature had been withdrawn; and that in consequence he had sent one of his aides-de-camp to tell Benedetti that the incident was closed and that he could not see him again on that subject. What had happened seemed to Bismarck and to his associates a humiliating surrender to France, and they were plunged in gloom. But Bismarck had been given permission in the message to communicate the event to the press, and he drew up a version and submitted it to the others. The new version certainly misrepresented the original, for it attributed the King's refusal to see Benedetti again not to the receipt of definite news of Leopold's resignation but to the nature of his demands. The new version was, in Moltke's words, not the signal for a parley, but a note of defiance in answer to a challenge. It was communicated to the press, and circulated to the Prussian legations in Germany the same evening and created profound excitement throughout Germany.

Equally disturbing was the effect of Bismarck's message on Parisian and French opinion. The war was brought about not by what happened at Ems but by the false report of what had happened. There was no effort to discover whether the report was false or true. The statesmen of France—even the pacific Ollivier—treated a question which involved the lives of millions in the temper of duellists. France had been insulted; she had received a box on the ear (*un soufflet sur la joue*) and honour demanded immediate war. At a council on July 14 all in the end voted for war. On the 15th the Assembly supported this decision. Hardly a voice was raised on the other side, though Thiers demanded further information as to the exact proceedings at Ems. Ollivier saw his deeply cherished hopes of peace disappear; but he accepted war, he said, 'with a light heart,' because his conscience was clear.

There were, of course, greater and deeper causes of war than Bismarck's 'doctoring' of the Ems telegram; but it was the communication prepared by Bismarck for the press at the Berlin dinner-table which actually set alight the flames of the great war which led up to the vastly greater war of 1914. A little delay to allow nerves to grow steady and passions to cool, the expedient of reference to an external judgment which might have appeased the sense of honour, these things might have prevented the war, at any rate in the shape in which it came.

CHAPTER XX

THE FRANCO-GERMAN WAR AND ITS EFFECTS

IT was generally believed in Europe that France would win in the great war which now began. French military prestige stood high; German soldiers were considered to be inferior in scientific training; and their success against Austria was discounted for various reasons. But in the actual fighting the French scored no success of any importance, and the war worked out very closely according to the German programme. The first attack, delivered with great impetuosity, so broke the French resistance that it never recovered. The siege of Paris was indeed unexpectedly prolonged; but Bismarck succeeded in bringing the war to the desired end without a European Congress, which of all things he most feared. Nor is it difficult to detect the main elements of the German success. The German army was scientifically organised and prepared, and all the problems of war had been thoroughly studied. The command was united in the hands of Moltke, already famous for his conduct of the Austrian War. Through its territorial organisation the German army was ready long before the French, and it had in the decisive early stages of the war a great superiority in numbers; the Germans are estimated to have had on the frontier in the first encounters five hundred thousand against two hundred thousand men. In artillery, in scouting, in geographical knowledge they were undoubtedly superior to their opponents. Moreover, a great enthusiasm swept over Germany and all party spirit was stifled in the ardour of the moment. On the side of France there were divided counsels. The Emperor nominally commanded, but his health was broken and his direction of the war was never more than nominal. The country would doubtless have been swept away by enthusiasm if victory had crowned the French arms, but, when defeat came, the divisions of the state were quickly seen. Thus unity, science, and concentration of purpose encountered division, tradition, and shifting plans. MacMahon commanded in Alsace; Bazaine in Lorraine. Bazaine was at first the national hero, though before the war ended he came to be regarded either as a fool or a traitor.

On August 6, 1870, the German Crown Prince attacked and defeated MacMahon at Wörth. The battle opened Alsace to the German invasion. MacMahon withdrew the shattered remnants of his forces towards Châlons. On the same day Bazaine and the army of Lorraine were defeated at Spicheren. These were serious and even terrible events. What line should the French commanders pursue? The first idea was to retreat on Paris and fight the next battle in the neighbourhood of the capital, and this plan has generally found the approval of military experts. But throughout the campaign military motives were constantly being overruled by political considerations, and it was so here. The bad news from the frontier had overthrown the Ollivier Ministry, and power was entrusted to Count Palikao, an old soldier, seventy-five years of age, with no political experience. Through him the Empress Eugénie exercised a preponderating influence on the course of the war until the Empire was swept away by disaster. It was believed that a retreat on Paris would be fatal to the new Government; and the Emperor and Bazaine were persuaded to attempt the defence of Metz. But the Germans struck blow on blow. First the French troops were driven in at Borny, to the east of Metz, and then the German armies marched round to the south of Metz with a view to encircling it and shutting up Bazaine and his troops. Bazaine made a half-hearted attempt to escape from the trap; but in a series of encounters, which are usually known as the Battle of Gravelotte, the effort of the French army to break away was defeated, and Bazaine was cooped up with an army of nearly 200,000 men. Napoleon himself had managed to get away and had surrendered the command which he was no longer able to exercise. The superiority of the Germans in the command and in the rank and file, in discipline and initiative, in weapons and in endurance had been demonstrated throughout the operations.

France was now threatened by a terrible catastrophe; but a wise policy might have given her hope and allowed her to prolong the war until other European Powers entered the arena. MacMahon was near Châlons with a force that was large but much demoralised. The Emperor had abdicated the command into his hands. MacMahon resolved to retreat on Paris, to gain what reinforcements he could, and to fight

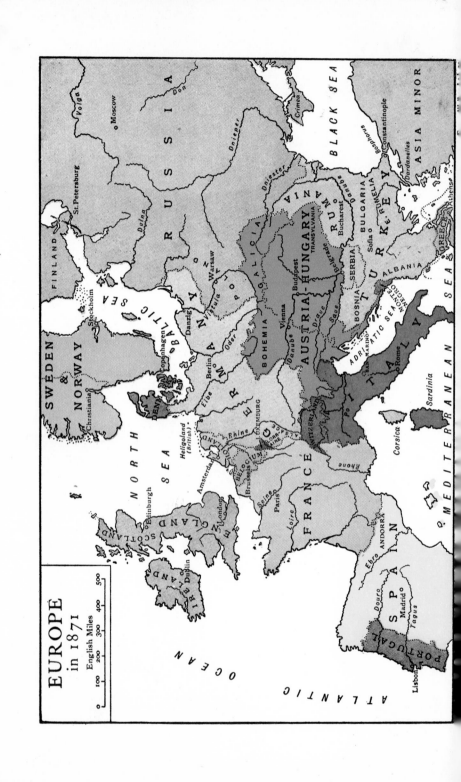

EUROPE
in 1871

English Miles

0   100 200 300 400 500

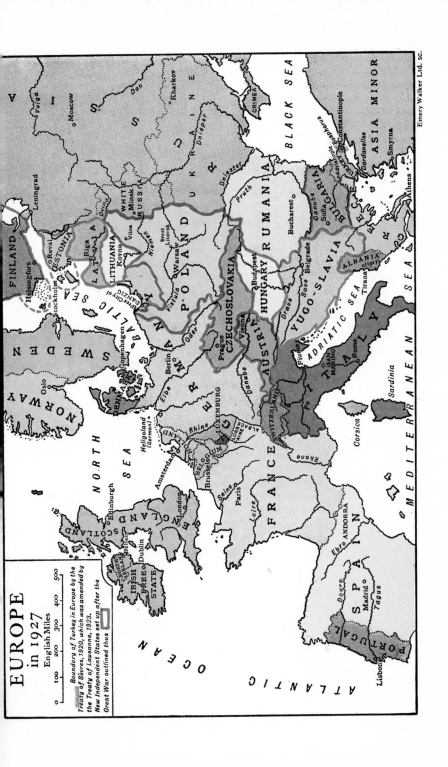

EUROPE
in 1927
English Miles
0   100   200   300   400   500

Boundary of Turkey in Europe by the
Treaty of Sèvres, 1920, which was amended by
the Treaty of Lausanne, 1923.
New Independent States set up after the
Great War outlined thus

Emery Walker Ltd. sc.

his next battle with the support of the guns of the Paris forts. The wisdom of this decision is admitted; but again it was overruled for political reasons. The Empress felt that a revolution was preparing and that the retreat of the Emperor and the abandonment of the popular hero Bazaine would precipitate it. She shrank from such a blow for her husband's sake, but above all for the sake of her son, the Prince Imperial. A decision was taken in Paris and communicated to MacMahon. Metz and Bazaine were to be relieved at all costs. MacMahon accepted the decision against his own better judgment. The series of operations which followed would probably in any case have been fatal to France. Their only chance of success lay in rapidity and definiteness of plan. But on the French side there were changes of plan almost beyond counting, while Moltke watched the German movements with an alertness which took advantage of every mistake of the enemy. MacMahon marched towards Sedan by the northern route, choosing such roads as seemed most likely to avoid the enemy, and reached Sedan on August 30. All hope of reaching Metz had now disappeared; the Germans were in greatly superior force and had occupied all the bridges. Moreover, Bazaine had done very little to help the army of relief. There was, however, still a hope that the army, or a large part of it, might get back to Paris by Mézières. But MacMahon, though he had determined on this plan, underrated the imminence of the danger. He waited when every minute was of importance. The Germans attacked on the morning of September 1. There was still one line of retreat open, and MacMahon was determined to take that. But he was wounded early in the battle, and the command was taken over, by order of the Paris Government, by Wimpffen, who still cherished the illusion of the possibility of victory. The French forces were driven into the town at every point, and the city was attacked by a constant artillery fire. Late in the day the Emperor and the whole army surrendered into the hands of the Prussian King; 104,000 prisoners were taken.

The news of the disaster was at first disbelieved in Paris. But on September 3 Palikao announced the receipt of a telegram from the Emperor: 'The army has been defeated and taken prisoner; I myself am a prisoner.' The Napoleonic dynasty lived on the traditions of military glory attached to the name and collapsed under defeat. A revolution of some sort was certain. The Assembly met, hoping to maintain the control of affairs in its own hands, though some desired to retain the power of the Empress at least in name. But while they deliberated, Paris boiled into insurrection. The National Guards should have defended the hall but joined with the insurgents, who invaded the body of the hall and the galleries. Amidst great confusion a vote, declaring the Napoleonic dynasty at an end, was about to be taken, when Jules Favre declared that the Hôtel de Ville was the proper place for such a revolutionary decision, and induced the crowd to march thither. At the Hôtel de Ville there was a moderate and constitutional republican party as well as a more violent section, which was later identified with the Commune. In order to exclude this latter party from power, a motion was made to form a provisional Government consisting of all the deputies of the department of the Seine, including those who, first elected for that department, had later adopted another constituency. Paris thus took the helm in her hands; the rest of France was not consulted. Trochu was Minister of War; Jules Favre took the Department of Foreign Affairs; Gambetta was Minister of the Interior. The title of the new Government was 'the Government of National Defence.' The Republic was not mentioned, nor was the Empress Eugénie threatened. But she was frightened by the memories of Paris revolutions, and the fate of Marie Antoinette had always been before her eyes. She left the palace and found a night's shelter with an American dentist in the suburbs, and the next day made her way to a life-long exile in England.

The Germans had won the war. Could the war end now? Bismarck had shown his diplomatic insight by bringing the war with Austria to an end at the earliest possible moment. Would he act in the same way in this greater war? Germany had overthrown the Empire; could it make peace with the Republic of France? There seemed no absolute reason against it. If the end had come at once Bismarck would have given Europe peace and made alliance between France and Germany not impossible. The stream of European history would have flowed down a different channel from that which has conducted Germany and Europe through three-quarters of a century of unrest. But Bismarck was already preparing the public mind for the annexation of Alsace and Lorraine, and that made a peace or reconciliation impossible.

When the German troops appeared before Paris Jules Favre determined to ask for an interview with Bismarck, and he met his great adversary at Ferrières, near Paris, on September 18. Bismarck made it clear that Germany demanded the Rhine lands. 'You would have had no scruple in seizing from us the banks of the Rhine, although the Rhine is not your national frontier. We recapture our own lands, and we believe that we thus assure ourselves of peace for the future.' Jules Favre had declared that France would not cede an inch of territory or a single stone of her fortresses; and thus peace was impossible. The two men met again later, and Favre shed tears before his iron antagonist; but he could win no concession, and the war went on.

The Germans made no notable additions to their military laurels during the rest of the war. They made no attempt to take Paris by assault, but were content to blockade it and to drive back the attempts of the garrison to break out. They believed that failure of food supplies would produce an early surrender, and they were amazed and exasperated by the long resistance, which lasted from September 30 to January 28. Paris had plenty of men: 80,000 troops of the line, including the naval brigade; 115,000 of the Garde Mobile, a sort of reserve, who elected their own officers and were soon notorious for their lack of discipline; and perhaps

350,000 of the National Guards, who also elected their own officers and were quite unwilling to submit to discipline of any kind. Trochu was in command. He was frightened of the Parisians, and did not attempt the rigorous measures which the situation demanded. There was plenty of courage, patriotism, and enthusiasm in Paris, but little discipline, and it was Trochu's great fault that he did not insist on it.

Outside Paris, France had two main sources of hope. Gambetta, one of the few young men in a Government which consisted largely of old men, left Paris in a balloon to organise the war in the provinces. He is the one heroic figure of the war on the French side. He could boast with truth that despair had never come near his heart, and he gave France hope as well. His efforts failed, but the memory of what he attempted has allowed France to look back on these tragic months with pride as well as humiliation. He was immensely helped by an engineer, Freycinet; but his own energy, eloquence, and contagious enthusiasm must be mainly credited with the great results achieved. He raised an army of 600,000 men and equipped it with arms and food, mostly purchased from England. He found some really good commanders—d'Aurelle de Paladines, Faidherbe, and above all Chanzy. On November 19 De Paladines attacked the Germans at Coulmiers, to the north of Orleans, and gained a considerable victory—the only real victory won by the French during the war. It vastly raised the *moral* of the troops, and Frenchmen began to dream of driving out the Germans from France, as the English had been driven out by Joan of Arc when the outlook for France was even worse.[1]

But there was a third factor on which everything depended—Bazaine and Metz. While they held out, a large German army was kept in inaction, and Bazaine's obvious duty was to hold out to the last possible moment. His actual conduct is still the subject of much controversy. He never accepted the new Government quite loyally, and thought less of the actual war than of what was to come after it. He spoke of his army as destined to become 'the palladium of order,' and hoped to play the part of Monk and restore the imperial dynasty. His conduct of the siege has found no one to defend it. The sorties that he attempted were conducted without energy. His army and even the civilian population of Metz were in favour of continuing the struggle; and provisions were not entirely exhausted when he capitulated with his army of 173,000 men on October 27, 1870.

Perhaps Gambetta's cry, 'Bazaine has betrayed us,' is not justified, but he was unquestionably right when he said that the avalanche of German troops that poured down from Metz was the ruin of all his

---

[1] This was the only occasion on which the Higher Command in the German Army wavered or mishandled the situation. Sir Lonsdale Hale pointed out in his book, *The People's War* that the curious and shambling movements of Gambetta's vast, though undisciplined, armies were harder to foresee or to resist than those of a more regular force.

schemes. After the war Bazaine was tried, and found guilty of not having done 'all that duty and honour prescribed.' He was sentenced to death, but the sentence was commuted to imprisonment for twenty years. He escaped and died in 1888 in Spain.

Henceforth, though the French fought hard, fortune never smiled on them. Chanzy showed high military qualities in his conduct of the war in the west, but his troops got out of hand. He was beaten at Le Mans and his army dissolved. Faidherbe had no better fortune in the north. He too is reckoned a really fine soldier, but his troops were demoralised, and on January 19 he was decisively and finally beaten near Saint Quentin. In the south-east Bourbaki, an old general of the Empire, tried to relieve Belfort, which was being besieged by the Germans and gallantly defended. He was associated with Garibaldi, who had come to the help of the French in their adversity. But the hero of Italian liberty failed entirely to realise the hopes that were attached to his name. Age had told upon him, and he found the trained German troops proof against the methods which had been so successful in Sicily and Italy. Bourbaki's effort in this region had already failed when the armistice came. Through the negligence of Jules Favre his troops were not included in its stipulations. They were driven into Switzerland, where 80,000 frost-bitten and famine-stricken men laid down their arms.

The avowed aim of all these operations in the provinces was to relieve the siege of Paris. Their failure inevitably brought about the surrender of the capital. The besieged troops had tried to break out, but in vain. The greatest effort was made on November 31 under the command of Ducrot, who declared that whatever happened, 'You will not see me retreat.' Some successes were gained, but were soon swept away, and Ducrot retreated in spite of his promise. The Germans decided at last to bombard the city, but with little effect on the temper of the population. The last attempt at a sortie was made on January 19, and it was a complete failure. There was no hope from the provincial armies, and the food supplies were nearly finished. Jules Favre went to meet Bismarck in Versailles and an armistice was signed on January 28. Bismarck could not recognise the Government of National Defence as capable of speaking for France. New elections were therefore to be held at once, and the Assembly that issued from them was to meet at Bordeaux to accept or reject the terms of peace.

Thus the war ended. But it had been accompanied and it was followed by important diplomatic and political movements which added still further to the significance of its history.

The war was fought out as a duel between the two great combatants. It was the constant fear of Germany and the hope of France that Europe would interfere, and that the war would develop into a European struggle which would call the German armies from the heart of France. Germany was well served by the friendship of the Russian Czar, which it had been one of the constant objects of Bismarck to secure. Later, Bismarck publicly thanked him for having prevented the war from developing into a general European struggle.

Of all the French statesmen of the day Thiers had far the highest European reputation. His great learning, his eloquence, and his aloofness from the policy of Napoleon III had made of him one of the foremost of European figures. In September 1870 he accepted the proposal of the Government of National Defence that he should make a tour of the Governments of Europe to secure sympathy and help for France. He was an old man, and the task was laborious, but he carried it through with energy, and it was not his fault that it was not successful. He found Austria-Hungary friendly, but weak; England determined to maintain her isolation from Europe; Russia pro-Prussian; Italy prodigal in friendly words, but anxious not to provoke the hostility of Prussia. On his return he attempted to negotiate an armistice so that the opinion of France might be consulted. The attempt failed, as the Germans would allow no revictualling of the besieged city.

There was a moment when it seemed that Russia might unintentionally contribute to the relief of France from her embarrassments. After the Crimean War the victorious Powers—and chiefly France and Great Britain—had forced on Russia a clause in the Treaty of Paris by which the Black Sea was declared neutral, and Russia was thus deprived of the right of maintaining there any military or naval establishment. Probably the clause could in no case have been enforced for long, but now that France was humbled in the dust Russia saw her chance. She denounced the treaty. France was powerless to enforce it, but some regarded the action of Russia as a direct challenge to Great Britain, which she could not fail to accept. The British Prime Minister, Gladstone, however, had other views, for he was determined to maintain the peace if possible. He sent a messenger to Bismarck at Versailles: it marks the prestige of Prussia that it was necessary to consult the great Prussian on a question in which Prussia was not directly concerned. A way out was found by means of a conference, which was called to London. The face of Britain was saved by a declaration that no one party to a Treaty could denounce it by herself, and by a re-statement of the rules governing the closure of the Straits of the Bosphorus and the Dardanelles; but no effort was made to save the neutrality of the Black Sea. A French representative only appeared at the last session, and France is thought to have neglected a great opportunity of presenting her case against Prussia before the conference, or bringing about a 'general European conflagration' from which she might have reaped advantage.

Just before the armistice, when the victory over France was already secure, Bismarck had realised one great aim of his life. The greater part of Germany was united in an Empire in which Prussia held the predominant position. The stupendous triumph of German arms had united north and south and effaced, at least for the moment, their long-standing jealousies. Before the matter could be accomplished there was delicate negotiation, which was of course undertaken by Bismarck. In 1849 the King of Prussia had refused the German Empire, when offered by hands which seemed to him tainted by democracy. That mistake must not be made again, and the King of Bavaria was induced to make the actual offer. But before the end was reached there were some difficult questions to be solved. The King of Prussia was proud of his royal title and did not relish extinguishing it under the more showy name of Emperor; only the insistence of Bavaria induced him to forgo his objection. Then there was the question whether the new ruler should be Emperor of Germany or German Emperor, which roused some politicians to great excitement, and was finally settled in favour of 'German Emperor' as implying no lordship over German soil. Men asked, too, what relation this Empire bore to the old Holy Roman Empire whose last shadow had disappeared in 1806. Was the German Empire to be established or re-established? No decision was given, but the general opinion of statesmen and historians was that there was real continuity between the old and the new. The final scene took place in the Hall of Mirrors at Versailles on January 18, 1871. William was acclaimed German Emperor. The Crown Prince declared 'the interregnum of sixty-five years is over and the kaiserless terrible time is past.' To the King himself it was no very welcome change. He is described as 'morose' during the whole day, and informed the Queen that he 'was inclined to abdicate and hand over everything' to the Crown Prince.

No constitutional difficulties were raised by the new title. The constitution of the North German Confederation had been drawn up with a view to the possibility of the accession of the states of Southern Germany. Bavaria and Würtemberg and Baden took their places along with Prussia and Saxony, and little protest was raised against the change. Blood shed in common in victorious battle is, declared a Prussian historian, a wonderful cement.

Bismarck had not perhaps desired a national and united Germany, but rather a Prussian leadership of German Princes. On that idea at any rate the structure was based, and the new constitution (1873) bore the impress of the particularism and sectionalism once rampant in the Confederation. It was an adaptation to all Germany of the constitution of the North German Confederation created after the Austro-Prussian War. The King of Prussia, as in 1866, and his Chancellor Bismarck, headed the new Federal League. The new organisation was termed the German Empire. Its head (termed the German Kaiser, not the Kaiser of Germany) was merely the hereditary President of a League. The key to his power lay in the fact that he was King of Prussia, a state as large as, and more important than, all the other members of the new Empire. It was like a number of animals formed into a hunting pack; the leader was Prussia, a huge grey wolf, at whose heels ran jackals, like Bavaria, Saxony, Würtemberg, and in whose train followed thirty-five smaller animals varying in size from large rats to small mice.

In theory the rights of the smaller states were strictly preserved. The *Bundesrat*, or Upper Chamber, was the powerful legislative body and consisted of fifty-eight members. Of these only seventeen were Prussian, though Prussia ultimately secured control of three more votes. Prussia could be voted down by a majority in ordinary legislation but, as constitutional amendments could be vetoed by fourteen votes (Article 78), Prussia had a permanent veto on constitutional change.[1] In practice the solid front of Prussian delegates, whom smaller states generally followed, was generally sufficient to enable her to get her way in ordinary legislation. In any case the *Bundesrat* was a thoroughly conservative institution.

The Reichstag, or Popular House, was Bismarck's masterpiece. It was elected by universal secret suffrage with the ballot and contained 397 members. But though in appearance democratic, it was, in reality, limited in all ways. It was much weaker than the *Bundesrat* and much less experienced in the conduct of business. The Federal Chancellor and his Cabinet Ministers attended in the Reichstag, but were not dependent on its support and did not resign if their legislative proposals were defeated. The quotas to the army were fixed by previous arrangement with each state and embodied in the constitution. They could not therefore be altered except by constitutional amendment. All that the Reichstag could do was to refuse to vote additions to these quotas. The navy and the Colonies hardly existed in 1873 so that, in later years, the Reichstag had power to vote supplies for them, and could have refused to do so at will. Over foreign policy the Reichstag had little control; for treaties, both diplomatic and commercial, were usually concluded for longer periods than the life of a single Reichstag, with the express object of preventing them from being criticised at an election. There was thus little scope for the assertion of parliamentary control over important matters. And this power was still further impaired by the fact that the Reichstag was always split into many parties, which rendered opposition to the Government difficult. The parliamentary habit of mind was not possessed by the German in 1870, and there was not much sign of his having developed one by 1914. The average Reichstag member varied between blind obedience and factious opposition to the Government. Yet, with all these disadvantages, the Reichstag was sometimes able to assert itself, and there were moments when neither Bismarck nor William II found it possible to override it.

Bismarck had thus settled the internal government of Germany by supplying it with an Upper House representing states, with a pseudo-democratic Lower House representing numbers, with a constitution excluding many matters from the competence of both bodies, and which could not be amended without Prussia's permission. He had built up the whole fabric of Germany on a firm conservative basis. Prussia,

---

[1] Voting in the *Bundesrat* was by states not by individuals, *e.g.*, Prussia's vote was cast as a whole, for or against a Bill, and was returned as seventeen votes.

through her prestige, her money, her power was emphatically the 'predominant partner.' The other members might be called rather the departmental managers of a business, than the directing heads of the firm of 'Bismarck and Co.' Bismarck, in fact, was, for half a generation, unassailable.

The armistice had been concluded in order to allow of the election of a representative French Chamber before which the terms of peace might be brought for rejection or ratification. France generally was weary of the war, though there were some voices raised loudly for its continuance. Gambetta believed in continuing the struggle; and his opposition had to be overcome by force. Faidherbe and Chanzy said, and perhaps believed, that it was still possible to fight on. But France was anxious for peace. No other issue was placed before the electors, and a large majority of the members were pledged to bring the war to an end. The 600 members met at Bordeaux, far from the possible influence of the German army. Thiers, who had been elected by twenty-six constituencies, was appointed 'Chief of the Executive Power of the French Republic'; Jules Favre still held the Ministry of Foreign Affairs, but the real conduct of negotiations was in the safer hands of Thiers. As soon as the Assembly was constituted in Bordeaux, Thiers went off to interview Bismarck at Versailles. There was little negotiation to be done unless he was willing to risk the renewal of war. Bismarck had made up his mind on the general features of the Peace. He was determined to annex Alsace and most of Lorraine. Though he personally would have been willing to hand back the city and fortress of Metz into the hands of the French, in the end he yielded to the urgency of the soldiers, and insisted on the cession of Metz as well as of Strasburg. France had to pay a great indemnity, though its figure was reduced from two hundred and forty millions to two hundred millions sterling through the efforts of Thiers. There were many stipulations as to the payment of the indemnity, the conditions of which were stiffened after the outbreak of the Commune in Paris, and as to the maintenance of a German garrison of occupation until the terms of the treaty were complied with. On one point Thiers had gained an important concession. It had originally been proposed that Belfort should be annexed to Germany along with Strasburg and Metz; and Belfort was of the utmost importance as controlling an all-important entry into France from the south of Germany. Thiers threatened the renewal of war rather than abandon this place. In the end Bismarck, after consultation with the King and Moltke, agreed to leave Belfort in French hands if Thiers would allow German troops to make a triumphal entry into Paris. It was a strange alternative for the realistic Chancellor to propose, and Thiers accepted it at once.

With these terms Thiers hurried back to Bordeaux and submitted them to the Assembly. It was impossible not to accept them, but some strong protests were made. M. Keller, on behalf of Alsace and Lorraine, had declared 'their immutable will to remain French.' Now, when the terms were heard, the representatives of the lost provinces declared that what was done was 'in contempt of all justice and an odious abuse of power.' 'We declare once more that a compact which disposes of us without our consent is null and void.' Violent protest, too, came from certain representatives of Paris. They declared that the Assembly had surrendered two provinces and had dismembered France, and that it was no longer the voice of the country. Several of them resigned as a consequence. Victor Hugo, too—a name venerable to all Europe— resigned. His summary of the situation is noteworthy: 'Henceforth there are in Europe two nations which will be formidable—the one because it is victorious, the other because it is vanquished.'

The Treaty was ratified on March 1. In its definitive form it was signed at Frankfort on May 10. Thirty thousand German troops entered Paris and stayed there a short time, irritating by their presence the passions of the Parisians which were shortly to boil over into a terrible insurrection.[1]

CHAPTER XXI

THE FOUNDATION OF THE THIRD FRENCH REPUBLIC

THE Assembly at Bordeaux had been elected nominally for one purpose only—to establish peace with Germany. Many maintained that it had no mandate for anything else and that when once peace was signed it ought to dissolve. But France was faced by many pressing questions, and it seemed dangerous to have another general election after so short an interval. The Assembly persisted in regarding itself as a sovereign assembly, resting on the choice of the people of France and competent to decide whatever questions presented themselves. The most important question was the form of government under which the country was to live for the future. Of the 600 members of the Assembly at least two-thirds were in favour of a return to some form of monarchy, Legitimist, Orleanist, or Imperial. Yet this predominantly royalist Assembly estab-lished the Republic. That is the paradox of the next decade of French history.

The rising of the Commune in Paris had an important influence. There had been, from the Revolution of 1789 onwards, a constant

[1] Note: As a result of the war the French troops left Papal territory (August 19, 1870), a large Italian force entered Rome (September 20), and a plebiscite united her to Italy on October 2.

contrast between Paris and the provinces of France; Paris had usually been progressive and radical, while the provinces were conservative. The peasants especially were always ready to reject any measure which seemed to interfere with or endanger the security of their land. Both Napoleons had been able to count on the support of the peasantry, of whom they constituted themselves the champions. Paris, in spite of all Napoleon III's efforts, had remained obstinately republican. The city had suffered severely during the siege, and believed itself to have been badly treated at the Peace. The entry of the German troops had exasperated public feeling, which was also alarmed by political fears for the future. For it was generally believed that the Assembly would establish a monarchy, and against this Paris solemnly protested. Of all the causes that produced the rising of the Commune the fear of the re-establishment of monarchy was, in the opinion of Thiers himself, the most operative. After the armistice a vast number of the more prosperous citizens had left the city, and thus the conservative element in the population was weakened. On the other hand, the National Guards had not been disarmed. They retained their weapons and their organisation and took the leading part in the outbreak, especially in its early incidents.

Paris had not ceased since 1848 to ferment with eager speculation on all manner of social questions. Saint-Simon and Fourier had each their supporters, but socialism was the favourite watchword, though as usual it implied different schemes to different people. Marx's *Das Kapital* had been published since 1867, but had not yet begun to exercise any great influence on the mind of France. Marx, indeed, acclaimed the Commune as the beginning of a great movement which should inaugurate a world change, but there is little trace of his ideas in the actual programme of the Communists. Hostility to the centralised state is a strong feature in the utterances of most of the leaders. 'Centralisation means despotism,' they said. The time was not favourable to clear thinking or careful planning; but the central aim of the insurgents was the independence of the communes or municipalities of France which should be formed by federation into a whole, and organised on a basis of collectivism. The manifesto of the Commune published on April 20, 1871, makes this clear.

What does [Paris] wish? The recognition and consolidation of the Republic, the only form of Government compatible with popular rights. . . . Absolute autonomy of the Commune extended to all parts of France. . . . The autonomy of the Commune will have as its only limit the right of autonomy equally valid for all other Communes. . . . They are deceived or deceive the country who accuse Paris of aiming at the destruction of the french unity accomplished by the Revolution. . . . Political unity as Paris desires it, is the voluntary association of all local initiatives.

Paris was a huge city in which many nationalities were to be found, and the Commune was essentially international in its character. Thus it is not surprising that among the prominent Communards (there was never a leader properly speaking) a number of foreigners are to be found. Delescluze and Félix Pyat were Frenchmen and represented the more moderate wing. Cluseret was a French-American and had fought in the 'north and south' war. A Pole, Dombrowski, and an Italian, La Cecilia, played for a time prominent parts.

The movement may be dated from March 18. The Assembly had, partly in anticipation of the coming outbreak, been moved from Bordeaux to Versailles. The number of troops at the disposal of Thiers was very small—not more than 20,000. He ordered them to remove a number of guns from Montmartre. These guns had been made during the siege by the people of Paris and they refused to surrender them. The troops were surrounded by a huge crowd and prevented from taking the guns. Thiers believed that the number of soldiers in Paris was quite insufficient to maintain order, and that they might themselves be overwhelmed. He ordered them to evacuate the city and by March 30 Paris was left to herself. The struggle lasted until May 28—almost exactly two months. Thiers as head of the executive Government had to bear the burden of the responsibility for the suppression of the rising and the re-conquest of Paris. He was seventy-four years of age, but he had always taken a keen interest in the organisation and conduct of military operations, and nothing seemed to diminish his confidence or his energy. He had served, as we have seen, the Orleanist dynasty and in theory preferred a constitutional monarchy of the English pattern to a republic; but he had solemnly promised that he would not influence the decision of the Assembly in any unfair way. The confidence which all parties felt in him was a valuable asset for France at this crisis. He induced Marshal MacMahon, recovered from the wound that he had received at Sedan, to accept the supreme command. Thiers refused without hesitation the offer of German help, but he brought home by sea from Hamburg 100,000 French prisoners of war, and it was chiefly with these troops that the rising was fought down, but he had never more than 150,000 with which to subdue the great city. If the Commune had ever any chance of success it was ruined by the unceasing quarrels and jealousies of the authorities. Nominally, power was in the hands of the Commune (or municipal council) which had been elected on March 26. It was wholly revolutionary in tone. It delegated its powers very largely to a committee of five persons called the Committee of Public Safety, in which Delescluze became later the one dominating personality. But the National Guards were in effect an independent force, and elected a central committee which refused obedience to the Commune.

The Communards were at first confident of victory. The miracles of the first French Revolution would be repeated. The other great cities of France would come to their help. The soldiers fighting for liberty and social regeneration would be inspired by their cause to superhuman efforts. But nothing of the sort happened; and from the first contacts with the troops of Versailles it was clear that the Parisians could not hope to defeat the trained soldiers of France, even though their *moral* had been shaken by defeat in the German War. MacMahon made careful preparation of artillery. The German troops were still outside Paris and watched the bombardment of the twice besieged city. The attack began in regular form on April 29. Two important forts were taken, and the general assault was arranged for May 23. But in Paris there was no possibility of resistance. There were proclamations in plenty, and some good projects of legislation. But there were also continuous quarrels among the leaders. Cluseret was followed in the highest military post by Rossel, and Rossel by Delescluze, a man of great courage and purity of aim, but the fighting force did not improve. The great mass of the Parisians took no part either for or against the Communards. Then on May 21 a signal was made from the fortifications to the soldiers that the walls had been abandoned, and Thiers superintended the entry of the troops into the suburbs of Paris without encountering any resistance.

Even then the worst was yet to come. The central streets of the city were closed by barricades and obstinately defended, and were only captured after fighting of great cruelty on both sides. Some noble buildings in Paris were set alight with petrol, and some of the most famous—the Hôtel de Ville and the Tuileries among them—were burnt down. On May 24 the Archbishop and some others who had been held as hostages by the insurgents were killed as a protest against the treatment of some of their men in the hands of the Versailles troops. It was not until May 28 that the last barricade was taken. Then followed a horrible revenge, sometimes under legal forms, sometimes without them. Many were put to death; multitudes were exiled to the penal colonies. Hanotaux, the French historian and statesman, has summed up the results in these words: 'It is reckoned that 17,000 men perished in this horrible *mêlée*. . . . Paris lost altogether 80,000 citizens.'[1] The memory of the Commune was, down to the first Great War, a permanent force in French politics, preventing reconciliation between the parties, and maintaining a spirit of alarm and bitterness in political life. On the other hand, it is probable that the events in Paris did much to secure the Republic. The Commune had shown the fierce determination of the capital of France not to see the re-establishment of the monarchy.

The defeat of the Commune brought the Assembly face to face with its great tasks. The first of these was the settlement of relations with the Germans. The Treaty had to be signed, and in order to secure the evacuation of French territory by German troops the indemnity would have to be paid. The personality and reputation of Thiers were of immense value to France in dealing with Bismarck, who was inclined to adopt a truculent and suspicious tone towards France. The definitive Peace was signed, as we have seen, at Frankfort on May 10, 1871; but

[1] Gabriel Hanotaux: *Histoire de la France Contemporaine*, vol. I. pp. 211–14.

German troops were still in possession of many departments and would remain there until France could raise the required money. Thiers had great financial knowledge and much credit with the financial world. The money required was raised with astonishing ease, and Germany regarded the unexpectedly rapid recovery of France with suspicion and dislike, for the evacuation took place two years earlier than was anticipated. But she carried out loyally the stipulations of the Treaty. The German troops left, and the Assembly declared that Thiers 'had deserved well of the country.'

It was a great triumph for the aged President, but it led at once to more violent opposition to him in the Assembly. He was so necessary for the negotiations with Germany that until those were completed there could be no thought of driving him from his position. But now there arose for definite solution the question of the future constitution of France. And here the attitude of the President satisfied only a small section of the members of the Assembly. He had promised that he would not exercise any unfair influence on the decision of the Assembly; but he did not think that that promise prevented him from giving advice. He availed himself constantly of the right, which his position as President gave him, to address the House on any topic. He spoke indeed so often and, perhaps we should add, so well that the right was later limited by definite enactment. Thiers's own views were quite clear. He preferred a constitutional monarchy after the English pattern to a republic; but he believed that the actual situation made a monarchy impossible. 'All governments,' he said, 'whatever their names, are now essentially republican in character'; and 'if you will not cross the English Channel you will have to cross the Atlantic'; and he insisted that events had in fact given France a republic, and that to establish any sort of monarchy would be, under actual circumstances, a real revolution.

The Assembly, however, was predominantly monarchist; and would not accept a republican solution willingly. The restoration of the Empire had few open supporters. If Napoleon III had lived there would perhaps have been some attempt in that direction, but he died in England. There were now two systems and two men who divided the allegiance of the monarchists. The Comte de Paris represented the constitutional traditions of the House of Orleans. He had seen much of the world and was believed to hold liberal opinions. The hope of the Legitimists, of those who clung to indefeasible hereditary right and the close union of the throne and the altar, was Henri, Comte de Chambord. He lived in the neighbourhood of Vienna and was without political ambition. He was not anxious to reign in France and quite unwilling to sacrifice his political or religious principles in order to do so. The relations between these two royalist parties raised insuperable difficulties later, but for the moment the first thing was to get rid of Thiers. A motion, which was practically a vote of no confidence, was moved 'regretting that the policy of the Government was not resolutely conservative.' Thiers answered by defending his acceptance of the Republic. 'My reason is,' he said, 'that to-day for you and for me, in fact, the monarchy is absolutely impossible. There is only one throne, and three people cannot sit on it at the same time.' The House voted against him by a small majority and he resigned.

He was succeeded in the Presidency by Marshal MacMahon, who had been wounded at Sedan and had commanded against the Commune. He had hardly mixed in politics at all; but his royalist sentiments and his devotion to the Church were well known. He had no brilliance of thought or speech, and stories of his awkwardness and social blunders were current in Paris; but all acknowledged his uprightness, honesty, and seriousness of purpose. The Assembly had suffered under Thiers's continual brilliance, and welcomed the change. His mission was clear. He was to preside over the process by which the monarchy would be established. That was his own wish and the wish of his followers. Yet in fact the Republic was founded during his presidency!

Even if the royalists had been united the monarchy would not have been founded without a sharp struggle. But all attempts to unite them proved unavailing. The Comte de Paris went to see the Comte de Chambord. As Chambord was childless it seemed a natural solution that he should reign first, and that he should be succeeded by the House of Orleans. But if Chambord became king, on what principles would he reign? Would he insist on repudiating all that the French Revolution meant, or would he accept some of its principles? The question was summed up in the symbol of the flag. Would the Comte de Chambord insist on using the traditional white flag of the Bourbon House—the flag of Henry of Navarre and of Louis XIV—or would he accept the tricolour, with all its associations of revolution and of military glory? It had waved at the Battle of Austerlitz; but it had also stood by the guillotine when Louis XVI was executed. The flag was only a symbol, but it was an important one; and to the Comte de Chambord it was a religious symbol, and he was as unwilling to adopt the tricolour as a Christian would be to substitute the Crescent for the Cross. Efforts were made to induce him to change his decision, and there were rumours that he had done so; but his final answer was that he could make no sacrifice of his honour. Men felt that the monarchy under such circumstances was impossible. MacMahon is reported to have said that if the white flag were run up on the Hôtel de Ville the 'chassepots would go off of themselves'—that is, insurrection would blaze out at once. The Count tried to cut the knot by coming himself to Versailles, half hoping for a miracle in favour of the cause that he represented. He hoped that MacMahon at least would visit him. But MacMahon, though personally devoted to the Count, believed that a visit to the royal claimant was incompatible with his honour and the oath he had taken as President of the Republic. So the Comte de Chambord received his adherents, visited Paris and looked at the ruins of the Tuileries palace, and then returned to Austria. The cause of monarchy was lost. But the Assembly only slowly and unwillingly came to take the unwelcome decision. First it gave Marshal MacMahon 'the executive power' for seven years and appointed a commission to examine constitutional projects. Various resolutions were brought forward and rejected; but the by-elections ran almost continuously against the monarchists and had a considerable influence on the Assembly. The decisive vote was taken on an amendment proposed by a deputy named Wallon, determining the method of election of the President of the Republic. On January 30, 1875, it was adopted by a majority of a single vote, and by this narrowest of majorities France was committed to a republic.

A series of measures established the form of this Third French Republic. The new constitution was not one of those clearly arranged logical constitutions that France has often loved. It was the result of constant compromises, unwillingly adopted, by an Assembly which hoped that they would not last long. '*Le hasard fût notre maître,*' said one who took a prominent part in the debate.

France was to be a republic, and the head of the Republic was to be a President elected by the two Chambers (the Assembly of Deputies and the Senate) in common session. There were strong arguments against this method; but the one argument in its favour was sufficient. The only alternative, that of a plebiscitary election, had brought Napoleon III to power in 1851, and might very likely produce similar results again. So a method was adopted which handed France over to a series of Presidents of small political power and importance. The President had in the French Constitution almost exactly the position and powers of the King in Great Britain.[1]

There was universal manhood suffrage of all over twenty years of age. The Chamber of Deputies sat for four years. The Senate was elected for nine years. It contained at first seventy-five members nominated for life, but this provision was soon omitted. The rest were to be elected by a curious method; chiefly by delegates appointed for that purpose by the municipal councils of France. Gambetta called it 'The Great Council of the Communes of France.' The provinces had a large measure of self-government, but the new Republic maintained the Prefects, the characteristic institution of the First Empire and the descendants of the *intendants* of the old monarchy. They were nominated by the central Government, which gave to France an administration more centralised and less influenced by the people than we are accustomed to in England.

---

[1] The differences are that the French President presided at the Cabinet while the British King does not, and that the former was elected for a period only while the latter is hereditary. It is significant that every President who essayed to take a more direct or personal part in politics, fell, *e.g.* MacMahon, Grévy, Millerand. The King may at times have a real influence on policy owing to his permanence and experience, and is therefore probably more powerful than the President.

The approximation to the English system was in general very close, and many members of the Assembly hoped that in time the President might give way to a constitutional monarch. It was hoped to establish the English ministerial and cabinet system almost exactly. But in fact the French parliamentary régime proved in many ways very different from that of England. The ministries were much more unstable than those in England. Between 1873 and 1888 there were nineteen ministries in France, which gives a duration of less than a year to each; there were five ministries during the same time in England. But not only did the French ministries last for a shorter time than the English: they also had much less control over their supporters and over the whole Assembly than is usual with us. The explanation of this is not to be found in the French temperament. In the seventeenth century it was usual to contrast the steady loyalty of the French with the restless and revolutionary tendencies of the English, and Louis XIV made it a rule for that reason to enter into no binding relations with the English Government. The instability of French ministries may at least in part be explained by the following considerations: (1) The organisation of French political parties has never been so rigid as in England. There is not the same sense of party loyalty. Members vote against their own party far more readily; and this tendency is both the cause and the consequence of the multiplicity of parties. The cause of this different attitude to party is another question with which we must not here deal. (2) The fall of a ministry in France was not followed by a general election. In theory the President might, with the consent of the Senate, order a dissolution, but in fact it was rarely done. The consequences therefore of throwing out a ministry were not so serious to the individual member as in England: he had not to face at once another election contest with its doubtful issue and its certain expense.[1] (3) This fact enabled the whole popular House in France to rule far more effectively than in England, where nearly the whole of the business is carried on by the dominant party. In France Bills were usually introduced by Ministers, but their subsequent development and failure or success depended much more on the whole House, working through its committees or bureaux, which were not chosen on party lines, and decisive changes in a measure which would be fatal to a ministry in England were often accepted in France. The Chamber, conscious of its powers, saw with comparative equanimity the fall of a party ministry to which it had for the moment entrusted the executive power.

The Republic was thus founded, and it survived until its destruction by the cataclysm of 1940. But it had come almost by accident and it had many secret enemies. The monarchical parties still existed, though after the death of the Prince Imperial the Imperialists could not agree on any candidate; and the death of the Comte de Chambord did not succeed

---

[1] M. Doumergue, who attempted to assimilate the French Constitution to the British in the power to dissolve, failed and resigned in November 1934.

in uniting the Legitimists and the Orleanists. The President, MacMahon, was by no means prepared to accept the equal and democratic régime which the Republic implied to most of its supporters. He hoped, in close alliance with the Church and by the help of all the agents of government, to maintain the control of the executive and to govern independently of the Chamber of Deputies. The ecclesiastical or Catholic party was very strong and did not accept the Republic. MacMahon was more closely identified with its ideals than with those of royalism itself, and he hoped to maintain the ascendancy of the Church under the Republic. Thus Church and State came into frequent rivalry and conflict, more indeed over educational questions than over politics. The task which the Republic had before it was to control the executive power, to assert its supremacy over the Catholic Church, and to defeat the efforts, secret or open, of the monarchists of every kind.

The general election of 1877 is a real landmark in the history of the political development of France. MacMahon had submitted to republican ministries, but he had not liked them. Thiers until his death, and then Grévy, and Ferry, and, above all others, Gambetta had agitated for a more democratic interpretation of the constitution. MacMahon protested against Gambetta's 'doctrine of the omnipotence of the Chamber,' and declared that 'the independence of the President within the limits of the constitution must be maintained.' In 1877 he dissolved the Chamber and submitted the issue between himself and the Chamber to the constituencies. He worked for a majority as Napoleon III had been accustomed to do, using every sort of influence in favour of the candidates that he favoured. The result was a complete failure. France decided by an overwhelming majority in favour of 'Gambetta's ideas,' and the democratic majority was especially strong in the south and east of France. MacMahon refused at first either 'to submit or resign,' and he remained in his presidential office a little longer. But the situation was impossible. In January 1879 he resigned, a year before he would have been compelled by the constitution to do so.

The Republic triumphed in the choice of his successor, which fell on Jules Grévy, a man of the middle class, in close sympathy with the peasantry, without any leaning towards monarchism or Catholic ascendancy. The country at this time was making great progress industrially and commercially, she embarked again on colonial and imperial schemes. The possibility of the acquisition of Tunis had been discussed at Berlin during the Congress, and Bismarck thought that foreign adventure would turn the mind of France from brooding perpetually over the past or future of Alsace and Lorraine. Tunis was occupied in 1881. Madagascar was brought under French control in 1884. The movement which brought Tonking into the hands of France began in 1882. The mass of the people of France saw these adventures with alarm, and compared them with the Mexican expedition which had done so much to ruin the power of Napoleon III. At home the

10

chief interest lay in the conflicts with the Church over the organisation of a national scheme of education. This scheme was chiefly the work of Ferry, whose ministry (from February 1883 to March 1885) was the longest that France had for many years. The work done was of the utmost importance. Following largely the example set by Germany, a complete system of state and lay education—primary, secondary, and university—was organised, the effect of which on the later development of France has been very great. We must note, too, that in 1880 the Chamber came from Versailles and took up its permanent seat in Paris. A year later an amnesty was issued to those who had taken part in the rising of the Commune. Thus something was done to bridge over the gulf that the rising of the Paris Commune in 1871 had made between parties and classes. The State, too, took gradually a more frankly democratic character. In 1884 the life tenure of seventy-five seats in the Senate, on which MacMahon had set such store, was abolished. All the seats in the Senate were henceforward to become elective, and the method of election was made more equal. The freedom of the press was extended and assured. Liberty of association was conceded, and led to the formation of trades unions on the English pattern. Municipal government was made freer, when, everywhere but in Paris, the municipal councils were given the right to choose their own mayors. But the administration was still far more centralised and authoritative than in England; and the prefects remained, as they still remain, one of the essential parts of the French machine of government.

Most of those changes had been advocated strenuously by Gambetta, who represented more than any other man the ideals of the radical republic. There had always been a conservative element in the ideas of the man whom Thiers had once called 'a raving maniac,' and his language had grown more moderate as time passed. In November 1881 he was made Prime Minister, but his Ministry lasted only for three months and left no permanent mark on the life of France. In the general election of 1885 there was no longer a straight fight between monarchists and republicans. The republicans were divided and the conservatives gained a considerable number of seats, but the Republic itself was not seriously threatened.

Grévy had been elected to a second presidential term, but in 1887, on the discovery of a financial scandal, which touched the honour of his son-in-law, he judged it wisest to resign. The last months of his presidency had seen the beginning of the Boulangist movement. This developed into greater importance under Grévy's successor, President Carnot, but had best be briefly noticed here. There is a good deal that is mysterious in the origins and organisation of the movement, but its general character is quite clear. It was a last effort of those who, for whatever reason, disliked the parliamentary and democratic Republic to procure a revision of the constitution. What should take its place was by no means clear; but all the supporters of Boulanger were agreed in desiring a strengthening of the executive and a reduction in the interference of the Assembly in the work of administration. This might have led merely to a republic more after the pattern of the United States of America; or it might have given an opportunity to another adventurer of the type of Napoleon III to make himself ruler; or it might have led to the restoration of one of the old monarchical families. General Boulanger himself would certainly not have controlled the movement for long. He was not the imbecile that he was represented by his opponents. He had distinguished himself as a soldier, and had been a respectable Minister of War. But his chief recommendation was his capacity for appealing to the popular imagination, his handsome personal appearance, his fine horse, his highly coloured and vague rhetoric. He first became a popular figure in connection with a frontier incident. A French officer (Schnaebele) had been illegally arrested by the Germans, and Grévy was thought to have accepted the incident too tamely. Boulanger made himself the spokesman of French nationalism and was supported by the League of Patriots. But he also demanded a change in the whole constitution, and his programme was summed up as 'Dissolution, and revision through a specially elected constituent assembly.' The danger to the republican constitution seemed for a time really great. The claims of Boulanger were pressed on the electors by methods unusual in France and borrowed from America. He became a candidate for every constituency where there was a vacancy, and was elected in many with large majorities. He was elected even in Paris, but made little impression on the resolute republicanism of the south and east. In the end the movement failed through the weakness of General Boulanger himself, and through the strong and even violent measures which were taken against him by the Government. The electoral law was altered and Boulanger was accused of 'plotting against the safety of the state.' He fled from France, and soon afterwards committed suicide in Brussels. The general result of his movement was to increase the sense of the strength and stability of the republican settlement in France.

PART IV

THE GREAT ALLIANCES AND THE BALANCE OF POWER

CHAPTER XXII

RUSSIA AND THE EASTERN QUESTION, 1856–86

THE situation created by Prussia's victory in 1870 did not immediately produce the changes which German hegemony in Europe seemed to suggest. In eight years Bismarck had humbled England, crushed Austria and France, and created Germany. But he was wise enough to see that Germany could do no more at present. He wanted peace and time to consolidate his gains and, during that necessary breathing-space, he was quite ready to let other nations take the lead, and snatch at opportunity in areas where German interests were in no way endangered.

At this distance it is easy to see what the lines of expansion for European Powers were. In Asia and in Africa there were still wide opportunities and still unappropriated lands, to which Bismarck could encourage the expansion of England and France and thereby divert their attention from Europe. In Europe itself the only field for expansion was offered by the unrest in the Balkans and the increasing decay of Turkey. Here Russia was alike the most interested and ambitious of Powers, and it was difficult for Germany to oppose her. For it was due to Russia's good will and support that Bismarck had triumphed over all his enemies. This chapter will show that the years between 1870 and 1878 were the opportunity of Russia in Europe. The next chapter shows that the years between 1870 and 1883 were the opportunity for France and for England in Africa. At the end of that period (as we shall see in a third chapter) Bismarck had fixed his alliances and felt sufficiently strong to intervene both in Europe and overseas. During 1884–5 he picked up colonies in two continents, and between 1885 and 1886 he settled the Bulgarian imbroglio in the teeth of Russia. But the result of this forceful intervention everywhere was to cause a regrouping of the Powers, and ultimately to produce the Dual Alliance between France and Russia.

In 1870 Russia had a great opportunity. She had just got rid of the obnoxious clauses of the Treaty of Paris forbidding her to fortify

Sebastopol or to keep a fleet on the Black Sea. She had subdued the Caucasian and most of the Turkoman tribes, and was therefore ready for intervention in Europe. But the effectiveness of such intervention and the probability of success depended on the moral and material condition of Russia. Had she been armed and ready, an athlete among the nations like Prussia, her success would perhaps have been assured.

During the first quarter of the nineteenth century, under the rule of the brilliant but unstable Alexander I, Russia had suffered from alternative doses of enlightenment and reaction. Czar Nicholas I, who succeeded him, had applied to his vast dominions a rule of stern repression and carried out his system with gigantic energy. During 1848–9 his methods seemed justified, for his peoples remained quiet and his army could leave his own dominions to repress revolution in Hungary. But the Crimean War revealed the true weakness of Russia. The mediocre generals and the modest forces of England and France humiliated and worsted the great military autocracy. Appalling revelations of corruption and inefficiency discredited the Russian Government, and drove Nicholas into his grave, just as his despotic world was falling in ruins about his ears (1855).

The problem before his son, Alexander II, was to secure peace, and when he got that, as he did at Paris in 1856, to build up a new Russia. Even reactionaries admitted that a return to the methods of Nicholas was impossible. War does sometimes bring benefits, and it impressed this conviction on the governing class of Russia. Unlike Nicholas, Alexander had been consciously trained for his task. He was not a liberal in his youth and perhaps never really imbibed liberal ideas; but he desired reform and improvements and timidly and vaguely sought to produce them. The halo of idealism, which has surrounded him, has concealed the true man. He was a conscientious ruler, who stumbled painfully along the path of progress, at times retracing his steps and at others repenting of his rashness. From such a man no continuous and clear policy could come, though his moments of idealism or sagacity were responsible for some great reforms.

Of these far the most important was the emancipation of the Serfs. It was a reform made in England in the fourteenth century and completed in every other European country early in the nineteenth. It was still opposed by the reactionary forces in Russia, but the chief force of the emancipating movement came from the Czar himself, and it was therefore successful. He believed emancipation to be inevitable and was prudent in thinking and bold in declaring 'that it is better for it to come from above than from below.' [1] The manifesto of emancipation was finally issued on February 19, 1861, though the actual measures were not completed for some half-dozen years. Over twenty million

---

[1] Speech of the Czar to a deputation of Moscow nobility, March 1856.

serfs were thus not only emancipated but were provided with land.[1]
Compensation was given to the masters, though probably on an inadequate scale. On the whole, it was a great, necessary, and enlightened
reform, and the best justification of autocracy ever provided by Russia.
During the 'sixties local self-government was also introduced, first into
the country districts, and next into the towns. Extensive judicial reforms also took place, and the foundations of popular and elementary
education were laid.

But every step forward only served to reveal the terrible backwardness
of the country. Civil service reform failed because there was a lack of
competent national or local administrators; legal advance was retarded
by the dearth of good barristers. The absence of an educated middle
class hampered political development, and depressed or retarded commerce and credit. The transport system and railway development met
difficulties unexampled in other countries. The military system, though
revolutionised, was little less corrupt and inefficient in 1878 than in
1856. The press was indeed freer than ever before, but in a backward
country freedom of opinion is not an unmixed blessing. The spasmodic
censorship alternately cowed and irritated the press; reckless and unjust
criticism weakened the Government and frightened the Czar. By 1860
Alexander had set his face against freedom of opinion and by 1862 he
had restored a thoroughly reactionary censorship. The hopes entertained of the new reign had vanished, and despair had succeeded to
enthusiasm. Conservatives were wondering if the vacillation of Alexander was better than the resolution of Nicholas, while revolutionaries
had already decided that he had abandoned and betrayed them. Revolutionary feelings and organisations developed, and secret undercurrents
swelled in volume. There was widespread pessimism and depression
and much occult opposition to the Government.

As if to express this discontent and to justify reaction, Poland broke
out in rebellion in 1863. The revolt was hardly justifiable, except on
the principle, dear to Polish hearts, that Russian rule could never be
tolerated. During 1862 and 1863 the real concessions, offered by the
Russian Government, served only to provoke a Polish revolt, which
was as ill-timed as it was heroic and hopeless. The Czar really had an
excuse for reaction now. His offers had been scornfully rejected, and
England and France had foolishly endeavoured to support the Poles.
Brutal repression followed, and the Lithuanians, the Livonians, and the
Finns soon suffered for the turbulence of the Poles. From that time
forward a period of gloom and reaction set in, and every non-Russian
nationality within the Czar's Empire was brutally oppressed.

In foreign policy, however, the Russian Government had at last hit
upon an illuminating idea. In Asia their expansion was due to penal
colonies, to military ambition, or to annexationist greed. In Europe

---

[1] The land settlement was not in fact a good one and had to be 'unsettled' by the
end of the century.

the persistent advance to Constantinople could at last be concealed beneath a cloud of high-flown national and racial aspiration. It was the adoption of a Pan-Slavist policy which made Russian officials romantic, hid Russia's age-long ambitions beneath a sentimental veil, and enabled her to rally the Slavonic brethren in all lands outside her own dominions. This powerful weapon for propaganda was first discovered and used by the Russian Government in the days of Alexander II.

Pan-Slavism did not arise in Russia, but in Austria-Hungary. In that area were seven Slav races, who possessed opportunities for learning and for culture such as did not exist in Russia itself, and subjection to the Teuton and the Magyar was just the kind of oppression to stimulate the imagination of the Slav. For it is 'the captive peoples who fill their dungeons with legends.' The dreamers dreamed, and the scholars toiled, that the shattered fragments of their race might be fused into one vast spiritual whole. It was in 1824 that Jan Kollár, a Slovak, wrote his famous poem of *Slavy Dcera* (the daughter of Slava). Two phrases of his show the warmth of his imagination and sum up his ideal: 'Scattered Slavs, let us be one united whole and no longer be mere fragments'; and again, 'All Europe would kneel before this idol, whose head would tower above the clouds and whose feet would shake the earth.' Two years later Šafarik, another Slovak, laid a scientific foundation for this poetic aspiration. His grammar of the Slav languages was the first scholarly investigation of the affinities between the varieties of Slavonic speech. His studies attracted the attention of that learned body of Czechs who were slowly building up the foundations of their nationality anew and seeking to drive out both the German speech and the German rule from Bohemia. This propaganda suited their ideas and their purpose, and it was not an accident that the first ethnic and linguistic conference, uniting all members of the Slav race, was held at Prague in 1848.[1] The same year was memorable because the Catholic Croats and Orthodox Serbs united under the leadership of Jellačić and Austria to attack the Magyars.[2] And when Nicholas sent Russian armies into Hungary, he was regarded by Slavs as assisting the Pan-Slavist ideal. Much sympathy was also aroused among all Slav nations, except Poland, when Russia became involved and was defeated in the Crimean War.

Up to this time the Russian Government had unaccountably ignored the Pan-Slav movement. Alexander I had been a cosmopolitan, Nicholas a Russian whose eye rested on Constantinople but who sought to win his way there by Russian arms alone. His defeat in the Crimea impressed his son and successor and the bureaucracy. Crippled in material force by France and England in 1856, Alexander II could only

---

[1] It is a curious irony that the different Slav races could not use any common tongue, and finally used German as the language of the Congress.

[2] In 1849 Archbishop Strossmayer took up his episcopal residence at Djakovo in Croatia and began his long struggle for the cultural unity of Yugoslavia. He was also, within limits, an ardent advocate of Pan-Slav ideals.

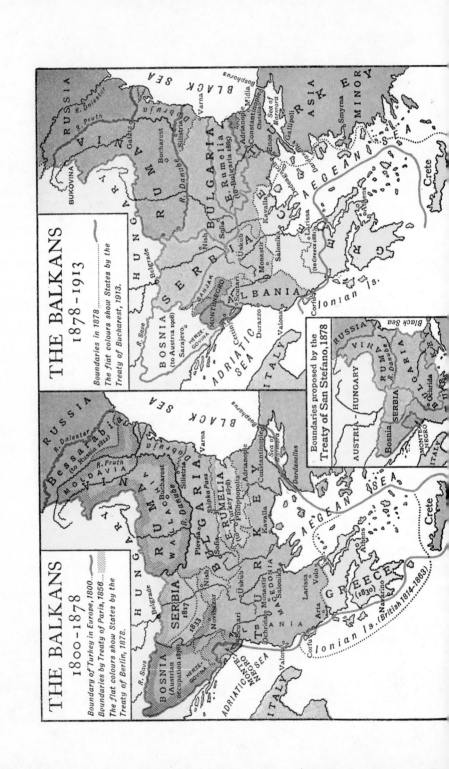

THE BALKANS
1878–1913

Boundaries in 1878 ....
The flat colours show States by the
Treaty of Bucharest, 1913.

THE BALKANS
1800–1878

Boundary of Turkey in Europe, 1800...
Boundaries by Treaty of Paris, 1856...
The flat colours show States by the
Treaty of Berlin, 1878.

Boundaries proposed by the
Treaty of San Stefano, 1878

make Russia's influence felt for a time by propagandist policies and by a general support of the Slav peoples outside his own Empire. In this way he might turn the Slav peoples of the Balkans into the satellites of the Russian planet.

In 1858 Montenegro, which had already shown strong sympathy for Russia, had beaten the Turks at Grahovo. But, during the next few years, her very existence was threatened by Turkey, and Russia came energetically to her support. Rumania, though not a Slav state, was assisted by Russia to complete her unity in 1861. In 1867 Russia interfered to remove the Turkish garrisons from Belgrade and other Serbian fortresses, and thus renewed her intimate connection with Serbia. Russia failed, of course, to win Poland, who revolted against her in 1863. But in 1867 she held a great ethnic exhibition at St. Petersburg, where delegates of all other Slav races (except the Poles) appeared, and where the Czar himself addressed the representatives of the other Slav races as 'brother Slavs.' [1] In 1870, as already related, Russia abrogated the Black Sea clauses of the Treaty of 1856. She announced not only that she intended to restore Sebastopol, the great fortress of Southern Russia, but that the Russian navy should again be rebuilt on the shores of the Euxine. As a demonstration of Russian power this was very impressive to brother Slavs, and no doubt greatly encouraged them to rise against the Turks. In reality the demonstration was an empty one enough, for Russia did not succeed in building a large fleet in time to affect the situation. Russia's advance against Adrianople was as much facilitated by her command of the Black Sea in 1829 as it was retarded by her lack of it in 1878.

The year 1870 was marked by an even more important and decisive step on the part of Russia. Up till this year the various Christian Slavs of the Balkans, as Bulgars and Serbs, were under the spiritual jurisdiction of the Greek Patriarch of Constantinople. Religion has always been the handmaid of politics in the East, and Russian statesmen thought that they would aggrandise the Slav element in the Turkish Empire if they could create a Slav Patriarch who would emancipate Slavs from Greek influences and from a Greek Patriarch. In seeking thus to create a new religious authority to rule over Slavs as a distinct nationality, Russia bethought herself of the Bulgars. Macedonia was inhabited by Greeks, Serbs, and Bulgars, but the latter were the most numerous. Hence Russia demanded the creation of a Slav Church and religious leader. The Sultan complied in a firman (edict) of March 10, 1870. He recognised the Slavs as a separate religious nation with a separate religious head, independent of the Greek Patriarch of Constantinople; this religious head was to be a Bulgar and was termed the Exarch.[2]

---

[1] A curious incident occurred. The Poles sent no representatives, but the Czechs expressed a hope that Russia and Poland might be reconciled.

[2] He did not actually function till 1872.

10*

Russia thought she had gained much by this concession. In reality the Turk showed a Machiavellian greatness in conceding it. *Divide et impera* had always been the motto of the Turk, and division between Greeks and Slavs in Macedonia was what he desired. No sooner was the purpose announced than the Greek Patriarch excommunicated the Bulgarian Exarch, and their followers took up the quarrel. Fights soon arose between the Greeks or Patriarchists and the Bulgars or Exarchists, and rival brigand-bands soon appeared who 'proved their doctrine orthodox, by apostolic blows and knocks.' The Turk rubbed his hands to see Christians at variance, and did everything to encourage their disputes. Moreover, though this policy certainly created a strong Slav bulwark to Greek influence in Macedonia, it also divided the Slavs themselves. There were Serb, as well as Bulgar, elements in Macedonia, and the Serbs hated a Bulgarian Exarch almost as much as they hated a Greek Patriarch. Hence the Bulgarian Exarchate divided not only Greeks from Bulgars but Bulgars from Serbs. And in the strife thus created between Bulgars and Serbs Russia was to find one of the gravest difficulties of her foreign policy in the Balkans. For the moment, however, these difficulties were not perceived, as the Serbs were much weaker in Macedonia than the Bulgars. And the creation of a Slav Exarchate certainly promoted a wave of Slav feeling and propaganda throughout the Balkans.

The first signs of revolt began in Bosnia and Herzegovina. The inhabitants there were nearly all Serbs in blood [1] and notoriously undisciplined and warlike. They adjoined Montenegro, whose inhabitants passed their whole existence in fighting the Turks, and the Montenegrin clan-chiefs planned raids to assist the risings in Herzegovina. The Turkish rule was relaxing, because Turkey was approaching bankruptcy. She could not maintain or arm her garrisons and yet at the same time demanded increased taxation from her already oppressed subjects. The Turkish cup of iniquity was full. A bad harvest in 1874 led to risings in both Bosnia and Herzegovina, which became formidable in 1875. [2] The Great Powers were anxious to localise the rising and to remove the causes of complaint, and a note, proposed by Count Andrássy, the Foreign Minister of Austria-Hungary, and circulated on December 30, 1875, was accepted by other Powers and by the Turkish Government early in the year 1876. It is quite certain, however, that the latter had no intention of carrying out the proposed reforms. On the contrary they had every intention of intimidating their Christian subjects by massacre and violence.

The Bulgars, who had been excited and encouraged by the grant of the Exarchate, now attempted an insurrection. The rebellion was easily

---

[1] About a third were Catholic, a third Orthodox, and a third Mohammedan or 'Turks.'

[2] Peter Karageorgević (King of Serbia in 1903) went out as a volunteer and took part in this rising.

put down, but was followed by a set of revolting atrocities, in which some twelve thousand persons (including women and children) were massacred. These incidents occurred in April, and it was long before the true facts or their import were realised in England.

Disraeli, the Prime Minister of Great Britain, was now confronted with a diplomatic crisis of the gravest importance. He was strongly drawn towards the East and had already shown insight in buying the Khedive's shares in the Suez Canal and in his policy towards India. But his view of the Turk was a mistaken one, based perhaps on his early travels in the Levant. He certainly admired the Arabs and perhaps confused them with the Turks. Certainly the Turk was gallant and a ruler of men, and Disraeli supposed him capable of progress and useful in resisting Russia. He did not understand that even the pettiest Balkan state could pay its way and could avoid massacring its subjects, and that therefore an increase in their territories tended to tranquillise areas previously seething with revolt against the Turk. He did not see that an Asiatic Power which massacred its Christian subjects, which never intended to sanction reform or progress, and defaulted on its debts, was an increasing danger to Europe.

Disraeli began by minimising the scale of the massacres and by suggesting that the anti-Turk agitation had been got up for political purposes, to cover the aggressions and advance of Russia. In this view he was apparently supported by his Ambassador at Constantinople.[1] But the facts had already been revealed by journalists, and a member of the British Embassy from Constantinople reported that the Bulgarian massacres were 'perhaps the most heinous crime . . . of the present century.' Disraeli's cynicism brought Gladstone from a temporary retirement and induced him to publish a pamphlet called *Bulgarian Horrors*. This lashed the British public to frenzy with its passionate descriptions of the atrocities. It concluded with the oft-quoted words 'Let the Turks now carry away their abuses in the only possible manner, namely, by carrying off themselves. Their Zaptiehs and their Mudirs, their Bimbashis and their Yuzbachis, their Kaimakams and their Pashas, one and all, bag and baggage, shall, I hope, clear out from the province they have desolated and profaned.' [2] The eloquence of Gladstone was supported by the serene wisdom of Lord Stratford de Redcliffe, now in extreme old age, who added the wise counsel that there would be no settling of Balkan problems unless protection was afforded not only to the Bulgars but to all the Christians of Turkey.

The excitement in Russia was naturally great, and the Pan-Slav

---

[1] By August 7 Disraeli was complaining of Elliot's 'deficiency of information' (Buckle's *Beaconsfield* [1920], vol. VI. p. 46). Kemal, the only reputable Turkish authority, admitted some 6000 dead.

[2] *Bulgarian Horrors and the Question of the East*, 1876, pp. 61–2. Note: it will be seen that the 'bag and baggage' policy, here expressed, is not expulsion of the Turk from Europe, but from Bulgaria, and (p. 54) from Bosnia and Herzegovina.

appeal was irresistible. Montenegro, whose subjects were always belli-cose, and Serbia, though ill prepared for war, could resist the popular pressure no longer. On June 30, 1876, Serbia and on July 1 Montenegro, plunged into war with Turkey. The Montenegrins won many successes, but the Serbs were badly beaten at the end of October, and only an ultimatum from Russia prevented the Turks from advancing on Bel-grade. It was now a problem as to whether Russia would not be com-pelled by popular sympathy to join her brother Slavs. At the end of October the Czar was informed by Great Britain that, whatever might be the feeling as to Turkish atrocities, England must protect her in-terests in the Suez Canal and Constantinople. Alexander II, on Novem-ber 2, gave a solemn assurance that he had no design of annexing Constantinople or Bulgaria. Disraeli, whose courage was unbounded, remained unconvinced and violently anti-Russian. On November 9 he spoke publicly at the Mansion House in this sense, and obviously ex-pressed disbelief in the Czar's pledges and Russia's disinterestedness. The Czar announced publicly, on the next day after Disraeli's speech (it does not seem certain he had heard its tenor), that he would act *inde-pendently* of the other Powers of Europe, if he failed to secure adequate guarantees from the Turk for the future protection of her Christian subjects.

Meanwhile cooler heads than those of Russian Czar or British Pre-mier had arranged for a Conference of the Powers at Constantinople. England sent to it the man who was to understand the problem best and was now to win his first diplomatic laurels—Lord Salisbury. His first experience was a study in disillusion. Abdul Hamid had become Sultan at the end of August, and, though young, was about to astonish the world with one of those transformation-scenes, of which he was to prove so consummate a master. The day before the Conference of the Great Powers met at Constantinople to demand reforms, Abdul Hamid endowed Turkey with a constitution. The Sultan, as a liberal and con-stitutionalist, blandly informed the Conference that Turkey was now a reformed state, and that he ought not to be asked to surrender his sovereign rights over his own subjects, when he had invited them to share in his Government. The Conference, thus nonplussed and baffled, broke up without accomplishing anything. Abdul Hamid, thus at liberty, ended the constitution in May 1877, disgraced Midhat Pasha, its champion, at once, and murdered him a few years later.[1]

It seems quite clear that the action of Abdul Hamid was governed by the belief that England would support him against Russia, as she had done in the Crimean War, for a British naval squadron was already in Besika Bay.[2] He was woefully mistaken. When Russia and England presented joint demands in April he rejected them, and Alexander re-plied to this rejection by declaring war. Rumania joined Russia in an

---

[1] Not till 1882, as England made efforts to protect him.
[2] It had been ordered there in May 1876.

alliance, and Montenegro again renewed the war. It was some two months before the Russian and Rumanian armies got into Bulgaria. There they were held up by the military genius of Osman Pasha at Plevna. Behind earthworks this dogged and heroic Turk repelled all assaults and immobilised the European forces of Russia for nearly five months. Finally Todleben, the forgotten hero of Sebastopol, an engineer as able as Osman, drew lines around him that proved too strong to be broken when the gallant Turk made his last sortie. Osman surrendered in December 1877, and before the end of January 1878 Skobelev, the most brilliant of the Russian generals, had opened the way to Adrianople, which fell on the 28th. The Turk was everywhere in retreat. The Serbs had re-entered the war and captured the important strategic centre of Nish, Prince Nicholas of Montenegro had seized Spizza and Dulcigno, and had burst into original poetry on his first sight of the sea. In Asia the Russians had been everywhere victorious and the great fortresses of Kars, Ardahan, and Erzerum, in fact all Armenia, were in their hands. Abdul Hamid sued for peace, and an armistice was agreed on January 31, 1878.

Peace was fairly well assured between Russia and Turkey. Was it assured between England and Russia? It was not certain. On January 23 the British fleet was ordered to leave Besika Bay and proceed to Constantinople,[1] and Parliament voted Disraeli (now Lord Beaconsfield) six millions. The Russian army moved within sight of Constantinople, only to see the ominous black hulls of the British fleet in the waters off Prinkipo island. The danger seemed great to the more timid of the British Cabinet and to the public, but Russia was really helpless. Her army was worn out and exhausted, her supplies were wretched, her finances were in disorder. It was quite impossible for the Czar to risk a conflict with a new enemy or enemies, for, in all probability, he would have had to fight Austria-Hungary on land as well as England on the sea. The dramatic touch, by which Beaconsfield ordered Indian troops to Malta in April, was not needed to prevent Russia from proceeding to extremities.

Russia took the wisest course under the circumstances, and signed a separate peace with the Turks on March 3 at San Stefano. By this she hoped to preserve most of her gains without offending England, for she did not enter Constantinople, and proposed to evacuate Adrianople. In Asia she proposed to annex Kars and Ardahan, but, in view of her conquest and evacuation of Erzerum, this was not an excessive demand and did not in fact give her control over most of Armenia. In Europe direct Russian gains were limited to the recovery of that part of Bessarabia which had been ceded to Rumania in 1856 and to a Russian advance to the mouth of the Danube. Russia proposed to compensate Rumania for depriving her of a fertile province by giving her

---

[1] This was countermanded, but the fleet was ordered to move up to Constantinople on February 9.

two-thirds of the barren Dobruja. This was not generous treatment to a gallant ally in the war, but Rumania was a Latin state and it was the aim of Russia to exalt the Slav.

In this aim she met with considerable difficulties, for the reason that Alexander had already promised Francis Joseph that Austria-Hungary might occupy Bosnia and Herzegovina.[1] Bosnia was the Serb country which Serbia dreamed of annexing. In denying this province to Serbia Russia practically abandoned the Serbs. She insisted indeed at San Stefano on the enlargement of the boundaries of Serbia and on her acquiring Nish. But Alexander could do no more for her, and even recommended her to go to Austria-Hungary for diplomatic help. He seems to have thought that Serbia must fall under Austro-Hungarian influence. For Montenegro he did more. He saw to it that she received accessions of territory—though not a seaport, nor contiguous boundaries with Serbia—and made it clear that he would support her independence against Austria-Hungary.

Russia's great card was to be the new state of Bulgaria, and the 'Big Bulgaria' she designed at San Stefano stretched the ethnic claims of Bulgaria to an extreme limit. Bulgaria not only included what is now Bulgaria, but added the modern Greek coast-line stretching west from the port of Cavalla to just short of Salonica, and nearly all of what is now Serbian Macedonia. Thus a new and great Balkan state of sturdy Bulgar peasants would have been erected. Liberated and (as was hoped) in future dominated by Russia, it would cover all the approaches both to Salonica and to Constantinople. In future Russia, having revived her sea power, could operate against Constantinople with the aid of a powerful land-ally on the Turkish flank.[2] The plan was obviously drawn in the Russian interest and based on the idea that Bulgaria, for whose freedom so many thousands of Russians had died, would be the obedient tool and pawn of the Russian Czar in future. In fact, as events proved, this would not have been the case, and both Disraeli and Alexander II were mistaken if they made any such calculation. The San Stefano agreement sinned indeed by giving Bulgaria somewhat too much, but it did not go far enough in justice to the Serbs, to the Greeks, to the Albanians, and to the Rumans. If (as was later done) Albania had been made independent, if Epirus and Thessaly had gone to Greece, and if Southern Bessarabia had remained to Rumania, the settlement would have been better.[3] Serbia might at this time have

[1] In the Agreement of Reichstadt, July 8, 1876, and in the Convention of Budapest, January 15, 1877.

[2] North-west Macedonia, Epirus and Albania, and Thessaly remained Turkish, but of course were severed by the Big Bulgaria from all connection with Constantinople. Greece, which had not fought, was not to have its boundaries increased. A programme of reform was drawn up for Thessaly and Crete.

[3] Dr. Seton-Watson's criticism of the San Stefano settlement as 'too Slavonic' in *The Rise of Nationality in the Balkans* (1917), pp. 107 *sqq.*, is interesting.

been induced to accept North-west Macedonia and been consoled by it for the loss of Bosnia.[1]

The British view was not determined by any consideration but that of resistance to Russia. Disraeli had got rid of the more timid of his Cabinet and made Lord Salisbury Foreign Secretary at the end of March. Though not entirely in agreement with his chief, Salisbury was prepared at any rate to oppose the creation of a 'Big Bulgaria,' which in the British view would have been a Russian stepping-stone to Constantinople. As soon as he became Foreign Minister, on the resignation of Derby, he issued a circular (April 1) to this effect; [2] and began to negotiate with Russia. Great Britain and Austria-Hungary had both already demanded a European Congress for revising the terms of San Stefano. Salisbury finally agreed to accept its main clauses on condition of Russia's abandoning at the coming Congress the plan of a 'Big Bulgaria.' The new Bulgaria was to comprise about one-third of that designed under San Stefano, and to extend merely from the Danube to the Balkans. Macedonia and its southern coast were to be restored to Turkey, and a third section immediately south of the Balkans was to be called Eastern Rumelia and to form an autonomous province directly under Turkish control. The real point of this arrangement was a purely military one. By holding Eastern Rumelia up to the Balkans the Turks would obtain a fortified mountain line which would defend Adrianople and Constantinople against any further Russian advance from the Danube. As this concession was made privately and beforehand by Russia, Great Britain consented to enter the Congress.

Disraeli seems to have thought that he had secured the Turks in Europe by these direct pre-conference negotiations with Russia, of which he did not tell Turkey. He secured Turkey in Asia and the British route to India by direct pre-conference negotiations with Turkey, of which he did not tell Russia. 'Austria will bring about a settlement of the Bulgarian situation,' said he at the Cabinet of March 27. 'It is the Armenian danger which is to be guarded against.' [3] The proposed Russian acquisition of Batum, Ardahan, and Kars was to be met by occupying 'some island or station on the coast of Asia Minor which will neutralise the presence of Russia in Armenia.' Cyprus was the 'key of Western Asia' and could be made a place of arms and a harbour, and was handy for landing at Alexandretta. So a short convention was secretly signed between England and the Sultan. If Russia annexed Kars, Batum and Ardahan, England was to occupy Cyprus, and to guarantee to defend by force of arms the Sultan's remaining Asiatic dominions against Russia. In return the Sultan promised to introduce 'necessary reforms' for the protection of 'the Christian and other

[1] The only flaw in this argument is that Serbia and Bulgaria might have quarrelled over their respective shares of Macedonia.
[2] In Hertslet's *Map of Europe by Treaty* (1891), vol. IV. pp. 2698 *sqq.*
[3] Buckle's *Beaconsfield*, vol. VI. pp. 266, 290, 299.

subjects of the Porte in these [the Asiatic] territories.' On May 26 it was known that the Sultan would accept this, and the formal Convention was signed on June 4. On the 2nd Disraeli and Salisbury had been appointed British representatives and had agreed to attend the Congress. Finally a secret agreement had been made with Austria-Hungary to the effect that she should occupy Bosnia and Herzegovina.[1] England was thus secretly in agreement with Russia, with Austria-Hungary, and with Turkey before the Conference opened, though neither Austria nor Russia knew of the Cyprus convention, nor Turkey of the Bosnian agreement. As Disraeli saw Bismarck before the Congress opened (June 13) and obtained a promise that the subject of Bulgaria should be taken first, there was not much fear as to the result, for the main concession there had already been made. Like most successful Congresses this one was successful because the principal items were agreed to beforehand.

Bismarck had offered Berlin as the seat of the Congress, and himself as 'an honest broker.' In reality his 'brokerage' was open to some suspicion, because he did everything to assist Austria-Hungary in the negotiations, and at times put pressure on her old foe, Russia. Andrássy, the representative of Austria-Hungary, gained most. He had actually declined to join Disraeli in a defensive alliance.[2] But his expenditure of ink and paper was more effective in gaining territory than Russian blood and treasure. Bosnia and Herzegovina were handed to Andrássy for political occupation, and the funnel or Sanjak of Novibazar was occupied by Austria-Hungary militarily. This occupation severed Serbia from Montenegro, and the latter, being pro-Russian, was greatly reduced from the boundaries granted it by San Stefano. Serbia was practically brought within the sphere of Austro-Hungarian influence. Serbia, Montenegro, and Rumania were all declared independent states. Russia, which had consented to the reduction of San Stefano Bulgaria to a third of its former size, now sought to deprive this concession of all value. She attempted to prevent the Turks from garrisoning Eastern Rumelia along the Balkan line, to which Disraeli naturally refused to agree. But it is probable that her attempt was an intrigue and not a threat to break the peace. At any rate Russia gave way quite early in the Congress, and the Big Bulgaria was trisected on the lines already agreed. Russia recovered Bessarabia from Rumania, and compensated her ally by giving her two-thirds of the Dobruja, which should more properly have gone to Bulgaria.

In Asia Minor the arrangements of San Stefano were startlingly altered by Disraeli's *coup* with regard to Cyprus. When Russia intimated her intention to retain Kars, Ardahan, and Batum, Disraeli revealed the Convention (July 7) and ordered the British fleet to Cyprus.

---

[1] It was already known that Russia would not oppose this. *v*. p. 302, n. 1.

[2] Buckle's *Beaconsfield*, vol. VI. p. 227, because, though Disraeli did not know it, he already had an understanding with Russia.

Russia showed irritation and, despite Disraeli's assertion to the contrary, seems to have got the better of him in the question of the Russo-Turkish boundary in Asia Minor.[1] Disraeli was really much exercised about the route to India, and, in private, made inquiries as to the possible defence of Mesopotamia against Russia. But his scheme of defence was rather unsuccessful in practice.

The Congress was thus over and the Great Powers were pacified. Queen Victoria offered Disraeli a dukedom, and gave Garters both to him and to Salisbury, amid the enthusiasm which the careful stage management had evoked and which the phrase 'Peace with Honour' embodied. It would be wrong to deny that Disraeli had shown great courage at the crisis, but courage in diplomacy should be accompanied by knowledge, and in this Disraeli was poorly provided, and he did not try to obtain it from the more instructed Lord Salisbury. He seems to have had no belief in the strength of nascent nationality in the Balkan peninsula and no idea of resisting Russia except by military force. His belief in the virtues of Abdul Hamid and the Turkish desire to protect and ameliorate the condition of their Christian subjects whether in Europe or Asia was woefully mistaken. His policy in Asia speedily came to nought. The despatch of British military consuls to Armenia to arrange for its defence against Russia proved useless. In 1880 Gladstone came into power and substituted political for military consuls, and Salisbury, on resuming office in 1886, like a wise man accepted the change in silence. But political consuls were no more effective in stopping massacres than military ones had been in organising defence. To crown all, in July 1886, Russia announced her intention of disregarding her expressed declaration (Article 69 of Treaty of Berlin) of considering Batum as a port 'essentiellement commercial' and proceeded to fortify it.[2] So neither Russia nor Turkey approved of, or regarded, or upheld Disraeli's Asiatic policy. Cyprus was never made a place of arms nor a naval base, and is anything but the 'Gibraltar of the Eastern Mediterranean.' The Sultan never attempted to keep his promises of reform in Asia, and after a time deliberately set to work to massacre his Armenian subjects, without paying any regard to British remonstrances. In 1896 British Blue Books set out the horrible story of these atrocities. In 1898 another Blue Book in recounting the guarantees or engagements of Great Britain, included our obligation to defend Asiatic Turkey and the Sultan's 'promise' to 'introduce the necessary reforms . . . for the protection of Christian . . . subjects.' In other words the Sultan still claimed, and could apparently enforce, the guarantee of Great Britain's protection of Asia Minor, though British Blue Books proved that he

---

[1] Buckle's *Beaconsfield*, vol. VI. p. 337; Lady G. Cecil's *Salisbury* (1921), vol. II. pp. 291–3.

[2] Even in the original bargain Russia got the better of Disraeli by persuading him that 'exclusivement' and 'essentiellement' commercial were the same thing, which they obviously were not. *Vide* Lady G. Cecil's *Salisbury* (1921), vol. II. pp. 291–3.

had in the most inhuman manner massacred those Christian subjects. He had promised to protect them in the same instrument which guaranteed his own dominions against attack.

In Europe Disraeli's policy, though not successful, was not irremediable.[1] Macedonia was indeed delivered over to terrible internecine warfare and suffering, but the blunder by which Bulgaria was separated from Rumelia was ultimately set right. At times Gladstone, by sympathetic insight, hit upon truths withheld from more professional diplomats. He had done so twenty years before the Congress of Berlin. 'Surely the best resistance to be offered to Russia is by the strength and freedom of those countries that will have to resist her. You want to place a living barrier between her and Turkey. There is no barrier, then, like the breast of freemen.'[2] Certainly the union of Moldavia and Wallachia in Rumania proved a more effective resistance to Russia than their separation. And the enlargement of Bulgaria produced, in the same way, her liberation from Russia.

Russia displayed colossal tactlessness in dealing with the new Bulgaria. In April 1879 Alexander of Battenberg became her Prince. He was a nephew of Alexander II, inexperienced in dealing with his subjects and subservient to Russia. A Russian general became Prime Minister and another one Minister for War. They attempted to dragoon the country and soon aroused the bitter resentment of Bulgars. In 1885 a conspiracy burst out in Eastern Rumelia, and the rebel Bulgars there expelled their Turkish governor and proclaimed the union of 'the two Bulgarias,' inviting Prince Alexander to be their ruler. Russia was hostile to this movement, but Stambulov, the strong man of Bulgaria, informed Prince Alexander that he would be expelled if he did not accept the Union. Prince Alexander capitulated and accepted. Russia was furious and withdrew all her officers from the Bulgarian army. Bulgarians were glad enough to see them go. Russia appealed to the other Powers to prevent the union of Eastern Rumelia with Bulgaria. Austria-Hungary, however, made no objection, because she realised that a strong Bulgaria would be anti-Russian. What would England do, England which had created Eastern Rumelia and risked war in 1878 rather than consent to its fusion with Bulgaria? Lord Salisbury was now England's Prime Minister and would surely support Russia. But, to the great surprise of every one, he did not do so. Lord Salisbury had learnt the lesson if others had not, and he quietly acquiesced in a union which he knew would make for permanent peace. And the 'living barrier' formed by the 'breast of freemen' was thus drawn across Russia's path to Constantinople.[3]

[1] Thus the Greek frontier was extended to include Thessaly in 1880, and Montenegro acquired a port at Dulcigno, as a result of Gladstone's aid.

[2] House of Commons, May 4, 1858.

[3] Lord Salisbury owed a good deal to the influence of Sir William White, for a time acting Ambassador at Constantinople and a truly great diplomat.

Bulgaria, though united, was not to escape entirely either the anger of Russia or the jealousy of her Slav neighbour. For Serbia now sought to intervene. One of the gravest defects of the Congress of Berlin was the disregard of the just claims of Serbia. She is said to have been told by Russia to apply to Austria-Hungary for support, and in 1881 she signed a secret Convention with Austria-Hungary which made her practically dependent on her. Now she suddenly declared war on the new Bulgaria (November 14, 1885). In a three days' battle at Slivnica the Bulgars were victorious. They began to advance into Serbia, when Prince Alexander received an ultimatum from Austria-Hungary which warned him to turn back.[1] He obeyed and went back to rule 'the two Bulgarias.' He soon found that he was not to rule in peace. In August 1886 the hapless Prince was kidnapped by the supporters of Russia and taken to Russian territory. There was a speedy reaction in his favour in Bulgaria, but he humiliated himself in a telegram to the Czar and was compelled by Stambulov and the Bulgarian patriots to abdicate. Thereafter, in 1887, Prince Ferdinand of Saxe-Coburg became the ruler of Bulgaria and pursued a strong anti-Russian policy.

In this fashion some of the worst consequences of the Congress of Berlin were liquidated in the decade following it. But certain ineradicable evils remained. There was suffering and atrocity in Armenia, but danger as well as misery in Macedonia. For, while the Great Powers ultimately allowed the Sultan to massacre at will in Armenia, they were not prepared to allow him the same freedom in Macedonia. For in Macedonia there were men of Greek, Bulgarian, and Serb blood, and in Macedonia there were endless opportunities for Russian and Austro-Hungarian intrigue. It was quite certain that these evils could not go on for ever, but the year 1886 marks roughly the period at which a temporary lull ensued, and when men could consider other great European problems.

'The true significance of 1878,' says a brilliant writer, 'lies in the fact that Bismarck made Andrássy his colleague and Disraeli his tool, and that he finally won and dominated Austria-Hungary without at the same time offending Russia.'[2] This statement is wholly correct as regards Bismarck's unswerving support of Austria-Hungary, but it is not wholly accurate as regards Russia. Alexander II was so seriously annoyed at Bismarck's attitude at the Congress that he wrote a letter to the German Emperor William I in April 1879, expressing doubts as to whether peace could be preserved between Russia and Germany. That irritation became much greater during 1885–6 when Russia found Bismarck would not support her in the Bulgarian crisis. So that in 1878 we have the remote origin of the estrangement between Russia and Germany, which divided Europe into two camps, the Franco-Russian

---

[1] Austria-Hungary, of course, could not allow a dependent Serbia to be laid in the dust by Bulgaria. During 1886–7 Bismarck's aid supported her against Russia.

[2] Dr. Seton-Watson, *The Rise of Nationality in the Balkans*, p. 115.

and the Austro-Italo-German Alliances. But, before we survey the con-struction of these great Alliances, which ultimately came into conflict, we must turn to other fields. This chapter has shown how Bismarck allowed Russia an opportunity in the Balkans, how she failed to make full use of it, and how in the end was compelled to restrain her activities. The next chapter will show how Bismarck permitted France and Great Britain to have their opportunities in the area of colonial enterprise, until he himself entered that field and limited their ambitions. The fact that even Bismarck thus in the end found himself limiting the activities alike of England, France, and Russia, may explain why his feebler successors ultimately succeeded in alienating all three Powers.

CHAPTER XXIII

THE GROWTH OF COLONISATION, OF TRADE, AND OF OVERSEAS EMPIRE, 1815–92

THAT great transmarine colonisation and activity took place in the seventeenth and eighteenth centuries is universally admitted. But it is often said that there was very little of it in the nineteenth century on the part of the European Powers, other than England. The great colonising career of France in Africa began in 1830, and colonisation, in the wider sense, was a policy actively pursued by all the European Powers, though it was not always pursued overseas. Colonisation for Russia meant the plantation of Siberia and penetration into Central Asia, and it was peculiarly active in the nineteenth century. For the German States, all active colonisers in the eighteenth and nineteenth centuries, it meant the plantation of waste areas in their own borders or in Europe herself[1] beyond which they did not look till the last quarter of the nineteenth century. Hence in the last decade of that century the entrance of Germany into the colonial field produced acute international controversy.

Colonising proper seems to mean the settlement of alien districts with white inhabitants. But there are other activities, which can hardly be classed under one head, and include everything from barter and huck-stering to military and economic imperialism. The arrival of traders, or travellers, or of missionaries is usually the first step. After that the situation leads gradually on to a sphere of influence, a chartered com-pany, a protectorate, or to full economic or political control. There are cases where the greed of a company, the enterprise of an individual, or

---

[1] During the eighteenth century the sand wastes of Brandenburg and Polish Prussia, and the areas re-won from the Turk in Hungary, were planted and peopled by settlers from all parts of Germany. The process was curiously analogous to French and British settlement on the North American Continent.

the decision of a naval or military officer in hoisting a flag, have determined the fate of provinces or of nations. There are yet others where the desire of a State to possess a strategic post like Kiao-Chau or Aden has led to direct governmental interference. But there is a real distinction between all these processes and that of colonisation. That has normally taken place only in deference to the overpowering need of a surplus population for fresh land, and we find generally that such a flow has moved only to the British Empire, to the United States, and to Siberia.[1] But nearly all European Powers have pursued a policy of trading with, exploiting, 'protecting,' or subjecting native races.

As our emphasis is rather on Europe than on England, the growth of the British Empire can only be outlined. In 1815, England could have taken all the colonies she wanted from either France or Holland. She concentrated on strategical protection of sea routes and commerce, and handed back the rich isles of Guadeloupe and Martinique to France and the immense wealth of Java to Holland. But she took care to retain the strategical outwork of St. Lucia in the West Indies, and secured the route to India by acquiring Cape Colony from the Dutch and Mauritius from France. Sir Stamford Raffles protected the route to China by acquiring Singapore in 1819, and the acquisition of Aden in 1839 still further ensured the route to India.

Meanwhile, as the routes were protected, colonial settlement proceeded apace and imperialist expansion in India was steadily pursued. The process was completed by the annexation of the Punjab just before the outbreak of the Indian Mutiny in 1857. From about this time we may date the vigorous life of our white colonies. Canada had led the way in self-government (1840), but before 1860 the colonies in Australia and New Zealand were developed enough to receive the grant of full responsible government. In 1867 Canada went further and united her different provinces in a federal system which provided full protection for the French settlers of Quebec.

The story of South Africa was less happy, and Cape Colony did not receive responsible government till late in the 'seventies. Her prospects had been injured by the abolition of colonial slavery (1834). Differences over native policy with the Boers led to their secession in 'the Great Trek' and to the foundation of Boer Republics (1848), repudiating the sovereignty of Great Britain. This situation, and the anomalous status of the Transvaal, caused three wars (1848, 1881, 1899–1902), but was ultimately solved by the combination of Dutch and English in the Union of South Africa (1909–10).

England had succeeded during the nineteenth century in peopling waste or sparsely inhabited areas with white populations. The sources of population were various. It had begun with the penal settlements and transport of political and other criminals to Australia. Then there had been a State-aided settlement in South Africa, mostly of ex-soldiers.

[1] The case of the French in Algeria is exceptional and is treated below.

Finally, and most important, the industrial revolution produced a surplus population in England, and want and distress, during the period of the 'hungry 'forties,' led to an immense emigration both to the United States and to Canada. England was so far ahead of other countries in her industrial revolution that she had already peopled parts of three continents before the rest of Europe began to send its stream of emigrants overseas. In 1881 Canada had a population of four millions and a half, Australia of two millions, New Zealand of half a million. Thus before the scramble for overseas possessions became general in the 'eighties, the main areas of white colonisation were already well settled by colonists of English blood or feelings, and formed, in fact, areas occupied by nascent white nations.

After 1815 France retained Guiana as well as most of her West Indian isles, but the 'Monroe Doctrine' and the attitude of Canning soon caused her to abandon any attempt at expansion in America. As expansion in Europe was impossible it was sought in Africa, while Syria and China were also considered as objects for the possible extension of French influence. Africa was selected as the point of attack, and the plan was formed by the Ministers of Charles X, the last Legitimist Bourbon King of France. As so often in French history, the foreign policy of the Legitimist Bourbons was inherited and continued by those who overthrew them. It has been said of the decision to take Algiers that 'the whole foreign policy of France in the last fifty years, and with it the policy of the other European states, has been turned into new paths by the fact that France again became one of the great colonial powers.' [1] There seems little exaggeration in this view, and it is to Wellington's credit that he recognised the importance of the step at the time.

The Algerian pirates, or 'Barbary Corsairs' as they were called, had a government of their own, but were technically subject to the Turks. They had for many centuries infested the Mediterranean as pirates, and robbed and enslaved Christian peoples. In 1814 a United States squadron released 500 Christian slaves, and in 1816 a British squadron bombarded Algiers and liberated 3000 more. The French had plenty of justification for interference on general grounds, but they seem to have intended from the first to use their opportunity to control and finally to annex Algeria. In the middle of 1830 a French expedition appeared and occupied the city of Algiers. France gradually extended her sway westwards and eastwards along the coast, and then began to press into the interior. The usual campaigns followed, in which Western science and persistence gradually overcame Oriental valour and indiscipline. Fugitive Algerine chiefs found refuge in Morocco and brought rein-

[1] E. Fueter, *World History* (1923), p. 116.

forcements from over the Moorish border. It was not until the French ships had bombarded Tangier and Mogador, and a French army had defeated the Moorish forces on land, that the Sultan of Morocco gave way and abandoned the Algerine cause. As a result the end came quickly and all Algeria was subdued by 1847. Thus the future was curiously foreshadowed, and the fate of Morocco seen to be involved in that of Algeria.

The French system of colonisation was a new and exceedingly interesting one. It was half-way between the English idea of white settlement by fortuitous individuals, and the ordinary idea of imperialism, *i.e.* economical control of the backward races and of their resources by Western companies or governments. It was, from the first, a system of colonising Algeria with a white population, which was to rule the Arab and other native races. The programme of the Molé Ministry in 1838, 'France is going to revive Roman Africa,' was literally and exactly correct. In complete contrast to the haphazard and individualistic methods of England, State support and State direction controlled the plan. First, roads were made and canals cut, legal security was given to foreign merchants and the native Jews were made French citizens. Then about 1841 colonisation, or a State-aided plan of importing true French citizens into the country, began. These Frenchmen were settled on the State lands confiscated from the Bey and from other leading Algerians, or in strategic centres, precisely as Roman colonists were planted by Rome in Spain or in Gaul. In the same way French soldiers in Algeria were encouraged to visit France towards the end of their period of service, to procure a wife and to bring her back to Algeria and settle there. Free land was given by the Government,[1] and intermarriage with the natives discouraged. The latter were treated with a judicious mixture of firmness and conciliation. The French manners, the Code Napoléon, the glittering splendours of their military displays, both attracted and impressed the natives. The population of France herself did not increase very rapidly or emigrate very willingly, and the lack of white settlers caused a partial failure of the original plan. What the French really aim at doing is shown by the population of Algiers itself, where there were in 1936, 149,549 Frenchmen, 25,526 other whites, and 77,246 Arabs and natives. This represents an ideal which France would be glad to have realised throughout Algeria, and perhaps elsewhere also.

The political conception underlying this colonisation scheme is clear. Algeria is nearly as much France as the department of Les Alpes Maritimes or of the Seine. At times efforts have been made to establish customs barriers between Algeria and France or to limit the franchise of white settlers. All such attempts have failed, and Algeria is a sort of overseas department or 'extension of France,' returning members to the Chamber, reading the French newspapers, and taking a modest part in

[1] *I.e.* from 1841–83, with a brief interval between the years 1860–71.

French internal politics.[1] Agreeably to the same conception the shipping between Algeria and France is reserved as a coastal trade. The whole principle is fundamentally different from the Anglo-Saxon one. The idea that British colonies were municipal corporations, inseparably connected with the motherland, was thrown overboard with the tea into Boston Harbour when the American Revolution began. A white colony, if planted by England, expects always and ultimately to develop a will and consciousness of its own. The French idea is to plant a colony which is an express image and counterpart of the motherland, and organically connected with it. So far the colony of Algeria has shown itself quite satisfied with its position as an outpost of France in Arab surroundings, and is the best example of a peculiar and interesting method of colonisation.[2]

The international implications of the conquest of Algeria were perhaps even more important than the system of colonisation pursued there. For a long time France did not try to advance her boundaries, but the very fact of her occupation tended ultimately to make such advance inevitable. Advance into the Sahara with the ultimate design of joining up with the French settlements in West Africa was a necessary result of establishment at Algiers. Friction with neighbours on both sides, that is with the Sultan of Morocco and the Bey of Tunis, was hardly avoidable. But these incidents had no serious consequences until Italy began to cast longing eyes on Tunis, and Spain (and ultimately Germany) began to think of securing 'a place in the sun' in Morocco. It was then seen that international questions of the first order had been raised by the French priority of settlement in Algeria. French expansion to the equatorial Sudan led to conflict with England and to the serious humiliation of France. And the French desire to possess Morocco seems to have had a dominant influence in bringing about the Anglo-French Entente.

During the 'thirties and 'forties some important French interests favoured a policy of active commercial enterprise in various quarters of the world. The French support of the rebellious Egyptian Pasha, Mehemet Ali, was obviously influenced by a desire to exploit, and perhaps to control, Syria. Palmerston defeated this attempt in 1840 and drove Mehemet Ali back upon Egypt. But the French interest in the Levant remained, and her commercial schemes and religious missions might at any time have been used to support active political projects. The strange genius of Michel Chevalier and other followers of Saint-Simon suggested the 'Mediterranean system' of communications which

[1] If Algeria had not a Governor-General she would be exactly like a French department. All French colonies (whether regarded as departments like Algiers or not) send deputies to Parliament.

[2] The difference between French and British ideas of treating the native races is equally interesting. The French arm, discipline, and therefore militarise their natives. The British reduce the armed forces of their natives and therefore demilitarise them.

led on to an actual project of cutting a canal through the Suez peninsula. The French consul at Tunis, Ferdinand de Lesseps, caught up the idea, reduced it to practice, and persuaded the Khedive of Egypt to grant him a concession (1854). He was bitterly opposed by England in the shape of Palmerston, who considered that the canal would open India to attack by a new route. But this opposition was fortunately vain, and De Lesseps completed his great work between 1859 and 1869. England had done almost nothing but oppose it, but in 1875 Disraeli suddenly intervened, bought the Khedive's holdings, and made his country the greatest of the shareholders. By 1880 England was deeply interested in Egypt, France in Algeria, and Italy in Tunis.

French imperialistic schemes were active in America as well as in the Levant, and the Suez was not the only canal which French enterprise thought of cutting. One of the motives of Napoleon III in his disastrous imperialistic venture in Mexico was to control Panama and perhaps to cut a canal through it.[1] As told elsewhere the Mexican enterprise failed in shameful humiliation, and from this time forward France abandoned any annexationist ambitions in Latin America.

In China and the Far East, French ambitions were conspicuous, whether France was Bourbon, Orleanist, Napoleonic, or Republican. The English were the first to try to break down the wall the Chinese Government opposed to Western commerce. After trade had been in an anomalous condition for many years, the British Government finally opened it by sending a small military and naval force to blockade the Canton river (1840). After some fighting Hong Kong was occupied and eventually (1843) ceded to England, and a number of Chinese ports (of which the most important was Shanghai) were definitely thrown open to British and other foreign trade. Other Powers were not far behind, and of these the most conspicuous was France. By brilliant diplomacy France secured for herself and for her Catholic missionaries and converts 'an undefined right of intervention on behalf of native Christians in 1844, and looked to establishing her influence on that basis.' [2] She further increased these concessions in 1858 and obtained what was virtually a religious protectorate over Catholic converts in China. This success probably had more effect than anything else in promoting that active hatred of Christian missionaries which the Chinese Government and people have so often shown. Various incidents led the British and French to co-operate in armed attacks on the Taku Forts in 1858 and again in 1860. About the same time Russia, which had already occupied the Amur Province of China and bordered on Korea, reached the Pacific and built a harbour at Vladivostock. As a result of all these measures China was more definitely thrown open to foreign commerce and the European diplomatic representatives were finally established at Peking. Up to 1880, therefore, no special attempt

---

[1] Napoleon III had written a pamphlet on this subject. For Mexico, *v.* pp. 241–3.
[2] Sir E. Satow in *Cambridge Modern History*, vol. XI. p. 812.

had been made, or success achieved, by any European Power in establishing special advantages for herself in China, though the French had
gained rights which might give them great advantages in the future. But
circumstances prevented their making use of it, and diverted their attention to an area south of China proper. As a result of the murder of
some French missionaries, Napoleon III sent an expedition, which conquered and annexed what is known as French Cochin-China (1862).
This led also to the annexation of part of Cambodia (1867). Difficulties
about the opening of Tongking, the chief port of Annam, led to a
further expedition which turned the whole of Annam into a French protectorate. The Chinese Government at Peking sent troops to reassert
their shadowy authority over these areas, but these were easily defeated
by the French, and China was forced to acquiesce in her loss of territory
in 1885. This anticipates events a little, but the year 1880 may be said
roughly to mark the period when China itself, apart from some outlying provinces of dubious loyalty, was still relatively untouched by
the conflicting ambitions of the Great Powers. But the signs were beginning to be ominous. The French were firmly fixed in Indo-China, the
Russians had annexed the Amur Province in the north, and the British
had long established a sort of Gibraltar at Hong Kong. All these were
within the bounds of the Chinese Empire. It was, therefore, hardly
possible to make any further moves against the integrity of China
without awaking the jealousy of one or other Great Power. The
Balance of Power had already extended its evil influence over the Far
East.

Nicholas I is once said to have asked Wellington to advise him as to
Russian policy in Central Asia. The Duke, who knew Asiatics well,
replied that short punitive expeditions by military commanders might
be undertaken without difficulty, but that, if civil officials once replaced
military ones in districts even temporarily occupied, Russian prestige
would forbid withdrawal and involve serious commitments. In other
words, if an advance into Central Asia was once begun, there could be
no thought of subsequent withdrawal. 'You could never go back.' And,
if you could never go back, you were likely to go forward.

The motives of Russian advance into Asia have been various. In
Siberia there has been colonisation by immigrant peasants, by convicts,
and by political criminals. In the Caucasus and in Turkestan frontier
disputes led to punitive expeditions and to Russian conquest. In China
the advance has been due mainly to conscious governmental policy and
to the search for an ice-free port on the Pacific. But, everywhere and
always, the truth of Wellington's dictum has been proved. The advance,
once undertaken, has gone on and has seemed to gain speed from each
fresh annexation. It has indeed never been stopped, or even momentarily arrested, except by war or by the threat of war made by a really
strong or civilised Power.

A factor of great importance in history has been the existence of

Tartar and Mohammedan tribes in the Caucasus. Russia had no difficulty in occupying the coast of the Black Sea, south of the Caucasus. But strategic reasons prevented her from attacking the Turks in Asia Minor from the rear, so long as the mountain tribes of the Caucasus were still unsubdued. The campaigns against them began in 1830, and seem to have been inefficiently conducted, for they were not subdued till 1859. Had this resistance been less stubborn, Russia might have scored important advantages in Asia Minor during the Crimean War. As it was, now that her communications were secure, she easily obtained the Province of Kars from Turkey in 1878. Disraeli's firm attitude in that year was unquestionably influenced by the fact that he realised the danger of Russian penetration into Armenia.

The colonisation of Eastern Siberia was persistent and led naturally to occupation of Chinese provinces, such as the Amur, in the way that has already been described. Russia advanced steadily and was only stopped by the sea when she built a port at Vladivostock (1860). As, however, it was not an ice-free one in winter, she began to think of acquiring a warm-water harbour. This could only be done by her advancing directly southwards into Korea or threatening Peking. But in 1880 she was diverted to Asia Minor and Turkestan.

In Central Asia the chief peoples to be subdued were the tribes of Eastern and Western Turkestan, the former a nominal province of China.[1] The raids of robber horsemen gave every Russian governor of a border province a perpetual excuse not only for punitive expeditions, but for policing (or annexing) territory contiguous to his district. But up till 1860 the spaces of desert between the Russian post of Orenburg and the Khanates of Khiva and Bokhara prevented any effective advance. Science and more geographical knowledge finally overcame these difficulties, and the first important step was the fall of Tashkend (1864). It was followed by the Russian capture of Samarkand, the famous city from which Genghis Khan and Tamerlane had ruled their immense empires. Russia enormously enhanced her prestige in Central Asia by this triumph, and all Eastern Turkestan soon fell into her hands. Western Turkestan held out longer, but the Khan of Khiva was finally compelled to cede his territories to Russia in 1873. One further tribe of Turkomans remained to be subdued. This was accomplished by Skobelev, the hero of Plevna, in 1880, and Russia and England seemed face to face.

Had not the time, prophesied by Palmerston in 1840, at last arrived? 'It seems pretty clear that, sooner or later, the Cossack and the Sepoy, the man from the Baltic and he from the British Islands will meet in the centre of Asia. It should be our business to take care that the meeting should take place as far off from our Indian possessions as may be convenient and advantageous to us. But the meeting will not be avoided

---

[1] Turkestan may be roughly described as the area south of European Russia and Siberia, and north and west of Persia and Afghanistan.

by our staying at home to receive the visit.' [1] In 1880 the British, Rus-sian, and Chinese Empires practically met at one point, for the British had not stayed at home. They had pushed westwards almost as rapidly as the Russians had pushed eastwards. The deserts of Persia and the mountains of Afghanistan were now the only barriers between Russian and British territory. All this Skobelev saw with the clear eye of a soldier and prepared a plan for the invasion of British India. Five years after the Russian diplomats had seen the plan, the moment seemed to have arrived for putting it into action.

Afghanistan was a buffer state dependent on Great Britain, and in 1885 Russian local forces got into dispute with the Afghans and occu-pied part of their frontier. Gladstone himself took a serious view of the situation. He asked Parliament to vote him eleven million pounds and accused the Russians of unprovoked aggression against a small and weak neighbour. Russia and England certainly came to the verge of war, though at the last moment the incident was smoothed over. The gravity of the crisis proved in the end to have been a fortunate thing, for it deeply impressed the Czar. During the crisis he had carried his head high in order to conciliate Russian public opinion. But he sought anxiously to avoid any similar incident in future. Lord Salisbury ad-vised people who feared the Russian danger to buy large maps to judge distances and to estimate the strength of mountain barriers. The Rus-sians, and the Czar among them, took that advice, and they found the line of least resistance to lie not towards India but towards China. For an advance depended on railway possibilities, and the deserts of Persia and the mountains of North-west India presented the most formidable barriers known to man, behind which lurked the troops of a well-armed Great Power. In comparison the physical difficulties offered to the rail-way penetration of China were small, while the power of the Celestial Empire was crumbling. So in 1892 the Czar turned his face away from India and towards China, and began to build a Trans-Siberian railway with French money. Russia thus took a step which she hoped would lead to a speedy conquest over an effete Asiatic Empire, but which, in fact, led to humiliating defeat at the hands of a virile one—that is, of Japan. But, whichever way it led, it led away from conflict with the British Empire in India. Hence the year 1892, when the Russian cloud shifted from the Himalayas and began to settle over Manchuria, is a year of supreme importance in Russo-British relations. It is also supremely important because Russia drew away from Germany and towards France.

Before the Russian advance had been diverted from Central Asia to Manchuria, a general scramble for territorial spoils had begun in Africa. France and Great Britain began the game, and they were fol-lowed at a short interval by Germany, and more distantly by Italy, by Belgium, and by Spain. The first definite acquisition in point of time, though not of importance, was the French annexation of Tunis. At the

---

[1] P. Guedalla : *Palmerston* (1926), pp. 225–6.

Congress of Berlin France had been reconciled to the British occupation of Cyprus by the suggestion that she should occupy Tunis. Lord Salisbury continued to favour this suggestion, and was supported by Bismarck, who wished to make France forget Alsace-Lorraine in Tunis. France therefore proceeded to negotiate with the Bey of Tunis. Like her neighbour, Egypt, Tunis was nominally under Turkish rule and actually in chains to her bondholders. A triple financial control by Italy, France, and Great Britain had been set up in 1869, but had not produced much result. Having concealed their aims from Italy, which also cast envious eyes on Tunis, the French Government massed a force on the borders of Algeria and attacked Tunis in April 1881—England was surprised, Italy was indignant, but Germany approved. Turkey tried to protest, but thirty thousand French troops were soon in the country, and by the Treaty of Bardo (May 12, 1881) Tunis became a French protectorate. Resistance by scattered tribes in the interior was soon ended and France congratulated herself on a new acquisition and a great stroke of policy. It is doubtful if it was the latter, and it is curious that Clemenceau was the only parliamentary deputy who voted against the new accession. He did so on the ground that 'it profoundly modified the European system and chilled precious friendships cemented on the field of battle.' The reference was to Italy, and Clemenceau saw further than anyone else in France. Italy's just resentment at her treatment over Tunis drove her into the Triple Alliance with Austria-Hungary and with Germany, and Italian hostility remained a danger to France for many years.

France had scored an acquisition by smartly anticipating a rival in one quarter. But in Egypt she was herself outwitted by another competitor, with the same result of establishing twenty years of bad feeling and hostility between victor and vanquished. England and France were both interested in Egypt, for it lay on the road to India. The genius of De Lesseps and his successful completion of the Suez Canal gave France the preliminary advantage. But Disraeli turned the tables on her when he bought the Khedive's shares in the company and made England the largest shareholder (1875). Next year, in view of the Khedive's approaching bankruptcy, Great Britain and France instituted a dual control of finance. Other interested Powers, *e.g.* Germany, Austria-Hungary, and Italy, exercised an important influence on the *Caisse de la Dette.* But England and France, by judicious wire-pulling and manipulation, gradually established a kind of joint-control over the whole country.

All might have gone well if hatred of foreign interference had not produced a kind of national movement, in the genuineness of which some foreigners believed, and which in any case deserved some sympathy. Khedive Ismail, who showed signs of independence, was deposed by the Sultan of Turkey (June 1879) at the suggestion of England and France. The new Khedive, Tewfik, was a mere puppet, and his subservience to

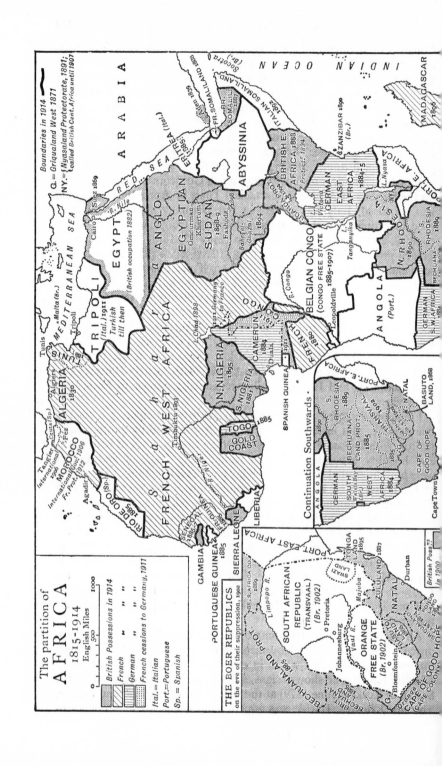

The partition of
AFRICA
1815–1914
English Miles
0   500   1000

British Possessions in 1914
French   "   "
German   "   "
French cessions to Germany, 1911

Ital. = Italian
Port. = Portuguese
Sp. = Spanish

Boundaries in 1914
G. = Griqualand West 1871
NY. = { Nyasaland Protectorate, 1891;
         called British Cent. Africa until 1907

MEDITERRANEAN SEA
Tangier (Ceuta (Sp.)
International Govt. 1906
MOROCCO ?Fez
International Govt.
Fr. Prot. 1912
Agadir
RIO DE ORO (Sp.)
1895

Malta (Br.)
Tunis
Algiers
TUNIS 1881
ALGERIA 1830
Tripoli
TRIPOLI
(Ital.) 1911
Turkish
till then

SINAI 1891

EGYPT
(British occupation 1882)
Cairo P. of Suez 1869
R. Nile

RED SEA
ERITREA (Ital.) 1885

ARABIA

Socotra (Br.)
BR. SOMALILAND 1884
FR. SOMALIL. 1892
ITALIAN SOMALILAND 1889

INDIAN OCEAN

ANGLO-
EGYPTIAN
SUDAN
Khartum
Omdurman 1898
1869–9
Fashoda 1898
Bahr el Ghazal

ABYSSINIA

S a h a r a
L. Chad 1898
1911 Germany
to France
Timbuktu 1893

FRENCH WEST AFRICA

R. Niger
GAMBIA
PORTUGUESE GUINEA 1885
SENEGAL 1885
GUINEA
SIERRA LEONE
LIBERIA

N. NIGERIA 1895
S. NIGERIA 1861
CAMERUN 1884 (Duala)
TOGO 1885
GOLD COAST
SPANISH GUINEA
FRENCH CONGO 1889
R. Congo
Leopoldville
Brazzaville

BELGIAN CONGO
(CONGO FREE STATE 1885–1907)
L. Victoria
L. Tanganyika

BRITISH E. AFRICA 1888
Uganda Protect. 1894
ZANZIBAR 1890 (Br.)
GERMAN EAST AFRICA 1884–5
L. Nyasa
NY.

ANGOLA
(Port.)

PORT. E. AFRICA
S. RHODESIA 1890
N. RHODESIA 1900
BECHUANA—

GERMAN S.W. AFRICA 1884

Continuation Southwards

ANGOLA
GERMAN SOUTH WEST AFRICA 1884
Walfisch Bay
BECHUANA
LAND PROT. 1885
S. RHODESIA 1890
TRANSVAAL 1877
NATAL
BASUTO LAND, 1868
CAPE OF GOOD HOPE
Cape Town

British Poss.
in 1900

THE BOER REPUBLICS
on the eve of their suppression, 1902

PORT. EAST AFRICA
BR. S. AFRICA CO. 1889
Limpopo R.
SOUTH AFRICAN
REPUBLIC
(TRANSVAAL)
(Br. 1902)
Pretoria
Johannesburg
Vaal R.
ORANGE
FREE STATE
(Br. 1902)
Bloemfontein
BECHUANALAND PROT. 1885
BECHUANA-
LAND 1895
TONGA 1895
SWAZI LAND
ZULULAND 1887
Majuba
NATAL
Durban
G.
Orange R.
CAPE
CAPE OF GOOD HOPE
CAPE COLONY

foreign Powers soon produced an ebullition of national feeling. Arabi Pasha, an Egyptian general, stirred up the army against the Khedive and made a *coup d'état*. On September 9, 1881, he led 5000 soldiers to the Khedive's palace, and demanded a change of ministers, an increased army, and a National Assembly. The Khedive yielded, and Arabi was thus supreme, though his dictatorship was decorously veiled for a time.

A collision between Arabi and foreign Governments, interested in preserving their property and protecting their subjects, was probably inevitable. At any rate a Franco-British Note, presented to the Khedive on January 8, 1882, rendered it so. It was one of those unfortunate attempts at intervention from outside, weakening the position of the Khedive whom it meant to support, and strengthening the resistance of the Nationalists whom it meant to intimidate. Arabi, from being a military dictator, now became a national hero. Previously he had played Monck to the Khedive's Charles II, now he would be supported by the Egyptians in the part of Cromwell. An Anglo-French naval squadron made a demonstration off Alexandria, which only served to irritate the Egyptians and to strengthen Arabi. On June 11 riots began in Alexandria, the mob killed fifty Europeans, and drove both Turkish and European residents from their great cities.

England for once acted vigorously and decided not to negotiate but to overthrow the military party in Egypt first. France refused to co-operate, so, on July 11, the British squadron alone opened fire on the forts of Alexandria and promptly destroyed them. Military action speedily followed upon naval. A British force under Sir Garnet Wolseley caught Arabi Pasha napping at dawn, stormed his trenches and utterly overthrew him at Tel-el-Kebir (September 13). Arabi was made prisoner and the Khedive, thus restored by British military action, again mounted his throne.

At the time only Bismarck and Germany supported Great Britain. Italy stood aloof, Russia agreed with Turkey in condemning British action, and France was the most indignant of all. She 'resumed full liberty of action,' a phrase well understood in diplomacy, and covering anything from sullen obstruction to almost open hostility. The consequences could easily have been foreseen. France had been invited to join with England in asserting a dual control and had declined. England had to act alone, but, as she bore the burden, she claimed the fruits of victory. Gladstone promised to clear out of Egypt as soon as affairs were settled. But they never were settled, and England, without perhaps meaning to do so, acquired Egypt 'in a fit of absence of mind.' She acquired with it the extreme enmity of France, and it was not till 1904 that she succeeded in conciliating her.[1]

---

[1] The revolt of the Mahdi in the Sudan in 1881 led, ultimately, to the reconquest of the Sudan by Lord Kitchener in 1898 in the names of the Khedive and of the Queen-Empress of Great Britain. The Fashoda crisis arose owing to the attempt of France to annex the equatorial or Bahr-el-Ghazal area of the Sudan. This was defeated by the firm stand of Lord Salisbury

The colonial appetites of France and Great Britain had been thus, to some extent, sated, when Germany very suddenly appeared as a Colonial Empire-seeker. Bismarck himself had long opposed a policy of German colonial enterprise. But German oversea commercial interests increased and gradually converted him to their views. Once having decided on the policy he acted with characteristic resolution. In April 1884 he proclaimed a protectorate over the whole of South-West Africa (except Walfisch Bay) from south of Portuguese Angola to the northern boundary of Cape Colony. In the same month he deliberately deceived the British Government as to his aims in the Cameroons, and in July (while the British Consul was on holiday) formally annexed its coastline as well as Togoland. In May of the same year a German New Guinea Company was formed, and this led, after further disputes with England, to a division of New Guinea into a northern or German sphere and a southern or British one.[1] During the years 1884 and 1885 similar methods resulted in the German annexation of Tanganyika or German East Africa. In about two years Germany became possessed of some millions of square miles of territory, 'without a fleet and without moving a soldier.' It was a strange contrast to the thirty thousand troops France had to bring to Tunis, to the pitched battle which England had to fight before Egypt yielded, and to her dozen years of desert fighting for the Sudan.

Another equally pacific conquest over even a vaster extent of territory was due to the ability and pressure not of a nation or a government but of a single man. King Leopold II of Belgium, who was as far-sighted as he was unscrupulous, had already seen the importance of Africa and had financed the famous explorer Stanley in expeditions which founded stations and persuaded chiefs to sign treaties to form a new state on the Congo (1878–1884). This Congo Association was technically international and commercial in character. Its development caused active apprehensions to France and to Portugal and produced a Conference of the Great Powers at Berlin (October 1884 to February 1885).[2] In result the Berlin Act, signed by the various Powers, handed over the vast basin of the Congo to this new organisation, which was termed the Congo Free State (or the Independent State of the Congo). King Leopold in fact personally ruled a state a million miles square. The provisions made for international control and international free trade were systematically violated by the unscrupulous monarch. He instituted a system of monopolies which prevented international competition and substituted Belgian for international control.[3] The system of government was corrupt and tyrannical, but it served the purpose of its author.

[1] The Dutch already occupied the north-west part.

[2] v. S. E. Crowe: *The Berlin West African Conference, 1884–1885.* (Longmans, 1942.)

[3] In 1889 his will, leaving his Congo estate to Belgium, was published. After much criticism during the next twenty years, Leopold finally made over the Congo State to Belgium during his lifetime. The accession of King Albert was marked by a striking improvement in the Congo administration.

By using those international sanctions (which he had no scruple in violating when it suited his own pocket or interests) he was able to prevent any single Power, great or small, from encroaching on the boundaries of the enormous territory he had acquired and ultimately bequeathed to his country.

The history of colonial development in Africa does not seem an edifying one. England accused the Boers, and the Boers England, of chicanery and deceit. And England, though promising that her occupation of Egypt was temporary, finally made it permanent. France deliberately deceived Italy over Tunis, and Germany England over South-West Africa and the Cameroons. Finally King Leopold, by a masterpiece of guile, tricked all Europe into giving him the richest of colonial plums. It does not appear at first sight as if masters, who used such means to acquire dominion, were likely to benefit those over whom they ruled. The only consoling thought is that the disputes, though acrimonious, were usually adjusted peacefully, and that the political control of a government is almost always better for natives than the rule of merchants or companies.

A general survey of colonial developments in the nineteenth century seems to bring out the following salient facts. England and Russia made white settlements and thus added to the strength and numbers of their white population. France, which partially failed in this attempt, was led to organise and to arm her black subjects for her defence. Colonisation or imperialist expansion was carried out peacefully for the first three-quarters of the century, while the waste spaces of the earth were still unexhausted by the three great expanding Powers, Russia, France, and Great Britain. But, after 1880, new competitors, especially the two newly resurrected nations of Germany and Italy, entered the colonial arena. The consequence was at once seen in the increase of tension all round. England quarrelled with France over Egypt, Italy with France over Tunis. Germany profited by these disputes to acquire large areas for herself. Italy was driven into the Triple Alliance by her colonial disappointments. Towards the "nineties,' however, more ominous signs appeared. Nearly all the waste spaces had already been staked out. The Empire of Morocco was the one independent kingdom of North Africa, and it was natural that both Germany and France should cast longing eyes upon it. Ultimately France gave up her claims on Egypt to secure British support in Morocco. And the origins of the Anglo-French Entente and its subsequent evolution were thus profoundly affected by colonial developments in North Africa.

No less striking was the situation produced by colonial or imperialistic expansion in Asia. Russia, after long treading the road to India, turned aside towards China in 1892. She thus postponed, though she did not avert, a conflict with England in Asia. England, finding Germany reluctant to assist her in stopping the Russian advance against China, accepted the Alliance of Japan (1902) for that purpose. And Japan declared war on Russia two years later. Expansion in Asia thus led directly to an alliance and to war. Expansion in Africa led to an Entente in 1904 and perhaps to war in 1914.

CHAPTER XXIV

BISMARCK AND THE FORMATION OF THE TRIPLE AND DUAL ALLIANCES, 1879–94

THE two preceding chapters have shown how the Eastern question revealed a gulf between Russia and Germany, and how this fact had not prevented Bismarck from securing colonial advantages at the expense of both England and France during the years 1884–5. The explanation lies in the system, originated by Bismarck in the early 'seventies, which continued developing until 1914, the system of the great European alliances. This remarkable arrangement of international checks and balances for a long time preserved peace among the peoples, but by the very fact of its existence ultimately engendered strife. For the system was one of competing alliances, not of a universal league. It was a Balance, not a Concert, of Power. As one combination strengthened or developed, its growth alarmed other states outside its orbit and mechanically produced a counter-combination. Competing alliances produced competing armaments, and the rivalry of hatred and of fear ended in the two opposed groups carrying their competition to the battlefield. In 1914, when it seemed clear that war was inevitable, the German Foreign Under-Secretary 'expressed regret that Germany, France "and perhaps England" had been drawn in—none of whom wanted war in the least and said that it came from "this d——d system of alliances, which were the curse of modern times." ' [1] He forgot that Bismarck had been the chief architect of the alliance system.[2]

Before 1870 the Great Powers in Europe were singularly divided. There was a close entente between Bismarck and Russia, but France was separated from England. Austria-Hungary and Italy hovered uneasily in the void. After the war of 1870, the three Great Powers of Eastern Europe drew together, and a meeting at Berlin of the Emperors of Russia, Germany, and Austria resulted in the entente known as the

[1] Gooch and Temperley: British Documents on the Origins of the War, vol. XI. p. 284.

[2] The best account of the relationships among the powers in Bismarck's time is that given by W. L. Langer in European Alliances and Alignments (New York, 1931) For texts of engagements, v. A. F. Pribram: The Secret Treaties of Austria-Hungary 2 vols. (Harvard, 1920–1).

Three Emperors' League. But the ideas of Austria-Hungary differed essentially from those of Russia. Austria-Hungary wished to absorb Serbia, to annex Salonica, but to preserve the Turkish Empire if she could. Russia wished to dominate Bulgaria, to annex Constantinople, and to break up the Turkish Empire if she could. Between these two views there could be no real reconciliation. Warning was given of that even in 1876, when the Czar had Bismarck asked this embarrassing question: Would Germany remain neutral in case of a war between Austria-Hungary and Russia? Bismarck was compelled to answer that Germany would have to see to it that neither belligerent lost her influence or independence as a Great Power. He meant, to put it in plain words, that Germany would never allow Russia to crush Austria-Hungary. The Czar did not forget the warning, and on January 15, 1877, he secretly promised to connive at the Austro-Hungarian occupation of Bosnia-Herzegovina, in return for Austria-Hungary's neutrality in the coming war. At the Congress of Berlin, when war had ceased, the Czar, already warned and suspicious, thought he perceived that Germany had weighted the scales against Russia. And his letter to the Emperor William in April 1879 even suggested to Germany that war might be the result of thus estranging an old friend.

The attitude of Russia brought Bismarck face to face with a very grave decision. The exposed position of Germany in Central Europe rendered a close alliance necessary with some one. Italy and England were hardly suitable, for he hated parliamentary states and did not think that any alliance with them could be permanent or stable. Austria-Hungary alone supplied him with what he wanted, so he was forced to approach her. Andrássy, the very able Austro-Hungarian Foreign Minister, was tottering to his fall. But he remained in office just long enough to conclude an arrangement. He played the gigantic fish with a master-hand. He knew that Bismarck feared a Franco-Russian combination and saw in this an opportunity to sell the Austro-Hungarian Alliance at a high price. He refused to engage to assist Germany against France, and treated the menaces of Bismarck with indifference. After a visit to Vienna in October, Bismarck came to an unexpected decision. 'If you will not accept my terms,' he said to Andrássy, 'I am forced (*ich bin gezwungen*) to accept yours.' And thus, for once in his lifetime, the Iron Chancellor capitulated. But he found it a difficult matter to convince William I, that 'old gentleman of eighty-two . . . with whom habit exercises enormous influence.' The aged Emperor was deeply attached both by sentiment and conviction to the old bond with Russia, but Bismarck prevailed with him at last, as he always did. The Treaty, held up by various preliminaries, was finally signed on October 7, 1879. It was, in form, simply a defensive alliance. By Article I each agreed to assist the other, if attacked by Russia. By Article II each agreed to observe 'benevolent neutrality,' if the other was attacked by 'another Power,' *i.e.* France. If Russia joined France, 'either by active co-operation or military measures,' however, Austria and Germany agreed to act together. The Alliance was to continue good for five years, with a possible extension for three more. It was renewed in 1883 and at subsequent intervals and, after 1902, was automatically renewed at the end of every three years until 1914. Andrássy succeeded in his great object by not committing Austria to war with France alone, but he failed to prevent the existence of the Treaty being made known to Russia before the end of the year. For the moment the effect was satisfactory, and Russia stopped 'breathing fire and flame.' But, taking long views, it ensured the estrangement of Russia from Germany, though the separation might be, and was, delayed. Even Bismarck's legerdemain could not prevent a result which lay in the logic of events.

Thus, secure in a firm alliance with Austria-Hungary, Bismarck felt strong enough to approach Russia once more.[1] On June 18, 1881, the *Dreikaiserbund* was defined by a treaty signed at Berlin. By Article I Austria-Hungary, Germany and Russia agreed to 'observe benevolent neutrality and to localise the war' if hostilities occurred between one of them and a fourth Great Power. This applied not only, of course, to France, or perhaps England, but also to Turkey. In the latter case it was, however, stipulated that the three Powers must reach a previous agreement as to the results of the war before Turkey was attacked. By Article II Russia recognised the Austro-Hungarian position in the Balkans as created by the Treaty of Berlin. By secret protocols attached to this Article, Austria-Hungary was to be allowed to annex Bosnia-Herzegovina whenever she chose, and to continue to occupy the Sanjak of Novibazar. Russia's compensation for this was that the other Powers undertook not to oppose but amicably arrange for the addition of Eastern Rumelia to Bulgaria, if and when produced by the force of circumstances. By Article III the three Powers agreed to compel Turkey to maintain the principle of closing the Straits of Constantinople to warlike operations.

The *Dreikaiserbund* Treaty was renewed in 1884, but expired in 1887, three years before Bismarck's fall. It unquestionably served a useful purpose, for it enabled Bismarck to intervene with effect whenever friction occurred, as it frequently did, between Austria-Hungary and Russia. But this arrangement could not be permanent, and in fact it broke down in the Bulgarian crisis of 1885-7. Article I of this *Dreikaiserbund* Treaty provided for the contingency of a Great Power or (Turkey) attacking one of the three Powers. But it stipulated for nothing more

---

[1] At one time he tried to sweep England into the net of his combination, and actually suggested an Austro-German-British alliance against Russia. Beaconsfield declined the overture. He let it be known that England would not take any step hostile to France, but would, in all probability, support Germany and Austria against Russia. Bismarck troubled no more about England, and during 1880 the project of an Austro-Russo-German *rapprochement* was taken up again. *v.* Buckle's *Beaconsfield*, vol. VI. pp. 486-94; Lady G. Cecil's *Salisbury*, vol. II. pp. 364-70.

than 'benevolent neutrality,' and was therefore far less strong than the Austro-German Treaty of 1879, which bound Germany to defend Austria against Russia by arms. For the 1879 Treaty was a real Alliance of two Powers, that of 1881 a vaguer Entente between three. And against the iron of the Alliance the earthenware of the Entente was bound to be shattered in the end.

By 1881 Bismarck was secure in Europe. He encouraged England and France in annexationist designs oversea, so that England occupied Egypt and France annexed Tunis. Italy had long had her eye on Tunis, but Bismarck had thoughtfully omitted to inform her of France's intentions. Italy, in some indignation, felt herself isolated and turned to her old enemy Austria-Hungary for help. But Bismarck turned to advantage even the irritation of Italy. He induced Austria-Hungary to put pressure on Italy, and obtained an invitation to Germany to form part of a new combination, and thus secured a further defence against France.

On May 20, 1882, Italy, Germany and Austria signed a Triple Alliance Treaty at Vienna, which may be described as one of neutrality and guarantee. In case of a French attack on Italy, Germany and Austria-Hungary would aid her. Italy agreed to help Germany against a French attack. In case one or two of the signatory Powers were attacked by two other Powers (*i.e.* Russia and France), all the signatory Powers would unitedly make war.[1] The arrangement was to hold for five years and to be kept secret. This treaty benefited Germany, for she obtained from Italy that promise of support against France which Austria-Hungary had refused. Italy gained even more, for she was not bound to aid either Austria-Hungary or Germany against an attack by Russia *alone*. And she *was* protected against Austria-Hungary by the very fact of the Alliance. Thus at one and the same time Bismarck had given Germany treaties of alliance or defence against Russia and France, and yet included Russia in one of his treaties, and extended his general system of control to Italy and Rumania.[2]

The efficacy of all these arrangements was tested in 1885. In that year Eastern Rumelia revolted from Turkey and threw in her lot with Bulgaria. The complications of this Bulgarian imbroglio have already been described elsewhere. It is enough to say here that Russia regarded Bismarck as having pursued a double-faced policy in the Balkans, and blamed him for a result which he had not desired and could not avert.

[1] Italy specially stipulated that the treaty was in no case to be directed against England.

[2] In 1883 Austria-Hungary also made a secret treaty with Rumania, by which the two Powers agreed to support one another against Russia if attacked by her. Bismarck acceded to this treaty at once, and Italy in 1888

The Czar Alexander III was deeply moved, and articles, openly advocating a Franco-Russian Alliance, began to appear in Russian papers in the autumn of 1886. To all intents and purposes, the *Dreikaiserbund* Treaty was already dissolved, though Bismarck was still secure by his Alliances with Austria-Hungary, with Italy and Rumania. But Russia was alienated and might soon become hostile.

The Reichstag received evidence of the gravity of the situation when a vote for the increase of the army for seven years was demanded in January 1887. Moltke openly said that Germany must be ready for war, and Bismarck declared that, while he did ' not expect an attack or hostility from Russia,' he had to be prepared. 'The difficulty is not to keep Germany and Russia but Austria and Russia at peace, and to ingeminate peace in both Cabinets.' The peacemaker, in Bismarck's view, would only be effective if he obtained new weapons of war. Turning then to France, he declared that he wished to be at peace with her ; that he would not attack her on the theory of 'preventive war,' *i.e.* because war was inevitable; but that, if war did occur, the war of 1870 would be child's play compared with that of 1890. In such case France 'would bleed us white, and, if we won, after being attacked, we would do the same.' [1]

The attitude of Russia had become almost menacing for Bismarck in 1887. The press attacks on Germany had continued, and Bismarck knew that the Czar had refused to repress them. But the *Dreikaiserbund* of 1881 expired in 1887 and thus provided Bismarck with an opportunity. For the triple bond he substituted a dual arrangement between Russia and Germany, which history knows as the 'Re-insurance Treaty.' It was signed on June 18, 1887, together with 'an additional and very secret protocol.' The chief provisions were (1) If one Power was at war with a third Great Power, the other would maintain benevolent neutrality and try to localise the conflict. (2) Germany recognised the preponderant influence of Russia in Bulgaria, and agreed to prevent the restoration of Prince Alexander. (3) Maintenance of the principle of closing the Straits of Constantinople, on the lines of the *Dreikaiserbund* Treaty of 1881.

Bismarck, by this Treaty, in effect, counterworked Austria-Hungary. He maintained that he was really benefiting her because he kept a certain restraining hand over Russia by the 'Re-insurance Treaty.' But Austria-Hungary and Russia were now on the brink of war, and the former suspected Bismarck, and with some reason, of duplicity. The inconsistencies of Bismarck's position become clearer if the 'Re-insurance Treaty' is compared with the Mediterranean Agreement signed in December 1887 by Britain, Austria-Hungary and Italy with Bismarck's encouragement, for this was founded on the principle of maintaining

---

[1] General Boulanger, as War Minister, had recently been agitating France, but Bismarck's coolness and prudence in refusing to take offence prevented serious consequences.

the 'independence of Turkey' from 'all foreign preponderating influence,' and referred specifically in this connection to the position of Bulgaria.[1]

Such were the complications of the international situation when Bulgaria selected Ferdinand of Coburg as her prince, and when that prince, having failed to obtain the consent of the Powers, proceeded to Bulgaria and took the oath as her ruler (August 14, 1887). Russia at once proposed to eject him; but this suggestion brought England and Italy closer to Austria, and made it clear that they might support her in her opposition to Russia's design to make Bulgaria a vassal-state of her Empire. The tension in Austria-Hungary and Russia became so great that Bismarck finally intervened. In February 1888 he published the Austro-German Treaty of 1879, thus announcing to the world that Germany would not permit Austria, if attacked by Russia, to lose her independence or her position as a Great Power. In the Reichstag he referred openly to the danger from France and to her connection with Russia. He said Germany was strong enough to defend herself, and to protect her 'safe friend' Austria-Hungary. 'Bulgaria is not an object of sufficient magnitude to set Europe aflame in a war whose issue none can foretell. I do not expect an early breach of the peace. But I advise other countries to discontinue their menaces. We fear God and nothing else in the world.' This proud speech evoked hearty cheers from the German Jingoes and was plainly intended to bring pressure to bear upon Russia.

For a few weeks Russia still pressed for the exclusion of Ferdinand from Bulgaria. Bismarck, bound by the 'Re-insurance Treaty,' hedged; but Austria, Italy and England showed no sign of yielding. Finally, therefore, Russia collapsed and accepted, though with an ill grace, the inevitable. Ferdinand remained as Prince of Bulgaria, and Bulgaria became in fact independent both of Russia and of Turkey. Austria-Hungary's position in the Balkans was stronger, for Serbia and Bulgaria both leaned on her for support. England and Italy were in the background. Germany still occupied the centre of the stage with her pledge of protection to Austria-Hungary, but she was no longer able to reconcile it with her 'Re-insurance Treaty' with Russia.

The old Emperor William told Bismarck that he was like a rider on a horse, who tossed five balls in the air and caught and threw them up again as they fell. The incomparable wizard had reached a time when he could no longer keep up all five. So long as no one except Russia knew of it, the 'Re-insurance Treaty' was useful enough. Though it had not prevented Russia from being defeated it had averted war over the Bulgarian affair. But Bismarck had only averted war by publishing the 1879 Treaty, which proved that, in the last resort, Germany would

[1] The Triple Alliance Treaty was renewed in 1887. Italy made agreements on two points with Germany and Austria separately: (1) Germany promised Italy to support by arms her claims to Tripoli and to check those of France in Morocco, in return for a renewed Italian offer to aid Germany against France in Europe; (2) Austria recognised Italy's interests in the Balkans, thereby making a great concession.

stand by Austria-Hungary. In that case Russia must find another ally who was not bound to Austria-Hungary and that ally could only be France. Bismarck's wizardry was not indeed exhausted and the Franco-Russian Alliance not yet concluded. In 1890 he renewed negotiations for a further Russo-German understanding, as the 'Re-insurance Treaty' was just expiring. They failed just after Bismarck's fall (1890). But it may be doubted whether even his jugglery could have kept the five balls still in the air. The 1879 Treaty and the Triple Alliance Treaty ultimately conflicted with the 'Re-insurance Treaty.' The time was now coming when the choice had to be definitely made. Was there to be a German alliance with Austria-Hungary and with Italy, or with Russia? There could not be one with both, and Bismarck had to stand by the Triple Alliance of Germany, Austria, and Italy. Bismarck's own policy therefore tended, in the long run, to throw Russia into the arms of France.

A general survey of the Bismarckian policy between 1870 and 1890 shows that it was primarily inspired by the idea of keeping France in order and enabling Germany to develop her new possessions and her enormous resources undisturbed. He encouraged Italy and England to rival France in colonial development so as to divert her attention from Alsace-Lorraine. He secured Germany against France by alliance with Italy, and against Russia by alliance with Austria. The problem Bismarck could not solve was how to remain on good terms, or in alliance, both with Austria and with Russia at once. The impossibility was made manifest in 1888, when he published to the world the German-Austrian Treaty of 1879 which pledged him to protect Austria against Russia. Russia knew, though the world did not, that the 'Re-insurance Treaty' pledged Germany to be neutral if Russia was at war with another Power (*i.e.* Austria). Genius can make black look like white for a time, but not for ever, and Russia at last knew in 1888 that the great diplomatic artist had tricked her. That he could have continued to trick her in the future seems highly improbable. Bismarck was bound more tightly to Austria-Hungary than to Russia, and the truth was out at last. It is true that Russia had not finally severed her connection with Germany when Bismarck fell in 1890. And it is probably true that his puny successors drove Russia into opposition more quickly than he would have done. But that the ways of Russia and Germany lay apart after 1888 seems morally certain. Indeed there is reason to believe that Bismarck himself recognised the fact and was looking for compensation elsewhere.[1] However that may be, the great Chancellor fell in 1890, and the

---

[1] A great controversy still rages as to Bismarck's ultimate intentions. The first school holds that he meant to maintain the connection with Russia, and the second that he meant to draw Great Britain into the Triple Alliance, *v.* B. E. Schmitt: *American Historical Review*, April 1924, p. 454, n. 41. Professor Schmitt wittily says that 'Bismarck's own utterances support each view.' In the Bulgarian imbroglio Bismarck only supported Austria-Hungary when he knew Great Britain was behind her, and

brilliant, impulsive and reckless William II became German Emperor in fact as well as in name.

Even in 1888 Russian policy had been tending in the direction of France, but Czar Alexander III was slow to move and hard to convince. His Ministers and relatives moved more quickly, and, as a result of the visit of a Grand Duke to Paris in November 1888, agreements were made for the supply of French armaments and munitions to Russia. The Grand Duke Nicholas assured the French Premier in 1889 that the two armies, 'will be one in time of war.' French diplomats and generals planned and executed a careful campaign of cajolery and flattery. And in 1891 Russia was revealed to all the world as absolutely isolated in Europe. For in that year the Triple Alliance was again renewed for six years, and England, still hostile to Russia, showed a friendly interest in this renewal. The French Government saw their opportunity, redoubled their attentions and floated Russian loans at Paris. In August 1891 the outlines of agreement were sketched out. (1) The two Powers agreed to an *Entente Cordiale* and to confer on every question of a nature to threaten peace. (2) If peace was in danger, and especially if one of the two were menaced by aggression, they agreed to concert measures. But the stubborn Czar was still reluctant to commit himself, and it was not until December 27, 1893, that a Military Convention, supplementing this agreement, was accepted. Russia agreed to assist France if attacked by Germany or by Italy supported by Germany. France agreed to assist Russia if attacked by Germany, or by Austria-Hungary supported by Germany. The French promised to employ 1,300,000 and the Russians 700,000 to 800,000 men against Germany. The Dual Alliance was thus practically complete.[1]

The Alliance was suspected at the time, but was not definitely revealed till 1895. It was an event of the greatest importance. The Dual Alliance was now opposed to the Triple Alliance and Germany thus had a formidable enemy on either flank. Europe was thus divided into two camps and each was necessarily an armed one. The balance was, for a time, fairly even, though in fact the Franco-Russian combination was probably the weaker. Italy was an uncertain and suspected ally to Austria-Hungary and to Germany. But, so long as England did not take one or other side, there was still a chance that European peace would be preserved. And a decade was to elapse before England's old hostility to France was overcome. During that period England approached both Russia and Germany with proposals for an alliance, and each time in vain.

he made a private overture towards England in 1889. For Bismarck generally, Langer: *European Alliances and Alignments* (N.Y., 1931), is admirable.
[1] All these documents are in Pribram: *Secret Treaties*, vol. II. pp. 204 *sqq.*

CHAPTER XXV

THE ANGLO-JAPANESE ALLIANCE AND THE FRANCO-BRITISH ENTENTE, 1895–1905

THE year 1895 witnessed a fateful decision. Japan had made war upon China and, to the astonishment of the West, the little athlete had utterly defeated his gigantic opponent. *Punch* produced a cartoon entitled 'Jap the Giant-Killer,' representing a tiny dwarf bestriding a huge Colossus and administering the *coup de grâce* with a sword. As a result of the Treaty of Shimonoseki (April 17, 1895) Japan obtained from China the independence of Korea, while she annexed for herself the island of Formosa and the peninsula of Liautung, including the harbour of Port Arthur. The latter was a warm-water harbour, was near to Peking, and was regarded with greedy eyes by Russia. The great Western Powers determined to read a lesson to the upstart mushroom Power in the East. Russia, France and Germany sent a collective demand to Japan demanding the evacuation of the Liautung peninsula and of Port Arthur[1] (April 23). Japan quietly obeyed, but she did not forget. She felt no anger against France, which had only acted with her ally, but she bitterly resented the action of Germany. The German Government, having already got Russia to promise to support her future claim to obtaining a port in China, had addressed Japan in terms of extraordinary rudeness, expressing her intention of 'removing all menaces to peace in the Far East.' Twenty years later Japan demanded the evacuation of the port which Germany had obtained in terms which repeated the exact words of the German ultimatum to herself. Over Russia Japan's revenge came sooner. Those who were in the confidence of Japanese statesmen knew that the events of 1895 made that Government resolve to humble Russia and to recover Port Arthur. And in ten years both ends were achieved. One Great Power in the West had abstained from taking part in the Franco-Russo-German demand. That Power was England. Her abstention was perhaps due to caution or to accident, but it made a most favourable impression on Japan. And from this moment Japan saw in the Island Empire of the West a possible ally against the militarist states of Europe.

In the New Year of 1896 the first signs of a rift between Germany and England began. At the end of 1895 Jameson led his famous 'Raid' against the Transvaal Republic. And on January 3, 1896, the Kaiser sent his even more famous telegram to President Kruger, congratulating him on the defeat of armed bands invading his territory.[2] This was

---

[1] The demand was collective, but the terms in which it was stated were different. Those of France were the most courteous, those of Germany the least.

[2] This telegram is almost as famous as the Ems telegram of Bismarck. It is charitable to suppose that the Kaiser's account in his *Memoirs* (1922), pp. 80–83 is due to his failure of memory. Other sources show that it was drawn up by his

interpreted in England as a German attempt to interfere with us in the Transvaal and provoked much indignation, especially among the British public. The German Government promptly retreated from their position, but left a lingering trail of suspicion behind them.

In the autumn of 1897 several interesting developments in German policy occurred. In June Admiral Tirpitz became Minister of Marine, in October Count (afterwards Prince) Bülow became Foreign Secretary (and Chancellor in October 1900), and at the end of the year the first extensive German naval programme was announced.[1] On November 14 Germany seized Kiao-Chau, thus obtaining a fine naval base in the Far East, and an incentive to future development.

Russia, which had reluctantly acquiesced in Germany's seizure of spoil, now looked about for compensation, knowing well that neither France nor Germany would oppose her. England approached Russia in January 1898 with proposals for an understanding with special reference to China and Turkey; but Russia, after some consideration, declined the overture.[2] She went ahead alone and seized Port Arthur. England showed herself bitterly hostile, sent a fierce remonstrance, and 'resumed full liberty of action.' By way of compensation England seized the harbour of Wei-Hai-Wei and France that of Kwangtschouan. Neither of these places were much of a compensation. Germany and Russia had been first in the field, and the latter had at last obtained a warm-water port on the Pacific.

England wished to preserve the Yang-tsze-Kiang valley as an economic sphere for herself.[3] But she felt it absolutely necessary to stop the pressure of Russia upon China. Russia accompanied her constant political advance with all sorts of demands for economic and financial concessions, which the miserable Chinese Government found it impossible to resist without the support of a European Great Power. Japan appeared as yet to be unimportant. Germany seemed the one Power strong enough to help. For other reasons as well England was beginning to feel her 'isolation' as less 'splendid' than it once had appeared. Lord Salisbury finally acquiesced in an unofficial approach to Germany, and

advisers and that he wished to strengthen the wording yet further, but he was overruled. *The Willy-Nicky Correspondence* (1920), p. 30, shows that on the same day as he sent the telegram to Kruger he wrote to the Czar, 'I have used very severe language in London' *re* the Transvaal.

[1] The Bill became law in April 1898. It added 12 ships of the line to the existing 7; 10 large cruisers to the existing 2; 23 small cruisers to the existing 7. It built 8 armoured coast defence vessels. All was to be ready in 1904.

[2] It is not usually recognised that England made this overture to Russia in 1898 (*v. Gooch and Temperley*, vol. I. pp. 5-18). Czar Nicholas (May 22, 1898) wrote of it to the Emperor William, 'Without thinking twice over it, their (the British) proposals were refused. *Two weeks later Port Arthur was ours,*' but it is clear that the Russian refusal was not as hasty as this.

[3] In reply to a question in Parliament, May 9, 1899, this British sphere was defined as the provinces adjoining the Yang-tsze-Kiang river and Ho-Nan and Chekiang.

it was conducted by Joseph Chamberlain during 1898.[1] It failed, partly because Germany made excessive demands, partly because she was unwilling to go so far as England in curbing Russia. This was indeed the first time the Sibylline books were offered to Germany. She might have had the English alliance at a price, but she refused.[2] Just after the failure of the negotiation a very ominous incident occurred. The Kaiser—who was going as a pilgrim to Jerusalem—made a speech at Damascus, in which he assured the three hundred million Mohammedans that he would always be their friend. This speech excited a good deal of attention, for a good many millions of these Mohammedans lived under British, French and Russian rule.

England was negotiating with Germany, but she was quarrelling with France. In 1898 Sir Herbert (afterwards Lord) Kitchener had at last begun the reconquest of the Sudan in earnest. On September 2 he broke the Khalifa's army at Omdurman, and entered Khartum immediately afterwards. He then heard that a French expedition of some 120 men under Captain Marchand had reached Fashoda and there hoisted the French tricolour. On September 19 Kitchener proceeded in person to Fashoda, but could not induce Marchand to lower his flag or to abandon his pretensions. The struggle was transferred from Khartum and Fashoda to London and Paris, and a crisis was soon at hand. The Marchand expedition had been sent by Hanotaux (the French Foreign Minister who had resigned at the end of June) in order to establish a claim on the Equatorial hinterland of the Sudan, and on the upper reaches of the Nile, principally on the province of Bahr-el-Ghazal. It was hard to expect the British Government, which had spent blood and gold in reconquering the Sudan with an army, to surrender some of its richest provinces to a French explorer with a platoon. On the other hand it was hard for the French to haul down the tricolour. Force, or the threat of force, was now to decide the issue. Lord Rosebery made a speech in which he pointed out that, when he was Prime Minister, England had declared that it would be an unfriendly act for France to make the claims it was now making. This—combined with the firm attitude of Lord Salisbury—proved decisive. On November 4 the French Ambassador intimated that Fashoda would be evacuated.

The crisis had passed. And, singularly enough, the difference was to lead to an entente. Russia and Germany had each just rejected

[1] Full details in J. L. Garvin: *Life of Joseph Chamberlain*, vol. III. pp. 254–95 (Macmillan, 1934); cp. *Grosse Politik*, vol. XIV. pp. 191–255.

[2] The only outcome of this negotiation was what is known as the Angola Agreement (30th August, 1898) between England and Germany. This defined the spheres of interest in Africa which England and Germany would occupy if Portugal abandoned her colonies. The effect of this was nullified by England giving an assurance to Portugal in 1899 that she would guarantee her colonies, in accordance with Article XV, and the secret article of a Treaty of 1661. This is incorrectly called the 'Windsor Treaty.' The text of the Angola Agreement is in *Gooch and Temperley*, vol. I. pp. 71–5.

England's proffered alliance, France had just avoided war with her. But Hanotaux had been anti-English, and Delcassé, though smarting in the midst of his humiliation, had the courage to speak of the need of a *bonne entente* with England. France—with relentless logic—recognised that there must be no intrusion into the Upper Nile, and that her differences with England had better be made up. Delcassé made clear his desire by deeds as well as by words, for he promoted two pro-English and anti-German diplomats, Barrère, whom he sent to Rome, and Cambon, whom he sent to London. And Cambon was in six years to be the French architect of the Entente.

In the middle of 1898 the Czar had issued his famous appeal for peace, which resulted in the First Hague Peace Conference (May to July 1899). The personal sincerity of the Czar has usually been admitted, though cynics have suggested that the backward state of the Russian artillery rendered a delay in armaments advisable. There was at any rate no serious attempt made to limit armaments. When it was proposed Germany made a vigorous opposition which negatived all possibility of success. But England at the last made a vigorous and successful effort to establish an Arbitration Tribunal. It was opposed to the last moment by Germany, and the Kaiser, when he finally gave way, remarked that he should depend not on arbitration, but on his own sharp sword, for safety.

The Hague Conference had hardly risen when war began between England and the Boer Republics of the Transvaal and Orange Free State (October). The war was one between combatants immeasurably unequal in resources. But the heavy losses of England in December 1899 made it seem for a moment as if success was doubtful. Much popular hatred was shown towards England on the Continent, particularly in Dutch, Belgian, French and German newspapers. But the more serious question was whether the three Powers, which had intervened against Japan in 1895, would intervene against England in 1899 or 1900. On the whole, it seems that Russia was the most unfriendly, and there may have been persons in her Foreign Office who contemplated intervention. France could not act alone, and Germany, while very willing to profit by our difficulties, certainly contemplated no active hostility, and dissuaded the other Powers from any such attempt.[1]

The Kaiser paid a personal visit to England in November 1899, when Chamberlain again pressed on him the prospect of an alliance, suggesting the United States as a third partner. The Kaiser refused, and subsequently aroused the displeasure of the Prince of Wales (afterwards Edward VII). His attitude was inconsistent; at one time he furnished the British Government with 'military aphorisms' or a military plan for the reduction of the Boer Republics to obedience; at another he

---

[1] Two attempts were made by Russia, in February 1900 and October 1901 (*v.* G. P. Gooch: *History of Modern Europe 1878–1919*, (1923) pp. 318–9), both of which were refused by Germany. But it is not clear that even Russia wanted intervention by force.

suggested that it was time to make peace with them. It is perhaps hardly fair to say that he represented German policy, which was neither friendly nor hostile until it was clear that England would win. The German public was overwhelmingly on the side of the Boers, and the Government sometimes trimmed its sails to the popular wind. But it committed no overt act of unfriendliness,[1] and from the end of 1900 onwards the Kaiser himself was personally friendly. Peace was made with the Boers in May 1902, and all danger of intervention was thus ended.

Events in China in 1900 caused a new offer to be made by England to Germany. In June the German Consul was murdered in China, and this was the prelude to a siege of the Foreign Legations in Peking, and to a pronounced anti-foreign movement (secretly encouraged by the Chinese Government) known as 'the Boxer' revolt. After much trouble an international force advanced and relieved the Legations at Peking. A German, Count Waldersee, was appointed Generalissimo of this force, and various indemnities and humiliations were exacted from the Chinese. The Kaiser, who had openly exhorted the German contingent to act towards the Chinese like Huns, was foremost in the work of vengeance.

England, which seems to have viewed the situation more calmly, sought to turn it to her advantage by making an agreement with Germany. This agreement (signed October 16, 1900) arranged for the joint action of the two Powers to maintain the 'territorial condition' of China, and the 'open door' in commerce wherever they could exercise influence. The terms were not clear, but England seems to have thought that she had at last got Germany to support her against Russia's aggression in North China. If so, she was soon undeceived, for on March 15, 1901, Bülow publicly stated that the Anglo-German Agreement applied to the Yang-tsze-Kiang valley and not to Manchuria.

This utterance did not help the negotiations which were once more taking place between England and Germany. They were handled by Lord Lansdowne (who had succeeded Lord Salisbury as Foreign Minister) and by the indefatigable Joseph Chamberlain. Germany seems to have wished to include England in her existing Triple Alliance (Germany, Austria-Hungary, and Italy). Lord Lansdowne, on the other hand, favoured a much more limited agreement. By this time England was getting dissatisfied and made it pretty clear to Germany that, if these negotiations failed, England would turn to France and Russia. This warning was regarded as 'bluff,' and once again Germany declined the Sibylline offer. By December 1901 all real chance of success in the negotiation had faded away.[2]

---

[1] She took advantage of England's preoccupation to drive a hard bargain as regards the partition of Samoa (November–December 1899), but the United States did the same on this occasion, as also in the Hay-Pauncefote Treaty.

[2] The record of this negotiation (unlike that of 1898) is in *Gooch and Temperley*, vol. II. pp. 60–88.

As Germany had proved a broken reed, England had again to search for a counterpoise to Russia's influence in North China. Just at this moment Japan renewed her solicitations to England, and Germany smiled on the negotiation. Within seven months the Oriental diplomats triumphed, and, without the knowledge of Parliament or of people, Lord Lansdowne signed a Treaty of Alliance with Japan on January 30, 1902. It was published at once, and its terms were as follows: Both Powers recognised the *status quo* in Eastern Asia, particularly in Korea and China. In case of war between Russia and Japan England promised to be neutral. But if a second Power (*i.e.* France) came to the aid of Russia (or of any other state at war with Japan), England promised to intervene and to support her ally with arms. The arrangement was to hold good for five years.

This Treaty was of epoch-making importance in every direction. Its intention, so far as Japan was concerned, must remain a little mysterious. The English diplomats seem to have thought that they would be able to keep Japan in order and to prevent her aggression against Russia. It is easy to see now that this was an entire mistake. Japanese military and naval organisation would be complete by the end of 1903, and, after that, England's alliance would (and did) enable them to attack Russia as soon as they found it convenient to do so. This was not the only British mistake. Her negotiators seem to have believed that the effect of this treaty would be confined to the local area of China. But the diplomacy of the Great Powers is world-wide in its action and extent, and an alliance affecting the Sea of Japan was found to trouble the Mediterranean and the North Sea. England's situation, however, was not so perilous as it appeared. She was not indeed on friendly terms either with Russia or with France, but then neither was she with Germany. Even after the Japanese Alliance England could have joined either the Triple or the Dual Alliance. Germany seems still to have expected or hoped for the former. As it turned out, England ultimately joined France and Russia in an Entente though not in an Alliance.

English statesmen, when they signed the Anglo-Japanese Alliance, saw one thing at least in a clear light. They knew they were departing from the system of 'splendid isolation'; they knew they were breaking from Canning's old tradition of eschewing alliances and avoiding guarantees. Yet they dared to do it and on this account these men deserved well of their country. It is idle to blame them for lack of foresight, a want from which all statesmen suffer. What they should be praised for, is for taking a step which they knew to be a daring one and a break with the past. How daring it was and how great was the break with the past they certainly did not know. But at least they dared and did something.

During the remainder of the year 1902 the dice fell unfortunately for Germany, as we can see now. The Anglo-Japanese Alliance tended to draw England away from Germany. For England had not asked

Germany to join in the Anglo-Japanese Treaty, since she found her German agreement about China to be worthless. The Triple Alliance began to break down in another direction. Peace was made with the Boers in May 1902, and England was stronger. Delcassé steadily pursued a policy of isolating Germany, and on 4th June, 1902, he got Italy to declare that the Triple Alliance was not directed against France.[1] He followed this up by a secret Neutrality Agreement (November 1-2) by which Italy pledged herself to remain neutral in a war in which France was engaged. So Italy was no longer bound by the Triple Alliance with respect to France, and she had already declared that she was not bound by it with respect to England.

The year concluded with a very unfortunate incident in Venezuela. Germany induced England to unite with her in a combined naval demonstration against Venezuela, undertaken in order to collect debts for British and German bondholders. As this incident came just after a visit of the Kaiser to Sandringham, public opinion was greatly excited in England. The neglect of popular feeling in England by her statesmen was quite as maladroit as the disregard for the views of the Government of the United States. In 1895 America had indicated clearly to England that she interpreted the 'Monroe Doctrine' as meaning that the United States was 'the predominant partner' who had to be consulted by European Powers before they interfered in America. Now two European Powers proposed to intervene without consulting her first. The British public viewed the affair as a German 'dodge' to embroil us with the American Government. Both considerations combined to make British statesmen retreat hastily from their positions.[2]

The year 1903 was memorable for the continental journey of Edward VII, who visited Lisbon, Rome, Paris and Vienna. All of these visits were connected by German journalists at the time, and by German historians afterwards, with the *Einkreisungspolitik* or 'encirclement policy' of this alleged Machiavelli among kings. In reality they seem to have been visits of ceremony or of pleasure. But the State visit made to London by the French President and by Delcassé (July 6-9, 1903) showed clearly that Franco-British relations were improving. The visit was the signal for some anti-German demonstrations in the British press. But, even so, the Rubicon had not yet been crossed. During the year the relations of Japan and Russia became steadily worse. The details need not concern us, for there was one cause of them, and one

---

[1] This was a return for the French secret undertaking (December 14–16, 1900) to give Italy a free hand in Tripoli. *v.* Pribram: *Secret Treaties*, vol. II. pp. 226–59.

[2] Before this time England had refused, largely owing to popular clamour, to join in the Baghdad railway scheme with Germany and France. The question came up finally in April 1903 and the British Government declined co-operation.

only: Russia had occupied Manchuria and was threatening Korea. Japan was resolved to fight if Russia occupied Korea, and unless she could get definite assurances against Russian aggression in Manchuria. When Russia would not give these pledges, Japan broke off the negotiations and declared war (February 1904).

During the autumn of 1903 Lord Lansdowne and Delcassé worked hard at a Franco-British Entente. The main aim of the British statesman was undoubted; it was finally to settle half a dozen old difficulties in Africa, America and Asia, on which France and England were at variance. These questions were due to old-time treaties or aggravated by recent hostilities, and on any one of them war might arise through a careless governor or an impetuous soldier. These questions Lansdowne meant to liquidate altogether, or, at any rate, to remove from the danger zone. The aim of France is less clear. But it seems certain that she wanted not only a settlement but an ally. Delcassé seems to have thought that, if she gave the one, he could gain the other. On April 8, 1904, the Franco-British Declaration as regards Egypt and Morocco was signed, the most important among a group of similar agreements dealing with special areas. From that date the Franco-British Entente was a virtual certainty.

There were concessions by one side or another in the minor questions, Newfoundland, Siam, West Africa. But the two main questions concerned Egypt and Morocco. England wanted a free hand in the one, France in the other, and, somewhat to England's surprise, France made little difficulty about Egypt. She secured some advantages in respect to the Suez Canal, but agreed not to obstruct our action by 'asking that a limit of time be fixed for the British occupation or in any other way.' [1] In return for this, France stated that she had no desire to alter the political status of Morocco, and Great Britain promised not to obstruct her action there. This was what was published. But secret articles were also signed on April 8, 1904, which were not revealed until 1911. One of these provided that, in case of modification of the status either in Egypt or in Morocco, there was to be as before freedom of trade, free passage of the Suez Canal, and prohibition of fortifications opposite the Straits of Gibraltar. The Capitulations were to be abolished in Egypt, if desired by France or England. Finally another secret article stipulated that, whenever the Sultan of Morocco ceased to exercise authority over it, a specified part of Morocco should be transferred to Spain.[2] In plain language, these secret articles provided for the annexation of part of Morocco by Spain. That meant, of course, that the

---

[1] Great Britain had stated originally that she would leave Egypt as soon as its financial affairs were in order. Lord Lansdowne now declared that he had no desire to alter the political status of Egypt, *i.e.* to annex it, but gave no hint of withdrawal now or in the future.

[2] Spain was informed of, and agreed to, these terms in a secret treaty with France of October 6, 1904.

rest of Morocco would or might be annexed by France, whenever she chose, and that England would have to give diplomatic support to this arrangement.

The secrecy of these arrangements is in itself suspicious. For, while France secured Italy's good will before April 1904 by promising her Tripoli, and Spain's good will shortly afterwards by promising her a part of Morocco, nothing was done by England or France to enlighten Germany as to the 'secret deal' over Morocco. German statesmen cannot have been ignorant of these secret arrangements for very long.[1] But they may not have known all about them and may well have feared that all German commerce—as well as political influence—was to be shut out from Morocco. That being so, Germany was certain to make herself unpleasant and to seek opportunities of testing the strength of this partially secret 'Entente.' It seems that the French statesmen saw farther than the English and recognised that this secret obligation was bound to produce a situation in which England would be led into the French camp, or at any rate be led away from the German one.

For some little time the German Government seems to have had no reasons for suspicion, although the coincidence of the Russo-Japanese war necessarily increased the danger of misunderstanding. In this war German sympathies were with Russia, and this was of great importance because of the alliance between England and Japan. On Trafalgar Day (October 21, 1904) the Russian fleet off the Dogger Bank shot at an English fishing-vessel, believing it to be a Japanese torpedo-boat. A tense situation ensued, which was eventually ended by the promise by Russia of full apologies and compensation. But in December of this year Germany took care to assure Russia of her support, in case of conflict with England. And, on the English side, the fleet in the North Sea was permanently strengthened. So that both Germany and England had become more irritated with each other than before.

As the year 1905 opened, the German Government began to get suspicious as to French designs in Morocco. By this time they seem to have known something of the secret articles and, even if they did not, the movements of France in Morocco were highly suspicious. France had given Germany, in 1904, the softest assurances as to 'the open door' and the integrity of Morocco. But early in February 1905 a French envoy was known to be making new demands on the Sultan of Morocco, which could only mean that France was attempting to obtain more control over the country, and therefore trying to alter the *status quo*. German statesmen at once suggested the project of sending the Kaiser himself as a kind of counter-envoy to Morocco. The suggestion was due to Holstein, that singular wire-puller; it was approved by Bülow;

[1] The secret was known to too many persons at Madrid and St. Petersburg for Germany not to learn something of the truth very soon. How much she knew is harder to say. Full revelations were not made until November, 1911, *v.* Temperley and Penson: *A Century of Diplomatic Blue Books*, pp. 497–9 (C.U.P., 1938).

and curiously enough was opposed, though vainly, by the Kaiser, whose opposition was certainly sincere, for he was actually rejecting an opportunity of appearing in the limelight. On March 29 Bülow spoke in the Reichstag, demanding 'the open door' for German trade and the political *status quo* in Morocco. On March 31 the Kaiser landed from his yacht at Tangier and made a speech. He declared that he recognised the sovereignty and independence of the Sultan, whom he considered as 'absolutely free.' 'I hope that under his sovereignty a free Morocco will remain open to the peaceful competition of all nations, without monopoly or annexation, on a policy of absolute equality.' This speech meant two things. It meant first, that Germany considered herself in no way bound either by the Entente or by the Franco-Spanish Treaties; next, that she would endeavour to safeguard the integrity and independence of Morocco. And these points were speedily emphasised. For on April 11 Bülow issued a circular demanding the summoning of an international Conference on Morocco. He was promptly backed up by the Sultan of Morocco, who now rejected all his previous concessions to France, and invited a conference at Tangier of those Powers who had signed the Treaty of 1880 which had settled the status of Morocco.

The time for testing the Entente had arrived. Delcassé wished to take a bold line and refuse a Conference. He asserted at a Cabinet on June 6 that England had made an offer to support him,[1] and that France by standing firm would cause Germany to 'back down.' But Delcassé found no support in the Cabinet except from the President of the Republic. He therefore resigned on June 11. The Kaiser celebrated his overthrow by visiting Count Bülow early one morning when he was still in bed, and saluting him with the title of 'Prince.' The incident caused an immense sensation. German interference had apparently caused the fall of a French Minister, and England had apparently failed to support France at the critical moment. It was a distinctly unpleasant incident. Rouvier—the French Prime Minister—who now took over French diplomacy, was conciliatory. But he strove desperately to avert a Conference. Finally, President Roosevelt, who was approached by both France and Germany, succeeded in getting all parties to agree to a Conference.

Before the Conference met, Mr. Balfour had resigned (December 4, 1905) and a Liberal Government was in office, with Sir Edward Grey as Foreign Secretary. He was to hold that office for a longer period

---

[1] The late Lord Sanderson expressed the opinion in private that this 'offer' was a mere delusion. The publication of the British and French documents of this period has made clear the source of Delcassé's statement. The British 'offer' was in fact one of consultation and not of alliance; but Paul Cambon had written to Delcassé giving a gloss on Lansdowne's words. If France accepted the proposal 'c'est entrer dans la voie d'une entente générale qui constituerait en réalité une alliance." v. *Documents Diplomatiques Français (1871–1914)*, 2nd Ser., vol. VI. pp. 557-60; cp. *Gooch and Temperley*, vol. III. pp. 76–8.

than any other man in the nineteenth or twentieth centuries,[1] and to be more severely tested than anyone except Castlereagh. As the Entente assumed a new aspect in 1906 it is well to sum up, so far as we can, the position reached at the end of 1905. Lord Lansdowne seems to have known that the Anglo-Japanese Alliance was indeed a departure from tradition, but he might claim that its existence alone prevented France (and perhaps Germany) from being involved in the Russo-Japanese war. The Treaty of Portsmouth, making peace between Russia and Japan, was actually signed on September 5, 1905. This surrendered Port Arthur, Manchuria, Korea, and half the isle of Sakhaline to Japan, while Russia refused to pay any war indemnity. Just before this, on August 12, 1905, the Anglo-Japanese Alliance was renewed for five years. England pledged herself in future to give help to Japan if attacked by only *one* Power (instead of by *two*). In return Japan agreed to defend India against attack. But Lord Lansdowne, while admitting that tradition had been still further abandoned, would probably have argued that England had kept the war from extending by her attitude during 1904–5, and that this new obligation would tend to preserve peace in the future in this local area of the Far East.

As regards the Entente with France a curious and interesting situation had arisen. Delcassé had called for British assistance and suggested that he had received guarantees for it. That the British Government emphatically denied, and in the form in which he stated it, there was, it is now clear, some unintentional exaggeration.[2] The Entente, however, meant something more in June 1905 than in April 1904. It had simply been a settlement with France of all dangerous or thorny questions. The official English view till the end of the Balfour Ministry seems to have been that this was still the case; but in fact the scope of the understanding had been widened by the conversations of April and May 1905, and an arrangement which seemed at first likely to be limited in effect to Morocco had become the basis of a general practice of cooperation between the two countries.

The main difficulty between England and Germany consisted in the rise of a dangerous popular prejudice on both sides. Popular opinion had embarrassed their relations in the South African War, had wrecked the Baghdad Agreement, had rendered difficult the Venezuela question, and had just inflamed the Tangier crisis. Repeated negotiations with Germany in 1898, in 1899, in 1901, had failed to create a working agreement or to promote an alliance between the two countries. England

---

[1] Grey held office from December 1905 to December 1916; Castlereagh, the next candidate, from March 1812 to August 1822. The reference is to a continuous period of office. Grey's policy is discussed in G. M. Trevelyan: *Grey of Fallodon* (Longmans, 1937), and G. P. Gooch: *Before the War*, vol. II. (Longmans, 1938).

[2] Curiously enough, the Kaiser wrote to Roosevelt (J. B. Bishop: *Theodore Roosevelt and his Time* (1920), vol. I. p. 476) in June 1905: ' My people are sure that England would now back France by force of arms in a war against Germany, not on account of Morocco, but on account of Germany's policy in the Far East.'

had indeed been more eager than Germany for an understanding. She had failed thrice, and popular opinion made it dangerous to renew the attempt at once. It was not possible to negotiate an Entente, for there were no outstanding diplomatic difficulties. There was only a dangerous popular tension on both sides. That being so, it was better to leave Germany alone for the present, and see if another Entente, another liquidation of long-standing grievances, could not be made. Here Russia was the obvious object of approach and France was the obvious intermediary. So the Franco-British Entente led naturally to a Russo-British Entente and away from Germany.

CHAPTER XXVI

THE STATES OF EUROPE BEFORE THE CATASTROPHE

As a result of the Morocco crisis, the Algeciras Conference met, and marked 'a milestone on the road to Armageddon.' [1] New and ominous developments appeared, and suddenly revealed Europe on the verge of a possible war, which might involve all the Great Powers. Since 1870 friction, leading to possible conflict between any two Great Powers, had often occurred. During 1886-8 there had been threats of wars between Russia and Austria-Hungary; in 1877, and again in 1885 and 1898, between Russia and Great Britain; between England and France in 1898; between Germany and France in 1875, in 1887, and again in 1905. But what made these incidents differ from the circumstances of the Algeciras Conference was that before 1906 the two protagonists were usually tranquillised by a united Europe acting as umpire. Now the Great Powers took sides even when not themselves involved and the outlines of the opposed combinations appeared. War was thus threatened not only between the two Powers directly at variance, but between the two armed combinations into which Europe was divided. Before 1906 war between two Powers might have been localised, as it was in 1870; after that date it seemed definitely improbable. From 1906 onwards crises regularly occurred every one or two years until 1914, and in each crisis the Anglo-French-Russian Entente faced the Austro-German Alliance, with Italy fluttering distractedly in the background. There were no longer any neutrals whose influence counted. The moderate and mediatory influence represented by the intervention between two potential combatants of a detached and independent Great Power or set of Powers was no longer present. And it seems to be clear now that these crises between armed groups could not go on recurring indefinitely.

[1] Winston Churchill: *World Crisis*, p. 36 (Butterworth, 1931).

At least, if armaments went on increasing with the crises, the probability of war became more certain with each successive crisis.

Whether the policy of 'Encirclement' (*Einkreisungspolitik*) increased the danger or not, this policy was not confined to one group. From 1871 to 1890 Bismarck was pursuing a policy of isolating France, just as (according to German views) Delcassé or Edward VII pursued a similar policy towards Germany in later years. There is no doubt indeed that Bismarck aimed in his later years at defence and not at aggression, but the same is probably true of England and France. The motive of combination in each group seems to have been primarily one of fear. Isolation, for instance, was desired by Grey neither for England nor for Germany. But an entente has a way of leading to the same ideas as those involved in an alliance. This has been very neatly illustrated by Professor Schmitt, who had drawn a parallel between Grey's letter to the French Ambassador of November 22, 1912, and the letter from Russia's Foreign Minister which constituted the first formal expression of the Franco-Russian combination.[1]

Sir E. Grey to Paul Cambon,
22 November, 1912.

'I agree that, if either Government had grave reason to expect an unprovoked attack by a third Power, or something that threatened the general peace, it should immediately discuss with the other, whether both Governments should act together to prevent aggression and to preserve peace, and if so what measures they would be prepared to take in common. If these measures involved action, the plans of the General Staffs would at once be taken into consideration, and the Governments would then decide what effect should be given to them.'

De Giers, Russian Foreign Minister, to M. de Mohrenheim, Russian Ambassador in Paris, 21 August, 1891.

'. . . the two Governments declare that they will take counsel together upon every question of a nature to jeopardise the general peace;

2. In case that peace should be actually in danger, and especially if one of the two parties should be threatened with an aggression, the two parties undertake to reach an understanding on the measures whose immediate and simultaneous adoption would be imposed upon the two Governments by the realisation of this eventuality.'

The comparison is not quite a valid one, for the second of these extracts was written at the beginning of an alliance, and the first of them after the thorough testing of an entente. But it is none the less highly instructive. It is hardly necessary to refer to the well-proved observation that defensive alliances have a way of becoming offensive ones. And the

---

[1] B. E. Schmitt: *American Hist. Rev.*, Ap. 1924, p. 459. Grey's letter is in *Gooch and Temperley*, vol. X. (2), pp. 614–5; De Giers' letter is in Pribram: *Secret Treaties*, vol. II. p. 211.

use of the words 'offensive' and 'defensive,' as applied to wars instead of to alliances, is admitted to have lost all meaning.[1]

It seemed certain, therefore, that there was ultimately, if not immediately, more danger in armed groups than there was in armed individual states. But the working out of this principle of group competition must be reserved to another chapter. Before we can trace the full working of tendencies in the groups, we must estimate the characteristic and individual tendencies in the chief states or nations of Europe. For one state may have influenced its group by its instability, its aggressiveness, its enthusiasms, or its conservatism. Thus the connection between a policy of internal unrest and external adventure is evident enough, and the influence of one such state might affect a whole group. The condition of Europe in the thirty years before 1914 is as relevant to the outbreak of war as the situation which preceded the Revolutionary War in 1792.

On the whole Great Britain was more interested in domestic than in external policy. The movements for the extension of the franchise and for Irish Home Rule absorbed public attention from 1885 to 1895, and Britain was 'isolated' in a real sense at the turn of the century. There was indeed an active policy of colonial and maritime development, but the advent of a Liberal Government at the end of 1905 discouraged annexationist tendencies and reduced for a time the competition of naval programmes. The public were, however, in no way disposed to allow the Government to cut down the Navy after Germany had launched her great naval programme in 1907. And the growing popular hostility to Germany proved a grave embarrassment to Lord Lansdowne over the Baghdad Railway, and to Sir Edward Grey over the Navy. Grey's management of popular opinion does not seem to have been very skilful, for, though he did not always keep it well informed, he at times gave way to its pressure. And the people and the press represented a growing danger to peace. It was said at a later date by Sir Austen Chamberlain,[2] 'we have no reason to flatter ourselves with the fond belief that the pride or vanity of a nation is less sensitive than that of a prince, or that in a moment of crisis the crowd will be cooler than the individual.' Lord Salisbury once caustically compared a foreign Minister in a democracy to a man playing a game of cards with others, while a very noisy person stood behind him and shouted out every card he ought to play. Sir Edward Grey must often have appreciated the truth of this remark.

The attitude of France throughout this period was at once inconsistent and perplexing. The Republic, which we last saw in the days of Jules Ferry and President Grévy, was a government of compromise and of the second-best. The life of its Cabinets was notoriously short, they

[1] *v.* Some very instructive quotations before and after the war of 1914 in Lowes Dickinson: *The International Anarchy* (1926), pp. 6–7 *sqq.*

[2] At Glasgow, November 2, 1926.

were 'lute-string administrations' fading with the summer or changing with the wind. Each of these flimsy Cabinets was liable to be swayed or overthrown by gusts of popular passion. One such gust forced M. Grévy to resign even the Presidency in 1887. During the same year the agitations, due to the Chauvinist and anti-German movement, led by General Boulanger, caused danger of war abroad and fear of a military dictatorship at home. The year 1889 saw the end of the Boulangist danger. But the year 1892 witnessed an appalling exposure of political corruption among parliamentary deputies in connection with the Panama Canal.[1] The 'group system' in the French Legislature favoured irresponsibility and instability in every sense, but the question was now raised as to whether any government or system could survive evidence of such terrible corruption.

None the less the dawn of the twentieth century showed that definite progress was being registered. Some of the old factions at least had 'ceased from troubling.' The Royalists, who had been so powerful in 1871 and even in 1879, were no longer of any real importance. Bonapartism, like Royalism, had been laughed out of existence by the follies of Boulanger. The Clericals, who had so often disturbed France, had been weakened by the Pope's Encyclical of 1892, which enjoined them to accept the Republic, and their opponents were about to unite against them. Even the notorious Dreyfus affair (1897–9), which threatened to produce a clerico-military reaction, was finally settled without bloodshed and without a *coup d'état*. Waldeck-Rousseau's Ministry at the turn of the century marked a new era in the history of parties and of parliamentary stability under the Republic. He had laid the old bogies of Empire, Royalism, and the Church, and now faced the new forces of Socialism, Syndicalism, and Chauvinism. His Radical Ministry, by appealing to the Socialists, formed a 'Bloc' with anti-Clericalism as their chief aim. During the years 1903–5 they treated the Church with such violence as to produce a slight reaction. Moreover, peaceful parliamentary evolution was interrupted by the progress of Syndicalism, a system aimed at the destruction of parliamentary institutions by 'direct action,' *i.e.* by strikes, by sabotage and by boycotts. In 1909 M. Briand was called upon to face a railway strike, inspired by Syndicalism, which he repressed by the drastic measure of calling up the strikers as reservists. Briand succeeded, but the power of the Government was seriously shaken. Threats and murmurs of war reconstituted the Government on a national basis in 1912 under M. Poincaré. Foreign policy and national defence became the order of the day. In 1913 M. Poincaré became President of the French Republic and a series of weak Coalition Ministries held office until the war of 1914.

---

[1] ' A hundred deputies and senators were said to be implicated,' six Cabinet Ministers were tried, and one convicted. ' The first Minister of the Republic . . . revealed his belief that the political society in which he lived was sapped with corruption.' J. E. C. Bodley: *France* (1899), p. 499.

A survey of external policy, in regard to both the French Government and the people since 1885, shows that this year ended a short period of friendliness towards Germany in which colonial expansion was held to compensate for the loss of Alsace-Lorraine. During the succeeding, or Boulanger, period the years of military service were reduced from five to three, but armaments were increased. Germany replied to these steps by a new Army Bill increasing her troops by 41,000 in 1887, and by other measures. So a dangerous competition in armaments began. The fall of Bismarck in 1890 slightly improved the situation, but a few unhappy incidents soon made it as bad as ever. The security given to France by the Russian Alliance (1893) diverted her attention from Germany, her rival in Europe, and enabled her to indulge her resentment against England, her rival in colonial development. The French press was exceedingly bitter, and the diplomatic defeat of France at Fashoda (1898) increased her hostility. But, as she did not take advantage of England's embarrassments in the South African War, the clouds gradually lifted and enabled the Anglo-French Entente to be negotiated (1904). Friction with Germany still continued, chiefly over Morocco, until the crisis of Agadir. The year 1912 witnessed the development at Paris of the anti-German influences of Russia, and the appearance of the resolute and vigorous Poincaré, who entered, hardly indeed as if he wished to provoke war, but at least as if he meant to provide for it when it came. The serious character of the crisis was shown in the new law of military service. In 1913 three years, instead of two,[1] was re-established as the period of universal military service. The Opposition was very violent and, but for the war, would almost certainly have repealed the three years' period. A strong development had taken place in the military interests and enthusiasms of France, and by 1914 a complete military reorganisation was taking place. Generally speaking, however, political troubles rendered far-reaching military plans unlikely or impossible of execution. While, therefore, the French public was during the years 1912–14 not only anti-German but more confident and more restless than at any period since 1871, both her generals and politicians knew that a war entailed very grave risks and should be averted as long as possible.

Russia and its Government certainly offered grave difficulties to peace. After the murder of Alexander II in 1881 a thoroughly reactionary régime ensued under his dull and well-meaning son, Alexander III. The Government was quite separated from the people and the Czar was influenced by the extreme doctrinaire reactionary, Pobiedonostsev. All sorts of unrest prevailed and the doctrines of Anarchism,

---

[1] The Boulanger reforms, 1887–9, reduced the period of military service from five years to three, but there were until 1905 many exceptions, permitting some conscripts to serve for one year only. In 1905 a new law made every one without exception liable to service for two years, a period raised to three years by the law of 1913, cp. R. H. Soltau: *French Parties and Politics* (1922), pp. 50–51.

preached by Bakunin from a safe seclusion at Geneva, found an echo in many cities. Brutal repression of ideas and attacks on the *intelligentsia* seemed the only policy of the Government. The sole material progress was made by Witte, who was Minister of Finance from 1892 to 1903 ; the nearest approach to a Minister like Colbert that Russia ever produced. By a vast extension of State monopolies, he made the State the universal publican, he dominated everything, and secured immense revenues from the liquor trade. He controlled the railway system and immensely developed its working. He greatly improved the currency system and thus enabled Russia to stand the financial strain of the Russo-Japanese War. But he was unable to emancipate Russia from economic dependence on Germany and in the tariff treaties the latter always maintained her superiority. Witte's influence in no way lessened the burden of armaments and he was unable to prevent the building of strategic railways.

The foreign and military policy of the country was conducted on thoroughly reactionary lines, and the accession of the last of the Czars, Nicholas II (1894), made little difference in this matter. And, though he summoned the First Hague Peace Conference, he undertook no serious measures for limiting armaments. He was personally sincere and desirous of peace, but a mere tool in the hands of his ambitious and irresponsible ministers and generals. Their policy was active and annexationist in Asia and culminated in the Russo-Japanese War. For this war the advisers of the Czar were largely responsible.

The Czar's advisers had brought on the war partly by bad faith in refusing to evacuate Manchuria, and partly because they felt certain of victory. They believed that war with Japan would enable the Government to atone for its intellectual bankruptcy and internal corruption by dazzling military successes. Defeat abroad therefore necessarily produced disorder and revolution at home. The 'Liberators' demanded a constitution, and Father Gapon organised the factory workers of Petrograd. He headed a procession to present a petition to the Czar which was fired on (January 22, 1905). All sorts of strikes, disturbances and assassinations then occurred. The agitation went on and the defeat of the Russian army at Mukden (March 23), and the destruction of their fleet at Tsushima (May 27–8, 1905) forced the Government's hand. In August an Act, providing for a Duma or Parliament, appeared. The Duma met next year, but neither on this, nor on any subsequent occasion, was it a successful or convincing body. Government continued in the hands of favourites or courtiers or generals, and Russia was only a little better prepared to stand the strain of war in 1914 than she had been in 1904. In foreign policy she drifted away from Germany from 1906 onwards, and the estrangement became greater after the Anglo-Russian Entente of 1907. Henceforward Russia pursued a strong Slavophile policy in the Balkans, and a strong anti-German policy everywhere. The internal instability of Russia, the ·unscrupulousness of her diplomacy,[1] and the fears and ambitions of her General Staff rendered her a serious danger to peace. It is certainly true that she did not want war in 1914, because her generals knew her military weakness only too well. But it cannot be truly said that a Government so constituted really made ultimately for peace. Russia's Government maintained and was increasing a great army, it built strategic railways as menacing as those of Germany in Europe, she was destroying the integrity of Persia in Asia, and was perpetually intriguing in the Balkans and stretching out a greedy hand towards Constantinople. Regarded by herself Russia was a distinct menace to European peace, and the counsels of her ally France, and of her friend England, were the only restraining influences upon her.

From 1903 onwards Russia once again bestirred herself in the Balkans and her activity was viewed with alarm by Austria-Hungary and Germany. For the Balance of Power was disturbed. Serbia, which had been pro-Austrian, was won over to Russia, and Bulgaria, which had been hostile, was reconciled to her. This situation was highly dangerous and, though the result of the Balkan war was to bring Bulgaria close to the Austro-Germans, Serbia was immensely increased in strength and Rumania attracted to Russia. So a policy of 'encirclement' had begun in the Balkans. It was to be met by drawing Bulgaria and Turkey into the Austro-German Alliance. These were the thoughts of the Austro-German statesmen in 1914, and they show how even the action of comparatively small Balkan States weighted the balances, and harassed the nerves of great European combinations. And the small Powers were quite willing to play great parts, and perhaps able to do so. The scales were so evenly held that even the plumping of a small Power on one side or the other might be decisive.

It was not, however, the small states which always decided the fate of Great Powers in Europe. Italy, which was near the stature of a Great Power, could and did exercise a restraining influence on the Austro-German Alliance or on the Triple Entente. Her constitution was based on a limited franchise, and serious social troubles were constantly feared by her Governments. Her colonial ambitions had been baulked at Tunis in 1881, checked in Abyssinia in 1896, and succeeded only in 1911 when she obtained the sterile area of Tripoli. Without coal or iron she feared a blockade from any Power with a strong navy. Her ties with the Austro-German Alliance were slight, for she had refused to contemplate an attack on England, and after 1902 had become exceedingly friendly with France. Her armaments were not such as to cause alarm to other powers, and her internal condition and the smallness of her resources rendered it impossible to increase them rapidly. Consequently her influence was always in the direction of moderation. In 1906 she stood for peace at Algeciras, and during 1908–9 and again

[1] The *Livre Noir* shows that a large number of French newspapers received Russian gold for pursuing Russian aims.

in 1912–13 she exercised a beneficial and restraining influence upon Austria-Hungary. Her Government, if sometimes cynical and interested, was at least very far from being bellicose. It was ready, as one of her Ministers jestingly said, to 'hold back by the coat-tails if necessary,' any Power likely to go to war. And this fact was at times a potent incentive to peace in the case of France, of Austria-Hungary and of Germany.

Italy hovered halfway between the Triple Entente and the Austro-German Alliance. The Central Powers presented a problem different from that in France and in Great Britain. For in Austria-Hungary and in Germany, as in Russia, military policy was not dependent upon parliamentary vote. In Germany the quotas of each state were part of the constitution and only additions or increases needed to come before the Reichstag.[1] The army was not in fact a parliamentary matter either in Germany or in Austria or in Hungary. It was therefore possible for Germany and Austria-Hungary to agree together on a military policy, which they could rely on being systematically carried out for a long period ahead. No such steady or consistent policy could be expected from the unstable and shifting parliamentarism of France or the party-ridden legislature of England. The Central Powers had in military affairs the advantage of unity in design and of constancy in pursuit. The difficulty in Germany was to stop an armament programme once begun, the difficulty in England was to execute it. The General Staff, or the chief military and naval authorities, were consequently much more important factors in the Austro-German Alliance than in France or in England. They were as powerful as the military leaders in Russia and incomparably more efficient.

The situation of Germany was very singular, particularly after the accession of William II in 1888. The German Empire was well established, Prussia was subservient to her King, the bureaucracy was intelligent, clean and pure. The people as a whole were docile and obedient to their rulers. Social organisation, as regards health and protection to workers, and particularly technical education, had been carried to a very high point, and the civic spirit showed itself in public works and in great municipal enterprises. It cannot be denied, however, that there was a surprising amount of social and political discontent. Social Democracy increased steadily, and the newspapers everywhere voiced the irritation of the public at the tireless labour and mechanical perfections of their internal government. Germany was a State controlled by officials and police rather than a nation formed of political men. The people feared political responsibility yet attacked those who assumed it. And the Government was much alarmed by this irresponsible and largely unreal criticism. Even the patriotism of the German, though deep and sincere, had a strongly flamboyant tinge. The nation consciously

[1] Money had to be voted, however, in the Reichstag for all naval and colonial expenses.

vaunted its victories, displayed its strength, and boasted about its self-sacrifice and devotion. The army, magnificent and ready as it was, claimed all the privileges of a military caste and showed insolence and disdain to civilians. No proposals for disarmament were ever seriously considered in Germany and the Government steadily opposed pacifist tendencies.

Had William II been a Frederick the Great he would have known, like him, how 'to move millions with inhuman harmony.' He could have forced their energies in almost any direction that he chose, and commanded their unquestioning allegiance. But harmony could only be secured if the purpose of the ruler was steady, unremitting, remorseless and fixed. Such a purpose was wholly lacking in the fickle, brilliant and easily swayed Kaiser. His religion, though sincere, led him towards absolutism. Yet he had much fear of the people, and assiduously courted them. At heart perhaps pacific, his reckless and impulsive public praise of his army and of war, his amazing private indiscretions to foreign diplomats, frequently produced the worst impressions and led to situations full of danger. He would always be a hero to himself and did not like contradiction or opposition in others. His admirers compared him (with his knowledge) to Siegfried or to Achilles, and his nostrils snuffed the incense of a truly Byzantine flattery. His nerves were unequal to a crisis as was shown in 1908, when the storm of wrath that arose against him for his *Daily Telegraph* indiscretion made him speak of abdicating and reduced him to a state of pitiable collapse.

The personal character of the Kaiser was a factor of very real political and international importance. For the German (and Prussian) system could only work if the nominal ruler was also the real one. The Chancellor and the Foreign Minister were not responsible to the Reichstag, and the General Staff and the Admiralty, embodied in Tirpitz, were directly dependent on the Kaiser. But the reins were never firmly grasped in the first decade after Bismarck's fall. The Chancellors were Count Caprivi and Prince Hohenlohe, the one being too much of a soldier and the other too much of a greybeard to exercise real power. Yet the Kaiser gave no consistent direction then or later.

Bülow, who succeeded Hohenlohe in 1900, offered the Foreign Office to Holstein,[1] who haughtily refused it. This sinister mystery-man planned countless diplomatic intrigues and inspired endless articles in the Press from the recesses of the Foreign Office, sitting in what Caprivi called his 'poison-shop.' His power was great, and he was able at times to overawe the Foreign Minister or Chancellor of the moment and to hoodwink or obstruct his imperial master. He spoke of the Kaiser as mad or as a fool to other Foreign Office officials, who retaliated by calling him a 'mad hyena' in private but did not dare oppose him to his face. He wrote out the draft of an imperial speech or

[1] There is an interesting article on Holstein in G. P. Gooch: *Studies in German History*, pp. 391–511 (Longmans, 1948).

interviewed a foreign ambassador without consulting the German Foreign Minister. All this the Kaiser knew, for he had warned Bülow against Holstein as far back as 1900. But Bülow feared Holstein because of the press campaigns he might inspire both against himself and against the Kaiser. When he offered to resign he usually got his way, and it was not till 1906 that the Emperor and the Chancellor summoned up courage finally to accept one of his often proffered resignations. Most of the bad decisions on foreign policy in the period were due to him, notably the refusal to accept England's overtures in 1898 and 1901, and the bellicose and undiplomatic attitude over Morocco in 1905 and till his dismissal in 1906.

Bülow was succeeded as Chancellor by Bethmann-Hollweg in 1909. Bethmann was a remarkable choice, for he had no experience of diplomacy and was called upon to handle at once diplomatic cases difficult and delicate enough to have perplexed Bismarck. He had a reputation for earnestness and sincerity, but he found it hard to impose his will either on the Kaiser, on the General Staff, on the turbulent Tirpitz at the Admiralty, or even on the boisterous Kiderlen Wächter at the Foreign Office. He says indeed in his *Memoirs*, pathetically enough, that he could do little for peace, as the two great lines of policy were fixed. He could do little to reduce the naval programme, for Tirpitz knew how to work the press and, whenever such attempts were made, the public always supported the Admiral, and the unchecked fleet building antagonised England. Similarly Germany had her eye on the Near East and the Baghdad railway and her friendship with Turkey antagonised Russia. Plainly in Bethmann's view it was the combination of naval armaments and Baghdad railway which united England with Russia and against Germany.

The building of the Baghdad railway, once begun, was certainly not easy to abandon. But the naval programme was a different matter. It is described in more detail elsewhere, but a few general remarks will be appropriate here. On the face of it Germany had as much right to build a fleet as any other nation, for she had colonies and seaborne commerce to protect. The principle was laid down in the memorandum to the German Navy Bill of 1900. 'Germany must have a battle fleet so strong that even the adversary possessed of the greatest sea power will attack it only with grave risk to herself.' The views of Tirpitz, the chief director of German naval policy, are not easy to fathom. Sometimes he speaks of possible aggression, sometimes of defence only, as the naval aim of Germany. Lord Haldane says Tirpitz 'would have accepted a two-to-three keel standard,' and adds that 'it would have been enough to enable them [the Germans] to secure allies and to break up the Entente.' [1] Great Britain may have been wrong in thinking this or

---

[1] Lord Haldane: *Before the War*, pp. 138–9 (Cassell, 1920). For Anglo-German naval rivalry, *v.* E. L. Woodward: *Great Britain and the German Navy* (Clar. Press, 1935).

in deciding to maintain a greater superiority in ships than that. But anyone who understood either her Government or her people knew that she would not accept such terms. In so far, therefore, as Anglo-German enmity contributed to the war, it was Germany's naval programme that was the actual cause. On this there seems no question, and there is likewise no question that Tirpitz had prevailed with his ship programme, whoever was Chancellor, ever since his appointment in 1897. The big programmes of 1900 and 1907 were carried through under Bülow, and Bethmann declares he could not stop their further development. Probably they could not have been carried through but for the Kaiser, who intervened more than once in the British negotiations for arresting shipbuilding, and who steadily supported Tirpitz. He seems genuinely to have believed an idea, which he expressed with an elegance foreign to Tirpitz himself, that 'with every new German battleship there was laid down a fresh pledge for peace, the golden.'

While her naval policy was pursued with unwavering persistency, Germany did not make war the aim of her foreign policy. Even after the fall of Holstein in 1906 her policy was full of inconsistencies; it used the language alternately of menace and flattery; it hovered uncertainly between England and Russia, and ultimately it alienated both. But it cannot truly be said that it aimed ultimately at, or worked for, war. Its chief peril lay in the fact that its direction was shared between Kaiser, Chancellor and Foreign Minister, a triplet of uncertainties. It has been well said that one bad general is better than two good ones, and one bad diplomat is certainly better than a trio of masters in diplomacy. Moreover, their only zealous ally constituted a considerable embarrassment to them. Austria-Hungary was too precious to be abandoned and was sometimes in a position to make Germany conform to her views. And the German General Staff, which was well aware of the weakness of Austria-Hungary, was always ready to urge vigour on the Austro-Hungarian General Staff.

Austria-Hungary was a Power in Europe compelled by her situation to form part of the great combinations. At any rate since 1878 Francis Joseph had avoided wars and evidently wished to go down to his grave in peace. He had observed the *Ausgleich* between Austria and Hungary; but he was stronger in the first than in the second. From 1880 onwards he had democratised the institutions of Austria and he finally introduced universal suffrage in 1907. He succeeded in conciliating the Poles of Galicia, but force or the threat of force had at times to be used to Czechs, Slovenes and Italians. None the less his polyglot empire held together, and in some ways his control over it was increasing rather than diminishing in 1914. It was in the Kingdom of Hungary, not in the Empire of Austria, that the difficulties and dangers both of his internal and external policy lay. Though the Magyars often made difficulties about the external aspects of the *Ausgleich*, they always adjusted them before differences became too sharp. But their rule over their subject races was a matter upon which they could take their own line. They could exclude Francis Joseph, a constitutional ruler dependent on a Ministry responsible to the Hungarian Parliament. And this fact was to be fatal to him and to them. The Magyars went on oppressing their subject races, Serbs, Slovenes and Rumans, imprisoning their journalists, suppressing their secondary schools, altering the languages taught in the elementary ones, everywhere and always aiming at denationalising or at 'Magyarising' them. It was here that the danger lay, for just outside Hungary over the Danube lay Serbia, a land of peasant warriors who viewed with indignation the oppression of their brother Serbs in Hungary, and sought by every means to convey sympathy and encouragement to them. The Government of Serbia was not so indiscreet as some of her individual subjects, but up to 1908 they certainly tacitly tolerated this violent propaganda.

Austria-Hungary viewed these manifestations with alarm. Aehrenthal, her Foreign Minister, proposed to make use of forged documents during 1908–9 to implicate Serb politicians within and without Austria-Hungary and thus provide a *casus belli*. Conrad von Hoetzendorf, the Chief of Staff, advised war in 1908 as on most subsequent occasions so as to finish with Serbia altogether. Aehrenthal had hoped that the annexation of Bosnia, which he had so rudely achieved in 1908, would end the Serb agitation. For he had substituted a permanent rule for a previous temporary occupation. He little knew the Serbs, for annexation only added fuel to the flame. And, after the Serb victories in the Balkan War of 1912–13, the flames blazed higher and higher. Conrad, who had been forced to resign his post for advocating war with Italy at the end of 1911, returned to it at the end of 1912 and celebrated his arrival by once more denouncing war against the Serbs. Franz Ferdinand, the heir to Francis Joseph, and Commander-in-Chief, certainly believed war to be inevitable at this moment. And the civilian element seemed at first insufficient to restrain these forces. Aehrenthal had died and been succeeded by Count Berchtold as Foreign Minister, which event meant that a strong, able and ruthless man had been succeeded by a weak, wavering and ignorant one. The old Emperor, however, was still for peace and he was supported from without. Italy and Germany strongly influenced him and Austria-Hungary for peace both at the end of 1912 and in the middle of 1913. The Emperor triumphed over the impetuous Conrad and the pliable Berchtold. But the Pan-Serb agitation went on, and the danger seemed greater at the beginning of 1914 than it had been in 1913. Conrad and Franz Ferdinand were bent on action. Their designs led to civil war within as well as to war without. For they wished to upset the Dual System and the Magyars, break the *Ausgleich* and erect a system of devolution all round, in which the Austrian Emperor would deprive Hungary of her equal status, and again be the centre of power. This could hardly have been attained without bloodshed, but they wished to add to it foreign complications. For they planned an active policy of settlement in Serbia, a settlement which could hardly end in anything but war. The forces were working against the old Emperor. The civilians, Berchtold the Foreign Minister and Tisza, Hungary's Premier, moved slower than Conrad, but they moved. All hope of reconciliation with Serbia had definitely been abandoned, and it was decided to bring her to book. Whether this was to be accomplished by war was perhaps at first doubted, but, as the action proposed was to be 'timely and energetic,' that makes very little difference. The risks of war were certainly to be run. Austria-Hungary was traditionally a 'timid' Power, and according to Gibbon 'the timid are always cruel.' Certainly they sometimes become desperate and make resolves under the influence of fear, and they did so in 1914. All through May and June Berchtold laboured at an exposé of future Austro-Hungarian policy. He finally finished it on the 24th June. Only four days later Franz Ferdinand was assassinated at Sarajevo by a Bosnian Serb who had hatched the plot at Belgrade. After June 28 all hope seems to have disappeared in Vienna. Conrad at last prevailed and Berchtold came over completely to his view. And at this crisis Germany, which had prevailed in keeping the peace a year before, offered Berchtold and Tisza a blank cheque. Even yet Berchtold had the old Emperor Francis Joseph to convince, and his stubborn resistance was at last overcome by discreditable means. One inducement was that he knew he would have Germany's support, and the reason for this was published to the world just as war broke out.

'. . . it was clear to Austria that it was not compatible with the dignity and the spirit of self-preservation of the monarchy to view idly any longer this [Serbian] agitation across the border. The Imperial and Royal Government apprised Germany of this conception and asked for our opinion. With all our heart we were able to agree with our ally's estimate of the situation, and assure him that any action considered necessary to end the movement in Servia directed against the conservation of the monarchy would meet with our approval.

'We were perfectly aware that a possible warlike attitude of Austria-Hungary against Servia might bring Russia upon the field, and that it might therefore involve us in a war, in accordance with our duty as allies. We could not, however, in these vital interests of Austria-Hungary, which were at stake, advise our ally to take a yielding attitude not compatible with his dignity, nor deny him our assistance in these trying days. We could do this all the less as our own interests were menaced through the continued Serb agitation. If the Serbs continued with the aid of Russia and France to menace the existence of Austria-Hungary, the gradual collapse of Austria and the subjection of all the Slavs under one Russian sceptre would be the consequence, thus making untenable the position of the Teutonic race in Central Europe. A morally weakened Austria under the pressure of Russian pan-slavism would be no longer an ally on whom we could count and in whom we

12

could have confidence, as we must be able to have, in view of the ever more menacing attitude of our easterly and westerly neighbours. We, therefore, permitted Austria a completely free hand in her action towards Servia, but have not participated in her preparations.' [1]

If this German utterance is to be accepted, it would mean that Serbia alone was the cause of the war. And we should have proof of the suggestion made earlier in this chapter, that the action or tendencies of one Power (and that a small one) could embroil all Europe. Obviously the matter is not as simple as that. For the real cause of Serbian agitation was that the independent part of her race resented the fact that two-thirds of their blood brothers were being oppressed by Austria-Hungary. Two states, and not one, were thus really involved. But the reason why a civilised state comprising fifty millions of men feared the agitation or hostility of one comprising only four is interesting. It was because other states had joined one or other of the contending groups, and the quarrels of two states involved all the Great Powers and three-quarters of Europe. France, dreaming of Alsace-Lorraine, had bound herself to Russia. Germany fearing both had joined with Austria-Hungary. England, disliking Germany's naval programme, had drawn close to Russia and to France. A series of antagonisms between pairs of states, none of them necessarily formidable in themselves, had divided Europe into hostile camps, and each great armed group watched the other with suspicion, till finally 'the guns went off by themselves.' The fact of the matter is that it was not the separate characteristics of each individual Power alone that were important, but their conjunction and inter-mingling with the vaster streams of European movement. Accordingly the next two chapters will show how the grouping of the Great Powers led from one difficulty to another, until all localisation of a conflict between two nations became impossible. For the principle of fear dominated the politics of individual states and of collective groups alike.

CHAPTER XXVII

THE THREE CRISES—ALGECIRAS—BOSNIA—AGADIR—1906–11

The International Conference on Morocco did not meet until 1906. And, as is often the case in Conferences, some preliminary agreement was reached before it met. France had agreed to the Conference and to the integrity of Morocco. Germany had accepted the public clauses of the Entente Agreement. Both parties had agreed to a scheme of reforms, which included an internationally organised police for

---

[1] *v.* German White Book, published on August 1, 1914. *Collected Diplomatic Documents* (1915), p. 406.

Morocco except on the side adjacent to French Algeria. Morocco was to have a State-Bank and not to have her public services worked to the advantage of any particular interest or nationality. Nevertheless the attitude of Germany appeared so menacing early in 1906 that Sir Edward Grey authorised conversations between French and British naval and military experts,[1] on the clear understanding 'that these conversations or plans . . . did not commit either Government, and involved no promise of support in war.'

The Conference met at Algeciras on January 16, and consisted of the representatives of twelve states. It soon became a diplomatic struggle between France and Germany. Throughout, France was steadily and openly supported by her old ally Russia, by her new friend England, by her neighbour Spain. She received more concealed but no less effective support from President Roosevelt, on behalf of the United States. Italy, already pledged by her neutrality treaty to France, really supported her and not her ally Germany. The Kaiser showed that he understood this, for he sent a telegram to the Austro-Hungarian Foreign Minister after the Conference, thanking him for having proved 'a brilliant second on the duelling ground' and suggesting that he would do so again. The implication was that Germany could not trust Italy, but could trust Austria-Hungary. In fact, however, even 'the brilliant second's' support of Germany at the Conference was lukewarm. It was somewhat of the Bob Acres type, for the second's courage had oozed as the duel approached.

Germany's aim at the Conference seems to have been to get the Moroccan police officered from the Minor Powers, or to permit the Sultan freely to choose his own police. In any case she wished to prevent France from organising them. After much discussion she did finally agree to entrust the police jointly to a Franco-Spanish *personnel* under a Swiss Inspector-General. In this all-important question of police France really triumphed, for she secured the predominant share of the control and excluded Germany and her Allies from it altogether. In a barbarous and disturbed area the police control was likely to be the lever of power.

As regards financial control and commercial opportunity Germany had more success. A State-Bank practically under the Four Powers— France, England, Germany and Spain—was created, with equal opportunities for each nation. There was, however, an ominous clause that the regulation of the Customs Act and of the traffic in arms was to be undertaken by France in conjunction with Morocco on the Algerian frontier, and by Spain and Morocco on the Riff frontier. While Germany had, therefore, established the theoretical principle that Morocco concerned all Powers equally, France had practically safeguarded her

---

[1] There was a similar series of discussions between British and Belgian military experts. For both series *v. Gooch and Temperley*, vol. III. pp. 169–203; also Grey: *Twenty-Five Years*, vol. I. pp. 69–93.

individual action in future. Germany had, in effect, been opposed by every one, except perhaps Austria-Hungary, and she had failed to obtain more than lip service to her demands. The 'peaceful penetration' of Morocco by France could be undertaken by that Power at once, and 'peaceful penetration' might change insensibly into aggression. If Germany wished to interfere, she could not do so again at a Conference with any hope of success, for she would be outvoted. She could only interfere by force, and that meant war. So Algeciras marked a stage, which meant that Germany was more isolated than before. There was another interesting little development. The fact that French and British soldiers and sailors had begun to discuss together contingent plans meant very little. The discussions of such experts are sometimes rash, sometimes vague, sometimes technical, sometimes hypothetical. But the fact that the civil authorities had *authorised* such discussions meant a good deal, for it meant that politicians viewed a war with a German army on one side and a Franco-British army on the other as a distinct possibility. This was a step, says Mr. Churchill, 'of profound significance and of far-reaching reactions . . . However explicitly the two Governments might agree and affirm to each other that no national or political engagement was involved in these technical discussions, the fact remained that they constituted an exceedingly potent tie.' [1] In 1901 England had offered an alliance to Germany; in 1904 she had settled her difficulties with France; in 1906 she was discussing possible measures of war with her against Germany. So events were moving, and more rapidly than the brains of diplomatists.

The last link in the chain of British engagements was to be Russia. It was difficult to annul suspicions on either side. For half a century Russia had been looked on as the Colossus moving slowly and irresistibly upon India. Her conduct in China had more recently been open to grave suspicion, and England had taken several anti-Russian measures of late. She had made an Anglo-German Agreement about China in August 1900, and a Japanese Alliance in 1902, which she renewed in 1905 in what seemed a more anti-Russian form. In 1903 England had shown she intended to exclude foreign warships from the Persian Gulf and in 1905 she had undertaken an expedition to Tibet with the object of substituting her own for Russian influence there. On May 11, 1905, Mr. Balfour, as Prime Minister, thought it necessary to warn Russia against further progress in the direction of Afghanistan and of the North-Western frontier of India. As has already been indicated the Kaiser took advantage of the various incidents of the Russo-Japanese war to inflame Russia's feelings against England and to offer her his help. Even as early as October 1904, the Kaiser was suggesting to the Czar that a League of Russia, Germany, and France should combine against England. And the Czar, who had just heard of the British feeling in the Dogger Bank incident, answered that he would like a draft

[1] Winston Churchill: *World Crisis* (1931 Edn.), p. 35.

treaty sketching such a League 'to abolish English and Japanese arrogance and insolence.' The Kaiser sent off a treaty at once, but the Czar then suggested that France should be consulted before it was signed. The Kaiser held up his hands in horror and the negotiation slackened. But the Kaiser managed to get an exchange of notes by December 12, 1904, by which Germany agreed to coal the Russian fleet, on condition that Russia 'stood by' her in case of England's interference on the ground that such coaling was an unneutral act.

In June 1905 negotiations for peace began between Japan and Russia, which ended in the Treaty of Portsmouth (5 September 1905). And in July the brilliant and impulsive Kaiser achieved what he considered a master-stroke. He paid a surprise visit in his yacht to the Czar's yacht at Björkö (July 24). There next day he persuaded the impressionable Czar, who had no political adviser with him, to sign a treaty 'before God, who heard our vows,' as the Kaiser afterwards said.[1] The Kaiser wrote that he felt a moisture all over him and saw the hand of God in this achievement. 'July 24,' said he, 'is a cornerstone in European history and a great easing of my dear country's situation.' This astounding treaty contained four provisions. First, each state promised to join the other 'with all its forces' if attacked by any European state. Second, neither would conclude a separate peace. Third, the treaty came into force on conclusion of peace with Japan and a year's notice was necessary for cancellation. Fourthly, Russia was to make its terms known to France and invite her to sign it as an ally.

This treaty, described by the Kaiser as 'a Continental combine'—'to block the way to the whole world becoming John Bull's private property' would indeed have been a triumph. It would have compelled France either to obey Germany or to abandon Russia, and have isolated England completely. But Russian statesmen were not quite mad, and soon made it clear to the Czar that Russia's ally France could not be treated thus. Even Witte, who was at first inclined to favour it, said that the pact was absurd. He became Prime Minister on October 20, 1905, and at once assumed a correct official attitude. The Czar wrote formally to the Kaiser through the ordinary official channels, and the Russian Ambassador at Berlin took the attitude, under instruction, that the treaty was inoperative as it contravened the Dual Alliance, and that France must agree to any revision of the latter. It took the Kaiser some time to realise that his plan though as brilliant as a soap bubble, was also as frail, and destined to the fate of all bubbles.

The poor feeble Czar had had a thorough lesson not to outrun his Ministers or to do anything against the French Alliance. For he now incurred new obligations. Early in 1906 France laid Russia under an obligation by raising on her account the largest foreign loan then known to the world. This enabled Nicholas II to set the Duma (his new

---

[1] Two officials—one German, one Russian, countersigned as witnesses but did not read the treaty. *Grosse Politik*, vol. 19, pp 458–65.

Parliament) at defiance in July and to dissolve it, and the service was not forgotten.

The influence of Russia at Algeciras in 1906 was exercised against Germany, as was that of England. Friendly feelings between England and Russia were thus fostered and soon bore fruit. And just at this moment the question of the Baghdad railway became acute and involved Germany and Russia. Lord Salisbury, when he heard of the suggested British share in the Baghdad railway, is said to have remarked, 'Anyone who has a share in that railway will have trouble with Russia. I propose to keep England out of it and to let Germany have the trouble.' This story, whether true or not, represents exactly what happened. Early in 1907 Russian Ministers had the good sense to recognise that the Baghdad railway had got too far for them to oppose Germany over it. But they bore Germany ill-will for promoting it, and gave England credit for standing aloof. While they came to no agreement with Germany even over this special point till 1910, they made a general agreement with England as to all outstanding difficulties in 1907. The chief one concerned Persia, and over that a convention was signed at St. Petersburg on the 31st August.

The object of this convention was stated to be the maintenance of the integrity and independence of Persia. In view of the fact that Russia appropriated a large zone to the North-West and England another to the East, this appeared optimistic. And, in fact, this agreement confined the really independent Persia (who was not consulted) within much narrower limits than before. It might perhaps be argued that England consented to a partial division in the hope of securing the real independence of the remainder and of acting as a drag on Russian aggression. But England was singularly unfortunate about this time in restraining the aggression of those with whom she signed agreements. She signed an agreement in 1902 and saw Japan at war with Russia in 1904; she signed one with France in 1904 and saw war threatened with Germany twice within two years; she now signed an agreement with Russia and saw the independence of Persia threatened in three or four years. The fact is that, when England emerged from her 'splendid isolation,' she necessarily encouraged the three Powers with whom she signed agreements to pursue their own ends. For the agreements were bound at least to remove the danger of British opposition. One thing is quite certain. England may have been, and probably was, honest in her desire to preserve the new *status quo* in Persia, but Russia was certainly dishonest. Every attempt to improve the status of the independent part of Persia met with her opposition and every attempt was made by her to penetrate into North-West Persia and to create pretexts for annexing it. Sir Edward Grey was obliged in the next few years to look on helplessly while Russia pursued her dark and dangerous intrigues against England's honour and Persia's integrity. A caricaturist pictured Sir Edward Grey in the embrace of the Russian bear, with a puzzled look on his face, as if wondering whether the caress would be changed to a hug.

The immediate results were very successful. Already on June 10, France had signed a treaty with Japan guaranteeing the integrity and independence of China, and a similar guarantee-treaty was signed between Russia and Japan on July 30. Defeated by Japan, and bribed by the hope of England's aid, Russia thus gave up her ambitions in China. She had already abandoned her ambitious designs in Afghanistan and confined them to North-West Persia, where the deserts of the centre separated her widely from British influence. Russia then was no longer dangerous to China or to India. Did this mean that she had abandoned her design of playing a great part in the world? By no means, but she had determined to play that part in an area where she would not have to meet England or Japan. It was on Constantinople that Russia once more fixed her gaze. If she had to meet Germany there, she did not expect to be alone.

Every year from 1878 onwards some sharp-eyed journalist or politician had foretold 'war in the Balkans in the spring.' After thirty years of false prophecies they were within an ace of being right in 1909. The Balkans had given Europe a good deal of trouble after 1878, and for obvious reasons. Bulgaria had refused to accept the influence or direction of Russia almost at once, and Serbia, which had tamely accepted vassalage under Austria, revolted at the turn of the century. The estrangement was confirmed when Peter, the head of a new dynasty, came to the throne on the murder of the last Obrenovič in 1903. The balance was altered in the Balkans. Rumania was pro-German and pro-Austrian, but Bulgaria, Serbia and Montenegro were all pro-Russian. And in 1903 Turkey in Europe seemed to be fast breaking up. Macedonia was worse governed than ever and Abdul Hamid was getting old and losing his grip. In 1897 Austria-Hungary and Russia had agreed on maintaining the *status quo* in the Balkans and on doing their mutual best to keep the peace and avoid raising difficulties. This pledge was renewed by what was known as the 'Mürzsteg Punctation' between Russia and Austria-Hungary on October 2, 1903, to meet a new situation. A revolt had broken out in Macedonia, followed by the usual massacres, and Great Britain had taken an active interest. Russia and Austria-Hungary finally secured the consent of the Great Powers to the creation of an international gendarmerie in Macedonia.[1] It was followed early in 1905 by efforts of Lord Lansdowne to secure a more effective collection of taxes under international supervision. Neither of these reforms worked without friction but both resulted in much

---

[1] It is significant that, though under this scheme all the other Great Powers controlled gendarmerie zones in Macedonia, Germany declined to undertake a zone.

good to the inhabitants and were accepted by both Austria-Hungary and Russia. But towards the end of 1907 both opposed Sir Edward Grey's attempt to increase the efficiency of the gendarmerie; and Germany flatly refused to help.

In January 1908 the harmony between Austria-Hungary and Russia over Balkan affairs, which had endured for a decade, was rudely disturbed. Aehrenthal—the masterful new Foreign Minister of Austria-Hungary—suddenly announced that he meant to build a railway through the Sanjak of Novibazar, to connect up with the Turkish terminus at Mitrovica. Vienna would thus be united by direct railway communication with Salonica, and Montenegro more than ever separated from Serbia. As a matter of fact the plan was crude to a degree and, because of its engineering difficulties, impracticable, but the spirit of aggression was evident. Izvolsky—Russia's new Foreign Minister—made a counter-proposal of a railway from the eastern boundary of Serbia on the Danube to San Giovanni di Medua in Albania. So a veiled Austro-Hungarian railway advance on Salonica was to be met by a veiled Russian railway advance through Serbia and Albania. Aehrenthal eventually accepted Izvolsky's counter-proposal, but neither railway was ever built. Had they been, war between Austria-Hungary and Russia could hardly have failed to ensue. But the really serious matter was, as Izvolsky complained, that Austria-Hungary had broken the agreement reached with Russia in 1897, which had been confirmed by that of Mürzsteg in 1903.

It was particularly unfortunate for the peace of Europe that Austria-Hungary's bold step forward came six months after the Anglo-Russian *rapprochement*, and naturally increased it. When King Edward paid a long overdue visit to Czar Nicholas at Reval the demonstrations of Anglo-Russian cordiality excited German and Austro-Hungarian anxiety. Bülow was assured that the Anglo-Russian Conventions of 1907 had not been directed against German interests. But both Bülow and the Kaiser made speeches suggesting that Germany was encircled on all sides and would have to defend herself. And these speeches were received with great applause.

Just at this critical moment the Turkish revolution occurred, and was certainly hastened by Turkish fear of an Anglo-Russian Entente. A secret Committee of Union and Progress (the 'Young Turks') had long been planning revolt among the officers of the Turkish army. And early in July Niazi and Enver Bey raised the standard of revolt against Sultan Abdul Hamid and proclaimed the Constitution. The hitherto invincible tyrant collapsed with hardly a struggle and professed (as he had once done before) that he would become the mildest of constitutional kings. The able soldiers, who had engineered the revolt, were profuse in professions of liberality. All Christian peoples—Greeks, Serbs, and Bulgars—were to be free under the Turkish flag and to fraternise with the Mohammedans. So monstrous and insupportable had been the tyranny of Abdul that for a time these professions were believed. Greek popes kissed Turkish dervishes, Serbs fraternised with Bulgars, and both walked in procession with Turks. The Great Powers at once seized the opportunity to abandon all Macedonian reforms, on the pretext that the 'Young Turks' were liberals and could manage their own affairs. It is improbable that even the Great Powers believed in this delusion,[1] for the 'Young Turks' proved to be as ruthless and as militaristic as Abdul Hamid, and incomparably more efficient. Their professed liberalism proved to be a mere sham, which they discarded at the first opportunity. Austria-Hungary at any rate, among the Great Powers, soon showed that she intended to exploit the 'Young Turkish' movement to her advantage, and Germany was not far behind her.

In April Izvolsky had begun some very curious negotiations with Aehrenthal, and had made a definite proposal at the end of July; that is, just after the Anglo-Russian meeting at Reval. He proposed, in short, to let Austria-Hungary annex Bosnia, Herzegovina, and the Sanjak if she would support the opening of the Straits of Constantinople to Russian warships. Aehrenthal appears to have assented in principle, and even got Germany and Italy to do so.[2] The negotiations were carried further in September, when Izvolsky stipulated for a European Conference, and Aehrenthal informed him that he meant to annex Bosnia early in October.[3]

Aehrenthal, who was a bold and determined man, resolved to strike as soon as he could, and to make assurance doubly sure invited Ferdinand—the Prince of Bulgaria—to Vienna. As he was received with great distinction and was a sufficiently artful person, quick to catch and to act upon a hint, there seems no reason to doubt that what happened in the first week of October was, in effect though not in name, a concerted movement. At any rate on October 5 Ferdinand threw off the suzerainty of the Sultan, and proclaimed himself King or Czar of an independent Bulgaria. The Austrian Emperor followed this up on October 7 by a proclamation to the effect that Bosnia-Herzegovina, which had been temporarily occupied since 1878, were now formally detached from the sovereignty of the Sultan and annexed to Austria-Hungary.[4]

These announcements came like a thunder-clap. They were unknown to, and apparently unsuspected by, England or France. They took

[1] The real reason was that the International control in Macedonia caused quarrels between the Great Powers.

[2] It was stipulated, however, that Constantinople should not be attacked and that the Straits should also be free to Rumanian and Bulgarian warships.

[3] There is much dispute on both sides—and Izvolsky's conduct was certainly tricky. He did not inform his ally or England of his negotiation at the time, doubtless scenting difficulties with both over the Straits. But it seems hard to resist the impression that he genuinely believed that Aehrenthal would support him over the Straits.

[4] Austria-Hungary, however, offered to withdraw, and did withdraw from her military occupation of the Sanjak, which had lasted since 1878. This was due to pressure from Italy.

12*

Izvolsky by surprise in some sense, they aroused a profound emotion in Serbia. In public Izvolsky spoke violently and demanded a European Conference, where he hoped doubtless to obtain assent to the free passage of Russia's warships through the Straits as compensation for Austria-Hungary's annexation of Bosnia. He was in England on October 9, and seems to have pressed this view upon Sir Edward Grey. Unfortunately for England, both now and later, her Foreign Minister understood very little of the Near East. At this time he seems to have been shocked by both Austro-Hungarian and Bulgarian actions, on the ground that they were breaches of the Treaty of Berlin of 1878. These they unquestionably were, but there had previously been half a dozen breaches of that agreement with the express or implied sanction of Great Britain, and several had been sanctioned without a European Conference. Was it worth submitting to a Conference a further breach, already approved in principle by Italy and Germany as well as by Austria-Hungary and, in some sense, by Russia herself?[1] Probably Sir Edward was ignorant of the facts of the case. At any rate, on October 7, before he saw Izvolsky, Grey announced in a speech that he meant to demand a European Conference to sanction this breach of engagement. After he had seen Izvolsky on the 13th, it was publicly announced that England and Russia were agreed in demanding a Conference. But Grey was not in a position to promise Izvolsky the revision of the Straits clause. For he could not sanction a further breach of the Treaty of Berlin until the Conference met.[2] As he also 'advised reconsideration' to Austria-Hungary it is plain that he hoped at this stage that she would return upon her steps, and thus avoid a Conference and therewith any question of 'compensation' to Russia. Izvolsky thus paid the penalty for not having consulted his friends beforehand.

England and Russia were partially at variance, and France was not anxious to go to war to support Russia in a matter on which she had not even been consulted. Aehrenthal judged the situation with brutal realism. The Franco-Russian Alliance was unlikely to fight; Germany had given him promise of support. Even in October Aehrenthal had made it clear that he would not go into a Conference unless it was understood beforehand that it was only held to sanction the *fait accompli* of the annexation. On December 25 Izvolsky had to explain himself in a speech to the Duma and he was anything but warlike. England, indeed, seemed more resolute than France or Russia but, as Aehrenthal remarked, 'What *can* England do to us?'

Aehrenthal thus made it quite plain that no useful purpose would be

---

[1] In the protocols to the *Dreikaiserbund* Treaty of June 18, 1881, Germany and Russia had agreed to Austria-Hungary's annexing Bosnia whenever she chose—and Italy was at any rate at a later stage cognisant of this and approved, provided Austria-Hungary evacuated Novibazar. *v.* Pribram: *Secret Treaties*, vol. I. p. 43.

[2] In a guarded reply to Izvolsky of October 14, 1908, Grey said that the Straits must be open to all nations, and Turkey's consent obtained. He also deprecated any action at the moment. *v. Gooch and Temperley*, vol. V. p. 441.

served by a Conference, and also that he was not likely to support Russia's claims to the Straits. Having done that, he finally offered a solution which did something 'to save the face' of the Powers demanding a Conference. He offered to pay two and a half million pounds compensation to the Sultan for the loss of his crown property in Bosnia. Bulgaria also arranged to compensate Turkey for her loss of sovereignty by paying five million pounds as her share of the Oriental railway. At this point—and at this point only—Izvolsky intervened with effect. He offered to pay for this to Turkey by remitting the same amount of Turkish unpaid war indemnity to Russia. He thus established a strong claim on the gratitude of Bulgaria. A secret pact between the two Powers had already been signed in 1902, and the closeness of their relations at this period is shown by the frequent rumours of new secret treaties.

England and Russia had been defeated in their desire for a Conference, Turkey had been compensated, Bulgaria cajoled, Serbia remained unappeased and resentful. One small state, solitary and scowling, was to cause a great commotion. The situation was extraordinary. Serbia like Bulgaria had recently become a satellite in the wake of the Russian planet. But Serbia felt that not only had she not done a wrong to Turkey like Bulgaria, but that she had received one from Austria-Hungary. For in 1878 Austria-Hungary had been allowed to occupy Bosnia and Herzegovina, a country identical in blood and speech with the Serbs.[1] The blow to Serbia had been softened by the word 'occupation,' which was of Turkish territory and thus might be temporary. 'Annexation' by Austria-Hungary meant a permanent alienation of a million Serbs from their mother country. They were now to be united to the five millions of Serbo-Croats already under Austrian or Hungarian rule. There was already a gigantic Alsace-Lorraine within the Austro-Hungarian dominions, now a new 'unredeemed' area was permanently added. The hot Serbian blood boiled to think that the Great Powers thus conspired to rob Serbia of her future and Serbs of their birthright. The Great Powers knew and cared very little about the matter. Even Izvolsky told the Serb representative in Paris that it was a gain that Austria-Hungary had evacuated the Sanjak, for such evacuation blocked her ultimate advance to Salonica. As if that compensated the Serbs for the loss of their great dream of uniting all Serbs beneath one throne and one flag!

The impassioned patriotism of the Serb constituted the chief danger to European peace. The agitation, which exceeded all bounds, was led by George, the vain and foolish Crown Prince of Serbia. A visit to St. Petersburg in the winter of 1908–9 did not cool his ardour, and his return lashed the people and press of Serbia to further transports.

---

[1] Even the Mohammedans or 'Turks' of these provinces spoke Serb and were Serb in blood. On the other hand the 'Turks' of Novibazar were real Mohammedans of Turkish or Albanian speech and blood.

Pictures were published showing the Crown Prince in the character of St. George plunging his sword into the Austro-Hungarian dragon, its coils relaxed in agony, to liberate the two fair maidens—Bosnia and Herzegovina—at the touch of the sword of this singular saint. The press compared him to Napoleon and suggested that one George had freed them from the Turks, and that his namesake and descendant would free them from the Hapsburgs.

Against these frantic and Chauvinistic outbursts the soberer element in Serbia, headed by King Peter, could for a long time do very little. When the Great Powers acquainted her with their proposals, Serbia replied by a clever note in which she demanded compensation. She thus put the Powers in the position of having to put pressure on a small state and, as that state was a Slav one, Russia at any rate would find the task a hard one.

On March 17, in order to solve the difficulty, the German Government proposed to the Russian that Aehrenthal should announce to the world that Turkey had accepted his annexation proposal. It also suggested that the Powers, instead of meeting in a Conference, should exchange notes recognising the whole transaction. Izvolsky gave an evasive reply, and, on March 21, Prince Bülow instructed his representative at St. Petersburg to demand a categorical answer to the previous proposal, thus in fact presenting an ultimatum. Izvolsky was then compelled to accept the annexation, though he still suggested a Conference. Russia was thus coerced by a not very carefully veiled threat of war. Bülow then at once circularised the Great Powers asking them to recognise the annexation, as Russia and Germany had now done. Izvolsky's humiliating surrender was made public. France and Italy accepted, somewhat under protest, the German proposal, but Sir Edward Grey still declared that recognition of annexation must follow, and not precede, an Austro-Hungarian settlement with Serbia. Everything thus now depended on Serbia.

The attitude of Serbia had already caused serious alarm in Austria-Hungary. The Emperor Francis Joseph was throughout for peace. But Franz Ferdinand, the heir to the throne and the Commander-in-Chief, was inclined to agree with Conrad, the Chief of Staff, who urged this as a favourable moment to stamp out this nest of vipers at their borders, and who declared that they would have to fight Serbia soon anyhow, and that the longer they waited, the more unfortunate would be the results. At the last moment, more peaceful counsels prevailed. Franz Ferdinand announced in the papers that he was not in favour of war, and Aehrenthal was induced by England to delay his ultimatum until the end of March. In Serbia itself a profound emotion was caused by the publication of Izvolsky's surrender to Germany, and an angry mob broke the windows of the Russian Embassy. The war party in Serbia had received a great blow and, under its stress, the Crown Prince announced that he abdicated his claim to succeed his father (March 28).

King Peter thereupon put pressure on his advisers, who sent a satisfactory note to Aehrenthal. Serbia admitted that the annexation of Bosnia did not infringe her rights; agreed to reduce her army to the level of 1908; and promised to accept the situation, to abstain from provocative propaganda within the dominions of Austria-Hungary, and to live on neighbourly terms with her.

The crisis thus ended, but it had deeply shaken the existing European system. Sir Edward Grey had strongly insisted upon two points, the sanctity of treaties, and the necessity of calling a European Conference to sanction the breach of any treaty. His views did not find much favour, but they are a noticeable anticipation of England's resistance to the German suggestion that a treaty was a 'scrap of paper.' The next important point is that the Austro-German combination had won a victory over the Triple Entente of Russia, France and England. A year later the German Emperor boasted of how Austria-Hungary had been helped by a loyal ally taking his stand at her side 'in shining armour at a grave moment.' He seemed to be gloating over Russia's humiliation. Both the action and the speech were intensely mortifying to Russia, and Russian statesmen and generals resolved to make Russia too strong to submit to any such humiliation again. Izvolsky in particular became the unsleeping enemy of Germany whether he was at St. Petersburg or Paris.[1] The manner of the defeat of the Triple Entente brought war a distinct stage nearer. Germany had been rebuffed at Algeciras after mutterings of war; Russia was defeated over Bosnia, because the sabre had been definitely rattled by Germany. If the Triple Entente and the Austro-German Alliance engaged in a diplomatic duel again, war was now more likely because the antagonists had learnt to dislike one another.

No one at the time would have said that the relations of Austria-Hungary to Serbia were anything like so important as those of the Great Powers to one another. Yet, if long views are taken, this may actually have been the case. Three millions of Serbs stood free and independent in Serbia; across the border were five millions of Croats and Serbs and now a million Bosnians stood waiting to be freed from the Hapsburg yoke. At the moment of the crisis, when he thought war with Serbia certain, Aehrenthal had made use of some documents, forged in the Austro-Hungarian Legation at Belgrade, to accuse some Serbo-Croat politicians in Austria-Hungary of conspiracy with the Serbs of Serbia. Their trial, with its shameful revelations of how Austro-Hungarian diplomats had acted as forgers, took place at Vienna in 1909, and served as an advertisement at once of Yugo-Slav unity and of Hapsburg credulity and trickery. Even had they wished, the Serbian Government could not now have stopped the Yugo-Slav propaganda inside Serbia, or its ramifications in Bosnia, in Dalmatia and in Croatia. The irredentist

[1] He was succeeded by Sazonov at the Foreign Office in 1910 and left to become Russian Ambassador at Paris.

propaganda went on, the leavening and the fermentation continued, and Austria-Hungary grew more and more alarmed at its growth. But neither the Great Powers nor Austria-Hungary had any thought in 1908 of how dangerous and explosive may be the result of disregarding the feelings or national aspirations of any people however small. They knew better in 1914, when the seed sown by the Bosnian annexation had grown like the prophet's gourd, and when Austria-Hungary staked her existence on annihilating Pan-Serb and Yugo-Slav propaganda at their heart and centre—the Kingdom of Serbia.

Germany's relations with England became decidedly worse in 1907. That year saw a second Peace Conference at The Hague, which lasted from June to October. A good deal of useful technical work was done at this Conference, but there was no advance whatever in the proposals for limitation of armaments. Towards the end of the Conference the British offered to keep naval armaments at their existing levels and promised to build no more ships, if other Powers agreed. This offer was not unlike that which was successful at the Washington Naval Conference of 1921. It marks the international tension and mutual suspicion that Germany opposed this project with vehemence and success. At the first Hague Conference she had equally opposed Russia's projects of military disarmament. Russia had wished to stop the race of armaments then, because her artillery was weaker: England wished to stop it now because her navy was stronger than the German. So the factors were complex and Germany's position a difficult one. But it seems that, while she could not have accepted both these offers, she might have accepted one of them. She was the only Power before 1914 that always and consistently refused all thought of limiting armaments. There was indeed more danger in accepting offers in 1907 than in 1899. For in 1899 Russia and England were bitter enemies and in 1907 they were negotiating an Entente. What, indeed, independent and neutral observers said about the Conference of 1907 was that the various Powers there seemed to proceed on the assumption that a war between England and Germany was likely, or certain, in the future. Events were evidently developing, for no one could have dreamed of such an assumption in 1899. It is worthy of note that these grave suspicions were entertained when a Liberal Government was in power in England, which was undoubtedly anxious to economise in naval expenditure and to repress jingoistic and imperialistic aspirations.[1] A visit of the Kaiser to Eng-

---

[1] This was the spirit of the Government, though the impetuous Admiral Lord Fisher says that, in January 1908, he recommended King Edward to 'Copenhagen the German Fleet à la Nelson,' *Memories*, pp. 18–9, 183. Some of his reckless utterances at The Hague Conference got through to Germany and provoked alarm in official circles.

land in November 1907 did something to allay suspicion. He proved unexpectedly conciliatory and even offered to hand over to England that part of the new Baghdad railway which was to end in the Persian Gulf. But Prince Bülow finally vetoed the proposal and this was probably the last chance Germany had of keeping on really friendly terms with England. The Entente with France was still only an entente, that with Russia had but just begun, and it was still possible for England to be friends with both Germany and Russia.

The Kaiser did much harm to Anglo-German relations in 1908. He wrote a letter to the English First Lord of the Admiralty, the substance of which got into the papers and provoked much hostile criticism and a great demand for naval activity in England. Tension was shown when Sir Charles Hardinge spoke to the Kaiser of the dangers of naval competition and the Kaiser replied that he would go to war rather than submit to dictation of his naval programme by a foreign Power. King Edward's visit to Czar Nicholas in June was more important for this reason. In August, King Edward met the Emperor Francis Joseph at Ischl and complained of the tension produced by the naval competition of Germany and, as Francis Joseph said, 'tried (without success) to detach me from the alliance with Germany.' At the end of October an extremely injudicious interview with the Kaiser was published in the *Daily Telegraph*. The Kaiser informed the British public that the majority of his people wanted war with them and that he alone stood between, and had, secretly and openly, been England's friend. This revelation provoked a violent explosion of protest in Germany and loudly expressed suspicion both of Germany and of the Kaiser in England. Suspicion was equally felt in British Government circles. The Bosnian crisis had just occurred in which Germany seemed to be supporting Austria-Hungary. And the Admiralty learnt in the autumn of 1908 that the German naval programme of 1909–10 was being anticipated.

In March 1909 these secrets of the British Admiralty were revealed to the House of Commons. The Government programme was considered inadequate and an agitation for eight Dreadnoughts to be laid down in the year began. It was crystallised in the popular slogan 'We want eight, and we won't wait.' After resisting the agitation for a time the British Government gave way to their public, and Germany was outdistanced in the race. England built eighteen Dreadnoughts between 1909 and 1911 and Germany nine.[1]

The Bosnian crisis passed and in July 1909 Prince Bülow laid down his office. Kiderlen-Wächter became Foreign Minister while Bethmann-Hollweg was made Chancellor. His difficulties as to stopping the Baghdad railway or the naval competition have been told elsewhere. It

---

[1] Lord Roberts inaugurated, by a speech in the Lords on November 23, 1908, a campaign for compulsory military service, avowedly because of the danger from Germany. He continued it by speeches in the country until the war of 1914, but met with small success.

is, however, to the credit of Bethmann that he instituted negotiations late in 1909 for reducing the naval programmes, or rather for retarding them. He declared that he could not repeal the naval law, which laid down a programme only to be completed in 1918. But he could arrange that fewer capital ships should be laid down in the earlier years and the number be equivalently raised in the later. This suggestion did not come to much, but it was something. For the retardation of the ship-building for a few years would have meant a certain relaxation of tension. In return for this somewhat shadowy naval arrangement, Bethmann demanded a very definite political advantage. He asked England to pledge herself to an agreement that 'in the case of an attack made on either Power [England or Germany] by a third Power or group of Powers, the Power not attacked should stand aside.'

This famous neutrality proposal was repeated, in one form or another, in the next two years and again in 1912. Its benefit to Germany was evident and substantial. If Russia or France (or both) attacked Germany, England would be neutral. But one Power (Japan) was bound to England by an alliance. Two others were bound by Ententes, and neither Russia nor France, nor Japan was in the least likely to attack England.[1] At the moment, so far as human probability went, Germany was the only Power ever likely to do so. The acceptance of the proposal therefore would have been, from the English standpoint, of no special advantage. It might indeed have been of grave disadvantage. What would happen, for instance, if France had attacked Germany, and Germany had replied by invading France *via* Belgium? Germany would certainly have claimed that England had pledged herself to neutrality, despite the violation of Belgium and the breach of the Treaty of 1839. As the new agreement would have been the later document, it would have been difficult to dispute this view.

The fundamental fact in the whole question of the 'neutrality formula' was that it would have been inconsistent with the assumptions underlying the Franco-British Entente; and this was reflected in the first reply made by England. She offered to give assurances in July 1910 that nothing in her agreements with any other Power was directed against Germany and that she had no hostile intentions towards her. As a result of further negotiations England asserted that there was nothing exclusive in her Entente system, and that a similar method of settling difficulties might be embodied in an agreement with Germany. The German reply to this in May 1911 promised well; but at this moment a rash action on her part produced the crisis of Agadir.[2]

---

[1] Italy and Austria-Hungary could, of course, have attacked England but no one believed that they would do so except at the instigation of Germany.

[2] Germany caused the neutrality offer to have precedence of the naval discussions, and agreement on the first had to precede agreement on the second. It ought to be noted here that the *pourparlers* as to naval retardation were throughout unsatisfactory. For instance, despite reassuring statements from Bethmann, in the latter part of 1910,

The root of the Morocco crisis of 1911 lay in Algeciras. Germany had been deeply wounded by the results of that Conference and showed it in 1908. A grave incident took place, that of 'the Casablanca deserters,' over which Germany tried to bully France. Clemenceau happened to be Premier and refused to be intimidated and was supported by England and Russia, and the incident ended in arbitration at The Hague Tribunal, which was unfavourable to Germany (November 1908). As the Bosnian crisis was then to the fore and the Kaiser was very unpopular because of his *Daily Telegraph* interview, Germany had no wish for further complications elsewhere. Accordingly she initiated *pourparlers* at the beginning of 1909, which resulted (February 8) in a Declaration being signed by France and Germany known as the 'Morocco Pact.' This practically assured to France special political influence in Morocco, while giving to Germany equal economic opportunities with France in that area. It seemed that a new order of things had begun, but, after a very annoying set of negotiations in which Germany was conciliatory, the two parties failed to reach any economic agreement either over the mines or railways of Morocco. By the end of 1910 Germany was thoroughly annoyed at the French inability to arrive at economic agreement, and by the beginning of 1911 she had real reasons for becoming alarmed at French political activity in Morocco.

The internal situation in Morocco was becoming impossible. The Sultan was overturned by his brother in 1908, and the usurper, though recognised by the Powers, was not obeyed by many of his subjects. In 1910 his request for French officers to reorganise his army was refused, and he found himself unable to defend his capital (Fez) against rebellious tribesmen. He appealed to France for aid and in April 1911 she agreed to organise and despatch a Moorish, and if necessary a French, column to Fez to relieve the Sultan from anxiety.

Even in March Kiderlen-Wächter had told the French that German public opinion would be excited by French operations in Morocco, which might appear to tear up the Act of Algeciras. When troops were actually sent in April both he and Bethmann saw the situation clearly enough. It is always easier to send troops into a disturbed area than to get them out again, and occupations by civilised Powers of barbarian territory, even if meant to be temporary and military, often become permanent and political. Spain agreed with Germany that the action of France endangered the Act of Algeciras, and with it the integrity of Morocco. Sir Edward Grey thought differently, or at any rate protested that he was satisfied with the assurances of France, and meant to stand

the Kaiser informed the British Ambassador that he would never consent to any agreement binding Germany not to enlarge her naval programme. When, however, the German Government subsequently examined this proposition they withdrew the offer of 'retardation.' The utterances of Bethmann in the Reichstag were also not calculated to soothe British suspicions. Sir E. Cook: *How Britain strove for Peace* (1914), pp. 18–28; G. Lowes Dickinson: *The International Anarchy* (1926), pp. 387–99.

by her. France tactfully suggested the resumption of the Franco-German railway negotiations in June, but these were interrupted by an extraordinary step on the part of Germany.

On July 1, Germany informed the Powers who had signed the Algeciras Act, that she had sent a German gunboat, the *Panther*, to the port of Agadir in Southern Morocco, in order to protect German interests and subjects there. Germany explained that she considered the Act of Algeciras to be now dead, and could not look on while France and Spain seemed to be disregarding the Act. The man who sent the *Panther* certainly produced the crisis of Agadir. But who was he? The Kaiser says he vainly protested against it, Bethmann does not seem to have been responsible, and Kiderlen appears to have been the culprit.[1] Kiderlen's idea seems to have been a mere 'bluff.' He did not really mean to attempt to partition Morocco, but he thought it a good opportunity to get rid of the Algeciras Act, and to press France to cede Germany a slice of Congo territory in return for her abandoning political designs in Morocco. He thought he could do this by holding Agadir until France surrendered. That seems the only intelligible explanation of so rash an act.

The act was unwise for several reasons. Sir Edward Grey was already known to be very sensitive about treaties, and here was one openly torn up without England being consulted or a Conference summoned. Next, to send a warship to dominate a port on the Atlantic was the best way to convince every Englishman that Germany was trying to secure a naval base at Agadir by violent means as she had done at Kiao-Chau. On July 4 Sir Edward Grey informed the German Ambassador that the action at Agadir created 'a new situation.' He seems to have expected information on the subject from Berlin, but Kiderlen chose to assume that this was unnecessary, and gave no assurances till July 23. During this period of three weeks there were important negotiations between Jules Cambon and Kiderlen at Berlin. Kiderlen asked for a direct negotiation, thus excluding England and other signatories of Algeciras, and enabling him to demand compensation for retiring from Morocco, from France alone and in French territory (French Congo). Cambon agreed to a negotiation *à deux*, but said he must keep friends and allies informed of the negotiation. Kiderlen then demanded practically all the French Congo, and his tone was so menacing that England and France began exchanging views as to the possibility of real danger. On the 21st Sir Edward saw the German Ambassador and in plain language made clear to him that England thought Germany's demands for the Congo excessive and that her attitude at Agadir needed explanation as she might even have hoisted her flag there. On the 23rd Germany gave the required assurance by telegraph. Had they been made earlier, these guarantees of good faith would have ended the crisis.

On July 21, and before the German reply had been received,

[1] v. *Kiderlen Wächter*, ed. E. Jäckh (Berlin and Leipzig, 1924), vol. II. pp. 122–3.

Mr. Lloyd George made a resounding entry into foreign politics. In a public speech at the Mansion House he stated that 'Britain should at all hazards maintain her place and her prestige amongst the Great Powers . . . [if she were to be treated as] of no account in the Cabinet of Nations . . . peace at that price would be a humiliation intolerable for a great country like ours to endure.' This statement was not suggested by Sir Edward Grey but had his full approval and he subsequently defended it in public by saying that, if ever the time came when we could not make such a statement, 'we shall have ceased to exist, at all events as a great nation.' But it is one thing to make statements like this in private. Cambon had used strong language to Kiderlen, but France had not openly protested. And it is quite another to make them in public. The sensation created was immense. The German public stated that Germany was flouted, menaced and defied. 'Stand firm, William!' called out the Berlin crowd to the Kaiser, as they saw him riding down the Unter den Linden one day. But William could not stand firm. On July 24 and 25 the German Ambassador complained about the speech to Grey, but found him very determined. On the 26th and 27th he made a very courteous communication from Berlin which ended the difficulties between England and Germany.

The difficulties between France and Germany were not yet ended. The undercurrents of military preparations, though not of mobilisation, might have been detected in July in Germany, France, England and Belgium. But these were precautions, and in fact most diplomats knew, after the Mansion House speech, that Germany must yield or fight. She had not fought. Very tedious negotiations took place between Kiderlen and Cambon, and on August 20 the latter thought war possible. But the acuteness of the crisis became known to the public, there was a run on German banks in September, and the Kaiser and Bethmann finally put the brake on Kiderlen. In the second week of October an accord was reached, and the final agreement signed on November 4.

In substance France turned the interior of Morocco from an internationalised area to a French Sphere. Early in the next year the Sultan agreed to a French Protectorate, and except for Tangier and the Spanish zone Morocco now became French. Germany retained only 'the open door' for trade. In compensation Germany obtained two large strips of French Congolese territory—running upwards from the German Cameroons, exactly as the horns of a cow spring from its head —and as it were transfixing the Belgian Congo with the two points. The aim was evidently to give Germany direct access to the Belgian Congo, in order to put her in an advantageous position to secure a pre-emption on that territory.[1] Germany had been defeated in the negotiation, and the extremely bitter debates in the Reichstag showed that the public realised the fact and put down the defeat to England. The British public

[1] At various times in the negotiations Kiderlen demanded this pre-emption, but Cambon always refused.

was somewhat more moderate on hearing the news in November that the two nations had nearly been at war in July.

Agadir was a crisis infinitely more serious than Algeciras and undoubtedly more critical than the Bosnian one. The Triple Entente had been defeated over Bosnia and Russia humiliated. But their defeat and humiliation were perhaps less public and anyhow less recent than that of the Triple Alliance, and of Germany in particular, at Agadir. This time England had appeared 'in shining armour' at a grave moment, to support her friend. An able publicist put his finger on the gravity of the new situation at once. He said that the bond of the Triple Entente is less close than that of the Triple Alliance, but for practical purposes Europe is divided by these two great combinations, and the tenseness of the situation makes crises inevitably recur. Russia and the Entente accepted defeat without war in the crisis of 1909. Germany accepted defeat without war in that of 1911; neither would accept defeat without war in any future crisis.[1] Both groups understood the danger, and both began to prepare. England had already been organising an expeditionary force of six divisions, now arrangements were made with the Admiralty to transport it rapidly overseas at need, *i.e.* to co-operate with France. Preparations of all kinds for press-censorship, for war legislation and the like were made. If a peace-loving country and government faced reality and made preparations like these, it is not surprising that military and naval activity developed elsewhere in a less liberal atmosphere. And the tensity of the situation was increased by military re-organisation everywhere and particularly by the designing and development of Russian strategic railways and of German strategic canals.

Russia and Italy used the crisis of Agadir to press demands on their respective Allies which they might otherwise have declined. Italy watched the crisis from June onwards with the full intention of obtaining Tripoli from Turkey, while France, Germany and England were too occupied to prevent her. She had indeed previously obtained the consent of all the Great Powers to her eventual occupation of Tripoli, but none of them approved of the moment she selected to execute her project. On September 26 Italy sent an ultimatum to Turkey and declared war three days later. Even as stated by herself Italy's reasons for war were pretexts. They were simply a cloak for a naked resolve to annex the territory of another Power which had done her no harm. The war reflected little credit on Italy from any point of view, but she eventually occupied the coastline of Tripoli and also the Dodecanese—twelve islands in the Ægean, of which Rhodes was the most important. The outbreak of the Balkan War, in October 1912, forced Turkey to conclude the Peace of Lausanne with Italy, and to cede to her these ill-gotten gains.

[1] Grey expressed the view before the outbreak of war in 1914 that Russia would not accept a second humiliation after Bosnia. *Twenty-Five Years* (1925), vol. I. pp 332-3.

Russia's action, while France and England were grappling with Germany, was less successful though even more discreditable. She intrigued so much in Persia, and showed so clearly her intention of annexing Teheran that Sir Edward Grey became extremely irate, and Cambon advised Russia to abandon her designs unless she wished to end the Entente. Russia also returned to the old idea of opening the Dardanelles to Russian warships and made a formal demand to this effect at Constantinople in December 1911. Turkey was informed by both England and France that they did not support this demand, and accordingly refused Russia's request.[1] But Turkey had become thoroughly suspicious of the Entente and was now more pro-German than ever.

In the beginning of 1912 the atmosphere between Russia and England had become so chilly that Germany made one more effort to break up the Triple Entente. The Kaiser asked 'his friend Lord Haldane' to pay an informal visit to Berlin. Lord Haldane had hardly arrived when Mr. Winston Churchill offended Germany by a speech (February 9) in which he described her fleet as 'a luxury' and England's as 'a necessity.' But the reactions to this speech were probably not the cause of the failure of the overture. Haldane proposed the 'two keels to one standard,' and said that our neutrality could not be reckoned on if Germany attacked France. Tirpitz tried to argue for a 10 : 16 keels' standard and communicated his *Novelle* or naval programme. Bethmann replied by the old neutrality proposal in the following form. 'If either of the high contracting parties becomes entangled in a war in which it cannot be said to be the aggressor, the other will at least observe towards the Power so entangled a benevolent neutrality, and use its utmost endeavour for the localisation of the conflict.' The English reply did not go even half-way to meet this view, and when Bethmann tried to secure what seemed to him an essential addition, Grey, in Bethmann's words, 'roundly refused' it.[2] It is clear that Germany hoped to bind England to a formula separating her from the Entente, and that Haldane and Grey both saw this and refused to accede to the proposal. But, if Grey's suspicions were to some extent aroused by the neutrality proposal, a study of the *Novelle* increased them. At the end of July Churchill indicated to the Commons that the new German programme meant an increase not only in ships and *personnel*, but also an unprecedented increase in the fighting efficiency of the forces available in peace time.

British public opinion was being prepared for a further increase of the fleet in the North Sea and for the abandonment of the Mediterranean to

[1] Sazonov added to his blunder by pretending that the overture was unauthorised and by appointing a new Ambassador at Constantinople.

[2] *v. Gooch and Temperley*, vol. VI. pp. 682–3, 713–4, 715. cp. Bethmann-Hollweg: *Reflections on the World War* (1920), vol. I. pp. 54–5; Lowes Dickinson: *International Anarchy*, pp. 389–99. It is clear that the Kaiser's influence at this stage was particularly unfortunate. *v.* E. Brandenburg, *Von Bismarck Zum Weltkriege* (2nd Edn. Berlin 1925), pp 353–4. On the whole question of the naval rivalry at this period, cp. E. L. Woodward: *Great Britain and the German Navy* (1935).

France. Franco-British naval conversations took place in the summer and autumn. In October the third French Battle Squadron joined the other two in the Mediterranean. England virtually left to France the defence of the Mediterranean against Austria-Hungary,[1] and the British Squadron based on Malta was much reduced by the despatch of several ships to the North Sea. England in return practically assumed the defence of the Channel. These arrangements were described by Sir Edward Grey, in a letter of November 22, 1912, to the French Ambassador, Cambon. 'We have agreed that consultation between [naval and military] experts is not and ought not to be regarded as an engagement that commits either Government to action in a contingency that has not arisen and may never arise. The disposition, for instance, of the French and British fleets respectively at the present moment is not based upon an engagement to co-operate in war.' That might be so, but it rendered co-operation infinitely more probable.[2] On August 2, 1914, when war between Germany and France was seen to be inevitable, Grey promised to protect the Northern French coast from being bombarded by Germany. That was not war with Germany, but it was an action which rendered war with her extremely probable. When the North Sea and the Channel were defended solely by England, and the Mediterranean mainly by France, each Power felt obligations when war broke out against the other. A common plan of defence in peace time can only rest on a close political understanding, and it is hard to conceive such an understanding without some obligation. So November 1912 seems to mark a decisive stage in British estrangement from Germany. The final failure to arrive at a naval understanding with her in the early part of 1912 caused England to concentrate her fleet in the North Sea and to rely on France to protect the Mediterranean. France was, in fact, though not in name, adding to British sea power. Germany, on the other hand, was compelling England to loosen her grip on the Mediterranean. The effect was to drive England away from Germany and towards France.

[1] It was not expected that the Italian fleet would side with Austria-Hungary and Germany.

[2] Winston Churchill: *World Crisis* (1931 Edn.), p. 81, says of the Mediterranean arrangement, '. . . the moral claims which France could make upon Great Britain if attacked by Germany . . . were enormously extended.'

CHAPTER XXVIII

FROM THE BALKAN LEAGUE TO THE WAR OF 1914

No single event influenced the outbreak of war in 1914 more than the Balkan War of 1912–13. Other incidents, as Algeciras, Bosnia or Agadir, disturbed the situation because they affected the Balance of Power in the future. But the overthrow of the Turk caused an immediate danger, for it affected the Balance of Power in the present. Serbia, Bulgaria, Greece and Rumania were revealed as conquering military states. The Turkish army—trained by Germany as a potential ally—was utterly beaten. Serbia added a million to its population, erased the humiliations of the Bosnian annexation, and triumphantly asserted her prestige in an outburst of Pan-Serb and Yugo-Slav enthusiasm, which swept Dalmatia and Bosnia like a prairie-fire. Serbia, hitherto rebuffed and discredited, appeared armed, victorious and triumphant. As Italy had arisen from Piedmont so a united Yugo-slavia was to arise from Serbia. The prestige gained by Greece and Rumania was only second to that of Serbia. All three states now looked forward to a time when each flag would cover all their kinsmen in the Balkans, a greater Greece, a greater Rumania, a greater Serbia. And their brethren beneath the Turkish or Hapsburg rule looked forward to the day when the arms of their free countrymen would break the hated yoke from off their necks. A perpetually increasing nationalistic agitation in Austria-Hungary and Turkey, where such agitation was so dangerous, was the direct result of the Balkan War.

The genesis of the Balkan War is an extremely simple one. Russia had temporarily reconciled Bulgaria with Serbia. But these two small states soon found that Russia was not prepared to support to the full their nationalistic designs of liberating their downtrodden brethren from Turkey. They found other Great Powers even less sympathetic; none of them was prepared to prevent the Young Turks from persecuting the Christians of Macedonia even more brutally than had Abdul Hamid. Bulgaria and Serbia decided to act together, and at the critical moment the appearance of a man of genius in Greece for the first time brought the three states into a Balkan League.[1] That League smashed the Turks, defied the Concert of Europe, and upset the Balance of Power. For decades the relations of the Great Powers had been rudely shaken by the transfer of even the smallest bit of territory or population in the Balkans; they were shattered altogether by the radical changes of the Balkan War and the conflict of 1914 was perhaps the result.

The Bosnian incident taught the Bulgars and Serbs that though Russia had been unable to help them then, she would try to help them in the future. The first idea seems to have been to attack the Turks,

[1] Montenegro was ultimately also a member of the League.

while Russia and France held Austria-Hungary and Germany in check. The Serbs, despite their promise of 1909, apparently tolerated a furious Pan-Serb or Yugo-Slav propaganda in Austria-Hungary to prevent her from interfering while the Balkan states attacked Turkey. It was not till the autumn of 1911, however, that the Bulgars listened to Serb overtures. By that time they had seen that the Young-Turkish persecution of Christians in Macedonia meant extermination unless there was some interference from outside. And, so early as August 1911, Venizelos, the Greek Prime Minister, pointed out to the Bulgars that a defensive alliance between Greece and Bulgaria would ensure the safety of both and save the Christians of Macedonia.

The Bulgars began their delicate task of negotiating with the Serbs in October 1911. A treaty was ultimately signed in March 1912, guaranteeing each party its territory and independence and promising mutual support if one of the Great Powers tried to annex or occupy any territory under Turkish rule. A secret annex arranged for common action against Turkey, subject to Russia's approval. And, after making some preliminary partitions of territory, the two parties agreed to leave the assignment of 'the contested zone' in Macedonia[1] to the arbitration of the Czar. A military convention was signed in April 1912. On May 29, 1912, Bulgaria signed a defensive alliance with Greece, followed by a military convention in September. The small independent Serb kingdom of Montenegro was also approached verbally in August, and agreed to join the League.

Sazonov, who came to the Russian Foreign Office at the end of 1910, probably hoped to control Serbia and Bulgaria, and warned them at an early stage that his Government would not approve action against Turkey. Poincaré, the active French Premier who visited St. Petersburg in August 1912, saw further than Sazonov. He pointed out that these agreements contained 'the germ of a war not only against Turkey but against Austria'—and 'was in fact *une convention de guerre* which not only revealed the ambition of the Serbs and Bulgars but encouraged them.' He was perfectly right. Hatred of Turkey and not love of one another was the tie uniting the Balkan League, and these fighting cocks were not to be restrained by the warnings of any Great Power. Austria-Hungary had some faint suspicions of the coming crisis, but did little to prevent it. In mid-September, Sazonov, at last alive to the military preparations of the Balkan League, sought to invoke the intervention of the Great Powers. He was too late. On October 7 the members of the Balkan League were informed that the Great Powers were opposed to a rupture with Turkey, and would, in any case, permit no change in the territorial *status quo* in the Balkans. The next day (October 8) Montenegro, disregarding altogether these menaces, declared war on Turkey, and set the Balkans aflame from one end to the other.

[1] The ' contested zone' was the Monastir area, very dear to Bulgarian hearts and full of pro-Bulgars.

What followed is one of the miracles of history. There can be no doubt that the Great Powers believed that the Balkan League would be beaten. Both they and the Turks were speedily undeceived. On October 22 the Bulgars won a great victory over the Turks at Kirk-Kilisse; on the 26th the Serbs opened the way into Macedonia by a resounding victory at Kumanovo, which they followed up by a victory in front of Monastir, where their troops fought for a day breast-high in the water. The Greeks, who had been temporarily checked at Florina, found only fleeing Turks to contend with when they advanced again, and on November 8 they entered the coveted town of Salonica. This was really the end of the Turkish Empire in Macedonia. Mr. Asquith, on November 9, in his speech at the Mansion House, brushed aside altogether the collective menace of the Great Powers to the Balkan League of only one month before. He said that the Great Powers would recognise the new facts and consent to the territorial changes already won by blood and sacrifice.

The position of the Balkan League was, however, by no means so strong, nor were the Great Powers so weak, as they appeared to be. The Serbs had reached Durazzo on the sea coast of Albania, or had 'brought their steeds to water in the Adriatic,' as King Nicholas of Montenegro poetically remarked. Austria-Hungary now threatened, in unmistakable terms of menace, that she would allow no Serbian annexation of Albanian ports; Italy supported her, and Sazonov reluctantly concurred. On December 3, 1912, an armistice was arranged between the Turks and the League, and it lasted till February 3, 1913. Three great Turkish fortresses still held out at the end of the year: Scutari in Albania against Serbs and Montenegrins; Janina in Epirus against the Greeks; Adrianople in Thrace against the Bulgars. The rest of European Turkey was in the hands of the Balkan League up to the lines of Tchataldja, which are but some thirty kilometres distant from Constantinople itself. There Bulgaria had penned the biggest Turkish army, but had been informed by Sazonov that she would not be allowed to enter Constantinople.

It is pleasant to record that France and Germany, for once, helped one another to keep the peace and to localise the conflict. In December Conrad certainly wanted to attack the Serbs, but the refusal of the aged Austrian Emperor to go to war was greatly strengthened by the attitude of Germany, which was extremely pacific. And Italy also assisted Germany to restrain her ally. Similarly Poincaré and France worked hard to restrain Sazonov, whose previous commitments could hardly avoid encouraging the Balkan League even when he professed to disapprove of their actions. Sir Edward Grey during this period at no time hesitated to throw his full weight into the scales of peace. Largely owing to his efforts, though heartily seconded by Poincaré and the Kaiser, the system of settling matters or rather trying to settle them by the European Conference was again adopted, and despite all difficulties, the method justified itself. The machine was bound to work clumsily, for the Great Powers often disagreed, though not to the point of fighting with one another. It was difficult therefore to put active pressure on the small and militarily triumphant League. But, though the Conference was at times hoodwinked and defied both by the Balkan League and by the Turks, it proved a good instrument for reconciling the Great Powers.

On February 3 the League resumed hostilities against the Turks, and the danger of conflict between the Great Powers became very great. Austria-Hungary had mobilised troops to threaten Serbia; Russia had mobilised in the Caucasus to threaten Turkey. On January 24, 1913, Enver Bey overthrew the relatively pacific Turkish Government at Constantinople, murdered the Turkish Commander-in-Chief and became a sort of military dictator. He promptly and contemptuously repudiated the arrangement for settlement made in December by the Ambassadors' Conference of the Great Powers, and resumed hostilities with the Balkan League. The results were at first disastrous to Turkey. The large island of Crete, which the Great Powers had so often denied to the Greeks, now surrendered quietly and hoisted the Greek flag. The Albanian city of Scutari fell to King Nicholas of Montenegro, and he refused to retire from it. But Austria-Hungary would not give way here, and, under her pressure, the Great Powers forced Nicholas to evacuate it by a naval demonstration. The great Epirot fortress of Janina fell before the Greeks, and Adrianople, the greatest prize of all, yielded to the combined efforts of the Serbian artillery and the Bulgar army. The situation in March may be described as follows: the Bulgars held Macedonia east of Salonica and all Thrace up to the Tchataldja lines, on which they made no impression. The Greeks held most of Epirus and Southern Macedonia including Salonica. The Novibazar area and all Macedonia hitherto unconquered had passed into the hands of the Serbs. The crucial question really concerned the 'contested zone' of Macedonia. This area, comprising Monastir and the heart of Macedonia, was the prize which Bulgaria had lost in 1878 and now trusted to regain. Unfortunately for her Serbia held it, and Serbia was not wholly satisfied with her share of the spoils. It is true that she had agreed that the 'contested zone' was to be assigned according to the arbitration of the Czar, but that was before she had conquered it. Force alone would make her or Bulgaria yield.

The Great Powers had already decided in principle that Albania should be independent, and, in this one instance, their show of power had taught Serbs and Montenegrins to evacuate territory. Austria-Hungary forced the Great Powers to act, and they incontinently bundled the Montenegrins out of Scutari. The Great Powers had also partially defined the boundaries of Albania to the north. They agreed on a northern boundary, which ran counter to all the dictates of common sense, and of which the result (doubtless suggested by Austria-

Hungary) could only have been to facilitate future conflicts between Serbs and Albanians. Of this fact the Russians and the Germans were fully aware, though Sir Edward Grey seems to have been wholly ignorant of it. He believed the European Conference to be such an excellent device, as to be incapable of drawing up an agreement contrary to common sense.

The Albanian question thus settled, the Great Powers, disavowing their utterance of October 1912, proceeded to cut off from Turkey all territory west of a line between Enos and Midia, thus confining her within a small corner of which the extremity was Constantinople. This area was ceded to the Balkan Allies *en bloc*, the island of Crete went to Greece alone, and the fate of other Turkish islands, Samothrace, Lemnos, etc., was left for the Great Powers to decide in the future. The further assignments of the Great Powers met with bitter opposition. Greece did very well in obtaining not only the great prize of Salonica but a stretch of South Macedonia which included many Bulgars. Serbia got Northern and (what was gall and wormwood to the Bulgars) Central Macedonia. Bulgaria was to obtain Thrace and the Ægean coast. After much protest and pressure the Balkan League and Turkey signed this Treaty of London on May 30. They all of them tore it up immediately afterwards.

The Bulgars were not prepared to surrender either Salonica to the Greeks or the 'contested Macedonian zone' to the Serbs. But these two nations held the disputed areas, anticipated the Bulgar refusal, kept themselves ready, and formed an alliance. King Ferdinand of Bulgaria secretly ordered one of his armies to attack the Serbs in Macedonia and another to move on Salonica. On June 29 the Bulgars secretly attacked the Serbs at midnight. It was in vain that the Bulgarian Premier protested that the attack was unauthorised and that the Bulgarian army had been ordered to cease hostilities. The wrath of Serbs and of Greeks was thoroughly aroused against their treacherous ally. King Constantine at the head of the Greek army captured the Bulgars in Salonica and undertook a brilliant but reckless campaign up the valley of the Struma. He was extricated from a dangerous situation by the Serbs, who utterly routed the Bulgars at the Bregalnica. Within six weeks 50,000 of the allies were killed. Meanwhile two Powers, who were not members of the Balkan League, improved the situation by triumphing bloodlessly over the already helpless and defeated Bulgars. Enver Bey led a Turkish army by forced marches out from the lines of Tchataldja and speedily recovered Adrianople. The city, which had cost so many thousand Turkish and Bulgarian lives, was surrendered without a blow. Secondly, Rumania, which had viewed the division of the spoil with angry eyes, mobilised her army, invaded the absolutely helpless Bulgaria, seized important strategic points, and menaced Sofia. On August 10 the Bulgars signed the Treaty of Bucharest, with Serbia, Greece and Rumania. Bulgaria was forced to cede to Rumania the fortress of Silistria commanding the Danube and the southern part of the Dobruja, which was ethnically Bulgarian.[1] The Serbs retained all North Macedonia and the 'contested zone' (the Monastir area) which was certainly pro-Bulgar. The Greeks retained South Macedonia from Florina opposite Monastir up to the borders of Western Thrace. They obtained the fine harbour of Cavalla, the only practicable opening for Bulgaria on the Ægean,[2] and the rich tobacco districts of the hinterland. Bulgaria still retained Western Thrace with the poor roadstead of Dedeagatch as her sole Ægean harbour. The Serbs, Greeks and Rumans thus ignored the Great Powers over nearly everything except Albania. The Turks under Enver Bey equally despised the Treaty of London, and calmly retained Adrianople, which, according to the decision of the Great Powers, was to become Bulgarian. The Greeks and the Turks equally refused to accept any decision of the Great Powers as to the fate of islands like Lemnos and Samos, and technically continued to fight one another. The Great Powers stomached these affronts as best they could. They dared not resort to force, for that would have ranged Austria-Hungary and Germany on one side and France and Russia (if not England) on the other. This difficulty enabled the small Powers to pluck their beards with impunity.

The actual gains in population meant something: Serbia added a million to its total or about one hundred thousand fighting men to its army; Greece did about the same; and Rumania gained important strategic advantages. Even Bulgaria got some territory. The actual loss of territory and population by Turkey affected that strange Empire much less than it would have done a Western State. Christian subjects were no loss, for they were not allowed to serve in the army, but the independence of Albania deprived Turkey of a fine recruiting ground for soldiers and administrators.[3] The defeat in the field was a positive gain, for the Turks set to work to reorganise their army in earnest, and it proved its worth in the coming war. The recapture of Adrianople also awakened the national patriotism of the Turks, which was stimulated by the fact that their rule in Europe was now confined to areas ethnically Turkish.

The best commentary on the Balkan War of 1912–13, and of its effects, is that none of the belligerents, whether defeated or triumphant, believed that the territorial decisions would be permanent. The victorious Serbs and Montenegrins thought they would have to fight Austria-Hungary before they could rest on their laurels. The defeated Bulgars made overtures for an alliance both with Austria-Hungary and

---

[1] Montenegro received a large increase of territory to the East—Djakovo, Ipek, etc.

[2] It is to the credit of Venizelos that he desired Bulgaria to have this port so that a Greco-Bulgar alliance might remain a possibility. He was overruled by King Constantine and the General Staff.

[3] Many Grand Viziers have been Albanians, as, e.g. the Kiuprile. So was Mehemet Ali, the most famous of all the modern rulers of Egypt.

with the Turks so as to be revenged on their former allies. The Greeks hovered uncertainly between the Entente and the Austro-German Alliance. All of them expected a new war very soon, and thought any treaties made in 1913 to be the merest 'scraps of paper.'

The attitude of Russia naturally became of great importance after the Balkan War. She controlled Serbia, was increasing her influence on Rumania, but had alienated Bulgaria. Moreover, Turkey had been so weakened that Russia might perhaps still have a good chance of further dismembering her. As early as April 1913 Turkey had appealed to Germany for a good German officer to reorganise her army, though it was agreed that he should not be sent till the Peace. Germany was anxious to build up Turkey in Asia, and decided to send General Liman von Sanders; he was to be given the status of a commanding general. On November 17 Sazonov indicated Russia's anxiety and disapproval, as Liman would command a Turkish army corps in Constantinople, and his protest was backed up by the Russian Prime Minister, who was visiting Berlin. Germany was at once explanatory and evasive. Russia, however, appealed to her Allies and suggested an identical note of re-monstrance to Constantinople signed by herself, France and England. Grey agreed to support this in principle, but wished to delay common action. His position was embarrassing, for a British Admiral was at Constantinople with a very similar naval mission to that proposed for Liman's military one. The Kaiser was for standing out, but the German Foreign Office instructed their Ambassador at Constantinople to come to terms.[1] France was ready to support Russia in any move which she might make, but Grey was more cautious.[2] On the last day of 1913 Bethmann obtained the Kaiser's assent to a compromise. Liman von Sanders became Inspector-General and a Turkish Field Marshal, but resigned his command over the first Turkish Army Corps in Con-stantinople. This ended the matter. It is often quoted as an example of Germany's moderation; but it was hardly that. Both Bethmann and the German authorities at Constantinople said that German prestige would actually gain. The functions of command and inspection could not be performed by one man, and Liman himself thought his position better.[3] The incident is, however, instructive because Russia and France came near to war with Germany.

A Council held at St. Petersburg decided not to go to war with Ger-many over this matter, especially as England's attitude was uncertain. But on February 21 a still more important Council took place, which discussed the question of the Straits.[4] It decided that Russia should try

---

[1] v. Grosse Politik, vol. 38, p. 260 n.; Siebert: Entente Diplomacy and the World (1921), p. 698.

[2] v. Documents Diplomatiques Français (1871–1914), 3rd Ser., vol. VIII. p. 869; Gooch and Temperley, vol. X. (1), pp. 394–6.

[3] v. Grosse Politik, vol. 38, pp. 283, 305.

[4] M. N. Pokrovsky: Drei Konferenzen (1920), pp. 32 sqq.; M. Montgelas: The Case for the Central Powers (1925), pp. 94–5.

to secure command of both Bosphorus and Dardanelles; that this command could only be secured by a European war and not by a localised conflict with Turkey; that for the moment a political atmosphere must be created favourable for 'operations leading up to the occupation of the Straits.' There is no doubt that this was a very serious decision, for the Czar's views, according to the French Ambassador, were that 'to reopen the Straits, I would even use force.'[1] At the same time he was begging him to assist in bringing about a close agreement with England.[2]

Sir Edward Grey was not thinking of agreements with Russia or of using force anywhere. He still believed in his idea of a European Conference, for he thought that it had averted war in 1913 and saw that the inclusion of Germany in such an organisation was the surest road to peace. He persevered in a pacific attitude towards Germany. In fact during the winter of 1913 and the first half of 1914 negotiations took place with Germany over the Portuguese Colonies and also over the Baghdad railway, which resulted in a considerable measure of agreement. A full power for signing the Baghdad Treaty was actually sent off to London on July 22 by Germany.

For reasons too long to note here the Portuguese negotiation was dropped in March, but it is pathetic to note that on July 28, 1914, Germany was preparing to resume this negotiation. Thus, up to the very brink of war, England and Germany were pursuing a settlement of their own private difficulties.[3] One unfortunate incident had occurred. When Sir Edward Grey accompanied King George on a state visit to Paris in April, pressure was put upon him to engage in naval conversations with Russia. France was asked and was ready to make a proposal which drew closer the ties of the Entente. England was at that time by no means on good terms with Russia and anxious to conciliate her. So the naval conversations took place. They became known and were reported in the press. On June 11, 1914, Sir Edward Grey, questioned in the Commons, replied in characteristic parliamentary style. 'The answer given,' he writes, 'is absolutely true. The criticism to which it is

---

[1] v. *Documents Diplomatiques Français* (*1871–1914*), 3rd Ser., vol. X. p. 200.

[2] The policy of Russia in 1914 is still obscure, in spite of the revelations in the documents. It seems clear that Izvolsky wanted war (but he was an Ambassador only) and that Sazonov did not. The material arguments were certainly against war till 1917. M. Bogičević in his *Causes of the War* regards Russia as aggressive in 1914, but his testimony, and that of most Serbs, is marred by party bias. The assertions in *Livre Noir*, vol. II. pp. 346–7, that Grey promised Sazonov aid in case of war against Germany in September 1912 were denied by Grey in *Twenty-Five Years*, vol. I. p. 298, and his statement is confirmed by documents in *Gooch and Temperley*, vol. IX. (1), pp. 749-72. But the whole attitude of Russia in 1914 shows that, despite temporary differences, she was anxious to improve relations with England, because English aid in a future war was still uncertain. Hence not only the naval conversations, but the curious fact that Sazonov suggested a mutual guarantee of Asiatic possessions to England, and even offered to include Japan (July 1914) (*Gooch and Temperley*, vol. X. (2), pp. 821–3, and vol. XI. p. xi.)

[3] *Grosse Politik*, vol. 37, pp. 137, 469.

open is, that it does not answer the question put to me. That is un-
deniable.' [1] But, unfortunately, his answer was widely interpreted as a
denial of all naval conversations whatsoever with Russia. This was
bound to cause a bad impression; for the German Government had
secret information not only of the British naval conversations with
Russia in 1914, but also of the British military conversations with
France authorised in 1912.[2] It seems that Grey would have done better
frankly to reveal the existence of both conversations to Germany. For
he denied there were any secret agreements and yet tried to conceal the
secret conversations. It is difficult to see how Germany could accept
Grey's assurance, and, though we cannot help sympathising with this
honourable gentleman in his grave difficulties, his solution of them had
unfortunate effects.

The real signs of the alteration to the Balance of Power made by the
Balkan War are seen in their effect on the soldiers. A memorandum of
December 1912, drawn up by Ludendorff for the German General Staff,
contemplated war as the result.[3] He was doubtful about Italy joining
the Austro-German combination and fairly certain that England would
side with France and Russia. He thought that it was necessary in case
of war to take the offensive against France and violate Belgium, and to
remain on the defensive on the Russian frontier. He insisted that it was
necessary to vote large sums to increase Germany's military strength,
and particularly to fortify the Russian frontier. It is interesting that he
regards the Triple Alliance as a 'defensive' combination and the Triple
Entente as having 'marked offensive tendencies,' though this may be his
way of putting things. On March 28, 1913, the money for this outlay
came before the Reichstag for the vote, in the shape of a capital levy
of fifty million pounds, and the news became public. It was of peculiar
significance, for people saw that so great a financial demand could hardly
be made again in peace time. On the 29th it was announced that the
German peace strength would be increased by 120,000 men.

Military developments were taking place, in the same period, elsewhere in Europe. The fruit of Haldane's reforms in the British Army
now matured. About the same time arrangements were made in the
Belgian Parliament for a considerable increase of her army. The French

---

[1] Grey, *Twenty-Five Years*, vol. I. p. 289.
[2] Bethmann sent a special message to Grey pretending to be convinced. Grey,
however, was hard pressed by Ballin in a private conversation. On this occasion
Grey hinted at the possibility of exchanges of views with France and Russia, but
added 'no such naval convention existed and that it was not England's intention to
agree to any such convention.' *Grosse Politik*, vol. 39, pp. 626–45; *Gooch and Temperley*, vol. X. (2), pp. 800–13, vol. XI. pp. 4–6.
[3] Ludendorff: *The General Staff and its Problems* (1920), vol. I. p. 57. There is a
further report which the *Temps* says is his, but of which he has denied the authenticity.

Government had already been planning a Bill for turning the military service from two years into three, and the German increases spurred on the French Government to carry this Bill in both Houses by August. At the same time France obtained an addition of strength by taking recruits at 20 instead of 21, and by extending the period of liability for military service from the age of 45 to 48 years. Here again the measure was ominous. France had no more to give either in men or in period of military service. And when a country has no more to give, it becomes nervous or is likely to gamble on its last card. Russia also was not to be behindhand; during 1913 she increased her effectives by 135,000 and raised her periods of service by three months.[1] What was ominous about all this was that, at the moment, Germany was in the best military position, but that year by year her advantages would decrease; so the temptation to her military men to go to war was great. Russia expected to knock two days off the time required for mobilisation in 1914, to increase her network of strategic railways on the German East frontier, and to be quite ready in 1917. At the end of 1912 Ludendorff had written that Russia was 'still very much behindhand with the reorganization, equipment and arming of her forces, so that for the time being the Triple Alliance need not be afraid of an armed conflict even with her, in spite of her numerical superiority.' As, however, Russia 'will be stronger with every year that passes,' one can understand that Germany grew nervous as Russia's armaments increased.[2]

Germany, or at least her General Staff, was nervous for another reason too. Ludendorff in his memorandum described Austria-Hungary as 'most threatened politically,' and says in a note that Moltke feared that she would take her own line and 'be swept along by overhasty measures which involved us without affecting our vital interests.' Ludendorff adds that Moltke had 'little confidence in our [German] diplomacy. He doubted whether it would adopt the right course at a critical moment.' We must bear these facts in mind in considering the motives which swayed the Kaiser, who considered himself a soldier and whose marginal notes of this period more than once exalted military at the expense of civilian judgments. On February 24, 1914, Moltke, the Chief of Staff, sent a long report to Jagow—the Foreign Minister, on

---

[1] This provoked a new report from Moltke; v. Grosse Politik, vol. 39, p. 219.

[2] In general, figures quoted for increase of armaments are very misleading and contradictory. The League of Nations' figures in Journal of the Institute of International Affairs, May 1926 pp. 123–4, do not seem to agree with those of Montgelas, Case for the Central Powers (1925), pp. 104–8. On paper Russia and France had been increasing armaments faster than Austria-Hungary and Germany since 1899. But men are the raw material of war, and Russia was even in 1914 very deficient in rifles and heavy guns. Further, as any soldier knows, statistics mean very little until critically examined. One wants to know the proportion of rifle to ration-strength, whether gendarmerie or colonial troops are included in strengths, and whether estimates include pensions and are really all spent (as they were certainly not in Russia) in improving efficiency.

the development of the Russian Army,[1] and about the same time the Italian Chief of Staff was reported as feeling anxious about it, though he did not believe that Russia would make an aggressive war. A report from Germany's Ambassador at St. Petersburg stated that Sazonov was friendly but weak, and that other, and darker, forces in Russia were working against him. The Kaiser annotated: 'In any case he neither can, will, nor wishes to alter anything. Russo-Prussian relations are once for all dead—We have become enemies.' A hot campaign in the German and Russian press on their respective armaments, which broke out in March, seemed to underline this. Curiously enough Kaiser William at this time, and Franz Ferdinand about two months later at Konopisht, refused to be alarmed by Russia's military preparations at the moment. The latter indeed held that her internal unrest prevented any real danger from her. Moltke, however, was reported to be gloomy on June 1, and to have said, in reference to Franco-Russian preparations, 'We are ready, and the sooner the better for us.'[2] And this report is probably true.

The most serious feature, however, was Rumania's apparent defection from the Austro-German Alliance. Hitherto Rumania had been bound by a secret treaty which was known only to the King and a few leading Ministers, and it was likely that it would not be honoured by the Rumanian Cabinet, Parliament, or people. For there were three million Rumans in Hungary who were abominably oppressed by the Hungarian Government. Ludendorff had drawn attention to the military danger of Rumania's defection in December 1912, and Conrad no longer doubted that she would default at the end of 1913. But the matter was not a simple one, for the Rumanian question affected the internal affairs of Hungary as well as the foreign policy of Austria-Hungary. As long as the Hungarians oppressed Rumans in Hungary, the Rumanian Government outside Hungary would not be won back into the Austro-German fold. Kaiser William went to Vienna in March 1914 and found that both Berchtold and the Emperor Francis Joseph thought Rumania 'virtually lost.' A few days later the Kaiser spoke with Franz Ferdinand, the heir to the throne, who criticised Berchtold for want of openness and attacked the Hungarians for ill-treating their Ruman subjects. The situation had become worse on June 12–14, when William again visited Franz Ferdinand (as it proved for the last time) to admire the roses in his garden at Konopisht. In the interval between this and their former meeting the Ruman subjects of Hungary had scorned Tisza's overtures, and a serious bomb outrage had occurred at Debreczen. Franz Ferdinand expressed himself in very violent terms against the Hungarians and reiterated the need for conciliating the

---

[1] *Grosse Politik*, vol. 39. pp. 533 *sqq.*
[2] Eckardstein: *Die Isolierung Deutschlands*, (Leipzig, 1921), pp. 184, 185 n. There had been a renewal of the military engagements of the Triple Alliance by a new military convention between Germany, Austria-Hungary, and Italy on March 10, 1914. But the rulers of Germany believed Italy's aid would be slight.

13

Rumans both within and without Austria-Hungary. He also spoke of the need of a diplomatic alliance with Bulgaria, thus isolating Serbia and putting pressure on Rumania.

Serious as was the threat to Austria-Hungary both internal and external, from the Rumanian danger, it could not compare with that from Serbia. The Government of that country had promised in 1909 to live in good neighbourly relations with Austria-Hungary and to repress hostile propaganda towards her. They were not anxious either in 1913 or 1914 for a new war, because they had much to gain by delay. Ammunition and rifles were deficient, their new territory needed consolidating, and Russia would not be ready for war until 1917. But the four millions of Serbian Serbs called to the eight million Serbo-Croats under the Hapsburgs.[1] Even had the Serb Government desired to do so, they could hardly have suppressed the incessant propaganda and habitual intercourse between their own Serbs and those beyond the Danube and Drina. There was no press censorship in Serbia, the newspapers could say what they liked, and availed themselves liberally of their freedom. Pan-Serb agitation, which had been at bloodheat in 1908, was at boiling point during 1913 and 1914. A feverish and furious agitation ran through Serbia, Bosnia, Dalmatia, Croatia.[2] Hundreds of students dreamed of the days when Yugoslavia should be free and of how to die for her freedom. In 1910 a student sought to assassinate the Governor of Bosnia, and committed suicide before being captured. He exclaimed with his last breath, 'I leave it to Serbdom to avenge me.' This incident was glorified in a notorious pamphlet which had a wide sale. In 1912 student demonstrations at Zagreb ended in bloodshed, and the Ban or Governor of Croatia was twice within an ace of being murdered by students. In January 1913 two young Bosnians planned to murder their Governor, abandoning their attempt only at the last moment, and in August another Zagreb student made an attempt on another Ban. In March 1914 a new attempt at Zagreb was discovered just in time to prevent the Ban and an Austrian Archduke from being assassinated. These attempts were due partly to propaganda, partly to criminal or terrorist organisations. But they were most of all due to the emotions aroused by the birth of new ideas. 'Thoughts burst forth, burning and irrepressible as lava. Do not demand of any new thought that it should be just to the thought that preceded it.'[3] That would have seemed treason to the cause. The whole educational life of Croatia, Dalmatia, and Bosnia was a seething mass of discontent and smothered rebellion, and the students of independent Serbia inflamed the agita-

[1] Six million Serbo-Croats, two million Slovenes. Even the proposed union of Serbia and Montenegro excited great apprehensions at Berlin and Vienna.

[2] It had different aspects. There was a Pan-Serb agitation and a Serbo-Croat or Yugoslav agitation quite distinct from it. In addition there were societies like the Narodna Odbrana which were merely propagandist, and others like the Black Hand which were criminal and terroristic.

[3] Castelar.

tion.[1] These activities were so flagrant that they could not be concealed from the authorities. But they were infinitely more active inside Austria-Hungary than in Serbia.

Berchtold, the Foreign Minister of Austria-Hungary, and Tisza, the Hungarian Premier, were well aware of the agitation. They knew that it could not go on for ever, and were naturally inclined to think that it was more due to propaganda from outside than to unrest from within. But Tisza was, in his own way, a great man and wished to move cautiously. For he knew the difficulties and danger Hungary would encounter in war to be more serious than Berchtold dreamed of. But the defection of Rumania urged both men to action against Serbia, and during April and May 1914 they moved steadily in this direction. It was at this point that Conrad, as Chief of the General Staff, intervened with effect. Like the Sybil he was perpetually offering the books of his wisdom which had hitherto always been repulsed. His views were summed up in his own epigram that war with Serbia would have been a safe game in 1909, that a similar war in 1913 was a game which still offered chances, that in 1914, though a desperate hazard, it must be undertaken as there was no alternative. The Serbs, he said, were led by irresponsible agitators, 'full of unquenchable hatred for us,' and only amenable to force. In the winter of 1913 and the spring of 1914 he repeated this view over and over again to Kaiser William, to Moltke, the German Chief of Staff, to Berchtold, and to Franz Ferdinand. The last, while not apparently concurring in Conrad's views of an immediate attack on Serbia, agreed to a diplomatic offensive, and recommended it to the Kaiser at Konopisht. Berchtold agreed, and the point of this offensive against Serbia was to bring Bulgaria into the Triple Alliance, and to inform Rumania of it. Serbia would thus be isolated, and Rumania might once more be won back. It was hoped ultimately to include Greece and Turkey in the new group. Russia would thus be effectively countered in the Balkans. After many revisions, Berchtold had at last finished his memorandum on June 24, and was about to forward it to Germany for approval and support. But, while he was putting the last touches, something occurred which converted him to Conrad's views at a blow. For on the afternoon of June 28 he and all the world learnt that a Bosnian Serb, who had just come from Belgrade, had assassinated Franz Ferdinand and his wife at the bridge of Sarajevo.

The story of events from the assassination of the Archduke till the outbreak of war is even yet not clear.[2] It is remarkable that the chief

[1] The only scientific description of these sinister activities is in R. W. Seton-Watson's *Sarajevo* (1926), pp. 63–79. But no one who saw Dalmatia, Bosnia or Croatia in 1912 or 1913, could doubt the prevalence of an extraordinary unrest.

[2] The fullest account and the one nearest to finality is that given by B. E. Schmitt in *The Coming of the War 1914*, 2 vols. (New York, 1930).

Austro-Hungarian investigator not only did not find any evidence of complicity of the Serbian Government in the assassination, but that he reported it as 'definitely improbable.' So the fact is that the Austro-Hungarian Government accused the Serbian Government of complicity in the plot, *when all the evidence to hand showed that they were guiltless.*[1] Whatever the facts may turn out to be, nothing can absolve the Austro-Hungarian Government from this responsibility.

The German Government was misled as to the facts by Berchtold and may have believed the Serb Government really guilty. It seems certain that the support of Germany was the decisive factor with Berchtold, and that he could not have sent the ultimatum without it. In fact he stiffened up his memorandum of June 24 by a demand 'for the isolation and diminution' of Serbia and then asked Kaiser William for support on July 5. It is important to note that, in deciding to support Austria-Hungary, Germany was fully aware that it meant war with Serbia. And the Kaiser and the Chancellor had very recent information that war with Serbia would mean war with Russia too. On June 17 the Rumanian Prime Minister reported a remark of Sazonov, who was then accompanying the Czar on a state visit to Rumania, to the effect that 'under no pretext would Russia admit an Austrian aggression against Serbia.' And Kaiser William wrote in the margin of the despatch 'Aha, then the Rumanians would help the Russians!'[2] Only three weeks before Germany had heard that war with Serbia meant war with Russia, and probably with Rumania also. Under these circumstances it was dangerous to give a blank cheque to Austria. That she gave it Germany publicly avowed.[3] This makes the question of whether she knew the contents of the ultimatum, or not, hardly relevant to the question of her responsibility.

There can be little question that Berchtold did not mean the ultimatum to be accepted, and therefore that he meant to provoke war with Serbia. Its drastic character and the demand for a reply in forty-eight hours seem to prove this. But when Serbia replied judiciously and moderately, the effect produced in Vienna was very different from that produced in Berlin.[4] Kaiser William at once expressed the view that all pretext for war had disappeared and took steps to ease the situation.

---

[1] From this point of view, therefore, the Serb guilt is irrelevant and academic. It has not been proved that the Serbian Government had any share in the plot. Their interests seem to have been against any such reckless move. But they unquestionably failed to warn the Austro-Hungarian Government of any such attempt, of which it has been asserted, though not proved, that they knew something. It is a fact that two Serbian officers, one of them Chief of the Military Intelligence, though strongly opposed to the civil government, had knowledge of, and lent support to, the plot.

[2] *Grosse Politik*, vol. 39. pp. 520–21.

[3] *v.* above, p. 353.

[4] On July 25 Serbia answered the note at 6 P.M., having already mobilised between 3 and 4 P.M. Austria-Hungary decreed a partial mobilisation (enough to deal with Serbia) at 9.30 P.M. on the 25th and declared war on Serbia on the 28th.

Probably it was too late to do anything, for, as has been well said, 'only a miracle' could have averted war after the ultimatum. But Germany deserves some credit for having made the attempt.

Germany's appearance in the rôle of moderator was partly due to England. On the 26th England's fleet was prevented from dispersing after manœuvres and thus in effect mobilised. And some strong remarks, made by Grey, reached Berlin at 4.37 P.M. on the 27th, asking Germany to restrain Austria-Hungary from 'a fool-hardy policy.' By 10 A.M. on the 28th the Kaiser had suggested a move on these lines to Bethmann, who sent off a wire that night. It reached Vienna at 4.30 A.M. on the 29th. Berchtold was asked to moderate his further demands on Serbia and to make a conciliatory approach to Russia. It seems clear that he never intended to do this, and his action was inconclusive and unsatisfactory till mid-day on the 31st, when he took steps leading to war.

On the 29th the General Staff began to be of importance in every country and in Germany Moltke was prevented from mobilising. The same evening Sazonov decided on a partial mobilisation of the Russian army, which the soldiers persuaded him to make general. But at 9.30 the Czar intervened and again made the mobilisation partial.[1] But between 3 and 4 P.M. on the 30th Sazonov won over the Czar to a general mobilisation, which was actually executed at 6 P.M. that night.

Germany had this great advantage over Russia that her mobilisation was the more rapid. Consequently she could afford to wait a little longer with safety, especially in view of the advantage of throwing on Russia the odium of causing the war. But Moltke, whether on his own initiative or not, intended to make sure. At 7.40 P.M. on the 30th (before he knew of Russia's mobilisation) he wired to Conrad at Vienna urging on him a general Austro-Hungarian mobilisation and stating that a German mobilisation would follow. Conrad took this at 10 A.M. on the 31st to Berchtold, who in a council decided on general mobilisation of Austria-Hungary at 11.30 A.M.

At exactly the same time on the 31st Germany received definite news of Russia's general mobilisation. At 1.45 P.M. she declared the state of *Kriegs-Gefahr*, the stage preceding mobilisation, and informed Vienna that mobilisation would follow. At midnight (31st July–1st August) an ultimatum went to Russia demanding the arrest of her mobilisation in twelve hours, and an ultimatum to France demanding her neutrality. Without waiting for an answer, Germany decreed general mobilisation at 5 P.M., and at 7 P.M. (6 P.M. German time) Germany declared war on Russia.

The part played by France was dictated partly by the obligations of her alliance and partly by an arrangement made by Viviani and Poincaré, who were visiting Russia and only left at 9.30 on July 23. Before

---

[1] The difference between a partial and a general mobilisation was very great. The former would be in the South and thus not threaten Germany. Moreover, if begun, it was hard to transform quickly into a general mobilisation.

leaving they had agreed that France and Russia 'should not leave any-thing undone to prevent a request for an explanation [from Austria-Hungary] . . . of such a kind that Servia might consider it as an attack on her sovereignty and independence.' [1] But before any steps could be taken the Austro-Hungarian ultimatum had been delivered. As it proved, Poincaré and Viviani did not actually reach Paris till the 29th, and on that evening at a Cabinet meeting appear to have decided to stand by Russia. On the 30th the French Minister of War suggested to Rus-sia's military attaché that there was nothing to prevent her from making secret military preparations even though mobilisation measures were temporarily relaxed.[2] This was a serious suggestion, if it was inspired by the French Cabinet. The Russians were fully conscious that their mobilisation was slower than the German, but secret military prepara-tions were dangerous in every sense. The French military preliminaries were begun on the 25th, and on the 29th five army corps took up posi-tions for defence on the frontier, though reservists were not summoned. On the 30th an important step was taken by drawing a cordon of ten kilometres round the French frontier, and withdrawing nearly all French troops behind it. In the military sense this was unimportant, but diplomatically it had excellent effects, especially on England. On July 31, on hearing of the German declaration of war on Russia, the five French army corps were authorised to take all necessary steps to defend the frontier. On August 1 general mobilisation was decided, and actually decreed at 3.45 P.M.,[3] about an hour and a quarter before that of Germany. France was careful to explain that mobilisation was not war, but it does not seem to have been doubted that it would follow. The German ultimatum to France had been delivered at 7 P.M. on July 31. It demanded an answer in eighteen hours as to whether France would be neutral in a Russo-German War. This time limit was ex-tended, for neither side was anxious to make the rupture, and each tried, by making use of petty frontier incidents, to put the other in the wrong. In result war was only declared by Germany on France at 6 P.M. on August 3. We may sum up by saying that France took no provocative steps, but made no obvious attempt to moderate Russia. She made several appeals to England for assistance, but always apparently taking care not to involve any pledge of honour. 'In these interviews, under all the strain of anxiety, Cambon never once hinted that any obligation or point of honour was involved; never suggested that, in such a crisis as this, if we stood upon the letter of the written communications ex-

---

[1] Telegram of Viviani, 1 A.M., Reval, July 24. French Yellow Book. *Collected Diplomatic Documents* (1915), p. 154, and *Documents Diplomatiques Français (1871-1914)*, 3rd Ser., vol. XI. p. 1.

[2] *Livre Noir* (1925), vol. II. p. 290.

[3] P. Renouvin: *Les Origines immédiates de la guerre* (1925), pp. 176-80. On p. 177 he shows that the 10-kilometre cordon 'n'était donnée qu'à titre indicatif.' For the errors in reporting this decision as to the cordon, *v. Gooch and Temperley*, vol. XI pp. 202 n., 214.

changed between us in 1912, we should be acting contrary to the spirit of them.'[1]

England's part in the outbreak of war is the last, and in one sense the most important, to be described. As told before, the fleet was prevented from demobilisation on the 26th, and on the same day a circular suggestion for a Conference was made by Grey.[2] But this proposal reached Berlin at the same time as a report from Prince Henry of Prussia that King George V thought England would be neutral, and this belief may have influenced events. The Conference suggestion was rejected by Germany. But a sharper tone from England on the 27th prompted her to suggest moderation to Austria-Hungary on the 29th.[3] Unfortunately on that evening Bethmann made a bid for neutrality to the British Ambassador, offering in case of war to preserve the integrity of France (though not of her colonies) and hinting at a possible violation of Belgium's neutrality. Grey refused stiffly on the 30th, saying it would be a 'disgrace' to make this bargain, but suggesting once more the possibility of a Conference at the moment, and for the future, as a panacea for Europe's ills. In consequence of the hint about Belgium Grey asked both France and Germany on the 31st for an assurance that each would respect the neutrality of Belgium so long as no other Power violated it. By 2.15 A.M. on the 1st France had given a definite assurance, while Germany gave an evasive answer by 3.30 A.M. Grey had already been pressed hard by France for support. He had also received on the 31st a strong private memorandum from Sir Eyre Crowe, advocating the maintenance of the Balance of Power, and the support of France on the ground that an 'honourable expectation has been raised,' which we could not repudiate 'without exposing our good name to grave criticism.'[4] Grey admits that if we did 'not decide at the critical moment to support France,' he himself would have had to resign.[5]

By August 1 the period of indecision was coming to an end, for Germany had refused the Belgian pledge. But the Cabinet still refused to send the expeditionary force overseas or to defend the northern coasts of France against German attack. Grey informed Lichnowsky, the German Ambassador, on August 1 that he was disappointed at Germany's evasive reply as to Belgium. When asked 'whether, if Germany

[1] Grey: *Twenty-Five Years*, vol. I. p. 340, but Cambon is reported as saying to Grey on August 1, 'Is there not a moral obligation on you to support us, at any rate with your fleet, since it was at your advice that we transferred our own?' Gooch: *Recent Revelations of European Diplomacy* (1930), p. 146.

[2] Or rather by the permanent Under-Secretary Nicolson in his absence. *Twenty-Five Years*, vol. I. p. 315; for Prince Henry's message, v. *Kautsky Documents*, p. 215, but cp. King George's letter published in *Gooch and Temperley*, vol. X. (2), p. 658.

[3] On the 29th Winston Churchill despatched the British fleet secretly to its stations in the North Sea and elsewhere.

[4] v. *Gooch and Temperley*, vol. XI. pp. 228-9.

[5] *Twenty-Five Years*, vol. I. p. 312.

gave a promise not to violate Belgian neutrality, we would engage to remain neutral, I replied that I could not say that; our hands were still free, and we were considering what our attitude should be.' And he suggested that much would depend on public opinion.

On the morning of August 2 the Cabinet met again. It knew that Germany had declared war on Russia, and probably that German troops had entered the neutral territory of Luxemburg and were likely soon to enter that of Belgium.[1] It had also received a promise of unconditional support from the Conservative Opposition. But the Cabinet remained undecided as to intervention. One point was settled, for at 2.20 P.M. Grey declared to the French Ambassador 'I am authorised to give an assurance that if the German fleet comes into the Channel or through the North Sea to undertake hostile operations against French coasts or shipping the British fleet will give all the protection in its power.'[2] This was to be subject to the consent of Parliament. Grey pointed out to Cambon that this 'did not bind us to go to war with Germany unless the German fleet took the action indicated, but it did give a security to France that would enable her to settle the disposition of her own Mediterranean fleet.' It is here that we realise the importance of Mr. Churchill's remonstrance with Grey as to the very disposition of that Mediterranean fleet two years before, and as to the consequences it might ultimately entail. 'But [consider] how tremendous would be the weapon which France would possess to compel our intervention, if she could say, "On the advice of and by arrangement with your naval authorities we have left our Northern coasts defenceless. We cannot possibly come back in time." Indeed [I added somewhat inconsequently] *it would probably be decisive whatever is written down now. Everyone must feel who knows the facts that we have the obligations of an alliance without its advantages, and above all without its precise definitions.*'[3]   So the French weapon was effective, and the consequences at length revealed.

There was a Cabinet meeting on the morning of the 3rd, when it was already known that Belgium's neutrality was almost certain to be violated and that Belgium herself would fight. The Cabinet ordered mobilisation of the army and Grey went down to the Commons. His speech was a great success, and it was clear that the violation of Belgium, the point which he emphasised, would be supported by Parliament as a *casus belli*. Grey now knew what to do. At 9.30 A.M. on the 4th he demanded an immediate reply from Germany as to respecting Belgian neutrality. At 2 P.M., having been informed that Belgian territory had been violated, he instructed the British Ambassador at

---

[1] The Luxemburg telegram was received 11.45 A.M.
[2] *Gooch and Temperley*, vol. XI. pp. 274–5.
[3] The italics are the Editors'. Minute to Grey of August 23, 1912. Churchill: *World Crisis* (1931 Edn.), p. 82; *Revue de France*, July 1, 1921, pp. 38–40. Cambon regards this decision as committing England to war, which cannot be waged 'by halves.'

Berlin to demand 'a satisfactory reply' and to ask for his passports if he did not receive it by midnight. And so at midnight England entered into war.

The British attitude was really assumed on the 2nd, with the decision to protect the north coast of France. For it is hard to see how war could have been avoided after this step. None the less Grey could not have taken even this step without the approval of the Commons, and it seems to have been the Belgian question which enabled him to carry this point with them. So in that sense it is true that Belgium was the real cause of the British entry into the war. It seems to be clear that Grey wished to stand by France anyway, and that he would have resigned in case we had not. But he got neither Cabinet nor Parliament to approve steps in that direction until the Conservatives offered their support and the Belgian question loomed large on the horizon. The criticism made by some, that Grey might have prevented war if he had offered to stand with France and Russia at an earlier date, is in reality a tribute to the moderation of the British Cabinet.[1] That England went to war on the question of Belgium alone is untrue, that without the violation of Belgian neutrality Grey might have failed to carry Parliament or Cabinet into war seems to be true.[2]

[1] The 'ifs' of history are naturally difficult to weigh. Grey himself has put up a strong opposition to this particular 'if.' *Twenty-Five Years*, vol. II. p. 43. For other criticisms on Grey *v.* Montgelas: *The Case for the Central Powers*, pp. 173, 184, 202–3; and for Paul Cambon, *v.* Gooch: *Recent Revelations of European Diplomacy* (1930), p. 146, and the 4th Edition of this work, published in 1940, pp. 294–5.

[2] Professor B. E. Schmitt in *Current History*, March 1927, pp. 847–8, thus summarises England's attitude with reference to Russia's mobilisation (the references are to Gooch and Temperley: *British Documents on the Origins of the War* (1926), vol. XI.):

'About the Russian mobilization, the British Government was fully informed. . . .

'The British attitude toward Russia was dictated by two considerations:

'(1) After the "reasonable" Serbian reply (minute on No. 171), the Russian defense of Serbia was held to be justified. To Nicolson's mind, it was "quite preposterous, not to say iniquitous," for Germany to argue that "all the Powers are to hold the ring while Austria quietly strangles Serbia" (No. 239). Grey, therefore, in his conversations with Lichnowsky, "assumed that a war between Austria and Serbia cannot be localized" (minute on No. 100), and said that he could "do nothing for moderation unless Germany is prepared *pari passu* to do the same" (minute on No. 103). It was understood that "if Russia mobilizes, . . . Germany will do the same"; but since "it seems certain that Austria is going to war, . . . it would be neither possible nor just and wise to make any move to restrain Russia from mobilizing" (Crowe's minute on No. 170). Possibly Grey later regretted this attitude, for on July 31 he remarked to the French Ambassador that the Russian mobilization, "it seemed to me, would precipitate a crisis, and would make it appear that German mobilization was being forced by Russia" (No. 367).

'(2) Much more was at issue than the fate of Serbia. "Russia is a formidable power and will become increasingly strong," Nicolson observed on July 20 (minute on No. 66). "Let us hope that our relations with her will continue to be friendly." Buchanan telegraphed that "for ourselves position is a most perilous one, and we shall have to choose between giving Russia our active support or renouncing her friendship" (No. 125). Crowe dotted the i's: [Continued overleaf

13*

The real question raised by the story of the last five weeks before the war is not whether war could then have been averted, but whether the preceding situation had made war certain. The impression of Colonel House on his peace visit to Europe in May 1914, was that the air was charged with electricity, 'militarism run stark mad,' and that everything betokened a readiness to strike. This impression from over the water is deepened by all that we see between February and June, the councils of Russia's Government, the threats in her press, the increases in her army, and in that of Germany and France, the contest between Entente and Alliance for the favours of Rumania, England's naval conversations with Russia, Moltke's words that the sooner war came the better for Germany, and finally the secret but ominous preparations by Austria-Hungary for a final reckoning with Serbia.

All these were symbols and signs of deeper and darker forces. At last what so many had feared had come about. The ambitions, the fears and the hatreds of the two groups had plunged the world in darkness. 'The lamps are going out all over Europe,' said Grey one evening. 'We shall not see them lit again in our lifetime.'

' "It is clear that France and Russia are decided to accept the challenge thrown out to them. Whatever we may think of the merits of Austrian charges against Serbia, France and Russia consider that these are the pretexts, and that the bigger cause of Triple Alliance versus Triple Entente is definitely engaged.

' "I think it would be impolitic, not to say dangerous, for England to attempt to controvert this opinion, or to endeavour to obscure the plain issue, by any representation at St. Petersburg and Paris. . . .

' "Our interests are tied up with those of France and Russia in this struggle, which is not for the possession of Serbia, but one between Germany aiming at a political dictatorship in Europe and the Powers who desire to retain individual freedom." (Minute of July 25, on No. 101).

'This point of view determined British policy. But Grey refused to promise assistance in spite of four appeals from Sazonov (Nos. 101, 125, 170, 247) and one from Izvolsky (No. 216); he left Russia to take her own course.' cp. S. B. Fay: *Origins of the World War* (New York, 1930), vol. II. chap. vi.

PART V

THE WAR AND ITS AFTERMATH IN EUROPE AND ASIA, 1914–23

CHAPTER XXIX

THE WAR, 1914–1918

I. 1914

EUROPE beheld a unique sight during the early days of the war. Huge columns of troops were on the move along its Eastern, Central, and Western plains. They were moving in numbers so great as to resemble a migration of the peoples. Europe had armed on an unprecedented scale and her mobilised millions were already on their march to death. From Germany grey columns passed across the Rhine and streamed towards France. Blue French columns, with a few khaki-clad British ones, were straining to meet them in Belgium. A few grey German divisions could be seen on the borders of East Prussia. Long yellow columns were pressing to the northern frontiers of Austria-Hungary and watching anxiously for the green waves of advancing Russians. Far away to the south, huge yellow columns were swarming across the Bosnian border, to envelop the little army of Serbia. Six weeks sufficed to decide the fate of all these movements. The tiny Serb host had repulsed the Austro-Hungarians. The Russians had been flung back from East Germany with enormous loss, but had routed the Austro-Hungarians and occupied most of Galicia. Paris was saved—and the blue-khaki columns had driven the grey ones before them from the Marne to the Aisne. Effects had been produced by one battle in the West, and by another in the East which lasted till the end of the war. The green waves never again submerged East Germany; the grey tide never again lapped the walls of Paris.

The Russian offensive may come first. It was not so important as the German thrust in the West, but none the less weighty in ultimate result. The German plan was to make their thrust for Paris, and to leave a very small garrison in East Germany hoping that the Austro-Hungarians could make head against Russia for six weeks. After that Paris would have fallen and German reinforcements could be sent Eastwards. This plan had one defect, it left East Prussia naked and exposed to a daring thrust. If the Russians overran East Prussia and combined this success with a victory in Galicia, the results would have been startling. The Silesian coalfields and their immense industrial population

would have been open, and the Austro-Hungarian flank would have
been rolled up and destroyed. The German General Staff had considered these possibilities and decided to face the risks. They despised
the Russian military machine for its slowness, inefficiency, and corruption.

The Russian Commander-in-Chief, the Grand-Duke Nicholas, was
perhaps the best choice Russia could have made. He had the advantage
of rank, of energy, and of devotion to his profession. Moreover, unknown to Germany, he had in his pocket the war plans of Austria-
Hungary, which had been betrayed to him by Slav officers in the service
of Francis Joseph. He had another advantage—which neither he nor
Germany expected. The first stages of the Russian mobilisation were
passed with unexpected rapidity and the green masses were soon flood-
ing not only Austrian Poland but East Germany. For the Grand-Duke
had resolved to make a bold effort to influence the campaign in France.
Originally the Russians had resolved to throw all their forces against
Austria-Hungary, but the Grand-Duke altered this plan in order to save
Paris. He sent two large armies to envelop the German force in East
Prussia. His plan might have succeeded had his choice of men been
more fortunate. One commander, Samsonov, was bold to the point of
rashness; the other, Rennenkampf, was cautious to the point of weakness. Had they been men like Ruszki or Brussilov the result would have
been different. Victory was certain in Galicia where the Austro-
Hungarian plan was known. It could have been secured in East Prussia
by bold and resolute leadership.

East Prussia had a legendary horror of the Slav barbarians, and
heard with terror the news of their invasion. Rennenkampf attacked the
Eastern border but made ground slowly, Samsonov pushed rapidly up
from the south. The two commanders were divided by distance and
did not act in unison, though each army was stronger than the whole
German force. It was little wonder that the German commander lost
his head and spoke of retreat. He was at once superseded and replaced
by a retired general, drawn from obscurity in Hanover, and by a staff
officer who had just won celebrity in France. Hindenburg and Ludendorff arrived on the scene too late to frame any plan of their own. But
they found one drawn up by Colonel Hoffmann, who had studied the
local conditions and taken the measure of the Russian commanders.
He calculated that Samsonov was advancing too quickly and Rennenkampf too slowly, and that they were out of touch with one another.
In that case each could be attacked separately, and destroyed by the
German force which, though smaller, was more efficient than either.
Any other course meant ruin or defeat, so Hindenburg and Ludendorff
swallowed the plan whole, and applied it with the utmost vigour and
resolution. They began by launching two-thirds of their whole force
against Samsonov. Thousands of Russians were slain or captured in
the marshes of Tannenberg, and Samsonov took his own life in the

agony of defeat (August 26–29). Then Hindenburg turned eastwards against Rennenkampf—and drove him beyond the German border, slaughtering thousands in battles by the Masurian Lakes (September 6–12). In all something like a quarter of a million Russians were slain or captured. The Russians had none the less caused by their invasion the recall of two German Army Corps to Prussia at a critical moment during the advance on Paris (August 25–26). It is possible to hold that this diversion produced the German defeat on the Marne.[1]

The relief to Germany was immense. The slaughter of myriads of barbarians in these 'dim weird battles' amid marshes and lakes fired the Teutonic imagination. It was at Tannenberg in 1410 that the Teutonic Knights had been overthrown, and the Grand-Duke Nicholas had boasted that the Slav sword, drawn there, had not rusted. On this twice famous field the verdict had now been reversed, and the Germans had been triumphant over the greatest odds. The names of Hindenburg and Ludendorff became linked, and this victory (which neither had devised) gave both immortal fame and led them ultimately to the highest positions of military command. Tannenberg became to the German what Salamis or Marathon were to the Greek, and Hindenburg became a living hero of legend.

The verdicts of the people are not always those of history, and even the defeat of Tannenberg was not necessarily decisive. The Russian troops were notoriously indifferent to losses, and had still a chance of overwhelming not only Galicia but East Prussia before the year ended. It took Russia only three weeks to pierce deep into Galicia. They had little superiority in numbers, but they had the priceless advantage of knowing the enemy's plans. By the end of August they had defeated the Austro-Hungarians in front of Lemberg and entered the town. In the early days of September they won a colossal victory in front of Grodek. Two-thirds of Galicia passed into their power, the great fortress of Przemysl was masked, and the Russian armies reached the passes of the Carpathians and approached the old royal Polish city of Cracow. Its capture would have been decisive, for it defends the gap which gives easy access at once to Silesia and to Austria. With Cracow in their grasp the Russians could have turned the whole German frontier line of defence by Posen and Thorn, and occupied Breslau and the Silesian coalfields.

Cracow was not saved by Austro-Hungarian or by German generals in Silesia but by Hindenburg. That commander had himself just had a narrow escape from defeat. He had crossed the border in pursuit of the flying Rennenkampf and in the eagerness of advance only just avoided falling into traps like those he had set for the Russians. He did avoid them however and eventually regained his own territory. In the early days of October he found that a unified direction had been arranged for the whole Austro-German line, and that he had the chief German

[1] B. H. Liddell Hart: *The Real War* (1930), p. 86.

command. He, or Ludendorff, had profited from experience. They had learnt that East Prussia was safe from invasion and that the Russian area east of it was dangerous for invaders. Looking at the front as a whole it was clear that there was only one way of saving Cracow. That was to threaten Warsaw, and he now attacked Warsaw at a moment when Austro-German power was increasing and Russian declining. The German reserves were arriving, along with ample supplies of munitions. The Russian mobilisation had been quicker than was anticipated, but the arrival of reinforcements and drafts was very slow. Curiously enough, the loss of Russian men had mattered little, but the loss of rifles and guns had mattered much. Russia could only produce munitions in small quantities and her supplies were already drying up. Her troops were feeling the strain of a continuous campaign in which they had not been relieved, they were imperfectly armed, and were undoubtedly outnumbered by the Austro-Germans during the late autumn of 1914 (not of course in actual ration strength, but in the number of men who could be efficiently armed).

In the second week of October Hindenburg moved on Warsaw with five converging attacks, extending from Thorn in the north to Cracow in the south. But his movements had been anticipated by the Grand-Duke Nicholas, who had secretly withdrawn the Russian armies so that they formed an almost continuously straight line, stretching from the extreme end of East Prussia (with a bulge defending the capital of Warsaw) to a point on the Carpathians some forty miles east of Cracow. This time the German attacks were a complete failure and were easily flung back to the frontier. The Austro-Hungarians for a time had some success and temporarily relieved Przemysl. But by the end of October the whole attempt had proved a costly failure and the Russians were again close to the German frontier. Two Russian offensives followed— one against Silesia and the other once more against Cracow. Neither succeeded, but a second attack by Hindenburg on Warsaw was held up some forty miles west of the town. The campaign closed in December, with both sides fought to a standstill. It also closed—and finally—the chance of an early decision in the East. The German frontier was intact, Cracow was saved, Silesia defended, and the Carpathian barrier still held. The long green line stretching from East Prussia to the Carpathians was, in future, one for defence not for attack. The Russian 'steam-roller,' as it was called, was no longer effective for advance. Russia might be important in immobilising masses of German and Austro-Hungarian troops, but there was neither hope nor possibility of the 'Slav Colossus' achieving victory. It was the old story of Frederick the Great and the Russians, the battle of the athlete against the giant. The Titan was already severely punished, though his vast strength enabled him to prolong the struggle. The athlete was too agile to be knocked out, but still did not carry enough weight to knock out his opponent.

In the West, as in the East, deadlock was reached by the end of the year. The struggle in the West had been more dramatic, and the failure of the German offensive against Paris is much less easy to explain than the failure of the Russian attack on East Prussia. Russia's plans had miscarried because she lacked patience, energy, science, intelligence, power of organisation and all sorts of *matériel*. Germany had all these and many other qualities too. Foch said her army in 1914 was the best equipped and most formidable that ever took the field. Yet this stupendous exertion of military energy, this supreme effort of intelligence and will by a most gifted people, came to nought. The supreme objective—the capture of Paris—failed, and with that failure everything was lost. Indeed, looking at ultimates, it seems to have involved the destruction of the German military system and dynasty. Was the campaign then a gamble or a miscalculation of chances? The stakes were so high that it was not worth playing unless Paris could be captured.

The German offensive plan against Paris had been perhaps more carefully studied than any military design in history. Count Schlieffen—then Chief of Staff—had finally evolved it in 1905, though it was not officially adopted until 1912. The French frontier—as left in 1871—offered formidable obstacles, unless the German advance violated the neutral areas of Belgium and Luxemburg. Northwards from Alsace stretched the Vosges and the Ardennes, a line of woods and hills which were militarily formidable. Art had supplemented nature by a second line of defence in the shape of a bristling row of fortresses from Belfort, Épinal, and Nancy to Toul and Verdun. In this restricted area the vast German masses had no room to deploy and would batter their heads against impregnable barriers. Belgium and Luxemburg offered ample space, while the French fortifications behind them were much less developed. Schlieffen left the ethics of violating neutral territory to statesmen and considered only the military problem. If they penetrated Belgium the vast armies of Germany could manœuvre on a wide circle, swinging round on the great German fortress of Metz as a pivot. Armies could be poured through Belgium and Luxemburg into North France and could then advance on Paris. The outermost army on the right was to pass Paris on the west (the side nearest to England) and to come round it from the south. The French armies would then be caught in a trap between Paris and the Vosges. They would either be immediately enveloped or driven across to the German armies in Alsace or over the frontier into Switzerland. Paris would fall and the war be at an end six weeks after it had begun. This was the Schlieffen plan, but when the younger Moltke became Chief of Staff he introduced serious modifications. He weakened the right or manœuvring wing and strengthened the left wing south of Metz, and this change, perhaps, in itself explains the German failure.

The first clash was at the Belgian frontier fortress of Liège, which the Germans sought to seize by a *coup de main*. On the 5th August the

Belgian garrison, fighting with great gallantry, defeated the attempt. Altogether they delayed the advance of the first German Army by two, if not three, days, and this delay was of great importance. But no Belgian valour could stem the German tide. By the 20th August Brussels, the capital, opened its gates. Most of the Belgian Army retired into Antwerp, where it constituted a formidable threat to the flank of the advancing Germans.

We must now leave the German hosts sweeping on through Belgium and Luxemburg to Paris and consider the French dispositions. General Joffre—the French Chief of Staff—was a soldier of strong nerves. But he had an army inferior both in numbers and in *matériel* to the German, and he had to guard every part of the frontier till he knew where the German blows would fall. The calculations of the French General Staff were at fault. They had rightly anticipated a German violation of Belgium and Luxemburg. But they had reckoned (and refused to be convinced until too late) that the line of advance would be east of the Meuse through Luxemburg and the Ardennes. They tried disastrous offensives in Lorraine and failed in their effort. They also hoped to get a British-French force up in time into Belgium to hold a line stretching south from Antwerp and Namur to Sedan. This was a good plan, but the Germans were too quick for it to be carried out. Joffre thereupon authorised a new plan. Namur was to be held as the apex of a triangle, with a western side ending at Mons and an eastern one stretching to Sedan. This manœuvre involved some danger, for it meant holding a sharp salient, but it had many advantages if Namur, the apex, could hold out for a fortnight. It was believed (though erroneously) that it could, and it was here that the Germans sprung on the Allies one of the first of their many military surprises. On the 21st of August they began to bombard Namur, and their immense guns caused its capitulation on the 25th. Its fall placed the allied troops, who were hurrying to their positions, in a situation of extreme peril. British troops had reached Mons on the 22nd and found the first German Army feeling round their left flank and threatening to encircle them. On the 23rd their neighbours the fifth French Army were flung back from Charleroi, and the fourth and third French Armies further eastward suffered still worse reverses, and fell back even more rapidly. The British, after a victorious rearguard action near Mons, followed the retreat of the fifth French Army on the 24th. The British won a small success against the first German Army at Le Cateau (26th) and the fifth French were victorious in a rearguard action at Guise (29th). The situation was, however, still grave; Amiens fell, and before the end of the month the British were cut off from the Channel ports and their supplies. Von Kluck's first German Army was sweeping on to Paris. Joffre, after seeing the failure of his original plan, was now at work on a new one. The second and first French Armies had resisted stoutly in front of Toul, Nancy, and Verdun. He therefore decided to hold on to this fortified area and swing back his exhausted armies in the west. The British, the fifth, fourth, and third French Armies were to retreat behind the Seine to prepare for an ultimate offensive. Meanwhile General Gallieni, with a newly organised army (the sixth) was to defend Paris. This plan involved certain dangers, for Paris was, or might be, isolated until the retreating troops could reorganise and advance to its aid. But it kept the armies (other than the sixth) united and intact.[1]

The German advance had apparently been triumphant everywhere, yet the High Command was in difficulties. Wastages had told on the strength of the advancing armies. Two corps had been detached to watch Antwerp, and by a grave decision two more had been hurriedly taken from the investing force of Namur and sent off to Russia (August 25–26).[2] None the less the German Headquarters considered that the programme had been carried out, and Moltke issued orders accordingly on August the 28th. Von Kluck with the first Army was ordered to circle round Paris and then to move southwards, Bülow with the second Army was to advance on Paris itself, and to keep in touch with the neighbouring third German Army. All this was according to plan, but not according to the ideas of Bülow. He had discovered one gap, which seemed to be widening, between von Kluck and himself, and another gap between himself and the third Army. The heavy French repulse of his army at Guise on the 29th shook his nerve, and produced an important decision. Bülow—without referring to Headquarters—implored the first and third Armies to close in to his support. Von Kluck agreed and closed rapidly in towards Bülow, hoping thus to catch the British or the fifth French Army. German Headquarters heard this news from von Kluck when it was too late to alter his movement. They approved it, though it entirely destroyed their plan. It would now be impossible for von Kluck to circle round Paris, or for Bülow to invest it. Von Kluck's extreme right wing was advancing so as to pass some thirty miles east of Paris. This blunder destroyed Germany's hope of victory, and gave France her opportunity.

Gallieni, who was Governor of Paris and commander of the sixth Army, had marked the advance from his watch-tower. By September 3 his anxiety was relieved. Von Kluck could not now attack Paris, and the capital could be in no immediate danger. The sixth French Army could therefore take part in the fighting. Gallieni considered that a sortie from Paris would be almost useless. But, as von Kluck's right flank was already exposed, he and his sixth Army could deal it a deadly blow if they fought in conjunction with the British and the French fifth Armies. It is a matter of dispute whether Gallieni himself devised the plan and forced it on Joffre, or whether Joffre took the initiative.

---

[1] In view of the Gallieni-Joffre controversy it is important to note that these measures were taken on August 24–25, and that Gallieni only became Governor of Paris on August 26.

[2] v. pp. 397, 405.

Anyhow, Joffre assumed full responsibility on September 4, when he issued his famous General Order for resuming the offensive. 'The time for looking back is past. Every effort must be made to attack the enemy and hurl him back. Troops which find advance impossible must stand their ground and die rather than give way.'[1] Joffre had realised that the supreme moment of decision had arrived.

On the same day the German High Command issued new orders. Von Kluck and Bülow were to defend the German flank, by forming a half circle facing west towards Paris and thus hold off the sixth French, the British, and the fifth French Armies. The third German Army was to attack in front. The fourth and fifth German Armies were to push past Verdun and take Nancy in the rear, thus separating the French Armies and placing them between two fires. The new German plan was a desperate attempt to pluck victory from defeat. Even now von Kluck did not obey orders and retire quickly behind the Marne. Hence when the sixth French Army attacked him on September 6 he was at a great disadvantage. On the 7th the British and the fifth French Armies joined in the attack. Von Kluck held the sixth French Army, but his forces were weakened at their points of contact with the British and the French fifth Armies. The gap in the German defences widened. Next to the fifth French Army, behind the marshes of Gond, a new French Army (the ninth) had been formed. It was weak in guns and men, but strong in its commander, General Foch. The German third Army hammered vigorously at his thin lines, and only Foch's extraordinary tenacity prevented a break through. Further eastwards still the French lines held, though the fighting was extraordinarily severe, especially round Verdun, Nancy, and Toul. The war of movement, of manœuvres, and of decisive action therefore centred round the Marne and the marshes of Gond. But even on the 9th the Germans were not yet beaten in fight, and their defeat was due to the weakness of their own commanders rather than to the strength of the Allies.

The German High Command was still at Luxemburg, and, by reason of the immense distance, had in fact lost touch with the situation. By September 6 those 'central determining orders, which moulded the battle . . . two hundred miles away,' had ceased to mould it at all. Moltke finally delegated his authority as Chief of Staff to a certain Colonel Hentsch. He instructed him to motor to the Headquarters of each German Army and, if he judged a retreat necessary after local examination, to order it on his (Moltke's) authority as Chief of the Great German General Staff. This motoring delegate, a mere colonel, thus invested with supreme power was able to use it. On the 8th he visited the fifth, fourth, and third German Armies and satisfied himself that they could stand their ground. The question was whether the first and second Armies could still do so. Bülow, as he learned, had declined to

[1] The best discussion in English of the Gallieni-Joffre controversy is by Sir F. Maurice in *The World Crisis: A Criticism* (1927), chap. iv, pp. 92–119.

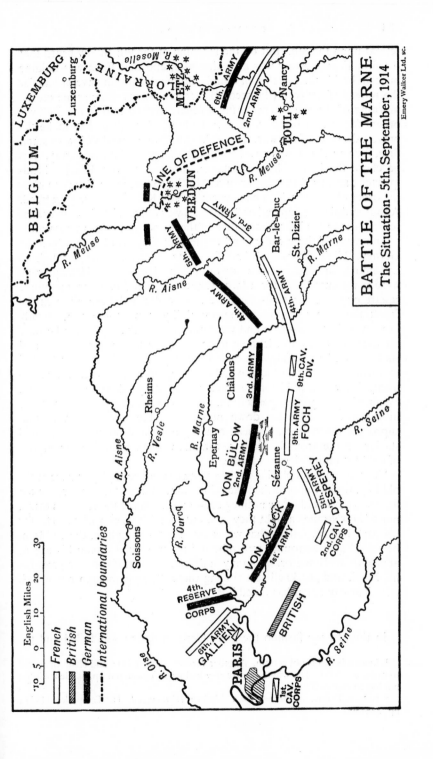

BATTLE OF THE MARNE.
The Situation - 5th. September, 1914

Emery Walker Ltd. sc.

retreat upon the 8th. But on the morning of the 9th Bülow heard that the fifth French Army was attacking him, and that Foch was holding his own beside the marshes of Gond. Bülow thereupon gave orders for the retreat of his own (the second) German Army. Some time on the morning of the 9th the motoring delegate arrived and found Bülow's orders for retreat being executed.[1] Colonel Hentsch had to make the gravest decision of the war. He could still have ordered Bülow to stand firm, for von Kluck was now actually overlapping Gallieni's army. But he chose the line of least resistance, motored to von Kluck's head-quarters, and used the authority of Moltke to force von Kluck to obey the order of retreat which he now gave. Von Kluck unwillingly agreed. About mid-day of September 9 the crisis was over. The German armies retired first to the Marne, and then to the Aisne, and Paris was saved.

The news of those orders and the fate of the great battle, which the German High Command had failed to control, came through to Luxemburg in the early afternoon of the 9th. The German Headquarters were in a house 'built for a large school and standing upon the public square opposite the post-office. . . . An order had been given at the front: the man upon whose responsibility it went—a man already broken with illness—rose and went out uncertainly, as though he were far older than his age, leaning upon the plain iron rail of the school staircase, as he painfully descended the steps . . . He came in his full uniform, this general officer, who had accepted and ordered the retire-ment. He was a nobleman, superior in military talent to his fellows, even amid that great organization, which was the best designed for war in Europe. . . . He sat down publicly on the low stone wall that supported the railings, his head bending more and more forward, and staring on the ground. He bore a name with very different memories of cold triumph. It was Moltke.

'A group of boys playing in the square ceased from play to gaze at the old boy, timidly approached the railings and stared at that poor, broken figure. They could know nothing of the traditions of the Prussian army, nor of how strange a sight they saw, but they felt its enormity. He, for his part, had forgotten what was around him—the place, the children; he stared at the ground, remembering as in a vivid dream his urgent appeal to his Emperor, his agony at defeat, his intelligence too great for his heart, and the knell still ringing there: "The campaign has failed. . . . The campaign has failed." '[2]

.   .   .   .

In this strange fashion the great German design was foiled and the

---

[1] Even this fact is not certain. Another version is that Bülow and Hentsch agreed to order a retreat. The whole controversy will never be cleared up, as Hentsch did not live to take part in it.

[2] Hilaire Belloc, in *Scenes from Modern History*, ed. H. Temperley (1931), pp. 228–30.

German armies turned back to the Aisne. There were still dangerous moments, there were still surprises in store for the Allies. In the first week of October the defences of Antwerp were smashed by the enormous guns of the Germans and the great fortress surrendered. But the Belgian Field-Army was successfully withdrawn and took its place in the Allied line. The Allies won the 'race to the sea,' protected the Channel ports, and ensured British communications by the heroic defence of Ypres. Both sides, exhausted by warfare, were digging themselves into entrenchments. France was defended for the first time by a continuous line of earth and iron stretching from the sea to the Vosges. A deadlock was established, which was not much disturbed till 1917, nor broken until 1918.

The year ended in the West as in the East with exhaustion and stagnation. But the failure of the German thrust at Paris is one of the mysteries of warfare as well as one of the problems of history. The Germans believed that, had they got to Paris, France would have been defeated and the war brought to an end, and in this view they were probably right. But the Germans also believed that the capture of Paris was a certainty, an assumption falsified by the event. Yet in some respects their military superiority was even greater than has usually been represented. The French General Staff miscalculated the direction of the German advance and the numbers of their divisions. They had an erroneous theory of the offensive, which rendered their counters to the German advance a series of bloody and useless failures. Up to the 28th August the German Command had fulfilled its programme to date, and success seemed within their grasp. Incidents like the detachment of two corps to East Prussia and of two more to Antwerp, or the resistance of Maubeuge, or the exhaustion of German troops are perhaps quite enough to explain the disaster. Yet the French had been decisively beaten at many points, and the Germans were still unbroken and victorious. The German failure began when von Kluck abandoned the original plan of marching round Paris, and struck south-east to join up the army of Bülow. This move enabled Gallieni and Joffre to launch a successful counter-offensive on the German flank. It is, of course, arguable that the gaps in the line were so serious that von Kluck was unable to act otherwise. But this assumption is doubtful. The German generals seem to have disregarded the High Command, when they did not agree with it. They did not seek to persuade it, but simply took action on their own. Thus von Kluck marched south-east at the request of Bülow on August 29 and Bülow gave orders for the retreat of his army on September 9, in each case without getting leave from the High Command. Indiscipline in the field was accompanied by a singular paralysis at Headquarters. The concentration of all power in the hands of Colonel Hentsch, who was sent as a travelling delegate by motor-car to settle the crisis on the spot, is an example of that palsy. Here was a colonel empowered to overrule generals and order retreats in the name and with the authority of a command which had already lost control of the situation. This display of impotence at the nerve-centre explains much. The Kaiser was, of course, quite unfit for supreme command, but the younger Moltke was also unsuited for it. His physical condition was poor, and his mental grasp appears to have been deficient. The Schlieffen plan required a right wing of overwhelming strength, the assumption being that (as events proved) French attacks on the centre in the Ardennes could easily be repelled. Moltke would not accept so bold a plan. Between 1905 and 1914 he added nine new divisions to the German Army, but placed only one on the right wing and eight on the left.[1] If seven of these divisions had been given to the right they might have filled the gaps and deterred Bülow and von Kluck from upsetting the Headquarters' plan. In the last analysis failure lay in a variety of complex and contingent causes, such as the too great independence of local commanders in the field, the weakness of the High Command which first modified the Schlieffen plan and then withdrew units from the fight at the crisis. The fact is the great ability of the German generals has blinded us to some of their defects, both in staff-work and in command in the field. They had learned almost everything from books and from manœuvres, they had had practically no previous opportunity of real service in war. At any rate the Frenchmen knew better how to combine local initiative with firm direction from the centre.

The French General Staff had blundered badly in their appreciation of the German designs. But Joffre, like Foch, Mangin and Gallieni, had had experience of war and therefore a power of observing realities and profiting by mistakes. It is certain that Joffre did not consider himself beaten even on August 25, a day when the news of defeat came from every quarter, of the fall of Namur, of the hurried retreat of the British and of three French armies. On that day of ill omen Joffre conceived the idea of an eventual counter-offensive and arranged to re-form his armies behind the Seine. If it be true that Gallieni, and not he, was responsible for the decision for the counter-offensive, the lesson is none the less instructive. Gallieni did not first lead out his army from Paris against von Kluck and then inform Joffre of his action. He persuaded or forced the High Command to agree with him, and only moved after orders for a general advance had been issued. Even if they were due to an impulse from below, the orders of September 4 took the form of a command from above. Thus the counter-offensive of Joffre was a properly concerted movement, in which the subordinate commanders thoroughly supported one another and their chief. Gallieni, when hard pressed by von Kluck, consoled himself by the thought that the British

---

[1] This is declared to have been a mistake by good critics both in France and Germany. But Moltke had to convince South Germany she was safe for political reasons. This fact is often forgotten. v. Sir F. Maurice: *British Strategy* (1929), pp. 91–2.

were relieving him from the south; Foch, clinging desperately to the
fringes of the Gond, reported the situation as 'excellent' and attacked,
in the belief that pressure on his front must mean a German retreat
before Gallieni and the British. It was in this manner that victory was
snatched from defeat before Paris. These methods are a complete contrast to those by which von Kluck or von Bülow coerced or defied von
Moltke.[1]

II. 1915

It is best to look at the campaign of 1915 through the eyes of Falkenhayn. Moltke had faded out of sight as the German armies fell back
from Paris, and Falkenhayn took his place as Chief of the German Staff.
He had to consider the whole problem of the war anew and to see what
courses were open to Germany. Though the Western thrust had failed
Germany still had the initiative. Falkenhayn thought the situation extremely serious, but did not, in his heart, abandon the belief that German victory in the West could alone be decisive. He rejected the idea
that he could get a decision there in 1915, as the Allies had a superiority
in men and *matériel*. The situation in the East in his view demanded
action. Turkey had joined Germany in the autumn of 1914, and England was preparing an expedition to force the Dardanelles and dictate
peace at Constantinople. Falkenhayn counted on its failure if ammunition, guns, and German expert military advice reached the Turks. But
a more formidable enemy was likely soon to be in the field. Italy had
been Germany's ally, but at the beginning of the war had declared her
neutrality. It was clear, however, even in the early months of 1915, that
Italy would not long remain neutral and would soon attack Austria-
Hungary. As soon as that event occurred large numbers of the Austro-
Hungarian troops in Galicia would have to be diverted to the Italian
front. This consideration was the decisive one with Falkenhayn. He
was not in principle an Easterner, nor did he believe that any defeat of
Russia would produce a real decision in the sense of ending the war.
But he thought a vigorous attack would push back the Russian armies
still further and render Austria-Hungary safe before she was attacked
by Italy.

Before April ended Franco-British attacks took place in the West,
and the first British landed at the Dardanelles. But Falkenhayn had
made up his mind and was not to be deterred. He had found an
admirable leader in Mackensen and directed him to break through
the Russian front—about 40 to 50 miles south-east of Cracow. On

---

[1] *Note on the Schlieffen Plan.* The plan as such—as in all modern military operations—aimed at the destruction of the enemy's army in the field, but it was assumed
that the fall of Paris would be the result of it. As regards Falkenhayn's plan for 1915,
that given above is his own account, but the German official history declares he
wanted to attack in the West but was overruled by the Kaiser. His statements are
questionable, though that quoted on p. 410 is probably exact.

May 2nd Mackensen's 'phalanx' pierced the Russian line between Gorlice and Gromnik. Its success could hardly have been greater and the Russians were completely routed. Falkenhayn exploited the success and diverted divisions from the West and from Hindenburg's part of the front for the purpose. Early in August Warsaw fell—and the Russians, despite furious struggles and counter-attacks, were pushed steadily backwards and expelled from Poland altogether. Their ammunition and rifles were so defective that they were hopelessly outclassed and the number of Russian prisoners taken was extremely large. By the end of September the Austro-German forces stood on a front stretching from the Bay of Riga in the north in an irregular line to the Bukovina and Eastern Carpathians in the south. Falkenhayn had a much shorter line to defend, and had relieved Austria-Hungary. It was believed, though, as events proved, wrongly, that all fear of a future Russian offensive had been removed.

Serbia's gallant little army had flung back the Austro-Hungarians in utter rout in August and again in December 1914. It was dangerous to leave them unsubdued when Italy was beginning to batter at the western border of Austria-Hungary. In September Bulgaria, hitherto neutral, decided to join the Austro-Germans and signed a secret military convention with them. Mackensen was withdrawn from Russian Poland to command a united force of Austro-Germans against Serbia with Bulgaria operating on the flank. The Serb army, weakened by typhus, could offer little resistance, and finally made its escape through Albania after suffering the loss of more than half its effectives (November). Franco-British troops had entered Greek territory, but they were unable to protect Serbia, and had to content themselves with holding Salonica as a base. There for three years they remained.

The Franco-British campaign in the West, undertaken chiefly to relieve the pressure on Russia, was expensive and useless. The most serious efforts were in Champagne in September. On the Italian side the results were almost equally disappointing. Operating in the Isonzo country the Italians, though superior in numbers, were hampered by inexperience and a difficult terrain. They had achieved almost no result by the end of the year except that of attracting a large number of Austro-Hungarians from the Eastern front.

It is impossible here to discuss why the Dardanelles expedition was decided upon. It is certain that the objective offered immense advantages if attained. If Constantinople fell and the Straits were opened, Russia would at once be relieved. Suffering cruelly from a German blockade she would be aided in the Black Sea by munitions, supplies and sea-power, while Russian grain and supplies would be available to the Allies. It is even possible that the glamour of obtaining Constantinople would have restored to the Russian Czar all the prestige he had lost by his defeats. Rumania and Greece would have been compelled to join the Allies, Bulgaria would have been defeated and Serbia restored. But such an enterprise required careful forethought and preparation, which could not be improvised. It required, above everything, secrecy and celerity, and neither of these factors was present.

Early in November 1914 British cruisers had most foolishly bombarded the Dardanelles' forts. The expedition was resolved upon in January 1915, and another bombardment took place at the end of February. An attempt to force the Straits by warships alone failed in the third week of March, and it was then decided to effect a landing with troops. But when the military expedition arrived in April the Turks, thrice forewarned, were at last forearmed.[1] Landings were effected both at the toe of the peninsula and at Anzac, but the troops found it difficult to advance much beyond the beaches and nowhere held the crest line. When in August landings were attempted at Suvla the British were nearer success, but still failed to achieve their purpose. It was a tragic failure and, though the British hung on with their usual tenacity, evacuation became inevitable when the heavy rains set in and swamped the trenches. The evacuation was carried out with almost no loss, owing to the masterly dispositions of General Birdwood.

On the whole it is probable that the risks of the Dardanelles expedition were too great to make success possible. Most of the troops were imperfectly trained, the maps were bad, and the experience of the past was not applied to the solution of the problem. Lord Kitchener's plan of landing in the vicinity of Alexandretta, though much less ambitious, was a more feasible project. It could not easily have been resisted by the Turks and it would have cut the connection between Constantinople on the one side and Jerusalem, Mecca, and Baghdad on the other.

The year 1915 closed in almost unbroken gloom for the Entente. Russia had been hopelessly defeated, Serbia and Montenegro had been annihilated, Bulgaria had joined the Austro-Germans, Italy had failed to win any real success, England had been beaten at the Dardanelles. Yet the prospect was not so bad as it seemed. Falkenhayn had succeeded in the East, but, as he well knew, the East was not the decisive front. The Italians, though still unsuccessful, were exercising a steady pressure on Austria-Hungary and absorbing the greater part of her energies. The French Army was still intact in the West, the British Army was steadily growing in strength and efficiency. The sea-power of England had already been effective in banishing the German commercial flag from the seas, and cooping the German Navy up in the Kiel canal. All the German overseas colonies, except Tanganyika, had been conquered, and Tanganyika was certain to fall if the war went on. Above all, the British blockade of Germany was beginning to be felt, the strangulation coils were tightening. The effect of sea-power and the blockade was slow—but certain, provided the war was sufficiently prolonged.

[1] The force was mainly British, but a French contingent under General Gouraud assisted.

III. 1916–1917

The year 1916 was intended by all parties to be a year of decision—and it was in the West that the decision was sought. Falkenhayn reported on the situation to the Kaiser at the end of 1915.[1] His memorandum viewed Russia as incapable of an offensive, Serbia as shattered, Italy as contained by Austria-Hungary, England as the chief enemy from whom 'Germany can expect no mercy.' England was 'obviously staking everything on a war of exhaustion,' with blockade as her weapon. It was therefore necessary to 'show England patently that her venture has no prospects.' It was useless to attempt to attack England herself and she would not be convinced by ventures against Salonica, Suez, or Mesopotamia even if they were successful. 'England, which has known how to swallow the humiliations of Antwerp and Gallipoli, will survive defeats in those distant theatres also.' But it was necessary to prevent England using weapons in Europe. She had already used several, Russia, Italy, and France. Two of these had been stricken from her hand, or rendered impotent. It was not worth while to attack the British lines in the West, for that was at bottom a 'side-show.' But, if the French were defeated, England's 'best sword' would be knocked out of her hand, our 'arch-enemy' would be deserted by her continental allies on the land, and might be coerced by a ruthless submarine campaign at sea. She might then be induced to make peace. Falkenhayn proposed to attack a limited sector of the French front at Verdun, to attract thither the best forces of France, and to 'bleed her to death.'

Here we see another great decision. The decision to aim at Verdun is as important, in its way, as Schlieffen's decision to pass through Belgium. It was equally a failure and is of peculiar interest because it is perhaps the last time that Germany had the free power of initiative. Her offensive in the case of Verdun was a matter of choice, all her subsequent operations were matters of necessity. It is probable that Falkenhayn adopted this plan from desire to economise his own men—and to save losses. He hoped that Verdun would prove a magnet of attraction and that Frenchmen would flock there from all parts of the front and be killed. But while it is true that many French divisions were badly damaged at Verdun, it was impossible to expect that a limited objective would put France out of action. Falkenhayn was not willing to take the risk of an offensive on the grand scale, and his more limited objective failed. It is true that the French were badly shaken, and lost more than the Germans. But what Falkenhayn had not realised was that the British Army was no longer 'a side-show.' Its power was now to be felt in the main theatre of war. The French resistance at Verdun enabled the British to prepare their offensive in comparative safety. On the 1st July a combined Franco-British offensive began on the Somme and raged with the utmost fury until October. In the month of September

[1] E. von Falkenhayn: *General Headquarters 1914–1916* (1919), pp. 209–18.

the British for the first time employed that valuable discovery of the war, the tank. Both the tank and the young British soldiers were in too experimental a stage to win decisive victories. But, none the less, the battle of the Somme was probably the greatest shock the Germans had hitherto received. It was fatal to Falkenhayn, who was compelled to hand over his authority as Chief of Staff to Hindenburg by the end of August. The German attempt to reach a decision had completely failed. Not only had the French defended themselves at Verdun, but the astonished Falkenhayn beheld a British Army equipped with abundant munitions and guns, and capable of contending on equal terms with the German. If the British had accomplished so much with an Army imperfectly trained, what were they likely to do in 1917 with more experience and greater supplies? The emergence of England as a first-class military power struck the Germans with amazement and dismay. England no longer needed to use France as a sword on the Continent: she had her own, formidable in weight and sharpness.

One of the most important events of 1916 was the offensive of Brussilov in the East. Germany had considered the Russians to be passive and, though not actually defeated, incapable of resuming the offensive. For they had lost millions of dead, and were still poorly armed and insufficiently equipped. But the Russian soldier had no hypersensitive feeling such as that possessed by more highly organised temperaments. Just as some savages need no chloroform when a doctor is amputating their limbs, so the Russian soldier viewed the losses of his own or of neighbouring armies with indifference. He endured the cold and hardships of winter with stoicism—and moved forward to this last of his great offensives without enthusiasm but without fear. In March the Russians had attacked near the Baltic without much success. Urgent appeals from France and from Italy caused them to hurry on their great planned offensive and begin on the first days of June. Brussilov, who advanced in the south against Lutsk, may have meant no more than a reconnaissance in force. But he broke so easily through the weak ramparts of Austro-Hungarian resistance, that he decided on a grand offensive. He was followed by the armies on both flanks, and once more, but for the last time, the great Russian hosts broke through and drove the Austro-Hungarians in utter rout before them. Hindenburg promptly came to the rescue and by a series of brilliant counter-attacks checked the Russian advance and restored something like the old line in August. The Austro-Hungarians had lost half a million in prisoners and dead, the Russians even more. For internal reasons Russia was already breaking under the strain of warfare, but this last desperate offensive further exhausted the resources and man-power of Austria-Hungary. Her difficulties were increased by the fact that her attack on Italy from the Tyrol had failed, and that the Italians had definitely passed to the offensive in the Isonzo area, and won a number of successes. Last of all, Brussilov's offensive and the resistance of Verdun definitely decided Rumania to enter the fray. In August she declared war upon, and invaded, Austria-Hungary. Had she succeeded, Transylvania and the cornlands of Hungary would have been overrun. Austria-Hungary could hardly have resisted such pressure and the end of the war would have been in sight.

Hindenburg and Ludendorff had been called to the High Command at a critical moment. They acted with promptitude and saved the situation then as so often later. Falkenhayn and Mackensen, than whom there could hardly have been better leaders, were despatched respectively to Hungary and Bulgaria to organise the offensive against Rumania. These two masters of warfare showed Rumania what Samsonov and Rennenkampf could have done in East Prussia, if they had acted in perfect time with one another. Mackensen pushed up the Dobruja with a German-Bulgar force, and thereby stopped the Rumanian attack on Transylvania. Falkenhayn, who had been watching his opportunity, broke through the mountain passes of Rumania's northern front in mid-November, and struck for Bucharest. Mackensen with admirable judgment crossed the Danube and attacked the Rumanian capital from the south. The two German leaders met in Bucharest. It was a real victory. The Rumanians were henceforth confined to Moldavia, Austria-Hungary was not only relieved from all danger on this front, but Russia had now to send troops to garrison Moldavia and to defend a longer line of front. Above all, the vast resources of Wallachia in corn and oil were now wholly at the disposal of the Germans and undoubtedly helped them to prolong the war.

The year 1916 thus closed with a gleam of triumph for Germany. But there can be no doubt that she had had the worst of the fighting. She had failed at Verdun and suffered defeats on the Somme. Austria-Hungary had been routed on the Russian front and beaten on the Isonzo. It was a poor compensation to have conquered half of Rumania.

At sea the only great naval battle of the war had been fought off Jutland (May 31). The Germans had claimed a victory and that Britannia no longer ruled the waves. No one believed them. The result was indeed indecisive and in the crisis Jellicoe had played for safety. He may have been wise, for he was the only commander whose operations could have lost both a battle and the war in a few hours. The British public showed no anxiety at the news, and the effect was equivalent to a victory. The stranglehold of the blockade increased in rigour, and the main German fleet never again sought battle on the high seas. The British command of the sea was wholly unshaken. Indeed the German resort to a ruthless submarine campaign was actually a confession that they could fight England under the sea but not above it.

There were indeed no illusions at Berlin and Vienna. Falkenhayn and Conrad—the respective Chiefs of Staff—had been removed from their posts, the privations of the peoples were alarming their rulers, and the actions on the Somme had confronted them with the new menace

of England as a formidable military power in the West. This appears
to have completed their dismay and the civilian rulers decided to speak
of peace. The Kaiser had indeed promised his soldiers that they should
have it 'before the leaves fall.' Many of them had found peace by the
waters of the Somme or in the marshes of Pinsk while the leaves drifted
down on them. Consequently the German Government published its
willingness to make peace in the last days of December. They had great
advantages if they had negotiated on the basis of *uti possidetis*. They
had captured and still held four enemy capitals, Belgrade, Cettinje,
Brussels, and Bucharest. They occupied Belgium and North France,
Serbia, Montenegro, Wallachia, all Poland and much other Russian
territory. These were strong bargaining counters to trade against their
lost colonies, a strip of Austro-Hungarian territory, the Turkish port
of Basra. Peace was, however, wrecked by the German militarists
who insisted on the retention of strategic advantages in Belgium and
North France. Nothing shows the determination of England and
France better than the fact that they put forward as their conditions of
peace demands which would have involved the break-up of Austria-
Hungary and the expulsion of the Turks from Constantinople. These
demands could not have been—and were hardly meant to be—accepted
by Germany. So the war went on—and Germany was driven into her
greatest blunder.

To Germany, however, the situation appeared so desperate that she
forced into the war the only neutral power strong enough to resent her
dictation. Wilson had won his re-election as President because the
American public thought him less bellicose than his opponent and more
likely to keep them out of the war. At the end of 1916 he had formally
approached both belligerents with a view to peace. Within four months
after his effort America was at war with Germany. The situation was
peculiar. England had begun by blockading the German coasts and the
pressure became worse and worse. She held on like a bull-dog and
every now and then tightened her grip and approached nearer to the
throat of her rival. It was a situation like that between Napoleon and
England. The struggle was so intense that neither side would suffer
neutrals gladly. Germany had cowed all those on the Continent, and
she now decided to cow the United States by the use of the submarine
weapon. The United States had always believed in the rights of neutrals
and in what they called the 'Freedom of the Seas.' They had had sharp
passages with the British. But the Franco-British market absorbed
endless supplies of American munitions. British naval commanders, if
they confiscated property, did not sink defenceless travellers. Since
1915 German submarines had at times sunk neutral ships and, as in the
case of the *Lusitania*, American passengers in British ships. From 1916
onwards the United States had shown signs of restlessness and had
made Germany promise (May 4, 1916) to restrict her submarine
activities. On the 31st January 1917 the German Government informed

the United States that the Entente Allies by 'brutal methods' compelled Germany to resume freedom of action (*i.e.* to break the promise). 'Under these circumstances Germany will meet the illegal measures of her enemies by forcibly preventing after February 1, 1917, in a zone around Great Britain, France, Italy, and in the Eastern Mediterranean, all navigation, that of neutrals included, from and to England and from and to France, etc. All ships met within that zone will be sunk.' No great neutral nation could accept such provocation. Diplomatic relations were severed at once. And in April the United States declared that 'a state of war' existed with Germany.

In this gravest of all decisions taken during the war on the German side, Hindenburg and Ludendorff accepted the naval view that the introduction of an absolutely 'ruthless' submarine campaign would destroy England's supplies and end the war. It was believed that six or at most twelve months of such warfare would starve England out.[1] This calculation explains why the Germans attempted no offensive in the West in 1917, and viewed the entry of the United States into the war with indifference. They thought that all would be finished in Europe before America could intervene.[2]

Viewed at this distance the German calculation seems absurd. The entry into the war on the side of the Entente of a great nation with almost unlimited supplies, wealth, and population seems absolutely decisive. But it took in truth a very long time before America's resources and energy told. America's soldiers had to be armed almost entirely with French and British rifles, big guns and fighting aeroplanes till the end of 1918. They took long in coming over and were not always fully trained. But they had youth and unbounded confidence and thus more than compensated for the loss of Russia. In two respects their aid was absolutely decisive, in their almost limitless supplies of money and of men. The most dangerous crisis of the war was during the German offensive of 1918. At that grave moment American troops were already in small numbers in the trenches, and the supply of munitions was practically unlimited. England lost nearly a thousand guns, but they were all replaced from reserve stores in three weeks! And the reason was this. British money had financed the Allies and pegged the American exchange up till America's entry into the war. From that date a series of expedients could have maintained the credit of England for a

---

[1] Ludendorff: *My War Memories*, vol. I. pp. 315–17, says the Chief of Naval Staff put it at six months—at the critical Council of January 9, 1917, and that he himself thought it safe to put it at twelve months. As will be seen by reference to p. 410, Falkenhayn had contemplated a submarine campaign in the future.

[2] Their calculations were ludicrously false. Thus they reckoned a million American troops would require five million tons of shipping, and that this amount could not be spared. In fact, three million troops were transported to Europe. *v.* Ludendorff: *My War Memories*, vol. I. p. 316. The chief American contribution after entry into war was not so much munitions as the raw material of munitions, which was worked up in England and France.

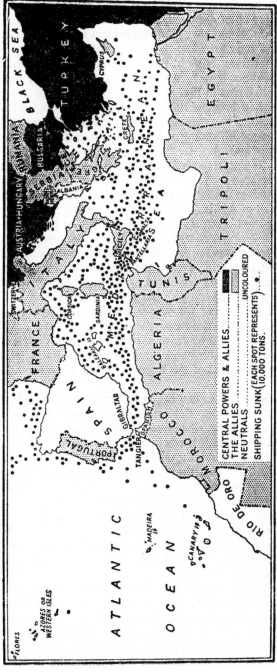

WAR MENACE IN THE MEDITERRANEAN 1914–1918.

Destruction of shipping carried out by Central Powers in the first World War.

time, but ultimately there would have been a collapse of credit and therefore a slowing up of the supplies of food and munitions from America. That 'slow-up' would have been very evident in March 1918, and during the next five months, when they were most needed, they would have been most lacking. Without the aid of America's men and money the Entente could not have been victorious and might have been defeated.

Ludendorff's plan in 1917 seems to have been simply to wait until the submarines had brought England to her knees. England and France were prepared to attack with vigour in the West before the strain was felt, and Ludendorff sprang a clever surprise on them by retreating from a large part of his front. He fell back to the famous 'Hindenburg line'—and left the Entente to push their offensive over a desolate area. Nivelle, who had replaced Joffre as generalissimo, engaged in a costly offensive which resulted in the failure of the troops and his own disgrace and retirement (end of April). What was worse, a most serious mutiny broke out among the French soldiers, disheartened by pacificism, by losses, and by blundering leadership. The danger was very real, a further French offensive was impossible, and the Germans might discover the truth and attack them. Pétain, the hero of Verdun, was put in command at the front and succeeded in the most difficult of all tasks, in reorganising and reinspiriting the sullen, discontented, and mutinous troops. He was blamed for over-severity to mutineers and for caution in the face of the foe. But Pétain accomplished the seemingly impossible and in the end nursed his froward children to victory. He was not the equal of Foch as a commander, but he deserves immortal honour for not having 'despaired of the Republic' when her own children forgot her.

The British offensive had begun before the French and was planned in combination with it. But in May the French offensive came to an abrupt stop, and Haig, who knew the reasons of cessation only too well, determined to continue a resolute offensive as long as his men could endure it. He thought it the only way of distracting the attention of the Germans. All through the spring, the summer, and the autumn the British Army hammered remorselessly and tirelessly at the Germans. Ludendorff compared the British advance to that of a 'mad bull,' and at times it was as blind as it was furious. This *via dolorosa* ended at last in November in the swamps and blood of Passchendaele. The German lines had been thrown back but not pierced; the French Army had been saved by the sacrifice of the British—for the best part of that gallant army lay in the mud of Flanders.

On the Eastern front everything went wrong except at Salonica, Baghdad, and Jerusalem. Under Entente pressure King Constantine of Greece abdicated in favour of his second son. Venizelos, returned to power, at last brought Greece into the field against Germany and enabled the Allies to prepare for an offensive against Bulgaria. In March the British forces avenged the capitulation of Kut, drove the

Turks before them in defeat, entered Baghdad, and occupied nearly all Mesopotamia. In Palestine Allenby showed himself superior to Falkenhayn, who commanded the Turks. He seized the port of Jaffa, and gave Jerusalem as a Christmas present to the delighted British public. These successes, though small and in outlying theatres, were significant. They were all in areas where the Entente had previously been defeated, and they all secured important strategic advantages, from which the spectacular victories of the next year were achieved.

Elsewhere there was unrelieved disaster. The Russian Revolution occurred in May, the Czar was deposed and the Monarchy overthrown. For a time the Russian front held, but the Revolution had completely demoralised the troops. Even Kerensky, who was pro-Entente, said that Russia was worn out and could not remain in the war after the end of the year. The end came even quicker. The army was demoralised and leaderless. It had been defeated in August, and thereafter it rapidly dissolved. The Bolsheviks overthrew Kerensky in October and made peace with Germany before the end of the year. Rumania, which had fought gallantly and defeated Mackensen himself, was compelled by the defection of her ally to accept a peace on most humiliating terms. It was hard on her, for her resistance at Marišesti was as heroic as that of the French at Verdun.

It had been supposed that Italy's successes on the Isonzo in 1916 would be improved in 1917, and that Austria-Hungary would be finally overthrown. In fact, Italy avoided complete disaster only by the narrowest margin. In September the Austro-Hungarian command thought the situation so desperate that they resolved on an offensive as the only possible chance of restoring the jaded *moral* of their troops. Ludendorff showed the coolest daring when appealed to for aid and lent them his only reserve, a force of six German divisions. These were however enough, for they were led by Otto von Below. That great commander found a weak point in the Italian defences, used the German divisions as the spear-head, broke through with ease and drove the vast Italian forces before him in complete and headlong rout. The precipitation of their flight actually saved the Italians. The victors had not expected such success and had no time to organise the pursuit. The Italians tried to stand on the Tagliamento, but finally had to fall back to the line of the Piave. There the Germans were held up. The line was shorter and easier to defend, and the Italians were heartened by the arrival of reinforcements from France. These French and British veterans were 'men who knew how to die,' and they were led by fearless commanders. Italy reorganised her shattered forces and found an Italian Pétain in General Diaz. None the less Caporetto had been a shattering disaster, and the weakness of Italy continued to be a grave preoccupation for the Entente during most of 1918. It was well that at this time both England and France were regenerated.

14

At the beginning of 1917 a strong government was just assuming power under Lloyd George in England. She had opened careers to the talents in a way impossible in hide-bound Germany or aristocratic Austria-Hungary. Lloyd George, the new premier, had been brought up on a village green; the Chief of Staff had served for years as a trooper; the First Lord of the Admiralty as a railway porter. General Smuts, the only member of the Cabinet who came from a Dominion, had been fighting against England fifteen years before. England's energies were enormously developed, her munitions were supplying even her Allies. France was cursed with a succession of ministers so weak as to be unable to prevent anti-war propaganda from spreading to the troops, and causing mutiny at the front. In the last days of 1917 these very disasters worked their own remedy. Politics had become worse and worse, but finally the fall of one feeble minister after another enabled Clemenceau ('The Tiger') to become head of the French Cabinet. The pacificists were at once assailed, Bolo Pasha was executed, Caillaux imprisoned, Sarrail, the dubious generalissimo at Salonica, recalled. A new spirit of resolution ran through France under a leader as patriotic and fearless as Danton. 'Je fais la guerre,' said the indomitable old man. 'I shall fight in front of Paris, I shall fight within Paris, I shall fight behind Paris.' 'No surrender' was at last the motto, and France feared the enemy within no longer.

IV. 1918

Ludendorff's thoughts, as he planned his campaign for 1918, ran somewhat as follows: 'The manhood of Germany has been bleeding to death these four years and the strain cannot go on beyond a fifth. We are stinted not only in men but in everything—horses, goods, chemicals, metals, rubber. Austria-Hungary is in still worse need and is visibly perishing. Our ruthless submarine campaign has failed. Limitless supplies and overwhelming masses of men in America, and our submarines cannot prevent them from being brought to Europe in ever-increasing quantities. But we still have a chance of victory. Russia is at last out of the war, and the whole forces of Germany can be turned against France. Nearly forty divisions and four hundred thousand men can reinforce the western front. With these we have at last a superiority of force which will last for about four months. We will strike for victory at the point of junction of the Franco-British forces, separate their armies and win the war. Once we have done this, no American reinforcements can affect the issue.' Ludendorff told the Kaiser that it was 'the greatest military task that has ever been imposed upon an army.' But his military brain could not conceive of any half-measures or of peace. 'It must,' he said, 'be victory or defeat.' He showed that the fate of the Hohenzollern dynasty and of Germany hung upon the event, by formally announcing that 'His Imperial Majesty the Kaiser' was in command of the offensive. There was a saying that 'William II was the only monarch in Europe who could not lead back a defeated army to his capital.' Ludendorff was to prove that the saying was true.

The Allies in the West had made some efforts to meet a German offensive by unifying their military policy. A supreme War Council had been created, which was intended to co-ordinate effort. Its chief advantage was that its first French member was Foch. They studied the situation and finally worked out a plan for controlling the reserves at the front. But neither Haig on the British sector, nor Pétain on the French, was willing to submit to an international committee dictating their use of reserves from the rear. Their objects were indeed different; Pétain had to defend Paris, Haig the Channel ports. Neither could think in terms of unity nor look far beyond his own needs. But if one man assumed control of the whole front, he would dispose of the reserves not according to French or British needs or prejudices, but as the general situation required. A few weeks after the establishment of the supreme command, Haig was protesting that Foch was neglecting British interests, Pétain that he was neglecting French ones. Could anything have more completely justified both Foch and the supreme command? Yet it was not until March 26th that he was appointed to 'co-ordinate movements' on the whole front. It was even longer before he was given the reality as well as the title of Supreme Command. By that time the Germans were in sight of Amiens.

The junction between two allied armies is always a weak point in their defences, and Haig's difficulties had been increased by having recently been forced to take over fifteen miles of the French lines at a time when his own forces were being reduced to supply men for Salonica and Palestine. He was more correct than the Supreme War Council in fixing both the date and the locality of the German offensive. But it so happened that he had placed his least experienced army commander with the smallest forces in the most important sector—that adjoining the French, and that no real reserves were immediately available. Pétain, on the other hand, was expecting a blow far away on the French front east of Rheims and his strategic reserve was not near enough to give immediate aid to the British.

On March 21st Ludendorff attacked on a forty-three mile front, between Arras and La Fère. On the Somme the fifth British Army was simply swept away and the Germans were soon within twenty miles of Amiens. But Ludendorff's main blow had been aimed at Arras, where he calculated on breaking through and then rolling up the British and forcing them towards the coast. Here the third Army under Byng— the most dogged of British commanders—offered a successful resistance and drove back the victor of Caporetto with loss from Arras on the 28th. Ludendorff thereupon stopped von Below's attack in this area and drove his forces onwards against Amiens. But this time he was too late. French reinforcements had aided the beaten British, and Foch had assumed command. His first public utterance was: 'The Boche is stopped. . . . I can guarantee Amiens.'

Foch was a remarkable character. He had been eminent as a professor of military science, and had produced a theory of the offensive which the French Army had adopted. But his practical application of it had discredited him in 1916. He was also objectionable to Republicans as a Catholic, and he had been for a time in retirement. Enforced leisure and his work on the Supreme War Council had helped him to view the war from behind the lines. He was accompanied everywhere by Weygand, a little bird-like man who never brought papers to a conference and carried the whole organisation of the army in his head. The staff methods of Weygand and his chief were difficult to penetrate, and caused amazement to the British. Foch had no popular gift of inspiring the troops, and was never loved as was 'Père Joffre' by the French or 'The old Plum' (Plumer) by the British. But he possessed a cold power like the elder Moltke, and, like Wellington, felt sure of beating the enemy as soon as he was called to command. In his view Ludendorff's methods were 'buffalo strategy.' He stuck one horn in at one place, and the other at a second without real calculation or thought. It would not be possible to beat this blindly goring animal at once. He must wait till the German buffalo had exhausted its strength, and until the Entente had recovered theirs. Till then no sentiment and no popular pressure must be allowed to interfere with his plans. He intended, for instance, to make the British Army resist until the last gasp, and to send them no reinforcements until their line was absolutely breaking. By being niggardly of assistance he would accumulate reserves. By sacrificing a part he would preserve the whole. Even if he had understood and explained his methods better they could hardly have been popular. He was acting the part of a matador in the bullring, who renders no aid to his assistants even when they are injured or tossed into the air by the bull. They risk their limbs as they worry the bull, but the matador risks his life as he gives the death-blow. To succeed his nerves must be cool, his strength unexhausted, and his hand sure.

Ludendorff disengaged his left horn from in front of Amiens, and stuck in the right one between Béthune and Ypres (April 9th). The Portuguese gave way in confusion, British units retired more slowly, and the Germans were soon on the Lys. Haig issued his famous order: 'Every position must be held to the last man. . . . With our backs to the wall and believing in the justice of our cause, each one of us must fight on to the end.' Haig's words—so different from his usual taciturnity—marked the crisis. This was on the 12th April, and the offensive lasted a fortnight longer. But even on the 14th Foch considered the battle as *finie*. He ultimately sent French reinforcements, but only allowed them to be used with the utmost sparingness. The Germans managed to capture Kemmel hill from a French division, but broke off their offensive before April ended.

Ludendorff had made two huge bulges in the British line—one upon the Lys and the other near Amiens. But he had not broken it. He decided, therefore, to attack the French in the Soissons-Rheims area; he would attract sufficient Allied reserves there by sticking one horn in west of Rheims, and the other east of it. He would then return to the British positions in Flanders and finally break through. On the 27th May—and for four days longer—the Germans burst over the Chemin des Dames and drove the French and some British troops before them. A huge gap appeared some forty miles broad, and twenty-five miles at its deepest point. There were over 60,000 prisoners. For the first time the German Crown Prince commanded an army which was successful, and for the second time the Germans reached the Marne. Ludendorff now decided to stick his left horn in east of Rheims. After that had again attracted reserves, he would begin his final offensive against the British. But east of Rheims was General Gouraud, who had learned from Pétain the principle of an elastic defence and how to hold the front lines with a mere screen of troops. On July 15th the blow fell, but it was parried with little loss of men to the French and little gain of ground to the Germans. Before Ludendorff had recovered from this surprise, Foch struck his first offensive blow.

The huge bulge in the French line, like the two bulges in the British, was not all to the advantage of the Germans. They had had to hold a longer line shaped like a deep half-circle, which could be attacked on both flanks. Just below Soissons, Foch found his opportunity and began his offensive. The leader was Mangin—the Hotspur of the French armies—a man absolutely impervious to losses, and with an extraordinary capacity for getting the most out of his men. Mangin struck at the neck of the bulge, hoping to catch the Germans before they could retreat. He did not succeed, but the Germans fell hurriedly back, pressed from all sides of the half-circle. There were 30,000 enemy prisoners, a third of what Germany took before Amiens, a half of what she took on the Chemin des Dames. But it was an authentic victory, and like a gleam of sunshine dispersed the gloom that had settled on the Allies. To experts in such warfare it meant much. Foch was not a man to pass to the offensive at all in half-hearted fashion. He meant to strike hard and to go on striking.

Ludendorff was still dreaming of breaking the British front, and was not going to be disturbed even by a big local reverse on the Marne. On the 2nd August he actually ordered preparations to be made for one offensive near Amiens, and a second in Flanders. Neither materialised, for on the 8th August, to the German amazement, Haig struck hard in front of Amiens. The material results were not astounding, though a fair amount of ground and 20,000 prisoners were gained. But the moral

effect was immense. August 8th was called by Ludendorff himself 'the
Black Day of the German Army.' The twice-defeated British had suddenly passed to the offensive, disorganised Ludendorff's plans, and
broken his spirit. Ludendorff saw all his schemes crumble. He could
no longer attack, and the enemy obviously could. The situation had
worked out in terms of mathematics. For four months the Germans had
held a slight numerical superiority over the Allies. That period had
ended—America's millions were pouring in, and the German reserves
had ceased to fill up the gaps. The longer the allied offensive went on,
the more certain was the ruin of Germany. Foch feared that Ludendorff
had grasped the lesson, and would retreat, while there was time, to
shorter and more defensible lines in the rear. But Ludendorff would
not confess to defeat, and refused to retire until too late.

Foch himself, though always yearning for the offensive, had not expected a decision till 1919. His aim had at first been to free lateral railways and to secure better positions for the Allies. But Foch learned
from Haig's victory of August 8th something that Ludendorff did not.
Haig considered it a proof that the German *moral* was affected, and
that further attacks would succeed. With iron tenacity of character, he
now pressed Foch along a path which he was already inclined to tread.
Foch had noted that Haig's converging attacks produced the effect of a
surprise on a small scale, and that the system could be used for offensives
on a grand scale. Foch now agreed to strike home, but even yet expected
no more than to inflict heavy loss on the retreating Germans. The
British and French commanders had, however, to win over General
Pershing, the American commander. He had scattered American forces
all over the front to help the Allies. He was now determined to unite
them and to fight with an American Army, and he had strong views as
to what his objectives should be. Ultimately, however, a series of grand
offensives was planned on the following lines for September. The British
had the hardest task, they had the mass of the German Army facing
them and the strongest defences. Haig was to strike at the Hindenburg
line and drive the Germans back. As soon as his offensive developed,
King Albert and the Belgians were to attack in the region of Ypres.
While the bulk of the German forces were thus held in Flanders, the
French under Mangin were to strike up from Soissons. The American
objectives were twofold. They were first to hammer out the salient of
St. Mihiel, near Verdun. When that was accomplished, they, with
French supports, were to attack in the Meuse-Argonne area and press
forward to Sedan, thus cutting the Germans' line of communications.
A last French Army, under General Castelnau, was held in reserve to
attack in the Ardennes, that area in which the French offensives of 1914
had failed so disastrously and in which they now meant to finish the
war. Foch calculated that Ludendorff's reserves were exhausted, and
that his armies, thus held fast to all parts of the front, must give way at
some points, and that a general German retreat must in any case result.

He proposed to produce the effects of surprise tactically by the use of
tanks, and strategically by a series of offensives arranged in a timed and
harmonious fashion. And during September the blows of Foch fell in
relentless succession.

On September 28th Ludendorff was sitting in his headquarters at the
Hôtel Britannique at Spa. The news was everywhere bad. The Americans had straightened out the St. Mihiel salient, and were attacking
with the French in the Argonne. The Belgians were attacking in their
own territory, the British had just broken the 'Siegfried line.' The
German prisoners numbered a quarter of a million in the Allied offensives of three months. They were speaking, too, of internal revolution
in Germany. Yet Ludendorff was still unconvinced by the news from
the home front and from the West. What finished him was the news
which reached him from the East. As he spoke of the Bulgarian disaster
before two officers, he gradually got worked to a frenzy and fell down
in a fit. 'Foam appeared on his lips and in a slow, gliding motion, the
heavy body of a giant fallen for Germany fell athwart the room.'[1]
When he recovered he gave orders to conceal the fact of his seizure and
to sue for peace. His decision was accepted on the 29th.[2] In the weeks
that followed he recovered his nerve and made attempts to stop the
peace-making that he had himself begun. But the forces once set in
motion could not be arrested, and peace once asked for came certainly
and soon. The final impulse to it came, as has been seen, from the
East.   .   .   .   .

Far away on the Salonica front was a tall, bare hill, which commands
so wide a view that the Macedonians say 'you can see from it all the
kingdoms of the world.' Up that hill, late in June 1918, rode and
scrambled a group of Entente officers. They consulted a plan and maps,
and studied the horizon long with their glasses. Before they rode away
the commander had adopted the proposed plan, and the decision made
him a marshal of France and the victor in the most successful of Allied
offensives. The plan was that of a Serb general, Mišić, but Franchet-
Despérey was bold enough to take the great risk of throwing his army
against immense mountain walls, relying on the effect of a surprise
attack on the centre. On the 15th September the offensive began, it was
all over in a fortnight, and on September 29th Bulgaria surrendered,
and was out of the war. That meant the collapse of the whole Eastern
front and of Austria-Hungary, and the news of this surrender broke the
heart and will of Ludendorff, and caused him to sue for peace.

[1] *Rhenische Westfaelische Zeitung*, September 28, 1928, on the evidence of an
eye-witness.
[2] The story of Ludendorff's fit on the 28th (not the 29th) has been denied, but not
convincingly. It is true that he did not receive the news of the Bulgarian Armistice
till early on the 30th. But he knew Bulgaria's surrender was inevitable on the afternoon of the 28th, and this was the cause of his decision to make peace on the 29th.
v. Ludendorff: *My War Memories*, vol. II. p. 721.

Germany sent out her first peace note to President Wilson on October 3rd. Her cause was already hopeless. By a strategic masterpiece, similar to that of Salonica, Allenby captured and destroyed the entire Turkish army in Palestine and entered Damascus on October 1st. Turkey signed an armistice before the end of the month. By that time the Italians had driven the Austro-Hungarians before them in complete rout at Vittorio Veneto. Early in November the British had passed all the German lines and reached open country in North France. The Americans had got to the French frontier at Sedan; the French reserve Army was threatening Lorraine. Foch himself still did not regard the war as finished in the West. He thought it might last even five months longer. Germany's armies had been defeated but even yet her front was not broken. What was broken was the nerve and will-power of her High Command. It was that which hastened the end. The armistice at the eleventh hour of the eleventh day of the eleventh month of 1918 merely registered the fact of Ludendorff's decision to sue for peace at the end of September.

The final defeat of Hindenburg and Ludendorff on the Western front in 1918 provoked surprise after their previous victories in Russia, in Rumania, in Italy, and in France. It is true that their material difficulties were great. They had no tanks, they lacked all sorts of supplies, from rubber and leather to chemicals and fats. Yet they succeeded in three great offensives, and in each case sprang tactical surprises on the Allies. Yet after each of his great offensives in 1918 Ludendorff hesitated. He had expected to break through in March and, having failed, turned to the Lys, where success was less easy. He succeeded at the Chemin des Dames beyond his hopes, but failed to appreciate the effect of Foch's counter-stroke. He displayed always the tactics of a master-fencer but, as Foch said, the strategy of a 'buffalo.' [1] It is at least interesting that Hindenburg when advised in the East by Hoffmann and Ludendorff was masterly in both tactics and strategy. When advised by Ludendorff alone in 1918 in the West he excelled only in tactics. In any case the German offensives of 1918 so nearly succeeded that they are their own justification. Nor was their strategy so much at fault as their disregard of Napoleon's maxim that you must draw up plans in case of defeat as well as to secure victory. What they lacked was an alternative plan once their offensives had failed. Here as elsewhere Hindenburg cannot avoid responsibility. Nor would he desire to do so, for, during the crises of 1918, and apparently at all times, he showed a greatness of character to which his subordinates never attained.

---

[1] This expression of Foch does not occur in his published works, but was heard by many Allied officers at different times. His general criticism on 1918, after reading Ludendorff's *War Memories*, is '. . . in the tactical details of his operations, Ludendorff planned his attacks admirably. The planning was perfect . . . . But— there were no after-plans. . . . He had no notion of the ensemble, and no plan on a large scale.' *v.* Raymond Recouly: *Marshal Foch* (1929), pp. 96-7, 101.

Some, if not all, of the deeper causes of German defeat are now evident. Lack of man-power was the first. The well of German manhood had run dry, as had the British and the French, but American man-power was an almost inexhaustible fountain. Military defeat was, however, only one side of the enormous reverse inflicted upon Germany. It was moral, political and, above all, naval. British sea-power worked by blockade and by hunger. The effect of this attrition finally coincided with, and greatly intensified, the military reverse. While the Allied offensives lessened the material power of Germany, insufficient food, defective equipment, and tales of the anguish at home sapped the soldiers' *moral*. Breaking point had been reached because of the strain imposed by the Navy at the time of the armistice negotiations. The German Government were so convinced of this fact that they would have accepted any armistice terms which the Allies had chosen to offer. Even the gallant German soldier was showing signs of indiscipline and demoralisation, and the German people were already in revolt. They were prepared to sacrifice Kaiser, dynasty, army, glory, everything for peace and food, and so were their Allies. Neither Bulgaria, Austria-Hungary nor Turkey had the hope, the desire or the power to resist longer. The mills of God, or of the devil, had ground slowly, but they had ground small and fine, at last.

During this war America played the old part history assigned to England in Europe. She decided the issue by throwing her weight against the strongest Continental Power. England had failed to decide the issue herself in spite of the fact that she excelled all her previous efforts in European wars. From the first she not only dominated the seas, but departed from her traditions by raising an army equivalent to a Continental one which she ultimately based on conscription. Yet, none the less, she failed to decide the issue. It is improbable that England would herself have been beaten and starved out, for she carried three million Americans to France during the strain of the submarine campaign in transports which could have been used for food. But the war might well have ended in defeat for France and a stalemate between Germany and England, if the United States had not intervened with her boundless resources. Philip II, Louis XIV, and Napoleon were baffled or destroyed when help came from over the Channel. Germany was not beaten in 1918 until help had come from over the Atlantic. That is the greatest testimony to her power and her valour.

CHAPTER XXX

THE PARIS CONFERENCE AND THE TREATY WITH GERMANY, 1919

On the afternoon of June 28, 1919, the fountains in the gardens of Versailles were playing in their famous cascades for the first time since the war had begun. Immense crowds were there, but they had not come to see the fountains. They were looking at four men who had left the palace and walked down past the *tapis vert* to gaze for a few minutes at the jets bursting forth from the largest fountain. As they returned, the crowds pressed so closely upon them that gendarmes and soldiers came to their aid. These four men had just signed an instrument which they imagined would give permanent peace to the world. That was a delusion, yet none the less the men were worth looking at. They had enjoyed more power over wider areas than any man then living on the earth. They had governed the world since the Armistice, and they had just laid the German Empire in the dust in the very place in which it had arisen in glory.

The 'Big Four,' as they were called, were Orlando,[1] Lloyd George, Clemenceau and Wilson. The peace and world settlement were theirs; their characters and their power had moulded them. Orlando had the face of a disillusioned idealist, worn, thoughtful and sad. He had an impossible task at the Conference, for Italy's part in the war had been real but her people's demands were large. Faced with stronger colleagues, and distracted by party politics at home, he found himself unable to gain his ends and was compelled to give way to events. The fate of everybody was really in the hands of a triumvirate, each of whom was, in Shakespeare's phrase, 'a third part of the world.' Of the three Wilson appeared to be the most commanding. His tall stature, his long Puritan head and firm jaw, suggested something at once narrow, resolute and formidable. He was one who could break but could not bend. His stiffness was indeed his bane as well as his merit. It provoked ridicule, it led alike to wrong decisions and unwise concessions. A magnificent orator, he had no legal precision of mind, and no sort of readiness in debate. In detail and in discussion he was unequal to Lloyd George or Clemenceau. Yet even they confessed to the weight of his character. The ablest Belgian statesman revealed the truth when he said that Clemenceau and Lloyd George were both men he understood, but that Wilson was beyond him. Wilson sometimes exercised a power (*une puissance*) which could be neither understood nor resisted. It is true that he gave way in some points, but also there were things in the Treaty which he alone could have won.

[1] Orlando was not present on June 28, but Sonnino deputised for him and walked down to the fountains.

Clemenceau was a complete contrast to Wilson. Short instead of tall, plump instead of spare, walking slowly through age and the wound he received during the Conference, he seemed old and tranquil. The serene expression of his face in repose, with his brown eyes and white hair, made him look like some grave Oriental sage. The aspect belied him, for his temperament could be volcanic. On one occasion he found too many expert advisers in the room and curtly ordered them to leave. Their last look was of him with his face suffused with fury, his moustache bristling like that of a tiger, demanding explanations of Pichon, his Foreign Minister, who literally cowered before him. At times he could be coarsely satirical and cynical, at others he showed a literary and artistic insight. But he knew when and where to indulge his moods. While he treated the smaller Powers and even Italy with such indifference as to provoke violent protests, he well understood that neither England nor the United States could be so handled. He understood Englishmen and Americans far better than most Frenchmen. His belief in France was noble and sincere, but she was the only thing in which he believed. It is certain that he laughed in secret at the 'fourteen commandments' of Wilson. It is hardly doubtful that he wished for a peace based on force, and on force only; but he knew—as other Frenchmen did not—that he could not obtain that. He had judged the limits of British and American concession, and was strong and wise enough to restrain his extremists. Moreover in debate he had a readiness and even a tact and delicacy which were at times invaluable.

The part of Lloyd George has not always been fairly described. The terms of peace (which he and his advisers drafted at a week-end party) are sufficient to show his real views and to prove that he possessed the instincts of a statesman.[1] He had no thought of exacting impossible amounts of reparation from Germany. 'Was it sensible,' he said later, 'to treat her as a cow from which to extract milk and beef at the same time?' But he was hampered by the ferocious demands of the British public, by the cries of 'hanging the Kaiser' and 'squeezing Germany till the pips squeak.' At the most crucial moment of the peace negotiations Lloyd George was confronted by a telegram from 370 Members of Parliament demanding that he should make Germany pay. Of course he had to capitulate, and he replied that he would keep his pledge (April 9). What else could he do? If it was possible to produce an arrangement such people would accept, it was not likely to be a considered one or a wise one. It is probably true to say that, in so far as Lloyd George had a bad influence on the Treaty, it was because he faithfully reflected these forces.

If these were the difficulties created for Lloyd George at home, they were equally great abroad. He had to reconcile two colleagues, one of whom wanted a peace to be based almost wholly on force, and the other

[1] v. H. W. V. Temperley: *A History of the Peace Conference of Paris* (1924), vol. VI. pp. 544 *sqq.*

a peace based almost wholly on idealism. Lloyd George had to adjust the two points of view, and the task was inconceivably difficult. It meant self-effacement on his part, sacrifice of his pledges, of his consistency, sometimes even of his dignity. Yet he succeeded in many instances. There are points, as will be shown, in which he is liable to severe criticism. But this fact should not exclude the services which his inconceivable adroitness and flexibility rendered to the common cause. It cannot be said that he neglected any purely British interests. The charge that will lie against him in history is that he neglected nobler and more universal interests.

The old world of Europe disappeared during the war. It went down fighting, but it went down. Consumed in the furnace of war, Europe had become a mass of molten metal, and had to be reshaped anew. The old political conceptions had many of them disappeared before the Peace Conference met. Hereditary military dynasties had ceased to exist in Russia and Germany, in Austria-Hungary, in Turkey. Constitutional kings had been deposed in Greece and Bulgaria. The 'balance of power,' that fundamental concept of European diplomacy, was called by President Wilson 'the great game, now for ever discredited.' Men spoke now of a 'Concert of Powers' and a 'League of Nations.' The limitation of armaments and the destruction of militarism were everywhere declared to be the aim. But the old forces, though weakened, were still there, and M. Clemenceau embodied these.

The basis of the Peace Treaty was not, as has sometimes been asserted, the Armistice, but the pre-Armistice negotiations. These resulted from Germany's suing for peace by the note issued, at Ludendorff's demand, on October 3, 1918. A correspondence ensued with President Wilson. In ultimate result the Allies made an offer on November 5, 1918. They stated that peace could be had on the basis of the terms laid down in Wilson's speeches of January 8, 1918 (the Fourteen Points), and subsequent addresses. The Allies excluded Point 2, 'the Freedom of the Seas,' from discussion, and added a definition of loss and damage to the terms in Wilson's speeches. Germany signified her consent to this whole offer of November 5 by approaching Foch and signing an armistice which was intended to be purely military and naval in character (November 11, 1918).[1]

The Peace Conference opened in January 1919 at Paris, with Clemenceau as President. The first great principle of the Peace Treaty was to found a League of Nations, and it was here that Wilson scored his greatest success. Clemenceau hardly owed even lip-service to the League. Lloyd George, though not unfriendly, thought it in 1919, and indeed until long after, secondary to other issues. Neither certainly desired to have the League and the Peace Treaty so tied up that one could not work without the other. This was exactly what Wilson in-

[1] One clause in it refers to Finance and Reparations, Art. XIX, but this is probably only an expansion of the loss and damage clause of the November 5th offer.

tended. Lloyd George and Clemenceau moved for a Commission to discuss it. Wilson, to the surprise of all, put himself on the Commission. It was therefore impossible to adjourn or ignore the Commission's report. When it was presented Wilson got it accepted, and the Covenant of the League was solemnly adopted. But even towards the end of March opposition revived, and attempts were made by Clemenceau and Lloyd George to separate the Covenant from the Treaty. Wilson this time showed his teeth, the two statesmen of the old world gave way, and the Covenant became part of the Treaty. Wilson seems to have reasoned thus: 'Europe is exhausted with war and excited by popular clamour. These facts make it impossible to make a good treaty. But, if the League once passes into law as the Covenant, it can be used as a means of revising the objectionable clauses of the Treaty itself. As racial hatreds die down, the power of the League will assert itself, wrongs will be healed and remedies applied. It matters little if some of the Treaty is bad, so long as the League is good. The one is temporary, the other permanent, the lesser instrument will ultimately be absorbed in the greater.' There can be little doubt that this reasoning was sound, and had America remained in the League its conclusions might well have been justified by time. There is no doubt that, but for Wilson, the League would either never have existed at all or have had little practical importance.

Connected with the League was the establishment of the great Mandatory system. This was a system enjoined on the Powers who undertook to govern the German colonies and the Turkish areas which were now at the disposal of the conquerors. Instead of annexing them, the Allies worked out a system by which the Power taking over any of these so-called mandated areas was bound to conduct the government in the interests of the governed, as 'the well-being and development of such peoples form a sacred trust of civilization.' [1] 'Securities for the performance of this trust' were embodied in the Covenant, and took the form of requiring each Mandatory Power to submit an annual report, and of constituting a permanent Mandates' Commission. The latter received the annual report, and could inquire into the working, of each mandate and demand publicity in any case that seemed necessary. The system was not perfect, but was infinitely preferable to mere annexation, and it was again largely due to Wilson.

The League organisation was to consist of a council of the Great Powers, including representatives of Minor States, and an Assembly including all members of the League. Ultimately, provision was also made for the constitution of a Court of International Justice. Thus the international executive, legislature and judiciary were constituted. Securities for the future permanent existence of international organs for the control and regulation and revision of the Treaty were thereby

[1] *v.* Article 22 of the Covenant. For the League generally, *v.* C. K. Webster and Sydney Herbert: *The League of Nations in Theory and Practice* (1933).

provided. The whole was an immense advance on the achievement of any international conference in the past. Akin to it was the creation of the International Labour Office, with its Labour Parliament of Governments, employers and workmen.

With the Covenant in his pocket Wilson paid a flying visit to America (February 14), not returning until March 14. This month was a very fateful one, as it showed exactly the position of the Allies to America. Wilson returned to find a new situation. Clemenceau and Lloyd George had no objection to Wilson and his international covenant or mandatory system as such; but their chief concern was that their own national interests should not be imperilled by his idealism.

From the point of view of military security, and this is the first of all national interests, England was in a very favourable position. The whole fleet of Germany had been surrendered and was soon to be at the bottom of the sea, and with that surrender the chief cause of Anglo-German enmity disappeared. Nor was there likely to be any dispute about the colonies which caused serious difficulties. Lloyd George could therefore view the European situation with tranquillity. Not so France. The German army had not surrendered en masse, nor had it yet been effectively disarmed. Thrice in a hundred years forces from Germany had passed over the Rhine, twice they had entered Paris, and the third time they had entirely devastated Northern France. No Frenchman could contemplate a fourth attempt without horror. Foch proposed a drastic solution: the permanent disarmament of Germany and the creation of a client Rhine Republic (really dependent upon France), which would interpose a demilitarised area between Germany and France for the next fifty years or more. Foch urged this plan with bitterness and intensity, but Clemenceau refused to put it forward. Wilson and Lloyd George were determined that the German area west of the Rhine should not be subject to France, and Clemenceau admitted their opposition. A compromise was agreed upon, a compromise which in the long run was to prove unworkable. The German area west of the Rhine was to be entirely demilitarised for ever. But in 1936 Hitler sent German troops into this demilitarised area, occupying and fortifying it, while France and England vainly protested. The Saar basin was to be held by an Inter-Allied force for fifteen years. At the end of that time a plebiscite was to decide whether the inhabitants wished to belong to France or Germany. The plebiscite, held in 1935, was for Germany. There was not much doubt as to how it would go, as only one per cent. of the Saar inhabitants was non-German.

As regards the other points of the frontier, the areas of Eupen, Moresnet and Malmédy were ceded by Germany to Belgium, though a show was made of consulting the wishes of the inhabitants. According to Wilson's eighth point, 'the wrong done to France by Prussia in 1871 in the matter of Alsace-Lorraine, which has unsettled the peace of the world for nearly fifty years, should be righted in order that peace may once more be made secure in the interests of all.' Alsace-Lorraine was accordingly to be ceded outright to the French by Germany. In these provinces France acquired nearly two million subjects and three-quarters of the German iron production.

Thus was the Western frontier settled. The North was soon settled, also by a plebiscite which returned the North Schleswig area to Denmark. The Eastern frontier offered much greater difficulties. By Point 13, Poland was to be allowed access to the sea, constituted as independent and guaranteed by international covenant. Now Poland must have a frontier, and the Polish and German elements were inextricably mingled on the whole frontier from Danzig to Upper Silesia. It was no more possible to distinguish them than to draw a line between colours in a piece of shot silk. No solutions could be exact. East Prussia (the area of Hindenburg's victories and the home of the Prussian junker) projected into Polish territory. Danzig, a German town surrounded by Polish villages, stands sentry over the Vistula, the river which carries the commerce, and therefore the life-blood of Poland. A Polish corridor was carried from the south separating East Prussia from Germany and ending in Danzig. As the result of an ingenious and fateful proposal made by Lloyd George, Danzig was put under control of the League of Nations, Poland remaining responsible for her foreign relations. A large area—West Prussia and Posen, containing many Prussians—was assigned *en bloc* to the new Polish state. Ultimately it was arranged to decide the fate of three other areas by plebiscite. Those of Allenstein and Marienwerder voted for, and were returned to, Germany. In Upper Silesia, an area rich in coal, the plebiscite took longer, and its results were fiercely disputed. It was not until 1921 that a dividing line was finally drawn, and it was contended that it would work out unfairly for Germany. As a result of these decisions Poland acquired a considerable number of Germans as well as Poles, and the best part of the mineral wealth in Upper Silesia. In result, much bitterness naturally remained. It may be said roughly that the Germans accepted, at least for a time, the Western frontier, with the demilitarised area of the Rhine, and the return of Alsace-Lorraine to France; but from the beginning they steadily refused to accept the idea that their Eastern frontier was a final settlement. The German's hatred of the Pole was even deeper than his hatred of the Frenchman, and the prospect of rich districts and large German populations remaining permanently to Poland was hateful to Germany. The situation of this frontier remained one of the dangers of Europe.

In addition to Poland, Czechoslovakia was erected into an independent state. This vigorous young state of Czechs and Slovaks took over from the old Austria the areas of Bohemia abutting on Germany. It was only in Bavaria, therefore, that Germany touched Austria. And as an additional security, it was provided that there should be no political union between Austria and Germany without the consent of the Council of the League of Nations. The protection to France on Germany's Eastern frontier was therefore the constitution of two new independent states (Poland and Czechoslovakia), which promptly allied themselves with France. Germany was deprived of something like two million subjects and a great source of wealth in the shape of coal. In addition, Austria was separated from Hungary and reduced to a state of some eight millions. She was surrounded everywhere by hostile states. The one exception was Germany, and with Germany she was forbidden to unite, though this did not prevent her annexation in 1938.

The securities so far required to render Germany less dangerous in future were either territorial, by readjusting the frontier, or economic, by reducing the wealth of Germany. The further security in the demilitarisation of the German area west of the Rhine disappeared in 1936. In addition, Luxemburg and Belgium were deneutralised in the west. On the east, Poland and Czechoslovakia were created, and Austria enormously reduced in power. So Germany was deprived of over four millions of population and much wealth in coal and iron. Her Austrian ally was rendered harmless, and four states created or strengthened on her flanks. All these, it was hoped, would be in alliance with the Entente.

It might be thought that these precautions, which strongly resemble those applied to France in the settlement of 1815, would have been enough. But the lesson of the war and of the enormous and increasing power of Germany had been thoroughly learnt by the French at least. The plan was a drastic one. It was to abolish Germany for ever as a military power by limiting her army practically to a police force. Lloyd George added the interesting innovation of a voluntary long-period service army. The existing forces were to be demobilised and conscription abolished in Germany. Instead soldiers were to serve for twelve years—and the total number was to be limited to 100,000 men. In this way no large numbers of recruits could ever be trained and, as the years went on, very few would have any experience of military service. The existing armaments were to be destroyed, and the production of munitions to be strictly limited in future. As an additional precaution, the German Staff was to be strictly limited in numbers and powers. The aim was to prevent the production of war materials, to limit effective forces, to defamiliarise Germany with militarism, and to prevent the brain (*i.e.* the General Staff) of the army from functioning in future. This system was also to be applied to the navy, and *similia similibus* to Austria-Hungary, Bulgaria and Turkey. It was an ingenious system—and only Turkey refused to have it forced upon her.

The first defect in the German disarmament was that the limitation of the army to 100,000 was too low a figure for Germany. It was four times less than what the British General Staff recommended. In result Germany and the others were tempted, or compelled, first to evade, and finally to repudiate, these clauses. All these four countries had, in less than twenty years, as many men trained or armed as they liked. These military, naval and air clauses were introduced into the German Treaty with the statement that they were enforced on Germany and her allies, 'in order to render possible the initiation of a general limitation of the armaments of all nations.' Germany (and Austria and Bulgaria and Hungary) complied with the demands, but awaited in vain any effective 'general limitation of the armaments of all nations.' Germany and the other states, in the result, rejected the clauses openly in 1936. In the end the feverish competition in armament production was resumed on a greater scale than that which led to the war of 1914.

Great severity was shown in the case of German rights and interests outside Germany. All German state property in her former colonies was confiscated, and all her trading privileges and rights in countries such as Morocco, China, Siam, Equatorial Africa, were abrogated. It was therefore made extremely difficult for her to trade outside Europe. Kiao-chau and German rights in Shantung province went on lease and the Marshall Isles on mandate to Japan, and all her other colonies in Africa and the Pacific to France, the British Empire and Belgium.[1] She also received very stern treatment as regards control of her ports, waterways and railways wherever they had an international character. The Rhine, for instance, by an extreme application of the doctrine of international rivers, was governed by an international board on which Germany was in a hopeless minority; Great Britain and Italy together had, actually, as many representatives on the Rhine Commission as Germany herself. The Kiel Canal, more justifiably, was neutralised and demilitarised. Both the internationalisation of the Rhine and the neutralisation of the Kiel Canal were later repudiated by Germany. These provisions, taken in conjunction with those relating to enemy property and debts, were of extreme severity. Indeed, those relating to private property, which enabled individual property to be confiscated in Allied countries as a set-off against national Reparation debts, were revolutionary in character. They were clearly most dangerous as a precedent in future treaties, and are a good illustration of how hard it is for experts, pursuing a formula, to do justice to a defeated enemy.[2]

The heated atmosphere of the Peace Conference led more than anything else to the Penal Clauses. These provided for the extradition from Holland of the German ex-Kaiser, and for his trial by a special tribunal 'for a supreme offence against international morality and the sanctity of treaties.' They also provided for Germany's surrender to the Allies, for trial by special tribunal, of certain German persons who had violated

[1] *Mandates:* To France, Cameroons (part); to Great Britain, Cameroons (part), Togoland, German South-West Africa, Tanganyika; to Belgium, part of Tanganyika; German New Guinea to Australia; Samoa to New Zealand; Nauru to Great Britain; Marshall Isles to Japan.

[2] The property clauses, Part X of the Treaty, were done by experts alone, and were the only section in which the 'Big Four' had practically no share and influence.

the laws and customs of war, or had been guilty of criminal acts against
Allied nationals. In the end these clauses proved unworkable. The
Dutch refused to give up the ex-Kaiser, on the very justifiable ground
that it was against international law for the Allies to demand the surrender of a political refugee from a neutral state. A vast list of war
criminals was drawn up, but it proved impossible to extradite them from
Germany in view of the ugly temper of the German people. A few of
them were tried and punished by German tribunals. When the President
of the German Republic was elected in 1925, the French thought of
declaring the election annulled by the Treaty, since the successful candidate was a war-criminal. They eventually desisted, and were wise to
do so—for the name of the old war-criminal and the new President
was Hindenburg.

The last and most important section of the Treaty to be mentioned
here was concerned with Reparation. Passions ran high. France, with
her devastated areas and desolated cities, clamoured for the amplest
indemnities. She held, too, that the exaction of huge sums from Germany was a kind of *revanche* for the indemnity of 1871. And there was
further a desire to cripple and injure Germany by fines and amercements. French hatred of Germany was so fierce, her demands so impassioned, that no moderation could be expected from her. Lloyd
George was unfortunately in nearly the same position. The British
election was won on the cry of 'making Germany pay to the last farth-
ing.' This cry conflicted with the legal basis of the Treaty, but Lloyd
George never denied that he advocated it. Unfortunately there were
different opinions as to how many farthings Germany possessed.
Before Lloyd George left for Paris a committee of British financiers,
headed by the Australian premier, Mr. Hughes, produced what was
known as the 'business-man's estimate.' They reckoned that Germany
could pay twenty-four thousand million pounds![1] The sum was
ridiculous. No one at the Peace Conference seriously suggested more
than a third of that sum as possible, few believed that more than a fifth
of it could be exacted. Keynes, the best British financial adviser, suggested two thousand million, in a lump sum, as the most that could
be got out of Germany. This was only one-twelfth of the 'business-
man's estimate,' which had been popularly acclaimed in England.
Lloyd George might well ask in private (as he frequently did), 'What is
a poor politician to do?' It was no use asserting too openly that 'the
business men' were drunk with passion and their 'estimate' moonshine.
For the politician who did that would quickly lose his job. Even as it
was he came near doing so. The telegram of 370 members of Parliament demanding that Lloyd George should make Germany pay to
the utmost was a danger-signal. It was a threat he could not openly
disregard, and it hampered all his subsequent policy. The most

[1] *v*, the document in Lloyd George: *The Truth about Reparations and War-Debts*
(1932), pp. 12–13.

extraordinary part of the whole affair is that the 'business men' never demanded an inventory of Germany's assets nor a calculation on a business basis. It was always an estimate based on passion and on prejudice, which eschewed contact with realities.

One chance, and one chance only, remained. President Wilson had said very nobly, 'America wanted nothing for herself' in reparations or money. But on his voyage to Paris he had said very naïvely that he was 'not much interested in the economic subjects' to be discussed at Paris.[1] That was just the tragedy. There is little on the subject in Wilson's speeches and addresses, which formed the legal basis of the Treaty. He himself was interested in enabling republics to be erected in Germany, Poland, Czechoslovakia, and drawing their frontiers for them. But the economics of Europe—and indeed of the war in Europe—were hard for him to understand, and still harder for him to settle. Keynes proposed a plan for cancelling Inter-Allied Debts, but this was too bold for America. But the question of Reparation was different. Some of Wilson's advisers prepared a business estimate of German assets. When that was rejected and a total of five thousand millions was proposed, Lloyd George showed complete frankness. 'Lloyd George admitted that this was all that could reasonably be expected, but objected that [British and French] public opinion would not accept it.'[2] This stand destroyed all idea of getting a lump sum out of Germany. And the settlement ultimately adopted was one which was extremely ingenious. A Reparation Commission was formed and endowed with very large powers of control to determine Germany's capacity to pay. The British and French public were satisfied, assuming that Germany would be made to pay enormous sums. The aim of Lloyd George (and doubtless also of President Wilson) was just the opposite. It was to get that sum down to reasonable limits, when the Reparation Commission sat in an atmosphere free from passion and in which it was safe to tell the public the truth. Also, if the United States had remained on the Reparation Commission, it is clear that its decisions and its conclusions would have been very different. The Treaty, even as it was, appeared to demand something like eight thousand million pounds.[3] But it was certainly the intention of Lloyd George and Wilson greatly to reduce this sum.

In connection with Reparation, however, a most unfortunate incident occurred. Lloyd George and the French had at first tried to make Germany 'pay the whole cost of the war.' This principle was knocked on the head by President Wilson, who declared, and rightly, that it was inconsistent with the legal basis of the Treaty.[4] This basis was not that

[1] R. S. Baker: *Woodrow Wilson and World Settlement* (1923), vol. II. p. 319.
[2] Baker, vol. II. p. 377.
[3] J. M. Keynes: *The Economic Consequences of the Peace* (1919), p. 207.
[4] A fact which Mr. Lloyd George never realised. *v.* his *Truth about Reparations and War Debts*, pp. 14–15: cp. B. M. Baruch: *The Making of the Reparation and Economic Sections of the Treaty*, New York (1920), pp. 25–6.

Germany should pay the whole costs, or even an indemnity; she had simply agreed to pay compensation 'for all damage done to the civilian population of the Allies and their property by the aggression of Germany by land, by sea, and from the air.' Now this definition would only have produced about three thousand millions from Germany. Moreover, it would have been enormously to the advantage of France as against England. Lloyd George therefore desired to find a basis by which more could be demanded, and a bigger share of reparations obtained for England. He found it in pensions to widows and orphans of persons killed in the war and in separation allowances during the war—a category which could not possibly be covered by the definition of loss and damage given. France agreed to this proposal, which meant adding some five thousand million pounds to the original three thousand million. But President Wilson had to be convinced—and it took much time. It was argued that pensions could not possibly be included in the loss and damage definition; it was argued much less reasonably that it could. Smuts submitted an argument that it was legal and logical. Wilson finally astonished everyone by saying: 'Logic! Logic! I don't give a damn for logic. I am going to include pensions!'[1] So pensions were included. There can be very little doubt that this decision was wrong. It is also hardly possible to deny that, if so, it was a breach of faith by the Allies of an international engagement with Germany of a sacred character. But it is not likely that Wilson included it because he did not realise the legal or logical objections to doing so.[2]

In this fashion the Treaty was completed and the Germans were asked to sign. By a very grave breach of international courtesy and usage, the German delegates were not allowed to discuss the Treaty in private with the Allies. They were restricted entirely to written intercourse. The result, curiously enough, worked out entirely to the Allied disadvantage. Had there been discussion in committee there would have been full explanations at close quarters of the whole meaning of the Treaty. There would also certainly have been modifications of some clauses. As it was, the Germans could not find out the true meaning of everything. They therefore misinterpreted Article 231, which begins the Reparation section of the Treaty, as charging them with war-guilt. It was, in fact, merely a technical verdict of guilty against Germany, in order to justify the exaction of money from her. But the Germans always interpreted it as fixing the guilt of the war upon Germany in the practical and moral sense. And this interpretation was repeated so often that even the Allies, or at least the Allied press and public,

---

[1] E. M. House and C. Seymour: *What really happened at Paris* (1921), p. 272.

[1] This is much disputed. A different interpretation is given by R. S. Baker (*Wilson and World Settlement*, vol. II. pp. 379–83), Keynes (*Economic Consequences, etc.*, pp. 48–9; *A Revision of the Treaty* (1922), pp. 134, 139–46) and Baruch (*Making of the Reparation*, etc., p. 29), who suggest that Wilson was convinced by legal arguments.

came to believe it.[1] It is perhaps the most impressive demonstration ever given that the denial of courtesy and a fair hearing even to a foe bring severe penalties with them.

•   •   •   •   •   •   •

By a sort of symbolic retribution carefully planned and designed by the French, the signature of the Peace Treaty took place at Versailles, in the Galerie des Glaces. This was doubly memorable. It was the hall where Louis Quatorze set up his motto, *Nec Pluribus impar*, which he decorated with the painted trophies of his victories, in which he received and humiliated the Doge of Genoa, in which he proclaimed his grandson King of Spain. In that same room William I, King of Prussia, had been proclaimed German Emperor by the warriors and princes of Germany, fresh from their triumph over France. And in the room where Royalist Germany had recorded her victory, Republican Germany was to record her defeat.

Here is the account of an eye-witness on the 28th June 1919: 'To-day I saw the Germans sign. The entrance to the Galerie des Glaces was up two lines of stairs, guarded by a line of troopers, with blue uniforms, steel breast-plates, and helmets with long horse-hair plumes, making a splendid appearance. . . . At three p.m. there was suddenly a tense interval and silence, and, preceded by four armed officers, the Germans appeared. One pale, bowed, with glasses like a student (Müller); the next head erect and hair like an artist's (Bell). Immediately after, I suppose by design, the cuirassiers all suddenly sheathed their swords . . . a symbolic and conscious act. The atmosphere of hate was terrible. They advanced and sat down on the fourth side of the square, near the table of rose and almond-wood, on which lay the Treaty. In a minute or two Clemenceau got up, and speaking in a sharp, clear, musical voice, like a succession of strokes on a gong, said: "We are in complete agreement. I have the honour to ask messieurs the German Plenipotentiaries to sign." At this point the Germans got up and bowed low. They were asked to sit down again and the speech was translated. After this they came forward and signed slowly amid a tense hush.

'Then came Wilson (and his plenipotentiaries), Lloyd George, who smiled broadly as he finished, the Colonial Premiers, and the Maharajah of Bikaner, looking magnificent in a pale khaki turban. After that Clemenceau, with Pichon and Tardieu behind him. Then Sonnino, on the last day of his reign, and then the Plenipotentiaries of Minor States. As Paderewski, with his tawny mane and stage-bow, signed, the guns began to boom outside.

[1] The German observations on the Draft Treaty make this interpretation of Art. 231. The Allied Reply (*v. German Treaty*, 1920, pp. 271–6) of June 16 generally charges Germany with War Guilt, and quotes Art. 227–30 (trial of Kaiser and war criminals) as 'Responsibility for the War.' It does not admit that Art. 231 bears this meaning. After reading this reply, the Germans signed.

'The ceremony ended soon, the Germans were carefully escorted out, and Clemenceau came down the hall slowly, beaming, shaking hands. As he went out the old man reached me his hand, or rather the hand covered as always in a grey glove. "Felicitations," said I. "Mille remerciments," said he. . . . A great moment, but I fear a peace without victory, just as we had a victory without peace.'

CHAPTER XXXI

NATION-MAKING IN THE NEW EUROPE

I. CENTRAL EUROPE

THE history of the war and the peace is overhung with dark clouds of delusion. It is assumed that the war was a purposeless agony, the peace treaties a series of penal measures and amercements. These half-truths obscure the real facts. For, whatever may be thought of the German Treaty, it developed international organisation to a point unknown before in human history. Whatever may be thought of the treaties with Austria, with Hungary, with Bulgaria, they satisfied national aspirations to an extent unprecedented in Eastern and Central Europe. These treaties enabled two nations—Rumania and Yugoslavia—to become great states and to reunite themselves to their long-severed kinsmen. It brought two others to life, Czechoslovakia and Poland, after centuries of extinction. Four others, Esthonia, Latvia, Finland and Lithuania, recovered their freedom. These achievements seem likely to be memorable in history. And, if they are, importance will attach to the treaties which made them possible.

Popular delusions abound with regard to the treaties with Austria, Hungary, Bulgaria and Turkey. It was contended, for instance, that the Entente Allies were legally bound to apply the Wilsonian principles to these treaties and to other countries as well as to Germany. To Germany the pledge was admitted. An offer was made on 5 November 1918, which Germany accepted by signing the Armistice, and this offer was a promise to make peace on the basis of Wilson's speeches from 8 January 1918 onwards (the Fourteen Points, etc.). Bulgaria signed an armistice on September 29, Turkey on October 30, and Austria-Hungary on November 3. Their terms all differed from the German, for each of these countries sued for peace after admittedly overwhelming defeat, and received it on the basis of unconditional surrender. Consequently the Entente Powers in no way made a contract (as they did by their offer of November 5 to the Germans) to apply Wilson's principles to these countries. Any such pledge was implicit and moral, not explicit and legal.

It will be best to take Austria-Hungary first. The last act of the old Common Monarchy was to sign the Armistice on 3 November 1918. Immediately afterwards Austria parted from Hungary and the two became separate and independent states.[1] Ultimately Austria signed one Peace Treaty (St. Germain, 10 September 1919) and Hungary another (Trianon, 4 June 1920), and peace negotiations with each were entirely separate. The population of Austria as distinct from Hungary was about 22 millions. The Treaty of St. Germain reduced Austria to less than half her old population. She surrendered seven and a half million Slavs in Galicia to the new Poland, and over a million other non-Germans. She gave up also nearly four million Germans, of whom three and a half millions went to Czechoslovakia. Austria's new boundaries confined her to the Austrian Archduchies, Styria and the Tyrol, with a population of about eight millions odd, nearly all of pure German race. The once proud Austria, which had ruled over twenty million subjects and fifteen different races, was reduced to less than half of her former size, and lost a third of her purely German population. She became miserably poor and dragged out a pathetic existence from this time, and was annexed by Germany in 1938.

Poland, on the principle of self-determination, had received the Slav populations of Ruthenes and Poles from Austria. But why was it necessary for Czechoslovakia to take three and a half million Germans from Austria? The reason was that some of these Germans were separated by Czech territory from Austria and faced Imperial Germany, while others were inextricably mingled with Czechs. If Czechoslovakia had a right to exist at all, she could only do so as a polyglot and multi-racial state. To be 'viable' at all, she must include all sorts of races and stretch her tentacles far. As finally constituted there were over six million Czechs, nearly two million Slovaks, three and a half million Germans and not quite a million Magyars. This was the only instance at the Peace Conference in which any state was deliberately formed on a multi-national basis. In other cases alien races were reluctantly admitted, not deliberately chosen as the basis of a state.

In history the Czechs had once been a nation, and it was held that they had a right to be so again. Their ability and organising capacity, like their hatred for the German, was great. Moreover, it was evident that, in so polyglot a state, the ruling race would not attempt, or if it attempted, would not succeed, in coercing the alien races. On the whole, Czechoslovakia justified these hopes. Under two great teachers, Masaryk, their first President, and Beneš, his successor, she showed a largeness of international outlook and a tolerance towards her subject races which was unique in Central and in East Europe. Certainly the Poles treated their Ruthenians (who were Slavs) much worse than the Czechs treated their Germans (who were Teutons).

---

[1] This was marked by the fact that Hungary signed a separate military convention with the Allied Powers (November 13, 1918).

Austria in one sense had more to suffer from Italy than from Czecho-slovakia. For, though she lost much less to Italy, the Hapsburg monarchy had been an eternal enemy, the tyrannical power reigning in Lombardy and Venetia and denying Italians their freedom. Such memories are not easily forgotten, and in 1866, when Austria finally abandoned Venetia to Italy, she retained the Trentino. The fact that the southern part of the Tyrol was inhabited by Italians provoked Italian patriots, who gave it the name of *Italia Irredenta*. But there was another provocation too. The Austrians had taken great care to retain spurs and tongues of mountains running down into the Italian plains. The territory thus re-tained projected like a bastion into Italy, protecting Austria from all assault and facilitating attack on Italy from this area. The Italians suc-ceeded at the Peace Conference in exactly turning the tables on Austria. They pushed the Italian frontier right up to the Brenner Pass, not only thereby annexing a quarter of a million Germans, but giving Italy an offensive advantage against Austria in the case of war. It was wholly needless to give her this power or to hand over so many Germans to her keeping. Two other frontiers were proposed which would have given her adequate defence, without sinning so much against racial ethics. But the fear of a revived Austria, the ghost of a dead past, prevailed.

The line thus conceded to Italy in the Tyrol was part of the price Italy demanded for siding with the Entente. The Secret Treaty of London, April 26, 1915, demanded territory in Istria, which meant ceding half a million Yugoslavs to Italy, and half of Dalmatia as well. England and France were agreed to cede Istria, but they tried hard to avoid ceding half Dalmatia as well. President Wilson, who was not bound by a secret treaty, stubbornly resisted. The Italian case was a bad one, for they wanted the port of Fiume as well, and the port of Fiume had not been included in the Treaty of London. Hence if they got half Dalmatia they would not get Fiume. If they got Fiume they would have no claim to half Dalmatia. Wilson took a strong stand against their having Fiume, and was supported by England and France. But the whole matter was not settled at the Peace Conference. It was ultimately decided by direct negotiations between Italy and the Yugo-slavs. In the end Italy got Fiume and one or two islands in the Adriatic and the town of Zara in Dalmatia, surrendering all the rest. Italy eventually included within her borders half a million Yugoslavs, in addition to the quarter of a million Germans in the Tyrol. It was not a good settlement, but it was better than none. If you are trying to absorb parts of other races, it is best to place them behind strong barriers, which will make it difficult for their brethren to free them. Italy had effectively done this. The quarter of a million Germans in the Tyrol and the half million Yugoslavs in Istria and the Julian Alps were separated from their kinsmen by enormous mountains, so the prisoners were behind walls which were strong, and Italy held the key.

As a result of the war the old kingdom of Serbia grew into the new state of Yugoslavia. During the war the Serb army under the Regent (later King Alexander) had suffered intensely and performed miracles of valour. They had their reward, and trebled the size of their country. To the old kingdom of Serbia were now added Montenegro, Dalmatia, Bosnia and Slovenia. The old kingdom of four millions swelled to thirteen, partly at the expense of Austria, but mostly at the expense of Hungary. The inhabitants of the new kingdom were nearly all Yugoslavs—of similar blood and speech to the Serbs.[1] Twelve out of the thirteen millions in the new kingdom were Yugoslavs. There had never in the past been a kingdom uniting all Yugoslavs, and this made its formation difficult. There were differences of religion and history, and old barriers of prejudice. The quarrels in Parliament and the disputes between the different parties or races finally became so bitter that King Alexander abolished the constitution of 1921, and governed as dictator. In 1931 he sought to set up a modified form of representative government, of which the success was moderate. Alexander was murdered in 1935 after having untiringly pursued the Yugoslav ideal. A Regency under Prince Paul followed and was still in office when war came again to the Near East.

Rumania, like Yugoslavia, derived enormous accessions of wealth and population from the war at the expense of Hungary. She was particularly fortunate, because she was late in entering the war and had to make peace at the end of 1917. She again took up arms very late in 1918. Her statesmen at the Peace Conference showed considerable truculence, and, in defiance of the Great Powers, sent their soldiers into Budapest in August 1919, and terrorised and looted it to their hearts' content. By the subsequent treaty with Hungary Rumania obtained enormous advantages. The whole of Transylvania, rich in forests and ores, fell into her hands; so did the great city of Temesvár and a large slice of the fertile cornland of Hungary. In addition Rumania regained the Bukovina from Austria, and the great province of Bessarabia from Russia. She more than doubled her old territory and population, obtaining over eight million new subjects, of whom more than half were Rumanians. The Rumanian kingdom, thus strengthened and reorganised, was not, however, an ideal state. Historical differences were very great, Bucharest was not well situated to be the capital, the government was intolerant and corrupt, and the lot of the subject peoples was hard. In one direction alone Rumania was far-sighted. Despite opposition from her landowning class of nobles, she insisted on a forced distribution of land to peasants. She did this not only in the conquered lands but in old Rumania also.

We are now in a position to estimate what the Treaty of Trianon (June 4, 1920) really did to the kingdom of Hungary. It cut off the Slovaks and some Magyars from her in the north and gave them to Czechoslovakia. It severed Rumanians and Magyars from her and gave

[1] The Slovenes speak a different dialect, but Croat and Serb are the same language.

them to Yugoslavia in the south. It left her with a population of seven
and a half millions, of whom over six million were Magyars. She therefore lost about three million Magyars in all. Czechoslovakia, Rumania
and Yugoslavia thus took from Hungary not only subjects of their own
race, but three million Magyars in addition; about half a million went
to Yugoslavia, one million to Czechoslovakia and a million and a half
to Rumania. It must however be remembered that Hungary before the
war had over half its subjects aliens, and the populations of Czechoslovakia, Rumania and Yugoslavia were distributed a great deal more
according to racial unity than was the case in any of these regions in
1914.

This is not the only argument to show that in Central and East
Europe at least the carving up and redistribution of races was, on the
whole, to the good. Pre-war Hungary had been ruled by a narrow,
aristocratic Magyar caste, able and courageous, but hostile to all non-
Magyar elements in the state. After an interval of revolution these
tendencies reasserted themselves. The rule of the Regent Horthy was
supported by a reorganised Magyar aristocracy, with a tight hand on
democracy and no disposition to make land free and easy for the
peasant to acquire. This was the real difference between Hungary and
the lands which surrounded it. In that part of the world the war was a
war for free land for the peasant. The Entente fought for the peasant,
Hungary for the landowner. Rumania, reactionary and corrupt as she
was, recognised this truth and compelled even her nobles to distribute
land to the peasants on a generous scale. In Czechoslovakia land was
freely assigned to the peasant by the new government. The Serbs have
never had any aristocracy since the Turks destroyed it. The Serbs applied their old policy freely and readily to the whole of Yugoslavia, and
distributed land to peasants in fair shares, taking care that it should be
inalienable. Without the Austrian and Hungarian treaties these experiments could not have been made. To the objective eye there can be no
doubt that Hungary, with its chivalric virtues, represented a vanishing
past, and that the new states represented the future. Whatever may be
said of treaty-making in the West, the new forces, created by the Treaties
of East and Central Europe, were stronger than the old and more in
touch with modern life.

II. THE BALTIC, POLAND AND RUSSIA

FOUR states of the Baltic coast had a most prominent share in the war,
and were, as a result of the peace, all of them enabled to realise their
national aspirations. These states were Finland, Esthonia, Latvia and
Lithuania. They had always in the past been the battleground between
Swedes, Russians, Poles and Germans. After the war they were at last
free and able to live their own lives. Finland was the most mature of

these countries as regards national status and evolution. Since Russia wrested her from Sweden in 1809 Finland's position always approached that of independence. For a time she actually attained it during the Russian Revolution of 1905; and, even when Russia resumed control, her separate position remained. She sent no members to the Duma and paid a tax in lieu of military service. A foolish and violent attempt was made to russianise Finland, but this broke down as soon as war began. In 1917 the Russian Revolution granted her complete autonomy. Finland was for a time in danger both from her own reactionaries and from the Bolsheviks in neighbouring Russia. It was, in fact, hard to say whether White or Red influences were more dangerous to her. Ultimately peace was made with the Bolsheviks in 1920, and from this time until 1939 Finland pursued her own national development untouched from without.

Esthonia and Latvia may be taken together. There are differences between them. The Esths, like the Finns, are Ugrian and primitive in race, while the Letts are a Slav people. None the less both in servitude and in freedom the two states have had a common history. In the Middle Ages they were both subjected to German landlords (the 'Baltic barons') and reduced to the conditions of mere serfs. Russia conquered both countries at the beginning of the eighteenth century. As the Russian Government did not like Germans it did something to raise the condition of the serfs as against their masters. At last in 1863 it emancipated all the serfs. In this way a new era for both countries began. Education was pushed forward, and national aspirations gradually took shape. The Esths soon became one of the best educated races in Europe. They were almost wholly homogeneous in race, and they were particularly active in expelling German influences in higher education. The Letts were not far behind them, and both were prepared for independence when the war began. Latvia was a theatre of war from the start, but in 1918 the Germans finally occupied Esthonia as well. During the years 1919–20 both countries had to struggle against Germans on the one side and Bolsheviks on the other. Both were ultimately successful, and were admitted as independent states into the League of Nations in 1921.

The same year witnessed the resurrection of Lithuania. That state was neither so homogeneous as the others, nor were its inhabitants so tough in fibre, nor were they trained so much to the sea. In Finland at Helsinki, in Esthonia at Reval, in Latvia at Riga, the capital was a port. Lithuania's capital was Vilna, in the interior, and it was threatened by Poland. During the war Germany had found it politic to allow the Lithuanians a considerable amount of freedom as a counterpoise to the Poles. After the armistice she was in a dangerous position, though she received friendly aid from Esthonia and Latvia in 1918. During 1919 she gradually disencumbered herself of Germany, only to meet with fresh threats to her independence from Poles and Bolsheviks. The former, not the latter, proved the more serious menace. The Poles, remembering the old medieval connection of Lithuania and Poland, fought desperately to preserve it. When that hope failed they decided at least to secure control of Vilna. They sent a Polish general, Zeligowski, to seize it. He did so and held it in the name of Poland and undoubtedly at the instigation of the Polish Government.[1] The Great Powers had recognised the independence of Lithuania in 1922. But they proved entirely unable to shake the Polish grasp on Vilna and finally acquiesced in its retention by Poland in 1923. Thus Lithuania, though deprived of its capital by Polish agency, recovered its independence.

All these four Baltic states may be described as states whose national independence existed 'on sufferance.' They were plainly not strong enough, either individually or collectively, to stand out against the attack of an armed Great Power. The Poles or the Bolsheviks might equally be a danger to them.   Their independence in fact was governed by the ability of Poland and Russia to counterbalance one another.

Lying outside and beyond modern Austria and Hungary, and the newer or enlarged states of Eastern Europe and the four Baltic states, the two Powers of Poland and Russia were of fundamental importance. Behind them there stood a long history of opposition. In the past Poland represented Catholicism and Latin culture, Russia Byzantinism and Orthodoxy. Poland thought Russians barbarous and, finding no defensible frontier between the countries, invaded and dominated and colonised many parts of Russia. She gradually grew stronger and pushed the Russians out. Finally in the eighteenth century Poland became weak, was partitioned by three Powers and destroyed. But nations do not die readily, much less a nation so gifted and brilliant and patriotic as the Poles. Poland had once been a great nation. She determined to be so again. As the three partitioning Powers, Russia, Germany and Austria-Hungary, suffered defeat in the war, they relaxed their grasp on Poland. The Poles seized their opportunity and were already a nation again before the war ended. The Peace Conference, in recognising Poland's independence, merely acknowledged a fact. But difficulties arose at once about drawing her frontiers. The German frontier was not easily settled, but was the least of the difficulties. It was soon found that in East Galicia three million Ruthenians had no desire to belong to the Poles. It was also found that Lithuania wished to be independent. The Poles knew what they wanted, and the Great Powers gradually wearied of the struggle. They obtained East Galicia and, by very questionable means, also got possession of Vilna, the capital of Lithuania.

Poland thus obtained territories to the west and the south, but what was to be her boundary to the east? The boundary in the past had never been the ethnic frontier, and the Poles may perhaps be excused

---

[1] This instigation was denied at the time, but was subsequently admitted by Pilsudski himself.

for wanting to keep Russia at as great a distance as possible from Warsaw. From 1917 onwards the Bolshevik Government of Russia had announced a policy of war against capitalists and the bourgeoisie and their intention of releasing the proletariate in bourgeois countries from the state of degrading servitude under which they laboured. The bourgeoisie in countries other than Poland received this news with calmness, as they were not directly affected by these threats. Poland, however, was near and therefore became excited. A conflict between her and Russia was inevitable, as soon as the Bolsheviks (or Reds) destroyed the Whites in Russia itself. For the Poles represented the armed patriotic bourgeoisie—the Russians the proletariate. Having overthrown their own bourgeoisie, the Russian Reds moved on the Poles. The Great Powers made some futile attempts to intervene, but neither side was disposed to listen to their demands. Foch, however, sent his *alter ego*, General Weygand, to act as military adviser to the Poles, and this one very small Frenchman was a reinforcement more valuable than thousands of soldiers. Pilsudski—the head of the Polish State—wisely took his advice. Poland seemed in extreme danger. For the Red army was commanded by the famous ex-Tsarist General, Brussilov, and was within a few miles of Warsaw. Then Pilsudski suddenly made a desperate counter-offensive. It was entirely successful (August 10, 1920). The victorious Poles pursued the fleeing Reds over three hundred miles. Finally, an armistice and treaty were signed at Riga (October 12, 1920). This established the Polish-Russian boundary on the Disna-Minsk-Ostrog line.

The Great Powers had studied ethnic data at Paris and produced a boundary for Poland which represented the eastern limit of purely Polish territory. This was known as the 'Curzon line.'[1] But the boundaries of 1920 were settled by the sword, and by Poland's own sword. By the treaty with Russia at Riga she acquired a population and territory about double that recommended by the 'Curzon line.' There were some twenty-seven millions in all, White Russians and Ruthenians and Lithuanians being the alien elements. In the year 1935 Poland lost Pilsudski, her strange, brilliant but sage dictator; his successors were not his equals in prestige or in actual power. But Poland continued the policy of friendship with Germany, inaugurated by Pilsudski in 1933, until the development of Hitler's offensive against Europe brought about a spectacular change. It is still too early to judge impartially the series of events which led to the eclipse of Poland in 1939 and to the changes which took place in her policy and outlook during the years of occupation. But it is well to remember the long history of Polish misfortune and resurgence and the peculiar strength of her national traditions.

[1] It was roughly from Punsk, in the North, to Grodow-Vlodava, north of Kholm; and thence to the boundary of Eastern Galicia. *v.* Temperley: *History of the Peace Conference of Paris*, Vol. VI, map opp. p. 282.

CHAPTER XXXII

WORLD SETTLEMENT AND NATION-MAKING IN THE
NEAR, MIDDLE AND FAR EAST

IF the nineteenth century was the age which produced nations in Europe, the twentieth produced them in Asia. The phenomena are most remarkable. They appeared indeed in different forms in the various countries, in Japan which early in the century became recognised as a Great Power; in China where freedom from the West was followed all too rapidly by other threats to independence; in India and Persia; in Turkey and throughout the Arab world. The phrases of nationalism and self-determination were everywhere. They were admitted at the Peace Settlement after the first World War, and this lent an enormous impulse to these movements. For the first time every one of the nations here mentioned met the nations of the West in an International Conference on equal terms. The Peace Settlement affected all three parts of the East directly, but principally the Near and Middle East.

The settlements under the Turkish Treaty fell into three parts: first, settlements in Europe, mainly in Thrace, which affected Greeks, Turks and Bulgars; second, the internationalisation of the Straits and Constantinople, which concerned Turkey, England, France and Italy; third, the problems of Asia Minor, Iraq, Palestine, Syria and Arabia, which concerned Greeks, Turks, Arabs and Jews, and raised the problem of nation-making in the East in an acute form.

For many centuries the Bulgars have been established in Bulgaria proper, Macedonia and Thrace. In the South they have conflicted with Greeks, in the East with the Turks, and in both cases with extreme bitterness. But at the Peace Conference Bulgars and Turks appeared as defeated and as detested enemies. Greece was radiant and victorious. But it was only for the moment. Venizelos, the great man of Greece, had but recently returned to power and his position was insecure. His territorial demands were needed to popularise him in Greece and were against his better judgment. Bulgaria was forced to give strategic advantages on the frontier to Yugoslavia. She was compelled to cede Western Thrace to Greece and was thus cut off from all access to the Ægean. In addition Venizelos secured Adrianople and Eastern Thrace from Turkey by the Treaty of Sèvres. He thus brought Greece within a few miles of Constantinople, a prize he one day hoped to gain for her.[1] The Straits from the Dardanelles to the Sea of Mar-

[1] The actual settlement proposed for Constantinople and the Straits was that they should be internationalised, and that the United States should take the Mandate as also for Armenia. This hope flickered out in September 1919, and thereafter both areas were assigned to Turkey.

mora were to be internationalised and demilitarised. The arrangement in reality enabled a British or Allied fleet to reach and, if necessary, attack Constantinople without difficulty in case of war.

Even these gains were not enough for Venizelos, and he aspired to a Greek dominion in Asia Minor based on the sea. Ever since the days of Troy Greeks had been active as settlers and traders on the west coast of Asia Minor which was called Ionia. Greek troops had been in occupation of Smyrna since May 1919, and in and around this province Venizelos designed to establish a permanent Greek dominion. He found there something like half a million Greeks or Ionians and doubtless hoped to attract more. This concession was embodied in the peace with Turkey signed at Sèvres on 10 August 1920.

Sèvres is the French factory for the most delicate china ware, as the wits did not fail to notice when the treaty was signed there. Ominous signs appeared from the first. The United States, Yugoslavia, and the Arab king of the Hejaz refused to sign at all. Turkey signed under protest. The Turkish army in Asia Minor began to look dangerous. There was no one to execute the treaty. Venizelos, with a British loan, undertook to do so. The Greeks easily defeated the Turks and captured Brusa, their old Asiatic capital. Very soon afterwards, however, Venizelos fell from power in Greece and fled the country. The ex-King Constantine returned from exile to Greece in triumph. The fall of her greatest statesman deprived Greece of the favour of the Allies and of her last chance of Asiatic dominion. The china-shop of Sèvres was entered and smashed by a bull. The bull was Mustafa Kemal Pasha, known later as Kemal Atatürk.

Mustafa Kemal appeared at this time to be simply a brutal and fearless soldier, but he stood for a principle and had all patriotic Turks behind him. The wretched Sultan and his ministers lived at Constantinople beneath the guns of the British fleet and had been forced to sign the Sèvres Treaty. But the humiliations of Turkey, above all the presence of the detested Greeks at Smyrna, had roused the best or worst feelings of patriotic Turks. Anatolia was their home and in its highlands they could defy the Allies. Mustafa Kemal, who had distinguished himself at the Dardanelles, openly revolted and stirred up the army. In 1920 he had been defeated in the first round by Venizelos and driven into the interior. But early in 1921 he held a National Assembly at Angora (now Ankara) and drew up what is called the 'Angora pact.' It demanded complete independence for the Sultan and Constantinople, and the union under Turkish sovereignty of all parts of the Ottoman Empire 'inhabited by an Ottoman Moslem' majority. In reality the manifesto amounted to a refusal to accept the Sèvres Treaty, and to an announcement that Mustafa Kemal and his soldiers would reconquer by force any part of Turkey that they could. One can hardly blame them for this attitude, especially in view of the fact that they had a fierce national patriotism behind them.

It was King Constantine, now restored to his throne, who decided the fate of the Greek Empire in Asia. Venizelos had shown no desire to venture much beyond the coast in attacking the Turks, and had even disapproved of going as far as Brusa. Constantine decided that it was necessary to attack the evil at its centre. He would penetrate to Ankara, the Kemalist capital, and dictate peace in the highlands of Asia Minor. It was a good scheme if it could be done. He was himself a general of repute, but his project was declared impossible by the best military experts, among whom were Sir Henry Wilson and Foch. But in the interests of his dynasty Constantine decided to make the attempt, backed by the moral support and financial aid of Lloyd George. The French troops in Cilicia had intimated that they would not attack the Kemalist Turks and would perhaps send them supplies and arms.

Mustafa Kemal was confident as to the situation. He said 'that the Greeks might beat him, but that he did not mean to be rounded up. He would retire to regions where the Greeks could not get at him and would continue the war until the Greeks gave in.'[1] In 1921 the great Greek offensive began. It was pushed with the utmost gallantry over difficult country by devoted efforts. But no valour could penetrate to the stony and waterless plateau around Ankara. The Greek offensive died away before it reached there, and the Greek army was left clinging to a precarious front stretched vertically across Asia Minor. No permanent frontier had ever run along the line the Greeks now held. The coasts have been dominated or protected by sea-power, but Ankara, or some such city, has always commanded the interior. The Greeks could not go forward and dared not go back, and the end was inevitable. In August 1922 Mustafa Kemal suddenly descended from his hills in great force. He broke the thin and wavering Greek line at several points, and drove their dispirited troops in utter rout before him. It was a complete and colossal disaster. In September Smyrna itself fell and was given to the flames. It was the end not only of Greek dominion but of Greek residence in Asia. For ultimately Mustafa Kemal expelled not only every Greek soldier but every Greek inhabitant.

Mustafa Kemal led his victorious troops onwards to the Straits, where they found sectors held by British, French and Italian troops. British troops still garrisoned Constantinople and British warships were in the Sea of Marmora. French and Italian troops hurriedly withdrew, but the British troops stood firm. Lloyd George stated that he would defend the 'Freedom of the Straits,' and prevent the Kemalist troops from crossing into Europe. His gesture was not so bold as it sounds, for he had already intimated to Mustafa Kemal that Eastern Thrace could be returned to Turkey. Still it produced an armistice (11 October 1922) and after nearly a year resulted in the Treaty of Lausanne (24 July 1923).

[1] C. à C. Repington: *After the War* (1922), p. 360.

So far as Bulgaria was concerned Turkey regained Adrianople, and got back Eastern (but not Western) Thrace from Greece. The Greeks were entirely expelled from Asia Minor whether as a government or as individuals. The neutralised zone round the Straits was much reduced in size, but preserved in essentials. It was still possible for them to be rushed quickly from the Mediterranean by French, British or Italian war vessels. Mustafa Kemal, triumphant in his military success, refused to submit to any limitation of his armaments. Turkey was therefore the only ex-enemy power not restricted in the manufacture or use of her armaments or in the number of her troops. This treaty was humiliating to the Great Powers of Europe, and simply registered the fact that, in everything except demilitarising the Straits, Mustafa Kemal was strong enough to defy them. And, in order that he might continue to defy them, he shifted his capital from the now vulnerable Constantinople to the impregnable hill fastness of Ankara.

Mustafa Kemal set a most striking example in Turkey after 1923. He was a man of great courage and determination. In the face of local opposition, he introduced wide-sweeping reforms, dealing with every aspect of the life of the people. His achievements include the complete overhaul of the administration, the introduction and enforcement of new legal codes, the improvement of communications, finances and agricultural and industrial methods, the emancipation of women, the Europeanisation of dress, and the introduction of the Latin characters. A law of 1934 compelling all Turks to adopt a surname resulted in his own change of name to Atatürk (the father of the Turks). Perhaps the most daring and symbolic of his reforms was the abandonment of Constantinople as capital, and the building of the new capital at Ankara. Atatürk was certainly ruthless in his suppression of all opposition, particularly in the early days of his régime. His methods were undoubtedly those of a dictator, but they were necessary if the chaos of centuries was to be reduced to order. Atatürk himself declared in 1932: ' . . . let the people leave politics alone for the present. Let them interest themselves in agriculture and commerce. For ten or fifteen years more I must rule. After that perhaps I may be able to let them speak openly.'[1] He died in November 1938, before this work was fully accomplished.

Yet, from a state which, in the nineteenth century, had been regarded as an intruder in Europe, Atatürk built up a Turkish state which gave to its citizens—men and women—greater freedom and security than any of their forefathers had enjoyed, and transformed Turkey into an independent sovereign state, free from foreign interference for the first time for almost two centuries.

The tragedy of Armenia was the saddest of all the countless horrors associated with the great war of 1914. History is not a censor of morals. Yet it is the duty of the historian to draw attention to any exceptional

[1] H. C. Armstrong: *Grey Wolf* (1932), p. 329.

event or departure from ordinary standards, and both were found in Armenia during the 1914 war. Unfortunately there is no doubt where the responsibility lies. On the Turks of this period of vigorous Young Turkish nationalism lies the blame for massacres and cruelties such as authentic witnesses had never before related. The Armenian tragedy is a page of history which the Turks dyed purple with innocent blood.

The sum total of massacred persons will never be known. But it can hardly be wrong to reckon that something like six hundred thousand perished out of twelve hundred thousand deported. Of the survivors a good many were forcibly converted to Islam. But these terrible events did not end the tragedy and it is still more appalling to record that the Turks found yet further means of wreaking their vengeance. The Russians captured Erzerum in 1916, but their army melted away with the revolution of 1917. Gradually the Turks recovered not only their own part of Armenia, but entered Batum, Kars, and even Erivan. Enver was gone, but Mustafa Kemal and his successors 'did not their work negligently.' Their progress was marked by a trail of blood. Even in Cilicia those Armenians who were left were massacred. At Sassun and Bitlis the Turks completed their destruction. Even Erivan itself, the heart and capital of Russian Armenia, had to pay its tax of blood. At least a hundred thousand more were added to the death roll.

The Armenians had been abandoned by the world in spite of the Treaty of Sèvres. After the Armistice British troops for a time kept order in Transcaucasia; when these retired the Republics of Georgia, Erivan, and Azerbaijan struggled vainly against the Turks. Finally the Bolsheviks came to the rescue, restored the situation somewhat, and signed an agreement with the Turks (16 March 1921). By this they surrendered Batum and Kars and therefore a good two-thirds of Armenia. All Armenia that was left, known as the Republic of Erivan, was absorbed into the Soviet system of Client Republics. This was the true settlement of Armenia. In the Treaty of Sèvres the Turks had agreed to a national home for Armenians. President Wilson was appointed as arbiter to draw the boundaries, and defined its boundaries as very wide, reaching so far as Erzingan to the west. But this was purely an agreement and an award on paper. Mustafa Kemal entirely disregarded this part of the Sèvres Treaty when it came to making the Treaty of Lausanne in 1923. The Powers of Europe, by acquiescing in the omission of all mention of Armenia, recognised the Soviet-Kemal agreement of March 1921.

The Soviet Client Republic of Erivan flourished. Canals were dug, copper was produced, and experiments in cotton-growing and textiles were developed. The remnants of the Armenian race, though not much over a million, showed once again inexhaustible elasticity and vitality. They were strengthened by refugees and immigrants from without. Indeed, if we are to believe their own and the Russian statistics, nature came to their aid. The rate of population increased faster than is recorded in any other instance in history.

It is a relief to turn from the sickening tragedy of Armenia, where the Turks massacred helpless victims before friendly nations could bring them aid, to Arabia which took arms against its oppressor and won freedom by the help of other nations.

Syria, Palestine, Iraq and Arabia had always been the home of the Arabs, a gifted and passionate people. The Arab had always hated and despised the Turk. Even a desert Arab can quote poetry, and Turkish culture owed everything to Arab art, architecture and literature. Each tribe had a tradition of hatred of the Turk or of victory over him. Each one had stories and legends of how they had cut off patrols or pashas' heads. They had sometimes even defeated a Turkish army, but it was a very different matter to overthrow Turkish rule altogether. The Arabs were brave, but they were scattered and quarrelsome like the Highland clans. It was difficult to organise or unite them or keep them together for a common object. They had a national object—the resurrection of the Arab race, but they wanted a religious sanction and a leader. They found both in the person of an old man at Mecca.

The only office the Turks had allowed to become hereditary was that of Grand Sheriff or Governor of Mecca. This Holy City was the birthplace of the Prophet, and the Sheriff belonged to his tribe, and was thus of the purest and noblest Arab descent. Hussein, the Grand Sheriff in 1914, had a lineage much older than that of the Sultan. Arabs had often questioned the Sultan's right to be Caliph (or successor of the Prophet): was that title not due to Hussein? When the war opened the British began by repulsing the Turks from the Suez Canal and seizing Basra, the port of Sinbad the Sailor. The time seemed to have come. Hussein might dream a true Arab's dream of driving the Turks back into Anatolia and of sending Arab horsemen to water their steeds in the old Arab city of Damascus. Hussein was spurred on by his two sons, Abdulla, an administrator, and Feisal, a man with a great moral influence over the desert sheikhs. 'He won over and inflamed new tribes,' said Lawrence. At length Hussein took his courage in his hands and in July 1915 sent a secret letter to the British at Cairo. He offered to revolt and to free the whole Arab race from the Persian Gulf to Mosul, from the Red Sea to Beirut and Damascus. He asked England to aid him in this grandiose plan.

The British had long known the Arab hatred of the Turk, and even played with the idea of using the Grand Sheriff.[1] The correspondence with Hussein has never been published in full by the British Government. The British Government claim that they reserved by implication

---

[1] Public Record Office, F.O. 78/1514. From Sir H. L. Bulwer to Lord Russell. No. 847 of December 12, 1860. This shows that the project of using the Grand Sheriff to counteract French influence in Egypt was discussed and vetoed by Lord John Russell so far back as 1860.

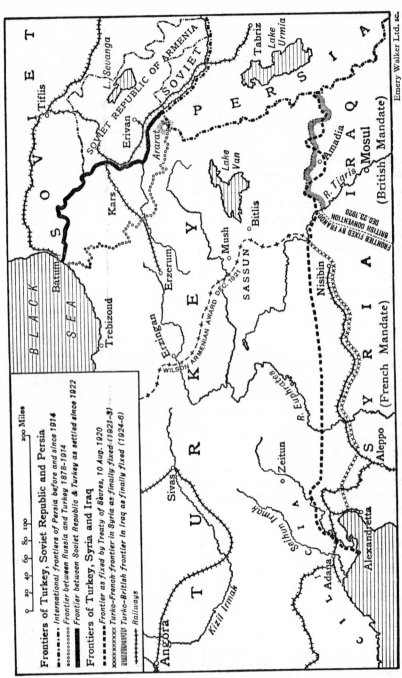

Frontiers of Turkey, Soviet Republic and Persia
‐·‐·‐·‐ *International frontiers of Persia before and since 1914*
ooooooooo *Frontier between Russia and Turkey 1878‐1914*
▄▄▄▄▄ *Frontier between Soviet Republic & Turkey as settled since 1922*

Frontiers of Turkey, Syria and Iraq
▪▪▪▪▪ *Frontier as fixed by Treaty of Sèvres, 10 Aug. 1920*
xxxxxxxx *Turko‐French frontier in Syria as finally fixed (1921‐3)*
ⅢⅢⅢⅢ *Turko‐British frontier in Iraq as finally fixed (1924‐6)*
+‐+‐+‐+ *Railways*

0 20 40 60 80 100   200 Miles

Frontiers in Asia Minor, Syria, Armenia, Iraq and Persia in 1926.

Emery Walker Ltd. sc.

the question of Arab independence in Syria and Palestine. Hussein claimed that they did not.[1] But they certainly encouraged him to revolt. They promised him money, arms, supplies, aeroplanes, instructors and, in extreme need, British troops. A small group of men studied the question and devised the plans: Hogarth an old scholar, Lawrence a young one, Storrs the Oriental Secretary of the British High Commissioner, and Admiral Wemyss. Lawrence, the youngest of them, carried out the design, became the friend of Feisal, the hero of the Arabs, and a prince of Mecca. Hussein was encouraged by British promises and soon proved that he was in earnest. He did not intend to risk anything and chose his own time to revolt. But the time that he chose was in itself a service to the British, and when he drew the sword he used it. In April 1916 the world was amazed to learn that three thousand British and six thousand Indian troops had surrendered to the Turks at Kut. But in June that event was eclipsed in importance for both Turks and Arabs by the astonishing news that Hussein had revolted in the Hedjaz, had announced himself as the true Caliph, and declared for the freedom of the whole Arab race. The effect in the Hedjaz, Akaba and the Median was immense. There, men saw the prospect of freedom for themselves and of vengeance on the Turk. In Iraq and Syria British gold and steel were the main influences.

In March 1917 the British avenged the defeat of Kut and entered Baghdad in triumph, and by the autumn of 1918 they had destroyed the last Turkish army and captured Mosul and all Iraq. They had not had much aid from Arab rebels; the Pan-Arab crusade had not disposed the local inhabitants to be friendly and to reveal the military secrets of the Turks. In the Palestine-Syrian area Arab resistance counted for a good deal. Arab spies were everywhere, Arab contingents, raised and drilled by the British, did good work against the Turks. Allenby learned their value when he captured Jerusalem in 1917. When he won his 'crowning mercy' at Megiddo in the autumn of 1918, he sent Lawrence and Feisal to act as a flying right wing east of Jordan. They won the race, and on October 1 the wild Arab horsemen galloped into Damascus a few hours ahead of the Australians. The first chief rode on a liver-coloured stallion, the finest Arab steed in the army. This knight of the desert had the privilege of entering first, because he had fought in over fifty battles against the Turks. That night Lawrence sat alone in the city and heard the muezzins call the faithful to prayer. 'One, with a ringing voice of special sweetness, cried into my window from a near mosque . . . ". . . God alone is great: there is no god—but God." . . . and softly added: "And He is very good to us this day, O people of Damascus." '[2]

[1] Hussein subsequently claimed that the British had promised the independence of the whole Arab race. In this case the evidence is obscure. v. Temperley: *History of the Peace Conference of Paris*, vol. VI. pp. 126–7, 131–2. Further information appeared, however, in G. Antonius: *The Arab Awakening* (1938), pp. 413–27.

[2] T. E. Lawrence: *Revolt in the Desert* (1927), pp. 434–5. He had added in the original, 'While my fancy, in the overwhelming pause, showed me my loneliness and lack of

It was six centuries since the Arabs of that city had enjoyed a "night of perfect freedom."

Some opportunists had proclaimed Feisal 'King of all the Arabs' before he arrived at Damascus. Waves of Pan-Arab nationalism swept rapidly over all parts of the Middle East. They conflicted soon enough with the ambitions of two great European Powers. With the independence of Arabia Proper no one wanted to interfere. But England had conquered Iraq and Mosul, Palestine and Syria. Since the days of Louis Quatorze France had coveted Damascus and Beirut and now received what England had conquered in Syria. Even Mustafa Kemal only slightly modified the Treaty of Sèvres in relation to French territory. By the Sèvres line (1920) the Franco-Turkish frontier ran from a point north-west of Alexandretta until it reached the British area of Mosul. By the Lausanne Treaty (1923) Mustafa Kemal pushed the French line a little further south. By 1920 France had expelled Feisal from Damascus since he had attempted to found an Arab kingdom there. Syria was finally constituted a French mandated area, including Damascus, Aleppo, Beirut. Further south England occupied Palestine, constituted as a mandated area, but with the special mission of making it the national home for the Zionist Jews, and reconciling the Arab inhabitants (who were in a great majority) to the process. Transjordania was organised as a state under British protection, with Abdulla, another son of King Hussein, as ruler. The settlement in none of these countries was satisfactory nor permanent. Disturbances followed in Damascus and the Lebanon; and in Palestine the reconciliation of Arabs and Jews proved well-nigh impossible.

In Iraq the situation was more satisfactory. When Feisal lost his Syrian kingdom the British obligingly found him another in Iraq. An Arab of Mecca was not entirely suited to Baghdad, but Iraq grew in power and in wealth under his rule and that of his successor King Ghazi. It ceased to be a mandated territory in October 1932.

The Arabs began by throwing off the yoke of the Turk, they ended by throwing off that of King Hussein. In 1915 the British Government, after making their compact with Hussein, found it convenient to make another with a second Arabian chief. His name was Ibn Saud and he ruled over the Wahhabis, an obscure inland tribe. No one thought that he would drive Hussein from Mecca in a decade. But his warriors were as devout, as fearless and as formidable as the Ironsides. In Ibn Saud they had found an Arabian Cromwell, and they now went forth to conquer. While Hussein fought the Turks with British aid, Ibn Saud fought the tribes of the interior with his own resources. In 1924 he had finished his task and decided to advance on Mecca, where King Hussein dwelt in fancied security. Since the abolition of the Sultanate he had

reason in their movement: since only for me, of all the hearers, was the event sorrowful and the phrase meaningless.' v. R. Graves: *Lawrence and the Arabs* (1927), p. 381. Yet nearly half the population of Syria is non-Arab and much non-Mussulman!

claimed the title of Caliph, and worn the black mantle of the office. It availed him little when Ibn Saud led his puritan warriors against the Holy City. Resistance was hopeless and Hussein fled in despair.[1] Ibn Saud entered Mecca, and for the first time for centuries brought Arabia beneath the sway of one man. The destiny of Ibn Saud was strange, but not so strange as that of Hussein. At the word of that old man of Mecca Arabia's horsemen set out on their thousand-mile ride to Damascus. One of his sons who rode with them gained a principality beyond Jordan, another son a kingdom by the Tigris. The father himself became a king in the Holy City which his ancestors had ruled for seven centuries. Then he became Caliph for six months, only to be driven from Mecca by a conquering puritan from the desert. The Holy City has already forgotten him, and Hussein, the last of the Caliphs, found a refuge and a grave in Jerusalem.

This brief survey will have made clear that the catchwords of self-determination and nationalism in their extreme form spread like fire in the East, and gave new ideals to old or dead nations. In each case there was an intense national pride and a desire to remove alien influences altogether. An evolution somewhat similar to the Turkish, though on a smaller scale, has been seen in Persia. The previous history of Persia is of some interest. For she had a reforming and constitutional movement in 1907, which promised well. It was checked partly by reactionary influences but largely by Russian interference from the north. Persia had been divided into British and Russian spheres of influence in 1907. Russia's interference ended with the war, but after it England made an effort to secure political control over Persia by the Anglo-Persian Agreement (9 August 1919). This arrangement was upset by the refusal of the revived Persian Parliament to accept it. The Russians then intervened and appeared to be threatening to conquer the country. But early in 1921 they not only withdrew their troops, but abandoned every attempt at influence in Persia altogether. They retired from all concessions, abandoned public works, harbours, railways and roads in which they had any interest or influence. The Persians were greatly encouraged by this attitude and proceeded in 1921 to remove all British supervisory influences. British advisers, civil and military, were promptly dismissed and every possible trace of foreign influence eradicated. The power behind this movement was again a successful soldier, Reza Khan. He ultimately deposed the feeble ruler and became himself Shah in 1925. Persia had long been a prey to feudal anarchy and brigandage in the provinces, which Reza Shah's military efficiency at length subdued. The modern enemy of the brigand and the rebel is the road and the aeroplane, and Reza Shah used both with effect. He ruthlessly executed or

[1] Ibn Saud entered Mecca in 1924, six months after Hussein had proclaimed himself sole Caliph. Hussein fled to Jerusalem, where he died in 1931.

imprisoned brigand and feudal chiefs. He made good roads and mod-
ernised the government, the army, the education and even the dress of
his subjects. He did much for Persia in the sixteen years of his rule.
Behind him as behind Mustafa Kemal was the idea of expelling the
foreigner and equipping his countrymen with weapons and improvements sufficient to resist the influences of the West.

The same influences and tendencies were to be seen, though working
more subtly, in the development of China and Japan between the wars.
Through the return of its students from abroad and the influences of
Western education, China became permeated with liberal and democratic ideas. These worked in the main as a disorganising force, dis-
solving the old fabric of empire and not substituting anything durable
in its place. Brigand-generals terrorised some areas till Chiang Kai-
shek and the Nanking government achieved relative stability. The
hatred of the foreigner became less conspicuous, and it was from their
own kinsmen rather than from Europeans that they had most to fear.
This was all the more disastrous because of the opportunity it gave to
Japan.

The problem cannot be said to have arisen from the war, but it was
immensely affected by it. During the seventies Japan accomplished the
work of six centuries in as many years. Great revolutions, abolishing
the old institutions of Japan, and throwing her open to Western progress, were carried out with amazing ease and almost without bloodshed.
In the nineties Japan was victorious over China, in the first decade of the
twentieth century over Russia. Her victories were won by a constitution and a class resembling the Prussian, with militarism, efficiency and
bureaucracy for their watchwords. The alliance with Great Britain,
however, tended for a time to assimilate Japanese diplomacy to European standards. During the war, however, Japan had no need to pay
attention to such influences; she extorted various concessions from
China, in particular the celebrated twenty-one demands of 1915. Then,
in 1919, some of these concessions were revoked, though she obtained
the province of Shantung on lease from China as a result of the German
Treaty. European and American diplomacy was again brought to bear,
and in 1922, as a result of pressure from the Washington Conference,
Japan signed a treaty with China providing for the Japanese evacuation
of Kiao-Chau and Shantung (4 February 1922). After that date, however, trouble in China increased and Japan sent into Manchuria and
even to Shanghai great military forces. The meaning of these movements is apparent. Japan had shaken off European tutelage. She
looked to the Asiatic mainland as a sphere of economic expansion.
Canada, the United States, and Australia ring round the Pacific. They
declared for white settlement only and protected their respective continents from Japanese immigrants. Japan had lost the restraining

influence of her alliance, which England herself terminated in 1921. There were no longer outside influences to temper her policy.

Although in the late nineteenth century Japan equipped herself with the machinery of constitutional government, it was a very superficial structure. The Constitution of 1889 established a legislature of two Houses and other trappings of constitutional government: but the Constitution, having been granted by the Emperor, could not be amended, since the Emperor remained infallible. There was in fact, no clear break with the past, and the government preserved its autocratic character behind a thin veil of liberal political institutions.

By the end of the 1914–18 War, Japan had acquired a veneer of Western civilisation, and was ready to shake off European tutelage and set herself up as the political and economic leader of Eastern Asia. It was this desire for hegemony that led Japan to attempt to subordinate China to the status of a vassal, first in the economic and later in the political sphere. Japan had developed enormously in the industrial field, and she was anxious that China should not rival her, but should provide a market for her goods. It was China's resistance to this absorption by Japan which provoked the Sino-Japanese War which broke out in 1937.

PART VI

THE GREAT POWERS OF EUROPE IN THE TWENTIETH CENTURY

CHAPTER XXXIII

MARXISM AND THE SOVIET UNION; ITALY AND GERMANY; BRITAIN AND FRANCE

I. Marxism, Origin and Evolution

The French Revolution did not end with the fall of Robespierre, nor with the crowning of Bonaparte. It started a continuing process which has not ceased even to-day. Any French historian will understand if you speak of 'la révolution' as a continuous phenomenon, unfolding or developing itself throughout the years. 1789, 1793, 1830, 1848, 1871: these are merely dates in a life history; but with the year 1917, the scene shifts from Paris to the old Russian capital of St. Petersburg. The Bolshevik revolution was the sequel to the Paris Commune of 1871, the Commune to the revolutions of 1848, 1848 a continuation of the expulsion of Charles X in 1830, 1830 was an aftermath of 1793. The movement changed its character as it developed, from Jacobinism to Utopian Socialism, to Marxism, and to Bolshevism, but it was an unbroken process.

The first indications of revolutionary Socialism may be found, perhaps, by nice investigators in Hébert's *Père Duchesne*, a very foul-mouthed extreme Jacobin organ of 1793. But its programme was only a vague but violent outpouring of hate by the poor against the rich. A more definite Socialist programme was put up by F. N. ('Gracchus') Babeuf at the very end of the revolution, in 1796. In that year, in consultation with a number of disappointed Jacobins, this young enthusiast organised a conspiracy which was broken by police spies just when it was about to break into insurrection. Its chiefs, including Babeuf, were guillotined; it is known in history as 'the Conspiracy for Equality.' Decrees which were prepared for issue in the event of success provided for the establishment of a voluntary National Community, in which private property should cease to exist, and all production and distribution should be run co-operatively. There was no suggestion of nationalisation, but all the power of the State was to be used to cajole, press and coax the citizens into the Community which would eventually extinguish private production quietly and peacefully.

This programme, which for its time was not unlike the programme applied to Russian agriculture under Lenin, remained as an inspiration to a number of secret societies which survived Napoleon and Waterloo. P. Buonarroti, one of the 'Equals,' published a history which was widely read, and which in a translation by Bronterre O'Brien exercised a powerful influence on the British Chartist movement. All the secret Republican and National societies, even including the Carbonari, were henceforward more or less infected with doctrines of social, as well as of political, equality. Their first opportunity to show their power came in 1830, when they had something at least to do with the chasing out of the last autocratic Bourbon, Charles X, from Paris and his replacement by the Orleanist Louis Philippe. But the latter monarch was strictly a nominee of the upper bourgeoisie, and after a short period of liberty the conspirators had to go underground again.

Underground, they had to discover for themselves why the 'bourgeois monarch,' with his green umbrella and frugal habits, was not enough. Their realisation of this was accompanied by a significant change in personnel, which de la Hodde, a police spy, dates from 1838: '. . . recruiting among the ill-conditioned members of the bourgeoisie was replaced entirely by recruiting from the scum of the popular class. . . . This is a noteworthy date, when the bourgeois element altogether abandoned illegal means.' These are the phrases a police agent used in his own record; translating them into normal English we see they mean that the middle class was slowly abandoning conspiracy, which was being adopted by members of the working class. Armand Barbès (1809–1870), a sentimental republican of the old type, and Auguste Blanqui (1805–1881), a far more important revolutionary and the first formulator of the theory of the dictatorship of the proletariate, were the chief leaders. They spent much of their lives in prisons, undeterredly organising secret societies in between, of which the most notable is one which is remembered because of its name—the Society of Seasons, in which each member was a 'Day,' each section of seven Days a 'Week,' led by a 'Sunday,' every four Weeks, a 'Month,' led by a 'July,' every three Months a 'Season,' led by a 'Spring,' every four Seasons a 'Year,' of which there were three. This society was broken up by a vain insurrection in 1839.

Outside France, there were other less important societies, in Belgium, Germany and Italy, holding more or less utopian and eccentric views. The German idealist Wilhelm Weitling, a tailor, deserves mention, because he slightly influenced two men destined to be of greater importance than any so far mentioned, Karl Marx (1818–1883) and Friedrich Engels (1820–1895). Marx was the son of a lawyer in Trier, a converted Jew, and had been educated at Berlin University, where he devoted himself to studying Hegel's philosophy instead of law. He barred the way to his own academic advancement by his liberal opinions. In 1842 he was appointed editor of the *Rheinische Zeitung*, and came into such conflict with the censor that he had to leave Germany and go to Paris the next year. There he met Engels, and their lifelong collaboration began. Engels was a Prussian, son of a manufacturer of the firm of Ermen and Engels, which employed him in Manchester.

The two young men endeavoured to reconcile the Socialist theories of Weitling and Babeuf, with which they were emotionally in sympathy, with the Hegelian philosophy which they intellectually supported. In so doing, in three years which they spent together in Brussels (1845–1848) they constructed a philosophy of 'scientific Socialism' which was in due course nearly to extinguish all others. This they did by inverting Hegel's dialectic and applying it to economic and political history, renaming it Dialectical Materialism.

The Hegelian dialectic represented in its day a considerable advance in the knowledge of the human mind, and through it of the external world. As Hegel was an idealist philosopher (holding that *ideas* were real) these two amounted to much the same thing. We may explain the only part of his philosophy which interests us here in the following way. Perhaps the longest step made by a savage mind towards civilisation is when it fixes for itself categories. Distinction is the beginning of knowledge: when the savage begins to use and recognise the idea of the earth, say, or of justice, he is becoming a reasoning being. But these fixed ideas are of necessity exclusive. The earth is the earth; it is not the moon, it is not the forest, it is not that mountain. Justice is not injustice. As philosophy becomes more complicated it entangles itself by trying to define these. What is justice? What is truth? Before the ancient world broke up these questions became interminable and the practical man, like Pilate, stayed not for an answer. Hegel solved the problem by making a further step. Ideas were not rigid; they were flexible and changing, each containing within itself its opposite and implying it. Life implies death, justice injustice. One idea gives birth to another, which arises out of it though it is its opposite; from their conflict arises an amalgamation of the two, a synthesis of both into a new idea, containing elements of both though it itself is new. The first is called the Positive, the second the Negation, the last step the Negation of the Negation. Alternatively the process is described as Thesis—Antithesis—Synthesis.

Marx and Engels declined to agree that ideas were real; their minds were strongly materialist, and rejected this as mystical nonsense. But they found (or considered they found) that the dialectic they had painfully acquired would still work, shifted to a material plane. In particular, they perceived a great dialectical process going on before them. The Capitalist system (Thesis) was producing its opposite, proletarian Socialism (Antithesis), and from their conflict would result a Communist society (Synthesis). The victory of the Socialists was thus part of an inevitable process, now for the first time philosophically explained.

More concrete arguments reinforced their case. The Marxist Theory of Value, first expounded at length in *Das Kapital* (Vol. I, 1867; other volumes posthumous), taught that by the necessary retention of surplus value in the production of commodities, capitalism produced recurrent overproduction crises of increasing violence in which it would eventually be overwhelmed. The course of Victorian industry made this view plausible enough, and armed with these philosophical and economic beliefs the two men promulgated a theory of history, the materialist conception of history, which unlike the other portions of their philosophy obtained some support from scholars outside the Socialist Movement.

This important theory, with all its consequences, was first expounded in November 1847 by Marx and Engels to the convention of the League of the Just, a predominantly German secret society, which adopted it by acclamation. It was embodied in the *Communist Manifesto*, a document which has been perhaps more influential than any other in modern history except the French *Declaration of the Rights of Man* and the American *Declaration of Independence*. It opened by declaring 'The history of all hitherto existing society is the history of class struggles,' and proceeded to describe in some detail, and almost with admiration, the exploits of the bourgeoisie, successors to the serfs, in subjecting the whole world to the rule of civilisation, breaking up the tyrannies of feudalism, inventing machinery and a system of manufacture and rescuing 'a considerable part of the population from the idiocy of rural life.' But with this magnificent development it had also unwittingly produced its own destroyer. It had thrown together in great factories vast masses of 'proletarians,' a wholly new class of human beings, deprived of all wealth, of distinctions of rank or craft, mere 'hands' though not slaves. Continually deprived, by recurrent crises and the fight for cheaper production, of what little resources they had, they were forced into ceaseless struggle against their oppressors, and as factories grew larger and the numbers of their masters decreased, organisation became easier. The conflict was bound to go on, and the workers were bound to win. The last words of the *Manifesto* became world famous: 'The workers have nothing to lose but their chains. They have a world to win. Workers of all lands, unite!'

The *Manifesto* appeared too short a time before the revolutions of 1848 for it to affect their course. When that storm was over, Marx and Engels had fled to England (the former in great poverty) and nearly all the hopeful secret societies had been swept out of existence. Blanqui almost alone persisted in the old method of organisation, making his new societies strictly disciplined, armed, and dependent upon himself as general. The complete collapse of '48 had broken the hearts of the innocent revolutionaries of Weitling's type. The League of the Just, Marx's own organisation, collapsed amid bitter internal quarrels. Only where nationalist sentiment reinforced revolutionary feeling, among Poles, Italians, and Irish, did secret organisations survive. The sole item on the credit side was a clarification in the minds of the revolutionaries. The sharp division, which had appeared in the moment of success between bourgeois and proletarian, seemed to underline the truth of the Marxist analysis. In Britain, where the government was firmly based upon the middle class, the attacks of both the proletarian Chartists and of the nationalist Irish failed to shake the stability of the State. Elsewhere, governments, which lacked the support of the middle class, and depended upon aristocracy or royalty, collapsed as speedily as one would expect governments dependent on a class surviving from a previous age to do. From the Pyrenees eastward to the Vistula every government was overthrown or forced to change itself into an apparent democracy. And after a month or less of rejoicing the middle class found itself embarrassed by fresh and menacing, if vague, demands for social equality from the working class whose support it had so lightly used to expel or to tame King, Pope, or Emperor. Rarely did it care to press home its new victory: it was content and even relieved to see old names in charge of army and police. It turned against its recent allies in Paris in a three-day fight, and elsewhere less dramatically, and as a result of the ensuing division the old authorities or similar ones came back to power. The Marxist analysis of class divisions seemed to have been exemplified in the neatest possible manner.

An important effect of the '48 was a further change in the personnel of the international revolutionary movement, which was eventually to play into the hands of Marx and Engels. The traditional Jacobin elements, whose objects were national freedom from foreign control (as in Poland, Italy or Ireland), national unity (as in Germany and Italy) and the political Rights of Man (as everywhere except in England, Scotland and Wales), found their demands more or less imperfectly granted in the next quarter of a century. Italy and Germany became united and independent. Everywhere constitutions were granted, except in the outlying corners of Europe—Spain, Ireland, Russia and the Balkans, and there the growth and policies of the Labour movements were profoundly altered by this fact. A tacit, wholly unspoken concordat had achieved this. The restored monarchies or oligarchies had abandoned great portions of their power to the middle class and had in any case undertaken the duty of fostering and protecting capitalist industry and trade, and removing the antiquated laws or customs which hampered development. Italian, Hungarian, German and other nationalist movements had accepted this compromise and Mazzini, Kossuth and others, who would not see the need for it, found themselves laid aside by their own followers.

The troops that still rallied to the call of international revolution— diminished in numbers—more and more came to call themselves Socialist, though the name was far from widespread before the eighties. The influence of Marx and Engels was least in the country where they lived—Britain—where the new trade unionism of the 'Amalgamated unions' was based deliberately on co-operation with the employers and on acceptance of the capitalist system. It was greatest in their country of origin, Germany, and had most serious rivals in the premier revolutionary country, France. Here Blanqui patiently organised his own private army, but the less desperate revolutionaries and working men listened to P. J. Proudhon (1809–1865), a philosophical anarchist, author of the famous book *What is property?* ('Property is robbery'),[1] who advocated a system of peasant proprietorship, credit banking, and federal anarchism.

After sixteen years of depression the revolution seemed to recover strength and the First International (the 'I.W.M.A.'—International Working Men's Association) was founded in 1864 as a result of a meeting in St. Martin's Hall, Long Acre, London, called to protest against the atrocities committed during the repression of the Polish revolt, and attended by working men of various nationalities. On the committee elected there to organise an international union of workers sat Mazzini's secretary, Marx and several British trade unionists. Marx produced an *Address and Rules* which would logically make the society into a class-conscious international alliance of workers: the Italian, on its being adopted, withdrew, realising its import; the Englishmen, not realising it, stayed.

For two years the International remained little but an idea. Marx was too ill to influence it continuously, and when its first conference met in Geneva in 1866 the delegates, few as they were, produced a discouraging cacophony of irreconcilable programmes. The French delegates put forward Proudhon's philosophy. The British advocated the universal adoption of respectable and cautious craft trade unions on the 'amalgamated' model. The Swiss delegates offered a fine confusion of small holdings, simplified spelling, and federalism. There were hardly any other nations represented. But the mere fact of an international meeting of working-class delegates, for the purpose of agreeing on a political programme, created unexpected excitement. It was a wholly new thing in history, and right-wing, as well as left-wing, papers regarded it as a portent. From that meeting the International began to spread with astonishing rapidity. Where Socialist or trade union movements existed, as in Germany, it took them up into its ranks; where they did not, it founded them, as in Denmark. In the year 1867 it extended itself to Belgium and to Austria; in 1868 a large part of the German organised workers—said to be 110,000—became members, and organisation was begun in Holland, Spain and Italy. Next year Denmark was brought in, and a beginning made in Portugal; the National Labour Union of America also joined, returning its membership as 800,000 (probably falsely).

Marx was by now the dominating figure on the General Council

---

[1] P. J. Proudhon: *Qu'est-ce que la Propriété ?, ou recherches sur le principe du droit et du gouvernement* (Paris, 1840).

in London, and both in the discussions there and in the large correspondence, official and unofficial, which he carried on with representatives of movements in other countries, he spread his ideas industriously
and successfully. Each Congress showed a further victory for him and
an elimination of reactionary or of merely freakish proposals. His most
notable victory was in 1869, when the Proudhonist programme was
voted down in favour of a Socialist one by 54 to 4. By 1870 he could see
large and powerful working-class movements, deeply influenced by his
own ideas, in every European country, and imagined the world revolution very near. 'Things are moving,' he wrote to Engels, in September
1867. 'And in the next revolution, which is perhaps nearer than it
appears, we (*i.e.* you and I) will have this powerful engine *in our hands.*'

Both Marx and Engels were throughout their lives rashly optimistic
about the date of the revolution. They seemed to think that once they
had discovered and explained the process which would lead to a victorious proletarian revolution, that process would forthwith begin.
Each decade they expected victory, and were repeatedly disappointed.
Two factors for which they had not allowed destroyed their immediate
hopes, and behind these was the more important fact that capitalism
was not yet, in Marxist language, 'a fetter upon production' but was showing itself capable of surprising expansion. The two immediate factors
were the outbreak of the Franco-Prussian war, which set the French and
German workers, the two chief hopes of the International, to shooting
each other down, and the appearance of an organised opposition to
Marx's direction within the International itself.

Among the recruits who joined in 1869 was a Russian refugee living
in Switzerland, Michael Bakunin, who brought with him a group of personal adherents, with whom he constituted a branch in Geneva. He
derived his principles from Proudhon, so far as he had constructive
proposals, adding to them only atheism. But in his methods Bakunin
was far different from his mentor. His political ideas were always vague
and veered rapidly, but his instructions on organisation were precise
and unchanging. Political action was forbidden; the State was an evil
thing and must be destroyed. The oppressors and their agents were to
be removed; half converts were to be tied firmly to the chariot of the
revolutionaries by every means available. Stolen letters, blackmail,
threats, secret organisations within open organisations—all these were
justifiable means, and the last indeed was his favourite method. 'Have
you never thought,' he wrote to his chief French lieutenant, 'what is
the principal cause of the power and vitality of the Jesuit order? Do
you wish me to name it? Well, it is the complete effacement of private
wills in collective organisation and action. . . . I shall die and the
worms will eat me, but I want our idea to triumph. I want not the more
or less dramatic growth of my person, not of *a* power, but of *our* power,
the power of our collectivity, in whose favour I am ready to abdicate
my name and personality.' With a group of disciplined followers, who

were on principle unscrupulous, Bakunin was soon able to set the International in an uproar. The Swiss federation was torn in half, the newly-founded Spanish and Italian movements came more under his influence than Marx's; and even the Belgian and North American sections began to lean towards Anarchism. Nor were the effects, except in Belgium, ephemeral. Italian anarchism remained very strong until Mussolini stamped out all working-class movements. In Spain anarchism was a great power even in the early twentieth century. In New York anarchism entangled itself with free love, feminism, and the desire of Mrs. Victoria Woodhull to run for the presidency of the United States, but in Chicago the movement grew to great influence, rising to a peak at the time of the famous Haymarket bomb.

Marx was as revolutionary in spirit as Bakunin, but his idea of the revolution was a mass movement of organised workers conscious of their purpose and not led like sheep. Armed raids by drilled conspirators, for whom the average worker was mere conspiracy-fodder, were in his view dangerous follies. The conflict between the two men became one of savage personal bitterness, and things were obviously moving to a climax when the Franco-Prussian war broke out and the controversy was forcibly silenced.

The war was followed by the Paris Commune, whose history will be found elsewhere.[1] The Commune, until the outbreak of the Russian revolution in 1917, was the most venerated episode in Socialist history. Every March every Socialist journal brought out special numbers to commemorate it, poets wrote their best (or at least their most well-meant) verses to celebrate it, annual delegations visited the famous Wall of Père Lachaise cemetery to lay red wreaths on the spot where the most famous massacre of its defenders took place. All this not because it was a successful political experiment (it was not) but because it was the first working-class Government and so considered to be precursor of the revolution. Its members consisted of three groups—the largest was made up of Blanquists, who were leaderless because their chief was a prisoner in the enemy's hands, the second largest was composed of members of the International, and the third included a 'mixed bag' of revolutionaries of various tendencies. All went down to a common ruin in the slaughter which followed the victory of the Versailles troops.

The International assembled in Conference the next year (1872) at the Hague. Bakunin did not attend, his spokesman being a Swiss delegate named Guillaume. Marx and Engels did. The proceedings were wholly occupied by the general quarrel between Socialists and Anarchists, and at the end the latter were expelled and the International split into two. Marx and Engels rejoiced too soon: the bloodletting of the Commune and the violence of the dissensions had in fact killed the International and their victory was empty. The Marxist sec-

[1] *v. supra*, pp. 281–4.

tion nominally existed until it was wound up in Philadelphia in 1876. The anarchist section claimed a little longer life, though its effective power was broken in the unsuccessful Spanish revolution of 1873. Separate sections survived. The Italian organisation remained strong; so too did the Russian. In France in 1890 and 1891 a series of systematic propagandas-by-deed (assassination of individual reactionaries) culminated in the murder of President Carnot. But this was the last effort of the anarchists: the world had almost forgotten their existence until the Spanish Civil War brought the Spanish anarchists back into importance.

Marxism had more vitality. The Parties which had been founded, or adopted, by the International did not vanish when it disappeared. Nearly all of them survived, weak at first but steadily growing in importance. Until their death, Marx and Engels continually corresponded with them and encouraged them with advice, support and, on occasion, acid criticism. In nearly all European countries, except Turkey, a powerful Marxist Social Democratic Party appeared, securing if not the whole allegiance of the politically-interested working class, at least the support of a formidable minority. Only in Britain was this not true; the Social Democratic Federation (afterwards the British Socialist Party), despite the support of men such as William Morris, Tom Mann and H. M. Hyndman, remained to the end of its days (in 1919) a small sect. This was partly due to personal quarrels (Marx and Engels disliked Hyndman and refused to help him) but more because the Marxists declared the existing trade unions to be hopelessly non-revolutionary and set themselves in opposition to the most cherished institutions of the workers to whom they wished to appeal. Further, they were so rigid in their interpretation of their master's doctrine that they seemed to declare that revolution would come independently of human will; they thus left their followers with no duties but to announce this fact and denounce all who disagreed. Workers preferred the Independent Labour Party (I.L.P.) and Labour Party, which, if doctrinally incorrect, at least offered some useful work to do. Social Democrats abroad combined orthodoxy with a more practical attitude. Their parties increased, and from 1889 onwards regular international conferences were held. To these conferences was given the name of the Second International, but so weak was the connecting link that only at the beginning of the century was a central Bureau formed, and even then, unlike the old General Council, it had no coercive or executive powers.

The parties of this period were of varying importance, some of very great weight indeed. Any observer who tabulated the results of the elections in European countries could not fail to notice one unvarying feature—the steady, if slow, growth of the Socialist vote. In town after town their numbers increased, and while other parties had fluctuations they alone (unless legal violence was used to suppress them) each time recorded a larger number of successes. One essential difference indeed passed almost unnoticed: the First International had been essentially international and revolutionary, in the Second International the parties, despite their assiduous repetition of Marx's phrases, were essentially national, and, as their experience of social reform and municipal administration increased, they became less and less revolutionary.

Their numbers and power were, however, impressive. In Germany Marx's ideas were supreme, and the German Social Democratic Party, led by pupils of Marx, such as August Bebel, Wilhelm Liebknecht and Karl Kautsky, was the richest, most powerful and successful Socialist Party in the world. Eduard Bernstein challenged the accuracy of Marx on a question of economic fact—the concentration of capital—and his heresy was named Revisionism, but it was triumphantly rejected by the Party. The Danish Social Democrat Party led by Thorvald Stauning, the Swedish Social Democratic Party led by Hjalmar Branting, the Dutch Social Democrats led by P. J. Troelstra, the Austrian Social Democratic Party led by F. Adler, the Belgian Labour Party and the Norwegian Party were similarly without serious rivals, and the leaders were in every case men whom it was impossible not to recognise as politicians of high importance. In France an older revolutionary tradition raised obstacles to the dominance of the pure Marxists led by Jules Guesde. There were Blanquists and Reformists as well as Syndicalists. But when all the political groups were united by the tact and under the leadership of Jean Jaurès it was clear that Marxism was the predominant philosophy. In Italy Turati and Modigliani and in Spain Pablo Iglesias had to admit rivalry from the Syndicalists, revolutionary trade unionists who had refreshed Bakunin's practice with a dose of industrial unionism ultimately derived from Proudhon. They declared not only that the Marxist parties had ceased to be genuinely revolutionary, but that the nature of political campaigning made it sure that every Parliamentary party would go the same way. Nevertheless, the Socialist parties of Italy and Spain were indisputably the most important working-class organisations of their countries; the former had in 1914 a rich and splendidly organised co-operative organisation behind it, and the latter was the only Spanish party which was an organised party in the modern sense. In the Balkans turbulent political conditions prevented much constitutional success, but every country except Albania and Turkey had its Social Democratic Party, and among outstanding leaders were Christian Rakovsky the Rumanian, and Plato Drakoules the Greek, whose paper *Ho Rhizospastes* (*The Tearer-up-by-the-Roots*, less sensationally translated *The Radical*) was the most influential Labour newspaper published south of the Danube. In Russia the Social Democrats (S.D.s) had to meet serious rivalry from the Social Revolutionaries (S.R.s), successors to the Nihilists, who approved of individual terrorism as a reply to Tsarist methods. The Social Democrats were themselves divided into Mensheviks (minority) headed by Martov and Bolsheviks (majority) headed by Lenin. But this division was regarded as of less importance

than that between S.R. and S.D. The personality of the unquestioned
leader G. V. Plekhanov dominated both groups, and the busiest
conciliator of all was a young Jew using the name of Léon Trotsky.

The outbreak of the war of 1914 shattered the Second International.
The Socialist parties in all the belligerent countries, except Russia,
called upon their supporters to rally to their national governments: the
Second International might not have existed. A small neutral group,
the 'Dutch-Scandinavian Committee' with Camille Huysmans, the
Belgian Secretary of the International Bureau, made repeated but useless efforts to bring the parties together. In 1915 at Zimmerwald, in
1916 at Kienthal, and in 1917 at Stockholm steadily increasing minorities who were discontented at this failure met together to consider
action to stop the war and start a Socialist revolution. Soon after the
Armistice, at a meeting in Moscow in March 1919, they decided that
the Second International was worthless, and started a Third International, the 'Comintern,' to replace it.

In its early years, working under the eye of Lenin, the Communist
International secured the allegiance of every social revolutionary,
syndicalist and Blanquist as well as Marxist. It reverted, however, to
the organisation of the First International, with a 'presidium' to take
the place of the General Council, and equally strict discipline for every
member and party. Each party had to re-name itself 'The Communist
Party of . . .'; some parties, with many years' honoured history behind
them, much resented this, and even more doubted whether a band of
Russian enthusiasts in Moscow possessed sufficient knowledge to direct
them competently on the road to world revolution. The 'Twenty One
Points' which were drafted, partly by G. Zinoviev, who was president
of the Third International from 1919 to 1926, included an insistence
upon 'illegal work' which in itself outlawed (if need be) the parties
which accepted it. Nevertheless the majority of the French Socialist
Party, nearly the whole of the Italian Socialist Party, and powerful
groups in the newly liberated Eastern European states joined the
new organisation. In Scandinavia, Spain, the Netherlands and Britain
the response was small, although for a while Labour supporters who declined to join it nevertheless maintained a benevolent attitude towards
its propaganda.

The surviving portions of the Second International, the parties in
each country which had supported the war, re-formed themselves into a
body which called itself the Labour and Socialist International. It had
behind it, as before the war, the International Federation of Trades
Unions, which secured far greater support than the Third International's
'Red International of Labour Unions' which outside Russia secured
only the backing of small sectarian groups. The working class of every
European country where the Third International was strong was torn

by the dissensions between the two bodies. Opportunities which were never to recur were lost in the conflict, and to the exhaustion and unappeasable bitterness of the two parties is directly traceable the annihilation of both at a later date by Fascism in Italy, and by Nazism in Germany.

The Communist International up to the time of the Franco-Russian alliance in 1935 maintained an intransigeant and revolutionary position. This it claimed to be the true Marxism: its leaders Lenin and Trotsky were continually referring to Marx's writings as an almost sacred guide. The ephemeral 'Two-and-a-half' International, which existed for a few years in the 1920's in a vain effort to unite all working-class political organisations, used the same language and appealed to the same authorities. The Socialist International had the more difficult task of producing a theory of non-revolutionary Marxism, and in this their chief standby was the veteran Karl Kautsky. His theory was most effective in a double counter-attack, claiming that the 'dictatorship of the proletariate' installed by Lenin was not in fact contemplated by Marx at all and was a contradiction in terms, and that Marx's economic theory postulated that any Socialist revolution could only occur in a highly advanced industrial country—in other words, that despite appearances it had not occurred and could not occur in Russia.

This dissension dominated and marred Labour development until after the Nazi victory, when its sinister effects were clear to the most embittered propagandist. The sharp change which followed in Communist International policy was announced in a joint statement signed by Stalin and Laval (then French Premier) in Russia, which declared the former's approval of the French rearmament and so automatically extinguished the French Communists' anti-militarist and anti-imperialist campaign. Before long the various Communist Parties were outdoing each other in efforts to conciliate the 'reformist parties' they had previously denounced as 'Social Fascists.' In France their new mansuetude was largely responsible for the victory of the Popular Front (Radical-Socialist-Communist) led by Léon Blum. But this remarkable move to the right was not made without discomfort to their own followers. For the first time a serious revolutionary opposition to the Communists appeared in Europe, fostered by resentment at their 'compromising' policy. The increasing number of executions as a result of the 'Trotskyite trials' in Russia shocked Labour opinion, and the attempts to diminish the power of the Anarcho-Syndicalists in the Spanish Government aroused a great resentment. By 1937 there was in existence even a 'Fourth International' owing its inspiration to the exiled Trotsky in Mexico, who claimed to be once again the only true exponent of orthodox Marxism.

It is thus clear that Bolshevism established itself in Russia as a professed doctrine, emanating from Marx, with Lenin and Trotsky as his avowed disciples and exponents. But it would be an error to suppose that this spark, arising from the French Revolution, nursed by Blanqui, and tended by Marx, was finally blown into flame in the Soviet Union. That would imply that Russia owed everything to the West. Borrowings from Western thought and use of Western instruments and ideas were no novelty in Russian history. Peter the Great, Catherine and Alexander I each attempted a cosmopolitan reconstruction of Russian society, and each of them relied largely on foreigners to introduce new ideas into their Empire. But, despite their efforts, they did not succeed in changing the fundamentals of Russian character. They sharpened the intelligence, they developed the middle-class, they supplied ideas in education, in service, in efficiency, ideas unfamiliar alike to moujik and to noble in the past. But they did not check the inevitable drift towards revolution, they did not change the noble nor transform the peasant. The latter, by his land-hunger and by his behaviour in the army, ultimately decided the downfall of Czardom. He permitted Lenin and Trotsky to seize upon power and to exploit the situation. But even Lenin proved only a partially successful innovator. He had to conform to the permanent and indestructible forces in Russia. He illustrated the maxim that it is the differences and not the resemblances between Russia and the West, which are really important in Russian history.

II. The Soviet Union from the Revolution to 1939

It is tempting to compare the Russian Revolution of 1917 with that of France in 1789. Both countries were ripe for revolution. The outbreak of war in both cases only added to the social abuses, the internal chaos whose origins lay deep in the past. In Russia a weak and corrupt monarchy fell under the stress of war, and was succeeded by a weak liberal coalition, representing parties as diverse as the humanitarian conservatives and the peasant labour party. Kerensky, the leader of the peasant labour party, was also a member of the Petrograd Soviet, an elected council of soldiers and workers, chosen to represent their comrades. From the beginning, the decrees of the Provisional Government were to be submitted for approval to the Soviet before promulgation. Eventually, the Petrograd or Central Soviet became the more powerful body, being supported by the Soviets which had been formed in almost every town, every important factory and every regimental unit throughout the country. The organisation of the Soviet was in fact the only efficient one among the inert and tangled mass of competing factions and interests. In October 1917 the Provisional Government was dissolved and Lenin, who had returned secretly from exile in February 1917, became head of the new Government of the Soviets.

The strength of the new Government was tried from the very beginning: the situation to be dealt with was nothing short of chaos. One of the Government's first acts was to conclude, in March 1918, the humiliating and unpopular Treaty of Brest-Litovsk with Germany.

Had the treaty not been invalidated by the victory of the Western Allies, Russia would have lost all her Western provinces including the Ukraine. During the years 1919 and 1920, there was, moreover, armed opposition from Czarist supporters. White Russians, under able commanders such as Denikin, Kolchak, Wrangel and Yudenić assailed the new republic from all sides. They received advisers, tanks, aeroplanes and munitions from the Western Allies. Simultaneously, the latter cut off 'Red Russia' by blockade from war and civilian supplies, even from medical supplies. Nevertheless, the White Russians were conclusively beaten and forced to retire from the soil of triumphant Red Russia. Contrary to all expectations, the Revolutionaries proved able 'to live of themselves,' and to construct a self-sufficient State. To the outside world, it seemed impossible that a country torn by civil war, famine and terrorism should survive: all was confusion and misery. Yet, even whilst all this was going on, some sort of economic policy was improvised. Almost immediately after the Revolution of October 1917, all industries were nationalised according to the Socialist principle. When, three years later, at the end of the civil war, the country was still in a state of chaos and famine, private enterprise on a small scale was re-introduced. This was known as Lenin's 'New Economic Policy,' and was continued until 1928, when the first of the Five-Year Plans of production and distribution was introduced.

Whilst this immense effort of economic reconstruction was going forward, the constitutional structure of the Soviet State was gradually being evolved. The political theory of the Bolsheviks had stopped short at revolution: neither Marx nor Lenin appears to have considered the political structure of the State which would follow a successful revolution. The Soviet State is thus the product of events. It was based fundamentally on the soviets elected by the factory and village. A recent writer describes the system thus: 'From different parts of the country the local soviets sent delegates to attend the Soviet Congress that met from time to time in the capital. At these meetings of revolutionary leaders and workpeople the Commissars (or Ministers) were elected and immediate policies agreed upon. Russia was to be henceforth a Soviet State. In the ensuing struggle with counter-revolutionaries the soviets could not exercise the democratic control over the Government that seemed at first to be their function and the Communist leaders in Moscow became more and more authoritarian. Nevertheless, the soviets remained ostensibly the machinery of government and this machinery was gradually developed and improved.'[1]

This system was finally embodied in a written Constitution which was adopted in 1936,[2] and which defined the U.S.S.R. as a federal state

---

[1] K. Gibberd: *Soviet Russia* (revised ed., Royal Institute of International Affairs, 1946), p. 44.

[2] The text of the Constitution is printed in S. and B. Webb: *Soviet Communism* (3rd ed., 1944), pp. 410 ff.

formed on the basis of the voluntary union of the eleven Soviet Socialist Republics, equal in rights. It was also defined as a 'socialist state of workers and peasants,' and it is significant that the first section of the Constitution is devoted entirely to the economic organisation of the State. Introducing the Constitution in November 1936, Stalin declared that the Soviet Union had attained Socialism, 'the lowest form of Communism.' In the new Constitution all the fundamental principles of democracy appear, and Stalin therefore claimed that the 'Soviet democracy' was the 'sole true democracy' in the world. There is in fact no strict separation of powers into legislative, executive and judicial departments, and the Constitution was not accompanied by any essential change in the executive government. So far, the Constitution has been modified only in one respect: in February 1944 it was decreed that each of the constituent republics of the Union might have the right to separate Commissariats for Defence and Foreign Affairs.

The building up of the Soviet State was not, however, accomplished without opposition or violence from within. Already by 1920 there was a serious divergence of opinion between the extreme revolutionaries, such as Trotsky, who still believed that a Socialist State could never be built in Russia until revolution had converted the whole world, and the more moderate members of the Communist Party, such as Stalin, who proposed to concentrate first on national revival. For some years the struggle went on within the Communist Party, culminating in 1927 with the expulsion of Trotsky from the Party and his exile from the U.S.S.R. in February 1929. Trotsky, however, refused to accept defeat and gathered round him all the malcontents in an attempt to overthrow Stalin's régime. The Trotskyite threats of disorder were considered to constitute a serious menace to the economic recovery of the country, and ruthless measures were taken to exterminate all opposition. The exile of Trotsky was followed by a series of purges in which all those suspected of Trotskyite leanings were discreetly disposed of, many without the doubtful benefits of a public trial. In August 1936 Zinoviev and Kamenev, who had formed with Stalin the 'triumvirate' which had governed Russia immediately after Lenin's death in 1924, were tried, condemned and executed, on charges of having organised terrorist groups for the assassination of Stalin, Voroshilov and other outstanding opponents of Trotsky. The 'heresy-hunt' continued, and early the following year a great purge of the Red Army was carried out. In June 1937, Marshal Tukhachevsky and seven other generals were tried in secret, sentenced to death and shot, whilst thousands of Red Army officers were removed. The trials were hailed by enemies of Bolshevism as an indication of the breakdown of the Soviet system and as proof of the weakness of the Soviet Army. Others, however, considered that the purpose of these purges was to suppress a certain reorientation of Soviet foreign policy, allegedly supported by these generals and former leaders. It was an orientation towards Germany and away from France, and it is perhaps significant that a similar purge of German officers suspected of favouring co-operation with the U.S.S.R. took place early in 1938. One important result of the trials was to make the French military authorities very reluctant to embark on talks for the closer co-operation of the French and Soviet armies, and, notwithstanding the efforts made by Soviet military chiefs, the General Staff talks did not take place.

The strength of the Soviet Union was at this time arousing a good deal of controversy outside Russia, for there appears to have been little reliable information from which an independent and objective judgment could be formed. It was almost impossible to tell whether the existing régime was so unpopular that resort had to be made to extreme and terroristic methods during a time of peace, or whether the rulers had so lost balance as to strike wildly at any semblance of opposition. It is clear that very drastic measures were certainly taken against those who, in other countries, might have been accepted as honest critics of the régime. On the other hand, many of those removed were without doubt actively working to secure the overthrow, by violent means, of Stalin's Government, and would have constituted those who were later known as 'quislings' or 'fifth columnists.' As it was, when war finally came to Russia, she was able to present a united front, securely organised industrially and politically, and able to depend absolutely on the strength and integrity of the Red Army. When the Germans invaded Russia in 1941, there was only one example throughout the Soviet Union of 'Fifth Column' activities on any considerable scale; and this was to be found in the Republic of the Volga.

Perhaps the key to the internal discipline of the Soviet Union is to be found in the Communist Party of Russia. The Communist Party is, in fact, 'the power behind the machine.' Although it is the only legal political party in Russia, membership of the Communist Party is very much restricted, and it has been estimated that in 1939 there were only $2\frac{1}{2}$ million members of the party out of a total population of $170\frac{1}{2}$ million. 'Admission to Party membership,' we are told by the authors of *Soviet Communism*, 'is, and always has been, conferred as a privilege, to which no one has any prescriptive right, and in conformity with definite rules, to which no exception is allowed. Applicants for admission must, of course, profess whole-hearted acceptance of the communist creed, as laid down by Marx and as interpreted by Lenin and Stalin. They must manifest this adhesion in their lives by being habitually politically "active" in their respective spheres; not only by displaying zeal in their daily work of production or service, but also by spontaneously undertaking extra duties of social influence.'[1] Thus, membership of the Communist Party carries with it great obligations, and those found wanting in the performance of their obligations lose their membership. The importance of the party in Soviet Russia may perhaps best be gauged by the fact that when Stalin drew up the Con-

[1] S. and B. Webb: *Soviet Communism*, p. 266.

stitution of 1936, he held no high official position in the state apart from being an elected member of the Congress of Soviets. He was, however, General Secretary of the Communist Party of the Soviet Union, and Party Leader, and was therefore responsible for the general well-being and success of the Soviet State.

The achievements of the U.S.S.R. in twenty years were considerable, particularly in the economic sphere, for politically there has been little change in Soviet Russia. These achievements were not attained without great hardships on the part of the people of Russia, but the ruthless exploitation of human material, without regard to life, loss or damage, did in fact produce remarkable developments. By the threat or reality of starvation or death, the Russian peasant was compelled to re-shape his agriculture on new and modern lines. All economics, all politics, all society was moulded to a series of plans. Vast industrial enterprises and whole new cities were created. In the cities, the poor received what was doubtless better treatment than they were wont to receive, as far as housing, education, wages and hours of labour were concerned. Science was developed to an extraordinary degree, especially industrial and agricultural science, physics and mechanics. The almost boundless natural resources of Russia were tapped. River, field and mine were used to increase the wealth and self-sufficiency of the new Soviet State. Materially, the Soviet experiment appears to have been successful, and from the chaotic, famine-stricken land of 1919 there grew a country economically almost self-sufficient from the point of view of food supplies and of the major industries necessary for war. Politically, it is even yet impossible to tell whether the great Bolshevik experiment has succeeded. The Russian revolution has not followed the general course of previous revolutions in the west: after thirty-three years it still shows no signs of mellowing into prescription and right, and it is too early to say what kind of political system will ultimately evolve.

III. Dictatorships in Italy and Germany

Before the war of 1914 it was from the side of socialism and communism that fundamental changes in the constitution of European states were usually expected, both by those who desired and by those who feared them. And it was from that source that the great revolution in Russia came. But no one foresaw what was the most striking development of Europe since the war—the rise of dictatorships in several of the great states of Europe and the influence of dictatorial ideas in many states which still nominally adhered to their old constitutions. The first World War became, before it ended, a struggle between democratic states and the strong monarchies of central Europe. President Woodrow Wilson declared that the object of America's participation in the war was to make 'the world safe for democracy.' The actual result was the very opposite. The democratic states won. Democratic constitutions were widely established and democratic principles proclaimed. But in a very few years the tide turned. The fundamental ideas of democracy were repudiated in Italy, in Germany, and in other countries which came under their influence. What has been called 'the necessary liberties of a civilised state'—freedom of speech, freedom of the press, freedom of association, the participation of the people in the government—were denounced as a source of weakness. The Parliamentary tradition was abandoned and the states of central Europe went back to the traditions of the benevolent despotisms of the eighteenth century or looked even further back for their inspiration. New features were added, but none that were favourable to liberty as it had been interpreted before the war. The movement took the world by surprise, but its roots are to be found in the past and its ideas were drawn from earlier writers.

Throughout history there has always been a sharp conflict between the authoritative and the free state; between the desire to secure the largest amount of independent action to the individual citizen and the desire to secure for the government of the state the completest obedience from all citizens and the most unlimited power. Such a conflict is observable in ancient Greece, in Rome, in the middle ages as well as in modern times. A condition of peace has usually been favourable to liberty; war and confusion, whether actual or threatened, have nearly always tended to limit the independence of the citizen and to strengthen the hands of government. During the English civil war in the seventeenth century Hobbes preached the doctrine of what would now be called the totalitarian state and his *Leviathan* makes interesting reading for those who study the dictatorships of the twentieth century. When the civil wars were over and more peaceful conditions prevailed, Locke developed the philosophy of limited and parliamentary government and Burke preached it with lyrical fervour and enthusiasm. The French Revolution has been regarded as the great victory for democratic principles; but this is only true with much qualification. The great reforms of the eighteenth century before the outbreak of the Revolution were the work of the enlightened despots. Voltaire praised enthusiastically the work of Frederick the Great and deprecated the idea of a democracy for France. The spirit and temper of Rousseau are usually regarded as the opposite of Voltaire's. But the *Social Contract* is no text-book of democracy. Rousseau declared democracy to be an impossible ideal for any great state and therefore for France. He refused to regard England as a free country. In more than one place he declared that the establishment of a dictatorship might be necessary, and the teaching of the *Social Contract* is quite as capable of a Fascist as of a democratic interpretation. The rather mystical doctrine of the 'General Will' corresponds very closely to the claims made by Mussolini and

Hitler, especially by Hitler. When the French Revolution came, though in its first stage it established a constitution corresponding in its main features to that of Great Britain, it turned after the outbreak of war to different practices and ideas and in the Reign of Terror set up the dictatorship of a small group. When the Republic gave way to the Consulate and the Empire of Napoleon, France had a régime which has many close parallels to the condition of Italy and Germany between the two wars. Power was concentrated in the hands of one man who declared himself to be the real representative of the people; representative institutions were swept aside; while the support of public opinion was secured by much that would now be called propaganda.

The twentieth-century dictatorships in Germany and Italy had nevertheless certain characteristics which marked them out from anything which had preceded them. In the first place the Germany and Italy of this period were 'totalitarian' states. The interest of the state was paramount, and not merely paramount, but exclusive of all other interests that might by any possibility be rivals. Religion in all its forms was subordinate to the state. The object of the administration of justice was not to uphold any ideal of right but to advance the interest of the state. The obligations of morality were clearly subordinate not only to the necessities but to the interests of the state.

Next, the shape assumed by the government was wholly personal. There was no attempt to make the government hereditary, as would almost certainly have happened in the nineteenth century, but all power was given into the hands of an individual, who proclaimed himself the representative and almost the incarnation of the people and of the state and allowed neither opposition nor criticism. Every form of parliamentary government was swept away and denounced. When elections were held no opposition candidates were allowed. Neither Frederick the Great nor Louis XIV nor any medieval ruler ever claimed such power. For a parallel to it we must go back to the Roman Empire or to the Oriental monarchies.

Further, every effort was used to control or to mesmerise public opinion in favour of this novel form of government. Earlier governments did something of the same sort by means of the control of the Church and the censorship of the press. But the modern dictatorships influenced the imaginations and opinions of men by means of every agency of modern civilisation. Education in all its branches, the newspaper press, the theatre, wireless were all used to this end.

Lastly, there arose in Germany the strange and unscientific idea of the state as the representative of a race dependent for its strength and efficiency on a blood-bond. Germany was the great advocate of this conception, although something like it was to be found in other countries. Except for Hitler's advocacy of it, it would not have been of any importance.

Events in Germany gave to two books a greater importance than they would otherwise have achieved. A French nobleman, Arthur de Gobineau, published just after the middle of the nineteenth century a book called *The Inequality of Human Races*. He was himself descended from Norman stock and the thesis of his book was the immense superiority of the northern or Nordic races over all others in character and intelligence. He regarded them as the foremost representatives of the Aryan stock and as innately superior to all other races, especially to the Arab and Semitic races. Thus a Frenchman exalted the historic mission of the Germans. And an Englishman and the son of an English admiral took up the same theme and carried it to considerable notoriety. This was Houston Stewart Chamberlain, who settled in Germany, assumed German citizenship, and identified himself wholly with the German state and race. His strange book is called *The Foundations of the Nineteenth Century*. It was received with much applause in Germany and was specially praised by the Kaiser and through his influence was widely circulated among the influential classes of the country. It is a survey and interpretation of universal history, full of digressions and not without inconsistencies. It regards history as embodying a conflict between the Teutonic and Semitic races. The writer recognises a certain greatness in the Jews and speaks with reverence of Christ; but ends with a fierce indictment of them as incapable of what is greatest in humanity and as guilty of intolerance and cruelty. Contrasted with the Jews stands the Teutonic race, which Chamberlain interpreted in the widest sense so as to include not only the Germans but also the Celts, the Scandinavians, and the English; but the highest representatives of the Teutonic race are to be found in Germany. France he regards as decadent. She rejected the Reformation which was an assertion of Teutonic characteristics against the Latin races and has fallen under the influence of the Jews. The future of mankind lies with the Germans, when they have found a religion worthy of them and have grown conscious of their destiny. An amusing feature of the book is the way in which all the great men of history are claimed as belonging to the Teutonic stock. Thus Isaiah was a member of a Teutonic immigrant race. Christ was of the Jewish faith but of Teutonic parentage—and race is more important than faith. The leading families among the Greeks were Teutonic, as is shown by the epithet of yellow-haired applied to them in Homer. Dante was of Lombard, and therefore of Teutonic, origin. The book came into line with what was already a strong current of feeling in Germany; and though its praise of liberty conflicts with Nazism there can be no doubt that Hitler drew many of his ideas and convictions directly or indirectly from it.

Until the outbreak of the first World War the current continued nevertheless to flow strongly in favour of parliamentary and democratic institutions. The liberation and consolidation of Italy were founded on democratic principles. The constitution granted to Germany by Bismarck was democratic in appearance though in its application it was much the reverse. Russia tried to find a way out of her troubles by granting representative institutions, and, though the Duma was suspended, it came to life again. Even in Turkey a phantom Parliament was set up. Japan and China paid western Europe the compliment of imitating her institutions. Parliamentary institutions seemed as much a part of civilisation as the steam engine. To make the world safe for democracy was no absurd ideal.

But then came the War and no nation or state was ever the same again in its outlook. Wars have always led to a concentration of the powers of government; but never before had the concentration been so universal nor so complete as between 1914 and 1918. Every state felt itself to be engaged in a life and death struggle and all considerations were subordinated to survival and to victory. Government everywhere tended to become a dictatorship and parliamentary assemblies were reduced to play a subordinate rôle. Traditions of individual initiative and independence were cast aside. The whole energies of the nation were enlisted in the service of the state. The economic life of the people was controlled in a way which would have seemed incredible before the war broke out. Freedom of speech, freedom of organisation and freedom of publication were limited where they were not destroyed. Recruitment of labour was for the first time in modern European history extended to women. By these means the war was carried on beyond the period that had at first been thought possible. In brief, under the pressure of the war the totalitarian state was established in fact though not in theory. And when the end of the war failed to bring the alleviation of conditions that had been too readily expected, when the hopes of the League of Nations became dimmed or disappeared, and each state felt that it must rely upon itself, the traditions of the war naturally suggested themselves. Among the causes making for dictatorships after the war the experience of dictatorships during the war was one of the most important.

IV. ITALY FROM THE *RISORGIMENTO* TO THE WAR OF 1914

The history of the rise of the authoritarian state in Italy is one of special interest. For at first sight all the probabilities seemed to be in favour of Italy's preserving the forms of that parliamentary rule by which it acquired national unity. Modern Italy achieved its unity less by its own arms than by its intense belief in nationality and by its sturdy support of constitutional liberty. But its nationalism was not selfish and its liberty not unrestrained. Mazzini, though an intense nationalist, was not an exclusive one. He was also a disciple of freedom. Indeed he parted company with Cavour and Victor Emmanuel, the future king of Italy, because they were not, in his view, sufficiently devoted to democracy and to liberty. Charles Albert, in proclaiming the *Statuto* or Constitution, added to it the demand for the Union of Italy. When he abdicated, Victor Emmanuel, his son, was intended by the Austrian victor to abolish or to destroy the constitutional liberties of Piedmont and Sardinia. He firmly refused to do so, on the ground that he had given his word, and earned the nickname of *Il re galantuomo* accordingly. Loyalty to the constitution preceded, implied and enforced loyalty to the nation. Cavour, far the ablest political leader that United Italy produced until the war, supported the bluff king's declaration by intellectual arguments and by liberal programmes. In the Italy of that day Cavour was, in all directions except one, a genuine promoter of English parliamentary ideas and of economic and constitutional freedom. By that means national unity was achieved, and the tradition continued. The *Risorgimento* was based, in its very essence, on liberty and on the constitution. It is very interesting and curious to inquire how and why these traditions were lost, and not only lost but derided and despised. Mussolini based his revival of Italy on the rejection of parliamentary and constitutional ideals. He trampled, as he himself said, 'on the rotting corpse of liberty.' He treated the members of Italy's Parliament when he first met them as dictator with more scorn than Cromwell treated those of the Long Parliament. For Cromwell showed his sense of their power by turning them out, while Mussolini contemptuously allowed his deputies to remain. He warned them, however, that the slightest sign of independence would result in their extinction. Of all the old liberties of Italy only the king and the dynasty of Savoy remained.

We have here a historical phenomenon of much interest. How came it that after two generations, a revolution, founded on liberty and on a constitution, and achieving national unity and independence, threw away the bases of its support? The explanations are manifold. It is actually doubtful whether the rigid adherence to constitutional forms, which distinguished the kings of the House of Savoy from 1848 to 1914, was really wise, though it was an honourable policy. For parties were numerous and divided and the exercise of strong personal influence by the king might at times have checked corruption or promoted efficiency. Italy felt that the monarchy was drab, just as France thought that Louis Philippe was bourgeois. If the monarchy wore hodden gray, the ministers certainly did not wear purple. Cavour's successors were satirically described as 'the generals of Alexander.' They were just as quarrelsome, just as set on particularisms, just as unable to think for the whole, and almost as far removed from their great predecessor. They were without the support of the two greatest living Italians. Garibaldi, the one military hero, denounced Cavour and wanted a republic, so did Mazzini, the mystic seer and prophet. It was they who took from the government the ideal hopes of Italy. Then came the shameful defeats of Italy by Austria on land and sea in 1866. Venetia was indeed won from Austria, but was won by the sword of Prussia. When Rome was entered in 1870, and the golden milestone of the forum at last reached by the king of Italy, it was again not an Italian victory. Everyone knew it was the Prussian victory at Sedan which had given the keys of St. Peter to Italy. It was victory on terms that were shameful. Italy was at last 'free from Alp to Ocean,' but no Italian was proud of the part he had played in the liberation. A period of genuine moral depression ensued.

A further cause, this time an economic one, added greatly to the public distress and to the detestation of the government. The unity of Italy had been achieved by diplomacy and, save for Garibaldi, by foreign arms. For that reason this unity made little appeal to the ardent and to the idealistic. And the practical arguments for a time also served to make the government unpopular. The peasant learned that the price of unity could only be paid by the imposition of the grist tax, or 'tax on hunger' (1869), and by the extension of the tobacco monopoly. Even internal free trade was not an unmixed blessing, for it takes time to break down century-old tariff barriers, and to adjust the relations of half a dozen previously self-sufficient economic units. The peasants, who numbered more than half the population, were not politically articulate or powerful. Matters got so bad that in 1876 murmurs of revolution were openly heard and Victor Emmanuel determined, as a desperate resource, to have a really Radical Cabinet, and then ordered Deprétis to head a Left Ministry. Deprétis professed to be a disciple of Mazzini, but in fact he was of the school of Machiavelli. He was merely the most adroit and skilful of parliamentary tacticians. If he was personally incorruptible, he was wholly incapable of checking the corruption and inefficiency of his followers. It was he who inaugurated those parliamentary tricks of finesse, management, 'log-rolling,' *formismo* and *combinazione*, which finally made the Italian parliament a byword for unscrupulous cleverness. Professor Okey says of Deprétis: 'In his hands, Italian politics degenerated into a welter of corruption unparalleled in the history of the monarchy.' Professor Villari, himself an active and honourable politician of these days, says of the period that it made people in Italy detest parliament men and civil servants. In fact the only officials of the crown for whom anyone had any respect were the army. For they, officers and men, lived hard and devoted themselves to the service of the crown without thought of gain to themselves.

The year 1887 was marked by the arrival in power of Crispi. As an old follower of Garibaldi, he might lend prestige to the monarchy and rally the Republicans round the throne. He was cast in more heroic mould than any of the parliamentary tacticians, but had a full share of faults. He showed harshness, unscrupulousness and impulsiveness, and it was the latter which proved his ruin. After almost two years' absence from office he returned to power in 1893, and with an illuminating idea which, under happier circumstances, might have given him immortal fame. Italy, like other Great Powers, had been bitten with Imperialism and had obtained Eritrea and Somaliland. Hitherto, however, she had pursued the policy of subsidising companies and leaving them to develop the settlements. Crispi had conceived a grandiose dream of giving King Humbert a new crown. In his first ministry he had obtained England's consent to expansion in Abyssinia, and he now pushed this policy still further. A forward colonial policy would give Italy a vast African Empire and distract her thoughts from internal affairs. But his ill-advised interference with the men on the spot, his demands by telegraph for 'an authentic victory,' his reproaches stung General Baratieri into action. He went forward with 20,000 men against 80,000 Abyssinians. The Emperor Menelek came out from church to head his army and, on March 1, 1896, the Italians were defeated at Adowa. Over 6000 of them were killed or captured. This defeat ended Italy's dream of conquering Abyssinia and it drove Crispi finally from power. The low state of Italian *moral* is shown by the fact that no efforts, either of king or of army, could induce the parliament to vote the money for a new colonial campaign. On that point the people, as well as the parliament, were agreed.

The year 1898 was marked by serious bread riots in Milan and elsewhere, and by severe repression of socialistic movements. It is perhaps significant that these events took place when the king and the ministers were uttering platitudes to celebrate the jubilee of the constitution, and when thirty provinces were placed under military rule. If that was the result of half a century of the constitution, it might be asked if the experiment were worth continuing. Troubled years followed, full of strikes and demonstrations, and King Humbert was assassinated by an anarchist. This tragedy, however, tended to strengthen the monarchy by producing a reaction in its favour. The dynasty had always suffered from the fact that it was not deeply rooted in popular affection, and that its rulers were strangers to two-thirds of Italy. But their disinterestedness was evident and the new king, Victor Emmanuel III, on the whole increased the prestige of the monarchy and showed more initiative than his father. He took the important step of appointing a left-wing ministry in 1901, the first Italian ministry to show sympathy with the aspirations of labour, and to do something effective for the right of free speech and of combination. The social unrest, however, continued right up to 1914, and successive prime ministers found that tactics in Parliament were no remedy for economic ills. One illuminating incident, however, occurred. In 1911 Italy picked a quarrel with Turkey and went to war with her, seizing Tripoli and occupying the Dodecanese islands in the Ægean. Strangely enough this singularly inglorious conquest of a barren Turkish province was hailed by Italians as a great achievement, holding out to them a prospect of a revived and glorious Roman Empire overseas. Gabriele d'Annunzio tuned his lyre to an imperialistic strain, and the bold note reverberated in the hearts of 'Young Italy.'

The war of 1914 proved an acid test for the tacticians, the card-sharpers and the masters of legerdemain, who had so long dominated and disgraced Italy's Parliament. When the war broke out Italy denounced the Triple Alliance and remained neutral. And neutral Giolitti, the greatest of Italian parliamentarians, undoubtedly wished her to remain. He could influence Parliament, but he could not control the people. D'Annunzio whipped up the Italian youth to wrest the Trentino from the hated Austrians and ultimately to enter the field against Germany. The war, produced mainly by popular enthusiasm, did not fulfil expectations. Despite superior numbers the Italian forces could make little progress across barren and waterless limestone crags, the high command was inert, the comforts and welfare of the soldier were neglected, and his *moral* sapped by socialist and pacifist propaganda. Finally, in the autumn of 1917 the Austrians, reinforced by six German divisions, swept away the Italian armies in headlong rout at Caporetto. The Duke of Aosta's army alone offered effective resistance; the others retreated in disorder. 'It was a military strike,' wrote a foreign general as he watched the horde of unarmed and panic-stricken fugitives stream by him. The Italians finally stood on the Piave, where British and French divisions soon arrived to stiffen their resistance. In June 1918 the Austro-Hungarians tried an offensive across the Piave. Resistance was now firmer, and the sudden swelling of the river in the Austro-Hungarian rear prevented their receiving supplies and reinforcements. The Austro-Hungarians were defeated and Italian *moral* revived. Finally in the last days of October, under urging from their Allies, the Italians took the offensive. The Austro-Hungarian army, denuded of food and clothing, was dispersed and routed and Vittorio-Veneto was claimed by the Italians as one of the great victories of the war.

Caporetto was, however, a much more important event than Vittorio-Veneto. The Italian *intelligentsia*, which was the cleverest in Europe, knew well enough that Italy's *moral* had cracked under the strain of war. The common folk remembered the disaster and panic at Caporetto, and thought Vittorio-Veneto no compensation for it. The end of the war in 1918 presented them with the same ghastly humiliation as they had encountered in 1866. The spoils of victory were theirs, but they had been won by the sword of the stranger. There was the added complication that Italy demanded more at the Peace Conference than her Allies were willing to give. They ceded to her indeed Istria and Trieste, the Trentino and a large number of Germans in the Tyrol. But they prevented her from obtaining half of Dalmatia, and they refused to grant her the city of Fiume. In addition, and very important for Italy, in view of her colonial aspirations, the Allies would grant her very little in the colonial sphere. She got nothing in Asia. In Africa England ceded a small scrap of Somaliland, France ceded nothing, in spite of her own enormous colonial acquisitions. There is a good deal to be said for Mussolini's statement that Italy got nothing from 'the rich colonial dinner'!

V. ITALY FROM GIOLITTI TO MUSSOLINI, 1920–1939

The situation in 1920 was in the highest degree painful for Italy in both the material and spiritual senses. Almost destitute of coal and iron she had acquired no new industrial resources at the peace. And the results of Versailles were, in fact, distinctly humiliating to her, and had aroused the nation to fury. During the actual negotiations they overthrew Orlando and Sonnino and substituted Nitti and Tittoni for them. But they were simply politicians of the old type and what Italy needed was something really new, leaders possessed of dash, of boldness and of decision. The first sign came in September 1919, when d'Annunzio, with a number of Italian bravos, seized Fiume, and induced the occupying French and British troops to depart at short notice. D'Annunzio held the town as an independent freelance, showering unspeakable insults on the existing Italian government who did not dare even to blockade him. This was a very significant episode, for the government was neither strong nor bold enough to subdue him. When he finally gave up the town it was with the knowledge that it would become a free city, and the secret belief that it would ultimately be absorbed into Italy.[1] But it was he, and not the government, who reaped the harvest of glory connected with Fiume. Giolitti, the last of the old school of parliamentary jugglers, had resigned from being Prime Minister in June 1921. He had done so just after an election, in which what was known as the Constitutional bloc secured 273 deputies as against 121 Socialists. Mussolini, who now led the Fascists, indicated that his followers, though reckoned as Constitutionalists, were not unconditional supporters of Giolitti. That very clever old gentleman then resigned, leaving to succeeding ministries the task of dealing with the frequent conflicts between Socialists and Fascists in all the big towns. The Ministers allowed these disturbances to go on unchecked, and seldom even attempted to punish the instigators. That negligence gave the Fascists their opportunity. Their better organisation and leadership finally enabled them to triumph over the Socialists, and made them begin to think of triumphing over the Government. The Ministers looked feebly on, alike impotent and timid. Bold leadership might have saved the situation, for the army as a whole was loyal. But that was not to be expected of Italy's breed of politicians. Giolitti hoped that Socialists and Fascists would destroy one another, and that he

---

[1] In fact the Free State of Fiume was partitioned between Italy and Yugoslavia by the agreement of January 1924.

could then step in and dictate peace. A well-informed English traveller in Italy at this time remarked that the combinations of politicians were so delicate and so carefully adjusted, that the existing Premier had already arranged not only who was to succeed him but who was to succeed his successor. Giolitti was the crafty brain behind these arrangements and meant to be the next prime minister but one. His calculations were parliamentary and not adjusted to reality, and were destroyed at one blow delivered by the strong hand of Mussolini.

At the end of September 1922 Mussolini declared in a speech at Cremona that he favoured a constitutional monarchy, thus making a strong appeal to the law-abiding members of the state. Then on October 24, at a great Congress of Fascists at Naples, estimated at 40,000, he made far-reaching demands on the Government. Facta, the last constitutional premier, resigned on October 27, and Mussolini took the decision to march with his followers on Rome. He arrived there on the 30th, having met with practically no resistance. The King made him his prime minister, and he at once secured the army by giving the War Office to General Diaz, the hero of Vittorio-Veneto. There was probably more luck in the way of Mussolini than is usually recognised, and he himself seems to have doubted, for a time, of success. But there can be no question of the failure of all other leaders except himself. The existing political régime had excited the contempt of most serious Italians, and all were agreed that radical changes were necessary. In fact the majority of people said of Mussolini's advent to power—what had been said of Canning's—'He is not all that we wish, they [those whom he had expelled] are all that we hate.' And in this whirlwind of contempt constitutionalism disappeared. Mussolini was left to direct the storm.

The period of Fascist rule was marked by some great changes and by some genuine improvements. Administration increased in efficiency. The draining of marshes was continued, and colonies were planted, with varying results, in what had been malarial swamps. Undoubtedly the claims of industrial development made at the time were exaggerated, but nevertheless something was achieved. Brigandage in Naples and Sicily was suppressed. On the other hand, little was done to solve the question of land-distribution, and, although strikes were banned, no solution was found for agricultural and industrial unrest. The original programme of the Fascists comprised justice to labour, a strong foreign policy and an attempt to increase national prestige. It carefully excluded extravagant economic professions like the abolition of unemployment, although it always paid great attention to economic factors. One of its dominant ideas was expressed by Mussolini himself in these terms: 'The key-stone of the Fascist doctrine is its conception of the State, of its essence, its functions, and its aims. For Fascism the State is absolute, individuals and groups relative.'[1]

[1] B. Mussolini: *Fascism, Doctrine and Institutions* (Rome, 1935), p. 27.

The Fascist party indeed became the State and destroyed all opposition to itself so completely that it appeared to believe itself both nation
and State in one. Thus in 1929 the election of an All-Fascist Parliament
was made an occasion for rejoicing. Yet it is difficult to believe that the
quarter of a million Germans in the Tyrol, and the three hundred
thousand Slavs on the Adriatic, willingly returned representatives of a
party which denied to them the elementary rights both of language and
of nationality. The idea of an authoritarian or totalitarian rule is, of
course, familiar to those dominated by the influence of Rome, whether
imperial or papal. And this is perhaps one explanation of the character
of Fascist rule. The idea of a corporate State, and the representation
of gilds or trade interests, has been advocated by socialists in a slightly
different form. But a careful analysis of the origins of Fascism seems
to show that it was originally opportunist in character, and that it was
only after it became settled and assured of power, that it developed a
philosophy of its own.

One result of first importance, however, was secured, and it was one
which exhibited not only the diplomatic skill of Mussolini but the fact
that he won a victory which every other ruler of united Italy failed to
secure. He reconciled the Quirinal with the Vatican, the Italian
nation with the Pope, and thus healed a festering and gaping wound
in the body politic. On February 11, 1929, a solemn Concordat was
signed between the Pope's representatives and Mussolini. The weak
point of the *Risorgimento* had been its treatment of the Church and of the
Pope. Cavour, with all his ability, failed to propose an acceptable settlement, and inaugurated a treatment of the Church which shocked even
liberal Catholics. According to Lord Acton he 'trampled on rights more
sacred than the crowns of kings.' His successors exaggerated his
methods and their treatment of monastic orders and of the Church
was drastic and oppressive. The Pope retaliated by disavowing and
condemning their acts, by asserting his undiminished rights to the
Patrimony of St. Peter, and by retiring into the Vatican and becoming
a prisoner there. In that capacity he excited the sympathy of the whole
Catholic world, and was able to cause endless difficulties to the Italian
State and monarchy. For to a large section of Christianity he represented the greatest moral force in the world.

The Pope's situation was a peculiar one. Before 1870 he was the
Vicar of Christ and as such the earthly head of the Roman Catholic
Church. He was also the sovereign prince of the Papal States, though
these had recently been reduced in size.[1] In October 1870, after Victor
Emmanuel had entered Rome, the subjects that remained to the Pope
voted by a plebiscite for incorporation with the temporal kingdom of
Italy. The voice of the people decided the fate of the Pope. Victor
Emmanuel's decree of October 9, 1870, declared Rome and the Roman

---

[1] A large part of these had already voted for union with Italy and been incorporated with Victor Emmanuel's kingdom in 1860.

Provinces to be an integral part of the kingdom of Italy. The King thus evidently deprived the Pope of his power as a temporal sovereign, though leaving him in unmolested possession of the Vatican. Legal opinion asserted that the Pope's person was inviolable and his residence immune, that he had 'rights of legation.' But he enjoyed all such privileges in virtue of the law of a particular state (Italy), and not by virtue of international law. Yet later practice is not wholly consistent in this view. Bismarck recognised the Pope as an arbitrator in a territorial dispute; the Hague Conference refused to admit his representatives in 1899; the League of Nations declined to accept him as a member.

The position of the Pope was unique, transcending all rules, and there was a great increase of his prestige during and after the first World War. His appeals for peace were considered seriously by the various belligerents. After the war, France found it expedient to resume diplomatic relations with the Pope; and in addition, Great Britain sent diplomatic envoys and in 1928 established a regular legation to the Holy See. It is obvious that he thus possessed or acquired an international status. Further, by the Concordat concluded with Mussolini in 1929, Italy recognised the Vatican as a State with access to the sea, and the Pontiff as an international person. Considerable rights and privileges were also granted to the Church throughout Italy, the exercise of which all Italian governments since 1860 had previously denied. In return a solemn reconciliation between the kingdom of Italy and the Papacy took place. This was the most important part of the agreement. The Pope conferred a lustre on the Fascist government, and gave an authority to its continuance, in a way that no other ruler could have done. The survival of Mussolini's dictatorship for over twenty-one years was due in no small measure to his reconciliation with the line of the supreme Pontiff. 'One could finally,' said Mussolini, 'be both a good Italian, which is synonymous with Fascist, and a good Catholic.'[1]

Theoretically, during the inter-war years, Italy remained a monarchy. The Constitution was still based on the *Statuto fondamentale del Regno* granted by Charles Albert to his Sardinian subjects on February 8, 1848. According to this Constitution, which remained in force until Italy became a republic in June 1946, the executive power of the State was vested exclusively in the Sovereign, and was exercised by him through his Ministers. In fact, during the Fascist régime, Italy was governed by the personal dictatorship of Mussolini. The comment of Sumner Welles is worth quoting:

Italy had prostrated itself before Mussolini. He was thus enabled to achieve an almost complete control over every form of activity in Italian life. From top to bottom the Italian social system had become wholly corrupt through the corroding influence of Fascism. The structure had already become so rotten by 1940 that no effective means existed whereby the will of the Italian people could combat the fatal determination of their dictator.

[1] B. Mussolini: *My Autobiography* (Revd. Ed. 1939), p. 312.

The members of what was politely termed the Italian Government, were no more than Mussolini's lackeys. . . . The will of the Duce, however perverse, however ignorant, and however blindly mistaken the Fascist leaders knew him to be, was law. For no one in Italy from the King to his ministers, from the generals to the industrial magnates, dared to oppose him.[1]

Comparison of the Fascist régime in Italy with the National Socialist régime of Germany is almost inevitable. The similarities are obvious, but there is one point of difference which is worth mentioning. The Fascist doctrine at first contained no theory of racial purity: anti-Semitism has never flourished in Italy, and Mussolini himself had on several occasions condemned any such movement. It was not until 1938, and then probably under German pressure, that a manifesto was issued, sponsored by University professors, defining the principles of a Fascist racialism. First, Starace, Secretary-General of the Fascist Party, and then, on July 30 in a speech at Forli, Mussolini himself affirmed these principles. At the same time, a violent anti-Jewish campaign was waged in the press, and in August 1938 the first measures were enacted against the Jews, excluding them from the teaching profession. Other measures, mainly aimed at excluding Jews from the professions and the public services, followed in swift succession, but the active persecution of the Jews in Italy never reached the depths of racial hatred or the attempts at extermination to be found under the National Socialist régime in Germany.

VI. GERMANY FROM THE VERSAILLES TREATY TO HITLER, 1919–1933

It is easier to understand the rise of Hitler in Germany than the transformation of Italy by Mussolini. For in the first place we have in *Mein Kampf*, written by Hitler in 1924, a sketch of the programme which he actually put into practice. And in the second place it is not difficult to explain why a proud and gallant people trained to obedience, to war, to victory, and to government by authority, objected to anarchy, to defeat, and to government by discussion; their objection was the more natural since all these seemed to be imposed by foreign dictation. The reaction was obvious if not inevitable. For the Treaty of Versailles had an even greater effect internally upon Germany than it had upon the rest of Europe. It was Germany's determination to upset and to revise the Treaty which armed the opponents of the Weimar Republic and nullified all the efforts of pacifists, democrats and men of good will in Germany.

The year 1918 was intensely tragic for Germany. The Kaiser sought safety and found humiliation in flight and thus destroyed the hopes of

[1] Sumner Welles's Introduction to *The Ciano Diaries, 1939–43* (New York, 1946), p. xxvii.

the Hohenzollerns. Twenty-two reigning princes abdicated. Thrones disappeared everywhere in Germany with lightning rapidity amid the undisguised contempt of the majority. The mobs rose, exterminated the Spartacists and more extreme Socialists and set up constitutional republics. Ebert and the Social Democrats were in power and, after the elections had taken place early in 1919, they made a Coalition Government with the Democrats and the Centre Party. Thus the bourgeois parties had obtained a certain amount of power and some guarantees for order. Then came the necessity for signing the Peace Treaty of Versailles. The Government resigned and a new Ministry replaced it, even more destitute of prestige and authority. Finally, on June 23, 1919, the Chamber agreed to sign, and the humiliation of Germany was completed on June 28 in the Palace at Versailles where the German Empire had first been proclaimed. The signature of the Treaty was followed almost immediately afterwards, in July 1919, by the adoption of a Constitution, known as the Weimar Constitution. Among the characteristics of this Constitution was an interesting tendency to abolish the separate states of Germany and to centralise and unify the whole nation. These tendencies were carried further by Hitler who developed and intensified them, when the rest of the constitution had perished. The general trend at this time was economic and socialistic, and the aim was clearly to facilitate the translation of socialist theory into practice. The future of the existing constitution therefore obviously depended upon Germany's continued attachment to socialism.

The Weimar Constitution really never had a fair chance. For, however moderate the Government and however reasonable their proposals, events told against their popularity and even against the whole-hearted acceptance of their rule. Germany was smarting from defeat in the field, and distracted by internal dissensions. She was confronted with an enormous burden of internal taxation, and with the still more enormous (because incalculable) burden of reparation for loss and damage to the victorious Allies. France was stern and uncompromising for the most part, and, by a most unfortunate chance, whenever an unusually moderate Government held office in France, an unusually unbending Government held office in Germany. The chances of agreement were therefore much lessened because the moderates never held office in the two countries at the same time. To suffering was added the sting of injustice. The French occupation of the Ruhr caused Germany deep humiliation. Great Britain finally avowed that it was illegal and admitted it to be contrary to the Versailles Treaty. In 1925 the Pact of Locarno gave a chance to the moderates, and inaugurated an era of appeasement and of hope. But Reparations, with their attendant evils of unemployment, of hunger, of inflation, and of taxation, pressed ever more heavily upon the people. In 1924 the first attempt to remove Reparations from the realms of fancy to those of fact was made under the Dawes plan. During 1927–8 the operation of this plan stressed the

16*

advantages of a final settlement, and this was, in principle, achieved by the Young plan in 1929. But the financial and economic situation was still very critical for Germany. Even in 1931 French financial pressure forced Austria to abandon her idea of a customs union with Germany and caused Germany to acquiesce in this decision by bringing her to the brink of ruin. This peril ultimately produced safety, for the intervention of England and the United States produced first a moratorium and, ultimately, the final liquidation of Germany's debts. But by that time it was too late to save the Republic and the Constitution of Weimar.

The above sketch gives an outline of Germany's troubles, but it makes no attempt to estimate her real anguish and suffering. Hunger, humiliation, hopelessness for the future, the prospect of eternal poverty and eternal disgrace, the reduction of Germany to the rank of a minor power, the restriction of her army to one hundred thousand men, the constant interference from outside, the hopeless inferiority to which she saw herself condemned, these were permanent features in Germany's life in the decade after the war. The rays of hope, which broke in upon her from time to time, lasted only for a moment and left her to a more enduring despair. Stresemann, the architect of Locarno, died; the Young plan, at first so hopeful, seemed nullified by the sinister and subterranean operations of international finance. The Germans had never been a people politically self-conscious or articulate, and they had no power of improvisation and not enough practical instinct to meet their difficulties half-way. They drifted gradually into a curious condition in which they were ready to surrender everything into the hands of an individual. The first sign of this tendency was the movement which ended in the election of Hindenburg as President in 1925. This was a very significant move towards the Right. None thought that Hindenburg was a socialist; he was known to be a monarchist and the most striking representative of the Junker class. At the same time he was a true soldier and, as he had taken the oath to the Constitution, it was believed that he would observe it. The whole incident showed at least that the forces of the old régime, militarism, junkerdom, and conservatism, were still powerful if latent. What was not perceived was that other forces, and new ones, were more powerful still.

Hindenburg, according to his lights, was a good President, at least until extreme old age rendered him helpless in the hands of his advisers. Like most soldiers he was a good judge of a man, and a bad judge of a political tendency. But it is only fair to say that the complexity of parties, the absence of clear-cut issues, the economic confusion, and the ever present threat of foreign intervention made a political choice difficult. Hindenburg was undoubtedly a promoter and a supporter of the Locarno Pact, and thereby made an important contribution to restoring tranquillity. He was also anxious to keep the army out of politics and yet at the same time amenable to pressure from the legislature and from public opinion. But his position as President was unfortunate and, like that of the Prince-President Napoleon in France in 1849, one in which it was difficult to observe the Constitution and yet maintain order and efficiency. For the form of the government was bad from a practical point of view. It had been struck out at a heat and the relations of executive to legislature were ill-considered and almost unworkable. The fact that Hindenburg was President alone ensured stability. He remained sphinx-like and impassive while a succession of embarrassed and transient Ministries passed like shadows before him. At last he saw a man, whom he had once rejected, who seemed a little less unreal than the others. He chose him for his Chancellor and speedily found his prediction a true one. The man whom he had chosen was Adolf Hitler.

The origins of Hitler and his movement do not seem to be of great importance. Nazism, or National Socialism, actually originated in Austria in 1918, about the time that Hitler, though an Austrian, was serving in the German army. What seems to have made the greatest impression on Hitler at the time of the armistice was the collapse of authority, the shameful flight of the Kaiser, the mutiny of the German fleet, the soldiers' and workers' councils in the army. Despair and disgrace had come from the absence of true leadership. All this misery was due to hereditary kings, to legislative assemblies, or to trades unions, and so all of them must be subject to the leader in the new German State. This lesson he thoroughly learnt and, without knowing it, he was in fact the imitator of Carlyle. Hitler wrote in *Mein Kampf*, 'The best Constitution and form of state is that which, with the most natural certainty, sets the best brains of the national community in posts of outstanding importance and influence.' The fundamental principle he asserted was: 'Authority of every leader towards those below and responsibility towards those above.' He makes the important addition, 'The stronger must rule and not fuse with the weaker and so sacrifice its own greatness.' Government should be in the hands of an *élite* of force. Here we have marked out clearly what is known as the Führer principle, essentially military in its application with executive efficiency as its aim. He thoroughly grasped, what political scientists have long known, that political victory goes to the force which is best disciplined and most intent on its object, and not to numbers. Hitler was right when he said, 'A company of 200 men of equal intellectual ability would in the long run be harder to discipline than one consisting of 190 of inferior intellectual ability and of ten more highly educated.'

A study of *Mein Kampf* shows that the hatred of the Jews, like the exaltation of Aryans, was a development of this same principle of superiority. Jews were, to Hitler, 'the lesser breeds without the law.' He said they were incapable of fighting and that they possessed a code of morals, thoughts and a world outlook entirely opposed to national patriotism. The Aryans alone had the steel-hard virtues of courage and self-sacrifice. It was easy and obvious to make the Jews responsible for the misfortunes of Germany and to point to the fact that they were now leaders in peace time though they had never been leaders in war. They were responsible for the 'pollution of our blood' and were 'a parasitic nation.'

Connected with the hatred of Jews was the hatred of Marxists and of Marxism with whom and with which they were wrongly identified. It would be easy to cite a number of Jews, such as Rathenau and Ballin, who opposed revolution in Germany, and it is probable that the majority of Jews were anti-Marxist. But these facts made no difference to the ideas suggested by Hitler for the education of the masses. These were that Judaism and Marxism were equally dangerous, that they were inseparably united, and therefore that they must be jointly resisted. A crusade against one should also be a crusade against the other. The most effective means of resistance was obviously the cultivation of a strenuous German nationalism and of the old military virtues of loyalty and obedience. Thus national socialism arose as it were from rejection of Marxism and antagonism to the Jews. It arose also from the bankruptcy of other elements in the State. The Hohenzollern monarchy had failed at a crisis and could not be restored, the old military Junkerdom equally failed because it was aristocratic and barred the way to promotion from the ranks. The new Germany which Hitler promised to the German people was to be one which could select its *élite* from the people themselves, for all doors were to be thrown open to efficiency and merit. In this sense the new Germany could appear to be a democratic society. But politically it was the antithesis of democracy. The State was strictly authoritarian, under the absolute command and direction of its leader.

To these ideas was added a determination to cure economic ills, and this was one of the most important of all the points in Hitler's programme. Of propaganda he was a master, and he said of it, 'the more modest . . . the appeal [of propaganda] to reason, the more exclusive its appeal to the emotions, the greater its success. . . . The power of reception of the masses is very small, their understanding limited, but their power to forget enormous.'[1] The framing of an attractive economic programme, the promise to destroy unemployment and to find work for all, was therefore of all appeals the most effective. After the great 'slump' of 1929 this programme was dangled before the eyes of Germans, some of whom had not eaten meat for two years. It was irresistible. The unemployed could hardly be worse off than they actually were, and it was little wonder that they believed in a brilliant orator who promised them a new heaven and a new earth.

After the war Hitler returned from the army and took up his residence in Munich. It was there that his political education was completed.

---

[1] The quotations are from the 1927 German edition of *Mein Kampf.*

Bavaria was the home of unrest, traditionally opposed to Berlin and to the existing Government, full of discontented soldiers, of broken and desperate characters, of dreams and of regrets. Hitler noted with deep indignation how the Majority socialists insulted the army, how Jews took the first places in society and politics, and how Communists threatened to upset the very basis of the State. For the Constitution of Weimar and the Republic he had nothing but contempt and hatred. The one institution which attracted his respect was the Reichswehr, a new long-period service army, set up under the Treaty of Versailles, admirably trained and disciplined and conspicuously free from politics. He seems to have dreamed of forming a party, reproducing in politics the same power and equally prepared to crush out all resistance. In this early period Ernst Röhm was the power behind the Reichswehr in Munich and deeply influenced Hitler by his brutal and masterful character. The German Workers, as Hitler's party was at first called, was soon recruited from soldiers as well as workers and students, and in February 1920 the party was launched with a programme of twenty-five points. This party, the precursor of the Nazis and Brownshirts, tried an open revolt or *putsch* at Munich on November 9, 1923, of which Ludendorff himself was the chief instigator. Hitler's followers were fired on and dispersed, and he himself had his arm dislocated and was carried away from the scene. He was ultimately arrested, brought to trial and imprisoned for nine months in 1924, during which he wrote *Mein Kampf*. This was to be the bible of the Nazi movement and is invaluable as disclosing his programme and ideas.

For some years after the *putsch* of 1923 Hitler was under a cloud. The Nazi party (the Brownshirts) was reconstituted in 1925, but it grew slowly. During that year, and for some time later, conditions in Germany were improving. Hindenburg as President stood for stability, and Stresemann's idea of co-operation with England and France was accepted by many. It was not until the year 1928 that the Nazis began to increase their activities, for their real opportunity only came with the 'slump' at the end of the year 1929. The German Government had accepted the Young plan for liquidating Reparations. Hindenburg had agreed to it and, with his official concurrence, all opposition seemed to have ceased. Hitler, in conjunction with Hugenburg and certain other representatives of big business (who thereafter clung closely to him), went to Berlin and opposed acceptance. A great political sensation was caused. In this year (1929) Hitler only had 800,000 electors in the Nazi party. But next year (1930) the number of unemployed rose to 3,000,000 and the Government became unpopular owing to its drastic measures of taxation and reduction of expenses. At the election of 1930 Hitler polled 6,000,000 votes and secured 107 deputies. He had thus already the second strongest party in all Germany. Henceforth his party grew—as did the unemployed—and in proportion to them. In July 1932 he more than doubled the number both of votes and of deputies, securing nearly

14,000,000 votes and 230 deputies, and 37 per cent. of the whole electorate. His single party was the strongest, actually stronger than the Social Democrats and Communists put together.[1]

Hindenburg was, in principle, a constitutional ruler who tried to work with the Reichstag and to adopt compromise measures and ministries. But he could not ignore the enormous electoral power of Hitler. During the year 1932 he first made von Papen Chancellor and then allowed General Schleicher to overthrow and to succeed him as Chancellor. But von Papen early in 1933 made an alliance with Hitler, hoping thereby to overthrow Schleicher. In this aim he succeeded and, to ensure his triumph von Papen urged Hindenburg to choose Hitler as his next Chancellor, hoping that he would be a mere tool. Hitler actually became Chancellor on January 30, 1933. It was the end of von Papen, and the beginning of Hitler's triumphs.

VII. HITLER

The steps by which Hitler finally obtained supreme power need not be described in detail. They followed almost inevitably upon the possession of vast electoral power and on his skilful use of propaganda at the election which took place almost immediately after his coming into office. The other parties were supine, inert or helpless before his ruthless activity and energy. After a new victory at the polls he abolished all the other parties, Social Democrats, Communists and the rest. He broke them up as political organisations, confiscated their funds and imprisoned their leaders or hunted them out of the country. He strengthened his power later by a series of plebiscites, in which every device of propaganda and intimidation was used. There is nothing really surprising in his victory. He had attained power in the first place by the consent of the electorate and owing to the discredit and divisions of all other parties in the state. The one formidable internal danger that he faced was of a different kind and was military rather than political. The storm troops of his party, the Brownshirts, were led by his old lieutenant, Röhm, and Röhm seems to have dreamed dreams of ambition. He desired to amalgamate his Brownshirts into the professional Reichswehr. Had he done so Röhm would have controlled all the armed forces of Germany and therefore been infinitely more powerful than either the Reichswehr or than Hitler himself. Hitler's relations with the Reichswehr had not always been happy, but he knew the advantage of a non-political army, and he had no intention of yielding control over it to a subordinate of his own. After some obscure manœuvring Hitler suddenly appeared in Munich and, at his orders, Röhm, General Schleicher and a number of others were shot out of hand (June 30, 1934). The Reichswehr remained non-political and Hitler was now supreme. Hindenburg died on August 2, one of his

[1] July 1932: Nazis 230; Social Democrats, 133; Communists, 89.

last acts being to approve these executions. Hitler seized the opportunity to amalgamate the office of President with that of Chancellor, and thus combined all functions in himself.

Hitler's internal policy was authoritarian and totalitarian in every sense. Economics and finance were subjected to and controlled by the State. Rigorous and ruthless measures did a good deal to improve the industrial situation. Unemployment was met by turning the unemployed into labour corps, and by an enormous programme of armaments. None the less the promises of economic relief were more specific and far-reaching than those made by Mussolini and an economic crisis could not have failed to react sharply on the existing régime in Germany. In the political sphere all organised opposition soon disappeared, but in the religious sphere there is a different story to tell. It was here that Hitler contrasted strikingly with Mussolini. The Jews, who were the first objects of persecution, proved indeed incapable of resistance in Germany and were speedily expelled, deprived of their rights, or cowed into silence or submission. But the attempts of Caesar to secure the absolute control of the Churches met with stubborn opposition both from Protestant and from Catholic quarters, and the religious policy of Hitler met with only partial success.

The most uncompromising opposition came from the Protestant Pastors, for at first the Roman Catholic bishops were not disinclined to support Hitler in his fight against Bolshevism. Both churches, however, stood firm against Nazi attempts to coerce them into approving the new racial theories, as defined in the 'Nuremberg laws' of September 1935. These decrees deprived Jews of all citizen rights, forbade their marriage with 'Aryans' and virtually excluded them from the official, political and cultural life of Germany.

The struggle between the Protestant Church and the State reached a climax in 1937 when the Church was deprived of the control of its finances, and all action on the part of the Protestant opposition was forbidden, and participation in Church affairs became illegal. During the summer, large numbers of Protestant Pastors were arrested and sent to concentration camps. Prominent among them was Pastor Niemöller, once famous as a U-boat commander, and one of the strongest leaders of the Protestant Church. He was arrested and imprisoned on a charge of 'misuse of the pulpit and incitement to disregard the laws of the German Government.'[1]

Despite protests from religious bodies outside Germany, the persecution of both Catholics and Protestants continued, but did not succeed in exterminating either sect and in fact one of its main results was to strengthen the moral authority of both Churches.

Meanwhile, the position of the Jews in Germany had further deteriorated, and 1938 saw yet another manifestation of the depths to

[1] Despatch from Sir Nevile Henderson to Lord Halifax, March 3, 1938. *A. and P.* [1938–9], xxvii [Cmd. 6120] 433.
'Papers concerning the Treatment of German Nationals in Germany, 1938–1939.'

which the German leaders and their followers had sunk. In April a decree was issued ordering all Jews in Germany to declare their property in excess of 5,000 Reichmarks (£250 approximately), and towards the end of October the first mass expulsion of Polish Jews was begun. The murder of vom Rath, a member of the German Embassy in Paris, by a young Polish Jew, provided the excuse for a barbarous attack on Jews throughout Germany, which shocked the western world. *The Times* declared on November 11:—

'No foreign propagandist bent upon blackening Germany before the world could outdo the tale of burnings and beatings, of blackguardly assaults upon defenceless and innocent people, which disgraced that country yesterday.'

The indignation in America was so great that President Roosevelt recalled the American Ambassador to Washington 'to report.'

The indignation of the outside world had, however, no effect whatsoever in Germany and, as if to express the utter contempt of the Government for it, still further measures against the Jews were decreed. The latter were deprived of their whole movable and immovable property, and every economic activity was made impossible for them. The object of these measures, as stated in *Das Schwarze Korps*, the official newspaper of the S.S., was to impoverish the Jews in order to drive them into the criminal classes, and then 'to extirpate them with fire and sword' as criminals. Within Germany, the only protests against this policy were those raised by those Protestant Pastors who had hitherto escaped the concentration camp, and many of them were severely punished for condemning the anti-Jewish excesses.

Hitler's policy led him to remarkable and speedy triumphs and placed him personally in a position of more absolute authority than any German since the days of Charles V. It was a real united Germany that he ruled over, not a miscellany of kingdoms, principalities and free cities. The slogan, 'One nation, one realm, one leader,' was adopted with enthusiasm by the majority of the people.

Whether the German people remained united until the final collapse of Hitler's régime is a question which it is not yet possible to answer. Correspondents of foreign newspapers in Germany, and British consular and diplomatic representatives provide instances of the opposition of individuals to the régime,[1] but there appears to have been no organised body of resistance. It is perhaps significant that, although several attempts on Hitler's life were made during the war, three attempts between September and November 1939, there does not appear to have been any previous attempt at his assassination.

A study of the authoritarian state, whether in the Soviet Union, in

[1] Cf. William Shirer: *Berlin Diary* (1941); Howard K. Smith: *Last Train from Berlin* (1942); *A. and P.* [1938–9], xxvii. [Cmd. 6120] 429–64.

Italy, **or** in Germany, reveals certain similar tendencies. In each case the direction and control of economics was supremely important, the idea of political opposition was unthinkable, and the censorship and police control of the dominant party appeared to be absolute. But here the similarities end. The Soviet Union controlled production, distribution and exchange in a far more absolute sense than Mussolini or Hitler attempted to do. Though possessing a formidably equipped army the ideal of the Soviet appeared before 1939 to be industrial conscription and control, and to that extent she was externally non-aggressive and prepared to accept the League. The ideal of Italy and Germany was rather the military virtues of loyalty and obedience and direct readiness for war, and hence imperialism and expansion. There was also the great difference that religion and its influence were regarded by the Soviet Union as a species of narcotic, while it had a sphere of its own, if limited, in Germany and a definite and assured position in Italy. The difference was, in fact, far-reaching.

One vitally important tendency remains to be pointed out. Few people would maintain to-day the full doctrine of the 'separation of the powers' as it was taught in the seventeenth and eighteenth centuries. Between the legislature and the executive there is, and must be, a close association. Yet, in a more limited sense, the doctrine of 'separation of the powers' still holds. It is as essential to liberty to-day as it was when Montesquieu formulated the doctrine, that the judiciary in a state should operate independently of both executive and legislature. Where there is no sphere of independence for the judges, there can be no justice and no liberty in any real sense. For, when the judges are not free, justice and liberty are necessarily controlled, defined and interpreted by the executive or legislature, in other words by interest or by expediency. Freedom of the judiciary can only be limited to a very small degree, if justice and liberty are not to disappear altogether from a state. The danger therefore of the authoritarian state is that it represents power, simple, pure and uncontrolled.

VIII. GREAT BRITAIN AND FRANCE

It is quite plain that, when the State is power and has totalitarian or authoritarian standards, it loses all or nearly all the advantages derived from freedom of opinion. Professor Bury, surveying the history of freedom of thought, commented as follows: 'A long time [in the historical sense] was needed to arrive at the conclusion that coercion of opinion is a mistake, and only a part of the world is yet [1913] convinced. That conclusion, so far as I can judge, *is the most important ever reached by men.*'[1] Since the time when Bury wrote, unfortunately, the 'part of the world' unconvinced of this truth has grown very much

---

[1] J. B. Bury: *A History of Freedom of Thought* (1913), p. 14. The italics are not in the original.

in size. And it is a fair question to ask whether freedom of opinion is likely to remain unchallenged even in those states where it still exists. Mr. H. G. Wells wrote in 1936, 'The present phase in human affairs is one of widespread distress, fear and suffering. Never before was it so much needed to assert faith in the freely thinking, freely speaking, freely writing mind.'

During the stress of war, the freedom of opinion possible in peace time cannot, of course, be tolerated by any belligerent government. Professor Bury himself recognised this fact and maintained that 'a certain censorship of opinion' during war was 'necessary,' because 'every social principle is subject to the general limiting rule that it must not endanger its own existence.' Freedom of opinion in wartime would destroy those liberal states which permitted it, and preserve those authoritarian states which forbade it. Every principle of freedom 'ceases to be valid at the point at which its operation would be suicidal.' This defence of restriction of opinion, while war lasts, is obviously sound even on pragmatical grounds.

But the disturbing fact is that restrictions necessary in time of war are all too liable to remain as a legacy to the times of peace. After the war of 1914–18 a severe press censorship was, for example, instituted in Belgium, which had been for so long before 1914 a home of free thought and of free opinion. Restrictions on freedom of opinion remained also even in France and Great Britain and the United States. The old liberal idea was well expressed by Lord Holland in a protest in the Lords in the year 1819. He said that large meetings acted as 'a vent, comparatively innoxious, of that ill-humour and discontent, which, if suppressed might seek refuge in secret cabals and conspiracies.' In other words, the best remedy against secret plots was to tolerate free opinions. On this theory all Governments, except despotic ones, acted in the early twentieth century to a more or less degree. Opinion was almost wholly free in France, England and Italy, Scandinavia, Belgium and Holland. Even in Germany the Kaiser was handled pretty freely, and Hungary was outspoken enough when it wanted to criticise Francis Joseph. Turkey, Russia—and to some extent Austria—were the only places where strong censorship existed. But this widespread toleration of adverse opinion was limited, in a greater or less degree, by all governments in the period between the two wars. All of them recognised the danger of certain forms of propaganda, of certain incitements to resistance, of certain appeals to popular passion, and all of them restrained and limited them.

One outstanding explanation of this situation is that in the twentieth century war has become far more rapid and sudden than in any earlier age. The mechanism of government, the machinery of war, is obviously, therefore, much more important. This fact became abundantly clear at the time of the outbreak of the first World War. Owing to its comparative freedom from legislative interference, the army of Germany which was mobilised in 1914, was the best equipped and most formidably armed that ever took the field. That of France was at a disadvantage in many important respects, but not primarily because of irremediable defects such as inferiority of man power. Its political machinery was remediable, but had not been amended. The evils were the weakness of the executive; the interference of parliamentary committees; the desire of democracies to oversee everything and their inability to control anything; the corruption and inefficiency of French political life. All these had disastrous effects on the preparation for war as well as upon the war itself. In the year 1914 the fortifications of France were imperfect owing to parliamentary interference; the military reorganisation was delayed for the same reason; and the French General Staff was caught unprepared, through no fault of the military advisers. England was in little better case. The warning of Agadir had resulted in a careful scheme being produced for making special legislation applicable in wartime. Haldane's foresight had provided a small expeditionary force for work overseas. But no one had imagined the creation of an enormous army on the Continental scale during the war itself, and the very effort involved enormous and unforeseen risks. Other defects appeared, again due to the necessity of securing the consent of the governed. The war had actually to be waged for nearly two years before military conscription became law; industrial conscription never did become law. Yet it is plain that in a despotic, or authoritarian state, all resources can be conscripted at the very moment of the outbreak of war. This can be and was done, to a considerable extent, by the French Government, but it was not done by the British Government at the opening of the war. Moreover, as conscription had not then been adopted by England in peace time, her military situation at the outbreak of war was necessarily precarious. As George Meredith wrote at the end of the nineteenth century:

> 'A land, not indefensibly alarmed,
> May see, unwarned by hint of friendly gods,
> Between a hermit crab at all points armed,
> And one without a shell, decisive odds.'

The danger for free states is likely to be greatest in the first shock of battle. If the war is to be decided in three or six months, their chances will not be good. On the other hand their staying power is considerable and even decisive. Count Andrássy noted that in the war of 1914–18 it was the parliamentary states which survived, while four Empires perished. But, as warfare is at once more sudden and terrific to-day, it seems to follow that parliamentary states must develop a more efficient government in peace time than before. Their chances of survival evidently depend on the efficiency they develop, and on the qualities of discipline and self-sacrifice that are inculcated during the time of peace.

In France, the period between the two wars appears in retrospect to have been characterised by frequent changes of ministry, excessive parliamentary bickering, by several unsavoury scandals involving politicians and even Cabinet ministers, and by the inability of successive governments to achieve anything. It is easy to forget in the light of the events of 1940, that during the first decade after the first World War, France recuperated to an extraordinary degree. Despite heavy war losses in men, extensive material damage to her agriculture and industry, and a heavy war debt, France became prosperous, and reconstruction of the devastated northern and eastern regions was accomplished with rapidity and thoroughness.

Politically, however, France was divided into many parties, whose only common feature appeared to be attachment to France. In England, there was, between the three major parties at any rate, substantial agreement on the political machinery through which the differing policies might be put into effect. In France, however, there was no such agreement. 'The fundamental paradox of the Third Republican constitution was that it was a system of parliamentary sovereignty in a country where very few of the political parties or the broadly accepted schools of political thought really believed in parliamentary sovereignty.'[1] Experienced politicians of all parties were aware of the fundamental defects in the working of the constitution of the Third Republic, but they were seriously divided on the remedy to be applied. The most serious weakness in the constitution appeared to lie in the capacity for irresponsibility allowed to the Chamber of Deputies, which was elected for four years and was never dissolved before its legal termination. The result was that members did not fear Ministers and overthrew them recklessly. Ministries were shifting and temporary, whilst the popular house remained unchanged for four years. The system tended to increase the multiplicity of parties, and the difficulties of forming and still more of maintaining a strong cabinet were almost insuperable. Even short-lived ministries were the result of bargains and compromises with the opposition parties. In 1934, the coalition cabinet of Doumergue attempted to revise the Constitution by conferring on the President of the Republic or on the Cabinet, the power to dissolve the Chamber and appeal to the country, as in England. Doumergue failed, and the iniquitous system persisted until the end of the Third Republic. It is, moreover, interesting to note that the Constitution of the Fourth Republic, which was promulgated on December 24, 1946, contains no general right of appealing to the country. It merely provides that, should two Cabinet crises occur during a period of eighteen months, a dissolution of the National Assembly may be decided upon by the Council of Ministers, after consultation with the President of the Assembly.[2]

[1] D. Thomson: *Democracy in France. The Third Republic* (Royal Institute of International Affairs, 1946), p. 75.
[2] Articles 51–2.

Yet a further defect in the constitution of the Third Republic lay in the facility with which French Governments could resort to rule by decree instead of by formal legislation. During the war, the President's *pouvoir réglementaire* had been freely exercised to make *règlements de nécessité*. The practice was continued during the inter-war years and was extended by the willingness of the French Chamber to confer on the Government plenary powers to deal with specific situations. The abuse of this authority by Laval's Government in 1935, when some 500 decrees were issued, led to the refusal of the Chamber to grant such extensive powers to Blum in 1937 and to Chautemps in 1938. In 1938 there were, however, thirty-two 'decree-laws' dealing with social reforms.

The inability of successive Governments to accomplish administrative reforms and to restore the financial equilibrium led many Frenchmen to support movements for a more authoritative form of Government. Early in the 'thirties, admirers of foreign authoritarian régimes increased in numbers.

Gradually, various forms of communism, Italian corporativism and, later, even German national-socialism found in France advocates, heralds, and agents who were not always benevolent. Absorbed without assimilation these dogmas from abroad were swallowed, hook, line, and sinker, by irresponsible groups, most of which did not realize at first that they might be political weapons in the hands of foreign powers.[1]

Prominent among these groups was the quasi-Fascist organisation, the *Croix de Feu*, which had been formed in 1935, and which numbered amongst its sympathisers Marshal Pétain and Laval. At first the policy of the *Croix de Feu* appeared to be concerned entirely with the preservation of the existing state of society in France, but in active opposition to the socialist and communist parties. Its extreme members, however, formed themselves into a secret organisation, the *Cagoulards*, which reached the scale of a private army. In June 1936, the *Croix de Feu* was dissolved and banned by the Socialist Government, but in November of the following year, a vast *Cagoulard* plot was discovered, aiming at the overthrow of the Republican form of Government and at the formation of a dictatorship which would eventually pave the way for a return of the monarchy.

Meanwhile, in order to combat what they considered to be the Fascist menace, the ten parties of the Left[2] had united to form the

[1] P. Maillaud: *France* (2nd Edn., O.U.P. 1945), p. 90.
[2] The ten parties are given in D. Thomson: *Democracy in France*, pp. 252–3, as follows:—

Communist Party.	Conféderation Générale du Travail Unitaire (C.G.T.U.).
Radical Party.	Conféderation Générale du Travail (C.G.T.).
Socialist Party.	Socialist-Republican Union.
Ligue des Droits de l'Homme.	Comité de vigilance des intellectuels anti-fascistes.
Mouvement d'action Combattante.	Comité mondiale contre le Fascisme et la guerre.

Front Populaire. The aims of the *Front Populaire*, stated in the Programme of January 11, 1936, ranged from the 'cleansing of public life' to serious economic reforms and social legislation. Unfortunately, the Spanish Civil War, which broke out in July 1936, caused a deep rift in the *Front Populaire*, between the Communists and their supporters who wished to assist the Republican Spaniards by active intervention, and the Socialists who were content with Blum's policy of non-intervention. Some attempts were made to introduce social reforms but with little result. The German remilitarisation of the Rhineland in March 1936 increased the French preoccupation with questions of military defence and security.[1] From 1936 to 1939, France was concerned primarily with the problem of rearmament and defence, whilst struggling at the same time against acute financial difficulties and growing internal dissensions.

On the outbreak of war in September 1939, all Frenchmen were no longer united by loyalty to France, as they had been in 1914: the cry of *la patrie en danger* failed to rally those who owed allegiance elsewhere. France, without outstanding leadership, entered the war politically in chaos. In France, as in England, the Communist Party and its associates refused to support what they considered to be a 'capitalists' war.' In France far more than in England, it fomented labour troubles and dissatisfaction. There existed, too, in France, a large body of opinion which was prepared to endure almost any humiliation rather than undergo the horrors of another war.

During the first few weeks of the war there was some activity along the Maginot Line: the Germans were compelled to evacuate Saarbrücken, and the French to retire from the Warndt Forest. There followed, however, seven months of almost complete stalemate on the Western Front—a period of acute boredom, which should have served as a time of intensive preparation for the German attack. 'The one thing which French public opinion and national morale could not stand after the rapid mobilization of five million men and the rigid censorship of war was nine months of waiting and boredom.'[2]

In May 1940 came the invasion and military defeat of France by the Germans. The controversy which still surrounds the French defeat makes it almost impossible to assess the responsibility for the weakness of France which was the primary cause of her defeat. That France's weakness was in part due to her political and constitutional shortcomings is borne out by the political capitulation which followed hard on the military collapse in June 1940. The capitulation led in turn to the extinction of the Third Republic in July of the same year, when a secret session of the French Assembly met at Vichy to pass a Bill investing Pétain's Government with plenary

---

[1] The first special credits for the construction of the Maginot Line were voted in December 1929.

[2] D. Thomson: *Democracy in France*, p. 214.

powers,[1] until a new constitution should be submitted to the people and promulgated.

Great Britain was more fortunate than France, and for many reasons. One has already been mentioned, the substantial agreement among political parties on the machinery of government in the interval between the wars. There was, it is true, considerable discussion as to the merits and demerits of the principle of the smaller cabinet of the 1914–18 war. At that time a small committee of half a dozen, without administrative duties, supervised, directed, planned, energised and decided everything. The retention of this principle with some modifications was advocated as a result of the Haldane Committee on the Machinery of Government, appointed in July 1917. It was then proposed that the Cabinet should not exceed twelve members. Ramsay MacDonald followed this recommendation when forming his first National Administration in the economic crisis of 1931, as did Neville Chamberlain on the outbreak of war in September 1939, and Mr. Churchill in forming his first Government in May 1940. In all these cases, however, there was one important difference which distinguished these Cabinets from the War Cabinet of the first World War. The divorce of Cabinet rank from departmental duties was not maintained.

With the extension of the scope of the Government's activities, the idea that fundamental change was needed in the machinery of Government became more prevalent. The present functions of the executive have come to it from two opposite directions, from above and from below. To those functions delegated by the Crown have been added a great variety of services previously undertaken by private enterprise or by voluntary organisations. But the system of Government has not been fundamentally altered:

Most of the men who are charged with the political leadership of the nation; who share the responsibility for all the multifarious decisions of the Cabinet, and must, therefore, study all its papers; who prepare and pilot through Parliament all the principal measures of each year; who are the chief exponents of its policy to their party and to the electorate—these same men are also called upon to direct day by day the vast and varied activities of great

---

[1] The text of the Resolution of July 10, 1940:—

'The National Assembly confers power on the government of the Republic, under the signature and authority of Marshal Pétain, with a view to promulgating, in one or more decrees, the new constitution of the French State. This Constitution should safeguard the rights of labour, family and fatherland. It will be ratified by the nation and brought into application by the Assemblies which it creates.'

D. Thomson: *Democracy in France*, Appendix I, p. 248.

Of the members of the Assembly present, 80 voted against the Resolution, 569 in favour, with 50 abstentions. The 'Vichy' Government did not promulgate a Constitution, and continued to exist, constitutionally, simply by not doing so.

Government Departments. And this in a period when economic and international difficulties of the most formidable character imperatively require constant watchfulness, intimate study and vigorous initiative. A recent leading article in *The Times* said truly, "The need for a small policy-making Cabinet, with time and ability to act as the power-house of planning, was never more evident." [1]

Such discussions, however, did not affect that fundamental stability of the constitution which enabled the country to survive the major crises of the inter-war period, such as the General Strike of 1926, and the abdication of King Edward VIII in December 1936, as well as the threat of invasion in the earlier part of the second World War. This stability is the second of the reasons for the comparative lack of turbulence in the development of Great Britain. Yet another is to be found in the association of this country with the Dominions. It is true that in the period between the two wars the constitution of the British Commonwealth grew notably looser and more flexible. Great Britain alone signed the Pact of Locarno; Canada, Australia, New Zealand, and South Africa abstained. In the second World War, Eire, then the newest Dominion, remained neutral. Between these two dates the Statute of Westminster of 1931 gave a new interpretation to Dominion status. Henceforth, its identity with independent nationhood was beyond dispute. Nevertheless the association of the Commonwealth, together with the growing practice of co-operation with the United States is one of the strongest bulwarks of British freedom. In the age-long struggle between the eternally opposed ideas of liberty and authority the battle has by no means been lost, and much of the basis for the hope for the future is to be found in the democracies overseas. The strategic position in this struggle is held by the New World and the growing number of the free states of the Dominions. So long as they survive, the odds against liberty are hardly greater than they were in earlier ages.

CHAPTER XXXIV

CO-OPERATION AND CONFLICT, 1920–1939

I. THE POWERS AND THE LEAGUE, 1920–1938

THE first World War represented in one sense the culmination of international strife, misrepresentation, and hatred. Yet at the same time it saw the greatest advance ever made up to this time towards the idea of European and human unity. Groups of men and women in England and America never ceased during the course of the war to work at a scheme which should make it possible to avoid the recurrence of war, all the more because it was already clear that in modern conditions

---

[1] Lord Samuel: 'A Cabinet of Ten,' *The Times*, p. 5, September 9, 1947.

war threatened not merely to degrade but to destroy civilisation. Thinkers and statesmen of the British Commonwealth were the first prominent representatives of the idea, but later it was championed by President Woodrow Wilson, and it was owing to his determination that the League of Nations was made in the end an integral part of the Treaty of Versailles. By this means what was then thought to be an important safeguard of peace was secured. To destroy the League would be to destroy the whole settlement that followed the war; to destroy this would be, it was believed, to destroy the hopes of the future of civilisation.

The activities of the League were from the beginning very varied in character. Generally speaking, it may be said that they increased in importance in the first years of its existence. It was not until 1924 that a British Prime Minister attended the Assembly of the League at Geneva, and from this time it became usual for the Foreign Secretary to attend all important meetings, whereas previously only minor ministers had attended. The League indeed provided, at first in increasing measure, machinery for the settlement of international disputes on an unprecedented scale. All the signatory Powers promised to refer their quarrels to some form of external inquiry before acting, and not to be judges in their own cause. It established, moreover, a true Parliament of the world, where questions could be discussed and where decisions taken could gain the support of an extraordinarily wide public opinion. Thirdly, it arranged for international co-operation on the many questions which clearly transcended the limits of any individual nation. Fourthly, it provided for a judicial court which worked out standards and principles of international justice, and obtained authority to settle all disputes between a number of states. Lastly, it established a permanent council to watch over the general interests of the civilised world, and especially to guard the peace of the world.

In the first five years of the League it was a useful, but subsidiary, instrument. The Conference of Ambassadors was still in existence at Paris, and it was only after the signature of the Locarno Pact in 1925 that the Council of the League can properly be said to have superseded the Conference as the central organ of European affairs. The comparative importance of the Conference and the League is well illustrated by the Corfu incident of 1923. An Italian general was murdered, as was alleged, by Greek assassins. Mussolini, who had just come to power, demanded reparation from Greece and occupied the island of Corfu until he obtained it. The matter came before the League, the Assembly of which was actually in session, and was much discussed there. But it was, in fact, settled by an agreement of the Great Powers at the Conference of Ambassadors at Paris, whereby Greece paid a large sum in compensation for the outrage and to secure Mussolini's evacuation of Corfu. The League had not gained in prestige, and an even more serious weakness was revealed at the Assembly in this same year.

Article X of the Covenant bound all signatory Powers to 'respect and preserve as against external aggression the territorial integrity and existing political independence of all Members of the League.' At the Peace Conference in 1919, and at the League in 1920, Canada had strongly protested against this article as pledging her to armed intervention. The result was a resolution of the Assembly, generally accepted by members,[1] which had the effect of allowing each member 'to decide . . . in what degree the Member is bound to assure the execution of this obligation by the employment of its military forces.' This meant that each member would decide for itself whether it would fight or not. The year 1923 was thus marked by a weakening of the protective bonds of the Covenant.

The French, who viewed with much alarm this 'flight from sanctions,' tried to restore the situation by a treaty of mutual assistance. This was ultimately superseded by a Protocol enjoining compulsory arbitration on members of the League. The Protocol was signed by seventeen states in 1924; it was favoured by Mr. Ramsay MacDonald, who was then in power, but it was rejected by the Conservative Government in England in 1925, partly at least because of the strong opposition of British self-governing Dominions, with Canada at their head. Thus so early as 1925 the League had definitely failed to produce a general system of sanctions. From this time protection and security were sought by regional agreements, and this system of obtaining security was aided by Germany's desire to secure the evacuation of the Rhineland, and to enter the League. A series of agreements was initialled at Locarno in October 1925 and signed on December 1 at London. Of these the most important were:

(a) A treaty of mutual guarantee of the Franco-German and Franco-Belgian frontiers, signed by Germany, France, Great Britain, Italy and Belgium;

(b) A Franco-Polish and Franco-Czechoslovak treaty for mutual assistance in case of aggression by Germany.[2]

To take the second treaty first, it is significant that Great Britain refused to sign it, though affirming that she recognised the obligations of Article X of the Covenant towards Poland and Czechoslovakia. Unreality showed its head here, for England's bond, as a result, differed as regards Covenant obligations and as regards the obligations of an ordinary treaty. In the case of treaty (a), England promised to defend France by arms if attacked by Germany or Germany by arms if attacked by France. This obligation was also an unreal and one-sided one. For, if Germany attacked France, England's small expeditionary force (say 80,000 men) might have rendered France some aid. But, if 3,000,000 well-trained and perfectly armed Frenchmen attacked

---

[1] Technically this resolution had to be passed unanimously and, being opposed by Persia, was not passed. But it is certain that all other Powers approved it.

[2] Summed up in Locarno Pact signed December 1, 1925.

some 100,000 imperfectly armed Germans, the fact that some 80,000 Englishmen aided Germany on land would obviously have been negligible, despite the aid of the British fleet. England had promised to defend Germany if attacked, but she could not really have enforced her guarantee by arms. Thus realism had been set aside, and an atmosphere of illusion began to descend on international politics.

The agreement of Locarno was not useless, though it was shortsighted. It did not fulfil Sir Austen Chamberlain's prediction that it marked 'the real dividing point between the years of war and the years of peace.' But it did produce an atmosphere of goodwill and a period of appeasement, which was actually of importance and might have been decisive. Austen Chamberlain in England and Briand in France worked hard for co-operation with Germany—Stresemann certainly brought Germany back into the orbit of the Great Powers and made her a member of the League. It is obvious now, though it was less obvious in 1925, that the future depended on the League's being able to negotiate a general disarmament all round. Limitation of armaments had been promised at Versailles. The Allies had justified the disarmament of Germany and other enemy Powers by the clause that it was 'to render possible the initiation of a general limitation of the armaments of all nations.'[1] This promise was now repeated and its observance would at once have made Locarno a real treaty. For if the German and French forces were approximately equal, England's force, however small, could guarantee one against the other. Under the Peace Treaty Belgium had as big an army as Germany, and that state of things obviously could not continue if Germany was ever again to be a Great Power. Mussolini, though anxious for armaments, was quite willing to accept parity with France. But France seems to have been always unwilling to accept anything like parity either with Italy or with Germany. As discussion progressed, attempts were made to substitute words for swords. The United States, on the hint of Briand, first agreed to a mutual engagement with France, in which both parties renounced war as an instrument of policy. Mr. Kellogg negotiated this pact, and finally invited all nations to sign the treaty, renouncing aggressive war. This Kellogg Pact had been signed by all important nations, including the Soviet Union, by the year 1930. It was not really as far-reaching a pact as appeared, for nations only renounced wars of aggression. It had a real propaganda value for peace, but it was unreal in another sense. Nothing would happen if a signatory Power broke its word, there was not even provision for consultation of the signatory Powers in case of a breach.

The acid test, that is of general agreement to disarm, remained. If this could have been agreed it seems clear that the Covenant, as subsequently interpreted by the Locarno agreement and the Kellogg Pact,

---

[1] Preamble to Part V (Military Clauses) of Treaty of Versailles. This was *not* a contractual bond, as the Germans later asserted, but was a moral obligation on the Allies.

would have ruled the world. The preparatory work for disarmament began so far back as 1925, but it was unduly and unfortunately delayed. There were some good reasons for this, *e.g.* the Soviet Union was not a member of the League until 1934, though she attended the Preparatory Commission. Delay proved disastrous. In October 1929 Stresemann died and, though the Rhineland was finally evacuated in 1930, that same year saw the increase of the Nazi vote in Germany from 12 votes in the Reichstag to 107. It was quite clear that in Germany, at least, the party which wanted to abolish the Treaty of Versailles altogether was growing stronger. So even in 1930 the chances of a satisfactory settlement were lessening.

Then in 1931 came the disaster of Manchuria. The importance of this great northern province of China to Japan was strategically very great. It was bordered by the Soviet Union and Japan did not wish it to be subject to Communistic influences. The province itself had been governed by a quasi-independent war lord, who was suspected by Japan of unduly favouring China. As a result of certain incidents Japanese forces entered Manchuria in the autumn of 1931 and set up a puppet state known as Manchukuo under Pu Yi, the ex-Emperor of China. The intention was to remove all the authority of the Chinese Republic and definitely to place the new state under Japanese influences. Japan completed these arrangements by officially recognising the new state on September 15, 1932. This really ended the matter, and the inability of the League to protect China's integrity, according to Article X of the Covenant, became completely and painfully evident. After a full investigation of the circumstances and the publication of the valuable Lytton Report, the Assembly of the League recommended a settlement by which Manchuria would be autonomous under China (February 24, 1933). Japan entirely disregarded this recommendation, continued her control over Manchukuo, and withdrew from the League. One day after the Assembly had given its final decision, the Japanese army made a further advance into Chinese territory and severed a whole vast new province, known as Jehol, from Chinese sovereignty, thus once more flouting the authority of the League. It was the more significant that she succeeded in doing so, as Mr. Stimson, the Secretary of State of the United States, had taken an active part in exercising diplomatic pressure. The attempt to impose sanctions had entirely failed. Moreover, Japan's easy triumph in Manchuria encouraged her, four years later, in July 1937, to attack China in the hope of acquiring, by similarly easy means, her five Northern Provinces. But this time, the Japanese miscalculated: China resisted, and Japan became embroiled in a major war which lasted for eight years and eventually became merged into the second World War.

Disarmament, however, remained and, though the omens were not favourable, there was just a chance of success if it became possible to reconcile Germany's claim to equality of rights with the French demand for security. One such moment occurred when Mr. Stimson, Mr. Ramsay MacDonald and Dr. Brüning, the German Chancellor, were all present. The German terms were extremely moderate,[1] but the French Premier, M. Tardieu, went away electioneering and the opportunity disappeared. He was succeeded by M. Herriot, who was anxious for agreement, but unfortunately Dr. Brüning had to give way to von Papen, who in turn was succeeded by General von Schleicher, who was speedily replaced by Hitler. The arrival of Hitler to power and the excesses committed by Nazis caused the French and British Governments to revise their terms. They felt unable to grant equality of armaments to Germany without a trial period. They accordingly proposed that for the first four years Germany should convert her long service army to a short service conscript army but that no reduction of other armies should take place. During a second period of four years equality of rights should gradually be conceded. Germany's reply was to withdraw from the Conference and from the League. Hitler was still prepared to offer favourable terms (November 1933), though they were a good deal stiffer than those of Dr. Brüning. He asked for an army of 300,000 men with twelve months' service.[2] He was prepared to accept a good deal less than parity in the air and would have agreed to a permanent and automatic supervision for his armaments. He did not ask for any reductions in the armaments of other states for five years. England and Italy thought these terms ought to be accepted. But a new French Cabinet, with M. Barthou as Foreign Minister, brusquely terminated the negotiations and in a speech at Geneva M. Barthou stated that France would never agree to any German rearmament whatsoever (30 May 1934).

From this time onward rearmament began everywhere, and full conscription was introduced into Germany in 1935. An Anglo-German Naval Pact arranged for a limitation on German naval construction equal to about one-third of the strength of the British fleet. With the collapse of the disarmament proposals everything became estimated in terms of force. Germany hastened to arm, France to ally with the Soviet Union; Hitler accepted naval inferiority from England in order to detach her from the Franco-Russian group. The old game of the Balance of Power was thus being played out.

As force was beginning to be the law in Europe, the League was beginning to recognise that moral suasion or at least pacific blockades were the limit of its activities. On May 2, 1935, a compact was signed between France and the Soviet Union. The Treaty conformed in

---

[1] *The German terms:* A Reichswehr of 150,000 with 6 years' service instead of 12 and a small conscript force of 50,000 men with 3 months' service. The principle of the possession by Germany of aeroplanes and the heavier weapons forbidden by the Treaty must be admitted, but she would be content with 'samples' only.

[2] This number was actually less by 100,000 than the figure of 400,000 proposed by the British military section as the standing army for Germany at Paris in 1919.

principle to the idea of a mutual guarantee and was within the frame-work of the Covenant, but it was really a thinly disguised military alliance. It caused great uneasiness both to Italy and to Germany and so also did the entry of the Soviet Union into the League. And at this moment Italy entered upon her Abyssinian campaign.

Italy, as appears from de Bono's *Memoirs*, had resolved to attack Abyssinia in the year 1933. She put her resolve into practice in the autumn of 1935, and was at once named 'an aggressor nation' by fifty nations assembled in the League, and economic sanctions were put into force against her. This very decision of the League reveals its weakness, for Article 16 of the Covenant said nothing of 'sanctions.' It spoke indeed of immediate 'severance of all trade or financial relations' with the covenant-breaking state. But this 'severance' was meant, in fact, to be merely the preliminary to military action by all the members of the League. In addition it is clear that a policy of 'sanctions,' which did not include the prohibition of oil, was very far from 'severance of all trade or financial relations.' Moreover, a limited policy of 'sanctions' could only operate on Italy slowly, while half-armed Abyssinia was immediately exposed to the full weight of the attack of a first-class Power armed with tanks, aeroplanes and poison gas. This was not the way to uphold the rule of law. In a few months the campaign was over. Mussolini had crushed Abyssinia and defied fifty nations. The fifty nations recognised their defeat and lifted the 'sanctions' in the middle of 1936, whilst delaying recognition of Italy's conquest of the territory involved.

Hitler, who had of course sympathised with Italy, and supported her against the League while it was busy outside Europe, secured, at this point, a victory inside Europe. On March 7, 1936, he announced in a speech that he proposed to re-occupy the Rhineland (hitherto a de-militarised zone under the Versailles Treaty) with German troops. They entered the zone that night. He was following a policy of 'risks,' as one of his lieutenants explained, but the 'risks' had been carefully calculated and he won. His advance was not an armed threat to France's safety, for in numbers his troops were, at first, not very menacing.[1] But it was a tearing up of the Versailles Treaty by force, and a repudiation of the whole Locarno settlement. The last was the most serious, for Hitler had hitherto maintained that Germany was not bound by the Treaty of Versailles which had been forced upon her, but was bound by Locarno and similar agreements which she had 'freely signed.' He now threw both on the scrap-heap. His argument that the French Pact with the Soviet Union had violated the Locarno Pact, and thus justified his *coup*, was inadmissible. For, three weeks after the Franco-Soviet Pact was signed (May 2, 1935) Hitler himself had re-affirmed the obligations of Locarno. France and England, as almost always at a crisis in this period, had different policies. France was not

[1] They were 36,500 in number.

ready to fight alone over the Rhineland, though prepared to defend herself. She would probably have fought if England had agreed to do so. But England was tempted by Hitler's offer in his speech to re-enter the League, if the Covenant was separated from the Treaty and Germany's colonial claims discussed. Also the League was distracted by the struggle with Italy. Unanimity in condemning Germany would not have been secured there. In the end nothing was done, but something came of Hitler's action. On March 26, 1936, Mr. Eden, as British Foreign Secretary, made it quite clear in a speech that England would defend either France or Belgium, or both together, if Germany attacked their territory or independence. For the first time in British history the guarantee of defending Belgium and France against attack was made clear and absolute and independent of circumstances.

The remilitarisation of the Rhineland had also a profound effect on the position of Belgium, which had ceased *de facto* to be a neutralised state in 1919. The German action now exposed her again to the threat of sudden attack from the east, in the face of which the Locarno guarantees were inadequate. At the end of 1936 the Belgian Government therefore determined to pursue a policy 'exclusively and completely Belgian,' and requested Britain and France to release them from the obligations of Locarno. Britain and France acceded to the Belgian request in April 1937, but maintained their guarantees of Belgian security under the Locarno Agreement, since the Belgian Government had expressed their intention to defend their country against aggression or invasion.

The year 1936 marks a definite stage in the descent to the abyss. The League had been discredited by its inability to intervene effectively either in the attack of Japan in Manchuria or in that of Italy on Abyssinia. It demonstrated its weakness to all the world by its failure to intervene over the Rhineland. And in the summer of this year, four months after Hitler's flouting of the League, another event took place which was to provide yet a further instance of the unwillingness of the powers to take effective action in the interests of peace.

This new event was the outbreak in July 1936 of the Spanish Civil War. Hitherto the chaotic internal condition of Spain had attracted little attention from other European countries. The military dictatorship of General Primo de Rivera ended in January 1930. In the ensuing anarchy, the Republicans obtained a majority in the local elections, King Alfonso was exiled, and the Second Spanish Republic formally came into being on 9 December 1931. In the four and a half years which followed, there were three changes of Government. The Liberal left-wing parties held office from 9 December 1931 until December 1933, when the Conservative right-wing party gained power and held office until defeated in February 1936 by the Popular Front, a coalition of Republicans, the Catalan Left, Socialists and Communists. The Popular Front at once proclaimed a mildly Socialistic policy of land reform and some measure of State intervention in and control of industry. There was, however, no immediate intention on the part of the Government to disestablish the Church or to institute State owner-ship of industry. At the same time, there was some violence and dis-order by extremists of both the Popular Front and their adversaries, which culminated on 18 July 1936 in a military revolt in Spain and Spanish Morocco. This attempt by the conservative elements to seize power by a *coup d'état* was foiled by the Government, who raised a sufficiently large army to embroil Spain in a civil war lasting two and a half years.

By the beginning of August 1936, the issue and the opposing parties were fairly well defined. On the one side were those opposed to the Republican ideal, although they did not necessarily favour a restora-tion of the monarchy: they consisted of the Monarchists, landowners, the Roman Catholic Church hierarchy and some of the more prosperous of the business and professional classes. They valued above all the preservation of authority, order and discipline, and supported the mutinous army-caste whose avowed purpose was 'to save Spain from Bolshevism.' This 'Nationalist' party, led by General Franco, received at the very outset of the 'rebellion,' German and Italian material sup-port, the first German aeroplanes reaching Morocco on July 28. On the other side were the Republicans, consisting of Liberals, some Roman Catholics, Socialists, Communists, Anarcho-Syndicalists and Basque Nationalists who had already been promised autonomy by the Re-publican Government. The Republicans received some help from Russia, but on nothing like the scale on which the Nationalists received assistance from Germany and Italy.[1]

Theoretically, the Spanish Civil War, as a purely domestic conflict, was not the concern of the League of Nations, and only limited use was in fact made of League machinery in the efforts of the Powers to pre-vent the Spanish conflict from developing into a general European war. On the initiative of Britain and France, an international committee, including Great Britain, France, Italy, Germany and Russia, was set up in London on September 9, 1936, to discover means of putting into effect the principle of non-intervention. This Committee usurped to a large extent the functions of the League of Nations, although the Spanish Republican Government continued to raise grievances at Geneva.[2]

---

[1] By the spring of 1937 it was estimated that there were some 2,000 Russian sub-jects, mainly airmen and technicians, serving with the Spanish Republican Army, whilst there were 10,000 Germans and 70,000 Italians, including whole Army corps under Italian officers, serving with the Nationalists. *v. Annual Register*, 1937, p. 239.

[2] On August 21, 1937, the Spanish Government appealed to the League under Article XI of the Covenant, against the repeated attacks by Italian submarines and aircraft on Spanish merchant shipping.

Article XI of the Covenant declared it 'to be the friendly right of each Member of the League to bring to the attention of the Assembly or of the Council any

It is worth noting that there was one instance of effective international co-operation during the Spanish Civil War. During the first half of 1937, acts of piracy in the Mediterranean increased alarmingly: neutral shipping and even four British warships were attacked by aircraft and submarines which were undoubtedly of Italian origin in the service of the Spanish Nationalists. Early in September 1937, Britain and France took the initiative in summoning a conference of the Black Sea and Mediterranean powers to concert measures against this threat to neutral trade. Germany and Italy refused to attend the Conference which met at Nyon, and, on September 14, 1937, agreed on measures to be taken for the defence of shipping routes and the destruction of piratical submarines, surface craft and aircraft in the Mediterranean. These measures were put into immediate operation, and from that time acts of piracy in the Mediterranean ceased.

In dealing with the situation created by the intervention of other powers in the Spanish Civil War, the members of the League failed to formulate a policy which they were prepared to put into effect. The complaint of the Spanish representative at Geneva that the only effective non-intervention applied to Spain was the non-intervention of the League of Nations was clearly justified. The embarrassment of the League was reflected in the vote of the Council, in May 1938, on the Spanish Government's resolution that members of the League should consider ending the 'legal monstrosity of the formula of "Non-Intervention",' which the open intervention of Germany and Italy rendered a mockery. The resolution was rejected by four negative to two affirmative votes, but there were *nine* abstentions.

It seemed as if the Spanish Foreign Minister, Señor Alvarez del Vayo, were justified in his declaration before the League Assembly, on September 19, 1938, that there had grown up at Geneva 'a strange theory according to which the best method of serving the League was to remove from its purview all questions relating to peace, and the application of the Covenant.' And the events of the autumn were left to provide the answer to his question as to whether the great western democracies, before acting within the framework of the League, intended to wait until half the European nations represented at Geneva had been paralysed by discouragement, panic or the fact that they had ceased to exist as independent states.

The Spanish Republican Government continued the struggle until March 1939, but the amount of assistance which Germany and Italy were openly giving to the Nationalist side made the victory of General Franco's party a foregone conclusion. The Spanish Civil War ended with the surrender of Madrid on March 30, 1939, and on April 20, 1939, the non-intervention committee in London was formally dissolved.

circumstance whatever affecting international relations which threatens to disturb international peace or the good understanding between nations upon which peace depends.'

II. HITLER'S DRIVE TO THE EAST, 1938

Before the end of the Spanish Civil War other events were dominating the attention of the European powers. Indeed, by March 1939 even the most optimistic and pacific observers were convinced that Germany would not long delay in bringing about a crisis which must lead to war. By that time the writing on the wall had become plain to all; for after the Rhineland had come Austria, after Austria the Sudetenland, and after the Sudetenland the rest of Czechoslovakia. Moreover Italy had joined Germany in the famous pact which became known as the Axis.

For the history of these events we must return to the critical year 1936. In that year, for the first time, Hitler unreservedly committed himself to the view that Germany must demand the restoration of her colonies. This had long been the view of certain Germans. But Hitler, like Bismarck, had opposed colonial expansion, though ultimately (as in Bismarck's case) his hand was forced by public opinion. Hitler's argument in *Mein Kampf* was as follows: Germany could get all the expansion she wished towards the East ' along the road of the Teutonic knights,' preferably against Russia in the Ukraine. He did not think that land or a suitable outlet for surplus population could be found in the colonies and, even if they could, it would mean war with England, 'a healthy and expanding state,' with whom he wished to be on terms of friendship and even of alliance. This was still his view in 1927, when the fuller edition of *Mein Kampf* appeared. So his demand for colonies nine years later was a *volte face* and, to all appearance, was due to the necessity to conciliate German public opinion. It was one more hint to England that, so long as her armaments were weak, she would not carry much weight in the cabinet of nations. On February 17, 1937, Neville Chamberlain proposed to spend four hundred millions in one year on rearmament, and to go up to fifteen hundred millions in five years. Chamberlain followed up this announcement a year later (1938) by declaring that Britain would not pledge herself beforehand to defend Czechoslovakia, though she might have to fight for her in the end. At the same time, he went much further than to repeat Mr. Eden's pledges that England would defend by arms France and Belgium. He added that Portugal and her colonies, Egypt, and Iraq would all be protected by Britain from external attack.

At the end of February 1938, Chamberlain announced his disbelief in the efficacy of economic sanctions, and in the protective value of Article X of the Covenant. 'If I am right, as I am confident I am, in saying that the League as consititued to-day is unable to provide collective security for anybody, then I say we must not try to delude ourselves, and, still more, we must not try to delude small weak nations, into thinking that they will be protected by the League against aggression and acting accordingly, when we know that nothing of the kind can be expected.'[1] His disclaimer received dramatic illustration within three weeks. On March 12 Hitler sent German armed forces into Austria, which they occupied and annexed without the League doing anything to deter him. It was a flouting of the League as well as a breach of the Versailles Treaty, in which Article 80 forbade the union of Austria and Germany without the consent of the Council of the League. The Council was never even consulted. Some seven millions of men were transferred and a state, formerly a member of the League, was absorbed in Germany.

Germany had outlawed the League; Japan and Italy had been outlawed by it. Three of the strongest military nations thus stood outside the League and were bound, in the end, to come together. They were united by hatred of the League, and by a still more violent hatred of Communism and of the Soviet Union. On November 25, 1936, Japan and Germany signed an Anti-Comintern Pact and though both denied that this was anything more than a moral bond, the assertion was not generally believed. Italy later acceded to this Pact, and a moral entente at least united the three anti-League Powers from that time. There was a still firmer basis for Italo-German relations. At the end of September 1937 Mussolini visited Germany—and the result was the vociferous proclamation of the Berlin-Rome axis, as a political combination of high importance and value.[2] Hitler, with his usual adroitness, made use of it to make Mussolini accept his *coup* in annexing Austria (March 1938). Austria weak, both through her economic conditions and her acute internal differences, could do nothing for herself. Her situation had indeed been one of successive crises since the end of the war. In May 1932 the brief socialist government was succeeded by that of the 'midget Chancellor,' Dollfuss. On July 25, 1934, Dollfuss was murdered, and this marked the first step towards Nazi penetration. Before the formation of the Axis the presence of Italian troops on the Brenner was the most effective bar to open action. From the conclusion of this pact there was no European state which had at the same time the will and the power to intervene. In these circumstances the last moment efforts of the Austrian Chancellor, Schuschnigg, could be little more than a demonstration, and Hitler's troops marched in to a cowed and silent capital, which had once been the capital of the greatest state in Europe. Vienna had indeed a new and tragic primacy to set against the memories of the old days of the Holy Roman Empire. For the fate that befell her in March 1938 was to be shared by many another capital city before the tide of war receded in 1944-45.

The annexation of Austria made the future of the three and a half million Germans grouped round the westward fringes of Czechoslovakia an acute question in Europe. Some nine millions of Austrians had been added to Germany, and the three and a half millions in

[1] House of Commons, February 22, 1938.
[2] *v.* E. Wiskemann: *The Rome-Berlin Axis* (O.U.P., 1949).

Czechoslovakia were next door to the Austrians on one side and to the Germans on the other. A caricature in the *News Chronicle* of March 14, 1938, hit off the situation well. It represented Germany in the likeness of a wolf's head, with the upper or Silesian jaw closing over the western end of Czechoslovakia from one side, while the Austrian or lower jaw encircled it from the other. 'The jaws of the German wolf are closing in,' ran the sentence below, and six months later the jaws did actually close and separated the Sudeten Germans from Czechoslovakia.

Historically, the Czechs have proved themselves to be a people of strong character, with energy, a capacity for industrial development and a remarkable strength of will. The inhabitants of the predominantly Czech territory are not, however, purely Czech. Many Germans penetrated inside the mountains which make Bohemia a natural fortress. In 1919 some three and a half million Germans in Bohemia and Moravia were included within the boundaries of the new Czechoslovak state. The Czechs themselves numbered some six millions. To these were added nearly two million Slovaks, who had previously suffered much under Hungarian rule. They were not lively, civilised or industrialised like the Czechs; but slow-thinking, stolid, peasant farmers. They did not like the Hungarians, from whose rule they were freed in 1919, but they did not mix very well with the Czechs. Of Hungarians or Magyars proper over nine hundred thousand were annexed, of whom more than half were so intermixed with Slovaks as to be inseparable from them. The last alien element was Ruthenian, about four hundred thousand of this uncultured race being assigned to Czechoslovakia.

It is easy now to criticise a settlement which constructed a state of thirteen millions of whom only eight millions were Czechoslovak, that is of the dominant race. The addition of Slovakia and of Hungarian Ruthenia to Bohemia made a long and unwieldy state. But Slovakia had actually been freed, and was in *de facto* possession of Czechoslovaks in 1919, and its agricultural supplies were needed to feed the industrialised Czechs. Ruthenia was added, partly at least to enable a railway connection to go directly through to Rumania. This iron road alone enabled the three states—Czechoslovakia, Rumania, and Yugoslavia—to be in direct contact with one another, and ultimately to form the military alliance known as 'the Little Entente.'

Could any modifications have been made? The partition of the Teschen area, assigning over one hundred thousand Poles to Czechoslovakia, was sound. It gave her an indispensable railway-route and certain mining areas. It was even more necessary to give the new State of Czechoslovakia an opening on the Danube. The old city of Pressburg (Pozsony) was ceded by Hungary and re-named Bratislava. This was a necessity as the new State had no access to the sea, and this was its only contact with a great river. But there does not seem to have been any equal excuse for assigning to the new State the area of the Grosse Schütt (Csallo-Köz)—ending in the historic Hungarian fortress of Komárom. This decision had the effect of adding three hundred thousand Hungarians to the six hundred thousand already ceded to Czechoslovakia, making over nine hundred thousand in all.[1]

The inclusion of the Sudeten Germans has now to be explained. At one point it was suggested that two Sudeten salients, respectively at Rumburg and at Eger, might have been cut off from Czechoslovakia. In such case, however, they could only have been given to Germany (not Austria), which had never possessed them. This suggestion was not received with favour. The proposal was put forward by both British and American representatives. Mr. Harold Nicolson says, 'We worked that out and we went to our chiefs, who both of them said, "But you are mad. You were going to give Germany territory for having made war against us. This was never German territory. [In such case] Germany will come out of this war with an acquisition of territory in Bohemia." And, of course, it was impossible to get it through.'[2] This revelation shows well enough the difficulties at the Peace Conference in 1919. But, as a matter of fact, the cession of the territory would have done very little good. It would have removed from Czechoslovakia some 350,000 Germans (only some ten per cent. of the whole) and not really conciliated Germany at all. It would have interfered with a frontier line some six centuries old, and therefore intelligible and known. It is, of course, true that the western frontier of Czechoslovakia, as ultimately settled, offered good possibilities for defence of which the French were well aware. But this was by no means the only reason for its adoption. The real reason was that the Germans on the outlying fringes inhabited districts rich in coal and timber. These were worked up into highly developed industries, such as the Skoda works at Pilsen and the various factories at Prague, which were controlled by Czechs. It was felt impossible on economic grounds to separate the raw material from the manufactured product. The two areas had always been united politically before, and they were connected by the strongest ties of economic interest. It was, in fact, believed that Czechoslovakia could not, in the economic sense, prosper or pay its way unless three and a half million Germans were included. Economic 'viability' was the cause of their inclusion, though the racial difficulties were fully realised. It was also seen that, in any case, separation would have been difficult as the population was, in fact, intermixed.[3] It has indeed been contended that the Sudeten Germans showed by a plebiscite in 1918

---

[1] Proportions between the races have altered considerably since 1919. The statistics here given, are those used at the Peace Conference in 1919, and were the figures of the last census in Austria-Hungary (1910).
[2] Speech in the House of Commons, October 5, 1938.
[3] This is shown by the fact that the Sudeten cessions of October 1938 to Germany brought at least 600,000 Czechs under German control as well

their desire to belong to Germany. But this plebiscite was of very dubious value. It is at least doubtful whether it represented the feelings of Sudeten Germans in 1918, and still more doubtful whether it did so in 1919. At any rate, the Austrians always strenuously denied that the real feeling of Sudeten Germans was for union with Germany.

The reasons for constructing the new State have now been given. It remains to examine how far the experiment was successful. Economically and financially it did quite well, paid its way, and established a strong position in the world. Textiles, glass, heavy industries, furniture, and beet sugar all increased their production. The State was well governed in the administrative sense. It had a good army, a strongly fortified frontier, an efficient police system. It showed great educational activity. The Ruthenes were systematically educated for the first time, and the standard of literacy was greatly raised in Slovakia, whose schools had been neglected by the Hungarians.[1] The Germans and Czechs of old Bohemia were already among the best educated of the peoples in Europe. But under the Czechoslovak régime these standards were further raised. In fact, in 1938 the Sudeten Germans were actually in a more favourable situation, from the standpoint of elementary education, and better off than the Czechs themselves. The Czechoslovak statistics for 1935–36 showed that the average number of children in a Czech class in an elementary school was 49, while in a Sudeten German class it was 36. The German official statistics of May 15, 1936, give 42·3 children in a class in Prussian schools, and 42·6 in a class in Bavarian schools. So Sudeten German children were actually better served, from the point of view of small classes in elementary schools, than Czech children or Bavarian children or Prussian children!

Statistics seldom tell the whole truth, and still more seldom give a complete view of the treatment of a racial minority. There is no question that, during the early years of the Republic, the Sudeten Germans had much to suffer from harshness and from unsympathetic Czech officials. But there was this very important difference between the Czechoslovaks and the other victorious Entente nations of Central and Eastern Europe. All of them, Poles, Yugoslavs, Rumans, and Czechoslovaks, signed Minority Treaties promising to accord justice and linguistic privileges to their racial and religious minorities. None of these powers made so real and genuine an attempt to carry out the minority provisions as did the Czechoslovaks. None of them ever welcomed, as Dr. Beneš did from the first, the inquiries of the League into Minority

---

[1] The following were the percentages of illiteracy:

	Slovakia	Ruthenia.
Hungarian census in 1910 –	– 27·8%	45%
Czechoslovak census in 1930	– 8·2%	30·9%

grievances. This fact was, in itself, significant. For the virtue of the League was that, whether anything substantial was done or not, the truth as to a racial or religious oppression was substantially revealed by a League inquiry. As such inquiries were opposed by other signatories to the Minority Treaties than the Czechoslovaks, and promoted by them alone, it is obvious that they alone did not fear inquiry or publicity.

The fact is that Masaryk the first President and Beneš his foreign secretary and (in December 1935) his successor as President, were profoundly convinced that a polyglot state of thirteen millions (of whom over five millions were aliens) must give substantial justice to its minorities. They spared no effort to do so. But the Czechs were not as wise as their leaders. The higher bureaucratic posts remained in the hands of Czech officials, and in education, social insurance, or police control or municipal and district government it was possible for dislike to be shown in a score of petty ways, none of them perhaps very serious, but all of them irritating and some of them humiliating.

For over five years the Sudeten Germans formed a working parliamentary group with Czechs and had their representatives in the Cabinet. But within some half-dozen years, the attitude of the Sudeten Germans had entirely changed. The more moderate of them did not indeed desire violence or active war, but in 1938 the majority at least appeared to look forward to eventual absorption into Germany, and only desired a temporary arrangement with the Czechoslovak state in order to achieve that end. The first and most evident cause of this change of attitude was economic. The great 'slump' in industry, during the year 1929, was felt severely in the world in general, and in Czechoslovakia in particular. It was most felt in the Sudeten areas, and even when better times began the Sudeten conditions did not much improve. Unemployment continued and the Sudeten population began to despair of permanent improvement. Moreover the land reform and agricultural policy of the Czech government in the last period before the crisis caused with some apparent justification discontent in the Sudetenland, where no similar remedial measures were inaugurated.

Far more powerful than the economic factor was the direct political appeal made by a revived German nationalism. Hitler was the leading spirit of a Germany which was alive, awake, powerful, strong, domineering, exultant. The German reoccupation of the Saar, of the Rhine valley, the annexation of Austria, all showed the strength of the new government. Above all, the power of propaganda, of mass-suggestion, was used. To direct German propaganda inside the limits of the Czechoslovak state was not the same thing as directing it in Germany. But such propaganda was so highly organised and so powerful, that it could be enormously effective even inside an alien state. Hitler's propaganda in South West Africa succeeded in converting practically all the German inhabitants to Nazi ideas within a very few years. In the Sudeten area he did not succeed so well, for, to the last, some 10 or 15

per cent. of the Sudetens were not convinced by him. Yet in Czechoslovakia Germany had enormous advantages, contiguous territory,
possibility for the Sudeten Germans to visit Munich and Nuremberg,
to take part in the Nazi parades, and to see the Führer acknowledge the
salute of Sudeten battalions of devotees. The new Germany was displayed to the Sudetens on films, on the radio, in pictures and in leaflets.
By every form of ingenious suggestion,the racial unity of German blood
brethren was brought home to them.

What particularly stimulated Sudeten feeling was the parliamentary
situation in Czechoslovakia. The Sudeten party withdrew from the
Cabinet and from coalition with the Czechoslovak government in 1931.
Thereafter they sat in the parliament—a strong party, not far off fifty
members, but they were always in opposition and always out-voted
when it came to a division. They had publicity, they could protest, and
they made full use of their powers. At the same time, there was always
at hand the suggestion from Germany that their grievances would all
be solved by union with the Fatherland. These different motives,
economic, political, psychological, transformed the Sudeten Germans
in half a dozen years. In 1931 practically all of them sought a *modus
vivendi* with an alien government. In 1938 there was no division among
85 per cent. of the Sudetens; all wanted union with Germany. The only
difference was in the means. The moderates wanted to go slow and
achieve their end by negotiation, the extremists to go fast and to
achieve it by war.

Before we describe the crisis of May to October 1938, it is well to
say a word on the foreign policy of Czechoslovakia. Few diplomatists
in this period exceeded Dr. Beneš in moderation or in ability, but
the limitations on his power were great. He could only act within a
limited field. He was bound to rely upon France. In 1925 Great Britain
had signed at Locarno an agreement to defend and to guarantee the
Western frontier (*i.e.* France and Belgium) against Germany. She
refused to guarantee the Eastern frontier (that is Czechoslovakia)
against Germany, and remained consistent in that attitude right up to
1938. France had given Czechoslovakia assurances of military support.
She was one of three allied states which France had designed to form a
continuous barrier against Germany's eastward advance. These were,
reading from north to south, Poland, Czechoslovakia and Yugoslavia.
All had signed military alliances of mutual defence with France. Dr.
Beneš went further. By the treaties of August 14, 1920, and April 23,
1921, with Yugoslavia and Rumania, he created the 'Little Entente,'
and thus secured a double insurance of alliances. All went well until
1933, the year when Hitler really consolidated his power. But in that
fateful year Poland showed unmistakable signs of withdrawing from an
active alliance with France and of making advances to Germany. The
fact is that Poland considered herself a Great Power. She was not
going to be dragged in the wake of France, like a boat in the track of a

great ship. She freed herself, in effect, and became independent, pre-- pared to strike either a French or a German note exactly as suited her interests best. Poland's decision made a great gap in the continuous band of states which closed the eastern frontier of Germany. Her de- fection or isolation was a blow to France, but it was a still greater blow to Czechoslovakia.

As Germany grew in strength under Hitler, Czechoslovakia stood more and more evidently in her way. As a contiguous and polyglot state, efficient and prosperous, parliamentary and democratic, she re- presented everything a totalitarian state disliked. Behind the Czecho- slovak frontier was freedom not authority, liberty not order, variety not unity, many races and languages, not one blood and one speech. Indeed Czechoslovakia was a democratic bastion projecting into authoritarian territory; an island of French and Slav influence sur- rounded by a Germanic sea.

The first signs of real trouble came in May 1938, some two months after the Austrian annexation. From the end of April 1938 till the third week of May movements of German troops went on. The Czecho- slovak Government became convinced that Germany was gradually but imperceptibly, moving ten to twelve divisions towards her frontier, preparatory to a surprise attack after incidents between Sudeten Germans and Czechs, which of course could have been provoked at any time.[1] Dr. Beneš, with his usual prudence, refused to be alarmed, and declined to have a general mobilisation, which might have meant war. He decided on a partial mobilisation, and late on the evening of Friday, May 20, issued the orders to man the frontier, to mobilise one class of reservists and call up 84,000 special troops. Of 174,000 sum- moned, about 70,000 were at their posts by 3 A.M. on Saturday, and by noon the whole number, except eighteen defaulters,[2] had arrived and reported. Thus any chance of a surprise German attack across the frontier was entirely defeated. Yet, since the mobilisation was only partial, no serious complaint could be made. For a partial mobilisation actually interferes with a general one later, and shows a belief that war will not take place. The partial mobilisation proved most effective. By May 24 Germany was officially complaining of Czechoslovak action and protesting her own pacific intentions. It was one of the most bold and telling of the many diplomatic strokes achieved by Dr. Beneš before the outbreak of war.

The final period before the catastrophe was marked by an unprece- dented display of the Sokols at Prague. These gymnastic or athletic unions were voluntary associations, founded in 1862 to promote the

---

[1] v. Documents on British Foreign Policy 1919–39 (Ed. E. L. Woodward and R. Butler) 3rd Ser., Vol. I, pp. 328–9, and Documents on German Foreign Policy 1918–45, Series D, Vol. II, pp. 294–313 (Washington, 1949).

[2] Of these 3 were Czechs, 8 Sudeten Germans, 3 Slovaks and 4 Hungarians, and it is certain that some of them did not receive the orders owing to absence from home.

physical and moral well-being of the Czech people. Their numbers were reckoned only in thousands for some twenty years, but in the early twentieth century they rose to millions.[1] The Sokols began on village greens, and in small towns, finally invading large towns, provinces, all Bohemia, and all Slavonic lands. They were originally athletic in conception, but they also developed a moral, an emotional and a patriotic side of great importance. In Bohemia they remained voluntary unions, though immensely aiding the Czechoslovak national cause. The tenth grand national meeting (fourth since 1919) was celebrated at Prague in July 1938. For a week, thirty thousand athletes, boys, girls, men and women, gave marvellous displays of grace and precision to music before great crowds of spectators. The meeting ended in a grand march through the streets of Prague of one hundred thousand Sokols from all parts of Czechoslovakia, to demonstrate their loyalty to President Beneš. Slovaks outdid Czechs in the splendour of their national costumes, and showed that, despite surface differences, they were really united. Ominously notable as absentees, who refused to participate in any of these displays, were the Sudeten Germans.

In July the conflict in parliament and elsewhere between the Sudetens and the Czechoslovak Government came to a head. There were open threats of secession by the Sudetens, and ominous signs from Germany across the border. Beneš, as always, was ready to negotiate and, as usual, proved the most skilful of negotiators. Early in August Lord Runciman was finally despatched from England, as a 'purely personal mediator,' to see if some method of adjusting differences could be found. The solutions, which he proposed and which Dr. Beneš was ready to accept, might possibly have succeeded if they had been offered two or three years earlier. But it was too late, and the propaganda of frenzied nationalism prevented any possibility of acceptance. It is not even necessary to suppose that Germany was directly and, at the last moment, the cause of the rupture. She was responsible originally for launching the propaganda, and this responsibility is a heavy one.

The external aspect of the situation demands examination. France and the Soviet Union had each promised to defend one another, and had each promised to defend Czechoslovakia, against attack. But the Soviet Union's control over its army and the *moral* of that army were both doubtful at the time and difficulties of communications were great. Soviet military aid could not be easily obtainable. At the same time France was not in a position to render direct aid to Czechoslovakia. Italy was in sympathy with Germany and probably prepared to support her at need. She would certainly have refused to allow French troops to go through her territory. Such being the case, it is not evident that

[1] Professor Temperley was present in 1905 at a Sokol at Zagreb in Yugoslavia when the Czech delegate said he represented 60,000 of his countrymen. The number rose to over a million before the war and between three and four millions after it.

Franco-Soviet military aid could have saved Czechoslovakia. As the British Foreign Secretary said, 'there was nothing which France, or Russia, or we, or any others, could together have done which would have saved Czechoslovakia from being overrun.'[1]

England, of course, remained. But England was not pledged to defend Czechoslovakia though she was pledged to defend France. On the contrary, not only had she made this point clear in the Locarno Treaties, but Neville Chamberlain had stated on March 24, 1938, that he would not guarantee Czechoslovakia, though there *might* be circumstances in which England would intervene to defend her. The critics of British policy said that there would have been no war if, in July 1938 just as in 1914, England had said she would support Russia and France in case of war. In both cases this statement still remains a matter of opinion. If, as was widely believed at the time, Hitler was prepared to pay the price of war, England would have had to fight, and for this she had small inducement and still less opportunity. The events of the early years of the war were to prove that English preparedness for war was far less advanced than the public knew. Only Shakespeare has given coasts to Bohemia, and the British navy could give Czechoslovakia no direct aid. On September 11 Neville Chamberlain issued a statement to the press that 'in certain eventualities' England might lend direct armed assistance to France. This utterance was much misunderstood. It is clear that what he meant was, that England was bound to support France and defend her frontiers if attacked.

Events were developing rapidly. The first days of September had seen the great Nazi Congress at Nuremberg, where Hitler worked his audience up to great enthusiasm for the German race, ending the Congress with a speech full of menace on September 12. On the 7th Henlein, the leader of the Sudetens, suddenly broke off all negotiations with Lord Runciman and Dr. Beneš. On the night of the 11th (and perhaps earlier) desperate though obscure struggles broke out between Czech gendarmes and Sudeten rowdies near the frontier, and at several centres of Sudeten influence in Czechoslovakia. The Czechoslovak Government acted with vigour, proclaimed martial law and had the local situation well under control by the 14th. But the moral effect produced by these incidents was disastrous. Sudeten blood had been shed, and Germany clamoured for vengeance. At this moment Neville Chamberlain dramatically intervened and, on the 15th, flew to Berchtesgaden to interview Hitler. The German leader made it quite clear that 'there was nothing that anybody could do that would prevent that [the German] invasion [of Czechoslovakia] unless the right of self-determination were granted to the Sudeten-Germans and that quickly.'[2] Chamberlain returned to London to consult his colleagues and the French.

[1] Lord Halifax in a broadcast address to the United States, reported in *The Times*, October 27, 1938.
[2] Chamberlain, House of Commons, September 28, 1938.

Neither Britain nor France was in fact prepared for war. On September 19 the so-called Anglo-French plan was presented to the Czechoslovak Government; it was followed by a joint *démarche* on the 21st. Both of these demands were for the 'transfer' of Sudeten territory from Czechoslovakia to Germany, wherever the population was more than 50 per cent. German. These communications were followed up by the 'Godesberg Memorandum,' a demand by Hitler on September 23 for larger concessions still, which he emphasised publicly in a speech on the 26th. He indicated complete distrust of the Czechs, and thus induced Chamberlain to guarantee the 'transfer.' As a result of further negotiations on the 28th Chamberlain informed Hitler that 'you can get the essentials without war and without delay,' and made the proposal of a Four Power Conference at Munich. This was agreed to by Hitler that night as well as by Mussolini.

What finally happened was that on the night of September 29–30 an agreement was concluded at Munich by Italy, France, Great Britain and Germany, arranging for the immediate transfer to Germany of certain predominantly German districts in Czechoslovakia, and for plebiscites under international supervision to be taken in other districts, and for the frontiers to be finally settled by an International Commission. On October 3 Chamberlain contended in the Commons that the terms of this Munich agreement were much more favourable to Czechoslovakia than were those of Hitler's Godesberg Memorandum. Among other things, a joint guarantee against unprovoked aggression was given by France and Great Britain to the new Czechoslovak state at once. It was arranged further to settle the questions of Hungarian and Polish claims on Czechoslovakia in three months and, after that, Germany and Italy agreed to join in the guarantee. Also it was claimed that the total areas of cession had been reduced. In fact, as the matter worked out there was little difference between the territories demanded under the Godesberg Memorandum and those finally approved by the International Commission.

Czechoslovakia had no choice but to submit. She received what was in effect, a third ultimatum from Great Britain and France on September 29, and had to yield. German troops crossed the border on October 1. On the same day Poland announced that Czechoslovakia had ceded the Teschen area to her, which Polish troops occupied on October 2. The Hungarians at once made claims on parts of Slovakia, and on November 2 these were adjusted by Italo-German arbitration.

The responsibility of the Four Powers who signed the Munich Agreement cannot be assessed on the basis of our present knowledge. Neither England nor France, owing to strategical difficulties and lack of preparedness, could have done much. France had direct pledges to Czechoslovakia but it is easy to see why she did not enforce them. Some further points are worth noting in this connection. There seems no doubt that Poland received most serious warnings from the Soviet

Union as to the effect of her presenting an ultimatum to Czecho-slovakia demanding the cession of Teschen for at least a week before she acted. Poland entirely disregarded these threats, presented her ultimatum, and occupied Teschen by force of arms. If the Soviet Union did not act to prevent Poland from entering Czechoslovakia, it seems doubtful whether she would have acted to prevent Germany from doing so. Nevertheless the exclusion of the Soviet Union from the Munich Conference was a fact of major significance in the European situation. It was the symptom, and perhaps in some small measure the cause, of the divided front presented by the non-Axis powers. In the face of this divided front Germany scored a resounding success, a success so great that it appeared to create again the possibility of a German hegemony in Europe.

The danger was the greater because the success had been secured in spite of a strong public disapproval in Britain and France and in the United States. It was the greater also because few people believed that Germany would be content with her new frontiers. Burke said of the three powers which partitioned Poland in the eighteenth century: 'If they breakfasted off Poland, where will they dine?' Germany had breakfasted off Austria; she had refreshed herself again by taking the Sudetenland. It was soon to be seen that she did not feel that she had yet dined.

III. FROM MUNICH TO THE WAR OF 1939 [1]

The Munich Agreement postponed war in Europe for nearly a year, a crowded interval of armed and arming peace. At the beginning of this period the most striking fact in the European situation was the great strength of Germany. Her territories, swelled six months before by the inclusion of Austria, now took in the fringe of Czechoslovakia, and few doubted that she had a stranglehold on the remnants of the Czechoslovak state. She had new frontiers with her ally Italy and with Hungary and Yugoslavia. Italy was still a staunch friend, and Italian prestige had been increased by Mussolini's successful mediation in September. Russia was quiescent; Britain and France had recognised German claims.

The Munich settlement was accompanied by the joint declaration signed by Hitler and Chamberlain on the morning of September 30. They recognised the 'first importance' of Anglo-German relations, the desire of the two peoples never again to go to war with one another, and 'resolved that the method of consultation shall be the method adopted to deal with any other questions that may concern our two countries.' This declaration was immediately published. One thing was made clear: there was no thought of weakening the Anglo-French entente. For, on October 1 and 4, the British and French Prime Ministers exchanged

[1] Cp. L. B. Namier: *Diplomatic Prelude* 1938–1939 (Macmillan 1948).

messages stating this plainly. A fortnight later negotiations were opened for a Franco-German declaration, and on December 6 the German Minister for Foreign Affairs, von Ribbentrop, visited Paris and signed a joint declaration with the French Foreign Minister, Bonnet. It asserted the value of peaceful relations between the two countries, and recognised the fact that there were no territorial questions to separate them. In Bonnet's own words it was 'a contribution to general appeasement.' One comment on these declarations may be made at once. In his speech to the Reichstag on April 28, 1939, Hitler made it clear that, in his view, the 'agreement reached between Mr. Chamberlain and myself' did not apply to such problems as the future of the Czechoslovak state, but 'exclusively to questions which refer to the mutual relationship between England and Germany.' On July 13 von Ribbentrop, in a personal letter to the French Foreign Minister, spoke in even plainer language: the Franco-German declaration of December 6 meant that eastern Europe was not the concern of France. The logic of the Munich Agreement was thus, in German eyes, that Britain and France would no longer intervene in the affairs of central and eastern Europe. Very different was the interpretation in Britain. In his speeches following the crisis Chamberlain repeatedly laid stress on Hitler's statement that the gains from Czechoslovakia were his last demands in Europe; there remained, of course, the colonial question, but that, Hitler had also asserted, was no matter for mobilisation or war. In this difference of underlying assumptions one explanation is to be found of the ultimate failure of the policy of appeasement.

The colonial question had two aspects in the winter months of 1938–39. On the British side German proposals were expected but did not come, and on December 7 Mr. MacDonald, as Secretary of State for the Colonies, made a statement in the House of Commons to the effect that to hand over to any other country colonies or mandated territories was 'not now an issue in practical politics.'[1] He asserted, at the same time, the readiness of the Government to consider proposals 'for the more equal distribution of raw materials.' But, if the colonial question was unexpectedly quiet as between England and Germany, in another aspect it was a more vital disturbance. One result of the Czech crisis was undoubtedly the prominence in the public eye of two countries, Germany and Britain, and it is hardly an exaggeration to say of two men, Chamberlain and Hitler; and the relations of these two countries provide one of the main themes of the eleven months of peace. But, second only to Germany and Britain as a focus of attention, there was Italy. The Munich Agreement had brought new prestige to Italy—the British Prime Minister repeatedly paid tribute to Mussolini's mediation —but would prestige be enough? And as if in answer to such specula-

[1] It may be noted that M. Coulondre, the French Ambassador at Berlin, expressed the opinion on December 15 that the colonial question was not at the moment occupying Hitler's mind; v. Le Livre Jaune Francais (1939), No. 33.

tions the month of November 1938 saw the raising of the colonial question in Italy, with France, not Britain, as the objective. On the 30th there were spectacular, if disputed, cries in the Italian Chamber—'Tunis! Corsica! Jibuti!' Franco-Italian relations were strained throughout the winter months, although Daladier's 'No!' of January 26 was firm. Perhaps the importance of the issue has been exaggerated. The demands were put forward in the Italian press rather than by the Italian Government,[1] and it was to the Balkans and not to Africa that Italy was to turn. It is significant that in the very period of the agitation Britain decided to recognise fully the Italian Empire in Abyssinia, and to bring into force the Anglo-Italian Agreement of 1937 (November 1938). In January Mr. Chamberlain and Lord Halifax visited Rome—and —according to the joint statement issued on the 13th—held conversations which 'led to a frank and full exchange of views.' In Chamberlain's own view at least this visit 'definitely strengthened the chances of peace.'[2]

The Italian-French tension over the colonial question synchronised with a period of internal difficulty in France, for there, in contrast to Britain, the aftermath of the Munich Agreement was a time of open internal conflict. The occasion was the publication on November 13 of the French three-year financial plan, dealing not only with increased taxation and other financial measures but with hours of labour and the regulation of industry. Four days later the Conféderation-Général-du-Travail at a meeting at Nantes described the plan as a 'policy of aggression against the working class.' Strikes began on the 21st, and a stay-in strike at the Renault works was dispersed on the 24th by the use of tear gas. Other strikes followed. Distrust of the foreign policy of the Government combined with social grievances to produce the unrest; but no change came in the direction of foreign affairs. On November 23 Mr. Chamberlain and Lord Halifax were in Paris discussing Anglo-French collaboration; on December 6 M. Bonnet signed the Franco-German declaration with von Ribbentrop; on the 10th a vote of confidence in M. Daladier's Government was carried by 315 votes to 241, with 54 abstentions.

There was another aspect of the aftermath of the Munich Agreement, this time in Germany. The Jewish policy of the Third Reich had long aroused anxious interest outside its frontiers, and had gained new seriousness in the spring of 1938 with the annexation of Austria, where the principle of race-discrimination was immediately applied. Then the acquisition of the Sudetenland added to the tale of fugitives, and the new Czech state could no longer act as a place of refuge. Three events, following close upon one another, gave world prominence to the

[1] On December 17, 1938, an Italian note was communicated to the French Government, and it was published in the French press on March 30, 1939, together with the French reply. It did not, however, contain specific colonial claims.
[2] v. K. Feiling: The Life of Neville Chamberlain (1946), p. 393, and Woodward and Butler: Documents on British Foreign Policy 1919–1939, 3rd Ser., Vol. III, pp. 458–540.

problem in the months of October and November 1938. In October
the German Government decreed the repatriation of Polish Jews resident in Germany, and in large numbers they were conveyed to the
frontier. They lived there, pending a settlement, in conditions of great
hardship. On November 7 a young Polish Jew, named Grynsban,
whose parents were among these exiles, shot and fatally wounded vom
Rath, the Third Secretary of the German Embassy in Paris. A few days
later new orders were issued in Germany imposing heavy penalties on
the whole Jewish community; arrests took place on an unprecedented
scale, and unofficial incidents of brutality multiplied. Emigration was
the only road to safety, and the flood of refugees roused public sympathy in Europe and America. It was the first great blow to the hardly
won European confidence. The effect in Britain was particularly
striking. On November 21 the House of Commons adopted an Opposition motion deploring the treatment of minorities in Europe; on the
24th the Home Secretary, in a speech at Cambridge, referred to the
recent set-back to the policy of appeasement.

Nevertheless, in the eyes of Britain and France, the period October
1938 to March 1939 was characterised predominantly by the search for
the way of peace. For the next great landmark on the road to war we
must turn to the post-Munich settlement of the country most directly
affected, Czechoslovakia.

The system established in Czechoslovakia, after her losses of September, retained the forms both of unity and of independence. The
new President, Dr. Emil Hacha, elected on November 30, was the head
of a Central Government, of which M. Beran became Prime Minister.
There was still, in form, a Central Parliament, but on December 14 it
virtually voted its own extinction by adjourning, *sine die*, having
granted to the executive the powers to legislate by decree. Under the
direct rule of this Government were the Czech provinces of Bohemia
and Moravia, and under its indirect control the two autonomous provinces, Slovakia and Ruthenia. Difficulties followed between the Prague
Government and Berlin. In February it became known that only on
certain conditions would Germany carry out the promise in the Munich
Agreement to guarantee the new frontiers; she could not, for example,
guarantee any state which did not exclude Jews or which remained a
member of the League of Nations. At the same time difficulties multiplied between the Prague Government and that of the autonomous
Slovak provinces. Officially this tension was ended by an agreement on
March 6; but further demands followed. In the early days of March,
moreover, negotiations were taking place between Dr. Tiso, Prime
Minister of Slovakia, and the German Government, and, it seems clear,
between Germany and Hungary. On the 10th President Hacha acted
with decision; Dr. Tiso and other Slovak Ministers were dismissed, and
the next day a new Government was formed for Slovakia under M.
Sidor. On the 13th Hitler received Dr. Tiso in Berlin. On the 14th

Slovakia declared her independence, M. Sidor resigned, and Dr. Tiso was reinstated. On the 14th, too, M. Hacha was summoned to Berlin, and Hungary invaded Ruthenia. On the 15th Hitler accepted Dr. Tiso's request that Slovakia should be henceforth under German protection, and President Hacha under duress signed a document which virtually surrendered Czechoslovakia to Germany. When M. Hacha returned in the afternoon he was received by German troops, and on the 16th the Czech provinces were annexed as a protectorate to the Reich. On the same day Ruthenia was incorporated in Hungary. Alone among the constituent parts of the Czechoslovak state, Slovakia had so far retained her autonomy, and this was reinforced by a treaty with Germany on the 23rd by which Germany gained certain military control and predominant influence in foreign affairs. Even with German protection, however, Slovakia had to submit to frontier rectification with Hungary (March 23–31).

The effect of the destruction of Czechoslovakia on the international situation was immense. Notes were delivered in protest by France, Russia, the United States and Britain. On the 17th Chamberlain, in his speech at Birmingham, said that 'Public opinion in the world has received a sharper shock than has ever yet been administered to it, even by the present régime in Germany.' From this time indeed a new tone is observable in British official utterances. In his statement to Parliament, on the 23rd, the Prime Minister spoke openly of the domination of Europe as a possible aim of the German Government. Resistance to aggression succeeded appeasement as the keynote of British policy. At this time the President of the French Republic, accompanied by M. Bonnet, paid a visit to London, and it was announced that Britain had asked the French, Russian and Polish Governments to consider the possibility of a joint declaration defining their attitude to acts of aggression. On the 31st Chamberlain referred in the House of Commons to these consultations, adding that 'in the meantime before those consultations are concluded, I now have to inform the House that during that period, in the event of any action which clearly threatened Polish independence, and which the Polish Government accordingly considered it vital to resist with their national forces, His Majesty's Government would feel themselves bound at once to lend the Polish Government all support in their power.' He added that he was authorised to say that France stood in the same position in this matter as Britain.

The date of this interim pledge to Poland is significant. European opinion had hardly rallied from the shock of the Czech annexation when attention was turned to the Baltic. Lithuania was the first objective. On March 20 the Lithuanian Minister for Foreign Affairs was received by von Ribbentrop in Berlin, and on the 21st the Government decided to cede the Memel territory to Germany. The agreement, signed the next day, provided for a free port zone for Lithuania and that neither partner should use or 'support the use of force' against the other. On the same day there were anti-German demonstrations in Warsaw; on the 27th the German press started a campaign against Poland. As the result of the visit of the Polish Minister for Foreign Affairs, Colonel Beck, to London, a new statement confirming the previous pledge and making it reciprocal was made by Chamberlain to the House of Commons on April 6. A French *communiqué* of the 13th confirmed the Franco-Polish Alliance 'in the same spirit.'

The 'new epoch' in British policy—to quote Chamberlain's own phrase—was followed by other important diplomatic and political moves. At the beginning of April rumours of an Italian move in Albania were followed by an actual invasion on the 7th. King Zog fled the country, Scutari surrendered, and on the 12th a constituent assembly offered the Albanian crown to King Victor Emmanuel. The union was to be a personal one, and henceforth the King was described officially as King of Italy and Albania, and Emperor of Ethiopia. King Zog and the Queen had fled to Greece, and public sentiment was roused by the Queen's illness. Greece, it was feared in some quarters, might be the next objective, but Greek anxieties were allayed by Italian assurances on the 10th, and on the 13th Britain and France issued declarations extending to Greece (and to Rumania) assurances of 'all the support in their power.'

At this point another Great Power made a significant move. The President of the United States on April 15 made the first of his interventions in the European crisis. 'Three nations in Europe and one in Africa have seen their independent existence terminated'; and in the light of these 'recent facts' President Roosevelt appealed to Hitler and Mussolini asking for assurances that their armed forces would not attack (for a suggested period of ten years) a long list of countries, great and small, extending from Finland to Iran. In the event of a favourable reply, he was 'reasonably sure' that a similar assurance could be obtained from each of these twenty-nine or thirty states. The bait held out was the co-operation of the United States in the peaceful discussion of 'two essential problems'—the relief from the burden of armaments and the opening of avenues of international trade. Hitler's reply—in his Reichstag speech of April 28—gave little reason to suppose that the projected conference would follow.

Behind Hitler's speech of April 28 lay not only President Roosevelt's appeal—it was not until the end of the speech that this was answered—but a number of European events. In the six weeks since the Czechoslovak coup Britain and France had opened conversations with Russia, Greece, Rumania, Poland and Turkey. In the Balkans Bulgaria was receiving (and rejecting) overtures to join the Balkan entente.[1] Germany

[1] The Bulgarian Prime Minister stated (April 20) that access to the Ægean must be granted first. It is worth noting that, according to the French Minister at Sofia (December 16, 1938), the Prime Minister was then of the opinion that Poland rather

herself had approached many of the smaller states on President Roosevelt's list, asking whether they felt themselves menaced by her, and had received, naturally, diverse but discreet and suitable replies. And immediately before the speech Chamberlain's Government had made a startling decision, bringing their policy far closer to the lines advocated by those of their critics (particularly Mr. Winston Churchill) most disliked in Germany. On April 27 the House of Commons learned that Britain was to have conscription. The decision, running counter to repeated parliamentary assurances, was based openly on the need for meeting the 'new liabilities' which Britain was accepting in Europe, and aimed avowedly at carrying conviction that the new pledges would be taken literally. It was a domestic decision of great international importance, for it brought home in a way which no speeches or figures could do Britain's determination to 'fill the gaps in her defences.' The adoption of conscription (however limited)[1] was the counterpart to the notification by Germany (April 28) that she no longer accepted as binding the Anglo-German Naval Agreement of 1935.[2] The reason assigned for the denunciation in the German note was that the 'political decisions' of the past few weeks had destroyed the basis of the Agreement—*i.e.* that war between the two countries was 'excluded for all time.' The 'new epoch' of British foreign policy of which Chamberlain had spoken on April 3 was thus interpreted as a challenge to Germany.[3]

The growing breach between Britain and Germany was made far more serious because of the simultaneous development of Polish-German tension. Conversations between these two states had been taking place ever since the last weeks of 1938. On one point, the position of the Polish Jews expelled from Germany in the autumn, a measure of agreement had been reached; for it was announced on January 24 that the two countries had agreed to suspend expulsion on either side of the frontier, and to examine together the plight of those who had been living precariously on the borders. At this stage, too, a general *détente* seems to have been reached in Polish-German relations, for in a speech to the Reichstag on January 30 Hitler once more referred to the friendship between Germany and Poland as 'one of the reassuring factors in the political life of Europe.' But the improvement did not last long. There were recurrent press campaigns in Germany, rising at the end of March to complaints that the treatment of the German minority in Poland amounted to 'intolerable terror.' The position of Slovakia raised new difficulties between the two countries, while the old

---

than south-east Europe would be the next German objective. He appears to have foreseen the Russo-German *rapprochement* on this basis. *v. Le Livre Jaune Français* (1939), No. 34.

[1] The Military Training Bill passed both Houses of Parliament in May.

[2] *v. supra*, p. 509.

[3] The German White Book, *Dokumente zur Vorgeschichte des Krieges* (Berlin, 1939), insists that the 'new policy' was one of encirclement, and dates it from February instead of March.

problem of Danzig remained. Danzig, indeed, was in the forefront in Hitler's speech of April 28.

But, according to Hitler's statement, the 'decisive fact' in the Polish situation was the Anglo-Polish Declaration of April 6. He seized upon this, and in particular on the Polish obligation under it to come to the aid of England should she be attacked, as a breach of the German-Polish Treaty. This Treaty, concluded on January 26, 1934, for ten years, provided that the method of direct negotiation should be followed in all disputes between the signatories, and that in no circumstances would either party use force for the solution of difficulties. The day of the Reichstag speech and of the denunciation of the Anglo-German Naval Agreement was also the date of the repudiation of the German-Polish pact. Germany was freed at one moment from two long-standing engagements by the simple method of one-sided repudiation. The Polish reply (May 5) denied the alleged inconsistency between the pact of 1934 and the new Anglo-Polish engagement, cited the proposals made to Germany on March 26—to which no official reply had yet been made—and expressed readiness to enter into new negotiations if the 'fundamental observations' in the present memorandum were recognised.[1]

Much depended on the events of the next few weeks. The Reichstag speech of April 28 and the notes to Britain and Poland had brought about a new phase in the international situation. One important point was that the German-Polish question, hitherto a matter of private negotiation, had become of public concern to all Europe. The French Ambassador at Berlin reported early in May that various offers had been made by Germany to Poland in the past months, such as the partition of the Russian Ukraine; that it was to the credit of Polish statesmen that they had realised that what was really at stake was the independence of their country, for Germany was seeking to bind her to complete dependence on Berlin; and that, perhaps, having failed to draw Poland into a combination against Russia, Germany might seek to reverse the parts and rouse Moscow against Warsaw.[2] The retirement of the Russian Foreign Commissar, M. Litvinov, at the beginning of May was thought in many quarters to make such a reversal of Russian policy more likely. It was the more significant that this change in the direction of Russian foreign affairs came in the middle of the conversations opened by Britain and France with Russia in March, and that these negotiations were clearly proceeding with great slowness. Russia had two suitors during this critical period; to which would she listen?[3]

---

[1] The texts both of the German note and the Polish reply are given in the British Blue Book, *Documents concerning German-Polish Relations and the Outbreak of Hostilities between Great Britain and Germany on September 3, 1939* (Cmd. 6106), Nos. 14 and 16.

[2] v. *Le Livre Jaune Français* (1939), No. 124.

[3] For a detailed study of the foreign policy of the Soviet Union v. Max Beloff: *The Foreign Policy of Soviet Russia, 1929–1941*, 2 Vols. (O.U.P., 1947–9.)

The Russian decision in favour of Germany,[1] the 'bomb-shell,' as Chamberlain called it, of August 21, marks a new break in European relationships and a new phase in the development of German policy. The destruction of Czechoslovakia in March had been a moral shock to Europe, not only because it proved the falsity of assurances that the Sudetenland was the last demand in Europe, but because it gave the lie also to Hitler's claim that his object was simply the 'recovery' of German populations for the Reich. If in October 1938 three million Sudeten Germans were 'freed,' in March 1939 eight million Czechs paid the price in enslavement. Here indeed was naked aggression, deprived of any disguise. In so far as the old object persisted it took, henceforth, a new and startling form, for it reappeared as the policy of wholesale exodus. In July an Italo-German agreement provided for the removal of Germans from the South Tyrol; later, on October 6, the application of a similar policy to the Baltic area was announced. But these lingering remnants of the old policy could not disguise the facts. For the doctrine of 'self-determination' for Germans outside the Reich was substituted the insistence on *Lebensraum* for the Reich itself—a claim for national self-fulfilment for which the plea on behalf of German minorities served only as a cloak. This claim knew no barriers of nationality; the German people must fulfil itself at whatever cost.[2] The Russo-German pact completed the transformation, and gave a new shock to Europe. For both countries it meant an abandonment of the ideological basis of policy, for which few people outside the circles of high politics were prepared. As recently as May, common ideologies had vied with solidarity of interests as the foundation of the Italo-German alliance[3]; and how could the new treaty be reconciled with the hatred of communism and of Russia which underlay the Anti-Comintern pact?[4] To the western democracies, at least, the logic of the situation was that German policy would henceforth be one purely of aggression.

As yet the position of Russia was an enigma. Negotiations for an Anglo-Franco-Russian treaty had been in progress since March, with the object of combined action to resist aggression. On May 31 the new Russian Foreign Commissar, M. Molotov, had sketched the terms on

---

[1] The Russo-German non-aggression treaty was finally signed in Moscow on August 23. It contained in addition a Secret Protocol defining German and Russian spheres of influence in the Baltic States, Poland and Bessarabia. *v. Nazi-Soviet Relations, 1939–1941*. Documents from the Archives of the German Foreign Office, (Washington 1948), pp. 76–78.

[2] Cp. Lord Halifax's statement of June 29, 1939, in his speech at Chatham House, British Blue Book (Cmd. 6106), No. 25: '. . . if *Lebensraum* is to be applied in that sense, we reject it and must resist its application.' The 'sense' to which he referred is 'action by one nation in suppression of the independent existence of her smaller and weaker neighbours.'

[3] A Treaty of Alliance was signed in Berlin on May 22, 1939. It provided for political and diplomatic support if vital interests were threatened, and for military support in the event of war.

[4] *v. supra*, p. 515.

which it might be successful. On June 12, Mr. William Strang, the head of the Central European Department at the British Foreign Office, set out on a special mission to Moscow. When the end came, in August, French and British military missions were in Leningrad holding conversations with the Russian General Staff. Even then, when a direct connection had proved impossible, an indirect link, it seemed, might still be found through Turkey. In May a joint Anglo-Turkish declaration provided for co-operation in the event of a war in the Mediterranean arising from an act of aggression, and a similar understanding was reached in June between Turkey and France.[1] The definitive treaty was delayed until after the outbreak of war (October 19), and throughout this period Turkey was in close contact with Russia. The Anglo-Turkish declaration of May 12 was preceded by a Russo-Turkish *communiqué* on the 7th; in September the Turkish Foreign Minister, M. Sarajoglu, set out for Moscow to undertake long negotiations which failed to secure a treaty. Yet, when the Anglo-Franco-Turkish Treaty was signed on October 19, a separate protocol safeguarded Russo-Turkish relations. The position is indicative of the peculiar relation of Russia to the war between the Western Powers and Germany.

One of the main difficulties in the way of a successful issue of the Anglo-Franco-Russian negotiations was the problem of the Baltic States.[2] The inclusion of these smaller neighbours of Russia in any system of guarantee or pact for joint action against aggression was constantly pressed by M. Molotov. His speech of May 31 made this point clear, and referred also, perhaps ominously, to circumstances in which these neighbouring states might find the defence of their own neutrality against aggression impossible. One of them, Lithuania, had already concluded a pact with Germany on March 22, when Memel was ceded, and was finally, after the outbreak of war, to make her own terms with Russia in the treaty of October 10, by which she secured her ancient capital of Vilna, formerly included in the boundaries of Poland. The others, Finland, Esthonia, and Latvia, as Chamberlain revealed to the House of Commons on June 7, had made 'several communications' to Britain, stating that they wanted to maintain strict neutrality and they did not want to be included in the proposed guarantee. Finland was, moreover, at this time in the midst of negotiations, which she had opened in January 1939, for the re-fortification of the Aaland Islands. Proposals, supported by Sweden, had been approved by all the signatories of the Aaland Islands Convention of 1921; but Russia, who was also approached, had not agreed, and separate negotiations were in progress on this subject. It should be noted, moreover, that early in

---

[1] The Franco-Turkish declaration was postponed pending the settlement of the question of Hatay (Sanjak of Alexandretta). On June 23 the conditions for the cession of this region to Turkey were agreed.

[1] *v. supra*, pp. 442–4.

June the other two states, Latvia and Esthonia, signed non-aggression pacts with Berlin.

Whatever the explanation, however, for the failure of the efforts of the Western Powers to secure a treaty with Russia, the fact remains that that failure was a substantial contribution to the worsening of the diplomatic situation in Europe on the eve of the Polish-German crisis.

The final stage in the Polish question may be dated from the beginning of August. Ostensibly it was the future of Danzig which was at stake. In this ancient Free City, where a German population had long depended for its livelihood on the Polish hinterland,[1] the post-war settlement had been to a large extent already nullified in the past few years by the steady decline in the power of the Commissioner of the League of Nations, and the assumption of control in the city by the German residents who proclaimed their adherence to the Nazi party. Between the Danzig Senate and the Government of Poland there were difficulties over the position and number of the Polish customs officers, and a vigorous exchange of notes had taken place throughout the summer. The simultaneous demand in Germany for the cession of Danzig to the Reich and for a settlement of German claims to the Corridor (Pomorze province), together with the general deterioration in the European situation, converted this issue into one of first-class international importance.

German-Polish tension grew steadily in the month of August, and the German press rose in a crescendo of violence over the treatment of the German minority in Poland, varying this by attacks on Britain. The impression deepened in all countries that a German *coup* against Poland was imminent. Then on the 21st, while hopes in some quarters were still fixed on the conclusion of the Anglo-Franco-Russian negotiations, the announcement came of the Russo-German non-aggression pact, to be signed two days later when von Ribbentrop visited Moscow. Several last-moment efforts were made for peace. Chamberlain sent a personal letter to Hitler on the 22nd, and Daladier on the 26th; and if any doubt remained of the determination of Britain and France, it must have been removed by the publication of the Anglo-Polish Treaty of the 25th. President Roosevelt took a new initiative in an appeal to the King of Italy for mediation (23rd), and to Hitler and the Polish President (24th) to proceed by peaceful means. The King of the Belgians, in the name of the Oslo Powers, broadcast an appeal for peace (23rd), and combined with the Queen of the Netherlands to offer good offices (28th). Pope Pius XII followed an appeal for peace on the 24th by another a week later.

Events in the last few days of peace moved swiftly. But they could not move quickly enough for Hitler. On the evening of August 29 he agreed, though with hesitation, to a British request that he would re-open

[1] *v. supra*, p. 431.

negotiations with Poland. But the stipulation that a Polish plenipotentiary empowered to accept German terms as yet undefined should arrive on the next day was ominously reminiscent of Czechoslovakia. The Polish attempt on the 31st to negotiate by normal procedure through the Ambassador at Berlin failed to satisfy Germany, and the wireless announced on that evening the terms which in the same statement Poland was deemed to have refused. On the 31st, at mid-day, Mussolini made known to Britain and France his readiness to call a conference for September 3, provided their agreement were secured. The news was only a few hours old when, at dawn on September 1, Germany invaded Poland. Both Britain and France sent warning notes to Berlin on the 1st; the British reply to Mussolini stipulated that before the conference was held German troops should withdraw from Poland. The condition was unacceptable; the conference was not called. On September 3 first Britain and then France presented ultimata to Germany. By the evening of that day a state of war had been declared.

CHAPTER XXXV

EUROPE AT WAR, 1939–1945

THE German invasion of Poland brought to an end the long period of the prelude to war. For five and a half years from that date the history of Europe was dominated by the war, for every European country felt its effects, even those few which remained throughout the period, either neutral or, in the new terminology, non-belligerent.

At the present time, only a few years after the close of the war, it is impossible for a definitive history of the period to be written. Each country and, to some extent, every part of each country, looks at events from a different angle, and there is much historical research to be done before a convincing account can be written, free from the distortions which this involves. Moreover, the war was by no means purely a European war, and before it could be fairly claimed to be even mainly European the basis of the statement would have to be defined. War in Europe opened in September 1939. The war in Asia, with which it became inextricably mingled, opened more than two years later, and yet had been in a sense in existence already for nearly ten years. The history of the war in Europe cannot be regarded as isolated, except perhaps in its origins and results. The other continents, for different reasons, were essentially a part of it. The North American contribution was particularly great, because of the early entry of Canada into the European war, only seven days after Great Britain, and the decisive part played by the United States both before and after the declaration of war upon her by Germany and Italy on the 11th December, 1941.

Australia not only participated in the European war, but from her geographical position had a special place in relation to the Asiatic one. The importance of the continent of Africa was threefold. The decision of the Union of South Africa to declare war upon Germany brought South African forces, like those of Canada, Australia and New Zealand, into the forefront of the struggle. At the same time, the presence of Italian colonies in Somaliland and Tripoli, and the existence of Italian rule in Abyssinia, gave an inevitable importance to African territories. Lastly, the dominance of the Mediterranean in Allied strategy in the central phase of the war gave to North Africa a double significance as its southern shore. Many parts of the Asiatic continent were affected in somewhat similar fashion. The concentration of the war with Japan in Eastern and South-Eastern Asia and the islands of the Pacific brought grave consequences to the whole continent from India eastwards, and at the same time, those aspects of the war which were predominantly European and Mediterranean affected profoundly the region from Persia to the West. The fact that the Arab world stretches on both sides of the African-Asian frontier further increased the importance of the Mediterranean area.

The history of the war clearly, then, belongs only in part to the history of Europe, while, paradoxically, the whole history of Europe was dominated by the war. The effects of the five and a half years of war were catastrophic. They were catastrophic in material destruction to degrees which varied greatly among the belligerent powers. They were catastrophic in their influence on the European state system; for the war did not only, as previous wars had done, revolutionise the balance of power in Europe, it destroyed the possibility of any such balance, at least for many years. In political and economic strength the Soviet Union emerged without a rival on the continent of Europe. The position of Great Britain, still indubitably in the first rank of powers, seemed more than ever dependent upon her association with other parts of the English-speaking world. France, when the war in Europe ended, had a long way to go before she could recover from the effects of occupation. Germany as a single political entity no longer existed, and Italy—never quite a power of the first order, though very nearly so—had had a setback which could clearly be expected to last for several generations. Among the powers of admittedly second rank in the inter-war period, Poland had undergone changes which were revolutionary in character, and Spain, although a non-belligerent, had had too much of her strength sapped by Civil War in the 'thirties to be able to profit from this, her obvious opportunity. The very idea of balance, which persisted in spite of all attempts to find a substitute in the period between the two wars, was dead, and as yet no certain alternative has been found. The one fact that appears incontrovertible is that Europe can no longer stand alone. In the post-war organisation, as in the war itself, we seem to be at the end of an era, or at the beginning of a new era in which the history and the problems of Europe are alike part of the history of other continents.

The history of Europe in the war years is partly, but not wholly, the history of a long struggle among European nations, fought out by military, naval and aerial warfare, and by diplomatic and economic contest. It is also the history of the differing experiences and developments of European states, leading to a series of revolutionary changes in political and economic organisation, which have transformed the Europe of the pre-war period into that of to-day. The new era which is now beginning will have its roots in the remoter past, as all new eras must, but it will be affected to a very large degree by the internal changes which took place during the war itself. It was not only in Britain that war was accompanied by social change. Similar or dissimilar processes took place everywhere else, both in Eastern and Western Europe. It is above all the full story of these changes that remains to be told when succeeding generations have examined the records of the period. It is above all this story, of which it is possible at present only to see a broad outline, which future generations will have to construct.

The first phase of the war began with the invasion of Poland, and ended with the fall of France. It began without declaration or formality, with the attack by the German Air Force on the 1st of September on Polish military targets, airfields, military bases, training centres and railway junctions, and with the march of the German Army at dawn on the same day. The declaration of war by Britain and France two days later did not save Poland. Shock tactics, a combination of mechanised forces and aircraft, the paralysing of the Polish air defences before the beginning of the war was known, all combined to force a Polish retreat. By the 7th of September the Silesian industrial basin had been completely overrun, the Polish line of resistance had been broken, and German columns were approaching Warsaw. On the 10th the Polish Supreme Command ordered a general retreat to the south-east, leaving behind the isolated garrison of Warsaw. At dawn on the 17th, in accordance with a secret protocol of the 23rd of August, Russian troops crossed the eastern frontier of Poland and took up positions already agreed with Germany. The remaining four Polish forces were trapped, and compelled to surrender either to the Russians or to the Germans. The heroic resistance of Warsaw continued until the 28th of September, and the moving appeal made by the Mayor of Warsaw to the countries of the West will live long in western memories. In Moscow, on the same day as the fall of Warsaw, a German-Russian pact was signed, the 'German-Soviet Boundary and Friendship Treaty,' which defined in detail the limits of the respective occupations of Polish territory. In a joint declaration, issued on that date, the two Governments claimed that they had 'definitively settled the problems arising from the collapse of the Polish state and have thereby created a sure foundation for a lasting peace in Eastern Europe.' For the fourth time in little more than a century and a half Poland had been partitioned among her powerful neighbours.

The fate of Poland in 1939, as on these earlier occasions in the late eighteenth century, was only indirectly affected by the events which were taking place in the West. Of these events a few only need to be mentioned. On the very day of the invasion of Poland, Germany's ally Italy announced that she would not take the initiative in military operations, and on the same day Hitler stated to the Reichstag that 'for the carrying on of this struggle we do not intend to appeal for foreign help.' Declarations of neutrality were issued by other powers. Even Russia, in the act of crossing the Polish frontier, professed her neutrality in the Polish-German war. In the West, Britain and France were in a state of war with Germany, and the first steps were being taken to convert a war of words into a war of material action. The French army was mobilised, and took up defensive positions along the north and east frontiers of France. A British Expeditionary Force began to move. On the 4th of September advance parties of the British Army landed, and by the 11th of October the British Secretary of State for War claimed that 158,000 men and 25,000 vehicles had been transported to France without loss. By mid-October two British Army Corps under the command of Sir John Dill and General A. F. Brooke, had taken up the positions assigned to them on the Franco-Belgian frontier east of Lille. The British Commander-in-Chief was General Viscount Gort, who, in contrast to the arrangements made in 1914, was definitely under the orders of General Gamelin, the French Supreme Commander.

The military situation in this period is of the greatest importance in view of the events which followed. The French frontier with Germany was strongly defended by the fortified Maginot Line, which 'represented the highest development of scientific defence that Europe had seen.' The Maginot Line, however, did not extend along the Franco-Belgian frontier, which was fortified only by a barbed wire belt, an anti-tank ditch, and a series of pillboxes. Furthermore, facing the Maginot Line the Germans had built the Siegfried Line or Western Wall, a zone of field fortifications similar to the Maginot Line itself. The existence of these fortified lines of defence rendered unlikely any rapid military movement on Germany's Western Front. Moreover, the concentration of German troops in Poland added to the unlikelihood of a German attack against France. At the same time, French military preparedness was not far enough advanced to make possible a major attack on the Siegfried positions. Thus, while Poland was being overrun, patrol activity was the main characteristic of the war in the West.

One other feature of this period must be mentioned. In October and November two *démarches* were made for peace—the first jointly by Hitler and Molotov on the 6th of October, in accordance with the joint Russo-German declaration after the fall of Poland, the second on the 7th of November jointly by King Leopold of the Belgians and Queen Wilhelmina of the Netherlands, in an appeal for peace to the belligerents on both sides. The second of these two movements is of special interest because it heralded the next stage in the development of the war.

Before that took place, however, further changes had been enacted in the East. The Russian occupation of the eastern part of Poland had been one stage in the consolidating process by which Russia was seeking to strengthen her position on the Baltic. On the 29th of September Esthonia signed a pact of mutual assistance with Russia, giving the latter naval and air bases. Early in October Latvia and Lithuania admitted Russian garrisons; and then Russia presented her demands to Finland. She asked for the northern half of the Karelian Isthmus, between Lake Ladoga and the Gulf of Finland, for the cession of several islands in the Gulf, for a lease of the Rybachi peninsula in the far North, together with Petsamo, Finland's only ice-free port in the Arctic, and for the lease of the Baltic port of Hangö as a Russian naval and air base. These were the demands which Finland refused, and which caused the breakdown of negotiations halfway through November. By the end of the month Russia had denounced her non-aggression pact with Finland, and Russian troops had attacked at several points along the frontier. Her air force bombed the capital, Helsinki, and other towns. The first weeks of fighting brought very little success to the Russians, except in the Petsamo sector, for the Finnish defences across the Karelian Isthmus were particularly strong. It was not until February 1940 that the Russians were able to attack in force, or until March that Finland was compelled to accept the Russian terms.

The transformation of the war in the West from its first and comparatively static stage to its second, which, from an Allied point of view, was not only dynamic but disastrous, dates from April 1940. Already before this time, however, German preparations had been in progress for the first substantial move. Germany was of necessity vitally interested in the situation in Scandinavia. It was from Sweden that she obtained supplies of iron ore, and, during the months when the Baltic was closed to shipping, these supplies were brought from the Norwegian port of Narvik by sea down the whole length of the Norwegian coast. It was natural in these circumstances that discussions should take place, both in Germany and in Britain, as to the position of the Scandinavian countries. The obvious importance of these countries from the point of view of the Russian struggle with Finland was an added reason.

The German plans for the occupation of Norway culminated on the night of the 8th/9th April. At almost precisely the same time a British and French naval force was laying mines in Norwegian territorial waters, through which the German vessels passed laden with iron ore, and plans were also ready early in April for an Anglo-French landing at Narvik.

The German initiative was successful. Early on the 9th of April German troops invaded and occupied Denmark, almost without opposition, and very early on the same day German landings were made at points along the whole length of the Norwegian coast, and attacks from the air were made at Narvik, Trondhjem, Bergen, Stavanger, Oslo and Kristiansund. After the war had begun the German Minister in Oslo presented his Government's demands to the Norwegian Foreign Minister. The demands were virtually for the control of the whole country, and, by the time they were rejected in the evening of the same day, German penetration made effective resistance impossible except in the far north.

Britain and France immediately promised assistance to Norway, but it was not until the 15th of April that a small British force was landed near Narvik, and not until the 16th that a combined British and French force landed at Namsos. The landing at Namsos and the subsequent landing at Aandalsnes had as the main object the capture of Trondhjem, but the main attack had to be abandoned for lack of air support, and on the 27th of April a decision was reached to withdraw the expeditions from central Norway. Operations round Narvik were continued by a joint force of British, French, Polish and Norwegian troops, which succeeded in capturing the town on the 28th of May. But by that date other events were happening in western Europe which made this limited success unfruitful. On the 8th of June 24,000 Allied troops and large quantities of stores and equipment were withdrawn from Norway, and King Haakon and his Government escaped to continue the struggle against Germany from Britain.

The dominance of the Western Front began on the 10th of May, for this was the date when Germany took the initiative by the invasion of the Low Countries and France. Reports of German troop movements on the Dutch and Belgian frontiers had been current repeatedly in April, and defence measures had been taken by both the Dutch and Belgian Governments, although both were maintaining an attitude of strict neutrality. Both countries had refused to take measures in concert with the Western Allies to meet a possible German attack. At the same time, the Supreme War Council meeting in Paris on the 23rd of April decided that, if Germany should invade Holland, the Allied Armies of Britain and France should immediately advance into Belgium without further consultation with the Belgian Government.

This was the preparation, such as it was, to meet the great German offensive. Shortly before dawn on the 10th of May, an attack, not preceded by any declaration of war, was levelled at Holland, Belgium and Luxemburg simultaneously. Luxemburg, who, like her two greater neighbours, declared her intention to resist, was not unnaturally the first to be overrun. Holland was not able to hold out much longer. On the 12th the Germans crossed the River Ijssel at Arnhem, and penetrated the main defensive line. On the following day an armoured column crossed the Maas and pressed on towards Rotterdam. Dutch towns were subjected to heavy and indiscriminate bombing, and on the 14th the memorable attack took place on Rotterdam, when a large part of the city was systematically demolished. It was after these disasters that the Dutch were driven to capitulation on the 15th of May, and Queen Wilhelmina and the Dutch Government were taken to England in a British destroyer.

The attack on Belgium and France developed simultaneously. British and French armies had advanced into Belgium according to plan and had taken up positions along a front extending from Antwerp through Louvain and Namur to Givet on the Franco-Belgian frontier. The Allied line was broken on the 14th of May, when strong German armoured forces under von Rundstedt broke through between Namur and Sedan, crossed the Meuse, and struck west towards Amiens and south to Rheims. Amiens was entered on the 19th of May, Abbeville on the 20th. On the 23rd Boulogne and Calais were attacked. The rapidity of the German advance left the Allies in a critical position. On the 20th of May the British Cabinet instructed Lord Gort to force his way south-west to avoid being cut off, and to join with the French in the south; but an attempt to carry out these instructions failed. The British, French and Belgian forces which had originally held the Givet line were completely cut off, and confined within a triangle with little possibility of advance.

The controversy as to the actions of the respective powers in this critical position has not yet wholly been settled, and perhaps its main importance historically lies in the effect which the disagreements had on the later position of France. By the 25th of May Lord Gort had been convinced that the extrication of his forces by sea was the only possible solution. At midnight on the 27th/28th the Belgian Army capitulated. On the 27th the famous evacuation began at Dunkirk, and in all 338,000 British and Allied troops were evacuated without their equipment. A British Expeditionary Force had been driven from France.

The defence of France was now under the control of General Weygand, who had succeeded General Gamelin as Supreme Commander of the Allied Armies on the 19th, and who had occupied the brief interval since that date in strengthening the French defences in the so-called Weygand Line on the North and North-east frontier of France. It was along this line that the Germans attacked on the 5th of June, and it was through this line that they broke on the 9th. The successful operation developed rapidly into a series of movements which threatened Paris. The French Government, since the 21st of March under the control of M. Paul Reynaud, now decided to evacuate Paris, and moved first to Tours and then to Bordeaux. Two days before this decision, on the 10th of June, Mussolini had turned his back upon the ways of peace, and declared war on Britain and France. Two days after it the Germans entered Paris.

France, torn by rival policies and threatened with complete destruction, made several desperate appeals in the last days before her collapse, appeals to President Roosevelt for American help, and appeals—the importance of which politically was very great—to Britain to send more air support. The British offer on the 16th of June that Britain and France should join together in 'indissoluble union' seemed no adequate reply to the plea for material aid. On the 15th, the same day as President Roosevelt's answer to the French appeal, France requested formal release from her obligation under the Franco-British Agreement, and received the reply that 'an inquiry by the French Government to ascertain the terms of an armistice for France' would be agreed to by Great Britain, '*provided, but only provided, that the French Fleet is sailed forthwith for British harbours pending negotiations.*' In its effect on Anglo-French relations the controversy over the French fleet was hardly even second in importance to the unsuccessful appeal for more air support. The new French Government (for Reynaud resigned on the 16th of June and was succeeded by Pétain) not only asked immediately for an armistice, but limited its assurances about the fleet to a promise that it 'would never be allowed to fall into German hands.' In the opinion of the British Cabinet, British security demanded that more positive action should be taken, and on the 3rd of July the French warships at Plymouth and Portsmouth were forcibly taken under British control. The French squadron was immobilised at Alexandria. Unsuccessful attempts were made to persuade the French Admiral in charge of the fleet at Oran, in French Morocco, either to continue the fight in conjunction with the British, or to sail to America to be demilitarised. When these attempts failed, the British Mediterranean Fleet bombarded the French ships and crippled a large number of them.

In the meantime, the French Government had accepted the German armistice terms, and on the 22nd of June, in the dramatic setting at Compiègne, in the very railway compartment in which the Germans had signed the armistice terms with the Allies in 1918, the French envoys signed the convention with Germany. An armistice convention with Italy was signed two days later.

By the terms of the convention with Germany, far removed from the 'honourable agreement between soldiers' which Pétain had hoped for, heavy humiliation was put upon France. The whole of France north and west of a line from Geneva to Tours and thence south to the Spanish frontier, was to be occupied by Germany. In this region, which included all the Channel and Atlantic ports, the Germans were to have all the rights of an occupying power, except local administration, and the cost of the occupation was to be borne by France. The French forces were to be disarmed and demobilised, except those necessary for maintaining public order. The French fleet, except a section left for safeguarding French colonial interests, was to be sailed to specified ports to be demilitarised and disarmed. Germany declared that she had no intention of using the fleet against England or of keeping it after the conclusion of peace. All German prisoners-of-war were to be released; all French prisoners-of-war were to remain in German hands.

The Italian terms were considerably milder. They provided for the demilitarisation of specified zones in Southern France, in Tunis, Algeria and French Somaliland, and provided that Italy was to have full rights over the port of Jibuti, and that the equipment of French forces on the Italian front was to be surrendered.

The independence left to unoccupied France was clearly only nominal. Such control as remained was vested in a French Government which transferred its capital to Vichy. Much of the French Colonial Empire, including Syria and North Africa, accepted the Vichy Government. General de Gaulle, who had held office under Reynaud, crossed to England and enrolled a French Volunteer Force to co-operate with the British in the continuation of the war. Some of the crews of the French warships in British ports and Alexandria volunteered to serve under him. The remainder were repatriated to France, together with a major part of those French troops who had been evacuated from Dunkirk, of whom only a small proportion wished to continue to fight after the French armistice. Thus there came into existence the dual system, which was to last until the end of the war, of two French Governments, one in France and one in exile, the Government of Vichy and the Government of the 'Free French.'

A year passed between the fall of France and the German attack on Russia. Among the events of this period, first in point of time, as well as in the memory of people in this country, was the offensive against Great Britain. Second came the attack, first by Italy and then by Germany, on the Balkans. Thirdly, there were important developments in the war in the Middle East.

There was widespread expectation, particularly in France herself, that the Franco-German armistice would be followed by the defeat of Britain, and indeed few impartial observers would have dared to prophesy a different result. Even at sea, where Britain's strength was traditionally great, the history of the first nine months of war had not been reassuring. There had been few spectacular incidents, for the German attack had been directed at British mercantile shipping, and the closing of trade routes essential for the import of food and raw materials. Counter-attacks on the same lines could not achieve so much, for Germany was far more nearly self-supporting than Britain, although some shortages such as oil, rubber and nitrates could be increased. Towards the end of 1939 Germany gained a new advantage in the struggle through the use of the first of her 'secret weapons.' Magnetic mines, dropped from the air, in the approaches to British harbours constituted a serious danger until the introduction of the degaussing cable neutralised in some measure their effects.

The first major success of the Royal Navy came in December 1939 with the attack on the *Graf von Spee*, one of the two German pocket battleships (the other was the *Deutschland*) sent into the Atlantic to raid merchant shipping. The *Graf von Spee* was driven into the harbour of Montevideo where she was scuttled by her crew. A second episode a few weeks later was the dramatic rescue of British prisoners from the German ship *Altmark* in Norwegian waters on the 16th of February 1940. But against such incidents must be set the greatly increased menace from Germany which resulted from the conquest of Norway. British forces managed to forestall the Germans in Iceland and the Faroe Islands, an important fact for the future conduct of the war; but the failure in Norway and the radical change in the naval balance which came from the collapse of France and the Low Countries made the British position at sea a critical one in the summer of 1940.

In the face of these grave dangers a new Government was formed in Britain. On the 10th of May Neville Chamberlain resigned and was succeeded by a new Coalition Government under Mr. Winston Churchill. It was this Government which ignored Hitler's offer of peace made on the 19th of July, and, more important than this, it was this Government which dared to proclaim that Britain would continue to fight even if she had to fight alone. The acute phase of the campaign to break British resistance did not start until the 8th of August, although large scale air attacks on British targets had been taking place for the preceding month. The first part of what has become famous as the Battle of Britain was marked by German attacks on convoys and coastal towns in the south-east. Then came concentrated attacks, mainly against air fields and aircraft factories; finally, there was the third stage of the struggle, which opened on the 7th of September with heavy daylight attacks on the London area. The Battle of Britain continued until the end of October, although very early in that month the Germans discontinued their daylight attacks by bombers, and resorted to the use of fighter-bombers escorted by fighters and flying at great height. The whole German plan was dependent for its success on the rout of the British fighter force, but, for the first time since the war began, the Germans were consistently held and frequently beaten. The numbers of German aircraft lost during this battle were much exaggerated at the time, but the official figures given since the end of the war are effective enough: 1,733 German planes were destroyed.

The failure of the German attempt to beat Britain to surrender remains, even when viewed in the comparatively cold light of ten years later, one of the major reasons for the ultimate German defeat. Germany was prevented by her failure from transforming her attacks by air into a full-scale invasion. For the first time Hitler's timetable had been upset. The fall of Britain should have preceded the development of

18

German attacks elsewhere. As it was, the other offensives had to take place with Britain still undefeated. In the meantime, however, the air warfare continued. Night bombing on a large scale was its outstanding characteristic, the attacks being directed first to London, which was heavily raided on 82 out of 85 consecutive nights, and to the chief provincial ports, Southampton, Plymouth, Portsmouth, Liverpool, Bristol and Hull. The 14th of November was memorable for the attack on Coventry, which made 'coventrate' a word in common usage, at least for a time. In this attack, as in those that followed on Birmingham, Manchester, Sheffield, and on the towns of Tyneside and Clydeside, it appeared that the Germans were deliberately destroying the civilian population rather than attacking specific military and industrial objectives. Civilian air raid casualties during the five months from August to December 1940, totalled 22,744 killed, and many more were injured. The German Air Force suffered severely in the struggle, while the British losses, serious though they were proportionately, were comparatively small.

The British offensive in the air started in the same period. Synthetic oil plants in Western Germany, industrial installations in the Ruhr, ports and dockyards were the first objectives. On the night of the 25th of August Berlin received its first bomb attack, and, in the same month, the war was carried to the territory of Germany's ally, Italy, by attacks on Turin and Milan.

Before the Battle of Britain was over a new move was made in Europe by the Axis powers. This time the initiative belonged to Italy. On the 28th of October Italian forces attacked Greece from Albania. The Italian attack failed, and within three weeks the Italian forces had been driven out of Greek territory. By the end of 1940 the tables had been turned upon the invaders and the Greeks had advanced thirty miles into Albania.

Mussolini's decision to attack Greece appears to have been taken independently of Germany, and at first Hitler made no attempt to assist him. Nevertheless, plans for the German political and economic control of the Balkans were already prepared, and the failure of the Italian campaign in Greece was both the cloak for German designs and a prelude to German advance. This advance was indeed important from three points of view. It would bring the countries of the Balkans politically and economically within the German orbit; it would be an additional blow to Britain; and it would be of great value as a preparation for the attack on Russia, for which preliminary plans were issued in December 1940.

In this month of December the massing of German troops in Hungary and Rumania began, although it was not until the following spring that the full scope of Axis plans in the Balkans was revealed. Then, after considerable pressure, Bulgaria joined the Axis powers, and was occupied by German troops. Yugoslavia, however, resisted similar pressure, and her pro-German Government was dramatically overthrown. On the 6th of April 1941, Germany declared war on Yugoslavia, and won victory after a campaign lasting eleven days. On the 6th of April also, German forces entered Greece, forcing the Greeks to withdraw from Western Thrace, and overwhelming them by vast superiority in numbers. British help, promised immediately upon the first Italian attack, was sent early in the German campaign, but was insufficient to save the Greeks. The Germans soon broke through the Monastir Gap, the most important gateway from the north, and at the same time they advanced along the line of the Vardar to the capture of Salonica. Greek, British and Dominion forces withdrew to the Olympus line, but found it impossible to hold it. An attempt to stabilise resistance along a shorter line from Thermopylae to the Gulf of Corinth failed, and, after a magnificent last stand at Thermopylae, in which New Zealand and Australian troops shared the credit with the Greeks, the Greek Army capitulated on the 21st of April. The rest of the country was rapidly overrun by the Germans, who entered Athens on the 27th. Then the defeated Italians swarmed into Greece over the Albanian frontier, and the Bulgarians accepted the German invitation to occupy Macedonia and Thrace. Of the 53,000 British and Dominion troops landed in Greece over 40,000 were safely evacuated, although most of their equipment was lost. On the 20th of May the last phase in the struggle for the Balkans came with the German attack on Crete, and, after eleven days of very heavy fighting, in which British and Dominion forces suffered heavy losses in men and material, Crete fell.

The result of the war in the Balkans was thus to all appearances that Germany and Italy had complete control of the Eastern Mediterranean. This, however, was never wholly true. Turkey maintained her neutrality, and in Syria and the Middle East Britain continued to gain some success. A pro-Axis *coup* in Iraq, supported by German and Italian aircraft, was successfully overcome, and, in July 1941, the British occupation of Syria and the Lebanon, formerly under the control of the Vichy Government of France, strengthened the position of Britain.

The story of the war in the Mediterranean, the Middle East and in East Africa forms one of the most spectacular aspects of the struggle of this period. The fall of France and the entry of Italy into the war left Britain with comparatively few material resources available for the protection of her Mediterranean communications. The first result of this situation was the new importance given to Malta. Almost immediately after the entry of Italy into the war Italian air attacks on Malta began and continued without intermission until the Axis powers were defeated in North Africa. The damage to harbours and dock installations made it impossible for the Royal Navy to operate from the island, and at times it seemed as if it might even have to be abandoned because of the impossibility of maintaining its defence.

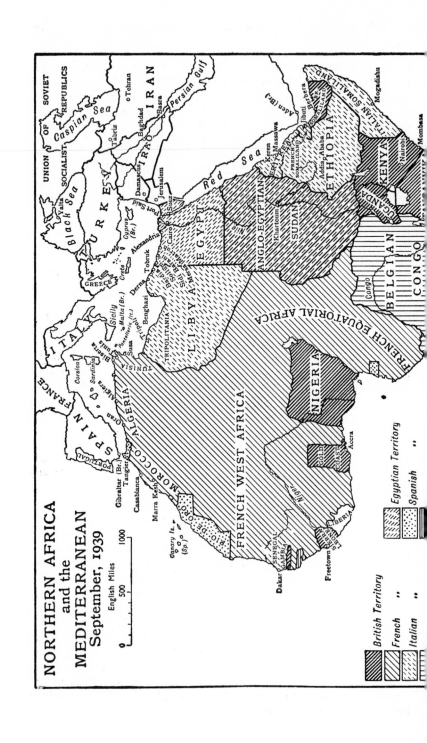

NORTHERN AFRICA
and the
MEDITERRANEAN
September, 1939

English Miles
0   500   1000

British Territory
French   "
Italian   "

Egyptian Territory
Spanish   "

In Africa itself, however, even during this difficult period of the war, British troops met with some success, in spite of the fact that reinforcements for Egypt had to be sent by the Cape route. The Italian attack on Egypt opened in September 1940, with the crossing of the frontier and an advance as far as Sidi Barrani. A few weeks later, at the beginning of December, British troops attacked the Italians and drove them out of Egypt. Tobruk, the chief Italian naval base in Cyrenaica, was captured on the 22nd of January 1941. By March 1941, the Italians had been driven out of Cyrenaica, and British units had reached El Agheila. In the dark days of the winter of 1940–41 the success of the British forces under the command of General Wavell was one of the few encouraging features of the situation.

At the same time British forces under Sir Alan Cunningham were advancing into Italian territory in East Africa. In July 1940, the Italians had penetrated into Kenya and the Sudan, and had overrun British Somaliland, thus threatening Aden and the Red Sea. Six months later (in January 1941) the British counter-attacked, and, after four months' fighting, the Italian East African Empire was destroyed. The heights of Keren, dominating the Eritrean stronghold, were captured on the 25th of March, after a battle the fierceness of which still remains memorable. Addis Ababa fell on the 6th of April, and on the 5th of May, five years after Mussolini had proclaimed his Empire in Abyssinia, Haile Selassie re-entered his capital. The surrender of the Italian Viceroy, the Duke of Aosta, occurred a fortnight later. Finally, at the end of November, the remaining Italian forces surrendered unconditionally.

By this time the war in North Africa had taken an unfavourable turn for the Allies. German forces had come to the assistance of the Italians, and at almost the same time the British position had been substantially weakened by the decision in the spring of 1941 to send troops and material to the help of Greece. This decision to divert British troops from North Africa to Greece was one of the most difficult that Britain had to face at this period. The result of these factors was that, at the end of March 1941, the Axis powers had been able successfully to launch a full scale counter-offensive, driving the British back into Egypt. A garrison, mainly of Australian troops, was left behind to hold Tobruk. Twice during the latter part of 1941 British forces took the offensive again, but with only limited success, and by the following June, when the Axis armies under Rommel again launched a counter-offensive, the British and Dominion armies had been weakened by the demands of the new theatre of war which had by then appeared in the Far East. Rommel drove the British armies as far back as Mersa Matruh, and on the 21st of June the garrison in Tobruk, which had held out through all the vicissitudes of the campaign, was forced to surrender. By the beginning of July 1942, it seemed as if all Egypt lay within Rommel's grasp.

By July 1942, the German attack on Russia was already more than a year old. The German offensive in the Balkans had indeed been a prelude to this great objective, for the Russo-German Alliance, based upon the partition of Poland, had been from the beginning an uneasy one. In the spring and early summer of 1940, while Germany was occupied in Western Europe, Russia, with German concurrence, had extorted Bessarabia and Northern Bukovina from Rumania. This was followed by the incorporation into the Soviet Union of the three Baltic States of Esthonia, Latvia and Lithuania. Other events soon confirmed the view that Russian confidence in Germany had been exhausted. Two days before the German attack on Yugoslavia the German Ambassador in Moscow had been told that Russia had agreed to sign a treaty of friendship and non-aggression with that state. Moreover, from the spring of 1941 onwards a series of border incidents had taken place, and complaints had been made by each of the two countries that the other was trespassing over the frontier, a familiar prelude to war.

It was on the 22nd of June 1941 that the German invasion of Russia began. Germany was joined by Finland, Hungary, Rumania and Italy. On the other side Great Britain lost no time in declaring her support for Russia, and on the 12th of July an Anglo-Russian Agreement was signed in Moscow, an agreement for mutual aid in the war against Germany. The attack took place along three lines: through Southern Poland into the Ukraine, through White Russia towards Smolensk and Moscow, and through the Baltic States towards Leningrad. The Germans made rapid progress, and it seemed at one time as if Hitler would achieve 'the ultimate objective' of his operations against Russia—the establishment of a defence line running approximately from the Volga to Archangel.[1]

In the North the Baltic States were quickly overrun, and German forces pushing towards Lake Ladoga reached the suburbs of Leningrad in October. The blockade of Leningrad, which was also threatened by the Finnish army from the North, lasted for nearly sixteen months. On the central sector of the Russian front German armies under Field-Marshal von Bock captured Smolensk on the 16th of July. Then they paused for a while to mass both men and materials for the assault on Moscow. In spite of Russian counter-attacks, this great offensive was launched by the Germans at the beginning of October. At first their advance was rapid. By the beginning of November the Germans were but sixty miles from Moscow, and a state of siege was proclaimed there. What was intended to be the final thrust was made on the 16th, but, after three weeks of intensely bitter fighting, the Russians held their ground, and von Bock, who had advanced 700 miles from Poland, was held within thirty miles of the suburbs of Moscow. After the German High Command had announced that operations were to be closed down

[1] Führer's Directive, No. 21, December 18, 1940, published in *Nazi-Soviet Relations*, p. 261.

for the winter, the Russians took the offensive for a time and recaptured some territory.

In the southern sector of the Russian front the German armies under Field-Marshal von Rundstedt had been equally successful. Profiting from the advance of von Bock's armies, which turned the Russian defences of the Rivers Pruth, Dniester and Bug, and by the successful advance into the Ukraine, von Rundstedt's army, aided by the Rumanians, swept through Bessarabia and along the Black Sea coast towards Odessa. Kiev fell on the 19th of September, Odessa on the 16th of October, and Kharkov on the 24th. Five days later the Germans broke into the Crimean peninsula, which they soon overran, with the exception of Sebastopol. Von Rundstedt's army advanced eastwards as far as Rostov-on-Don, which was captured on the 22nd of November, but retaken by the Russians a week later. The German armies in the south halted in early December on the line of the Donetz river.

The German successes, since the initial attack in June 1941, had been most spectacular, and Russian losses apparently catastrophic. The rich cornlands of the Ukraine, together with the important industrial areas both in the Ukraine and in the Dnieper Basin, had been abandoned by the Russians. The coalfields of the Donetz Basin and the whole of the Crimea except Sebastopol were in German hands. The two largest cities of Russia, Leningrad and Moscow, were threatened and declared to be in a state of siege.

In the late spring of 1942 the German army in the south, now commanded by von Bock, renewed the offensive and captured Kerch. Further north the Russian forces under Marshal Timoshenko opened an offensive at the same time and threatened Kharkov, but were beaten back by von Bock's counter-offensive across the Donetz. It is to be noted that, whereas in 1941 the Germans had taken the offensive on the three main sectors of the Russian front, in 1942 they were concentrating their forces and material in the southern sector. Here the big offensive opened on the 28th of June. Clearing their right flank with the capture of Sebastopol, and thus completing the conquest of the Crimea, the German armies struck eastward between the Donetz and the Upper Don. The two spearheads of their offensive were directed in the south towards the Caucasian oilfields and further north against Stalingrad, an industrial centre of first importance. The Germans were at first outstandingly successful, although they were unable to keep to their ambitious timetable, which included the capture of Stalingrad by the end of July. They succeeded in driving the Russians back to the west bank of the Don by the middle of August, and during the same period the German armies had reached the foothills of the Caucasus. By the end of October they had reached the Georgian Military Road which led to Tiflis, and at one time it seemed not improbable that the German armies might make a thrust towards the Middle East *via* the Caspian. In November, however, their advance was checked, and later

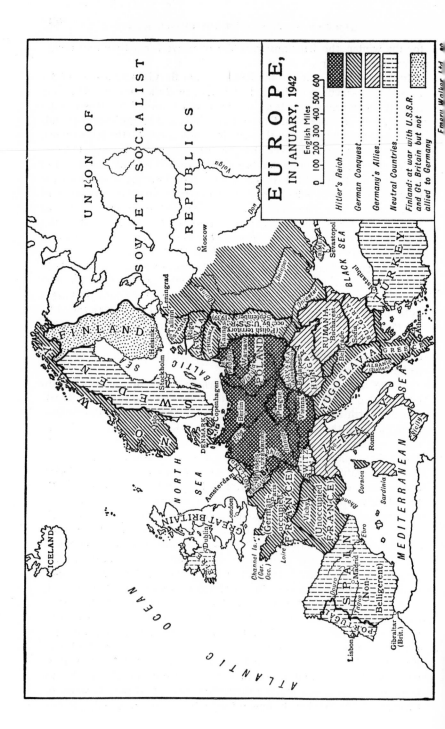

EUROPE,
IN JANUARY, 1942

English Miles
0 100 200 300 400 500 600

Hitler's Reich..........
German Conquest..........
Germany's Allies..........
Neutral Countries..........

Finland: at war with U.S.S.R.
and Gt. Britain but not
allied to Germany

Emery Walker Ltd

the requirements of the other sectors of the Russian front led to their withdrawal from the Caucasus.

Meanwhile, after a slight pause, the advance had been renewed towards the Volga on the 21st of August. A few days later the German armies crossed the Don, and drew near to the elbow bend of the river at Stalingrad. On the 5th of September German units were reported to be fighting in the streets of the city. Thus began the epic defence of Stalingrad, which ultimately spelt disaster for the German campaign. The Russians resisted street by street and house by house. Most of the city was indeed captured, but at a cost which Germany could ill afford. In 1942 she had lost more than a quarter of the four million troops engaged on the Russian front, and this was already beginning to have an effect upon the force of her advance. On the 19th of November the German armies round Stalingrad received a most unpleasant surprise. A Russian army took the offensive under General Zhukov, who had been transferred from the Moscow sector, and, attacking from three directions, cut the communications of the beleaguering armies and finally surrounded them. The desperate effort of the Germans to relieve the Stalingrad force failed, and by the end of 1942 there were no German troops within a hundred miles of Stalingrad, except for what was now a beleaguered garrison. The final surrender of these forces took place on the 31st of January 1943. The significance of this disaster for the Germans was heightened by the coincidence of defeat in Russia with defeat in North Africa, where the Battle of El Alamein in October 1942 marked the change of Allied fortune. The surrender of the German forces in the Stalingrad sector coincided almost precisely with the entry of the 8th Army into Tunisia.

A year before these events, the whole magnitude of the struggle had been altered by the entry of America into the war. America, indeed, had already been ranged on the side of the Allies, while nominally preserving her neutrality. Her attitude had been slowly changing since the outbreak of war. In 1939 President Roosevelt had placed an embargo on all shipments of arms to belligerents, in accordance with the provisions of the Neutrality Act. This measure was disadvantageous to Britain and France, for whereas Germany was militarily prepared for war, they were not. President Roosevelt, whose sympathies were quite clearly with the Allies, therefore urged the amendment of the Neutrality Act to permit the sale of arms, a measure which was carried by Congress on the 3rd of November 1939, and became law on the following day. The 'cash and carry' system was then instituted, which permitted America to sell arms to the belligerents on strictly cash terms and provided they were not carried in American vessels. This was as far as American opinion was prepared to go to help Britain and France at that time.

After the fall of France, the interest of America in preventing the annihilation of Britain was much greater, for events in Europe had shown that neutrality alone was no protection against aggression. President Roosevelt indicated his policy in a speech at the University of Virginia on the 10th of June 1940, when he declared: '. . . we will extend to the opponents of force all the material resources of this nation . . .' His words received practical application shortly afterwards, when, on the 2nd of September 1940, an Anglo-American agreement was reached by which Britain leased naval and air bases in the West Indies and Newfoundland to the United States, in return for the loan of fifty American destroyers.

By this time Britain's dollar and gold reserves were fast becoming exhausted, and by the end of the year she was unable to place new arms contracts in the United States. America had done much to help, but the obvious methods had come to an end and a new departure was necessary. This took the form of the Lease-Lend Act, which finally passed both Houses of Congress and was signed by President Roosevelt on the 11th of March 1941. The Lease-Lend Act authorised the President of the United States to 'sell, transfer title to, exchange, lease, lend, or otherwise dispose of . . . any defense article' to any nation whose defence he found vital to the defence of the United States. The act was put into immediate operation, and aid was at once given to Britain and China. Three months later, when Russia was attacked by Germany, she too came within the scope of lease-lend, and at the end of September 1941 a conference of British, American and Russian representatives met in Moscow and agreed on the provision of supplies from Britain and America for Russia. From this time to the end of the war America was, indeed, 'the arsenal of democracy.' War materials, food and equipment of all kinds were transported across the Atlantic in convoys which were subjected to constant U-boat attacks. The 'Battle of the Atlantic' was from the point of view of the ultimate issue one of the decisive battles of the war.

America was neutral when the Lease-Lend Act was passed; the immediate cause of her entry into the war is to be found in events in the Far East, and in particular in her relations with Japan. Throughout the year 1941 these were characterised by bitterness and friction. In December 1940, the Japanese Foreign Minister had declared that Japan's foreign policy would 'revolve round the Three-Power Pact,' and early in the following year it became clear that Japan was making preparations for an ultimate entry into the war. In July 1941, she had demanded and received from Vichy France bases in Indo-China. By October she had absorbed the whole of French Indo-China, although continuing negotiations with the United States. These negotiations came to a sensational close on the 7th of December. Without warning or declaration of war she carried out an air attack on the American naval base of Pearl Harbour in the Hawaiian Islands, destroying at a stroke American naval supremacy in the Pacific. A declaration of war against America and Britain followed immediately.[1] Simultaneously, Japanese forces landed in Thailand and north-east Malaya. Thailand's resistance ended on the following day, giving the Japanese army a free passage to Malaya. Moreover, the American Pacific bases of Wake Island and Guam, together with the greater part of the Philippines, were attacked and captured, although Corregidor in the Philippines still held out.

For the next eight months one disaster succeeded another in the Far Eastern war. The Allies suffered heavily in naval operations. On the 10th of December two British warships, the *Prince of Wales* and the *Repulse*, were sunk by Japanese air attack, and on the 27th of February 1942, the much depleted allied naval force was further weakened when a squadron engaged a superior Japanese force in the Battle of the Java Sea. After three days' fighting the allied fleet of five cruisers and six destroyers was annihilated. These victories gave Japan absolute naval superiority in Pacific and East Asian waters; she had also superiority in the air, and she exploited her advantage to the full against British, American and Dutch possessions. Hong Kong surrendered on Christmas Day 1941, and the Dutch East Indies in March 1942. In Malaya the Japanese armies made swift progress, for they were able to make unopposed landings behind the flanks of the defence. Kuala Lumpur was captured early in January; by the end of the month the Japanese had penetrated into Johore, and British troops had completely evacuated the mainland of Malaya. Singapore fell on the 15th of February. After the conquest of Malaya the Japanese turned to Burma, where they made steady progress in the face of determined opposition from allied troops, which included Chinese units under the command of General Stilwell, the American Chief of Staff to General Chiang Kai-shek. Japanese forces quickly reached the Gulf of Martaban, compelling British troops to withdraw across the Sittang river. Rangoon was evacuated on the 7th of March, Mandalay on the 1st of May, and a week later the Japanese armies reached Akyab on the Bay of Bengal. The expected invasion of India did not, however, take place. The force of the Japanese onslaught was stopped, mainly by the monsoon and by the necessity of consolidating the gains of five months' fighting.

In the Pacific, too, the Japanese had fought to a standstill. They had successfully attacked New Guinea and the Solomon Islands in March, and finally, on the 8th of April, they had landed on the Admiralty Islands. They had established themselves within a perimeter formed by Burma, the Netherlands East Indies, New Guinea and the Solomon Islands; they were in a position to threaten not only India but Australia as well. But the limits of Japanese expansion had been reached; and despite the claims of the European war, substantial reinforcements and supplies, including aircraft, were sent by the Allies to the Far East. The American victory at the beginning of May in the Battle of the Coral

[1] Germany and Italy declared war on the United States on 11 December.

Sea, a naval and air battle off the Solomon Islands, was the first major defeat of Japan. Exactly a month later the Americans won another decisive battle off Midway Island, when the Japanese lost sixteen warships, including four aircraft carriers. Early in August American forces landed in the Guadalcanal area of the Solomon Islands, and by the end of the year the fortunes of war in the Far East, as in other theatres, had changed.

Victory for the Allies in North Africa was the work of seven months, from October 1942 to May 1943. The plan was of much longer standing, for it was the result of a conference in Washington during Mr. Churchill's visit to President Roosevelt in December 1941, and of discussions which took place in the succeeding six months. The decisions then taken were confirmed after the costly raid on Dieppe in August 1942. A joint Anglo-American invasion of French North Africa was to take place, and at the same time the British forces in Egypt were to advance westwards. General Eisenhower was appointed to command the North African operations, with General Alexander as Commander-in-Chief in the Middle East and General Montgomery in operational command of the British 8th Army.

The attack by the 8th Army opened on the night of the 23rd of October 1942. It penetrated the main defences of the German forces under Rommel at El Alamein, beat off a counter-attack, and on the 12th of November entered Tobruk. In a little over three weeks Rommel was driven back to El Agheila. Then, after a halt of three weeks, while new supply lines were organised through the captured and damaged port of Benghazi, pursuit was resumed. El Agheila fell on the 14th of December, and the opposing forces were compelled to retreat another 250 miles before making their next stand at Buerat. Early in January 1943, they were driven from this position, and Tripoli fell to the 8th Army on the 23rd of the month. Rommel's armies had been chased 1,350 miles in eighty-two days. He fell back behind the Tunisian frontier to the Mareth line, a fortified zone which the French had formerly constructed for defence against the Italians.

The British and American landings in French North Africa took place near Casablanca, Oran and Algiers on the 8th of November. There was little French opposition in Algeria, except from naval and coastal batteries, and the capture of Algiers was swiftly followed by the fall of Oran and Casablanca. Within four days all fighting in the area west of Algiers had ceased. But the Allies were disappointed in their hope that the French authorities in North Africa would co-operate with them. Personal and political differences were alike hampering. Neither General de Gaulle nor General Giraud commanded sufficient support. Admiral Darlan, a leading member of the Vichy Government and a representative of that Government in North Africa, played a part which is not yet wholly clear in rallying the French forces to the allied side. On Darlan's assassination he was succeeded by Giraud, but by that time the main object had been achieved and most of the French forces had joined the Allies.

The German reply to the Allied landings was not only to send troops to Tunisia, but also to occupy what was hitherto unoccupied France. On the 11th of November the whole of this region except Toulon was occupied; a fortnight later German forces entered Toulon with the intention of seizing the French fleet, only to find that the fleet had been scuttled by the French themselves.

The main opposition to the Allies in North Africa came from the German army under Rommel. In the east, behind the Mareth line, the Germans faced the British 8th Army; in the west, they were opposed by the British 1st Army, the American 2nd Corps and the French troops under General Giraud. The combined strength of the German armies made possible a serious attempt in February 1943 to turn the allied line in Southern Tunisia; but this attempt failed, as did a further attack early in March. Then, on the night of the 20th of March, the 8th Army attacked and breached the Mareth line, on the 6th of April it broke through Rommel's next line of defence, and on the following day American troops of the 2nd Corps made contact with the 8th Army. In the west also allied troops had gone over to the offensive at the end of March, and early in April occupied Cap Serrat to the west of Biserta. The final assault began on the 5th of May, and two days later the American 2nd Corps entered Biserta and the British 1st Army captured Tunis. Within a week the entire Axis forces in Africa surrendered The total number of German and Italian troops taken prisoner reached a quarter of a million, and included some of the finest German and Italian units, and much of their equipment and material.

The significance of the victory in North Africa was threefold. In the first place, successful co-operation in the field strengthened the single-ness of Anglo-American purpose. Secondly, the victory led to the establishment of a provisional Free French administration on French soil, and marked the beginning of the revival of French military prestige. Thirdly, the North African campaign broke the spirit and fighting strength of Italy, and was the prelude to the collapse of Mussolini's régime.

The plan for the next phase of the war was decided by President Roosevelt and Mr. Churchill at a meeting at Casablanca in January 1943. But before it could be carried out it was essential to clear the Mediterranean, so that it might be used freely by allied shipping. The struggle for the Mediterranean had indeed never been wholly abandoned, as is shown by the British air attack on the Italian fleet in Taranto harbour in November 1940 and the British victory off Cape Matapan in the following March. A year later a convoy with material urgently needed in Malta arrived only after a famous three days of battling with the enemy. The losses suffered by British convoys for the Middle East were so great that supplies had to be sent by the long sea route by the Cape.

The assault on the Mediterranean began with the capture of the small but heavily fortified islands of Lampedusa and Pantellaria early in June 1943. A month later, British and American forces landed in Sicily. The British 8th Army, together with a Canadian division, attacked at the eastern end of the island; the American 7th Army in the west. German forces were concentrated in the northern part, barring the approach to Messina. The American army thrust in two directions —westwards to Marsala and northwards to Palermo, which was captured on the 22nd of July. The 8th Army, after rapid progress at the beginning, was halted by stiff resistance in the plain of Catania, and it was not until August that Catania was entered. On the 17th Messina fell.

Before this date there had been dramatic happenings in Italy. Mussolini resigned on the 25th of July and was succeeded by Marshal Badoglio, who formed a government with the object of making peace with the Allies. Secret negotiations were opened with the Allied High Command. Mussolini was imprisoned by his own party, then rescued by the Germans, and finally recaptured and ignominiously executed by Italian partisans in Milan on the 28th of April 1945. The armistice terms were signed by Italy on the 3rd of September 1943, but the announcement was delayed for five days in the hope that the Allies would have gained a foothold on the Italian mainland. The terms were unconditional surrender, immediate cessation of hostilities by Italian forces, the transfer to the Allies of the fleet and the air force, and the guarantee of the use of all airfields and ports. The Italian fleet, or such as was left of it, sailed to Malta on the 10th of September. But, while the armed resistance of the Italians had practically ceased even before the armistice was concluded, the German armies in Italy had still to be reckoned with. German forces occupied Rome on the 10th of September, and German control was made effective over the greater part of the country, particularly in the north. It was in these circumstances that Marshal Badoglio and his Government fled to the Allies and declared war on Germany. Thus Italy became a co-belligerent in the allied cause.

The first landing in Italy had been made on the 3rd of September at Reggio in Calabria by the British 8th Army. Six days later a further landing was made by the American 5th Army at Salerno, south of Naples. The Germans immediately concentrated their forces in the Salerno area and counter-attacked. After intensely bitter fighting the Americans maintained their position, supported by fire from warships, until the advance of the British force from the south relieved the pressure.

To the south, units of the 8th Army had already entered Taranto, Brindisi and Bari. The main body of that army now turned eastwards from Salerno to capture the important airfields at Foggia, which constituted one of the two great initial objectives of the Italian campaign. The second major objective of this period, Naples, fell to the American 5th Army on the 1st of October. After this the Germans fell back to the line of the Volturno river, and allied progress, both in the east and in the west, was slow. In November British forces secured a passage of the Sangro river. By the end of the year they had crossed the Moro river. In the west the American army crossed the Volturno in mid-October, and pushed the Germans back behind the Garigliano. The allied front in Italy now ran along a line from Ortona in the east, through Orsogna, and along the east bank of the Sangro and Garigliano rivers. At this time General Eisenhower went to England to take charge of the planning of the invasion of Western Europe, leaving General Alexander in command of the Allied forces in Italy.

Early in 1944 an attempt was made by the 5th Army to break the deadlock in the west. On the 20th of January allied forces crossed the Garigliano river, and two days later a landing was made further north, at Anzio, in order to cut off the Germans in the rear. This operation, however, was only partly successful, and the German Commander, Field-Marshal Kesselring, was able to block the advance. Next month the Allies made a further effort, this time in the mountainous region round Cassino, to the east of the Garigliano river. They failed, and it was not until May that they were sufficiently strong to break the enemy's positions. The main body of the 8th Army was then moved secretly to the support of the 5th Army in the west, and the offensive began. Allied forces broke through the German defences across the Garigliano and Rapido rivers, were joined by troops from the Anzio bridgehead, and drove the Germans in headlong retreat northwards. Rome fell to the 5th Army on the 4th of June, two days before the Allies were to land in Normandy. After this, progress was steady rather than rapid. Siena and Leghorn fell in July, Florence on the 11th of August. Early in September the opposing armies faced one another on the next German defensive line, 'the Gothic Line,' which extended across Italy in the northern Apennines, from the Arno river to Rimini. Pisa fell at the beginning of the month, Rimini on the 22nd. Ravenna was taken early in December, but a combination of bad weather and an able defence by Kesselring held off the Allies from Bologna. The final phase of the war in Italy opened on the 10th of April 1945, with attacks on both sides of the peninsula. Bologna was taken, then Spezia, and Genoa. By this time the defence had completely collapsed, and German forces surrendered in large numbers. Moreover, Italian patriots were seizing the industrial cities of the north. Thus it happened that on the 29th of April two German officers signed a convention at Field-Marshal Alexander's Headquarters—a convention which provided for the unconditional surrender of the German armies in Italy. In accordance with the provisions of this convention, the whole German army group in the Italian theatre of operations laid down its arms on the 2nd of May.

Russian offensives on Germany's eastern front coincided with the campaigns in Africa and Italy. The front was still at the end of 1942 deep in Russian territory. But the material preliminaries to attack had been long prepared. Russian production, from factories transported far to the east, was reinforced by large quantities of war supplies from America and Britain. Transport *via* Persia and the Caspian Sea was made possible by the occupation by British and Russian troops of strategic points in Persia in August 1941. The normal route *via* the North Sea and the Arctic was maintained, despite the severe losses suffered by British merchant shipping, and large numbers of convoys reached their destination. By the end of 1942 the tide had turned. The German defeat at Stalingrad marked the beginning of Russian recovery. A retreat from the Caucasus was forced and the Russians pressed home their advantage. Kursk, north-west of Stalingrad, was recaptured in February 1943, and then Rostov-on-Don. The Germans were driven out of the Donetz Basin and lost Kharkov. It is true that these initial successes were followed by a German counter-attack, in the course of which Kharkov was lost again; but even then the balance of victory lay with the Russians.

In the north, too, the Russians had passed to the offensive. On New Year's Day 1943, they captured Velikiye Luki at the hinge of the two great blocks of German forces which were facing south-east towards Moscow and north towards Leningrad. By the middle of January the siege of Leningrad was raised. At the end of February Marshal Timoshenko attacked the Germans to the south-east of Lake Ilmen, and freed Moscow from the threat of German conquest under which it had existed from the end of 1941. After a lull on all sectors, during which both sides prepared for the next offensive, the great struggle was resumed in July 1943, by a German attack on the Kursk salient. A Russian counter-attack further north against Orel was followed by a larger movement on the whole front from Orel to the Black Sea. By the end of August Orel, Kharkov and Taganrog were among the towns once more in Russian hands. A further offensive opened in front of Moscow before the end of September, and Smolensk was taken. An outstanding success was secured in the south. There the Germans had decided to retire for the winter to the line of the Dnieper, abandoning their conquests in the Ukraine to the east of the river, with the exception of the region between the bend of the river and the Crimea. Early in October, after severe fighting, the Russians forced this line and secured three bridgeheads over the river. Dnepropetrovsk was retaken on the 25th of October and Kiev on the 6th of November. The Russians were also successful further south, and drove the Germans back to the line of the Dnieper. A German counter-offensive in the Kiev salient was finally halted, and a major Russian attack west of Kiev was successful. By the end of 1943 the Russian army had in fact liberated two-thirds of the occupied territory.

In the following January the Russians switched their main offensive to the north front, where they broke through the German lines round Leningrad, and drove the German Army back from positions which they had held since 1941. Novgorod was captured, and the Germans were pushed back to the River Narva and Lake Peipus and into the Baltic provinces.

At the same time the Russian advance was continuing in other sectors. Rovno and Luck were captured early in February, and further south the Germans were being driven out of the Ukraine. Nikopol and Krivoi Rog, two industrial centres of first importance, were captured in February, and the Germans suffered a major disaster near Korsun, where ten divisions were encircled by the Russians. In March the Russians made spectacular progress before the thaw or rain ended operations until the summer. By that time their Army had crossed in turn the Rivers Bug, Dniester and Pruth. On the 10th of April Odessa was captured.

The Russians then invaded the Crimea and re-conquered the whole peninsula in a week, with the exception of Sebastopol which held out until the beginning of May. Thus, by the late spring of 1944, the Russian armies were dangerously near to German territory and to the German satellite countries in the Balkans. In the north they stood on the Esthonian frontier, in the centre they were already within the 1939 frontier of Poland, and in the south they had crossed the frontier of Rumania. By this time, then, when the Western Allies were fighting their way up the Italian peninsula, the Russian advance was bringing the war within striking distance of the borders of Germany.

The war had indeed already come to Germany, for during the preceding two years there had been attacks by air on targets in Germany and in the German-occupied countries. The scale of the air-offensive against Germany had grown steadily since the spring of 1942. The R.A.F. daylight attack on the Diesel engine factory at Augsburg in April marked the beginning of a new period; and on the night of the 30th of May came the raid on Cologne, the first of the 1,000 bomber raids on German targets. Essen, Bremen and Osnabrück were struck next. It was not long before American strength made itself felt. In January 1943, the United States air force opened a series of large-scale daylight attacks with heavy bombers against industrial targets. Moreover, new methods, as well as more destructive bombs, were being employed, and the allied successes in the Mediterranean provided air bases nearer to targets in central Germany and in the Rumanian oilfields.

The raids on industrial targets and installations continued throughout 1943, and increased in intensity in the following year. One of the results was that Germany had to turn from the production of bomber aircraft and concentrate on fighters. Another was the destruction of the synthetic oil factories on which Germany depended after the capture of the Rumanian and Polish oilfields by the Russians. The number of German civilian casualties was large. In air warfare the Allies had undoubtedly won the initiative, and maintained it to the end, despite the fact that in the winter of 1943-4 serious attempts were made by Germany to renew night raids on Britain.

In the last phase of the struggle in Western Europe German attacks on Britain took the then novel form of long-range pilotless projectiles, popularly known as 'V' weapons, the jet-propelled flying bomb or 'V.1' and the rocket bomb or 'V.2.' These weapons were launched from sites along the French coast and in the Low Countries. The installations as well as the main experimental stations in Germany were attacked systematically by R.A.F. bombers, and before the allied invasion of France over a hundred launching sites had been discovered and destroyed. In spite of all precautions, however, flying bomb attacks on London and south-east England began on the 13th of June, 1944, seven days after the first landing in Normandy. The first attacks by rocket bombs took place on the 8th of September. Considerable damage to life and property was inflicted, but the extent of the gain from the German standpoint is debatable. Industry had been diverted from the production of fighter and bomber aircraft, and in the final struggle in Europe the numerical inferiority of the German air force was an important factor.

The invasion of Western Europe began on the 6th of June 1944. The approximate date had been agreed as far back as the Conference at Teheran in November of the previous year. In December General Eisenhower had been appointed Supreme Commander of the invasion force and Air Chief Marshal Tedder became Deputy Supreme Commander. General Montgomery commanded the British group of armies under General Eisenhower's control, and in the initial stages was also Commander of Land Forces. The landings took place on the north coast of France between Cherbourg and Le Havre. British engineers had designed and constructed two great prefabricated harbours, known as Mulberry harbours, which were transported across the Channel in sections and assembled on a stretch of open coast. All facilities for landing troops, supplies and equipment were thus provided, without the necessity for the immediate capture of a port. The first task was to establish a beach-head through which the resources needed for a decisive battle could be built up. The Allies had two great assets—air and sea superiority; their air superiority enabled them to disrupt the enemy's supply and communication lines, and their naval superiority made it possible to keep their own armies supplied and reinforced. Caen and Cherbourg were the next objectives, when the beach-head had been consolidated. Cherbourg fell to the Americans on the 26th of June, but the capture of Caen—the task of the British forces—proved more difficult and was accomplished only after severe fighting on the 9th of July. Within five weeks of the landing, the Allies were in possession of the two main ports of Normandy.

In July an American army under General Patton broke through the German lines, capturing St. Lô and Avranches. Nantes fell on the 10th of August, and a week later General Patton's forces had liberated Chartres, Orleans and Chateaudun, and had reached Dreux. Meanwhile, the battle in Normandy had turned in favour of the Allies. When the Germans counter-attacked near Mortain, General Montgomery ordered part of the American force to swing north in the direction of Falaise to join the Canadians and the British. As a result, large numbers of German troops were enclosed in the Falaise pocket. The Germans managed to extricate some of their troops, but at a terrific cost in equipment and casualties; eight infantry divisions and two Panzer divisions were captured. In August General Patton's forces reached Mantes on the Seine below Paris; British units crossed the Seine on the 25th and raced for the Somme. Paris was liberated from within by members of the French Resistance Movement on the 23rd, and two days later General Leclerc's armoured division arrived to complete the victory. On that day, too, General de Gaulle entered the French capital.

At almost the same time as the break through to the Seine, a landing had been made on the French Riviera, between Toulon and Nice. Enemy opposition was comparatively slight, and the Franco-American force was able to consolidate its position and join in pursuit of the German armies. Toulon and Marseilles were captured within a few days. Valence fell to the American 7th Army before the end of August, Lyons to French and American troops on the 3rd of September, and Besançon a few days later. By the middle of September most of France except the Atlantic ports and Alsace-Lorraine had been liberated and the Allies were pressing on through Belgium and into Holland. Shortly before this date General Eisenhower had assumed direct command of all allied land forces in France. General, now Field-Marshal, Montgomery was appointed to command the British 21st Army Group, and General Bradley the American 12th Army Group.

After the victory in Normandy British and Canadian forces had captured Amiens and crossed the Somme. They took Arras, crossed the Belgian frontier and liberated Brussels and Antwerp on the 3rd and 4th of September. A day later American troops linked up with British forces after liberating Charleroi and Namur. By the end of the first week of September the British army had crossed the Albert Canal, and after another week had pushed on to the Escaut Canal and the Dutch frontier. Only the River Maas and the Lower Rhine separated them from German territory, and here the Germans had determined on their final stand. Allied airborne forces were dropped in south-east Holland in order to secure a crossing of the two rivers and to outflank the defences of the Siegfried Line. The attempt was unsuccessful, for the bridge-head which was established at Arnhem could not be held, although that over the Waal was. By the beginning of October the first phase of the assault on Europe was over. Perhaps one of the most outstanding successes was the least spectacular: the efficient supply of the allied armies in the rapid sweep across France, Belgium and Luxemburg up to the frontiers of Germany. General Eisenhower has recorded that this profoundly impressed even the Russian generals. After four months of rapid progress, however, the supply lines were beginning to feel the strain, and shortage of petrol and ammunition slowed down the advance. The gains were nevertheless substantial: British troops had liberated south Holland, French forces had reached the Rhine at Mulhausen, and the Americans had captured Strasbourg, crossed the German frontier, and were pressing on into the Saar.

Germany in 1944 was indeed suffering the dreaded war on two fronts, for the Russian armies were moving at the very time of the Anglo-American invasion in the west. Early in June they crossed the Karelian Isthmus, broke through the Mannerheim Line, and captured Viborg. Further north still they attacked with equal success between Lake Ladoga and Lake Onega. The Finns were obliged to give up the struggle before the end of August. Under the terms of the armistice, signed on the 19th of September, Finland undertook to withdraw behind the frontiers laid down in 1940, to hand over Petsamo to Russia, and pay $300,000,000 of reparations. Russia undertook to forgo her claims to the lease of the Hangö peninsula.

Parallel with this movement there was another on the White Russian front where the offensive opened before the end of June. Vitebsk fell on the 26th, and five German divisions were trapped and either killed or forced into surrender. Then again, at the same time, the Russians made a powerful attack in the sector to the south in the direction of Central Poland. Mogilev was captured and then Minsk, the capital of White Russia. The advance was along a 200 mile front, and there was no sector from which the Germans dared withdraw large reserves to meet an immediate need elsewhere. Soon the Russian armies were surging through the Baltic States and Poland. The fortress towns of Poland were captured one after another—Lublin, Lwov, Bialystok and Brest-Litovsk. The Russian armies reached the Vistula, and at one point were within ten miles of Warsaw. Unfortunately, the rising in Warsaw organised by the Polish underground forces came before the Russian army under Marshal Rokossovsky was ready to advance. In spite of initial success the rising of the Poles was suppressed, and the remnants of the city were ruthlessly destroyed. To the north of Poland, in the Baltic States, on the other hand, the Russians had made great strides. Pskov, Narva and Dvinsk were captured in rapid succession, and on the 1st of August Kaunas, the capital of Lithuania, fell. On the frontiers of East Prussia, however, the Germans rallied and even counter attacked; and for a time the Russian advance was checked.

A new offensive opened in August in the Balkans. The Russians started the campaign by the capture of Jassy, and the forcing of the line of the River Dniester. Rumania immediately announced her acceptance of armistice terms, and two days later declared war on Germany. The armistice was signed in Moscow on the 13th of September. Before this, however, Russian troops had entered Bucharest, and continued their march up the Danube, reaching Bulgaria and Yugoslavia in the first days of September. Bulgaria followed Rumania's example, declaring war on Germany, and asking Russia for an armistice. Belgrade was liberated, and Bulgarian troops co-operated with the Yugoslav partisans led by Marshal Tito to harass the German troops withdrawing from the Balkans. Hungary was the last of Germany's allies in Eastern Europe to desert her, but after the defection of Rumania her position had become impossible. Earlier in October the Russian army crossed the frontier from Rumania, advancing rapidly to within 65 miles of Budapest. German and Hungarian troops put up a fierce resistance, although part of the Hungarian army and the Commander-in-Chief soon joined the Russians. The armistice in the case of Hungary was not signed until the 20th of January 1945, and then only after the government had been overthrown. In the meantime, British troops had landed in Greece, at Patras, in October 1944, and the Germans had rapidly abandoned the country, their retreating forces harried by British troops and Greek partisans. By the end of the year the whole of Greece was liberated.

Thus, from east, west and south the German armies were at the end of 1944 forced back relentlessly within the boundaries of the German state. The war in Europe was entering upon its last phase, and although the Germans were yet capable of effective resistance, the ultimate issue was quite clear.

The final assault began early in 1945. The Germans, it is true, in the middle of December launched a heavy counter-offensive in the Ardennes, and succeeded in checking the American advance towards Cologne, and penetrated the American positions to a depth of 44 miles. The attack was a serious one, with its objective the capture of Liège, where the Allies had accumulated vast quantities of supplies in preparation for their next offensive. After very bitter fighting and very heavy losses on both sides, the German attack was finally repulsed early in the New Year. This offensive was indeed a last desperate gamble, and it failed. Nevertheless, it not only inflicted severe casualties on the allied forces, but it also delayed the allied offensive on the Saar for six weeks, as well as the general offensive which had been timed to coincide with the Russian attack from the east early in January.

On the 8th of February the attack was begun by British and Canadian forces south-east of Nijmegen, and this was followed by offensives along the whole of the western front. The capture of München-Gladbach was succeeded by that of Trier and Krefeld, and then by that of Cologne. The American 1st Army crossed the Rhine at Remagen, by the only bridge left intact. Coblenz fell in the middle of March, and by this time the western bank of the Rhine north of the Moselle was clear of German troops. In the south French and American forces had crossed the Moselle south-west of Coblenz to attack the pocket of German resistance in the Saar. Worms, Ludwigshafen, Kaiserslautern, Saarbrücken and Zweibrücken were taken in turn. By the 25th of March organised resistance west of the Rhine had ended. To the north, the 21st Army Group under Field-Marshal Montgomery crossed the Lower Rhine at four points, and secured a bridge-head from which they advanced north and east, covering 100 miles in eleven days. The object of this attack was the complete encirclement of the Ruhr, which was achieved by the beginning of April, although it was not until the 18th that German resistance in the Ruhr pocket ended. The Allies were now firmly established at three points east of the Rhine, at Wesel in the north, at Remagen, and at Oppenheim, south of Mainz. Thence they pushed forward into the heart of Germany, where bombing added to the general confusion. There were three main lines of attack : a powerful thrust eastwards through the Kassel area across the centre of Germany, an advance to the north to cut off Denmark and overcome resistance in the whole area north and west of Kiel and Lübeck, and an advance south-eastwards to join the Russians in the Danube valley and prevent the establishment of a Nazi stronghold in southern Germany. By this time co-ordinated German resistance was ceasing, and until the final surrender the story becomes a mere catalogue of captured German towns and cities.

The Russian offensive had been renewed a little before that in the west. Warsaw was taken early in January, and the Russian armies swept across Poland, and drove into German territory in a four-fold movement. In the same period Russian forces in the south had entered Budapest, and advanced up the Danube into Austria by the end of March, reaching Vienna in mid-April. The attack on Berlin was launched on the 16th of April; five days later Russian troops were fighting in the suburbs. The western Allies had by this time already reached the Elbe, and the two armies advancing from east and west met at Torgau. Berlin surrendered to the Russians on the 2nd of May, after furious battles in the streets and houses. Two days earlier Hitler was reported as having committed suicide. Everywhere German resistance had by now almost completely collapsed. On the same day as the capture of Berlin the German armies in Italy surrendered, to be followed three days later by the German armies in north-west Germany, in Holland and in Denmark. On the 7th of May, the final capitulation took place, and the instrument of surrender was signed by General Jodl, the German Chief-of-Staff, at General Eisenhower's headquarters at Rheims.

It had been decided as far back as the time of the first Washington Conference between Mr. Churchill and President Roosevelt, in December 1941, that the full weight of allied power should be directed first against the European enemy, and that, after the victory had been secured in Europe, the full resources of America and Britain should be concentrated against Japan. By the date when this change was possible, substantial gains had already been achieved in the Far Eastern War. The Japanese had reached the limits of their expansion by the end of 1942. In the following year the main theatre of British operations in the East was in Burma, where the Japanese had been consistently harried, mostly by attacks on their communications carried out by small units of British troops, the Chindits. When early in February 1944, the Japanese attacked on the Arakan front, they were beaten back. A month later the Japanese launched an offensive in Assam in an attempt to penetrate the Brahmaputra Valley and carry the war into India. After three months of very bitter fighting they were routed and in full flight across the Chindwin River, pursued by the British 14th Army. Then followed six months of hard fighting, which went on even through the monsoon. By the New Year the 14th Army had crossed the Chindwin River, and at the same time British forces were advancing along the Arakan front. In January the Ledo road across Burma from India to China was declared free from Japanese troops, and the land route to China was reopened to traffic. Further south Lashio and Mandalay were taken in March, and Rangoon early in May. The result of this long struggle was that the Japanese were decisively beaten in Burma. Preparations were then made for an allied landing in Malaya, but the general Japanese surrender came before these plans were put into effect.

In the Pacific, too, the Japanese hold had weakened. By the latter half of 1943 allied forces, mainly American, New Zealand and Australian, had begun the process of re-occupying the smaller Pacific Islands. Progress was necessarily slow, and in many of the larger islands isolated pockets of Japanese resistance managed to hold out until the end. Early in September 1943, General MacArthur launched an offensive in New Guinea, where Australian and Dutch troops had contrived to maintain a foothold in the south-east, in spite of the Japanese occupation of the island. This offensive was followed by the capture of the Gilbert Islands in November, and early in 1944 by that of the Marshall and Admiralty Islands. The Allies had at last won naval, air and land superiority, and were in a position to threaten Japanese communications and supply lines. In October 1944, American forces landed on Leyte Island in the Philippines, and secured a strong foothold, and the Japanese fleet was routed off Luzon, in the second naval battle of the Philippines, on the 23rd of October. It took two months of very severe fighting before the Japanese were finally defeated in Leyte Island, but towards the end of the year further landings were made on other islands of the Philippine group, and Luzon, the main island, was successfully attacked early in January 1945. American troops entered Manila, the capital of the Philippines, on the 4th of February. Finally, on the 5th of July 1945, General MacArthur was able to announce the complete liberation of the Philippines.

The Japanese had now definitely been on the defensive for six months. The Americans were gradually approaching the main Japanese islands. The capture of Iwojima in March brought them only 775 miles from the Japanese main island of Honshu. In mid-June the Americans completed the conquest of Okinawa in the Ryukyu Islands between Formosa and Japan. In New Guinea and New Britain, in Borneo and in the Philippines, Japanese troops were being driven back despite fanatical resistance. In Japan itself great destruction had been wrought in heavy aid raids by American bombers. More than half of Yokohama had been destroyed, and immense damage inflicted on Tokio, Osaka, Nagoya, Kobe and other Japanese towns. At the time of the victory in Europe the position of Japan was critical, and, although she was still able to inflict severe casualties on the Allies, the end was clear. In April Russia had denounced her neutrality pact with Japan, declared war on the 8th of August, and almost immediately sent troops across the Manchurian frontier. In July America, Britain and China issued a declaration from Potsdam, where an allied Conference was being held, setting out the terms on which they were prepared to make peace. The terms were those of unconditional surrender, and the alternative was utter destruction. The Japanese ignored the ultimatum, only to find that the threat was no empty one, for on the 6th of August, two days before Russia declared war, the first atomic bomb was dropped on Hiroshima. The destruction was indescribable. Four square miles of the city were reduced to rubble, and the number of casualties is said to have exceeded the total of British air raid casualties in six years of war. Still the Japanese made no offer of surrender. Three days later a second atomic bomb was dropped on Nagasaki, again with devastating effect. On the day after this the Japanese asked for peace on the basis of the terms laid down at Potsdam, and on the 14th of August the Japanese Government accepted the allied demands. The instrument of surrender was signed on the 2nd of September by Japanese envoys on board the U.S. battleship *Missouri* in Tokio Bay.

It was almost exactly six years since the war opened with the German attack on Poland. A torch lit on the frontiers of eastern Europe had set the whole world aflame. In Europe itself the effects varied from country to country, politically, economically and in material destruction. It was on this basis that statesmen and peoples had to set about the task of the construction of a new world.

CHAPTER XXXVI

THE POLITICAL STATE OF EUROPE, 1945–50

THE events of six years of war presented to the people and statesmen of Europe problems on an unprecedented scale. Many of them, at the present time, five years after the end of the war, are still unsettled. It is true that in contrast with the situation at the end of the first World War there was comparatively little re-drawing of the frontiers of Europe. Nation-making on the scale then practised was neither necessary nor desired. Nevertheless, in the Europe which emerged from the second World War the balance had shifted. In the east, Russia was the dominant power; in the west, both the greater and the lesser states looked to America, and the Atlantic Ocean seemed to have been reduced to the dimension of a narrow sea. Germany had in effect been partitioned, and her future rôle in European affairs was and remains unpredictable. During the period covered by this book, it was the practice for major wars to be followed by a general peace conference. Certainly, after the two most widespread conflicts, the Napoleonic wars and the first World War, conferences were summoned to re-draw the map of Europe. Five years after the end of the war, no general conference had been convened to consider the re-settlement of Europe after the second World War. The situation had become too complex to be resolved by this method, and the issue was dominated by the wishes of the three great Powers—Russia, Britain and America. When these Powers failed to agree, no settlement was possible.

From a very early stage in the war the problem of the re-settlement of Europe had been considered by the Allies. Even before the German attack on Russia on the 22nd of June 1941, the British Government, in concert with the European Governments which were exiled in Britain, and the provisional Governments formed by anti-Nazi statesmen from Czechoslovakia and France, had issued a declaration of their joint purpose and of their resolve to work together for 'a world in which . . . all may enjoy economic and social security.' In August 1941, this action was followed by the Churchill-Roosevelt declaration, more generally known as the Atlantic Charter, which set forth 'certain common principles in the national policies of their respective countries on which they base their hopes for a better future for the world.'

The principles laid down in the Charter were eight in number. First, there was the renunciation of aggrandisement; secondly, agreement that no territorial changes were to be made without the freely expressed wishes of the peoples concerned; thirdly, the recognition of the right of all people to choose their own form of Government, and restoration of sovereign rights and self-government to those who had been forcibly deprived of them. The fourth and fifth points enunciated the principles of equality of access of all nations to raw materials and trade, and the improvement of material conditions of life. Then followed the hope that a peace might be established which would assure to all men 'freedom from fear and want' and the freedom for all men to 'traverse the high seas and oceans without hindrance.' Finally, the declaration expressed the belief that all nations 'must come to the abandonment of the use of force.' This declaration was formally adopted at a meeting of the allied nations, which by that time included Russia, held in London on the 24th of September 1941.

Up to this point the allied nations had confined themselves to general declarations of principle. But, as victory became more assured, and it became possible to speculate on the pattern of post-war Europe, the Allies turned to more specific issues. They came, too, to consider the form of a comprehensive organisation of machinery for the maintenance of peace. Ultimately this consideration led to the growth of the United Nations Organisation. It is also relevant to the steps that were taken towards a political re-settlement of Europe.

The surrender of Italy and her later recognition as a co-belligerent with the Allies led to the next step forward. At the Conference held by Russia, Britain and America in July to August 1945, it was agreed that the preparation of a peace treaty with Italy should be 'the first among the immediate important tasks to be undertaken by the new Council of Foreign Ministers,' and, at the same time, Italy's membership of the United Nations was contemplated as a possibility. This Council of Foreign Ministers was established at the same Conference under the terms of what is known as the Potsdam Agreement. It held its first meeting in London in September 1945, but reached no agreement on the Italian question. At another meeting which began in Paris on the 25th of April 1946, and later, by adjournment, in June, an agreement was reached on some points but not on all. Further discussions took place at the Conference of Twenty-one Nations in Paris in July to October 1946, and at a further meeting of the Council of Foreign Ministers in November and December in New York. At the end of this meeting on the 12th of December 1946, it was agreed that the treaty with Italy should be signed in Paris on the 10th of February 1947. Signature took place accordingly by the representatives of Russia, Britain, the United States, China and France, and the fifteen other members of the United Nations who had taken part in the war against Italy. It was ratified by the four Great Powers on the 15th of

September and came into operation forthwith. By the terms of the treaty Italy was deprived of all the conquests of Mussolini's régime and was bound to recognise and respect the sovereignty and independence of Albania and Abyssinia. Her European frontiers were defined as those of the 1st of January 1938, except for certain modifications in favour of France and Yugoslavia and the cession of the Dodecanese Islands to Greece. Trieste and the surrounding territory, which had been a bone of contention between Italy and Yugoslavia since 1919, formed the independent 'Free Territory of Trieste,' to be administered by a Governor appointed by the Security Council of the United Nations. The inability of the Security Council to agree on the nomination of a Governor prevented this clause from being put into effect. Italy was also deprived of her colonies, and a final agreement on their administration was ultimately reached by the General Assembly of the United Nations in November 1949. Libya is due to become an independent state not later than the 1st of January 1952, with the help of a United Nations Commissioner and an advisory council; the date fixed for the independence of Somaliland is 1960, and in the meantime it is administered by Italy under the terms of a United Nations trusteeship agreement; a commission of inquiry is due to report on the wishes of the inhabitants of Eritrea. For the rest, the Italian peace treaty conformed to a pattern common to other peace treaties concluded in the five years following the war; the figures for reparations were prescribed and the strength of land, sea and air forces was limited.

One of the earliest declarations on post-war policy made by the Allies was in respect of Austria. At the Conference held in Moscow in October 1943, it was agreed that Austria should be 'liberated from German domination,' and the three powers declared their wish 'to see re-established a free and independent Austria.' At the same time, Austria was reminded that she must bear responsibility for taking part in the war on the German side. Despite the latter clause, it was decided at the Potsdam Conference of July to August, 1945, that reparations should not be exacted from Austria. Later there was some disagreement between Russia and the Western Powers on the interpretation of this decision, and this proved one of the main obstacles to the conclusion of a treaty of peace with Austria.

By May 1945, the whole of Austrian territory was in the occupation of Allied troops. At the end of April a provisional Government had been set up under Dr. Karl Renner, a former Social Democrat leader. This Government, originally set up under the aegis of Russia, was enlarged by the addition of three members of the People's Party (Catholics), and was formally recognised by the United States, Britain, Russia and France towards the end of October. The country itself, however, had been divided into four zones of military occupation, one allotted to each Power, and Vienna itself was similarly divided. An

STALIN

Allied Control Commission was established with the duty of setting up 'as soon as possible' 'a central Austrian administrative machine.' At the beginning of the following year the occupying Powers announced their recognition of Austria as a State, and recognised Dr. Renner as head of it. In April it was announced that the Austrian Parliament had decided on a return to the constitution of 1929, and on the 28th of June the Allied Control Commission handed over to the Austrian Government full authority, except in certain matters directly concerning the occupying Powers. Nevertheless, the inability of the great Powers to agree upon a peace treaty made impossible the achievement of full Austrian independence. Russia refused to include a discussion of the Austrian peace treaty on the agenda for the meeting of the Conference of Foreign Ministers in Paris in 1946, and again at the time of the meeting in New York in the following November. Further difficulties occurred in the discussions in 1947, partly because, in spite of the Potsdam decision that reparations should not be exacted from Austria, Russia advanced claims for reparations both for herself and for Yugoslavia. A Treaty Commission met in Vienna in the summer of 1947 but failed to reach any agreement, and this failure was repeated at a Conference in London in December; other discussions were equally fruitless. In May 1948, Britain, the United States and France declared that there could be no further discussion of the Austrian treaty until there was acceptance of two principles: that is, that Austria's frontiers should be those of 1938, and that reparations should not be exacted. No attempt was made to break the deadlock that resulted until, on the 7th of December 1948, Austria formally requested the Big Four to resume negotiations on the peace treaty. After many discussions a limited agreement was reached in June 1949, but this limited agreement has not yet borne fruit. In the meantime, Austria has applied for membership of the United Nations, but this, like the application of Italy, has been vetoed by Russia, and Austria also remains outside its scope.

The long history of the negotiations for a settlement of the German problem also goes back to the middle period of the war. At the Casablanca Conference in January 1943, President Roosevelt and Mr. Churchill issued a declaration, to which Russia later subscribed, announcing that the objective of the war was to be the 'unconditional surrender' of Germany, Italy and Japan. The declaration continued: 'Unconditional surrender by them means a reasonable assurance of world peace for generations. Unconditional surrender means not the destruction of the German populace, nor of the Italian or Japanese populace, but does mean the destruction of a philosophy in Germany, Italy, and Japan which is based on the conquest and subjugation of other peoples.' The future of Germany was further discussed at the Teheran Conference in 1943, and, although Stalin is reported as having favoured the adoption of a more specific policy, no conclusions were formulated.[1] At Yalta in February 1945, plans for the occupation and control of Germany were drawn up, but, since the war was not then ended, these plans emphasised the military rather than the political aspect of occupation.

It was agreed at Yalta that Germany should be divided into zones of

The Division of Germany into Zones, 1945.

occupation, one allotted to each of the three Powers, and that France should also be invited to take over a fourth zone. Co-ordination of administration and control was to be effected through a central Control Commission, consisting of the Supreme Commanders of the three Powers, with its headquarters in Berlin, and here again France was to be invited to supply a member. It was further decided that drastic measures were to be taken for the complete demilitarisation of Germany as well as for the total eradication of Nazism from every sphere of German life. It was also agreed that just reparation in kind should be paid by Germany.

The final capitulation took place on the 7th of May 1945, and by the end of May the whole of German territory was occupied by the Allies within the zones agreed upon at Yalta. Early the following

[1] v. Robert E. Sherwood: *The White House Papers of Harry L. Hopkins.* 2 Vols. (London 1948-9). Vol. II, pp. 777–8.

month the 'requirements arising from the complete defeat and unconditional surrender of Germany' were announced, including the surrender of land, sea and air forces, equipment and stores, the surrender
of the principal Nazi leaders and those guilty of war crimes, the recognition of the right of the Allies to station 'forces and civil agencies' in
Germany, and the steps to be taken to secure complete disarmament
and complete demilitarisation.

On the same day (the 5th of June 1945) the machinery for the government of Germany was outlined. The country was to be divided into
four zones, the area of Greater Berlin was to be occupied in sectors or
zones by the forces of the four Powers, and administered by an Inter-
Allied Governing Authority. An Allied Control Council, consisting
of the four Commanders-in-Chief, was established to exercise supreme
authority in Germany as a whole. The four Powers announced their
intention to consult with the Governments of the other members of
the United Nations about the exercise of the supreme authority which
they had assumed in Germany.

Allied policy towards Germany was further discussed at the conference which assembled at Potsdam on the 17th of July 1945. Many
decisions of great interest were made at this conference, and amongst
other things, it was determined that in the first stages of occupation,
'the administration in Germany should be directed towards the de-
centralisation of the political structure and the development of local
responsibility.' Detailed political and economic principles were also
laid down, and agreement was reached *in principle* to the modification
of Germany's pre-1938 eastern frontiers. Königsberg and the surrounding region of East Prussia was to be transferred to Russia, and all other
German territory east of the Oder-Neisse line was to be ceded to
Poland. Both these modifications were expressly subject to the final
delimitation of Germany's eastern frontier by the peace treaty.

No attempt was made at this stage to draw up a peace treaty with
Germany, and indeed this was hardly practicable, for there was no
government with which a treaty could have been concluded. Moreover,
as later negotiations were to show, the allies themselves were divided
on the terms of such a treaty, and agreed on only one point—a formal
declaration that the 'Prussian state' had *de facto* ceased to exist.

The failure of the allied Powers to reach agreement on even the
initial stages of a German treaty led to separate action by the Western
Powers on the one hand, and Russia on the other. Economic difficulties led to the economic integration of the British, American and French
zones. Differences between Russia and these Powers led in 1948 to the
complete breakdown of the four-power machinery for the control of
Germany. The three western zones became cut off from the Russian
zone, and, in east and west, preparations were set on foot for the
creation of independent German governments. These preparations
resulted, in May 1949, in the formation of the Federal Republic of

Western Germany with its seat at Bonn, and in the east, of the German Democratic Republic, set up in October 1949, with its seat in the Russian sector of Berlin. Berlin itself was excluded from both republics.

Germany was in effect partitioned. Two new German states came into existence, although neither was a sovereign state, for in both east and west, the occupying Powers reserved control particularly over military affairs and foreign relations.

The position in eastern Europe is dominated by the strength of Russia.[1] For here, since the end of the war, Russia has created and consolidated for herself a position of great influence. Her geographical proximity combined with political and economic conditions to strengthen her ties with the former Axis satellite states, Rumania, Hungary and Bulgaria, and the history even of those states which played an active part during the war on the allied side has been profoundly affected by Russian action.

Treaties of peace between the Allied Powers and Hungary, Bulgaria and Rumania were signed in Paris on the 10th of February 1947. For the most part, the terms of these treaties were identical, and were largely concerned with promises to secure to their nationals the 'human rights' and 'fundamental freedoms.' In addition, the Rumanians and Hungarians were bound to ensure that their Jewish subjects should enjoy equal rights. The frontiers of Rumania and Bulgaria remained as they were on the 1st of January 1941, except that Transylvania was returned to Rumania. Hungary was confined within her frontiers of the 1st of January 1938. The navigation of the Danube was declared to be 'free and open for the nationals, vessels of commerce, and goods of all States.'

In all these countries, 'People's Republics' have been set up, with constitutions based on that of the Soviet Union, and consistent efforts have been made to build up states politically and economically on the Soviet model.

The problems in the other east European countries present many aspects of great complexity. In general, Czechoslovakia, Poland, Albania and Yugoslavia have come to one degree or another under Russian influence. In Greece, on the other hand, the anti-Communist forces, after a long struggle, managed to hold their own. Poland was the only one of these countries whose frontiers were radically changed. After prolonged negotiation, she agreed to accept the 'Curzon line' of 1919 with slight modifications in her favour, as her eastern frontier, receiving in compensation territory in the north and west from Germany. These boundaries were, however, of limited importance, for in Poland Russian influence is particularly strong, and the Russian Marshal Rokossovsky has been appointed as Supreme Commander of the Polish Army and Polish Minister of National Defence (November 1949).

In Czechoslovakia the form of government established by Thomas

[1] v. H. Seton-Watson: *The East European Revolution* (Methuen, 1950).

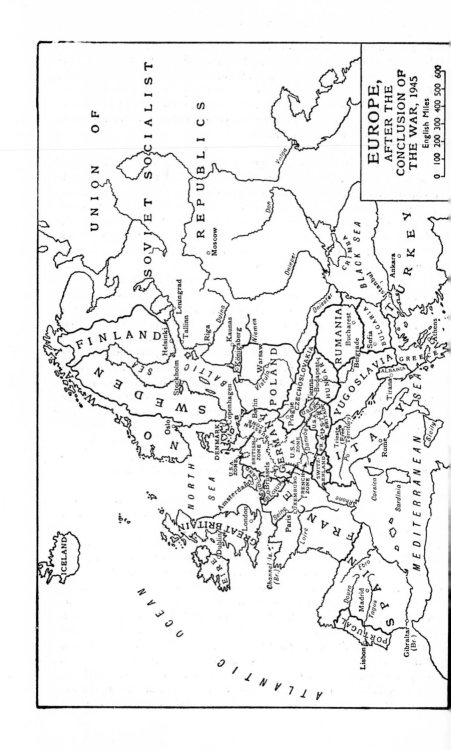

EUROPE,
AFTER THE
CONCLUSION OF
THE WAR, 1945

English Miles
0 100 200 300 400 500 600

END of RUSSIAN PERIOD

Masaryk after the first World War, has disappeared. The attempt to re-establish the republic, with Beneš as President, after the defeat of Germany had only temporary success, for the Communists seized power with Russian assistance by the *coup d'état* of February 1948. Czechoslovakia ceased by this act to form the bridge between East and West, and became completely assimilated into the 'Slav bastion.' A similar fate seemed at first to have befallen Yugoslavia, but fundamental differences with the Soviet Union led to an estrangement the measure of which it is not yet possible to judge.

It appears indeed that in eastern Europe, the dream of the nineteenth century Russian panslavs has become a reality. From the Baltic to the Ægean a long line of states is linked under Russian protection and control. In eastern Europe, Greece and Yugoslavia in varying degrees and with widely different constitutions stand outside the orbit of the Soviet Union.

At the northern end of the line is Finland whose withdrawal from the war took place in the summer of 1944. She finally signed a peace treaty with the Allies in Paris on the 10th of February 1947. By its terms the cession to Russia of the Karelian Isthmus and of the Petsamo district, was confirmed. Russia renounced her claim to the lease of Hangö, but in return acquired the lease for fifty years of the naval base of Porkkala-Udd. Finland, realising that her survival as an independent state depended largely on the maintenance of friendly relations with her powerful neighbour, accepted in April 1948 the Russian invitation to conclude a pact of 'friendship, co-operation and mutual assistance.'

In western Europe the problem of economic recovery demanded immediate attention in the period following the war, and a contribution of great significance has been the assistance of the United States. In the first two years, various expedients were tried, and finally, in June 1947, General Marshall, the American Secretary of State, took the initiative by inviting all the European countries to examine their problem in concert with the United States.[1] From this invitation grew the Economic Recovery Programme, or Marshall Aid Plan, which has been applicable to those countries which accepted the invitation, and has been of political as well as economic importance in western Europe.

At the same time, plans were evolved for the co-operation of the west European states with the United States and Canada in the defence of the west. The Brussels Treaty of collective defence (March 17, 1948) between Britain, France, Belgium, the Netherlands and Luxembourg, was followed a year later (April 4, 1949) by the North Atlantic Treaty whose signatories included the United States, Canada, the Brussels

---

[1] The following countries were represented at the conference held in Paris in July 1947, at the invitation of France and Britain, to consider General Marshall's offer: Italy, Belgium, the Netherlands, Luxembourg, Austria, Norway, Sweden, Denmark, Iceland, Greece, Portugal, Switzerland, Eire and Turkey.

19

Treaty Powers, Italy, Denmark, Norway, Iceland and Portugal. These treaties were indicative of the pre-occupation of western Europe and the North American continent with the economic and financial as well as the military aspects of security and defence. They provided not only for an integrated plan of defence, but also for regular and constant consultation, and a special body—the North Atlantic Treaty Organisation—was established to consider the implementation of the terms of this treaty.

Political conditions in these countries have moved slowly towards greater stability. In each state there have been dominant problems which caused serious internal controversy; the Indonesian question for the Netherlands; in Belgium, the division of opinion over the proposal for the return of King Leopold; and in France rapid political changes reminiscent of the inter-war years. France alone had no desire to return to the constitution in force before its supersession by the Vichy régime. A new constitution was therefore drawn up, and the Fourth French Republic came into being on the 24th of December 1946.

A movement towards unity has developed in western Europe as a whole and bore fruit in May 1949 in the establishment of a bi-cameral Council of Europe, with a Council of Ministers as the executive organ, and a Consultative Assembly, purely advisory in character. The first session of the Assembly met in Strasbourg in August and September 1949, and initiated an inquiry into the changes which would be required in the political structure of Europe, as a preliminary step towards unity in the west. No definition has been reached of the part which the Council of Europe, and the Assembly in particular, might play in European affairs. The whole structure is still in a tentative and preliminary stage of development.

The fundamental differences that have divided eastern and western Europe postponed the conclusion of a peace treaty with Japan,[1] and had serious effects in other parts of the Far East. China, Britain and the United States declared, as far back as 1943, that it was their intention to deprive Japan of all her conquests in the Pacific since the outbreak of the first World War in 1914, and to restore to China those territories which Japan had taken from her. On the surrender of Japan, the Allies carried out this policy as far as Japan was concerned. An Allied Council for Japan was established in Tokio, and supported by allied troops. The declared objective was the reform of Japanese institutions in the hope of setting up a more liberal régime. The situation in China was dominated, from the conclusion of the Sino-Japanese war, by an internal struggle, which led to the victory of Communist armies under Mao Tse-tung over the Nationalist armies of Chiang Kai-shek. A 'People's Republic' was set up, and in February 1950 a treaty of friendship, alliance and mutual assistance was signed with the Soviet Union.

[1] The Treaty was finally signed at San Francisco on 8 September, 1951. Russia was not a signatory.

EPILOGUE

THE period covered by this book is full of wars, which were progressively more destructive of life and property; for the development of science has put into the hands of combatants means of destruction incomparably greater than any possessed by earlier generations. But these years also saw a series of efforts to avoid war and to link together the nations of Europe and the world, which were more serious and more conscious of the goal than anything that the world had previously seen.

The project of a world union of Christian States was put forward at the close of the Napoleonic Wars by the Czar Alexander I, though it soon became overlaid by other motives—fear of revolution and ambition for power. It had not the slightest influence on the public policy of Europe, and is usually treated as unworthy of serious consideration. It can clearly be riddled with practical criticisms. Its motives were too narrow and indefinite; it took no account of the non-Christian world; it lacked entirely organisation and machinery. Before this time another and a more practical project had been inaugurated. When the Allies were pressing upon Napoleon after the Battle of Leipzig and had followed him on to the soil of France, a treaty of permanent alliance was signed at Chaumont on March 9, 1814. The moving spirit of the time was Castlereagh, the English Foreign Minister, so bitterly hated in his own time as a reactionary and supporter of tyrants. He proposed that the Four Great Powers who were fighting against Napoleon should not separate when hostilities came to an end. His ideas were expressed later in the terms of the Quadruple Alliance of 1815. The words of the all-important clause, which owes its origin to Castlereagh, deserve quotation:

'To facilitate and to secure the execution of the present Treaty, and to consolidate the connections which at the present moment so closely unite the Four Sovereigns for the happiness of the world, the High Contracting Parties have agreed to renew their Meetings at fixed periods, either under the immediate auspices of the Sovereigns themselves, or by their respective Ministers, for the purpose of consulting upon their common interests, and for the consideration of the measures which at each of those periods shall be considered the most salutary for the repose and prosperity of Nations, and for the maintenance of the Peace of Europe.'

Here at least was the recognition that the peace of Europe required and deserved regular attention. There was no effort to secure the co-operation of the states of Europe in matters of common interest; there was no appeal to arbitration or to international law. It was just such an alliance of Great Powers as Europe had frequently seen. None but the Great Powers had part or lot in it. But the meetings at regular intervals, and the hope of securing permanent peace in Europe by dealing with difficulties before they became too serious for conciliation were new and fertile ideas. There was no effort to win for it the support of public opinion; that would have seemed a dangerous imitation of the methods of the French Revolution. The Great Powers went their own way without any attempt to justify themselves in the eyes of the outside world, and very soon this attempt, which was genuinely intended to secure the 'peace and prosperity of Europe,' came to be regarded with the most vehement hostility by all that was progressive and humanitarian in European thought.

It is important to note that in 1818 at the Congress of Aix-la-Chapelle the Czar made an attempt to carry the idea of European unity further and to create something which would have borne fairly close resemblance to an embryonic League of Nations. He proposed a general alliance of all the signatories of the Treaty of Vienna, to guarantee to every legitimate sovereign his throne and his territory. Such an alliance the Czar contended, would be favourable to both order and liberty, for the security of governments would be assured if international law were placed under a guarantee similar to that which protected the rights of the individual. In such an event, the governments would be relieved of the fear of revolution, and would then be able of their own free will to offer constitutions to their subjects. It was a grandiose but not impossible scheme, containing perhaps elements that might be dangerous to popular causes, but capable of development and reform, had the times been favourable to its growth. The tendency of the age that was beginning was, on the contrary, towards national movements, often revolutionary in character.

While the world thus turned its back on the ideals of the Holy Alliance and went forward to new wars, which sprang from the very principle of nationality, the problem was becoming more urgent. For the era of invention had come, and the contacts between nations and states were being multiplied with amazing rapidity. It is hardly possible to exaggerate the gap which separates the twentieth century from the early nineteenth in the material and mechanical sides of life. Invention soon turned its attention to weapons of war and gave soldiers powers of destruction beyond anything that even Napoleon had dreamed of. The world, moreover, was linked together as never before. England knew more of Austria, Italy, or America than Kent had known of Yorkshire a hundred years previously. Since the beginning of the nineteenth century the movement has gone on with constantly increasing acceleration. It is many-sided and has had many different results, but its chief effects have been to produce rapidity of transit and of communication beyond all that was dreamed of in an earlier age; and with these results has gone a proportionate increase in the destructive powers of man. The need for some method of avoiding war was immensely greater than in any earlier age.

In the period immediately following the Napoleonic Wars, the emphasis in Europe lay on nationalism rather than on international co-operation, and it was not until the Crimean War that the problem of the preservation of international peace was again raised. The Congress of Paris provided no adequate solution, although on the initiative of Clarendon, the British Foreign Secretary, a protocol was issued declaring '. . . the Plenipotentiaries do not hesitate to express, in the name of their Governments, the wish that States between which any serious misunderstanding may arise, should, before appealing to Arms, have recourse, as far as circumstances might allow, to the Good Offices of a friendly Power.' The pious wish of the Paris plenipotentiaries remained quite without effect, and in the next fifteen years three European wars were fought. The period of comparative calm which followed in western Europe saw the revival of international feeling and organisations, and in commercial, labour, cultural and scientific fields there was in Europe, in the period 1871–1914, a real unity, but this unity did not extend to politics or governments. The most constructive proposal of the second half of the nineteenth century was for the development of the practice of arbitration. The idea of international arbitration was indeed as old as Periclean Athens, or older; but it is during the past century only that it has been seriously and almost continuously urged. Between the Battle of Waterloo and the outbreak of war in 1914 arbitration in some form was applied to nearly 300 international disputes. The universal acceptance of the idea was prevented by the refusal of the great States of the world to admit any procedure which even seemed to encroach on their complete independence. No European Government was willing to adopt arbitration or to appeal to any authority except force 'upon issues in which the national honour or integrity was involved.' So, though arbitration smoothed many diplomatic difficulties and provided useful machinery for the settlement of many secondary disputes, it did nothing to remove the tension between the Great Powers out of which the war of 1914 came, or to reduce the burden and expense of armaments.

A great effort—emanating from and really supported by the Czar of Russia—was made to regularise and extend the application of international arbitration in the two Peace Conferences held at The Hague in 1899 and 1907. The origins of the movement are somewhat obscure, and some Russian statesmen may have hoped to use the Conference for the advancement of certain narrow Russian plans; but without question there was in the Czar's mind, and in the minds of many who supported him, a genuine humanitarian desire to lighten the burden of armaments which weighed on all Europe, and to find if possible some means of removing from Europe the menace of war. The attempt to secure disarmament failed completely, as all attempts up to the present time have failed. Neither France nor Germany nor Great Britain, nor probably Russia herself, was really ready to take any effective steps or to run any risks to secure the desired end. The large number of Powers assembled at The Hague would only declare that 'the restriction of military charges, which are at present a heavy burden on the world, is extremely desirable for the increase of the material and moral welfare of mankind,' and this was something far weaker than the words which the Czar had used in sending out his invitations to the Conference. The armies of Europe increased rather than diminished during the next ten years. But though the movement for disarmament failed there was a unanimous belief that something might be done to maintain peace among the nations by the development of the practice of arbitration and the definition of its methods. And here something of real importance was done. The arbitration movement was given definite shape. A permanent arbitral system was set up, which could be called into action whenever two Powers wished to use it for the settlement of any disputes. Various methods were suggested to meet various circumstances. In some instances mediation might be used; in others a mixed commission of inquiry might examine and report on matters of fact; disputes which lent themselves to such treatment might be submitted to a court of arbitration, which was set up in a permanent form and was to be governed by fixed rules of procedure. The Conference also met in 1907, and again upon the initiative of the Czar; but the second Conference was something of a disappointment. It was seen once again that nothing could be done to disarm Europe, and many saw that without disarmament there could be no permanent peace. The wisdom of arbitration was reaffirmed, and the methods were reconsidered and improved.

The Conferences at The Hague gave a great impetus to the signing of arbitration treaties among the States of the world, and these were of real use in promoting a peaceful atmosphere among the smaller Powers of Europe. Not only had the number of arbitration treaties increased but a most important advance was also made in their form. It was hopeless, however, to expect that arbitration would maintain the peace of the world while the most important questions were formally excluded from its scope. Most of the great wars in history have been fought, not for the interpretation of clauses in a treaty, but for what were considered to be 'affairs of honour and vital interests.' The movement to include these matters within the scope of arbitration began in America. It encountered much opposition even there, but by September 1914 arbitration treaties between the United States and both France and Great Britain were drawn up, accepted and duly signed.[1] By these treaties all disputes of whatever kind which could not be settled by the ordinary procedure of diplomacy were to be submitted to a joint Inter-

[1] It is significant that Germany declined a treaty with the United States in 1914. Kaiser William II told President Wilson's trusted envoy, Colonel House, that he relied on his sword and not only on treaties. Had he relied on treaties he would have been much safer. For had Germany signed the arbitration treaty with the United States, the latter could not have entered the war for a year after she severed diplomatic relations (*i.e.*, till about March 1918!).

national Commission, whose constitution and procedure were carefully defined and regulated. The Commission was to report within a year, and during this time the signatory Powers were to take no step of any kind towards any other solution of their difficulties. The acceptance of these treaties would, under different circumstances, have attracted much attention, and would perhaps have been recognised as a step towards international peace almost as important as the Hague Conferences themselves. But in September 1914 Europe was at war.

With the ratification of the Treaty of Versailles in January 1920, the movement towards world organisation was carried into the political sphere by the establishment of the League of Nations, and the mechanism for the preservation of peace and for international co-operation in several fields other than the political, came into force. It was an event of first importance, and formed the next logical step in the movement for arbitration in international disputes which had its origin in the previous century. The League of Nations was the first practical attempt at international organisation aimed at the preservation of world peace. In the political sphere it failed in its main purpose. Even before the outbreak of war it was seen to represent, in its political functions, only the hopes of a vanished world, and to be a body without either authority or interest in taking action against aggression. The fundamental reason for its ineffectiveness is to be found in the unwillingness of nations to subordinate their own interests to the peace of the world. No nation was prepared to take the initiative. 'What was everybody's business in the end proved to be nobody's business. Each one looked to the other to take the lead, and the aggressors got away with it.'[1]

From the failure of the League and the embroilment of the whoïe world in war for the second time within a generation, grew the determination of the Allied Powers to create an international organisation capable of taking action in the face of a threat to peace. Britain, Russia and the United States decided, in October 1943, not to wait until the war was over, but to start at once to build up such an organisation. Draft proposals were drawn up by the representatives of Britain, Russia, America and China at conferences held at Dumbarton Oaks, Washington, between August and October 1944. From these proposals, the United Nations Charter was drawn up by the delegates of fifty states who met at San Francisco from April to June 1945.[2] The Charter set up the United Nations Organisation, to maintain international peace and security, to develop friendly relations among nations and to achieve international co-operation in solving international problems of an economic, social, cultural or humanitarian character. Six

[1] General Smuts: 'Thoughts on the New World.' A speech to members of the Empire Parliamentary Association, 25 November 1943.

[2] v. Sir Charles Webster's Creighton Lecture of November 1946, 'The Making of the Charter of the United Nations,' published in *History*, vol. XXXII, March 1947, pp. 16–38.

principal organs were created to carry into effect these objectives. The General Assembly, composed of all the members of the United Nations, has the right of discussing all matters within the scope of the Charter and making recommendations on them. Eleven members of the United Nations form the Security Council, on which five of the seats are permanently allotted to America, France, Britain, Russia and China, whilst the remaining six places are held for two years by members of the United Nations elected by the General Assembly. The Security Council is primarily responsible for the maintenance of peace and security: its functions are more specific than those of the Council of the League of Nations and it is given the means of enforcing its decisions relating to the pacific settlement of disputes and the prevention of aggression. Decisions in the Security Council on all matters, other than those of procedure, require an affirmative vote of seven members, including all the permanent members. This in effect gives the permanent members the right of veto. The Economic and Social Council of eighteen members elected by the General Assembly, is to promote 'respect for, and observance of, human rights and fundamental freedoms for all.' The Trusteeship Council replaces the Permanent Mandates Commission of the League, although the territories within its competence are not named. The International Court of Justice is based on the Permanent Court of International Justice set up by the League, and its statute follows very closely that of its precursor. Finally, a Secretariat completes the organisation, supervised by a Secretary-General appointed by the General Assembly on the recommendation of the Security Council.

The United Nations was created in the light of the experience of the League of Nations, and an attempt was therefore made to avoid the errors inherent in the constitution of the League. The Charter is thus a much longer and more explicit document than the Covenant, and the powers and functions of the United Nations are considerably more extensive than those of the League. Moreover, the Covenant formed an integral part of the Treaty of Versailles, and was drawn up in the aftermath of war. The Charter of the United Nations, on the other hand, was drafted before the conclusion of hostilities, and signed, ratified and in operation before the conclusion of the peace treaties. The membership of the United Nations is also more representative of all continents than that of its precursor, and its members include all the Great Powers which emerged from the war. On the other hand, even those ex-enemy states with which treaties have been concluded, are excluded from membership by disagreements between Russia and the Western Powers in the Security Council. And this remains so despite the fact that, in the preambles to the several treaties, the Allies envisaged their support for the inclusion of the ex-enemy states within the United Nations. There are, too, differences in the machinery of the United Nations which reflect the failures of the League. It is, for example, hoped that the powers vested in the Security Council will provide adequate machinery for countering aggression at its early stages. Nevertheless, the organisation of the United Nations owes much to the League of Nations, and the origins of its aims and basic principles are to be found even further back, in the thought and ideas of the nineteenth century.

The working of the United Nations since its inception in October 1945 hardly falls within the purview of this book, and it would be premature to attempt either to assess or to enumerate its activities. After the disappointments of the League of Nations, the hopes for the United Nations were more restrained and less optimistic. '. . . it was never contemplated at San Francisco,' wrote Mr. Trygve Lie, first Secretary-General of the United Nations, 'that the United Nations would or could abolish differences of interest and ideology such as we see in the world to-day. It was not believed that the great Powers would always act in unity and brotherhood together. What the founders of the United Nations did believe was that the United Nations would make it possible to keep disputes between both great and small Powers within peaceful bounds, and that without the United Nations this could not be done. Finally, they rejected the idea of an irreconcilable conflict that could be settled only on the field of battle, and proclaimed on the contrary the principle that all conflicts, no matter how fundamental, should and could be settled by peaceful means. . . . The United Nations has not been able to resolve great Power differences, but the conflict has been kept within peaceful bounds and the way prepared for further progress towards a settlement.'[1]

[1] 'Introduction to the Annual Report of the Secretary-General on the work of the Organization, 1 July 1948–30 June 1949.' Printed in *International Conciliation* (New York), September 1949, p. 589.

INDEX